Heath
Biology

James E. McLaren
Biology Teacher
Newton South High School
Newton Centre, MA

Lissa Rotundo
Biology Teacher
Formerly with Baltimore City
  Schools
Baltimore, MD

Content Reviewers

Lincoln P. Brower, Ph.D.
Professor of Zoology
University of Florida
Gainesville, FL

Karsten E. Hartel
Curatorial Associate
Museum of Comparative Anatomy
Cambridge, MA

Malcolm Jay Kottler, Ph.D.
Associate Professor of Biology
University of Minnesota
Minneapolis, MN

Welton L. Lee, Ph.D.
Curator of Invertebrate Zoology
California Academy of Sciences
San Francisco, CA

Paul LeFevre, Ph.D.
Professor of Physiology
  and Biophysics
State University of New York
Stony Brook, NY

J. David Robertson, Ph.D.
James B. Duke Professor
  and Chairman
Duke University
Durham, NC

Lawrence Slobodkin, Ph.D.
Professor of Biology
State University of New York
Stony Brook, NY

Fredrick J. Stare, Ph.D.
Professor of Nutrition, Emeritus
Harvard School of Public Health
Boston, MA

Richard W. Thorington, Jr., Ph.D.
Curator, Department of
  Vertebrate Zoology
Smithsonian Institution
Washington, D.C.

Claude A. Villee, Ph.D.
Andelot Professor of
  Biological Chemistry
Harvard University Medical School
Boston, MA

Walter R. Wilson, M.D.
Associate Professor of Medicine
Mayo Clinic
Rochester, MN

D.C. Heath and Company
Lexington, Massachusetts   Toronto

The Heath Biology Program

Heath Biology, Pupil's Edition
Heath Biology, Teacher's Annotated Edition
Heath Biology Laboratory Investigations, Pupil's Edition
Heath Biology Laboratory Investigations, Teacher's Annotated Edition
Heath Biology Tests, Copy Masters and Spirit Duplicating Masters
Heath Biology Chapter Worksheets, Copy Masters and Spirit Duplicating Masters
Heath Biology Computer Test Bank
Heath Biology Computer Test Bank, Teacher's Edition
Heath Biology Overhead Transparencies

Executive Editor: Roger R. Rogalin
Editorial Development: Ellen M. Lappa, Julia A. Fellows, Anne G. Jones, Pamela A. Cunningham
Project Design: Laurel J. Smith, Ellen Knox Coolidge, Leli Sudler
Illustrators: Leo Abbett,Arvak, Lori Baker, Michael Carroll, Nancy Kaplan, Ellen Knox Coolidge, John Hamburger, Bruce Sanders, Lisa Sparks, James Teason
Production Coordinator: Donna Lee Porter
Copyediting: Kathleen K. Harvie
Cover Photograph: Red-eyed tree frogs native to Central America by Z. Leszczynski
Readability Testing: J & F Incorporated

Field Test Teachers and Reviewers

George Bonnorris
Biology Teacher
University High School
West Los Angeles, CA

Ray Braswell
Biology Teacher
Denton High School
Denton, TX

Reid Harvey
Secondary Science Supervisor
Palm Beach County, FL

Dennis Kucinski
Biology Teacher
T.F. South High School
Lansing, IL

Sheila Nan Matus
Biology Teacher
St. Anthony's High School
Smithtown, NY

Claudine R. Morgan
Biology Teacher
Thomas Jefferson High School
Dallas, TX

Barbara Neel
Biology Teacher
Denton High School
Denton, TX

Susan Offner, Ph.D.
Biology Teacher
Plymouth-Carver Regional
Plymouth, MA

Nancee Ryan
Biology Teacher
Reading High School
Reading, PA

Julia Stevens
Biology Teacher
Sanderson High School
Raleigh, NC

George A. Tinker
Science Department Chairman
Marshfield High School
Coos Bay, OR

David Truelsen
Biology Teacher
Buffalo Grove High School
Buffalo Grove, IL

ISBN 0–669–06920–5

Preface

This course begins your first real experience with the subject of biology: the science of living things.

First, you should recognize that biology, like any science, consists of facts, principles, and theories that are based on research and experimentation. A large part of biology concerns theories on how living things have changed or evolved over millions of years. Evolutionary theories provide the best scientific interpretations for the data available. As new findings come to light, science dictates that these theories be modified or refined to continue to reflect the best scientific explanations. Keep in mind that evolutionary theories conform to the criteria set for a scientific theory. They are not to be treated as fact.

Heath Biology will be one of the primary tools you will use in your study. Before trying to use this tool, you should become familiar with how it can be used to make your work easier.

Heath Biology is organized to present a phylogenetic approach to biology. This type of approach means you will study the different groups of plants and animals according to their evolutionary relationships. Biological principles will be covered by studying representative organisms.

Each chapter of the text is divided into lessons. The first lesson heading is shown on page 3. The *Concepts* for this lesson are listed to the right of the lesson title. The *Concepts* can help you focus on what you will be expected to learn from the lesson. An expanded form of the *Concepts* is found in the *Summary* for each chapter. The *Summary* for Chapter 1 is found on page 16.

A lesson is further divided into short numbered sections, as shown on page 3. The headings highlight the major topics of the chapter. They can be used in helping you organize information in preparing an outline for review purposes.

An understanding of scientific terms is essential to a successful study of biology. Terms you should know, such as the word *microscope* on page 5, are highlighted in boldfaced type. Pronunciations are included for difficult terms, as with *hypothesis* on page 9. A listing of important terms for each chapter is found in the *Vocabulary* section of each Chapter Review. The *Vocabulary* list for Chapter 1 is on page 16. The *Glossary* at the back of the book can be used to find definitions of new terms quickly.

The *Checkpoints* and *Chapter Review* questions will help you in reviewing the important points in the chapter. *Unit Reviews* cover the major concepts of the unit. Answering all of the questions should adequately prepare you for a test.

Biology is both interesting and practical. *Do You Know?* notes, such as the one on page 3, reveal interesting practical sidelights about the topic you are studying. The basic unifying themes of biology are presented in the *Biology Insights*, such as the one on page 31. These *Insights* will often highlight the interrelationships among the material covered in several chapters. A broad understanding of these *Insights* should be one of your goals for the course.

At the end of each unit, you will find a brief overview of careers that require some knowledge of biology. The first of these career features is found on page 126. Since the study of biology is an ongoing process, topics of current biological research are covered briefly in the *Newsbreak* features like that on page 40.

Now that you are familiar with **Heath Biology**, you've completed your first step toward a successful year.

The Authors

CONTENTS

Unit Two
The Succession of Life

Unit Three
Monerans, Protists, and Fungi

Unit Six
Chordates

Unit Seven
The Human Body

Unit Eight

Organisms and the Environment

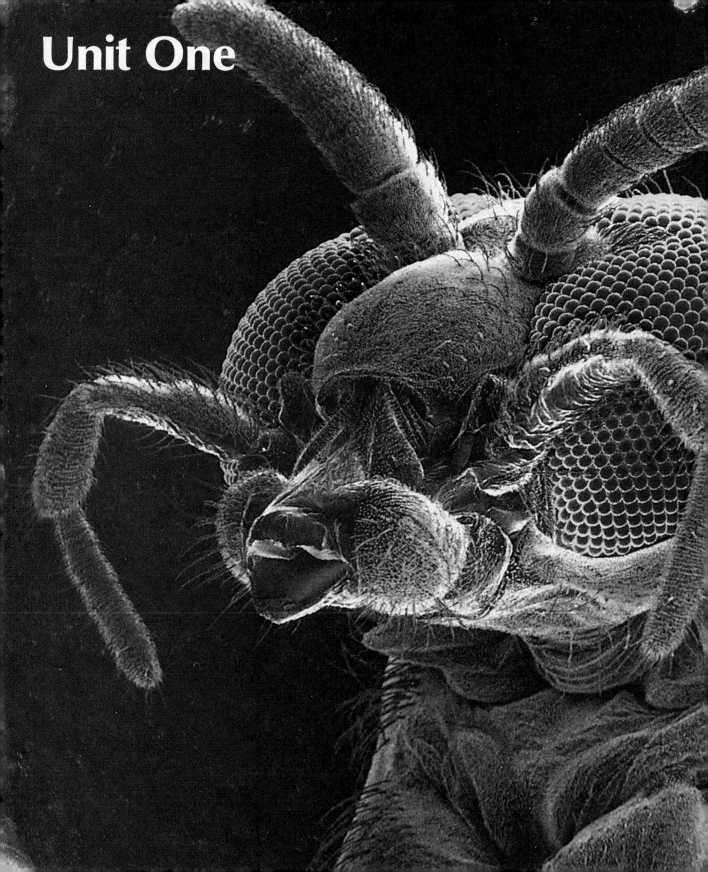

Unit One

The Science of Life

Head of a black fly photographed
with a scanning electron microscope
(color added)

1 The Process of Science

White storks nesting on a rooftop

If a bird the size of this one nested on your roof, you might be upset. In some parts of Europe, it happens all the time and people like it.

The bird is a white stork. Ever since the Middle Ages, the stork has been considered a sign of good luck in many countries. The stork is also famous for the legend that it delivers human babies. Such ideas are examples of superstitions. A superstition is a belief that two unrelated events are actually related.

Science, on the other hand, does not accept such explanations. Science is a way of finding out if one event actually causes another event. Science looks at explanations based on demonstrated relationships rather than on belief.

Although scientists have discovered many things about the stork, they have found no evidence that storks bring good luck or deliver babies. It is interesting that in countries where people do not believe this bird brings good luck, storks are not allowed to nest on houses and have become rare. Where storks are respected, they have remained common. So this human superstition has brought good fortune . . . to storks, at least.

Explanation through Science

Figure 1.1 shows a human skull many thousands of years old. Since this skull is older than human written records, scientists cannot be certain about what caused the hole in the skull. They think, however, that it was made on purpose and that the individual undergoing the surgery survived for many years after the hole was drilled. Scientists draw this conclusion because the bone around the edges of the hole shows signs of healing.

Some early cultures left written records about why they did this kind of surgery. They believed that severe headaches were caused by evil spirits. Drilling a hole in the skull supposedly allowed the evil spirits to escape. In the days before pain-free surgery and clean operating rooms, such surgery must have been difficult at best. Faced with such a "cure," these people probably did not often complain about headaches.

Evil spirits may seem to you to be a bizarre explanation for a disease. But in the absence of scientific knowledge, superstition was the only way ancient people could explain the cause of many events.

1–1 Characteristics of Science

Unlike superstition, science is knowledge gained through careful observation of objects and events. In order to explain events, scientists seek logical connections between observed facts. These connections often lead to general rules of cause and effect. But science is not just a set of facts and rules. Science is primarily a way of learning about the world. Of course, no one person could hope to understand everything about how the world works, so science is divided into many different branches. **Biology** is the branch that studies living things. **Biologists** are scientists who investigate life.

One of the most important characteristics of science is that *its conclusions are based on evidence*. In science all statements must be backed up by careful observation. You may believe that taking vitamin C prevents colds. Before scientists would accept this idea, however, they would need evidence to support it. Perhaps they would compare the frequency of colds among people who take vitamin C with the frequency of colds among people who do not.

A second characteristic of science is *objectivity*. That is, the results of a scientific investigation should not be influenced by the beliefs of the person making the observation. Other

CONCEPTS
- the unique characteristics of science
- the structure of a light microscope
- advantages of the electron microscope

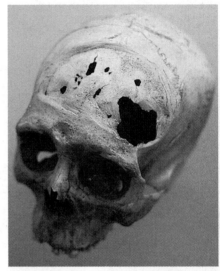

Figure 1.1 What caused the hole that you see in this prehistoric skull?

Do You Know?
The bark of the cinchona tree was used in primitive societies as a treatment for malaria. The bark contains quinine, a drug still used to treat the disease.

The Process of Science **3**

Figure 1.2 During the Middle Ages many people believed that strange animals existed. Drawings documenting their existence appeared in authoritative books of the time.

Figure 1.3 An excerpt from *Micrographia*, a publication by Robert Hooke. Hooke was an early scientist who made studies using a microscope.

Figure 1.4 Some units of measurement in the metric system

scientists using similar methods should reach the same conclusion. If a scientist is objective in measuring the number of people who get colds after taking vitamin C, anyone else should get the same results. Results obtained scientifically can be repeated.

A third characteristic of science is that it is the *result of the work of many scientists around the world*. Developing scientific explanations requires many more observations than one person can make.

Since the work of each scientist builds upon the work of others, new information is continually added to existing knowledge. Evidence for new and better explanations is reported in writing. Scientific observations must be recorded because human memory is often inaccurate. Today scientists publish the results of their investigations in journals.

There are several reasons for publishing. Publishing saves time. Scientists can read what others have learned instead of having to do all the work over again. Publishing also allows other scientists to check each other's work. If different scientists cannot repeat a set of results, the conclusions will not be accepted. Another important reason for publishing is to ensure that those who make discoveries will receive credit for their work.

A final characteristic of modern science is the *use of tools* to aid investigation. Scientists use tools because they recognize that their senses are limited. For example, because it is hard to see long distances, biologists may use binoculars to observe the behavior of birds. Many tools used by scientists detect and precisely measure details that human senses might miss. By using a balance, a scientist can compare the masses of objects with great precision. Modern scientists use the international system of metric units to record their observations.

Length			Volume or Capacity		
base unit: meter (m)			base unit: liter (L)		
			1 liter = 1000 cm³		
unit	*symbol*	*equivalent*	*unit*	*symbol*	*equivalent*
kilometer	km	1000 m	milliliter	mL	0.001 L
decimeter	dm	0.1 m			
centimeter	cm	0.01 m			
millimeter	mm	0.001 m			
micrometer	μm	0.000001 m			

Mass		
base unit: kilogram (kg)		
unit	*symbol*	*equivalent*
gram	g	0.001 kg
centigram	cg	0.00001 kg
milligram	mg	0.000001 kg

1–2 The Microscope

One of the most important tools used in biology to extend the senses is the microscope. The **microscope** is a device that provides an enlarged image of small objects. With a microscope biologists can often observe objects or details that would otherwise be too small to be seen.

The microscope has been in use for over 300 years. Some early microscopes are shown in Figure 1.5. Early microscopes were primitive compared to those used today.

You have probably used a hand lens to magnify, or enlarge, small objects. People have used such lenses for many hundreds of years. As you may know, the greater the curvature of a lens, the greater the magnification provided by the lens. In the late 1600s a Dutchman named Anton van Leeuwenhoek developed a way of making very tiny but strongly curved glass lenses. He mounted each lens in a metal support. A single lens magnifier like Leeuwenhoek's is called a **simple microscope**.

 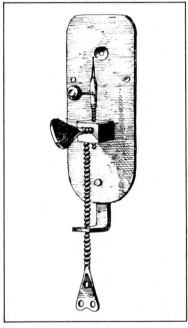

Figure 1.5 Some early microscopes. *Left:* One of Hooke's microscopes; *Right:* One of Leeuwenhoek's microscopes

Leeuwenhoek's microscopes could magnify objects to appear as much as 300 times actual size, but they all had a serious drawback. Strongly curved lenses bring objects into focus very near the lens itself. Such a microscope must be placed right up against the eye. The specimen must be held right against the other side of the lens. These microscopes were painful to use and very limited in how much could be seen. It was also difficult to illuminate the object being studied.

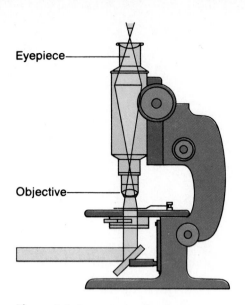

Eyepiece

Objective

Figure 1.6 A compound microscope

Figure 1.7 How far away can you move and still see two distinct lines?

Other biologists living at the same time as Leeuwenhoek began to use the first compound microscopes. A **compound microscope** has two lenses. One lens magnifies the object being observed. This lens is called the **objective**. A second lens, called the **ocular** [AHK-yuh-lur] or **eyepiece**, magnifies the image produced by the objective. The lens arrangement of such a microscope is illustrated in Figure 1.6.

The total magnification of a compound microscope is the product of the objective magnification and the eyepiece magnification. For example, on many microscopes a typical objective lens has a magnification of 43 times (43×). A standard eyepiece has a magnification of 10 times (10×). The total magnification of the objective and the eyepiece combined is 43 × 10, or 430 times.

Compound microscopes can be illuminated by a light beneath the specimen. In some compound microscopes a mirror reflects light onto the specimen. Thus, compound microscopes have a wider field of vision and better illumination than simple microscopes.

In modern microscopes most of the problems of the early microscopes are solved. But there is one limitation on the performance of compound microscopes that cannot be overcome. A compound microscope has a maximum useful magnification of about 1,000 times. Although it is possible to build a microscope that magnifies far more than 1,000 times, this is rarely done. No matter how high the magnification, a compound microscope can never show any more detail than is visible at 1,000 times.

Limits on the ability of a lens to show detail are set by the resolving power of the lens. **Resolving power** is the ability of an instrument to separate and distinguish two objects. All lenses have a maximum resolving power. You can test the resolving power of a very handy lens — the one in your eye. Look at the two parallel black lines in Figure 1.7. You should have no difficulty telling that there are two separate lines. Keep your book open to this illustration and prop it up on a desk. Now slowly move away while gazing at the lines. You will soon get to a point where the two lines appear to fuse into a single line. At that point, your eye can no longer resolve the two lines.

Because of the characteristics of visible light, it is impossible for a compound microscope to resolve objects closer than 0.0002 mm, no matter what the magnification. Under ideal conditions, at 1,000 times the compound microscope will show objects as separate if they are more than 0.0002 mm apart. They will appear to be a single object if they are closer together. Therefore, detail that is less than 0.0002 mm long cannot be seen under any compound microscope — its image cannot be separated from its surroundings. Further magnification would give a bigger image but would show no more detail. In fact, any magnification greater than 1,000 times makes objects appear fuzzy. Unfortunately, many things that are of interest to biologists are smaller than those the best compound microscope can resolve.

1–3 The Electron Microscope

The problem of limited resolving power was largely solved in the 1940s with the invention of the **electron microscope**. Instead of directing light through an object, the electron microscope directs a beam of tiny particles called electrons. Instead of using glass lenses to focus an image, the electron microscope uses special doughnut-shaped magnets. Because the human eye cannot see electrons, the magnified image produced by an electron microscope must be projected onto either a television screen or photographic film. In order to produce this image, the electrons must pass through extremely thin slices of the material being viewed.

The major advantage of the electron microscope is its resolving power. It can resolve two objects as close together as 0.0000005 mm. Such resolution requires magnifications of close to 1 million times.

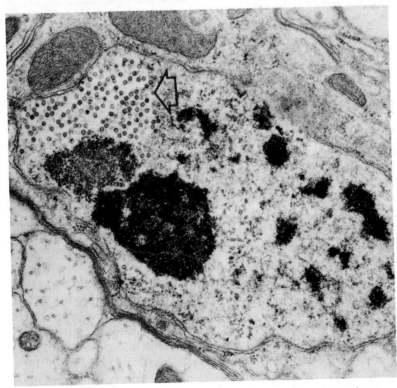

Figure 1.8 This photograph taken through an electron microscope shows a fruit fly nerve cell magnified 26,000 times. The arrow points to viruses within the cell.

One limitation of the electron microscope is that it cannot be used to study living specimens. This is because all specimens must be sliced very thin to allow the electrons to pass through. Specimens must also be prepared with special chemicals that kill organisms.

A more recently developed instrument is the **scanning electron microscope**. It is somewhat different from the electron microscope. The scanning electron microscope takes pictures of surfaces rather than of thin slices. The pictures have an almost three-dimensional quality, as shown in Figure 1.9.

Throughout this book you will see photographs taken through the different kinds of microscopes in use today. Each kind of microscope is useful for particular kinds of observations. Microscopes have allowed biologists to make observations that would otherwise be impossible.

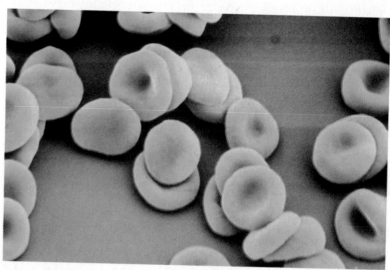

Figure 1.9 Blood cells as seen through a scanning electron microscope

Checkpoint

1. What are four important characteristics of science?
2. What are two reasons scientists use tools to help them make observations?
3. How many lenses are there in a simple microscope? In a compound microscope?
4. If the eyepiece of your compound microscope has a magnification of 7.5× and the objective has a magnification of 10×, what is the total magnification of your microscope?
5. What is the term that describes the ability of a lens to show two objects as separate images?
6. What kind of microscope can be used to view the smallest objects?

Methods of Science

One way biologists increase their understanding of living things is by making observations. Accurate observation plays a central role throughout all of science.

It has been only in the last 20 years, for example, that scientists have learned how chimpanzees and gorillas behave in the wild. Biologists have spent many thousands of hours watching and recording how these animals act in their natural setting. Such observations give scientists important information that is not available until someone collects it.

Sometimes observations lead to questions that cannot be answered simply by further observation. Then it may be necessary to find another way to investigate the problem.

1-4 Hypotheses and Experiments

Suppose you grow geraniums. Although you have had your geraniums for several months, they have never blossomed. In this case, your observations have identified a problem that cannot be answered by more observation. Why haven't your geraniums blossomed?

You suspect that your plants need fertilizer. This is your hypothesis. A **hypothesis** [hy-PAHTH-uh-sihs] is a temporary explanation for a set of observations. A good hypothesis is stated in a form that suggests a way to test the explanation. One such form is an "If . . . then" statement. In the case of your geraniums, your hypothesis could be restated as "*If* my geraniums are fertilized, *then* they will blossom."

Scientists think of the most reasonable explanation for their questions and then look for evidence to support or reject their explanations. One way to find evidence is by an experiment. An **experiment** is a way to test a hypothesis.

To test your hypothesis about geraniums and fertilizer, you could design the following experiment:

1. You select the two geraniums that are closest in size and place them next to each other on your windowsill.
2. Once a week you give one plant a glass of plain water. At the same time you give the other plant a glass of water that contains a measured amount of fertilizer.
3. Every week you record your observations.

The observations that you record during your experiment are your data. **Data** are information collected in an experiment. (A single piece of information is a datum.) The number of blossoms, appearance of the plants, and number of leaves are all data you might record.

- the importance of hypotheses, experiments, and theories in science
- the design of a controlled experiment
- the unpredictability of scientific research

Figure 1.10 Often careful observations are made and experiments carried out in places far removed from conventional laboratories.

The Process of Science **9**

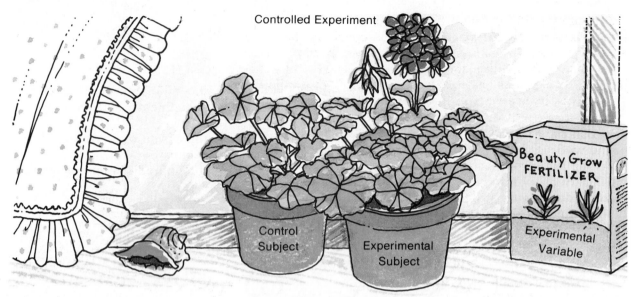

Controlled Experiment

Control Subject

Experimental Subject

Beauty Grow FERTILIZER

Experimental Variable

Figure 1.11 Testing a hypothesis

After a month you observe that the geranium receiving the fertilizer has developed buds. Two weeks later it has a bright red flower. During the next six weeks it produces three more flowers. During the same three month period, the geranium without fertilizer shows no flowers.

At the end of your experiment you conclude that your data support your hypothesis. Your experiment has shown that your geraniums do need fertilizer to blossom.

Scientists would say that the experiment you performed with your geraniums was a controlled experiment. In a **controlled experiment**, only one factor is changed. All other factors remain the same. Any factor that can be changed is called a **variable**.

By selecting geraniums of the same size, you made sure that any difference in their growth would not be due to the size of the plant. So size was not a variable in your experiment. By placing the plants side by side on the windowsill, you made sure they would receive the same amount of sunlight. So sunlight was not a variable and could not cause differences in the plants. By giving the plants the same amount of water at the same time, you made sure that water would not be a variable that could affect the plants. Your only **experimental variable** was the fertilizer. Because you were careful to control the variables, any differences in the plants could be attributed to the single experimental variable — the fertilizer.

In your experiment the plant without the fertilizer was the **control subject**. The plant with the fertilizer was the **experimental subject**. In a controlled experiment the control and experimental subjects are treated in exactly the same way except for the experimental variable.

Suppose that the geranium with the fertilizer had not blossomed in your experiment. You would conclude that your hypothesis was probably incorrect. Then you might develop another hypothesis. Perhaps your geraniums need more sunlight. You could design another experiment with a different experimental variable (sunlight) to test your new hypothesis.

When scientists want to answer a question, they often start out with the same steps described in the geranium experiment. These steps are part of the **research method**. The steps of the research method are

1. observing;
2. defining the problem or question;
3. forming a hypothesis;
4. testing the hypothesis with an experiment or observation;
5. observing and recording results;
6. drawing conclusions;
7. reporting or publishing results.

A list like this may suggest that scientists follow the research method as they would a cookbook recipe, but this is not so. The "steps" of the research method are just a description of a good problem solving procedure.

Some hypotheses cannot be tested by laboratory experiments. Comparing the numbers of smokers and nonsmokers who get cancer is not a laboratory experiment, but it does support the hypothesis that smoking causes cancer. Biologists can observe the migration routes of birds, but they cannot test their findings in a controlled experiment.

Figure 1.12 Using a computer to record and analyze data

1–5   Scientific Theories

An artist will often make a number of rough sketches before doing an oil painting. Hypotheses are like these rough sketches. They are working ideas that are constantly changed to fit new experimental data. If many scientists test a hypothesis over and over again and the experimental results always support the hypothesis, it becomes widely accepted as a correct explanation. When a hypothesis explains many observations and leads to predictions that are continually supported by experiments, it may be called a **scientific theory**.

The word *theory* is defined carefully in science. People often use the word to mean an idea that is uncertain. In science the word *theory* means something quite different. A scientific theory is an idea that is widely accepted as a correct explanation because it has been supported by many observations and experiments and continues to explain new observations.

Figure 1.13 Doctors in the nineteenth century theorized that men and women breathe differently. They thought that men expanded their chests, using the diaphragm (a layer of muscle below the ribs), and that women raised their ribs. The observations of many doctors supported this theory until a woman doctor discovered that women could also breathe using the diaphragm. They did not, only because the current fashion was to cinch the waist so tightly that the diaphragm couldn't move.

Figure 1.14 Louis Pasteur

A scientific theory can be changed if new and contradictory evidence is uncovered. But scientists do not expect theories to be completely thrown out. It is more common for theories to be modified slightly in the light of new evidence.

Notice also that scientists generally avoid the use of the word *proof*. Evidence can support a hypothesis or a theory, but it cannot prove a theory to be true. It is always possible that in the future a new idea will provide a better explanation of the evidence.

One theory that is accepted by biologists today is the germ theory of disease. It was first suggested as a hypothesis just a little over 100 years ago.

Before the germ theory people did not know the causes of disease. For thousands of years people tried many different "cures." Unfortunately, few of these "cures" were useful, since they were not directed at the actual cause of diseases.

When biologists first began to use microscopes, they discovered tiny living things called **microorganisms**. As biologists used microscopes more and more, they realized that microorganisms were everywhere. Scientists began to notice the connection between microorganisms and disease.

In the nineteenth century a great French biologist, Louis Pasteur, showed that some human diseases are caused by microorganisms growing inside the human body. When Pasteur first suggested that microorganisms can cause disease, the idea was only a hypothesis. Very few people accepted it. As scientists did more experiments and made more observations that supported the hypothesis, it became the germ *theory* of disease. Scientists now agree that Pasteur's original hypothesis explains much about some human diseases.

Once biologists understood the cause of many diseases, they were able to develop methods to prevent them. Diseases that were once greatly feared, such as typhoid fever and polio, are now rare in many countries.

Today when scientists try to cure a disease, they first look for a microorganism that causes the disease. No one expects that the germ theory of disease will turn out to be wrong. Many thousands of observations fit the theory. It is extremely unlikely that new observations will result in rejection of the germ theory.

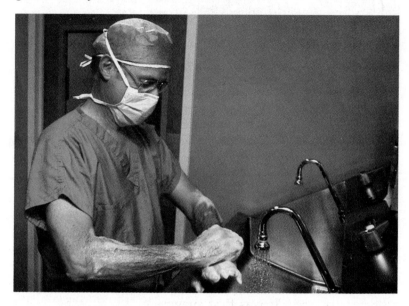

Figure 1.15 An understanding of the germ theory led to methods of disease prevention. Surgeons now scrub their hands and arms thoroughly with special soap to protect their patients from infection.

1–6 Science Is Unpredictable

The course of scientific research is not always predictable. Designing hypotheses and experiments that convince other scientists is not easy.

Research on a particular question may produce unexpected results that raise new questions and send research in a new direction. New equipment, such as the electron microscope, can open up whole new areas of scientific research. Then the amount of information in those areas will grow explosively.

Sometimes a correct hypothesis is made before there is enough information to support it. Consider the story of the Hungarian doctor, Ignaz Semmelweis. Semmelweis worked in a hospital in Vienna, Austria, some 40 years before the germ theory of disease was even suggested. At that time, many women died of a fever after delivering children.

Semmelweis observed a connection between women who died of childbed fever and doctors who did not wash their hands before assisting in the delivery. Semmelweis then insisted that the doctors in his hospital carefully wash their hands before assisting in deliveries. The number of women who died of fever dropped dramatically.

Today Semmelweis's conclusion may seem obvious, but the doctors of his day resisted it. Doctors were, perhaps, unwilling to admit that they were the cause of the problem. Remember that the germ theory was still some 40 years in the future. With no theory to explain how dirty hands could cause fever, the idea was difficult to accept. Semmelweis died in 1862, a defeated man who had failed to convince more than a few that his ideas were correct.

Just as the steps of the research method do not take resistance to new ideas into account, neither do they recognize the importance of luck. Sometimes accidents play an important role in science. In 1928 a British scientist named Alexander Fleming was growing microorganisms on plates of food material. Such plates have a cloudy appearance when microorganisms grow evenly across the surface. One day Fleming noticed that one of his plates had fuzzy green spots on it. This contamination interfered with Fleming's experiments. Though many researchers might have simply thrown out the contaminated plate, Fleming studied it closely. He noticed that there was a clear area around the green fuzz, as shown in Figure 1.16.

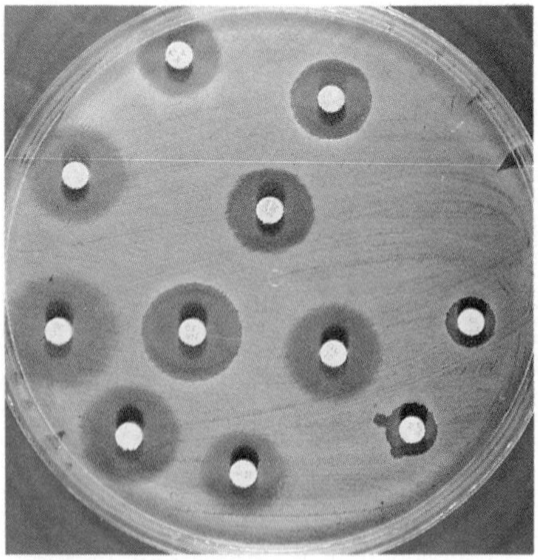

The clear area on the plate was free of microorganisms. Evidently, the green material produced something that killed the microorganisms on the plate. That observation led to the discovery of **penicillin**. Today penicillin is one of the most important substances used by doctors to kill microorganisms that cause human diseases.

Figure 1.16. How can you explain the clear areas where no microorganisms are living?

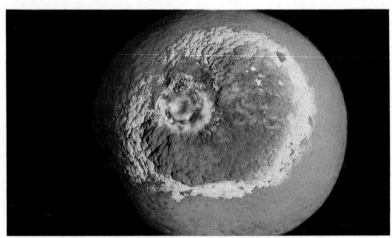

Figure 1.17 The moldy growth on this orange can easily be grown in a laboratory to produce penicillin.

Figure 1.18 In 1839, Charles Goodyear accidentally discovered a way to make rubber tougher and more heat resistant. This discovery made rubber a much more useful material.

Chance observations such as Fleming's are surprisingly common in the history of science. But as Louis Pasteur once said, "In the field of observation, chance favors only the prepared mind." Fleming was prepared to recognize the significance of the clear area on the plate. Other observers might have missed it completely.

Keep two things in mind as you study biology. First, the facts and theories presented here represent the efforts of thousands of scientists over hundreds of years. These scientists have tried to create the most reliable picture possible of the way living things work. Most of the theories presented here are valid because they have been repeatedly tested and confirmed.

Second, biology is a constantly growing and changing body of knowledge. Some of the theories presented here will change as new information becomes available. Perhaps you will think of questions that are not answered in this book. You may be able to find the answers to your questions somewhere else, or perhaps the answers are not yet known. The excitement of biology lies in its continuing search for a more thorough understanding of how living things work.

Checkpoint

1. Scientists devise temporary explanations for questions they ask. What is the term for such temporary explanations?
2. What is the information collected in an experiment called?
3. What do you call an experiment in which only one factor is allowed to vary?
4. A hypothesis that has been tested many times and has been found to explain many different observations may become a _____ .
5. Which theory states that microorganisms cause certain human diseases?
6. What important discovery was the result of an accidental observation in Alexander Fleming's laboratory?

CHAPTER REVIEW

Summary

- Science is a way of finding out how the world works. Scientists obtain much of their information from observing the world carefully and precisely. Science is objective; the results of scientific investigations can be repeated.

- Scientists use tools to help them gather information. One of the most important tools of the biologist is the microscope. Various kinds of microscopes are used to magnify objects that are too small to be seen by the eye alone. Compound microscopes are useful for magnifying objects up to 1,000 times. Electron microscopes have greater resolving power than compound microscopes.

- Much information of scientific interest can be obtained by collecting observations. Often, however, observations lead to questions that must be answered by experiments.

- Scientists frequently use the research method to solve problems. They form a hypothesis to explain an observation or answer a question. A controlled experiment is done to test the hypothesis. The results of the experiment determine whether the hypothesis should be accepted or rejected.

- Results of experiments and observations are published in journals so that other scientists can have access to them.

- A hypothesis that has received a lot of experimental support and continues to make reliable predictions may become a scientific theory.

- Although the research method is a general description of what scientists do, it is not a set of instructions to be followed rigidly. Often luck plays a part in scientific work.

- Science is constantly changing and growing as new information becomes available.

Vocabulary

biologist	hypothesis
biology	microorganism
compound microscope	microscope
controlled	objective
experiment	ocular
control subject	penicillin
data	research method
electron microscope	resolving power
experiment	scanning electron
experimental subject	microscope
experimental	scientific theory
variable	simple microscope
eyepiece	variable

Review

1. What is the name of the procedure that scientists often follow to solve problems?
2. How do scientists share the information from their observations?
3. What group of living things was discovered with the aid of the microscope?
4. Which lens of a compound microscope is closest to the specimen being viewed?
5. The lenses of an electron microscope are made of _____.
6. How is the electron microscope an improvement over the compound microscope?
7. What kind of electron microscope is used to look at surfaces of objects rather than through thin slices?
8. What do scientists call the preliminary explanation they give for a particular question?
9. In any experiment, what is a factor that changes?
10. An explanation supported by a large number of experimental results may become known as a _____.

Interpret and Apply

1. Name a common superstition and explain why it is a superstition.
2. Your compound microscope has two objectives; one is 10× and the other is 43×.
   a. Which would you use to locate an object?
   b. Which would you use for examining the object in more detail?
3. What would happen to the total magnification of a compound microscope if a 5× objective were substituted for a 10× objective?
4. State Semmelweis's hypothesis in an "If . . . then" form.

Questions 5–9 are based on the following:

A group of scientists are interested in testing a new chemical as a mosquito repellent. Two volunteers participate in the experiment. In part I of the experiment each volunteer places one arm in a container for two minutes with 100 hungry mosquitoes. In part II the other arm of each volunteer is sprayed with the new chemical repellent. Then each volunteer places the sprayed arm into a second cage with 100 new hungry mosquitoes. The following data are collected:

	Number of Bites without Spray	Number of Bites with Spray
Volunteer A	20	2
Volunteer B	35	10

5. State the hypothesis being tested by this experiment in "If . . . then" form.
6. What variable is being tested in this experiment?
7. What is the control in the experiment?
8. What variables were *not* controlled in this experiment?
9. Do the data support the hypothesis?

Challenge

1. Human memory tends to be selective. People often remember events that seem to fit patterns and forget events that don't fit patterns. How might this tendency allow many superstitions to remain in our culture?
2. Explain what is wrong with the following: Photographs can be enlarged as much as you want. It is possible, for example, to enlarge a snapshot to the size of a billboard. If you enlarge a snapshot of your pet dog enough, you should be able to see the fleas on the dog's fur. Even greater enlargement should show microorganisms on the legs of the fleas.
3. Two plants are placed in a window. Both get the same attention, but one of them dies.
   a. State a hypothesis that you could test to find out what happened.
   b. Describe an experiment to test the hypothesis.
   c. Describe results of such an experiment that could support your hypothesis.

Projects

1. Find out how a lens magnifies an object. If you can find two simple magnifying lenses, try to make a compound microscope out of them.
2. Investigate the process of taking photographs through a microscope. If you have access to standard photographic equipment, you might want to try some photomicrography.
3. Form a hypothesis about the effect of sunlight on plant growth. Design and carry out a controlled experiment to test your hypothesis.
4. Research the history of a particular discovery in biology and describe how the scientists involved arrived at their conclusion. You might want to look at the discovery of cells or the discovery of the circulation of blood.
5. Interview several people in your community who use science in their jobs. Find out how the scientific methods described in this chapter apply to their work.

2 The Characteristics of Life

Lion at sunset

As you know, there are obvious differences among living things. A one-year-old child has no difficulty distinguishing a cat from a caterpillar or a lion from a dandelion. In fact, on quick inspection, a lion and a dandelion appear to have nothing whatsoever in common.

One captures its food; the other manufactures its food from sunlight. One stalks across the landscape in pursuit of its prey; the other remains stationary in the grass. One is a tawny mass of several hundred kilograms; the other is a few grams of bright yellow petals and green leaves.

Yet, because the lion and the dandelion are both living things, they are similar in many ways. All living things have certain features and activities in common. What characteristics do cats and caterpillars, lions and dandelions, share that make them different from a rock or a rocking chair? Just what does it mean to be alive?

Recognizing Life

There are many nonliving objects that look or act like living things. For example, some plastic plants look real from a distance. But close inspection reveals that they are imitations.

Certainly, living and nonliving things have some features in common. Other characteristics, however, are found only in organisms. **Organism** is another name for a living thing, whether plant or animal. The following sections describe the features all organisms have in common.

2–1 Movement and Response

Movement is a characteristic of living things. Animals walk, crawl, hop, fly, and swim. Plants don't seem to move in the obvious ways that animals do. Yet many flowers open and close daily. In some plants, leaves move during the day as they follow the sun across the sky.

When the leaves of a plant follow the sun, they are reacting to the stimulus of the moving sun. A **stimulus** [STIHM-yuh-luhs] is any change in the surroundings that causes a reaction in an organism. All organisms react to stimuli (plural of *stimulus*).

The reaction of an organism to a stimulus is a **response**. When a dog comes running at the sound of its owner's whistle, it is responding to the stimulus of a sound. Responses to stimuli are usually less obvious in plants than in animals. One plant that does show an obvious and rapid response is the mimosa, shown in Figure 2.2. If you touch a mimosa leaf, all the small leaflets on the branch fold upward.

- characteristics common to all living things
- how living things obtain food
- adaptation and response to the environment

Figure 2.1 Some nonliving things, such as these glass flowers, can look very alive and real.

Figure 2.2 This mimosa responds dramatically to touch.

Response to stimuli is not unique to organisms, however. A waving flag is responding to the wind. A piece of iron moves in response to a nearby magnet. Therefore, response to a stimulus does not necessarily distinguish living from nonliving things. There must be other characteristics of life in addition to movement and response.

2–2   Energy from the Environment

Energy is the ability to do work, and all organisms require energy. Organisms get energy from their surroundings in the form of food. You can probably think of many examples of the ways animals get food. Plants also require food, but they can make their own with the aid of sunlight.

Because plants can manufacture their own food, they are called **autotrophs** [AW-tuh-trohfs]. Autotrophs produce their own food within their bodies. Most autotrophs are plants. Given enough sunlight, autotrophs make food from carbon dioxide and water by a process called **photosynthesis** [foh-toh-SIHN-thuh-sihs].

Organisms that cannot manufacture their own food are called **heterotrophs** [HET-ur-uh-trohfs]. Because heterotrophs cannot make food within their bodies, they must eat other organisms to stay alive. Cows and caterpillars are heterotrophs that get food by eating plants (autotrophs). Cats and coyotes are heterotrophs that get their food by eating other animals (heterotrophs).

Remember that life would not be possible if organisms did not get a constant supply of energy from their environment. The **environment** [ehn-VY-ruhn-muhnt] is all living and nonliving things that make up the surroundings of the organism. For autotrophs, energy to make food comes from sunlight. For heterotrophs, food comes from other organisms.

Figure 2.3 Energy for living things comes either directly or indirectly from the sun.

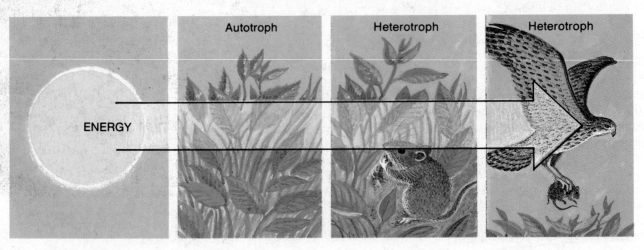

ENERGY

Autotroph   Heterotroph   Heterotroph

2–3 Production of Wastes

When living things take energy from food, they release waste energy. Waste energy leaves organisms in the form of heat. Organisms also get rid of chemical wastes. For example, one of the most common waste chemicals is carbon dioxide.

Yet the use of energy from the environment and the production of wastes are not unique to life. Many nonliving things also use energy and produce waste products. For example, a car engine releases energy from gasoline ("food") to make the car move. Waste heat is lost to the environment. Waste chemicals, including carbon dioxide, leave the engine through the exhaust pipe.

Figure 2.4 The fennec is a desert fox that gets rid of waste heat through the large surface area of its ears.

So far you have seen that movement, response, energy use, and waste production are characteristics of life. Yet these features are sometimes found in nonliving things as well. Are there characteristics that are unique to living things?

2–4 Growth and Reproduction

Children grow, pets grow, plants grow. All living things grow at some time in their lives, but some nonliving things seem to grow, too. If you live in a cold climate, you have probably seen icicles growing on buildings in the winter. Like the characteristics discussed earlier, growth in size cannot alone define life.

In addition to growing, organisms reproduce. **Reproduction** is the process by which organisms produce offspring that are similar to themselves. In fact, growth and reproduction go together. Organisms produce offspring, which themselves grow and reproduce. It is characteristic of living things that offspring are similar to their parents.

Figure 2.5 Stalactites and stalagmites, like icicles, appear to grow but are, in fact, nonliving.

Is reproduction a characteristic that alone defines living things? Think about a candle flame. Such a flame can reproduce as often as you hold the wick of another candle to the original flame. Each new flame will grow and be able to produce other flames.

The flame also shows other characteristics of living things. It moves in response to a breeze. The flame requires "food" from the environment. If the flame's supply of wax runs out, the flame "dies." Furthermore, the flame produces waste heat and waste chemicals, including carbon dioxide. A flame seems to have all the characteristics described so far — movement, response, energy use, waste production, growth, and reproduction. But of course a flame is not living. To find out why a flame is not alive requires close observation of living things.

2–5 Presence of Water and Organic Chemicals

Scientists have made several generalizations about living things based on centuries of careful observations. For example, every living thing ever studied requires water to stay alive. This characteristic alone eliminates the candle flame as a living thing.

Figure 2.6 Every living thing ever studied requires water to stay alive.

All organisms contain certain kinds of chemicals that are not naturally produced anywhere else. These are called **organic chemicals**. Many organic chemicals are complex and highly organized. Complex organic chemicals can be made in test tubes by scientists, but only living things produce them under natural conditions.

2-6   Presence of Cells

Every living thing is made of microscopic units called **cells**. Some organisms are made of many cells; others have just a few or only one cell. But cells are unique to living things. No nonliving thing is made of live cells. (A dead organism may still have cells, but the cells have stopped working.)

Each individual cell in an organism is alive. It has all the characteristics of life mentioned in this chapter. In fact, within cells you can find the characteristics that separate living things from nonliving things.

A cell is a complex structure made of many smaller parts. Like a complex piece of machinery the parts of a cell must work together in an organized way if the entire cell is to function smoothly. Cells use much of the energy they get from food to maintain the organization of all their parts.

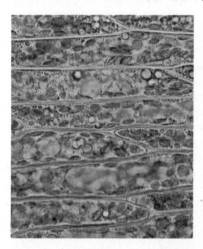 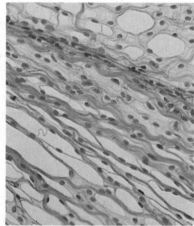

Figure 2.7 *Left:* Cells in water plants; *Right:* Human skin cells

2-7   Metabolism

Organisms require energy to grow and reproduce. Organisms and their cells do not grow as icicles do. Icicles get larger as ice is added to their outside surfaces. Organisms grow by adding living cells inside their bodies or by increasing the size of individual cells.

Organisms use energy to make new cells, to fuel growth, to repair cells, and to control the activity of each cell. The chemical processes of getting energy from food and using it to maintain the structure and function of a cell is called **metabolism** [muh-TAB-uh-liz-uhm].

In order to stay alive, organisms must release energy from food constantly. A running car engine stops when no more energy is available. If more energy is supplied later, the engine will work again. A cell cannot stop using energy. When a cell runs out of energy, it dies.

Figure 2.8 Babies need much food energy to make new cells and fuel growth.

2–8 Inheritance and Development

The reproduction of a living thing is very different from the reproduction of a candle flame. Living things inherit from their parents a coded set of "instructions" on how to develop into a new organism. **Inheritance** means passing characteristics from one generation to the next.

The stages that an individual organism goes through from the moment it begins life until it reaches adulthood are called **development**. The history of an organism from birth through reproduction and death is called the **life cycle** of that organism. Development and life cycles are not found in nonliving things.

2–9 Adaptation to the Environment

The instructions that an organism inherits from its parents allow it to live in its environment. A fish inherits gills and fins that allow it to live in water. The gills and fins are adaptations. An **adaptation** is a structure or behavior that allows survival in a particular environment.

You know, for example, that a cactus cannot live in the ocean, nor can a starfish live in a desert. Each is adapted to live in a particular kind of place.

The cactus lives where water is rarely available. It is adapted to store large amounts of water. Some other adaptations are shown in Figure 2.9. Adaptations are so universal in living things that biologists consider adaptations to be an important characteristic of life.

Figure 2.9 *Left:* These flowers are specially adapted to attract insects. *Right:* The shape of a dolphin's body is streamlined so it can move through water smoothly and easily.

As you can see, the candle flame fails many of the tests for being a living thing. It does not require water. It does not have cells. It does not use energy to maintain structure and organization. When a flame grows, it does not undergo development. When it reproduces, its "offspring" do not inherit a complex set of coded instructions. Finally, flames are not specifically adapted to any particular environment.

2–10 Summarizing the Characteristics of Life

You have seen that there is no single characteristic that defines living things. Recall the discussion of the lion and the dandelion at the beginning of this chapter. No matter how different these organisms appear, they share many characteristics that separate them from nonliving things. While a nonliving thing may have one or a few of the characteristics of life, only living things have all of them. All organisms

1. move;
2. respond to stimuli;
3. require energy from the environment;
4. produce waste energy and chemicals;
5. carry out metabolism and maintain internal organization;
6. grow from within;
7. require water;
8. make organic chemicals;
9. are made of cells;
10. inherit characteristics from parents and reproduce by passing coded information from one generation to the next;
11. have adaptations that help them survive in their environment.

Checkpoint

1. The reaction of an organism to a stimulus is called a
   _____ .
2. What is the name of the process by which plants make their own food with the aid of sunlight?
3. What is the name of the process by which cells use energy to maintain organization, to grow, and to carry out other activities?
4. What kinds of organisms are autotrophs?
5. What is a structure or behavior that allows an organism to survive in a particular environment?

Biogenesis: Life Produces Life

CONCEPTS
- living things are produced only by other living things
- the experimental evidence that finally disproved the notion of spontaneous generation

The idea that living things are produced only from other living things has not always seemed obvious. After spring rains, frogs, insects, and plants seem to materialize from the dried out mud of ponds. A piece of meat left outside will soon be covered with wormlike organisms. Three hundred years ago people took such observations as proof that some living things could appear from nonliving sources. People also once believed that one kind of organism could give rise to another completely different kind of organism. Such beliefs were common at a time when people did not understand the differences between living and nonliving things.

2–11   Spontaneous Generation of Animals

The idea that living things can arise from nonliving material is called **spontaneous generation** or **abiogenesis** [ay-by-oh-JEHN-uh-sihs]. Aristotle, the ancient Greek scientist and philospher, concluded that spontaneous generation was a reasonable explanation for the origin of some organisms. For almost 2,000 years after Aristotle, people saw no reason to doubt his authority.

As late as the 1600s most people accepted the idea of spontaneous generation of some animals. A well-known Belgian doctor of the time, Jan Baptist van Helmont, even wrote a recipe for making mice by throwing grain and some old rags

Figure 2.10 This early woodcut illustrates the incorrect notion that one kind of organism can give rise to another.

into the corner of a room! What eventually happened to the idea of spontaneous generation is an excellent example of how science works.

In the 1660s an Italian doctor named Francesco Redi challenged the idea of spontaneous generation. He became interested in the question of how decaying meat produces "worms" called maggots. Before doing controlled experiments Redi made careful observations. He let some decaying meat stand in an open box for a long time. As he expected, maggots appeared.

Most people would have stopped watching at that point, but Redi continued. After about 20 days the maggots formed hard shells around themselves. In another week or so, adult flies emerged from the shells. Redi recalled having seen flies of the same type landing on the meat in the early days of his observations. The maggots were actually young forms of the fly. Until Redi's study no one had ever observed the entire life cycle of flies.

Redi proposed a hypothesis to explain the origin of maggots. He said they were not spontaneously generated but came from eggs that flies laid on meat. Redi's hypothesis was testable. He set up an experiment in which his hypothesis and the idea of spontaneous generation predict different results.

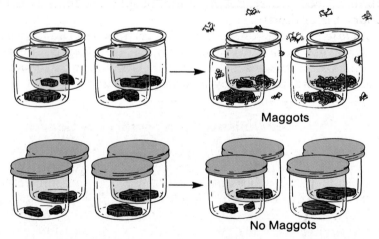

Maggots

No Maggots

Figure 2.11 Redi first compared sealed jars of meat with jars of meat left open to the air.

Redi's experiment is illustrated in Figure 2.11. He put four different kinds of meat into separate containers and sealed them tightly. He put the same kinds of meat into four other containers, which he did not cover. (How is this a good example of a controlled experiment?) If spontaneous generation were true, maggots should have appeared in all eight containers. But if the maggots came from flies' eggs, the maggots should have appeared only in the open jars where the flies could land on the meat. In fact, maggots appeared only in the open containers, confirming Redi's hypothesis.

Redi was a good scientist. He repeated the experiment many times with different kinds of meat, different kinds of jars, and at different seasons of the year. He always got the same results. (And he must have been a dedicated scientist, since he had to live with the awful smell of rotting meat!)

Redi even anticipated a possible objection to this experiment. Those who believed in spontaneous generation could say that air must be allowed to circulate freely into the closed jars. Air might carry some "active principle" necessary for spontaneous generation to occur. Figure 2.12 shows a setup in which jars containing meat samples were covered with a fine mesh cloth. The cloth allowed air to enter the containers but prevented flies from reaching the meat. Redi observed flies landing on the cloth and even laying eggs on it. Some of the eggs on the cloth hatched into small maggots. But the meat itself never grew maggots.

As a good scientist, Redi never claimed that his experiments disproved spontaneous generation in general. He had shown only that it does not take place in the case of maggots on meat. In fact, Redi himself believed that spontaneous generation produced wormlike animals inside galls, which are swollen growths on plant stems and leaves. Valisneri, a pupil of Redi, showed that many plant galls are caused by wasps that lay eggs on the plant.

In the century after Redi's death other scientists did experiments similar to his. They showed that spontaneous generation could not explain the origin of any animal that could be seen without a microscope. However, the idea of spontaneous generation was not yet totally rejected.

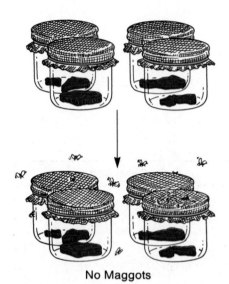

No Maggots

Figure 2.12 When Redi covered jars of meat with fine mesh, no maggots appeared on the meat.

2–12 Microorganisms and Spontaneous Generation

As you recall from Chapter 1, Anton van Leeuwenhoek was one of the first people to make and use microscopes. With his simple microscopes he looked at pond water, rainwater, scrapings from his teeth, and hundreds of other substances. In 1676 Leeuwenhoek made a remarkable discovery. Wherever he looked through his microscope, he saw organisms by the thousands — all too small to be seen without magnification.

The idea of spontaneous generation gained new support with the discovery of microorganisms. To test the idea, eighteenth-century scientists made mixtures called **infusions** [ihn-FYOO-zhuhns]. These consisted of water and food material heated to form a clear broth. Within a day or two almost any infusion became cloudy. The microscope revealed that the cloudy infusion was teeming with millions of microorganisms. These organisms truly did seem to appear from nonliving substances.

In 1748 a Scottish scientist named John Turberville Needham performed an experiment like those of Redi. He boiled an infusion of meat to kill any microorganisms in it. Then he sealed the container with a cork. As a control, Needham left another container of boiled meat infusion open to the air. In both containers microorganisms appeared! Since heating kills microorganisms and since the experimental container was sealed, Needham seemed to have found evidence that supported the idea of spontaneous generation of microorganisms.

Several decades later an Italian scientist named Lazzaro Spallanzani read about Needham's experiments and decided to do some of his own. Recall that in science repeating the results of an experiment is important. Spallanzani performed an experiment similar to Needham's, but with some important changes. The two experiments are compared in Figure 2.13. Spallanzani believed that microorganisms were carried in the air. He did not think Needham's corks provided a good enough seal to keep out such small organisms.

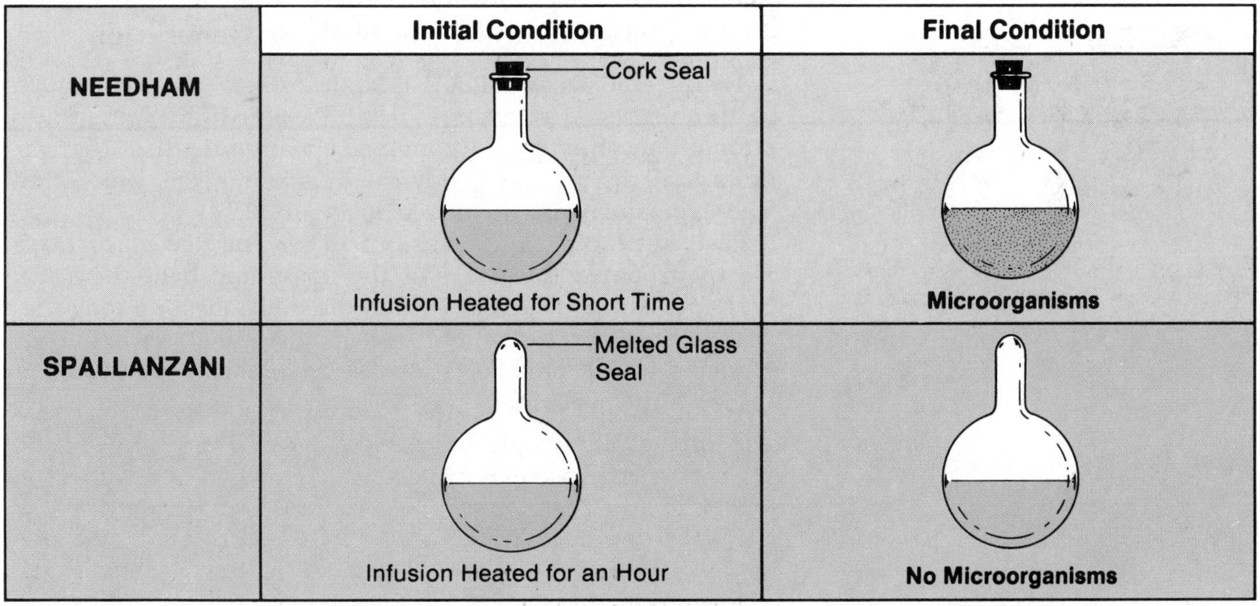

	Initial Condition	Final Condition
NEEDHAM	Cork Seal Infusion Heated for Short Time	Microorganisms
SPALLANZANI	Melted Glass Seal Infusion Heated for an Hour	No Microorganisms

Figure 2.13 The experiments of Needham and Spallanzani

Spallanzani placed infusions of plant materials in glass containers. He then heated the mouths of the containers until the glass melted and sealed the openings completely. Spallanzani knew that microorganisms can be very resistant to heat. He had shown in earlier experiments that boiling infusions for five or ten minutes did not destroy all the organisms in an infusion. So Spallanzani boiled his sealed containers for almost an hour. (CAUTION: Do not try this experiment yourself. Steam pressure could cause the containers to explode.)

After boiling, Spallanzani's sealed containers stayed free of microorganisms as long as he kept them sealed. If the top of a container was broken, however, microorganisms could be found in the infusion within hours. These results supported the idea that microorganisms are present in the air and multiply when they fall into an infusion.

Although Spallanzani's experiments were well designed, well controlled, and well carried out, the idea of spontaneous generation did not die then. In fact, the argument continued for another 100 years.

One major objection to the Spallanzani experiments was similar to an objection Redi had encountered. In Spallanzani's case, critics said that heating destroyed some "active principle" in the air. Spallanzani could not refute this objection, because he believed that fresh air carried microorganisms and heating the air killed them. He could not think of an experiment in which he could kill microorganisms and at the same time show he had not destroyed some active principle. As you know, ideas in science rarely change easily.

2–13   Pasteur and Spontaneous Generation

The French scientist Louis Pasteur is one of the great figures in the history of science. In 1861 Pasteur did a remarkably simple experiment that convinced many scientists that microorganisms are not produced by spontaneous generation. The experiment is illustrated in Figure 2.14.

Pasteur placed clear infusions in long-necked glass flasks. He then heated the necks of the flasks and bent them into S-shaped curves. Pasteur heated the infusions for a long time at high temperatures. This procedure killed any microorganisms inside the flasks. Unlike Spallanzani's sealed containers, however, these flasks let air pass in and out easily. No one could object that an "active principle" in the air had been kept out of the flasks.

Figure 2.14 Pasteur's experiment

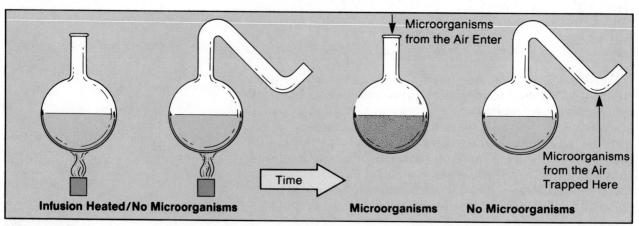

Figure 2.15 Pasteur's original flasks, still free of microorganisms

Although air could pass through the necks of the flasks, dust particles carrying microorganisms could not get through the S-shaped curves without being trapped in water droplets. (These droplets accumulated on the necks of the flasks during the heating of the infusion.)

As a control Pasteur broke the necks of several flasks to remove the curve. In every case, dust from the air settled into the flask and the infusion turned cloudy. The same thing happened when he tipped the flasks to permit contact between the infusion and the water droplets in the neck.

Pasteur's flasks stayed free of organisms as long as they were undisturbed. In fact, flasks from Pasteur's original experiments have been preserved in Paris. They are still crystal clear.

By his experiments Pasteur demonstrated that there are microorganisms in the air, the water, the soil, and everywhere. If care is taken to prevent the growth of these organisms, they cannot appear in nonliving material.

Within 20 years after Pasteur's experiments the idea of spontaneous generation was dead. In 1870 the English scientist Thomas Henry Huxley first used the term **biogenesis** [by-oh-JEHN-us-sihs] to mean that all living things arise from other living things of the same type. We now know that biogenesis is the only way organisms are produced and that it is, in fact, a characteristic of life.

 BIOLOGY INSIGHTS

Biological science depends upon evidence gathered by many different scientists over many years. The establishment of the principle of biogenesis is an excellent example of this process. The controlled experiments performed by Redi and Pasteur can be repeated by scientists today.

Checkpoint

1. What are two names for the belief that living things can arise from nonliving matter?
2. Who showed that spontaneous generation could not explain the appearance of maggots on decaying meat?
3. What were the two major differences between Needham's and Spallanzani's experiments?
4. What was the major difference between Spallanzani's experiment and Pasteur's experiment?

CHAPTER REVIEW

Summary

- Living things show many characteristics at the same time. Nonliving things may show one or a few of these characteristics but never all of them at once. These characteristics include
  1. movement and response;
  2. energy use and the production of wastes;
  3. growth and reproduction;
  4. need for water.
- Characteristics found only in living things include
  1. cells;
  2. presence of complex organic chemicals;
  3. metabolism, or the use of energy to carry out body activities and maintain cell organization;
  4. inheritance and development;
  5. adaptation to the environment.
- Spontaneous generation, the belief that some living things can be produced from nonliving things, was once a widely accepted idea. Experiments by Redi, Spallanzani, and Pasteur showed that organisms could arise only from other, similar organisms. This idea is called biogenesis.

Vocabulary

abiogenesis	life cycle
adaptation	metabolism
autotroph	organic chemical
biogenesis	organism
cell	photosynthesis
development	reproduction
environment	response
heterotroph	spontaneous
infusion	generation
inheritance	stimulus

Review

1. An organism responds to a _____.
2. What kinds of organisms carry out photosynthesis?
3. What group of organisms cannot make their own food?
4. What kind of energy do plants need in order to carry out photosynthesis?
5. The living and nonliving things surrounding an organism make up the _____.
6. List at least four characteristics that are found in all living things but not in nonliving things.
7. Name one observation that was used to support the idea that spontaneous generation occurs.
8. Who was the ancient Greek scientist who stated that some animals arose by spontaneous generation?
9. Francesco Redi was the first person to observe the life cycle of what organism?
10. What was the objection to Redi's first experiment?
11. Who discovered the existence of microorganisms?
12. The experiments of Redi, Needham, Spallanzani, and Pasteur were described in this chapter. Which of these scientists had evidence that supported abiogenesis? Biogenesis?

Interpret and Apply

1. In general, how does movement in plants differ from movement in animals?
2. What happens to the energy taken into an organism?
3. How is reproduction of a candle flame different from reproduction in living things?
4. What two observations caused Redi to suspect that flies were somehow involved in the appearance of "worms" on decaying meat?

5. In Redi's first experiment with the eight jars, what was the experimental variable?
6. What did Redi claim that the results of his experiments showed?
7. In Needham's experiment, what was the control subject?
8. What observation did Spallanzani make that indicated to him that Needham's experiments were not controlled carefully enough?
9. How did Pasteur's flasks keep microorganisms from entering the infusion?

Challenge

1. How does the movement of an animal differ from the movement of a windup toy?
2. How is the use of energy by a candle flame different from the use of energy by living things?
3. Using the characteristics of living things, what distinction can you make between something that is dead and something that was never alive?
4. Occasionally, when you open a bag of flour, you find some mealworms. Give a reasonable explanation of how these organisms might have gotten into the flour bag.
5. Scientists now know that many microorganisms can form spores that are extremely heat resistant. How could this fact have led to the apparently contradictory results of Needham and Spallanzani?

Questions 6–10 are based on the following information:

Even though Pasteur's experiments sound conclusive today, they did not convince all of the supporters of spontaneous generation who lived during the nineteenth century. Many other experiments were necessary to finally discredit the idea of spontaneous generation of microorganisms. Some of these experiments were preformed by the British physicist John Tyndall.

To perform his experiments Tyndall constructed a special glass box. The top of this box could be sealed from the outside air, but from the side projected a curved glass tube that was open to the air.

By shining a light through the glass sides of the box, Tyndall could see whether dust was floating in the air inside. When he allowed the box to remain motionless for several days, the air in the box would be free of dust.

Tyndall then placed test tubes filled with boiled infusions in the bottom of the box. He tried this when there was dust in the air and when there was none. These were his results:

a. Whenever there was dust in the air, the infusions in the test tubes became cloudy.
b. If there was no dust in the air, the infusions in the test tubes remained clear for months, as long as the air in the box was not disturbed.

6. What hypothesis do you think Tyndall's experiment was testing?
7. What was the experimental variable in his experiment?
8. What was the control in his experiment?
9. What conclusion would you draw from Tyndall's results?
10. Why do you think Tyndall built a glass tube on the side of his box?

Projects

1. In 1976 two robot spacecraft called *Vikings* were sent by the United States to look for life on the planet Mars. Find out what the experiments were designed to do and what the results of the experiments were. How do scientists explain the results that originally indicated that there may be life on Mars?
2. Find out how people do home canning of vegetables that grow in their gardens. Explain how these procedures relate to the experiments on spontaneous generation described in this chapter.
3. Pasteurization is a process named after Louis Pasteur. Find out what the process is, how it is done, and why it is done.

3 The Chemistry of Matter

Iceberg in Lancaster Sound,
the Arctic

Water is all around us. No other planet in the solar system has so much liquid water. All living things contain water and depend on the unusual properties of water to survive.

What is so unusual about water? Compared to other substances, water can absorb or give off large amounts of heat while changing very little in temperature. During an average day heat from sunlight can heat up the air, soil, or rocks by a large amount while the temperature of water in a lake will barely change. If water temperature changed as fast as the air temperature, many organisms living in water would die.

Most liquids shrink when they freeze. But water expands when it freezes. For this reason ice floats on water. Even though a lake is frozen on top, organisms can survive winter in the liquid water at the bottom of the lake.

You will see that water has many other properties that make it essential to life. Water has these characteristics because of its chemistry. An understanding of the chemistry of water and other substances is necessary to an understanding of living things.

Atoms: Building Blocks of Matter

By the early part of this century biologists realized that they could never understand living things unless they could understand the smallest parts of organisms. Cells are small, but they are made of even smaller parts. These parts themselves are made of particles too small to be seen. All the characteristics of life, such as growth, movement, and response, are a result of complicated changes in these particles. To understand what goes on in cells requires an understanding of some basic principles of chemistry.

3–1 Matter and Energy

According to modern physics, everything in the universe is either matter or energy. **Matter** is anything that has mass and occupies space. The three common forms of matter, shown in Figure 3.1 are called the **states of matter**. Solids have a definite shape and occupy a definite volume. Liquids have a definite volume but change shape to fill their containers. Gases have no definite shape or volume but instead spread out to fill whatever space is available.

Most substances can exist in any of the three states of matter. A change from one state to another is called a **physical change**. After a physical change the particles that make up the substance are the same. For example, ice, water, and water vapor are all made of the same kind of particles.

In all the states of matter the particles of a substance are in constant motion. Temperature is a measurement of how fast the particles are moving. The higher the temperature, the faster the particles move. The state of a substance depends on its temperature. For example, below 0°C water is a solid (ice). From 0°C to 100°C water is a liquid. Above 100°C water is a gas (water vapor).

Different substances undergo physical changes differently. At a temperature of −183°C, oxygen changes from a gas to a liquid. Gold does not melt into a liquid until it is heated to over 1000°C.

CONCEPTS

- three states of matter
- difference between physical and chemical changes
- properties of the electron, proton, and neutron
- atomic mass and atomic number
- isotopes and radioactivity

Figure 3.1 Particles in a solid are close together and move very little. In a liquid the particles are farther apart and move more. In a gas they are even farther apart and move freely.

Figure 3.2 The colors in autumn leaves are the result of chemical changes in the leaves.

If you heat sugar very carefully, the sugar will melt. Cooling will return the sugar to a solid state. These are physical changes. If you continue to heat melted sugar, it becomes a dark brown substance called caramel. Caramel is not sugar and will not turn back into sugar when cooled. When the particles of a substance are changed into different kinds of particles, the substance has undergone a **chemical change**.

Producing a chemical or physical change always involves energy. **Energy** is the ability to do work. You cannot weigh energy nor does it take up any space. Yet you are surrounded by energy and its effects. It takes energy to move your body and to move objects around you. Heat, electricity, and light are some of the different forms energy can have.

Any moving object has **kinetic** [kih-NEHT-ihk] **energy.** Kinetic energy is sometimes called the energy of motion. This motion may not be visible. Heating a substance causes the particles of the substance to vibrate faster, so the kinetic energy of the particles increases.

Figure 3.3 A cliff diver has potential energy when at the top of the cliff, and kinetic energy when diving.

An object does not have to be moving to have energy. Energy can also be stored, or **potential** [puh-TEHN-shuhl] **energy.** Figure 3.3 shows how a diver on a cliff has potential energy. As he dives, his potential energy is transformed into kinetic energy. Gasoline also has potential energy. Energy is stored in the gasoline. When a car engine burns gasoline, energy is released from the gasoline and the car can move. The food you eat has potential energy, which is released by your cells to do work.

3–2 Elements and Atoms

Everything in the universe is made of one or more elements. An **element** is a substance that cannot be chemically changed into a simpler substance. Oxygen, copper, and gold are familiar elements, but most elements are very rare. You have probably never heard of scandium and samarium, for example.

Scientists use a one- or two-letter **chemical symbol** to represent each of the elements. Figure 3.4 shows how common some of the elements are on Earth and in the human body. Next to each of the elements is the chemical symbol for that element. Only about 20 elements are common in living things. Over 95 percent of the matter in living things is made of the four elements carbon (C), oxygen (O), nitrogen (N), and hydrogen (H).

Each element is made of a single kind of **atom**. An atom is the smallest particle of an element that has the properties of the element. Atoms are incredibly small. A nugget of gold the size of the period at the end of this sentence contains more than 1,000,000,000,000,000,000 atoms.

A scientific model can help you imagine how atoms look and behave. Until 1911 the best scientific model for an atom was the billiard-ball model. Scientists thought atoms were like hard billiard balls that bounce off each other when they collide.

In 1911 scientists discovered that each atom is made of still smaller particles. In the center of each atom is a structure called a **nucleus**. The nucleus is made of particles called **protons** and **neutrons**. Spinning around the nucleus are much lighter particles called **electrons**. Figure 3.5 shows this model of an atom.

Element	Earth	Human Body
oxygen (O)	49.52	65.0
silicon (Si)	25.75	trace
iron (Fe)	4.70	0.004
calcium (Ca)	3.39	1.6
sodium (Na)	2.64	0.3
potassium (K)	2.40	0.4
magnesium (Mg)	1.94	0.05
hydrogen (H)	0.88	10.2
chlorine (Cl)	0.188	0.3
phosphorus (P)	0.12	0.9
carbon (C)	0.087	17.5
sulfur (S)	0.048	0.2
nitrogen (N)	0.030	2.4

Figure 3.4 Percentage of several elements in the earth's outer layer and the human body

 BIOLOGY INSIGHTS

The chemical composition of living things is very different from that of their environment. Organisms require energy to maintain this difference. The maintenance of a highly organized internal structure is one of the characteristics of life.

Figure 3.5 Electrons move around the nucleus, forming an electron cloud.

3–3   Properties of Atoms

The number of protons in the nucleus of an atom is called the **atomic number**. This number determines what kind of element the atom is. Hydrogen has the simplest atom. Each hydrogen atom has only one proton, so the atomic number of hydrogen is 1. A helium atom has two protons, so the atomic number of helium is 2. Each number from 1 through 106 is characteristic of a different element.

Many properties of an atom are determined by the **electric charge** of its particles. The electric charge of the protons and electrons is the property that causes these particles to attract or repel each other. Each electron has a negative charge, and each proton has a positive charge. Two particles with the same charge repel each other. Particles with opposite charges attract each other. Neutrons have no electric charge.

Figure 3.6 Like charges repel each other. Opposite charges attract each other. Neutral particles have no electric effect.

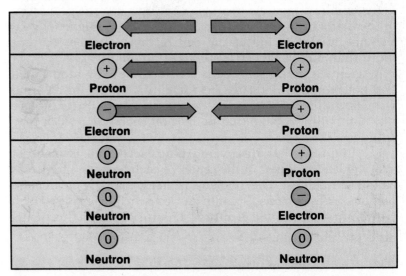

Each atom in any element has an equal number of protons and electrons, so that the atom is electrically balanced, or **neutral**. In other words, positive and negative charges are equal in number, and the atom has no net charge. Therefore, the atomic number is also the number of electrons in an atom.

Mass is another important property of atoms. Atomic particles are so small that it is not practical to measure them by everyday units of mass. For example, a single proton has a mass of only 0.0000000000000000000000002 g. Instead of using grams to measure the mass of atoms, scientists use a quantity called the **atomic mass unit**. The mass of a proton is almost exactly 1 atomic mass unit (amu). Neutrons have almost the same mass as protons. Electrons are far less massive. Electrons are so light that the mass of an atom is due almost entirely to the nucleus. The **atomic mass** of an atom is equal to the number of protons and neutrons in the nucleus. Common hydrogen has one proton and no neutrons. It has an atomic mass of 1. Helium has two neutrons in its nucleus, so its atomic mass is 4.

If you know both the atomic mass and the atomic number of an atom, you can determine the number of protons and neutrons in the nucleus. Copper (Cu) has atomic number 29, so copper must have 29 protons in the nucleus. Since copper has an atomic mass of 63, there must also be 34 neutrons in the nucleus (63 − 29 = 34).

	Location	Mass (in amu)	Charge
p	nucleus	1	+1
n	nucleus	1	none
e	outside nucleus	1/2000	−1

Figure 3.7 Atomic particles

Figure 3.8 The element sulfur has an atomic number of 16 and an atomic mass of 32. How many protons, neutrons, and electrons does it have?

3–4   Isotopes and Radioactivity

Common hydrogen has one proton in its nucleus. Both the atomic number and the atomic mass are 1. Figure 3.9 shows another form of hydrogen with a neutron in its nucleus in addition to the proton. This atom has twice the mass of ordinary hydrogen but is otherwise identical. Additional neutrons do not change the identity of an element. Figure 3.9 also shows a third form of hydrogen with two neutrons. It has three times the mass of ordinary hydrogen. All these forms of hydrogen, including common hydrogen, are **isotopes** [EYE-suh-tohps]. All isotopes of an element have the same atomic number, but each has a different atomic mass.

Carbon-12 is one of the carbon isotopes. Carbon has the atomic number 6, so carbon-12 has six protons and six neutrons. About 99 percent of the carbon atoms in nature are carbon-12. The rest are carbon-13 and carbon-14. Carbon-13

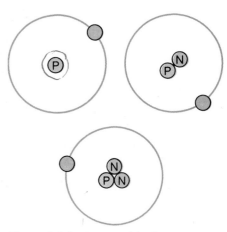

Figure 3.9 Isotopes of hydrogen

has six protons and seven neutrons. Carbon-14 has six protons and eight neutrons. Most elements have two or more isotopes.

Some isotopes are **radioactive**. A radioactive isotope is one with an unstable nucleus. Particles within such a nucleus break apart and throw off other particles. When the nucleus breaks apart, some of the energy that held the neutrons and protons together is released. Hydrogen-3 and carbon-14 are examples of radioactive isotopes.

Too much radiation is dangerous to living things. There is always a small amount of radiation in the environment, but fortunately most elements are not radioactive.

NEWSBREAK

Until recently, the only way to see inside a human body was through surgery or X rays. Both methods were potentially dangerous, and neither revealed how the body was functioning. Several new methods are giving doctors more information about the internal functioning of the human body, safely and without disrupting its activity.

One such method is positron emission tomography, or a PET scan. To perform a PET scan, radioactive isotopes are introduced into the body. These isotopes give off positrons, or positively charged electrons. When positrons collide with electrons, they produce gamma rays. Special instruments are used to detect these rays.

Different radioactive isotopes are useful for observing different organs. Nitrogen-13 can be inhaled to reveal the activity of the lungs. If oxygen-15 is injected into the blood, doctors are able to locate areas of heavy blood flow. This technique is useful in identifying cancerous tumors, which may have a high supply of blood.

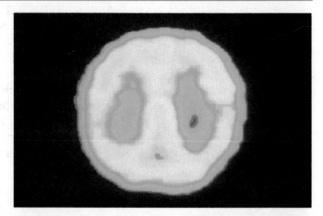

Doctors using PET scans have discovered that the flow of blood to the brain may be abnormal in patients with mental disorders. Some patients show increased blood flow to areas of the brain that govern vision. This may indicate that a patient is hallucinating. Doctors hope that the use of PET scans will help determine the cause of various mental illnesses.

To learn about recent developments in the field of radiology, ask your librarian to help you find current articles.

Checkpoint

1. What is the scientific term for anything that has mass and takes up space?
2. What are the three states of matter?
3. Atoms with the same atomic number but different atomic masses are called _____ .

Molecules and Compounds

Elements can combine to form new substances that have properties different from the elements that make them up. Because elements can join together in many different ways, an almost infinite variety of substances is possible.

3–5   How Do Atoms Combine?

The oxygen you breathe does not exist in the air as single atoms. Instead, oxygen occurs as pairs of atoms that are attached by chemical bonds. A **chemical bond** forms when two or more atoms attach or are attracted to each other. A group of two or more atoms held together by chemical bonds is called a **molecule**.

Molecules of some substances, such as ammonia, sugar, and water, contain atoms of more than one element. Such substances are compounds. A **compound** is a substance made of two or more chemically bonded elements. Molecules of some compounds contain as few as two atoms. In many biologically important compounds the molecules are made of thousands of atoms.

Figure 3.10 Combinations of many different compounds account for the variety of colorful and flavorful foods you enjoy.

The properties of compounds are always different from the properties of the elements that comprise them. The element sodium (Na) is a soft metal that can be cut with a knife. If it touches water, sodium reacts violently. If you were to touch sodium, you could be badly burned.

Chlorine (Cl) is another dangerous element. Breathing this green gas can be fatal. But sodium and chlorine combine to form a compound called sodium chloride, commonly known as table salt. Table salt is neither a poison gas nor a soft metal. It has none of the properties of the elements that make it up.

Just as elements are abbreviated by chemical symbols, the composition of a compound is indicated by a chemical formula. A **chemical formula** indicates the kinds and numbers of atoms that are bonded together in a compound. For example, NaCl is the formula for table salt. This formula indicates that there are equal amounts of sodium (Na) and chlorine (Cl) in table salt. H_2O is the formula for water. Each molecule of water has two atoms of hydrogen (H) and one atom of oxygen (O) bonded together. Each molecule of table sugar, $C_{12}H_{22}O_{11}$, has 12 carbon atoms, 22 hydrogen atoms, and 11 oxygen atoms.

Atoms combine, or react, to form compounds in specific ways. As you remember, every atom has a characteristic number of electrons equal to its atomic number. When atoms **react**, they form new chemical bonds by rearranging their electrons.

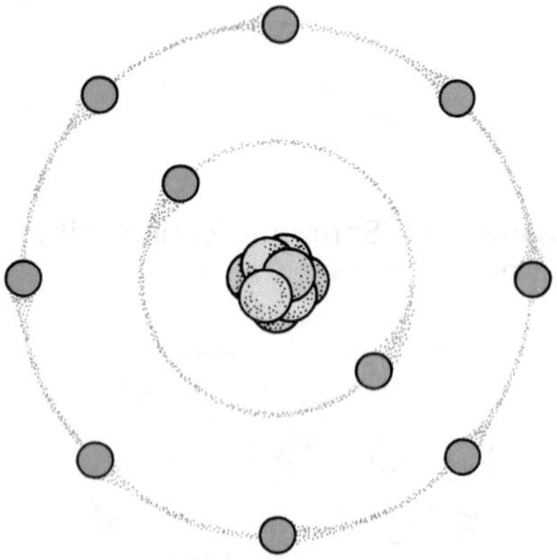

Electrons do not orbit the nucleus. As shown in Figure 3.11, electrons occupy certain regions of space outside the nucleus called **energy levels**. Each energy level has a capacity to hold a certain number of electrons. The energy level nearest the nucleus has a capacity of two electrons. The next energy level has a capacity of eight electrons. Other energy levels further from the nucleus can hold more electrons. For an atom such as sodium that contains eleven electrons — two are located in the first energy level. Eight are located in the next energy level and the remaining electron is in the third energy level.

The number of electrons in the outermost energy level of an atom determines how that atom will combine with other atoms. Each energy level can be further subdivided into **energy sublevels**. Some elements with filled energy sublevels show a special stability. These elements generally do not form bonds with other atoms. Elements that do not normally have filled energy sublevels combine to fill these sublevels. It is the rearrangement of electrons to fill energy sublevels that causes the formation of chemical bonds between atoms.

Figure 3.11 The electron energy levels are really spherical though they are often represented in only two dimensions.

Figure 3.12 Neon, an element used in colored lights, has filled energy sublevels.

3-6   The Covalent Bond

Most of the compounds you will learn about in biology are held together by covalent [koh-VAY-lehnt] bonds. A **covalent bond** is a bond between two atoms that share a pair of electrons. In a covalent bond the shared electrons provide the "glue" that holds the atoms together.

The atoms in a molecule of hydrogen (H_2) are held together by a covalent bond. As you can see from the model of a hydrogen molecule in Figure 3.13, each of the two atoms in the molecule shares its electron with the other atom. Remember that hydrogen needs only two electrons to have a filled energy level. By sharing electrons the two hydrogen atoms each have a full energy level. Both electrons count toward filling the outer energy level of each atom.

The atoms in water molecules are also held together by covalent bonds. Since an atom of oxygen has six electrons in its outer energy level, it needs two more electrons to complete the level. Therefore, it is capable of forming two covalent bonds. When an oxygen atom reacts with two hydrogen atoms, it forms one covalent bond with each atom of hydrogen. Then each atom in the water molecule has a full outer energy level.

Figure 3.13 Some molecules with covalent bonds

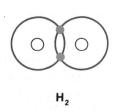 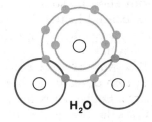 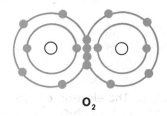

H_2 H_2O O_2

In the water molecule the atoms share a single pair of electrons. Such bonds are called **single bonds**. Covalent bonds sometimes involve more than one pair of electrons. Figure 3.13 shows how two atoms of oxygen can combine. The atoms share two pairs of electrons and form a **double bond** to give each atom eight electrons in its outer energy level.

An atom of carbon needs four electrons to fill its energy level. Therefore, it forms four covalent bonds. When one carbon atom and two oxygen atoms react to form carbon dioxide (CO_2), each carbon atom forms a double bond with each oxygen atom.

Covalent bonds between atoms can be shown in shorthand with a single straight line connecting the symbols for the two atoms. The line represents one shared pair of electrons. Figure 3.14 shows how several molecules can be represented in this way. Notice that double bonds are shown with two lines.

Substance	Molecular Formula	Bond Structure
Water	H_2O	H—O—H
Oxygen Gas	O_2	O=O
Hydrogen Gas	H_2	H—H
Carbon Dioxide	CO_2	O=C=O

Figure 3.14 A single covalent bond is represented by one line. Two lines represent a double covalent bond.

The Chemistry of Matter   **43**

3-7 Ions and Ionic Bonds

In molecules held together by covalent bonds atoms share electrons. But in some kinds of compounds atoms gain full energy levels by losing or accepting extra electrons.

Look at the electron arrangement of sodium in Figure 3.15. Sodium has 11 protons and 11 electrons. There is one electron in its outer energy level. If sodium were to lose this electron, the next energy level in would have eight electrons and become a full energy level.

A chlorine atom has seven electrons in its outer energy level. If this atom could gain one electron, its energy level would be filled, with eight electrons.

Figure 3.15 Sodium and chlorine form an ionic bond.

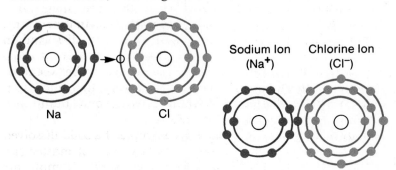

When sodium and chlorine react, each chlorine atom takes an electron from a sodium atom. Then both atoms have full energy levels. But when sodium gives up an electron, it has 11 protons and 10 electrons, and it is no longer electrically neutral. Its overall charge becomes +1. After taking an electron, chlorine has 17 protons and 18 electrons. Its overall charge is −1.

Any atom that has extra positive or negative charges is not electrically neutral. An electrically charged atom is called an **ion**. The symbols for sodium and chlorine ions are Na^+ and Cl^-.

Elements that have one, two, or three electrons in their outer energy level, such as potassium (K), magnesium (Mg), and aluminum (Al), usually form positive ions (K^+, Mg^{2+}, Al^{3+}). These elements transfer electrons to elements that have five, six, or seven electrons in their outer energy levels, such as fluorine (F), sulfur (S), or phosphorus (P). Elements such as these usually form negative ions (F^-, S^{2-}, P^{3-}).

Because sodium and chlorine ions are oppositely charged, they attract each other. This attraction between oppositely charged ions is called an **ionic bond**. An ionic bond results whenever electrons are transferred between atoms of different elements, forming ions. A compound in which the atoms are attracted by ionic bonds is called an **ionic compound**.

3-8 Solutions

If different substances react when they are mixed together, new compounds are formed. If there is no chemical change, however, the combined substances form a **mixture**. Sand stirred in water is a mixture. Sand and water separate quickly when you stop stirring. Some mixtures will not separate as easily. If you stir sugar and water, the sugar seems to disappear. You can taste the sugar, so you know it is still there. Unlike sand, dissolved sugar will not settle to the bottom of the water. Such a mixture is called a **solution**. A solution is a mixture in which the individual molecules or ions of substances are uniformly distributed. Solutions are made up of two parts. The **solvent** is the substance in which the other material is dissolved. The **solute** is the substance dissolved in the solvent.

In a solution of sugar and water, sugar is dissolved in water. Sugar is the solute and water is the solvent. This means that the sugar molecules are tucked in between the water molecules. If you could become very tiny and jump from one water molecule to another, you would bump into some sugar molecules along the way.

A sugar and water solution is an example of a solid dissolved in a liquid. However, substances in any state of matter can form solutions. Gases can dissolve in gases. For example, air is a solution of oxygen, nitrogen, and other gases. Gases can dissolve in liquids. Most lakes and streams have oxygen gas (O_2) dissolved in the water — in fact, this is the oxygen that fish breathe.

3-9 Water as a Solvent

Water has unique properties that make it an excellent solvent. Figure 3.17 shows a water molecule. Notice that the hydrogen atoms are not directly opposite each other. The relatively large oxygen nucleus (with six protons) attracts the electrons more than the two hydrogen nuclei attract them. Therefore, the electrons in the covalent bonds spend more time around the oxygen atom than around the hydrogen atoms. As a result, the oxygen side of the molecule has a slight negative charge, and the hydrogen side has a slight positive charge.

Even though the entire molecule has the same number of protons and electrons, the distribution of these charges is unbalanced. This unbalanced charge makes water a polar molecule. Any molecule with an unbalanced charge distribution is a **polar molecule**.

Because water molecules have positive and negative sides, they tend to attract each other as well as other polar molecules and ions. This attraction causes almost any polar or ionic

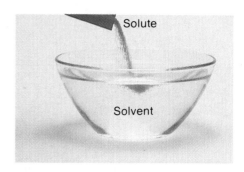

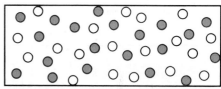

◯ Solute Molecule ◯ Solvent Molecule

Figure 3.16 In a solution the solute and solvent molecules are evenly distributed.

Hydrogen Side (+)   Oxygen Side (−)

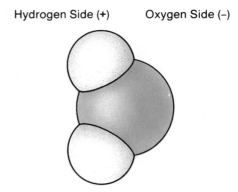

Figure 3.17 Water is a polar molecule.

compound to dissolve in water. Sugar is a polar molecule that readily dissolves in water. Oils are not polar compounds, so they do not dissolve in water.

3–10   Acids and Bases

Two common groups of compounds that dissolve in water are acids and bases. An **acid** is any substance that releases hydrogen ions when mixed with water. A strong acid is one that separates completely in water to release many hydrogen ions. A weak acid does not separate completely in water, so it releases fewer hydrogen ions. A **base** is a substance that separates in water forming ions that react with hydrogen ions. The strength of a base is determined by how completely it separates when added to water.

Scientists measure the acidity of an acid or a base on a pH scale. Pure water is neutral and has a pH of 7.0. The pH of an acid can range from 0 to 7. A low pH indicates a large number of hydrogen ions in solution. Therefore a concentrated acid solution will have a low pH value. Bases have pH values between 7 and 14. A concentrated base solution will have a high pH.

Figure 3.18 The pH scale

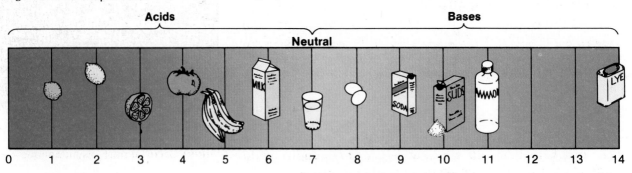

3–11   Chemical Reactions

A **chemical reaction** occurs when ionic or covalent bonds between atoms are broken or formed. Symbols can be used to indicate a chemical reaction. For example,

$$4Fe + 3O_2 \longrightarrow 2Fe_2O_3$$

These symbols are an abbreviated way of saying that four atoms of iron (Fe) and three molecules of oxygen react to produce two molecules of iron oxide. Iron oxide is more commonly known as rust. The numbers to the left of each atom or molecule show the number of atoms or molecules involved. The arrow means "yields" or "reacts to give." Substances to the left of the arrow are called **reactants**. Substances to the right of the arrow are called **products**.

If you look carefully at this equation, you will see that the total number of atoms is the same on each side of the arrow. For example, there are six atoms of oxygen in the reactants (two atoms in each of three molecules). There are also six atoms of oxygen in the products (three in each of two molecules of iron oxide). Similarly, the number of iron atoms is the same on each side of the arrow. During a chemical reaction the number of each kind of atom remains the same, although the atoms recombine into new compounds.

When the numbers of atoms on each side of the arrow are the same, the equation is a **balanced equation**. The following are further examples of balanced equations:

$$2H_2O \longrightarrow 2H_2 + O_2$$

(Two molecules of water react to give two molecules of hydrogen and one molecule of oxygen.)

$$C_{12}H_{22}O_{11} + H_2O \longrightarrow 2C_6H_{12}O_6$$

(One molecule of table sugar and one molecule of water yield two molecules of simple sugar.)

Writing a chemical equation does not necessarily mean that the chemical reaction it describes will occur. The top equation shows water breaking down into hydrogen and oxygen. But a glass of water will not break down into hydrogen and oxygen gas. Most chemical reactions occur only under certain conditions. To understand what happens in living cells, you must understand what kinds of chemical reactions occur in them. You will see how cells create conditions in which chemical reactions occur in a controlled way.

Figure 3.19 *Top:* Some chemical reactions occur slowly. *Bottom:* Others occur almost instantaneously.

Checkpoint

1. What is the smallest part of a compound that still has the properties of the compound?
2. Of the three particles that make up atoms, which is most directly responsible for forming chemical bonds?
3. Name the two basic kinds of chemical bonds.
4. What is a mixture in which the molecule or ions of the substances are uniformly distributed?
5. What property of water makes it a good solvent?

CHAPTER REVIEW

Summary

- A substance can exist in three common forms of matter — as a solid, a liquid, or a gas. The state of a substance depends upon its temperature.

- Atoms are the basic building blocks of all substances. Atoms are made up of electrons, protons, and neutrons. Elements are substances made of a single kind of atom.

- The atomic number of an atom is the number of protons in the nucleus. Protons are balanced by an equal number of electrons moving about the nucleus. Therefore, atoms are electrically neutral.

- Most atoms also have neutrons in the nucleus. The atomic mass of an atom is the number of protons and neutrons in the nucleus. An element may have several isotopes, or forms with different numbers of neutrons in the nucleus. Some isotopes are radioactive.

- Elements can combine chemically to form compounds. A molecule is the smallest part of a compound that still has the properties of the compound. Atoms react to form compounds by achieving full energy levels. Covalent bonds are formed when atoms share electrons. Ionic bonds are formed when atoms transfer electrons.

- If molecules do not chemically change when they are brought together, they form a mixture. One kind of mixture is a solution. A solution consists of a solute dissolved in a solvent. Since water is polar, it is a good solvent for both polar and ionic substances.

- Acids and bases are substances that dissolve in water. Acids release hydrogen ions when they dissolve; bases combine with hydrogen ions. The pH scale is used to measure the acidity of acids and bases.

- A chemical reaction occurs when the bonds between atoms change or rearrange. A chemical equation is a way of writing what happens in a chemical reaction.

Vocabulary

acid	mass
atom	matter
atomic mass	mixture
atomic mass unit	molecule
atomic number	neutral
balanced equation	neutron
base	nucleus
chemical bond	pH scale
chemical change	physical change
chemical formula	polar molecule
chemical reaction	potential energy
chemical symbol	product
compound	proton
covalent bond	radioactive
double bond	react
electric charge	reactant
electron	single bond
element	solute
energy level	solution
ion	solvent
ionic bond	state of matter
ionic compound	
isotope	
kinetic energy	

Review

1. What is another name for stored energy?
2. Name the three particles that make up all atoms.
3. Write the chemical symbols for hydrogen, carbon, and chlorine.
4. What elements do the symbols O, N, and Na represent?

5. What are the electric charges on the three atomic particles?
6. What is the significance of the outermost energy level of any atom?
7. What do chemists call a substance made of different elements combined chemically?
8. In what kind of a chemical bond are electrons shared?
9. What is the meaning of the arrow in a chemical equation?
10. What is the pH of pure water?

Interpret and Apply

1. If you know the atomic number of an element, what do you know about the element?
2. What is a radioactive isotope?
3. How is the number of electrons in the outer energy level of an atom related to the chemical reactivity of the atom?
4. What is the difference between an element and a compound?
5. What is the basic difference between an ionic and a covalent bond?
6. Write out the following chemical reaction in words:

$$2H_2 + O_2 \longrightarrow 2H_2O$$

7. A solution has a pH of 9.0. Is it an acid or a base?
8. The pH of tomato juice is about 4; that of lemon juice is about 2. Which acid contains more hydrogen ions in solution?

Challenge

1. Approximately what percent of the mass of a uranium atom (atomic number 92 and atomic mass 238) is due to its electrons?
2. Why do all isotopes of an element react chemically in the same way?
3. Methane (CH_4) combines with oxygen to form carbon dioxide (CO_2) and water. Write a balanced chemical equation for this reaction.

Projects

1. The amount of a substance that can be dissolved in a given amount of solvent is called its solubility. Compare the solubility of salt and sugar. Does their solubility change with a change in the temperature of the solvent? Perform an experiment to answer these questions.
2. Investigate the effect of dissolved salt on the temperature at which water changes state. Does the change in boiling or freezing point of water depend on the amount of dissolved salt? How do the results of your experiments explain why salt is placed on roads during snow or ice storms?
3. Read about the history of alchemy. In what ways were the early alchemists like modern chemists? In what ways were they different?
4. What is the half-life of an isotope? Find out how half-lives are used to determine the age of objects.
5. Find a recipe for making rock candy. You might want to make some and then explain what you observe. Apply what you know about solutions and the states of matter. Find a book in the library about crystals and crystal growing. Try to grow some of your own crystals following the instructions from a book.

4 The Chemistry of Life

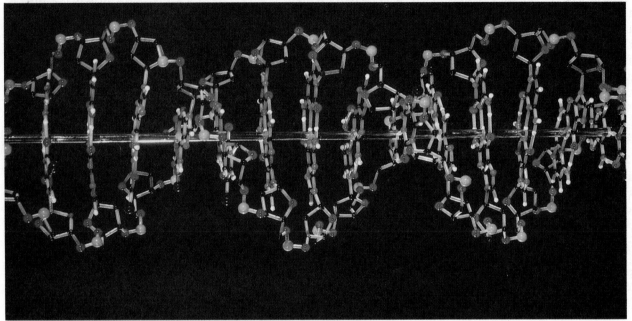

Three-dimensional model of
deoxyribonucleic acid (DNA)

The model in this photograph represents an enormous molecule, one made of thousands of atoms. Molecules this large and complex are unique to livings things. Even the smallest organisms make such molecules routinely.

Such molecules are based on the element carbon. Living organisms could not exist without carbon. Sixty to seventy percent of a typical cell is water, and about one percent is ions. The rest of the cell is made of carbon compounds.

Before the early 1800s scientists thought carbon compounds could be produced only by organisms. But in 1828 a German chemist named Friedrich Wöhler showed that carbon compounds could be made in the laboratory without the aid of living things. Since the time of Wöhler thousands of carbon compounds have been synthesized. Many of these substances, such as plastics, dyes, and synthetic fibers, are compounds never made by any organism. Yet no molecule made by chemists is nearly as complex as the molecule shown above.

The Chemistry of Carbon

Before Wöhler, scientists divided chemistry into two branches. They called the chemistry of carbon compounds in living things **organic chemistry**. The chemistry of nonliving matter was **inorganic chemistry**. Although scientists now know that carbon compounds are not associated only with living things, they still refer to the chemistry of carbon compounds as organic chemistry. Noncarbon chemistry is still called inorganic chemistry. Of course, carbon obeys the same laws as the other elements, but carbon and its compounds do have unique properties.

4–1 Properties of Carbon

Figure 4.1 shows the electron structure of the carbon atom. A carbon atom has six protons and therefore six electrons. There are two electrons in its inner energy level and four electrons in its outer energy level. Since carbon needs four more electrons to fill its outer energy level, one carbon atom can form four covalent bonds.

Carbon can form covalent bonds with four hydrogen atoms. This compound is called **methane**. Methane is a major component of natural gas. Figure 4.2 illustrates four ways to represent methane:

1. The *bonding diagram* shows how the electrons in the outer energy level form covalent bonds.
2. The *molecular formula* tells the number of each kind of atom in a molecule of the compound.
3. The *structural formula* shows the bonds connecting the atoms and the arrangement of the atoms within each molecule.
4. The *space-filling model* shows how the atoms in the molecule are arranged in space. (Notice that the methane molecule is not flat but is shaped like a pyramid.)

Any of these representations may be used to illustrate any carbon compound.

CONCEPTS

- the bonding properties of carbon
- four methods of representing the structure of carbon compounds
- the molecular structure of the amino, organic acid, and alcohol functional groups

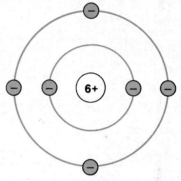

Figure 4.1 Carbon has four electrons in its outer energy level.

Figure 4.2 Methane

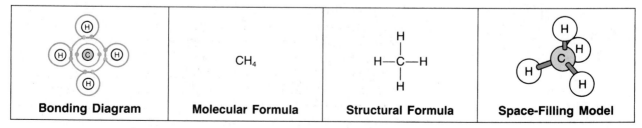

| Bonding Diagram | Molecular Formula | Structural Formula | Space-Filling Model |

Methane is the simplest of a group of compounds called **hydrocarbons** [hy-druh-KAR-buhns]. Hydrocarbons are molecules made of hydrogen and carbon. Coal, oil, and natural gas are mixtures of complex hydrocarbons. Figure 4.3 shows several simple hydrocarbons. As you can see from the structural formulas, carbon atoms can bond to other carbon atoms to form chains and even rings. In each carbon compound every carbon atom shares four pairs of electrons.

Figure 4.3 Some simple hydrocarbons

Hydrocarbon	Ethane	Ethylene	Propane	Benzene
Molecular Formula	C_2H_6	C_2H_4	C_3H_8	C_6H_6
Structural Formula	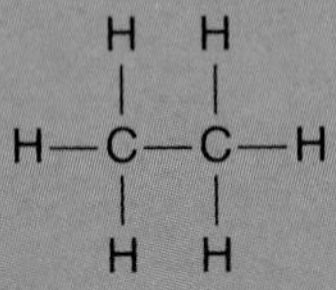	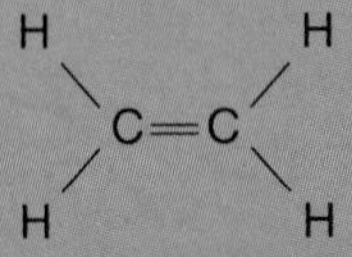	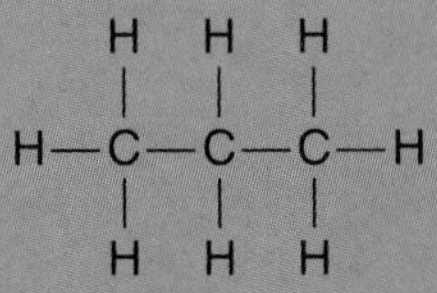	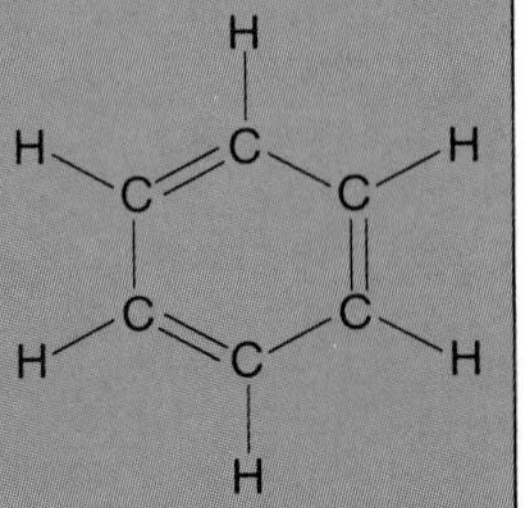

As you can see from the structural formulas, carbon does not always share four pairs of electrons with four different atoms. Notice the double bonds in the molecules ethylene and benzene. Double bonds are quite common in organic compounds. Molecules that have no double bonds and that have the maximum possible number of hydrogen atoms bonded to each carbon atom are said to be **saturated**. That is, the molecule is saturated with hydrogen. Molecules that have double bonds, and therefore fewer hydrogen atoms, are **unsaturated**.

4–2   Alcohols, Organic Acids, and Organic Bases

In addition to forming covalent bonds with other carbon atoms and hydrogen, carbon can form covalent bonds with many other elements, including oxygen and nitrogen. Look at the compounds **methanol** [MEHTH-uh-nawl] and **ethanol** [EHTH-uh-nawl] shown in Figure 4.4. Compare these molecules to methane (Figure 4.2) and ethane (Figure 4.3). They differ only in the addition of a single oxygen atom. Methanol and ethanol are examples of compounds known as **alcohols**. An alcohol has an –OH attached to one or more carbon atoms.

The –OH is an example of a special group of atoms attached to carbon atoms in organic molecules. Such special groups

Alcohol	Structural Formula
Methanol	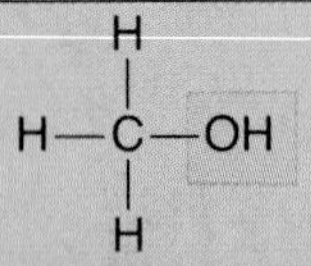
Ethanol	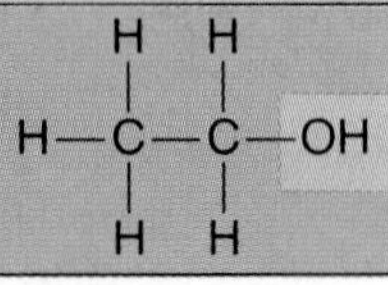

Figure 4.4 Alcohols have an –OH group. The bond between the O and H in this group is not shown but is understood.

are called **functional groups**. Functional groups give molecules distinctive properties. For example, organic molecules with alcohol groups (–OH) are more soluble in water than similar molecules without the alcohol group.

Two other functional groups that occur in many organic compounds are the **organic acid** group (–COOH) and the **amino** group (–NH$_2$). The –COOH and the –NH$_2$ groups are illustrated in Figure 4.5. Recall that an acid is any substance that releases hydrogen ions in water solution. A base is any substance that accepts hydrogen ions in water solution. The –COOH group releases hydrogen ions, so it is an acid. The –NH$_2$ group accepts hydrogen, so it is a base.

Although elements other than carbon, oxygen, hydrogen, and nitrogen are not abundant in organic compounds, they are still important to living cells. Sulfur and phosphorus are found in several important kinds of organic molecules. Magnesium, zinc, and cobalt are essential to the structure and function of molecules in many cells.

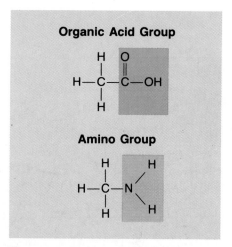

Figure 4.5 *Top:* An acid; *Bottom:* A base

Figure 4.6 The element magnesium is present in chlorophyll, the substance responsible for the green color of leaves.

Checkpoint

1. What do scientists call the study of carbon compounds?
2. Compounds that are made only of carbon and hydrogen are called _____ .
3. In compounds, how many pairs of electrons does each carbon atom share with other atoms?
4. What is the molecular formula for methane? The structural formula?
5. Draw the structural formulas for an alcohol group, an organic acid group, and an amino group.

Macromolecules

- synthesis of macromolecules from smaller molecules
- structure and function of major classes of carbohydrates, including sugars, starches, cellulose, and glycogen
- structure and chemical properties of lipids

Recall from Chapter 2 that one of the characteristics of life is the presence of organic molecules. All living things synthesize enormous molecules called **macromolecules**, such as the one shown on page 50. But even molecules this large are far too small to be seen in detail by a microscope, even an electron microscope. Scientists use complex methods to determine the shapes of macromolecules.

Understanding the structure of macromolecules is made easier by the fact that they are all synthesized from smaller molecules. The properties of a macromolecule are determined by the kinds of smaller molecules that make it up.

4–3 Carbohydrates

Sugars and starches are examples of organic compounds called **carbohydrates**. Carbohydrates are made of carbon, hydrogen, and oxygen. Most carbohydrates have two hydrogen atoms for every oxygen atom. In living things the main function of carbohydrates is to provide a source of energy.

The smallest carbohydrates are the simple sugars called **monosaccharides** [mahn-uh-SAK-uh-rydz]. Monosaccharides usually contain five or six carbon atoms. They are usually ring-shaped molecules with several carbon atoms and one oxygen atom in the ring. Monosaccharides also have many alcohol groups attached to the carbon atoms. One monosaccharide used for fuel in nearly all living things is **glucose**. Figure 4.7 shows glucose and several other monosaccharides. Notice how similar these monosaccharides appear. Some even have the same molecular formula, but minor structural differences make important differences in the chemical properties of the compounds.

Figure 4.7 Several monosaccharides. Notice that although glucose, fructose, and galactose have the same molecular formulas, their structural formulas are different.

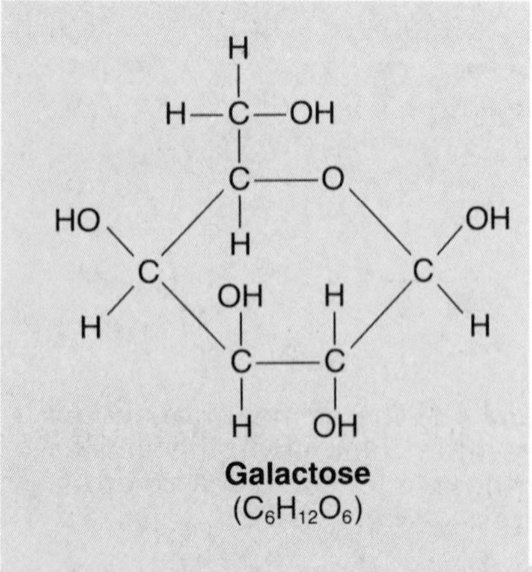

Galactose
($C_6H_{12}O_6$)

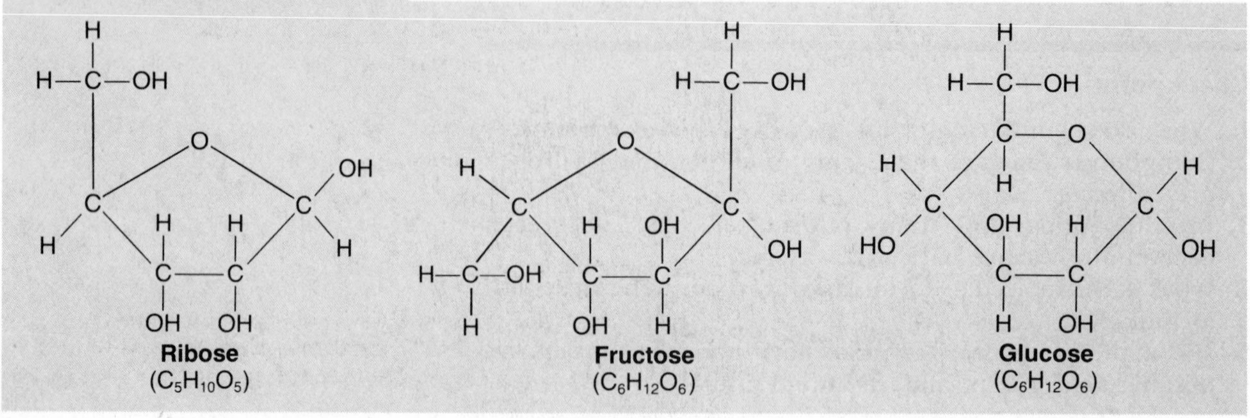

Ribose
($C_5H_{10}O_5$)

Fructose
($C_6H_{12}O_6$)

Glucose
($C_6H_{12}O_6$)

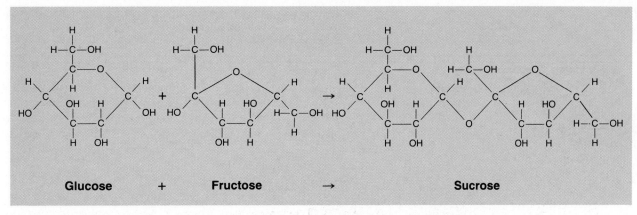

Glucose   +   Fructose   →   Sucrose

A single molecule containing two monosaccharides is called a **disaccharide** [dy-SAK-uh-ryd]. The disaccharide sucrose, which you know as table sugar, is formed from glucose and another monosaccharide, fructose. Almost any two monosaccharides can combine to form a disaccharide. For example, two glucoses combine to form a disaccharide called **maltose** or malt sugar. Lactose, or milk sugar, is a disaccharide made of glucose and galactose.

More than two monosaccharides can be joined into large carbohydrate molecules called **polysaccharides**.

Starch is a polysaccharide made of hundreds or even thousands of glucose molecules linked together. Plants make starch as a way of storing sugar molecules. Seeds such as rice, corn, and wheat contain starch that is used as food by the young plant.

Cellulose [SEHL-yuh-lohs] is another polysaccharide made by plants. It is also made of thousands of glucose molecules linked together. Starch and cellulose differ in the way the glucose molecules are linked together. Cellulose does not store food for the plant, but it gives plant cells structural support.

Glycogen [GLY-kuh-juhn] is a food storage molecule produced by many animals. Glycogen is also made up of glucose molecules. The structure of glycogen is similar to that of plant starch, but glycogen is more highly branched. Animals that make glycogen store it in their livers and muscles.

Figure 4.8 Sucrose, a disaccharide, is formed when glucose and fructose join.

Figure 4.9 Plants produce the polysaccharide cellulose. Animals produce the polysaccharide glycogen.

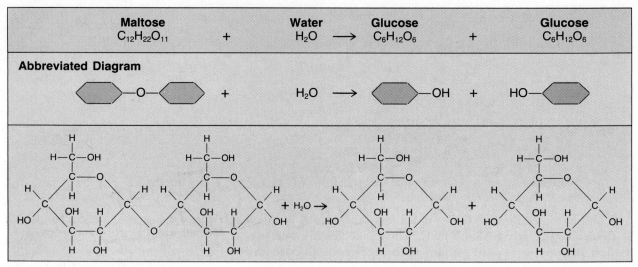

| Maltose $C_{12}H_{22}O_{11}$ | + | Water H_2O | $\longrightarrow$ | Glucose $C_6H_{12}O_6$ | + | Glucose $C_6H_{12}O_6$ |

Abbreviated Diagram

Figure 4.10 The hydrolysis of maltose. The abbreviated diagram makes it easy to see what is happening.

Polysaccharides and disaccharides can be broken down into monosaccharides by a chemical reaction called **hydrolysis** [hy-DRAHL-uh-sihs]. Figure 4.10 illustrates a hydrolysis reaction. In hydrolysis, a large molecule is split into two smaller molecules by the addition of a molecule of water.

4–4 Lipids

Bacon fat, vegetable oil, and furniture wax are examples of lipids [LIHP-ihdz]. **Lipids** are organic molecules that will not dissolve in water but will dissolve in nonpolar substances such as alcohols. Recall that water is a polar substance and in general, only polar or ionic substances will dissolve in water. Because lipids are nonpolar molecules, they do not dissolve in water. Lipids have many functions in cells. For example, lipids are part of the structure of all cells, especially cell membranes. Lipids also store energy in the cell.

Figure 4.11 shows the structure of an important kind of lipid, a fatty acid. **Fatty acids** have a long chain of carbon atoms with an organic acid group at the end. The carbon chain may be saturated or unsaturated. The carbon chain is nonpolar, so it is not soluble in water.

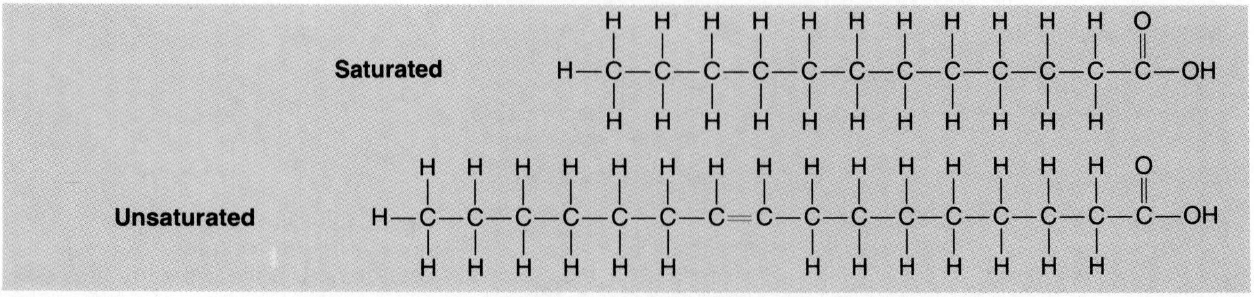

Figure 4.11 Two fatty acids. The unsaturated fatty acid has a double bond joining two carbon atoms.

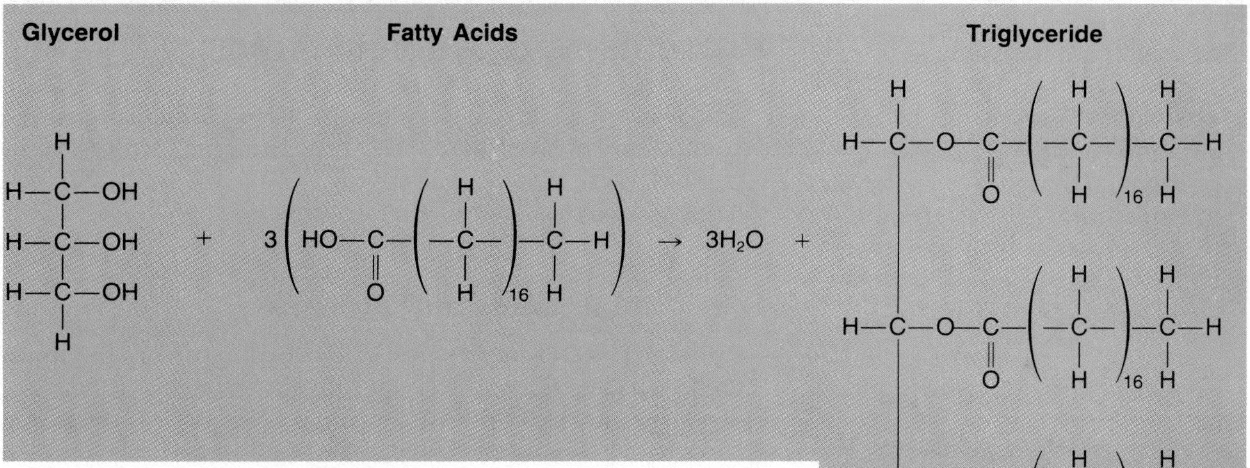

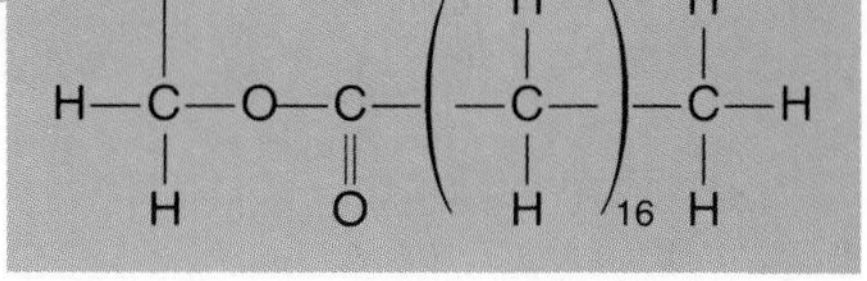

Glycerol **Fatty Acids** **Triglyceride**

Figure 4.12 shows three fatty acid molecules combined with a three-carbon alcohol called **glycerol** [GLIHS-uh-rawl]. The molecule that results from this synthesis is a **triglyceride** [try-GLIHS-uh-ryd]. When triglycerides are broken down by hydrolysis, they produce three fatty acids and glycerol. Because of their long, nonpolar fatty acids, triglycerides do not dissolve in water.

The three fatty acids in a triglyceride can be identical or each can be different. They can vary in length and can have varying numbers of double bonds. If the fatty acids have more than two double bonds, they are **polyunsaturated**. Triglycerides such as butter and lard are made from saturated fatty acids. They are solid at room temperature. A triglyceride that is solid at room temperature is called a **fat**. A triglyceride that remains liquid at room temperature is called an **oil**. Oils usually have unsaturated fatty acids. Oils are more commonly made by plants than by animals. Corn oil and peanut oil are some familiar examples.

Waxes are fatty acids combined with an alcohol that has a single –OH group. Beeswax, which is produced by honeybees, is an example of a naturally produced wax.

Figure 4.12 The formation of a triglyceride

Figure 4.13 Beeswax is a naturally produced wax.

Checkpoint

1. What substances have one oxygen atom and five or six carbon atoms in a ring with –OH groups attached to the carbon atoms?
2. Name three polysaccharides. What organisms make each kind of polysaccharide?
3. What property do all lipids have in common?
4. From what molecules are triglycerides made?

Proteins and Nucleic Acids

The most complex molecules in a living organism are the proteins and nucleic acids. Because these molecules are so complex, their structure has only come to be understood during the second half of this century.

4–5 Amino Acids and Proteins

Proteins [PROH-teenz] are the most common organic molecules in living things. They perform a variety of functions. Egg yolk is an example of a protein that stores energy for the embryo growing in the egg. Hair and fingernails are also made of protein. Many parts of cells are made of protein.

Like other macromolecules, proteins are made from smaller molecules linked together. In proteins the small molecules are **amino acids**. Figure 4.14 shows the structure of a common amino acid. In all amino acids a central carbon atom is bonded to a hydrogen atom, an amino group, and an organic acid group. The amino and the acid groups give amino acids their name.

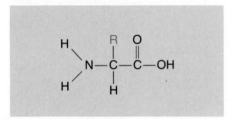

Figure 4.14 The generalized structure of an amino acid

In the molecule of an amino acid the fourth covalent bond of the central carbon atom can be shared with another organic group. The letter R represents the different groups that can occupy this position. Each different **R group** makes a different amino acid. Examples of R groups are shown in Figure 4.15.

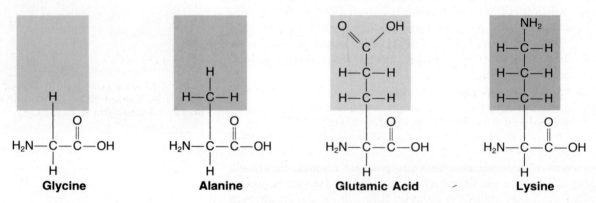

Glycine   **Alanine**   **Glutamic Acid**   **Lysine**

Figure 4.15 The R groups of some amino acids

Some R groups are ionically charged (plus or minus). Some are polar and some are nonpolar. The R group gives each amino acid its own characteristics. Although almost any organic group could occupy the R position, in fact only 20 different amino acids occur commonly in proteins.

Figure 4.16 shows that amino acids can be joined together by peptide bonds. **A peptide bond** is the bond that forms

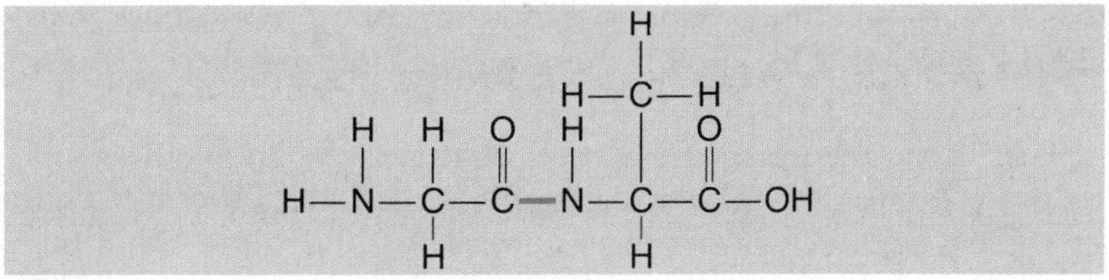

Figure 4.16 A peptide bond (shown in blue) joins two amino acids forming a dipeptide.

between an organic acid group and an amino group. Notice that the R groups of the amino acids are not included in the peptide bonds.

If two amino acids join, the molecule that results is called a **dipeptide**. More than two amino acids joined together, as in Figure 4.17, form a **polypeptide**. Proteins are long polypeptides. An average protein is about 200 amino acids long.

Proteins are distinguished by the order of their amino acids. Different proteins are made by arranging the 20 amino acids in particular sequences. With 20 different amino acids that could possible occupy any place in a chain of 200 amino acids, the number of possible proteins is enormous.

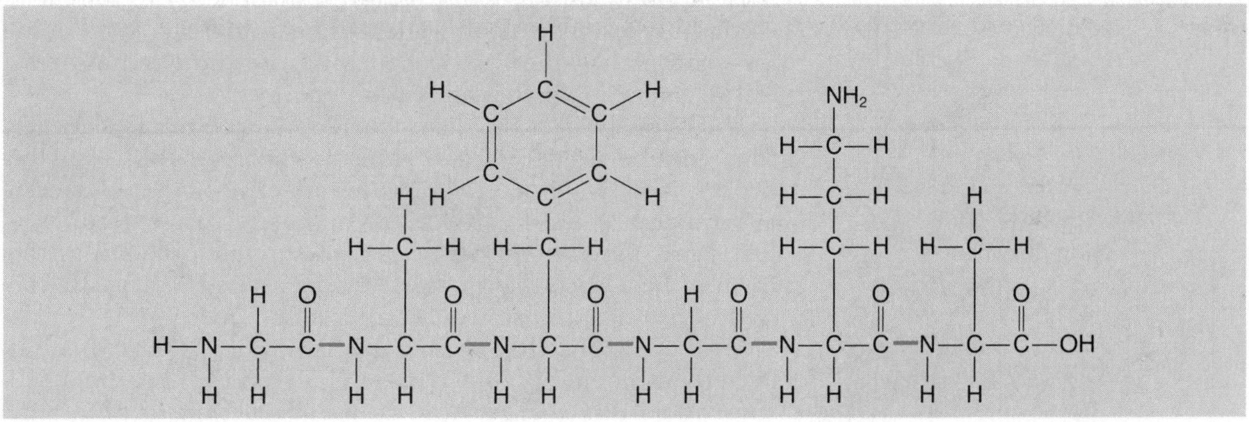

Figure 4.17 In a polypeptide as in a dipeptide, the amino acids are joined together by peptide bonds (blue).

4–6 Protein Shape

The three-dimensional shape of a protein is determined by the order of its amino acids. Each chain of amino acids folds in a unique way. The R groups of the amino acids interact with each other to bend the polypeptide chains. Positively charged R groups are attracted to negatively charged R groups of other amino acids in the protein. R groups with like charges repel each other. Water soluble R groups move closer to the water molecules that surround the protein in the cell. R groups that are insoluble in water move closer to each other and away from the surrounding water molecules.

Forces of attraction and repulsion between the R groups cause the protein to bend and twist until each R group is as "comfortable" as possible. Protein molecules with the same

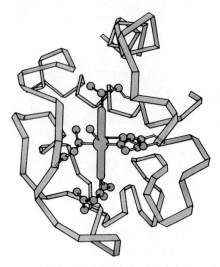

Figure 4.18 The chain of 86 amino acids in this protein molecule is folded many times. (The red-colored parts represent special chemical groups.)

amino acid sequence have exactly the same three-dimensional shape. Figure 4.18 shows the complex folding of the amino acid chain in a protein.

The three-dimensional shape of a protein molecule is extremely important. Shape determines the function of a protein in the cell. If even one amino acid is out of order or changed, the entire protein can fold differently. This change may totally alter the function of the protein.

4–7 Enzymes

Enzymes [EHN-zymz] are proteins that speed up chemical reactions in cells. Enzymes act as biological catalysts. A **catalyst** is a substance that changes the rate of a chemical reaction but is not used up in the reaction. Usually a catalyst speeds up a reaction. Almost all the chemical reactions that take place in living cells require a specific enzyme. Therefore, enzymes coordinate all the chemical activities in the cell.

Most chemical reactions require some energy to get them started. Before the potential energy in gasoline can be released, for example, a spark is needed to ignite the gasoline. This initial energy is called **activation energy**.

The hydrolysis of the disaccharide maltose releases energy that can be used by an organism. Before maltose can be broken into two glucose molecules, an initial input of energy is required. If the hydrolysis of maltose is carried out in a test tube, activation energy can be supplied quickly in the form of heat. But the amount of heat needed to activate the hydrolysis of maltose would kill a cell.

Most reactions that occur in cells require a large amount of activation energy. Since there is not enough heat in a cell to provide this energy, how do these reactions get started? The answer is enzymes. Enzymes reduce the amount of activation energy required to start a chemical reaction. With an enzyme present, the reactants need only the energy of normal cell temperatures to react. Without enzymes the reactions would take place, but so slowly that the cell could not live.

An example will show how enzymes reduce activation energy. **Maltase** is the enzyme that hydrolyzes maltose. On the surface of maltase is a small area called the active site. The **active site** of an enzyme is the place where the reaction occurs. The shape of the active site is maintained by the rest of the enzyme molecule, somewhat as the wooden framework of a roller coaster maintains the shape of the track. (Remember that enzymes are proteins and that the shape of a protein determines its function.)

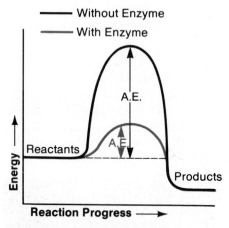

Figure 4.19 The amount of activation energy (A.E.) necessary for a chemical reaction to proceed is reduced when an enzyme is involved.

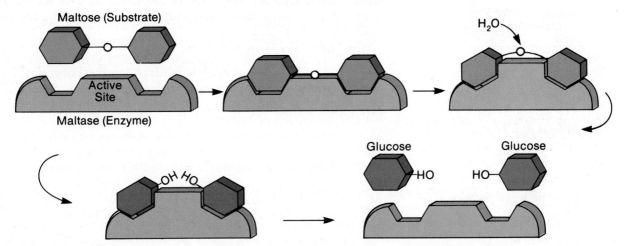

Maltose (Substrate)

Active Site

Maltase (Enzyme)

H_2O

Glucose   Glucose

HO   HO

Figure 4.20 The enzymatic hydrolysis of maltose

The active site of maltase matches the shape of the maltose molecule, so that the maltose can fit into it. Although maltose fits into the active site, the fit is not perfect. After it enters, the maltose molecule is slightly distorted. This distortion makes the bond between the two glucose portions of the maltose easier to break. This is like bending a piece of metal back and forth at one place to make it break more easily.

When the bond between parts of the maltose molecule breaks, two glucose molecules are released. Then the active site of the maltase is ready to accept another maltose molecule. Thus the enzyme speeds up the hydrolysis of maltose but is not used up in the reaction.

Each kind of enzyme has an active site that matches only a specific molecule. The molecule on which an enzyme acts is called the **substrate** of that enzyme. Maltose is the substrate of the enzyme maltase. Amylase is an enzyme that accepts only starch molecules as a substrate. Because the active site of a particular enzyme can combine with only one set of substrate molecules, there is a different enzyme for every type of reaction in a cell. Thousands of different chemical reactions occur in every cell, and every cell needs thousands of different enzymes to control these reactions!

Not all enzymes are solely protein. Some enzymes contain a nonprotein molecule attached to the amino acid chain. This nonprotein molecule is called a **coenzyme**. Coenzymes are attached near the active site. Certain proteins will not catalyze a reaction unless they are combined with a coenzyme.

Enzymes determine what a cell is and what it does. By producing a particular group of enzymes at a particular time, the cell controls what reactions will take place. The sum of all the chemical reactions that occur in a cell determines the structure and function of the cell.

BIOLOGY INSIGHTS

Structure determines function. The three-dimensional shape of each protein determines its function in the living organism. The relationship of structure and function is one of the unifying themes of biology.

Nitrogen Base (Adenine)

Figure 4.21 The three parts of a nucleotide

Guanine G

Thymine T

Cytosine C

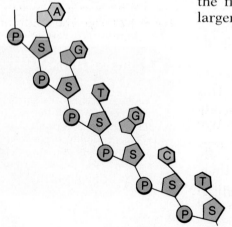

Figure 4.22 *Left:* A single nucleotide chain; *Right:* DNA as seen through an electron microscope

4–8 Nucleic Acids

In 1869 the Swiss chemist Johann Friedrich Miescher discovered a new class of molecules in living cells. Because he found these acid-like substances in the center, or *nucleus*, of the cell, he called them **nucleic acids**. Miescher knew nothing of the function or importance of these molecules. Scientists now know that nucleic acids contain the program that controls all the activities of the cell.

Like other macromolecules, nucleic acids are made of smaller molecules linked together. The basic unit of nucleic acids is the **nucleotide**. As shown in Figure 4.21, each nucleotide consists of three parts: a five-carbon sugar, a phosphate group, and a nitrogen base. Nucleotides may have one of several different nitrogen bases; several are shown below.

Figure 4.22 shows how nucleotides join together in a long chain to form nucleic acid. The sugar of one nucleotide is bonded to the phosphate group of the second nucleotide. Such a chain leaves the nitrogen bases exposed.

One nucleic acid is **deoxyribonucleic** [dee-ahk-see-ry-boh-noo-KLEE-ihk] **acid**, or **DNA**. This long name is based on the five-carbon sugar in DNA, deoxyribose. DNA is much larger than any other molecule in the cell. Figure 4.22 also

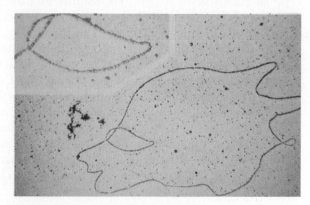

shows an enormous DNA molecule as seen with an electron microscope. DNA contains the code for the inherited information of the cell. This code is based on the order in which the nucleotides occur.

4–9   ATP and ADP

Figure 4.23 shows the structure of a molecule called **adenosine** [uh-DEHN-uh-seen] **triphosphate**, or **ATP**. ATP transfers energy within the cell. ATP is not a nucleic acid, but it is a nucleotide with two additional phosphate groups added to it. Figure 4.23 shows how ATP is formed by adding a phosphate group to **adenosine diphosphate**, or **ADP**. When ATP is formed in this way, potential energy is stored in the bonds between the phosphate groups. When ATP is hydrolyzed to ADP and P, energy is released. The cell uses this energy in metabolism.

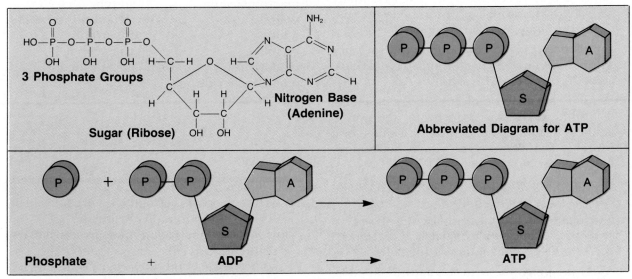

Figure 4.23 *Top:* The structure of ATP; *Bottom:* The formation of ATP

Checkpoint

1. Name the five parts of an amino acid.
2. What determines the shape of a protein?
3. What is a substance that speeds up a chemical reaction but remains unchanged itself?
4. What is the term that refers to the amount of energy needed to begin a chemical reaction?
5. The subtrate fits into what part of an enzyme?
6. What are the nonprotein portions of some enzymes called?
7. What is the name of the molecule that transfers energy in the cell?

The Chemistry of Life   **63**

CHAPTER REVIEW

Summary

- Carbon always forms four covalent bonds with other atoms. It can bond with other carbon atoms, with other elements, or with functional groups such as the organic acid and amino groups. There is a huge variety of organic molecules based on chains and rings of carbon.
- Carbohydrates are made of carbon, hydrogen, and oxygen; they usually have two hydrogen atoms for every oxygen atom. They range in size from the monosaccharides to huge molecules of starch, cellulose, and glycogen. Many carbohydrates store energy for use in the cell. Others provide structural support.
- Lipids are organic compounds that are not soluble in water. Typical lipids include fatty acids, fats, oils, and waxes.
- Proteins are macromolecules built of chains of amino acids. The sequence of the amino acids determines the identity and shape of a protein. The shape of a protein determines its function in the cell.
- Enzymes are proteins that catalyze chemical reactions in living things.
- Nucleic acids are macromolecules based on sequences of nucleotides. Nucleic acids contain the inherited information of the cell.
- ATP is a nucleotide with two additional phosphate groups. ATP transfers energy within the cell.

Vocabulary

activation energy
active site
adenosine diphosphate (ADP)
adenosine triphosphate (ATP)
alcohol
amino acid
amino group
carbohydrate
catalyst
cellulose
coenzyme
deoxyribonucleic acid (DNA)
dipeptide
disaccharide
enzyme
ethanol
fat
fatty acid
functional group
glucose
glycerol
glycogen
hydrocarbon
hydrolysis
inorganic chemistry
lipid
macromolecule
maltase
maltose
methane
methanol
monosaccharide
nucleic acid
nucleotide
oil
organic acid
organic chemistry
organic compound
peptide bond
phosphate group
polypeptide
polysaccharide
polyunsaturated
protein
R group
saturated
starch
structural formula
substrate
triglyceride
unsaturated
wax

Review

1. What element distinguishes organic chemicals from inorganic chemicals?
2. Hydrocarbons are all made from what two elements?
3. In a double bond, how many pairs of electrons does carbon share with another atom?
4. What characteristics does an amino group give to a molecule?
5. What kind of molecule is made of many simple sugars linked together?
6. When a macromolecule is broken down into a number of small molecules, what chemical reaction is involved.?
7. What is the function of cellulose?
8. What is the function of glycogen?
9. Starch, cellulose, and glycogen can all be broken down into the same subunit. What is this molecule?
10. List two functions of lipids in cells.

11. What kinds of organisms tend to make saturated fatty acids?
12. What is the major difference between fats and oils?
13. What is the function of ATP?
14. How do the 20 amino acids found in proteins differ from each other?
15. What kind of bonds join amino acids together in a protein?
16. An enzyme reduces the _____ of a chemical reaction.

Interpret and Apply

1. What is the difference between hydrolysis and chemical synthesis?
2. Name an element that is found in nucleic acids and some lipids but not in carbohydrates and proteins.
3. Write a simple chemical equation showing how a cell makes ATP.
4. What makes some amino acids water-soluble and others insoluble in water?
5. Which of the following compounds does not belong with the others in the list? (a) water (b) sugar (c) fat (d) starch
6. Which of the following compounds does not belong with the others in the list? (a) starch (b) wax (c) cellulose (d) glycogen

Questions 7 to 9 are analogies. Fill in the missing word or phrase to complete each analogy.

7. Saturated is to single bond as _____ is to double bond.
8. A spark is to gasoline as _____ is to a chemical reaction.
9. Proteins are to amino acids as nucleic acids are to _____ .

Challenge

1. Look up the electron arrangement of silicon. How many bonds and what kind of bonds would you expect silicon to form with other atoms?
2. Most animals make an enzyme that hydrolyzes starch into a molecule of maltose. Could this enzyme hydrolyze cellulose into maltose? Why, or why not?
3. What common feature is there in the way cells make polysaccharides, triglycerides, nucleic acids, and proteins?
4. In what two categories of macromolecules does the sequence of components determine the function of the molecule?

Projects

1. Find out how the simple hydrocarbons are named. What are some of the rules used to name organic compounds?
2. Look at the labels of some of the insecticides and painting compounds in your home. Write down some of the names of the organic chemical ingredients. See if you can identify any parts of the compounds from their names. Most of the compounds are very complex, but they usually contain some recognizable groups.
3. Find out what kinds of foods are rich in carbohydrates, lipids, and proteins. What kinds of organisms provide us with these foods?
4. Most living tissues contain an enzyme called peroxidase. The function of this enzyme is to break down a toxic molecule that is sometimes formed in cells called hydrogen peroxide (H_2O_2). The peroxide is broken down into water and oxygen according to the following equation.

$$2H_2O_2 \longrightarrow 2H_2O + O_2$$

Since peroxide is poisonous to cells, it is important that cells have a way of quickly getting rid of it. You can observe the effects of peroxidase. Add a small piece of uncooked potato to a small amount of hydrogen peroxide in a saucer. What happens? Try other kinds of living tissue and see if they all react in the same way. You can use plant tissue or different kinds of uncooked meat.

5 Cell Structure and Function

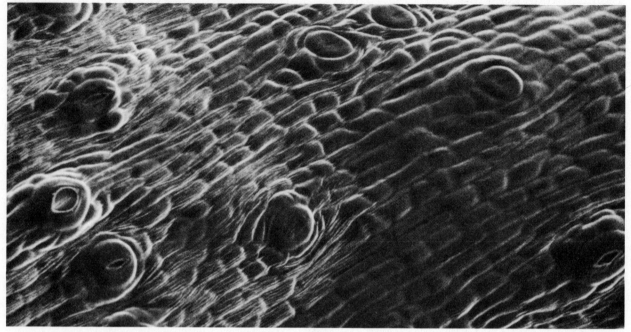

Scanning electron micrograph of stomata and guard cells on underside of a leaf

When you look at the wall of a building, you can tell at a glance that it is made of thousands of bricks. Our bodies, too, are made of many smaller units. The "bricks" of our bodies and those of all other living things are countless tiny units called cells. Unlike bricks, though, cells usually cannot be seen by the unaided eye. And far from being lifeless pieces of clay, cells are alive with activity. Within each cell, an astounding amount of activity goes on. Although we may not be aware of it, this activity never stops.

All living things, from bacteria to buffaloes, are built of cells. In some ways the cells of all organisms are alike, having many similar structures and functions. Yet in other ways bacterial cells are quite different from buffalo cells.

In the three centuries since the discovery of the cell, scientists have gained a vast amount of knowledge about how cells work. New techniques for studying cells become available each year. With these new techniques, scientists are able to discover more and more about the basic building block of life — the cell.

Cells: Building Blocks of Life

As you learned in Chapter 2, all living things are made up of cells. Many microorganisms are **unicellular**, containing only one cell. Most plants and animals are **multicellular**, or composed of many cells. You are an example of a multicellular organism. In fact, your body is composed of trillions of cells.

5–1 Development of the Cell Theory

In 1665, Robert Hooke, an English scientist, examined a thin slice of cork under a microscope. Hooke could see that the cork was composed of many small compartments. Because the compartments resembled the little rooms, or cells, of a monastery, Hooke named these compartments *cells*. The cells that Hooke observed were not living. Hooke did not pursue his discovery by investigating the structure or function of living cells.

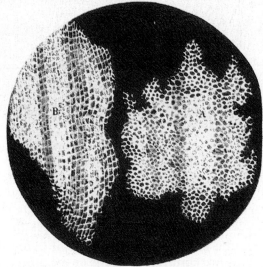

Almost 200 years passed before biologists came to understand the importance of cells. In 1835, the French biologist Felix Dujardin determined that many microorganisms are composed of a single cell. Dujardin also observed that the internal substance of all living cells was similar.

Three years later, Matthias Schleiden, a German botanist, stated that all plants are composed of cells. Shortly thereafter, Theodor Schwann, a German zoologist, concluded that all animals are composed of cells. Schleiden and Schwann then suggested that cells are the basic living components of all organisms.

CONCEPTS
- cell theory
- functions of cells

Do You Know?
The yolk of an egg is composed of one enormous cell.

Figure 5.1 A thin slice of cork viewed under the microscope shows small compartments called cells.

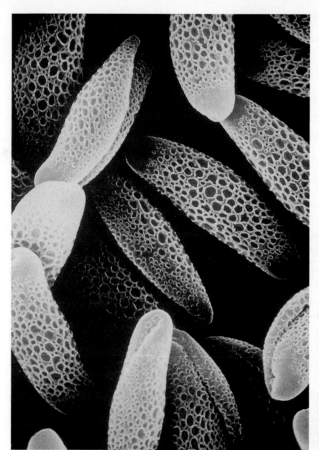

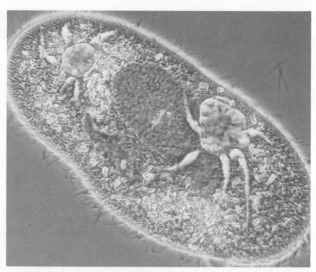

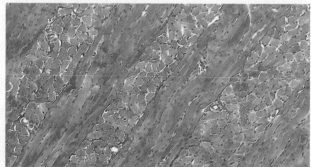

Figure 5.2 Cells come in a variety of shapes and sizes. The function of a cell is based on its structure.
Left: pollen grains; *Top right: Paramecium; Bottom right:* muscle cells

Twenty years later, Rudolf Virchow, another German biologist, wrote that the body is "a state in which every cell is a citizen." From his observation of dividing cells, Virchow concluded that cells can arise only from other cells.

The observations of these and other scientists formed the basis of the cell theory. The cell theory states that

1. The cell is the basic unit of structure of living things. All living things are composed of cells or the products of cells.
2. The cell is the basic unit of function of living things.
3. All cells come from other cells by the process of cell division.

Since Hooke's discovery of cells, scientists have developed a wide variety of techniques to study cells. The earliest tool used was the light microscope. Scientists discovered that treating cells with various chemicals, or stains, would color certain cell parts so they could be distinguished under the microscope. This allowed biologists to investigate the internal structure of cells.

More recently, the electron microscope and other tools have been used to study cells. Modern tools and techniques have allowed biologists to increase greatly their knowledge of cells. All current findings continue to support the cell theory.

5–2 Cell Functions

Each cell has all the characteristics of life described in Chapter 2. In addition, the cells of multicellular organisms may carry out specialized functions.

All cells require energy from food. **Nutrition** is the process by which organisms obtain and use food. Some cells are able to manufacture their own food, while others must obtain it from their environment.

Cells obtain energy by processing food molecules such as glucose. In the process of **cellular respiration**, cells convert the energy of food molecules into a form of energy usable by the cells.

Cells absorb water, minerals, and other materials essential to life from their environment. This process is called **absorption**.

As a result of metabolism, waste chemicals accumulate within the cell. For this reason, cells must eliminate, or excrete, waste products into the environment. If allowed to accumulate, waste substances would eventually poison the cell. Thus **excretion** is necessary to life.

All cells synthesize complex chemicals from simple chemicals. This process is called **biosynthesis**. For example, all living cells synthesize proteins from amino acids.

All cells can respond to conditions around them. They can alter their functions in response to changes in their environment.

As stated in the cell theory, all cells come from other cells. In reproduction, cells give rise to new cells. Multicellular organisms must produce new cells to replace worn-out cells. Cell reproduction also causes an increase in the number of cells, resulting in the growth of an organism. Adults are larger than infants because adults have more cells.

 BIOLOGY INSIGHTS

The cellular processes of all living things are fundamentally similar. This extension of the cell theory is one of the unifying principles of biology.

Checkpoint

1. Who was the first scientist to use the word *cell* to describe the components of organisms?
2. What term is used to describe an organism composed of many cells? What term describes an organism composed of one cell?
3. How are chemical stains useful in the study of cells?
4. What is the process in which the energy of food is converted to a form that is usable by the cell?
5. By what process does a cell rid itself of waste products?

Parts of a Cell

CONCEPTS

- structure of membranes
- contents of the nucleus
- organelles in the cytoplasm
- structure of the cell wall
- characteristics of eukaryotes and prokaryotes

Figure 5.3 The principal organelles of a plant and animal cell

Early biologists, limited by the resolving power of the light microscope, were able to see only a few structures within the cell. More advanced tools, particularly the electron microscope, have enabled biologists to explore the structure of the cell in great detail.

Within every cell are many smaller structures. These structures are called **organelles** [or-guh-NELZ], a word meaning "little organs." Not all cells contain every kind of organelle. The functions of the cell depend upon the number and kinds of organelles present.

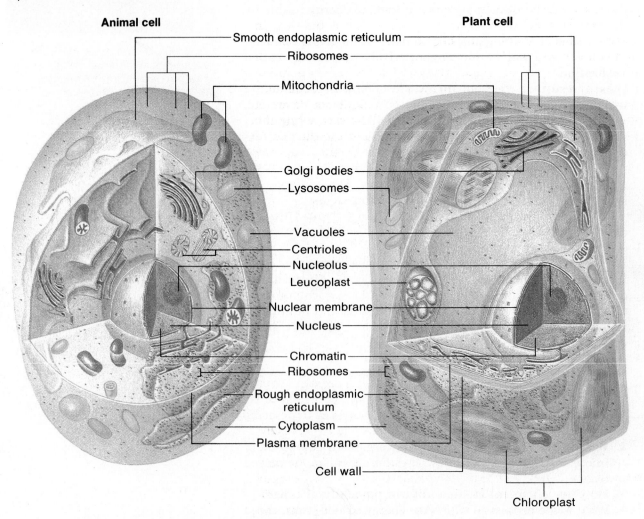

Animal cell

Plant cell

Smooth endoplasmic reticulum
Ribosomes
Mitochondria
Golgi bodies
Lysosomes
Vacuoles
Centrioles
Nucleolus
Leucoplast
Nuclear membrane
Nucleus
Chromatin
Ribosomes
Rough endoplasmic reticulum
Cytoplasm
Plasma membrane
Cell wall
Chloroplast

5–3   Membranes

Surrounding all cells is a thin layer called the **plasma** [PLAZ-muh] **membrane**. The plasma membrane is more than just a boundary between the inside and outside of the cell. It is an active area of the cell. Among other functions the plasma membrane determines which molecules may enter or leave the cell.

Because it is difficult to observe, the structure of the plasma membrane has been debated for many years. When examined with an electron microscope, the plasma membrane appears as a double line. According to the most widely accepted hypothesis, the membrane is made up of a double layer of **phospholipid** [fahs-foh-LIH-pihd] molecules. Each phospholipid is composed of a lipid and a phosphate group.

As you learned in Chapter 4, lipids will not dissolve in water. Unlike the lipid end of the molecule, the phosphate end is polar and will dissolve in water. The lipid ends of the phospholipids tend to "avoid" the water of the cell by pointing in toward the middle of the membrane. The phosphate ends point outward. Thus the phosphate groups of one layer of phospholipids point toward the inside of the cell, while the phosphates of the second layer point toward the outside of the cell. Each double layer of phospholipids makes up one unit membrane.

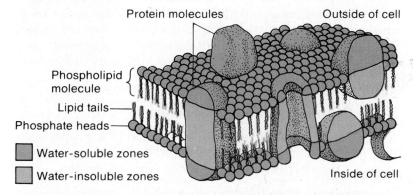

Figure 5.4 Phospholipid molecules of the plasma membrane align according to their solubility in water.

Embedded in the phospholipids are protein molecules. Thus the membrane is composed of both protein and phospholipid molecules, a bit like the pieces of tile in a mosaic.

The molecules in the plasma membrane are not stationary. The phospholipid molecules can move sideways within the membrane. Certain proteins stay in the membrane for only a few hours. When they leave the membrane, they are replaced by other protein molecules. Thus the components of the membrane are constantly moving, or fluid. For this reason, the membrane is described as a fluid mosaic. Because the plasma membrane is fluid, it can seal itself if it is broken.

The plasma membrane is not the only membrane in a cell. Protein and phospholipid membranes are found throughout the cell. Biologists estimate that only about one tenth of a cell's membranes are part of the plasma membrane. Many organelles are enclosed by membranes.

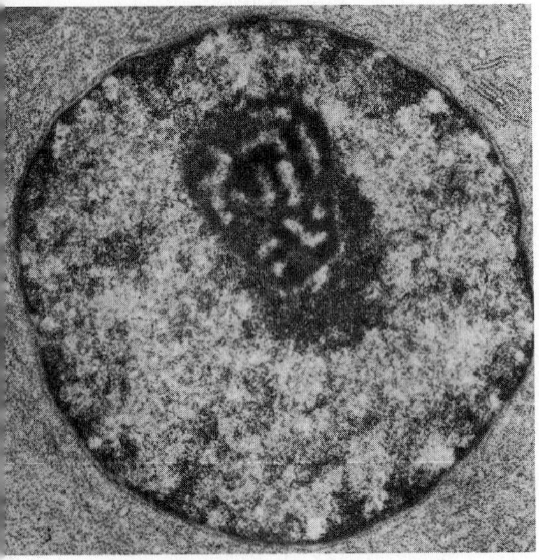

5–4 The Nucleus

The first organelle that biologists observed was the **nucleus** [NOO-klee-uhs]. The nucleus is a spherical structure that is usually located near the center of the cell. The nucleus directs the production of proteins in the cell.

The nucleus is bounded by two unit membranes called the **nuclear membrane**. The nuclear membrane contains pores through which only certain substances can pass. The nuclear membrane keeps the contents of the nucleus separate from the rest of the cell.

Within the nucleus is a material called **chromatin** [KROH-muh-tihn]. Chromatin is more readily stained than the rest of the nucleus. The chromatin contains the hereditary information of the cell. When a cell reproduces, the chromatin becomes visible as long strands called **chromosomes** [KROH-muh-sohmz].

One part of the chromatin is condensed into a darker area called the **nucleolus** [noo-KLEE-uh-luhs]. The nucleolus is involved in the production of ribosomes, which are organelles involved in protein synthesis. (Ribosomes are described later in this chapter.) Some cells have more than one nucleolus.

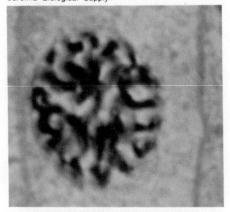

Figure 5.5 The cell nucleolus is contained inside the nucleus as shown in this electron micrograph of a cell nucleus.

Carolina Biological Supply

Figure 5.6 Cell chromatin is easily seen under the microscope when a cell is in the process of dividing.

5–5 Cytoplasm and Organelles

Many types of organelles are suspended in a gel-like substance called **cytoplasm** [SY-toh-plazm]. Cytoplasm consists of many types of proteins and other macromolecules.

Mitochondria **Mitochondria** [my-toh-KAHN-dree-uh] contain enzymes that release the energy stored in food in the process of cellular respiration. For this reason, mitochrondria are sometimes called the powerhouses of the cell. Each mito-chondrion (singular of *mitochondria*) is surrounded by two unit membranes. The outer membrane separates the mito-chondrion from the cytoplasm. The inner membrane is typically folded into shelves that stretch across the mitochondrion.

Some cells, such as those in heart muscle or the growing buds of plants, require much energy. Such cells have many more mitochondria than cells that require less energy. A single muscle cell may contain thousands of mitochondria.

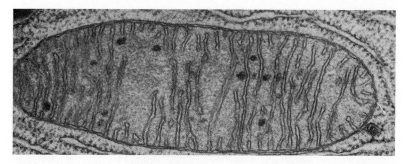

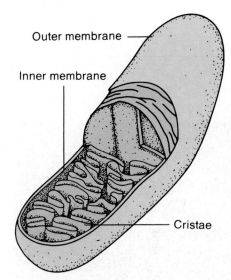

Ribosomes Throughout the cytoplasm are tiny, round or-ganelles called **ribosomes** [RY-bo-sohmz]. Ribosomes are composed of nucleic acids and proteins. The synthesis of proteins occurs on the ribosomes. Some cells contain as many as half a million ribosomes.

Endoplasmic Reticulum Ribosomes are often attached to long strands of membrane called the **endoplasmic reticulum** [ehn-doh-PLAZ-mihk reh-TIHK-yoo-luhm], or ER. The en-doplasmic reticulum forms a network of tiny canals through the cell. These canals connect the nuclear membrane and the plasma membrane. One function of the endoplasmic reticulum is to prepare proteins for secretion.

Endoplasmic reticulum to which ribosomes are attached is called rough endoplasmic reticulum, or rough ER. Ribo-somes attached to the endoplasmic reticulum usually syn-thesize proteins that will be secreted, or released from the cell. Unattached ribosomes in the cytoplasm synthesize pro-teins that will be used within the cell.

Endoplasmic reticulum without ribosomes is called smooth endoplasmic reticulum, or smooth ER. Smooth ER is not involved in the synthesis of protein.

Figure 5.7 This electron micrograph and cross sectional model of mitochondria show the double membrane and inner folding.

Figure 5.8 *Left:* This electron micrograph of the endoplasmic reticulum shows its rough structure. *Right:* The locations of ribosomes are shown on this 3-dimensional model of rough ER.

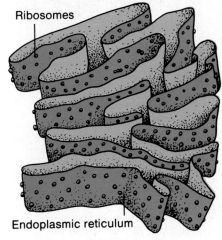

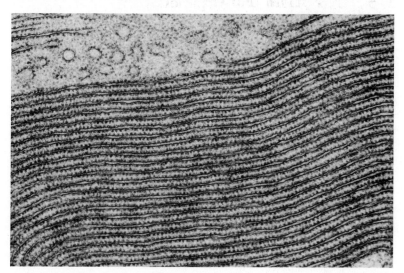

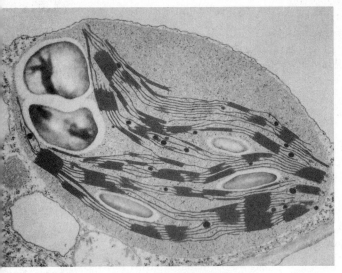

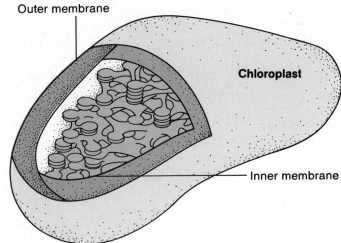

Outer membrane

Chloroplast

Inner membrane

Figure 5.9 The choloroplast model shows a structure similar to mitochondria. Chloroplasts give plants their green color.

Figure 5.10 A Golgi body can pinch off small vesicles filled with protein.

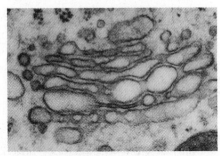

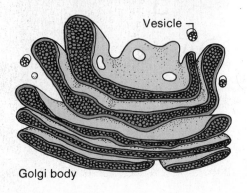

Vesicle

Golgi body

Plastids Plants and some unicellular autotrophs contain membrane-bound organelles called **plastids**. Plastids may store food for the cell or carry out other specialized functions. **Chloroplasts** [KLOR-uh-plahsts] contain the green pigment **chlorophyll** [KLOR-uh-fihl]. Chlorophyll is essential in capturing the energy of sunlight for the manufacture of carbohydrates.

Chromoplasts [KROH-muh-plahsts] contain red, orange, or yellow pigments that give many flowers and fruits their distinctive color. Chromoplasts in tomatoes contain the red pigment that makes tomatoes look red. **Leucoplasts** [LEW-kuh-plahsts] are colorless plastids. In leucoplasts, large starch molecules are synthesized from sugar molecules. Leucoplasts also store starch.

Golgi Bodies Flat membrane-bound sacs called **Golgi** [GOHL-jee] **bodies** are often associated with the endoplasmic reticulum. These structures are named after their discoverer, the Italian microscopist Camillo Golgi.

Golgi bodies prepare proteins for secretion after they are released from the endoplasmic reticulum. In the process of **secretion**, certain proteins are surrounded by pieces of membrane that pinch off the Golgi body. These pieces form tiny, membrane-bound spheres called **vesicles**. The vesicles carry the protein to the plasma membrane. Each vesicle then fuses with the plasma membrane, thus pouring its contents out of the cell.

Cells that secrete large quantities of protein usually contain more Golgi bodies than cells that secrete less protein. Cells that produce hormones often contain many Golgi bodies.

Vacuoles The cytoplasm of many cells contains fluid-filled spaces that are surrounded by membranes. These spaces are called **vacuoles** [VAHK-yoo-ohlz]. Vacuoles contain mostly water. In mature plant cells the vacuole may be so large that the nucleus and organelles are pushed against the plasma membrane. Vacuoles may also contain food molecules, salt, or pigments not contained in the plastids.

Lysosomes The **lysosomes** [LY-suh-zohmz] are also membrane-bound organelles. They contain enzymes that are capable of digesting the cell's proteins. For example, certain proteins stay in the cell membrane for only a short while. These proteins may then enter the lysosomes, where enzymes break them down and recycle their amino acids. The cell uses the recycled amino acids to make other proteins.

If lysosomes released their contents into the cytoplasm, their enzymes would destroy the entire cell. This occurs in only a few special cases. One such case occurs in the tail of a tadpole, which degenerates as the adult frog develops.

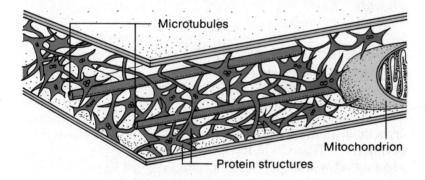

Figure 5.11 The cytoskeleton is a complex network of microtubules and proteins.

Cytoskeleton Until a few years ago scientists thought that the organelles were floating freely in the cytoplasm. Recent research, however, has revealed that the cytoplasm contains a **cytoskeleton**. This miniature internal support system is made up of **microtubules** and other tiny protein structures. Together these structural elements give the cell its shape, much as steel girders give shape to a large building. The cytoskeleton divides the cell into tiny spaces, thus limiting the movement of organelles through the cytoplasm. Certain molecules in the cell move only along paths established by the microtubules, much as railroad cars move along a railroad track.

Centrioles The cells of most animals and some simple plants contain two structures called **centrioles** [SEN-tree-ohlz]. The centrioles are cylindrical organelles containing bundles of microtubules. The centrioles often lie near the nucleus. Centrioles are important in cell division.

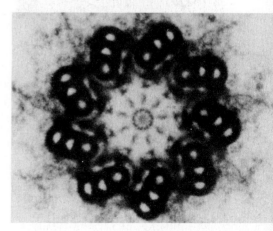

Figure 5.12 Centrioles also contain microtubules as shown in this electron micrograph cross section.

5-6 The Cell Wall

The cells of plants, fungi, and some single-celled organisms are protected and supported by a rigid **cell wall**. The cell wall lies outside the plasma membrane. In plants, the cell wall is composed largely of the polysaccharide **cellulose**.

The cell wall is a complex structure, as shown in Figure 5.13. A **primary cell wall**, laid down when the cell is formed, expands as the cell grows. After the cell reaches its full size, a **secondary cell wall** is laid down inside the primary cell wall. The secondary cell wall adds extra strength. The primary walls of neighboring cells are not in direct contact with one another. They are separated by the **middle lamella** [luh-MEL-uh], a layer composed of a jellylike polysaccharide called **pectin**. Unlike the plasma membrane, the cell wall does not determine what may enter and leave the cell.

The cell wall often remains intact after the rest of the cell has died. For example, the wood of trees is composed of the thickened walls of cells that are no longer living. The cells of cork that Hooke first observed were actually only cell walls.

Figure 5.13 The structure of a plant cell wall

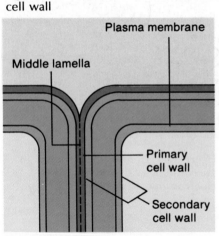

Plasma membrane

Middle lamella

Primary cell wall

Secondary cell wall

5-7 Eukaryotes and Prokaryotes

Although there are several important differences between the cells of plants and animals, the structure of these cells is surprisingly similar. In the cells of all plants and animals, the chromatin is contained within a well-defined nucleus. Cells that contain a nucleus are called **eukaryotes** [yew-KAHR-ee-ohts].

Not all organisms have cells containing the organelles found in plants and animals. The cells of bacteria, for example, do not contain a nucleus. Instead, the chromatin is stretched out in the cytoplasm of the cell. Cells without membrane-bound nuclei are called **prokaryotes** [pro-KAHR-ee-ohtz]. Prokaryotes also lack other membrane-bound organelles, such as mitochondria, Golgi bodies, and chloroplasts.

Checkpoint

1. In what organelle is the chromatin of plants and animals located?
2. Name the two main types of molecules that make up the plasma membrane.
3. Of what polysaccharide is the cell wall of plants composed?
4. What organelle contains enzymes that destroy protein molecules?
5. What is the cytoskeleton made of?

The Arrangement of Living Matter

Some organisms contain only one cell. Other organisms contain trillions of cells. In the human body, there are over 200 different types of cells. Each of these cells is slightly different from the other cells in the body, and each is specialized for a particular purpose.

5–8 Variety of Unicellular Organisms

Unicellular organisms are complete within a single cell. Some examples of unicellular organisms are bacteria and some simple plants. In these organisms one cell is capable of carrying out all the functions necessary for life. It can obtain and digest food, manufacture proteins, excrete wastes, respond to changes in its environment, and reproduce.

Unicellular organisms display a wide variety of specialized structures. For example, some have long threadlike flagella or cilia that are used to propel them through the water. Others have specialized cell walls for protection, or eyespots that are sensitive to light.

5–9 Tissues to Systems

Unlike unicellular organisms, the cells of most multicellular organisms are specialized to perform only particular functions. This specialization of cells is like the division of labor in a human society. In modern societies, everyone depends upon the work of other people. Some people grow food. Others perform tasks such as building houses, making clothing, or caring for the sick. As in a modern society, the survival of a multicellular organism depends upon the coordination and division of labor among its specialized members.

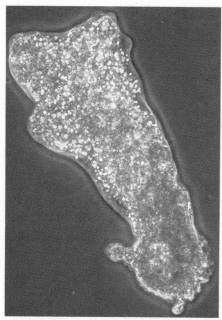

Figure 5.14 The amoeba is a unicellular microorganism found in pond water.

Figure 5.15 Assembly-line work requires the skills of many people doing specialized tasks to produce one product, such as a car.

Cell Structure and Function **77**

You are an example of a multicellular organism. Cells within your digestive system process food, which your blood carries to other body cells. Your body can perform complex activities because all your cells work together.

These specializations are reflected in the structure of your cells. For example, red blood cells specialize in transporting oxygen to cells. Their flattened shape allows them to pass easily through narrow blood vessels. If red blood cells were irregularly shaped, they might clog the blood vessels.

Nerve cells are specialized for communication between body parts that may be distant from each other. Some are over one meter long. Skin cells are specialized in protecting the cells beneath them. They contain a waterproofing material that prevents fluids from leaving the body too rapidly.

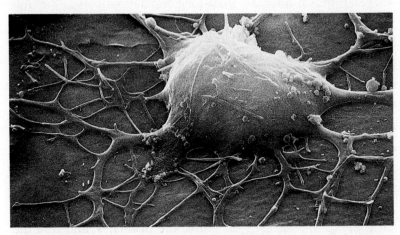

Figure 5.16 This scanning electron micrograph shows portions of long nerve fibers.

Plants, too, have different types of cells, each with different functions. One kind of cell is long, hollow, and thick-walled. It transports water and other substances throughout the plant and provides support for the plant. Other cells are small and reproduce at a very high rate. They specialize in making new plant cells.

When a group of many similar cells work together to perform a function, they are called a **tissue**. For example, nervous tissue is composed of many nerve cells, muscle tissue of muscle cells, and bone tissue of bone cells. Plants also contain tissues. One such tissue is the wood of trees, which contains cells that are specialized to support the tree and transport water.

In many organisms, several different types of tissues work together to perform a common function. The muscle, blood, and skin tissues that compose your stomach, for example, work together to store and digest food. The stomach is an example of an **organ**. An organ is composed of several different types of tissues working as a unit. Some of your other organs include your brain, liver, kidneys, and heart.

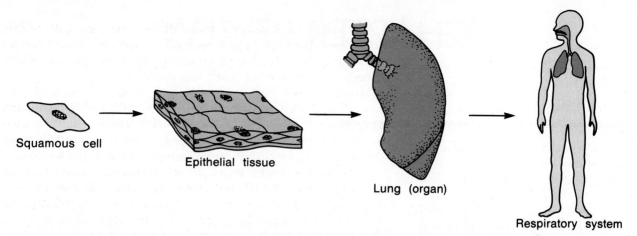

Squamous cell

Epithelial tissue

Lung (organ)

Respiratory system

Plants also have organs, such as roots, stems, flowers, and leaves. Each organ is made up of several different types of tissues, and each performs specific functions.

In many organisms, several different organs may work together to perform a particular function. Such a group of organs is called an **organ system**. Your nervous system, for example, contains your brain, spinal cord, and all the nerves that carry information to and from the parts of your body. Your respiratory system, which includes your nose, windpipe, and lungs, allows you to take in oxygen and excrete carbon dioxide.

An example of an organ system in plants is the vascular system of trees. The vascular system conducts water and dissolved minerals and food throughout the tree. It extends from the roots, through the trunk and branches, and into the leaves.

In any living organism, all the systems function together. Think about how your body functions when you hit a softball. Your muscular and skeletal systems allow your body and arms to move. This movement is coordinated by information from your nervous system. It is fueled by energy from food processed by your digestive system. Without the coordinated input of all these systems, you would be unable to hit the ball. All the systems working together make up the organism, or complete living thing.

Figure 5.17 Levels of organization for a complex multicellular organism: cells form tissues, which are part of organs, which are part of organ systems.

Checkpoint

1. Define a tissue.
2. Several different types of tissues working together to perform a common function compose a _____.
3. List the levels of organization in a multicellular organism, beginning with a cell.

CHAPTER REVIEW

Summary

- The cell theory was established by the work of many biologists over many years. Matthias Schleiden and Theodor Schwann concluded that cells are the basic component of all organisms. Rudolf Virchow concluded that cells can arise only from other cells.

- The cell theory states that
  1. The cell is the basic unit of structure of an organism.
  2. The cell is the basic unit of function of an organism.
  3. All cells come from other cells.

- All cells possess the characteristics of living things. Among those processes carried out at the cellular level are nutrition, respiration, absorption, excretion, biosynthesis, secretion, response, and reproduction.

- The nucleus contains the hereditary information of the cell. The nucleus also controls the activities of the cell.

- The plasma membrane is the living boundary of the cell. It determines what will enter and leave the cell. The structure of the plasma membrane is a fluid mosaic composed of a double layer of phospholipids in which proteins are embedded.

- Between the plasma membrane and the nucleus is a dense gel called the cytoplasm. Within the cytoplasm are a number of smaller structures called organelles. The cytoplasm contains a cytoskeleton composed of microtubules that determine the position and movement of many organelles.

- The cytoplasm contains numerous membrane-bound organelles. Some of these organelles are the mitochondria, which carry out respiration; Golgi bodies, which package and secrete proteins; and plastids, which contain pigments and store food.

- The cells of plants and some other organisms are protected by a cell wall.

- Eukaryotes are organisms in which the chromatin is surrounded by a nuclear membrane. Prokaryotes are organisms that lack a nucleus and other membrane-bound organelles.

- The cells of unicellular organisms must be able to perform all the functions necessary for life. In multicellular organisms, cells usually have specialized functions.

- A tissue is composed of a group of similar cells that perform a similar function. Organs are composed of groups of tissues that work together to perform a common function. An organ system is composed of a group of organs that perform a particular function.

Vocabulary

absorption	multicellular
biosynthesis	nuclear membrane
cellulose	nucleolus
cell wall	nucleus
chlorophyll	nutrition
chloroplast	organ
chromatin	organelle
chromoplast	organ system
chromosome	pectin
cytoplasm	phospholipid
cytoskeleton	plasma membrane
endoplasmic	plastid
reticulum	primary cell wall
eukaryote	prokaryote
excretion	respiration
Golgi body	ribosome
leucoplast	secondary cell wall
lysosome	secretion
microtubule	tissue
middle lamella	unicellular
mitochondrion	vacuole
	vesicle

Review

1. What are the three parts of the cell theory?
2. Name three structures of the nucleus.

In the following list, match the cell part to the correct description.

3. leucoplast
4. Golgi body
5. plasma membrane
6. cell wall
7. ribosome
8. vacuole
9. lysosome
10. chloroplast
11. mitochondrion
12. chromatin

a. prepares proteins for secretion
b. synthesizes proteins
c. contains hereditary information of the cell
d. stores liquids
e. performs cellular respiration
f. contains chlorophyll
g. contains digestive enzymes
h. supports and protects the softer parts of the cell
i. regulates which materials may enter and leave the cell
j. stores starch

Interpret and Apply

1. How does the cell theory support the concept of biogenesis?
2. Why is the plasma membrane described as being a fluid mosaic?
3. Name five cell parts that are bounded by membranes.
4. State two differences between the plasma membrane and the cell wall.
5. Why were lysosomes once called death sacs?
6. What is the difference between excretion and secretion?
7. Would you expect a unicellular organism to be more or less specialized than a single cell from a multicellular organism?
8. Place the following events in the proper sequence. (a) The protein is secreted. (b) The protein is manufactured on the ribosome. (c) A vesicle transports the protein through the cytoplasm.

9. Which of the following structures are found in the cells of most plants? Which are found in the cells of animals? Which are found in both?
   a. plasma membrane
   b. nucleus
   c. chloroplast
   d. cell wall
   e. centriole
   f. middle lamella
   g. ribosome
10. Which of the following are found in the cells of eukaryotes? Which are found in prokaryotes? Which are found in both?
    a. plasma membrane
    b. nucleus
    c. chloroplast
    d. cytoplasm
    e. chromatin

Challenge

1. Most animals are motile heterotrophs. Most plants are stationary autotrophs. Explain how the differences in the structure of plant and animal cells contribute to these characteristics.
2. Hormones are chemicals that are produced in one part of an organism, then transported to another part of the organism where they cause a response. The pancreas is an organ that secretes hormones into the bloodstream. One of these hormones is the protein insulin. What specializations would you expect to find in the cells of the pancreas? Explain.
3. Some organisms have structures that are not made of living cells. For example, your hair and fingernails are not alive. Does this observation contradict the cell theory? Explain.

Projects

1. Visit a laboratory at a nearby university or other institution. Ask to see some of the newer equipment that is used to study cells. Find out what the equipment is used for and how it works. Report your findings to your class.

6 Homeostasis

Sailboats in a brisk wind

Have you ever been sailing? It's a sport that requires great skill. Sailors must respond quickly to changes in their environment. The force and direction of the wind are never constant. Each time the wind changes, the sailor must adjust the position of the sail in order to remain on course. When the wind is brisk, a boat will tilt, or heel, toward the waves. In strong winds, sailors may have to move to the opposite side of their boat in order to keep the boat upright. You could think of sailing as a balancing act between the boat and the wind.

Like a sailboat, living things are subject to constant changes in their environment. Organisms that live in the ocean are subjected to changes in the chemicals dissolved in the sea water, in the amount of sunlight, and in the temperature. Organisms that live on land encounter even greater fluctuations in their environment. As the environment changes, organisms must adjust accordingly. Survival is a continual struggle to maintain a steady state while external conditions are changing.

Passive Transport

The chemical substances inside living organisms are very different from those found around them. For a cell to live, it must maintain the concentrations of certain chemicals within very narrow limits. The process of maintaining a relatively constant internal environment despite changing external conditions is called **homeostasis** [hoh-mee-oh-STAY-sihs].

Single-celled organisms maintain a relatively constant concentration of many ions and organic compounds. The cells within a multicellular organism, such as a human, also maintain a relatively constant concentration of substances.

Homeostasis occurs at the multicellular level as well as the cellular level. For example, when you are healthy your temperature stays close to 37°C, whether the outside temperature is 5°C or 30°C. If it is too hot outside, you cool down by perspiring. If it is too cold, you warm up by shivering. Homeostasis is necessary for life at both the cellular and the multicellular level of organization.

6–1   The Cell's Environment

Most cells are surrounded by fluids. Organisms that live in the ocean are surrounded by sea water. Organisms that live on land contain fluids, such as blood, that bathe most of the organisms' cells in liquid. The cytoplasm of a cell is composed mostly of water, with various substances in solution. The fluids outside the cell are also composed mostly of water, but with different substances in solution. Maintaining the proper balance of all these substances is part of homeostasis.

If the cell is to keep its identity and remain alive, it must maintain an internal environment that is very different from its surroundings. The plasma membrane separates the chemicals of the cell from those of the environment.

Yet in order to function, a cell must allow certain substances to pass through the plasma membrane. Cells require nutrients and oxygen, which must enter the cell from the outside. Cells also produce waste products, such as carbon dioxide, that must be removed from the cell. How do all these substances enter and leave the cell?

6–2   Diffusion

To answer this question, it is useful to understand the movement of molecules. As you learned in Chapter 3, molecules in gases and liquids are not stationary. Instead, they have

CONCEPTS

- definition of homeostasis
- process of diffusion across a permeable membrane
- movement of water by osmosis
- effects of osmosis on plant and animal cells

 BIOLOGY INSIGHTS

A watery environment is essential to the functioning of all cells. The only organisms that are truly successful on land are those that are able to maintain an aqueous environment for their internal cells. Most unicellular land organisms are confined to living in wet places, such as damp soil or decaying matter.

kinetic energy and are constantly moving about. As molecules move, they bump into each other.

A molecule will move in a straight line until it strikes another molecule. Then, like one billiard ball hitting another, it will change its direction. The molecule will then continue in the new direction until its next collision.

Collisions tend to scatter molecules apart. Molecules that are crowded together collide more often than those that are spread out. If many molecules are concentrated in a small area, they will gradually spread out until they are evenly distributed throughout the space available. The movement of molecules from an area of higher concentration to an area of lower concentration is called **diffusion**.

Figure 6.1 Over time the dye molecules diffuse throughout the water.

You are probably already familiar with the effects of diffusion. If you put a spoonful of sugar in a cup of tea, it will dissolve. At first the sugar molecules will be very concentrated in the bottom of the cup. But if you wait long enough, the sugar molecules will eventually diffuse throughout the entire cup of tea.

Molecules diffuse through air as well as through liquids. When you bake bread, some of the wonderful-smelling molecules bounce away from the dough. If you are sitting in the kitchen, the molecules will reach your nose rather quickly. If you're in the next room, it will take longer for the smell to reach you. Eventually the aroma will fill the entire house.

6–3   Permeability

In addition to moving through liquids and gases, molecules can diffuse through a more structured material if it contains spaces through which molecules can pass. A material is said to be **permeable** [PUR-mee-uh-buhl] to certain molecules if it allows them to pass through. The plasma membrane is permeable to certain kinds of molecules.

You can demonstrate diffusion through a membrane by using a sack made of cellulose. Cellulose is permeable to water and small molecules, such as the molecules of food coloring. First, fill the sack with water and blue food coloring. Then tie the open end of the sack and place it in a beaker of pure water. What do you expect to see?

The molecules of blue food coloring and water can pass readily through the cellulose. The water in the beaker can also enter the sack. Because the food-coloring molecules are more concentrated inside the sack, they will tend to spread out and move out of the sack. Water molecules, which are more concentrated outside the sack, will move into the sack. Eventually the water inside and outside the sack will be uniformly pale blue.

Like the cellulose sack, the plasma membrane of a cell is permeable to small molecules. Molecules such as water, oxygen, and carbon dioxide easily pass through the membrane. When a waste product such as carbon dioxide accumulates inside a cell, its molecules are more highly concentrated inside the cell than outside. Therefore, carbon dioxide molecules tend to move out of the cell.

The diffusion of molecules through a membrane does not require any energy from the cell. **Passive transport** is the movement of molecules through a membrane without the use of cellular energy. Diffusion through the plasma membrane is a form of passive transport.

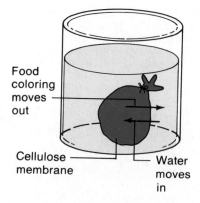

Food coloring moves out

Cellulose membrane

Water moves in

Figure 6.2 The cellulose sack is a permeable membrane. The diffusion of substances through this membrane is passive transport.

6–4   Selective Permeability and Osmosis

Sometimes a barrier allows only certain molecules to move through it. A window screen is such a barrier. It permits air to enter and leave a room, but it does not let flies pass through. Thus, a screen could be said to be permeable to air but not to flies. A barrier that allows only particular substances to pass through is said to be **selectively permeable**.

The plasma membrane is selectively permeable. Small molecules, such as oxygen and carbon dioxide, move easily between the molecules of the protein and phospholipid membrane. Certain large nonpolar molecules can also cross the membrane.

To investigate how selective permeability affects the cell, imagine a slightly different experiment with the cellulose sack. Fill the sack with a solution of water and starch. Starch, as you learned in Chapter 4, is a large molecule. What will happen when you place this sack in a beaker of pure water? The starch molecules are too big to pass through the cellulose, so they remain inside the sack, as shown in Figure 6.3.

Figure 6.3 Starch molecules cannot pass through the cellulose membrane. The osmotic pressure increases as water enters the sack at a faster rate than it leaves the sack.

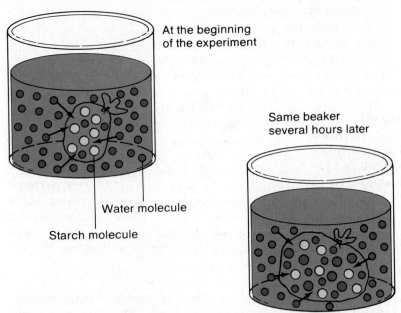

At the beginning of the experiment

Same beaker several hours later

Water molecule

Starch molecule

Because it contains starch molecules, the liquid inside the sack contains less water than the liquid outside the sack. Thus the concentration of water molecules is greater outside the sack than inside. Water molecules will move through the sack in both directions, but more tend to move into the sack than out of it. This movement of water is called **osmosis** [ahz-MOH-suhs]. Osmosis is the diffusion of water molecules through a selectively permeable membrane from an area of greater concentration to an area of lesser concentration. In both diffusion and osmosis the molecules are moving down a gradient from higher concentration to lower. Therefore the process does not require energy from the cell. Since osmosis does not require cell energy, osmosis is a form of passive transport.

As water molecules continue to enter the sack faster than they leave, pressure builds up inside the sack. The pressure caused by osmosis is called **osmotic pressure**. The increase in osmotic pressure changes the shape of the sack in much the same way that increasing the air pressure in a bicycle tire causes the tire to change shape. As a result of osmotic pressure, the sack swells.

As the osmotic pressure increases, the molecules inside the sack will collide more frequently. These collisions will tend to push some of the molecules out of the sack. At a certain point the colliding molecules will be pushed out of the sack at a rate equal to that of molecules entering the sack by osmosis. The point at which the rate of molecules leaving the sack equals the rate of molecules entering the sack is called **equilibrium**.

The movement of molecules through the cellulose does not cease at equilibrium. The molecules continue to move as before. But since the rate of movement in both directions is equal, there is no change in the concentration of the molecules on either side of the sack.

The direction in which water molecules move during osmosis depends upon where the water molecules are more highly concentrated. The cellulose sack in Figure 6.4a contains 10 percent starch and 90 percent water. The liquid surrounding the sack is 100 percent water. When compared to the liquid surrounding it, the liquid in the sack is said to be **hypertonic**. A hypertonic solution contains a higher concentration of dissolved substances, or solutes, than a solution to which it is compared. As the arrows show, water molecules tend to move into the hypertonic solution where the concentration of water is lower.

The sack in Figure 6.4b contains 10 percent starch and 90 percent water, but the surrounding liquid is 20 percent starch and 80 percent water. In this example, the water in the sack is said to be hypotonic. A **hypotonic** solution contains a lower concentration of solutes than the solution to which it is being compared. Water molecules tend to move out of a hypotonic solution.

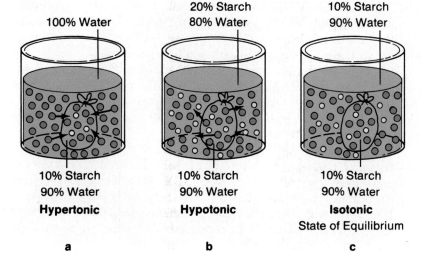

100% Water

20% Starch
80% Water

10% Starch
90% Water

10% Starch
90% Water
Hypertonic

10% Starch
90% Water
Hypotonic

10% Starch
90% Water
Isotonic
State of Equilibrium

a

b

c

Figure 6.4 All of the cellulose sacks were filled with the same proportions of starch and water. The type of solution in the sack depends on the proportions of substances outside the sack.

Figure 6.4c shows a sack containing 10 percent starch and 90 percent water. The composition of the fluid surrounding the sack is identical to the solution inside the sack. The two solutions are described as being **isotonic**. In this case, the sack and the surrounding fluid are in equilibrium. As you would expect, water molecules enter and leave the sack at the same rate.

Note that hypertonic, hypotonic, and isotonic are relative terms. In all three cases illustrated, the cellulose sack contains a solution that is 10 percent starch and 90 percent water. Depending on the solution to which it is compared, this solution may be hypertonic, hypotonic, or isotonic.

6–5 Animal Cells and Osmosis

Animal cells behave in much the same way as the cellulose sack. A red blood cell is about 80 percent water. If a red blood cell is placed in pure water, the contents of the cell will be hypertonic. More water molecules will tend to enter the cell than leave the cell. As shown in Figure 6.5, the blood cell will swell. Eventually the increasing osmotic pressure may cause the red blood cell to burst.

If a blood cell is placed in water that is 30 percent salt and 70 percent water, the contents of the blood cell will be hypotonic. Water molecules will tend to leave the cell. With fewer molecules, the osmotic pressure will drop. As a result of the loss of water, the cell will shrink.

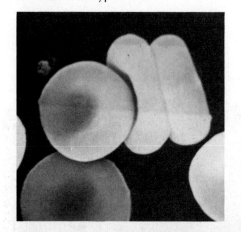

Figure 6.5 *Top:* Normal blood cells · are disc-shaped in an isotonic solution. *Bottom left:* The same cells swell to the point of bursting when the contents are hypertonic. *Bottom right:* The cells shrink when the contents are hypotonic.

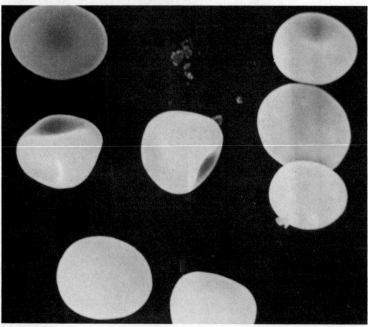
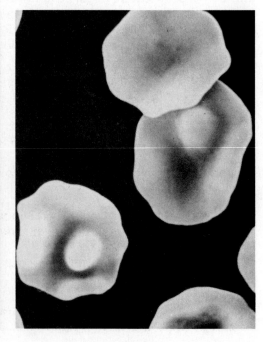

6–6 Turgor Pressure and Plasmolysis

Unlike animal cells, the cells of plants are surrounded by a rigid cell wall. Because of the cell wall, the effect of osmotic pressure on plant cells is somewhat different from its effect on animal cells.

When a plant cell is placed in a hypotonic solution, water molecules enter the cell, causing it to swell. But the cell does not burst. Instead, the cell wall resists the osmotic pressure. Osmotic pressure within a plant cell is called **turgor pressure**. Turgor pressure gives the soft tissues of plant stems and leaves their firm, rigid form. Plant cells that are swollen with water are said to be **turgid**.

If a plant cell is surrounded by a hypertonic fluid, water molecules will leave the cell. As water molecules leave, the turgor pressure drops. This causes the cytoplasm to shrink away from the cell wall. This loss of turgor pressure is called **plasmolysis** [plaz-MAHL-uh-sihs]. Plasmolysis causes plants to wilt.

Figure 6.6 *Left: Elodea* cells are turgid in fresh water. *Right:* When these cells are placed in salt water, plasmolysis occurs.

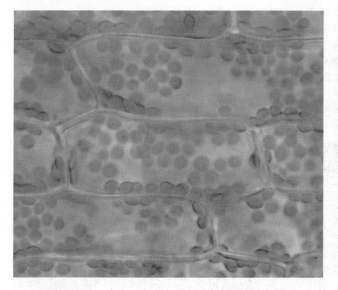
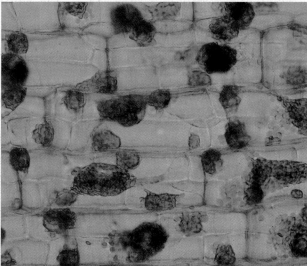

Checkpoint

1. What is the name of the process in which molecules tend to move from an area of higher concentration to an area of lower concentration?
2. What kind of membrane allows some, but not all, molecules to pass through it?
3. Define *osmosis*.
4. The point at which water molecules enter and leave the cell at the same rate is called _____.

Active Transport

Substances diffuse through the plasma membrane as a result of differences in concentration. This movement does not require the expenditure of energy. For a cell to achieve homeostasis, however, it must maintain high concentrations of substances that may be present in very low concentrations in the surrounding liquid. For example, cells contain high concentrations of certain amino acids and ions. Thus it is often necessary for a cell to move molecules across the plasma membrane against the direction of diffusion. For such movement to occur, the cell must expend energy. Movement of molecules that requires cellular energy is called **active transport**.

6–7   Transport Molecules

Water-soluble molecules such as amino acids are taken into the cell by one form of active transport. In this process, the cell manufactures a specific protein called a **transport protein**. The transport protein is embedded in the plasma membrane. When a needed molecule touches the cell, the transport protein attaches to it and aids its entry into the cell.

Transport proteins are highly specific — they attach only to certain molecules. Like enzymes, transport proteins are not used up in the transport process. Unlike enzymes, transport molecules do not produce a chemical change in the molecules to which they are temporarily bound.

CONCEPTS

- difference between active and passive transport
- function of transport proteins and transport vesicles

Figure 6.7 Transport proteins use energy to move amino acids and other substances across the plasma membrane by active transport.

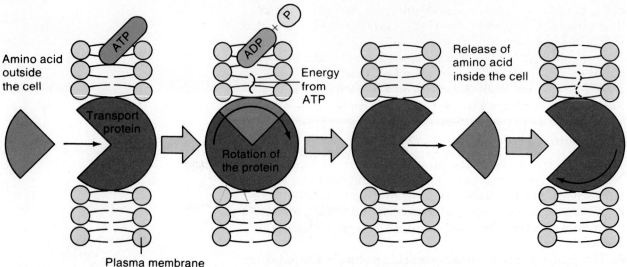

6–8 Transport by Vesicles

Certain large molecules may enter the cell without the involvement of transport proteins. These molecules enter indented areas within the membrane. As shown in Figure 6.8, parts of the fluid membrane surround the molecule, forming a vesicle. When the vesicle pinches off, the remaining membrane seals itself.

The vesicle then moves into the cytoplasm of the cell. Once inside, the vesicle releases its contents into the cytoplasm. The molecules of membranes around the vesicle then recombine with other membranes within the cell. The transport of molecules into the cell by means of vesicles is called **endocytosis** [en-doh-sy-TOH-suhs]. Endocytosis requires cellular energy.

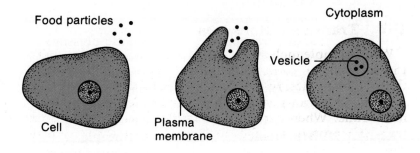

Figure 6.8 Endocytosis occurs when the plasma membrane surrounds particles such as food. The membrane pinches off within the cell to form a vesicle which carries material into the cytoplasm.

Some unicellular organisms feed by a kind of endocytosis called **phagocytosis** [fag-oh-sy-TOH-suhs]. Animals such as amoebas have flexible cell membranes. When these organisms encounter a particle of food, they surround it by extensions of their cytoplasm. Once the food is surrounded, the molecules of the plasma membrane join together, so the food is enclosed in a vesicle. Once inside the cytoplasm, the food is digested by special enzymes.

Large molecules may also be released from a cell by means of vesicles. The transport of macromolecules out of a cell by means of vesicles is called **exocytosis**. Proteins packaged by the Golgi bodies leave the cell by exocytosis. Both endocytosis and exocytosis require cellular energy.

Checkpoint

1. What kind of molecules allow amino acids to enter a cell?
2. What are vesicles composed of?
3. By what process do vesicles transport large molecules into a cell?
4. By what process do proteins packaged by the Golgi bodies leave a cell?

CHAPTER REVIEW

Summary

- Organisms exist in changing environments. Yet if a cell is to function properly, its internal environment must remain relatively constant. For life processes to continue, the concentrations of various substances within a cell can vary only slightly. The maintenance of constant internal conditions despite a changing environment is called homeostasis.

- The plasma membrane determines which molecules may enter or leave a cell. The plasma membrane is a selectively permeable barrier.

- Some small molecules can cross the plasma membranes by passive transport, which requires no cellular energy. Diffusion and osmosis are forms of passive transport.

- The direction in which a substance diffuses through a membrane depends on the concentration of the substance on each side of the membrane. *Hypertonic, hypotonic,* and *isotonic* are terms that are used to describe the relative concentrations of solutions.

- Osmosis is the diffusion of water through a selectively permeable membrane from an area of higher concentration to an area of lower concentration.

- In animal cells, an increase in osmotic pressure may eventually cause the plasma membranes to burst.

- In plant cells, an increase in osmotic pressure is counteracted by the rigid cell walls. Plant cells that are swollen with water are said to be turgid. Loss of turgor pressure in plant cells causes plasmolysis. Plasmolysis causes wilting.

- In active transport, substances are transported across a membrane against the direction of diffusion. Active transport requires the expenditure of cellular energy. Transport proteins and vesicles are involved in the active transport of molecules.

- In endocytosis, vesicles transport molecules into the cell. In exocytosis, vesicles release molecules from the cell.

- Some unicellular organisms feed by a form of endocytosis called phagocytosis.

Vocabulary

active transport	osmotic pressure
diffusion	passive transport
endocytosis	permeable
equilibrium	phagocytosis
exocytosis	plasmolysis
homeostasis	selectively
hypertonic	permeable
hypotonic	transport protein
isotonic	turgid
osmosis	turgor pressure

Review

1. As a result of what process do molecules tend to become evenly distributed in a given space?
2. Name two types of molecules that can pass easily through the plasma membrane.
3. Why are starch molecules unable to pass through a cellulose sack?
4. Does the movement of molecules stop when equilibrium occurs? Explain.
5. When comparing two liquids, the liquid with more solute dissolved in it is
   (a) hypertonic, (b) hypotonic, (c) isotonic, (d) equilibrium.

6. Will a plant cell burst if placed in a hypotonic solution? Explain.
7. Name a molecule that crosses the plasma membrane with the aid of a transport protein.
8. What is a vesicle?
9. Name two types of movement of molecules across membranes that require vesicles.
10. What condition causes wilting?

Interpret and Apply

1. When healthy, the human body maintains the amount of sugar in the blood at a relatively constant level. Of what principle is this an example?
2. What principle is demonstrated when the fragrance of uncapped perfume gradually fills a room?
3. Distinguish between diffusion and osmosis.
4. Which of the following processes require the expenditure of cellular energy?
    a. osmosis
    b. exocytosis
    c. diffusion
    d. phagocytosis
    e. active transport
    f. endocytosis
5. What would happen to a red blood cell if it were placed in a hypotonic solution?
6. What would happen if you placed a plant clipping in a solution of very salty water?
7. Why is the plasma membrane essential to the cell and its function? Why is it important for the membrane to be selectively permeable?
8. Describe an example of homeostasis in humans.
9. How would the response of a plant cell to a hypertonic solution differ from the response of an animal cell? Explain.
10. Describe the way in which an amoeba takes in food.

Challenge

1. Suppose that the level of carbon dioxide in the fluid outside the cell became higher than the concentration of carbon dioxide inside the cell. What would happen?
2. Why doesn't turgor pressure exist in animal cells?
3. You have a sack that is not permeable to starch molecules. A sack containing 20 percent starch and 80 percent water is placed in a container of 100 percent water. (a) Is the fluid in the sack hypotonic or hypertonic compared to the surrounding solution? (b) In which direction will the water molecules tend to move?

Projects

1. Investigate osmosis by using a white potato. Cut two equal slices from a potato, each about 3 centimeters thick. Place one slice in a glass of pure water. Place the other in a glass of heavily salted water. After waiting 30 minutes, take both pieces out of water and compare them. Explain your results on the basis of the principles explained in this chapter.
2. Very few organisms are able to live in environments that contain extremely high concentrations of salt. Research the organisms that are able to live in the Great Salt Lake in Utah or the Salton Sea in California. What adaptations allow these organisms to live in such environments? Report to your class on your findings.

7 Cell Energy

Sunlight reaches the understory of the Olympic rain forest, Washington

Life on Earth depends on the energy produced by our closest star, the sun. Energy from the sun travels through space in the form of light. Here on Earth sunlight filters down through the forest, eventually falling on green leaves. Leaves are able to trap this sunlight and use it to manufacture food.

When you eat, you are getting energy that originally came from the sun. The energy in fruits, vegetables, and grains is captured by plants. Since cows and hens eat grains, when you eat milk and eggs you are getting energy from the sun second-hand.

Your body uses energy continuously. When you opened this book, you used energy. As you move your eyes across the printed pages, you are using energy. The ultimate source of this energy is sunlight. In fact, sunlight is the source of energy for all energy-requiring activities of life. The conversion of energy from one form to another is accomplished by many chemical reactions. Energy conversion is a basic biological process upon which all living things depend.

Energy from Food

The activities of all living things require energy. Swimming, flying, capturing prey, and even the flash of a firefly use energy. Most of the activities of cells require energy too. Cell growth and the active transport of molecules across membranes require energy. The synthesis of carbohydrates, proteins, and lipids also requires energy.

The immediate source of energy for cells is the energy stored in the chemical bonds of organic molecules. Energy may be stored in many organic molecules, especially carbohydrates such as sugars and starches. These molecules are called food molecules. The most common food molecule is the sugar glucose.

7–1 ATP: The Energy Currency of the Cell

A cell may have a large supply of energy stored in the chemical bonds of sugars. However, a cell cannot use these sugars directly to fuel its energy-requiring processes. In order to use this energy, a cell must transfer the energy in its sugar molecules to a substance called adenosine triphosphate, or **ATP**.

To understand the function of ATP in a cell, it may help to compare energy to money. Have you ever tried to buy something from a vending machine with only a dollar bill? If so, you know that vending machines will accept only certain forms of currency. Although a dollar bill has the same value as four quarters, you have to exchange your dollar bill for four quarters before you can operate a vending machine. A similar situation exists in the cell. The sugar molecules are like dollar bills, while ATP is like the change in your pockets.

As shown in Figure 7.1, each ATP is composed of the base adenine and the sugar ribose. The ribose is bound to a chain of three phosphates. The phosphate molecules are connected by energy-containing bonds.

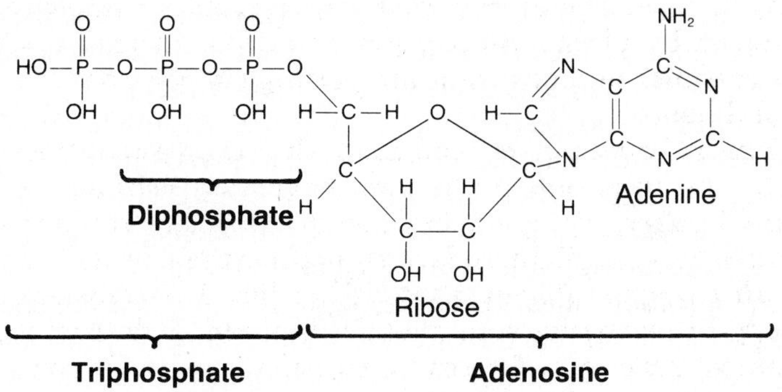

CONCEPTS

- ATP and cell energy
- general equation of respiration
- anaerobic and aerobic stages of respiration
- products of glycolysis
- citric-acid cycle and electron transport chain
- two pathways of fermentation

Figure 7.1 The structural formula of a molecule of ATP

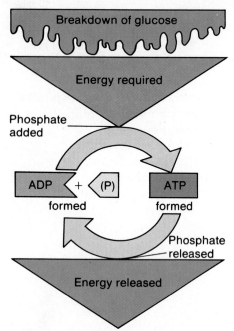

Figure 7.2 The ADP-ATP cycle. Energy released from glucose is stored in the phosphate bonds of ATP. When the cell needs energy, it can break the last phosphate bond of ATP, thus forming ADP again.

If the cell needs energy, it can break the last phosphate bond, thus liberating the energy that held the second and third phosphates together. When the last phosphate bond is broken, the molecule of ATP becomes a molecule of adenosine diphosphate (ADP) and a molecule of phosphate (P). The reaction can be expressed by the following equation.

$$ATP \rightleftharpoons ADP + P + energy$$

The double arrows indicate that the reaction is reversible.

ATP contains the principal form of energy that is usable by cells. When the cell has extra energy, it can be stored in ATP. This energy can easily be released from the ATP later. Almost all energy-requiring processes in cells, and therefore in organisms, require ATP as an energy source. Where does this ATP come from?

7–2 Cellular Respiration: Energy Transfer

Most cells produce ATP by breaking the energy containing bonds of glucose. The production of ATP from the complete breakdown of glucose is called **respiration**. Respiration uses oxygen to break sugars down into carbon dioxide and water.

In everyday language, people often speak of breathing as respiration. But breathing is simply a mechanical process that provides oxygen to the cells of animals. Once in the cells, this oxygen is used in cellular respiration. Although breathing is necessary for respiration, the two processes are quite separate.

In respiration, oxygen and glucose combine to release energy. Water and carbon dioxide are given off as waste products. The chemical equation that describes respiration follows.

$$C_6H_{12}O_6 + 6O_2 \rightarrow 6CO_2 + 6H_2O + energy$$
$$\text{(sugar)} \qquad\qquad\qquad\qquad \text{(ATP)}$$

Respiration occurs in the numerous mitochondria of each cell. Every mitochondrion has an outer membrane and an inner membrane folded into **cristae.** Surrounding the cristae is a dense fluid called the **matrix.** Enzymes in the mitochondria can transfer chemical energy from sugar to ATP.

To understand respiration, it may be helpful to think of the mitochondria as miniature fireplaces and the molecules of sugar as logs. When logs burn in a fireplace, they release energy as heat and light. The fire requires oxygen, and gives off carbon dioxide and water as waste products.

In respiration, sugar combines with oxygen, releasing energy and giving off carbon dioxide and water. This reaction cannot begin without an initial input of energy. This initial input is a bit like a match used to start a fire. The energy provided by the match allows the wood to start burning. The initial energy of the match is far less than the amount of energy released from the burning log.

Unlike a fire in a fireplace, though, the reactions in the mitochondria occur gradually. As you know, the heat of a fire is intense. If such heat were generated in a cell, the cell would die. Special enzymes in the mitochondria allow a stepwise release of energy.

There are two major stages of respiration. Scientists refer to these stages as the **anaerobic** [an-air-OH-bik] stage and the **aerobic** [air-OH-bik] stage. The anaerobic stage may take place without oxygen. The aerobic stage requires oxygen.

7–3   Glycolysis: the Anaerobic Stage

The first stage in the breakdown of glucose occurs in the cytoplasm of the cell. This stage is called **glycolysis** [gly-KAHL-uh-sihs]. During glycolysis a molecule of glucose is split into two molecules of a 3-carbon compound called **pyruvic acid**.

Two molecules of ATP provide the energy to split a molecule of glucose in half. When a molecule of glucose splits, it releases enough energy to form 4 molecules of ATP. The ATP is formed from ADP and phosphate already in the cell. Since 2 molecules of ATP were required to initiate glycolysis, the net result of this phase of glycolysis is 2 molecules of ATP.

In the conversion of glucose to pyruvic acid, hydrogen is released. This hydrogen is picked up by a coenzyme called nicotinamide adenine dinucleotide, or **NAD^+**. NAD^+ is a **hydrogen ion acceptor** and an **electron acceptor**. When the NAD^+ accepts hydrogen and two electrons, it becomes NADH. Two molecules of NADH form for each molecule of glucose split. NADH is an energy-rich compound that is used in the aerobic stage of respiration.

Figure 7.3 Glycolysis, or the anaerobic stage of respiration, consists of a series of complex reactions represented by the large arrow in the diagram. Two ATPs are required to start the reaction; four ATPs are produced.

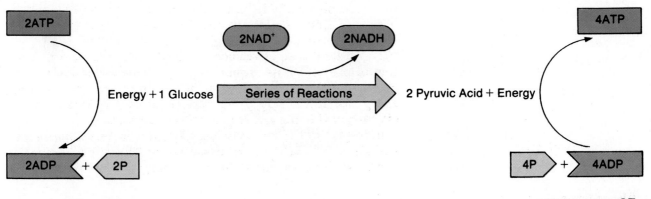

7–4 The Aerobic Stage

After glycolysis, the chemical bonds of pyruvic acid are broken down in a series of reactions. These reactions, which occur in the mitochondria, require oxygen. As you read about the steps of aerobic respiration, refer to Figure 7.4.

The pyruvic acid that was formed in glycolysis is transported into the mitochondria. In the presence of oxygen, pyruvic acid breaks down into the 2-carbon compound **acetic acid** plus a molecule of carbon dioxide. This carbon dioxide is released from the cell as a waste product.

The acetic acid combines with a coenzyme called coenzyme A to form **acetyl CoA**. In this step NADH is formed. Acetyl CoA then enters the citric-acid cycle.

Citric-Acid Cycle As the word *cycle* suggests, the **citric-acid cycle** is a series of reactions that begins and ends with the same compound. Citric acid is the first compound formed in this series.

In each turn of the citric-acid cycle, one molecule of the 2-carbon compound acetyl CoA combines with a 4-carbon compound present in the mitochondria. The resulting 6-carbon compound is citric acid. Citric acid is then broken down in a series of reactions. Each reaction is controlled by a separate enzyme, and each reaction results in a different intermediate compound. During the reactions of the citric-acid cycle, 2 molecules of carbon dioxide are removed, leaving the 4-carbon compound at the end of each cycle. The 4-carbon compound may then combine with another molecule of acetyl CoA, beginning another turn of the cycle.

Figure 7.4 Aerobic respiration. The aerobic stage of respiration includes the conversion of pyruvic acid to acetyl CoA and the citric-acid cycle.

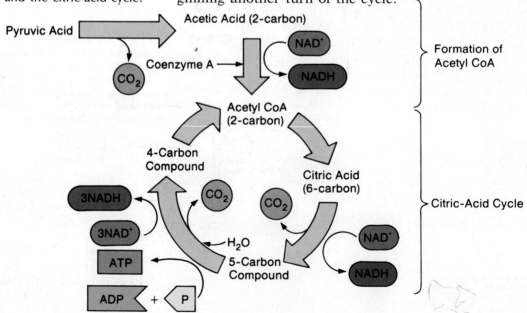

For each molecule of acetyl CoA that enters the cycle, 8 atoms of hydrogen are released by the intermediate compounds. The hydrogen atoms are trapped by NAD^+, forming NADH. Therefore, each turn of the cycle yields 4 molecules of NADH.

Electron Transport Chain In the second phase of aerobic respiration, NADH releases the electrons and hydrogen atoms trapped during glycolysis and the citric-acid cycle. Thus NADH becomes NAD^+ again.

The electrons contained in the hydrogen atoms pass through a series of coenzymes located on the cristae. These coenzymes are electron acceptors. Each time an electron moves from one acceptor to another, energy is released. The energy released is used to form molecules of ATP from ADP and P.

The series of electron acceptors make up the **electron transport chain**. As an electron is passed from coenzyme to coenzyme, some of its energy is trapped as ATP. At the end of the chain, the electron still exists, but it has less energy than at the beginning of the electron transport chain.

The NADH formed during the citric-acid cycle feeds electrons into the electron transport system. The electron transport chain releases energy with each transfer of electrons.

Electrons supplied by NADH at the beginning of the electron transport chain must be removed at the end. Otherwise, the

Figure 7.5 The electron transport chain. As electrons are passed along a series of coenzymes, they release energy. This energy is captured as ATP.

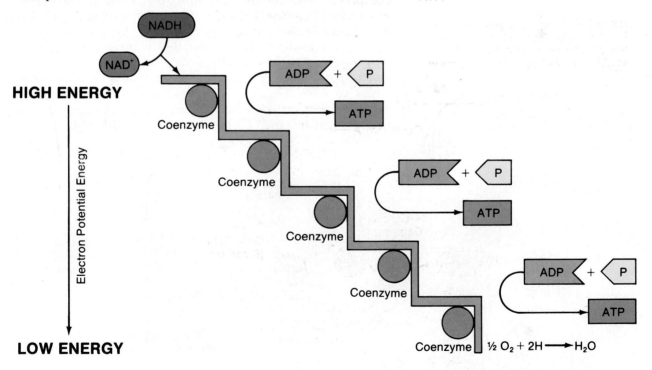

Reactions	ATP Made per Glucose Molecule
ANAEROBIC RESPIRATION (GLYCOLYSIS) 2ATP + Glucose → 2 Pyruvic Acid + 4ATP	−2 +4
AEROBIC RESPIRATION 2 Pyruvic Acid → 2 Acetic Acid Citric-Acid Cycle (2 cycles per glucose molecule) Electron Transport Chain	0 +2 +32
Net Yield of ATP	+36

Figure 7.6 ATP yield from the complete breakdown of glucose into carbon dioxide and water.

system would be clogged by electrons. New electrons could no longer pass down the electron transport chain, and electron transport would cease.

The last member of the chain of electron acceptors is oxygen. When the electrons reach the end of the electron transport chain, they combine with oxygen and hydrogen to form water. This water is released from the cell as a waste product.

At the completion of glycolysis and aerobic respiration, glucose has been broken down into carbon dioxide and water, and energy has been released.

For every molecule of glucose that is broken down in glycolysis and respiration, 38 molecules of ATP are formed. But remember that glycolysis requires an initial input of 2 molecules of ATP. Thus for every molecule of glucose that is completely converted to carbon dioxide and water in glycolysis and respiration, the cell has a net gain of 36 ATPs.

Figure 7.7 Location of the stages of respiration in a mitochondrion

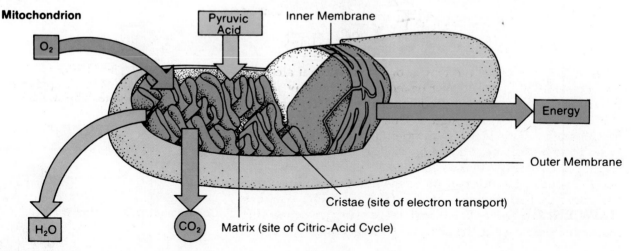

Mitochondrion

Pyruvic Acid

Inner Membrane

O_2

Energy

Outer Membrane

Cristae (site of electron transport)

H_2O

CO_2

Matrix (site of Citric-Acid Cycle)

7–5 Fermentation

Glycolysis does not require oxygen, but the aerobic reactions that follow glycolysis do require oxygen. Some organisms do not contain the enzymes necessary to break down pyruvic acid through the aerobic phase of respiration. These organisms obtain all of their energy from anaerobic reactions. When glucose is broken down without oxygen, a process called **fermentation** occurs. Fermentation is the conversion of glucose to lactic acid or alcohol. Like aerobic respiration, fermentation begins with glycolysis.

Fermentation produces no ATP in addition to that produced in glycolysis. Fermentation does, however, remove pyruvic acid from the cell. If pyruvic acid accumulated in the cell, glycolysis would stop. By removing pyruvic acid from the cell, fermentation allows glycolysis to continue to produce a net product of 2 ATPs for every molecule of glucose.

There are two kinds of fermentation. **Alcoholic fermentation** occurs in microorganisms such as yeasts. **Lactic acid fermentation** occurs in the cells of bacteria and animals.

Alcoholic Fermentation In alcoholic fermentation, pyruvic acid combines with the hydrogen from NADH to produce ethyl alcohol. The equation is shown below.

$$CH_3COCOOH + 2NADH \rightarrow CH_3CH_2OH + CO_2 + 2NAD^+$$
(pyruvic acid)   (ethyl alcohol)

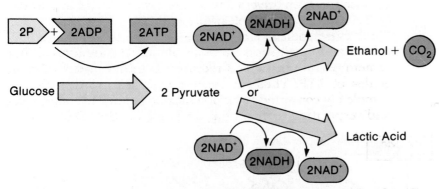

The yeast that is used to leaven bread carries out alcoholic fermentation. If you have ever baked bread, you may already be familiar with some of the products of alcoholic fermentation.

Bread dough contains sugar. This sugar is broken down by the yeast cells in alcoholic fermentation. As the yeast cells grow, they produce more and more carbon dioxide. This carbon dioxide forms tiny bubbles in the dough, which make the dough increase in volume. As fermentation produces more and more carbon dioxide, the dough rises. Dough rises best if kept in a warm place because the rate of enzyme-controlled reactions increases as the temperature increases.

Figure 7.8 Two pathways of fermentation. The enzymes present in an organism determine which pathway is followed.

Figure 7.9 During strenuous activity, lactic acid may build up in the muscles of an athlete.

Figure 7.10 The products of cellular respiration and fermentation

Lactic Acid Fermentation In lactic acid fermentation, no carbon dioxide is given off. Instead, pyruvic acid combines with hydrogen from NADH to produce lactic acid according to the following equation:

$$CH_3COCOOH + 2NADH \rightarrow CH_3CHOHCOOH + 2NAD^+$$
(pyruvic acid)   (lactic acid)

Lactic acid fermentation can occur in the cells of humans when there is not enough oxygen available for the aerobic stages of respiration. When you are exercising strenuously, glycolysis occurs at a high rate. In your active muscles, much pyruvic acid is produced. At this time your muscle cells may not receive enough oxygen to process all the pyruvic acid through the steps of aerobic respiration. Instead, your muscle cells produce lactic acid. The production of lactic acid permits glycolysis to continue to supply ATP to your muscles.

When lactic acid builds up in your muscles, it causes the muscles to ache. After strenuous exercise, you must continue to breathe heavily. The oxygen you take in as you catch your breath allows your cells to convert the accumulated lactic acid back to pyruvic acid.

As a result of fermentation, each molecule of glucose yields only 2 molecules of ATP. Compare this to the 36 molecules of ATP produced in aerobic respiration. In fermentation the rest of the energy remains in the chemical bonds of the waste products.

Fermentation	
Lactic Acid	Glucose → Pyruvic → Lactic + 2 ATP Acid Acid
Alcoholic	Glucose → Pyruvic → Carbon + Ethanol + 2 ATP Acid Dioxide
Cellular Respiration	Glucose → Pyruvic → Carbon + Water + 36 ATP Acid ↑ Dioxide Oxygen

Checkpoint

1. How many phosphates does a molecule of ATP contain?
2. What two molecules are formed when the last phosphate bond of ATP is broken?
3. What are the two major stages of respiration?
4. Which chemical substance is formed during glycolysis?
5. Which type of fermentation do yeasts carry on?

Photosynthesis: Capturing the Sun's Energy

All cells depend upon the energy stored in the chemical bonds of food to power their activities. But where does this energy come from?

Energy from the sun arrives on Earth in the form of light energy. Autotrophs such as plants and many single-celled organisms can convert light energy into chemical energy in the process of **photosynthesis**. In photosynthesis solar energy is stored in the chemical bonds of food molecules. Autotrophs use the food they make during photosynthesis to fuel their life processes. Heterotrophs are unable to produce their own food. Instead, they obtain their energy by eating autotrophs.

The raw materials of photosynthesis are simple, low energy molecules — carbon dioxide and water. The general equation for photosynthesis follows.

$$\text{energy} + 6CO_2 + 6H_2O \longrightarrow C_6H_{12}O_6 + 6O_2$$
$$\text{(light)} \qquad\qquad\qquad\qquad \text{(sugar)}$$

This formula states that carbon dioxide and water combine in the presence of light to form sugar and oxygen. Oxygen is a waste product of photosynthesis, which is released into the atmosphere.

Actually, the process of photosynthesis is not nearly as simple as this equation seems to suggest. Instead, photosynthesis consists of a series of complex reactions. These reactions can be divided into two groups: the **light reactions** and **carbon fixation**. During the light reactions, energy from the sun is captured as chemical energy. During carbon fixation, carbon dioxide is converted into sugar molecules.

7–6 The Light Reactions

Light travels as waves of energy. Sunlight is actually a mixture of different wavelengths of light. Each wavelength of light has a characteristic amount of energy and color. The wavelengths of light that humans can see are called the visible spectrum. The colors that compose the visible spectrum are red, orange, yellow, green, blue, and violet. You can see all these colors if you observe sunlight passing through a prism.

When sunlight strikes the leaf of a plant, the energy of light waves is absorbed by special photosynthetic pigments. A **pigment** is a substance that absorbs light. Different pigments absorb different wavelengths of light. Wavelengths that are not absorbed are reflected, giving each pigment a characteristic color.

CONCEPTS

- general equation of photosynthesis
- function of pigments
- products of the light reactions
- products of carbon fixation
- comparison of photosynthesis and respiration

Figure 7.11 Sunlight is composed of many different wavelengths of light.

Figure 7.12 The chlorophyll and accessory pigments give each leaf its characteristic color.

Chlorophyll [KLOR-uh-fil] is the major photosynthetic pigment. Chlorophyll absorbs large amounts of red, orange, blue, and violet light, but very little yellow and green light. Because it reflects green and yellow light, chlorophyll appears green.

In addition to chlorophyll, autotrophs contain other pigments called **accessory pigments**. Two common groups of accessory pigments are the carotenoids and phycobilins. Phycobilins, which are red and blue, and carotenoids, which are yellow or orange, absorb some green light.

The photosynthetic pigments of plants are contained in the chloroplasts. The internal structure of a chloroplast is shown in Figure 7.13. Each chloroplast contains many stacks of tiny, membrane-bound sacs called **thylakoids** [THY-lah-koydz]. Each thylakoid contains from 200 to 400 molecules of chlorophyll. Surrounding the thylakoids is an enzyme-containing fluid called the **stroma** [STROH-muh].

The light reactions occur in the thylakoids. When red or blue light strikes a molecule of chlorophyll, it causes electrons to absorb energy. This energy causes the electrons to become excited, or move to a higher energy level. The excited electrons bounce from one chlorophyll molecule to another. At the same time, the accessory pigments can capture the energy of green light, causing some of their electrons to become excited, too. Thus light from all wavelengths of the visible spectrum can be captured by electrons.

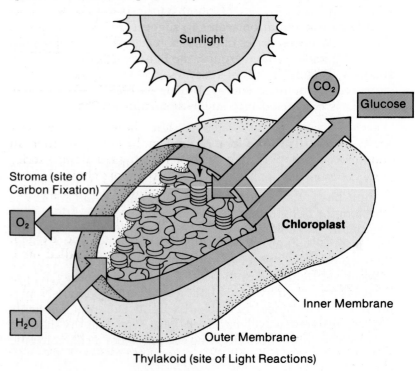

Figure 7.13 Location of the stages of photosynthesis in a chloroplast

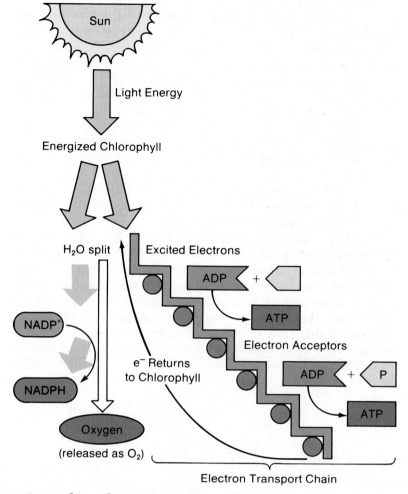

Figure 7.14 The light reactions of photosynthesis

A number of reactions occur while the excited electrons are bouncing from one chlorophyll molecule to another. In one series of reactions, the electrons are passed along a series of electron acceptors in an electron transport chain. As they move along the electron transport chain, the electrons give off energy. This energy is captured as ATP.

During the light reactions the chemical bonds of water molecules are also split, producing hydrogen and oxygen. The hydrogen then combines with a coenzyme called nicotinamide adenine dinucleotide phosphate, or **NADP⁺**. NADP⁺ is a hydrogen acceptor and an electron acceptor. When NADP⁺ accepts hydrogen and electrons it becomes NADPH. The oxygen from the water molecules is released from the cell as gas.

The light reactions last less than a millionth of a second. But in this short time, the energy of light is transformed into chemical energy.

Do You Know?

About 21 percent of Earth's atmosphere is oxygen. Evidence indicates that this oxygen has accumulated over the past two to three billion years due to the process of photosynthesis. Thus, humans are dependent on autotrophs not only for food, but also for oxygen.

7–7 Carbon Fixation

The NADPH and ATP formed in the light reactions are used as sources of energy in the next set of reactions. In these reactions, carbon from molecules of carbon dioxide is combined with hydrogen from NADPH to form glucose. This occurs in a series of reactions called carbon fixation.

Carbon fixation does not require light. Instead, it relies upon the ATP and NADPH produced in the light reactions. For this reason, carbon fixation cannot occur until the completion of the light reactions. Since they do not require light, the reactions of carbon fixation are sometimes called the dark reactions.

Carbon fixation is catalyzed by enzymes in the stroma of the chloroplasts. As you read about the carbon fixation reactions, refer to Figure 7.15.

The chloroplasts contain molecules of a 5-carbon sugar called ribulose diphosphate, or **RDP**. When carbon dioxide enters the chloroplast, its carbon atom combines with RDP to make a 6-carbon sugar. This sugar is chemically unstable. The 6-carbon sugar immediately splits into 2 molecules of phosphoglyceric acid, or PGA. Each molecule of PGA has 3 carbon atoms.

Each molecule of PGA combines with hydrogen from the NADPH produced during the light reactions. This combination of PGA and hydrogen produces a 3-carbon sugar called phos-

Figure 7.15 Carbon fixation, or the conversion of CO_2 to glucose. Light is not necessary for these reactions. Instead they use the energy of ATP and NADPH produced in the light reactions.

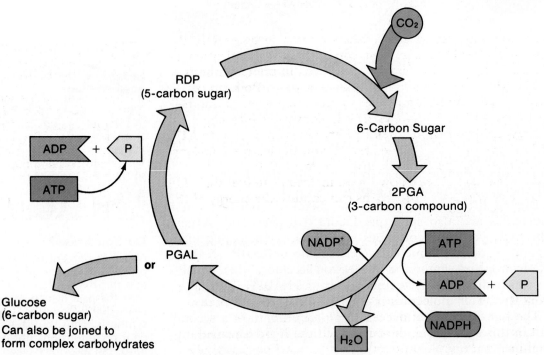

phoglyceraldehyde, or **PGAL**. NADPH becomes $NADP^+$ again. Water is released as a waste product.

PGAL is an intermediate product of photosynthesis. Some of the PGAL is used as food directly, and some is used to produce glucose. The cell also converts some PGAL back to RDP to be used in the next round of carbon fixation. If the cell spent all its PGAL to make food and never replaced any RDP, the dark reactions would soon stop.

PGAL is also used as the basic carbon skeleton for building many organic molecules. For example, two molecules of PGAL may combine to produce a molecule of fructose. Fructose is a 6-carbon sugar that can be converted to glucose, another 6-carbon sugar. Using PGAL as a basic building block, the cell can synthesize more complex carbohydrates. The energy needed for building these molecules comes from ATP.

7–8   Comparing Photosynthesis and Respiration

Although the processes of photosynthesis and respiration include many complex steps, it may help to compare these processes. The basic formula for photosynthesis is given below.

$$\text{energy} + 6CO_2 + 6H_2O \rightarrow C_6H_{12}O_6 + 6O_2$$
$$\text{(light)} \qquad\qquad\qquad\qquad \text{(sugar)}$$

The basic formula for respiration contains the same compounds.

$$C_6H_{12}O_6 + 6O_2 \rightarrow 6CO_2 + 6H_2O + \text{energy}$$
$$\text{(sugar)} \qquad\qquad\qquad\qquad\qquad \text{(ATP)}$$

As you can see, these reactions appear to be exactly the opposite of each other. You could think of respiration as releasing the energy that was captured in photosynthesis.

The processes are similar in several ways. Both processes involve the conversion of energy from one form to another. In photosynthesis, light energy is converted into chemical energy. In respiration, chemical energy is converted to ATP. In both photosynthesis and respiration, an electron transport chain uses energy from electrons to form ATP.

All organisms break down food molecules to fuel their life processes. But only autotrophs can capture the energy of the sun to manufacture food.

 BIOLOGY INSIGHTS

The similarity of the internal structure of mitochondria and chloroplasts reflects their similarity of function. The electron transport chains in both respiration and photosynthesis depend upon the arrangement of the inner membranes of these organelles.

Checkpoint

1. What is the general equation for photosynthesis?
2. Where in the chloroplast do the light reactions occur?
3. Name two kinds of accessory pigments.
4. What is the hydrogen acceptor in the light reactions?
5. What is the final product formed in carbon fixation?

CHAPTER REVIEW

Summary

- Most cellular activities require energy stored in ATP. ATP is composed of the base adenine, the sugar ribose, and three phosphates. The bond between the second and third phosphates is easily broken to provide energy for the cell.

- The phosphate bond in ATP is produced from the conversion of other forms of energy.

- In the process of respiration, sugar molecules are broken down in the presence of oxygen to produce carbon dioxide and water.

- The first stage of respiration occurs in the cytoplasm of the cell and does not require oxygen. In this stage, molecules of glucose are broken down into molecules of pyruvic acid. This stage is called glycolysis or anaerobic respiration.

- Aerobic respiration, which follows glycolysis, occurs in the mitochondria. Aerobic respiration requires the presence of oxygen.

- Aerobic respiration consists of the citric-acid cycle and an electron transport chain. In aerobic respiration, pyruvic acid is eventually converted to carbon dioxide, water, and energy. The energy is used to make ATP.

- Some organisms carry on fermentation in the absence of oxygen. Lactic acid and alcohol are the products of fermentation. In fermentation, each molecule of glucose yields only 2 molecules of ATP. In aerobic respiration, each glucose molecule yields 36 ATPs.

- Autotrophs use light from the sun to make chemical energy, or food, in the process of photosynthesis. In addition to light energy, photosynthesis requires carbon dioxide, water, and chlorophyll. Photosynthesis produces sugar and oxygen. Photosynthesis consists of the light reactions and carbon fixation.

- The light reactions occur in the thylakoids. In the light reactions, light energy excites the electrons of chlorophyll and the accessory pigments. These excited electrons are passed along an electron transport chain, where some of the energy is captured in ATP.

- During the light reactions the bonds of water molecules are split, producing hydrogen and oxygen. The hydrogen is accepted by $NADP^+$, thus forming NADPH. The oxygen is released from the cell as a waste product.

- Carbon fixation occurs in the stroma of the chloroplast. In carbon fixation, the NADPH and ATP formed in the light reactions are used to power a complex series of reactions. In these reactions, carbon dioxide combines with compounds in the cell.

- The intermediate product of carbon fixation is PGAL. PGAL may be converted into glucose, or used by the cell as a food molecule.

Vocabulary

accessory pigment	glycolysis
acetic acid	hydrogen ion acceptor
acetyl CoA	lactic acid
aerobic	fermentation
alcoholic	light reactions
fermentation	matrix
anaerobic	NAD^+
ATP	$NADP^+$
carbon fixation	PGAL
chlorophyll	photosynthesis
citric-acid cycle	pigment
cristae	pyruvic acid
electron acceptor	RDP
electron transport	respiration
chain	stroma
fermentation	thylakoid

Review

1. What is the overall equation for respiration?
2. In which step of photosynthesis is the energy from an excited electron captured as ATP?
3. What type of molecule passes electrons down the electron transport chain?
4. What type of fermentation occurs in muscle cells?
5. What holds ADP and P together in a molecule of ATP?
6. What are the two products of photosynthesis?
7. Which process occurs in the anaerobic stage of respiration?
8. What 5-carbon compound combines with CO_2 at the beginning of carbon fixation?

In the following questions, select the letter that best answers the question.

9. Which of the following events occurs in the carbon-fixation reactions of photosynthesis?
   (a) Water is split. (b) ATP is formed.
   (c) Chlorophyll becomes excited.
   (d) PGAL is formed.
10. Which of the following may *not* be formed by PGAL?
   (a) fructose (b) chlorophyll (c) RDP
   (d) glucose

Interpret and Apply

1. Define cellular respiration. How is it related to breathing?
2. In which part of the cell does glycolysis occur? Where is the electron transport chain located? Where does the citric-acid cycle occur?
3. Why must glycolysis occur before the steps of aerobic respiration begin?
4. Compare the process of aerobic respiration with fermentation. Which process releases more energy from a molecule of glucose?
5. Compare alcoholic fermentation with lactic acid fermentation. How are they different?
6. Name two ways in which photosynthesis and respiration are alike. Name two ways in which they are different.

7. What two organelles produce ATP?
8. Why do chloroplasts appear green?
9. Which photosynthetic pigment reflects orange light?
10. Place the following terms in order from smallest to largest: autotroph cell, chlorophyll molecule, chloroplast, electron, thylakoid.

Challenge

1. How many molecules of CO_2 would be necessary to produce three molecules of glucose?
2. How many molecules of CO_2 would be necessary to produce eight molecules of PGAL?
3. Does respiration occur in the light or in the dark?

Projects

1. Look up the experiments on plant growth carried out by the Belgian scientist, Jan Baptist van Helmont. Design an experiment to demonstrate his results using a fast-growing plant such as an avocado.
2. Recently organisms have been discovered that rely on the energy available from chemicals in deep sea vents. This energy is captured by chemosynthetic bacteria. Investigate this subject in your library. Where do these organisms live? What are the chemosynthetic reactions? What kind of heterotrophs rely on these organisms for food? Report on your findings to your class.
3. Devise and perform an experiment to test the hypothesis that autotrophs need light in order to make food.
4. Try baking a loaf of bread, using yeast as a leaven. When letting the dough rise, divide the dough into two portions. Keep one portion in the refrigerator and allow the other one to rise in a warm area. How can you explain the different results?

8 Cell Regulation and Reproduction

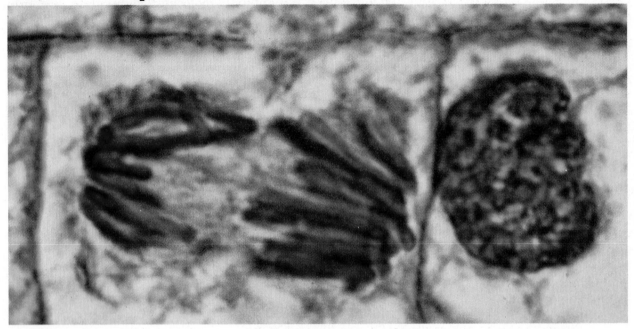

An onion cell during late anaphase

In the photograph above, the nucleus of an onion cell is dividing in half. Normally the chromosomes of a cell are so long and thin that they are invisible under a light microscope. During the division of the nucleus, though, the chromosomes become tightly coiled. These thicker chromosomes can be stained so that they appear red. In fact, the name *chromosome* means "colored body."

Although the chromosomes look unwieldy, their movement is surprisingly precise. Their positions in the nucleus are coordinated, so that they move with the precision of a formal dance. This precision ensures that every new cell will receive a complete set of instructions for producing proteins. The pattern of chromosome movement is the same in all plants and animals.

Clearly, some type of signal within the cell is directing the tiny parts to move as they do. Yet despite great advances in cell biology, scientists still do not know what controls this movement. The mechanism that coordinates nuclear division remains one of the unsolved mysteries of cell biology.

DNA, RNA, and Protein Synthesis

Proteins are important components of every living cell. As you know, the metabolism of cells is controlled by proteins called enzymes. Without enzymes, the various reactions in each cell could not take place. Proteins are also important in the structure of the plasma membranes, the cytoplasm, and the organelles. Obviously proteins are essential to life.

Each protein is a highly individual molecule with a complex shape that determines its function. Every cell is capable of making all the thousands of different kinds of proteins it needs. How does each cell synthesize such an enormous variety of proteins? And what determines the kinds of enzymes present in each cell?

8–1 DNA: The Double Helix

Only in the past few decades have scientists begun to decipher the chemical code that controls the production of proteins. Breaking this code has been the major achievement of molecular biology.

The molecule that controls the production of proteins is a nucleic acid called **deoxyribonucleic** [dee-ahk-see-ry-boh-noo-KLEE-ihk] **acid**, or **DNA**. In eukaryotes, DNA is contained in the chromosomes in the nucleus. DNA is like a library that stores the vital information of the cell. Like the books in a library, DNA's instructions can be used over and over again by the cell.

DNA was first isolated by the Swiss chemist Johann Friedrich Miescher in 1869, but over 80 years passed before the function of DNA was understood. By the early 1950s, scientists knew that DNA carried the information for running the cell. But they did not know how this information was coded or how it was passed from cell to cell. In order to break the code, it was first necessary to determine the structure of DNA.

Chemical analysis had shown that DNA is composed of nucleotides. Each nucleotide is, in turn, composed of three parts: a 5-carbon sugar called deoxyribose, a phosphate group, and a nitrogen base. Each nucleotide in DNA contains one of four different nitrogen bases — **adenine** [AD-neen], **guanine** [GWAH-neen], **thymine** [THY-meen], or **cytosine** [SY-tuh-seen]. The four nitrogen bases are shown in Figure 8.1. The bases are often abbreviated by the first letter of their name: A, G, T, or C.

Many capable scientists using many different methods competed to be the first to figure out the three-dimensional

CONCEPTS
- structure of DNA and RNA
- DNA code for protein synthesis
- function of messenger RNA, transfer RNA, and ribosomes
- advantages of polysomes

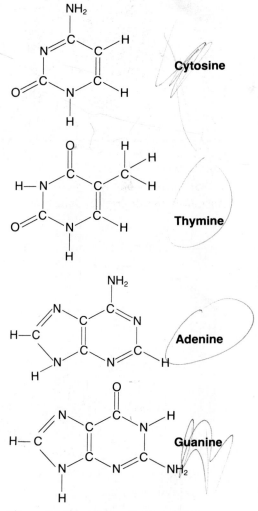

Figure 8.1 The four nitrogen bases found in DNA

structure of DNA. The race was won in 1953 by James Watson, an American biologist, and Francis Crick, a British physicist. Watson and Crick, who were working at Cambridge University in England, solved the puzzle by putting together scale models of nucleotides. Their success depended upon the evidence collected by other biologists — especially the data of the British biochemists Maurice Wilkins and Rosalind Franklin. For their contributions to the understanding of DNA, Wilkins, Watson, and Crick received the Nobel Prize in 1962.

Watson and Crick concluded that DNA is composed of two long nucleotide chains. Each chain has a backbone of phosphate and sugar. The backbones of the two chains are parallel to one another, as shown in Figure 8.2. The bases of the two chains face each other and fit together. Hydrogen bonds hold the nitrogen bases together.

The bases of one chain attach to those of the other according to the **base-pairing rule**. The base-pairing rule states that adenine always pairs with thymine (A:T or T:A), and cytosine always pairs with guanine (C:G or G:C). Thus a strand of DNA with the sequence T-A-G-C-A-T must have a partner strand with the sequence A-T-C-G-T-A. The matching pairs of bases are said to be complementary.

Watson and Crick showed that the sugar-and-phosphate backbones are twisted in a spiral, a bit like a twisted ladder. This structure is called a **double helix**. The sides of the ladder are the sugar-phosphate chains, and the rungs of the ladder are complementary pairs of nitrogen bases.

Figure 8.2 Nitrogen bases attach to each other by hydrogen bonds according to the base-pairing rule. The DNA strands are twisted into a double helix.

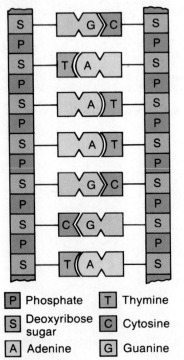

P	Phosphate
S	Deoxyribose sugar
A	Adenine

T	Thymine
C	Cytosine
G	Guanine

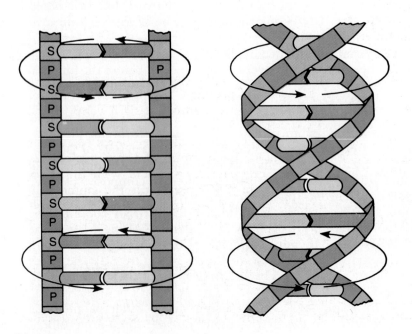

A single DNA molecule may be millions of base pairs long. The order in which the bases are arranged accounts for DNA's ability to run the cell.

8–2 The DNA Code

Once the structure of DNA was known, biologists began working to figure out how this structure carried the information for building proteins. Biologists performed many experiments in an effort to decipher the DNA code. From these experiments, they concluded that the code of DNA is carried in the sequence of the nitrogen bases. The sequence of bases determines the sequence of amino acids in a protein.

Amino Acid	DNA Codons	Amino Acid	DNA Codons
Alanine	CGA, CGG, CGT, CGC	Phenylalanine	AAA, AAG
Arginine	TCT, TCC, GCA, GCG, GCT, GCC	Proline	GGA, GGG, GGT, GGC
Asparagine	TTA, TTG	Serine	AGA, AGG, AGT, AGC, TCA, TCG
Aspartic Acid	CTA, CTG	Threonine	TGA, TGG, TGT, TGC
Cysteine	ACA, ACG	Tryptophan	ACC
Glutamic Acid	CTT, CTC	Tyrosine	ATA, ATG
Glutamine	GTT, GTC	Valine	CAA, CAG, CAT
Glycine	CCA, CCG, CCT, CCC	(initiator codon)	CAC
Histidine	GTA, GTG	Termination	
Isoleucine	TAA, TAG, TAT	codons	ATT, ATC, ACT
Leucine	AAT, AAC, GAA, GAG, GAT, GAC		
Lysine	TTT, TTC		
Methionine (initiator codon)	TAC		

Figure 8.3 DNA codons for amino acids

To understand how this code works, it is important to remember the structure of proteins. As you read in Chapter 4, proteins are made of chains of amino acids. Twenty amino acids commonly occur in proteins.

In a strand of DNA, each group of three bases represents a particular amino acid. Each group of three nucleotides constitutes a **codon**. For example, a strand with the bases cytosine–adenine–guanine (CAG) represents the amino acid valine. Each codon is like a three-letter word. The long strands of DNA are actually composed of a series of codons. Thus a molecule of DNA is like a sentence written in three-letter words.

Figure 8.3 shows all the codons that can be formed from the 4 bases of DNA. There are 64 such combinations. Most of these codons represent a particular amino acid. As you can see, several codons may represent the same amino acid.

Since they have the same meaning, these redundant codons are like words that are synonyms.

Certain codons do not code for any amino acids. These codons may carry other information, such as when to begin or end the building of a protein. A codon that signals the beginning of a protein is called an initiator codon. A termination codon signals the end of a protein.

8–3 RNA Structure

In addition to DNA, cells contain several smaller nucleic acids called **ribonucleic** [ry-boh-noo-KLEE-ihk] **acids**, or **RNA**. The structure of RNA, shown in Figure 8.4, is similar to that of DNA but the molecules are much shorter. In addition to length, there are three important differences in the structures of DNA and RNA.

1. Nucleotides of RNA contain the sugar ribose instead of deoxyribose.
2. RNA contains the base **uracil** [YUR-uh-sihl] instead of thymine. Like thymine, uracil forms a complementary pair with adenine. Thus the four bases in RNA are cytosine, guanine, adenine, and uracil.
3. RNA usually has only one strand of nucleotides and does not form a helix.

Each cell contains several different types of RNA. Each type of RNA has a different structure and therefore a different function.

Figure 8.4 Three major forms of RNA — messenger RNA, transfer RNA, and ribosomal RNA

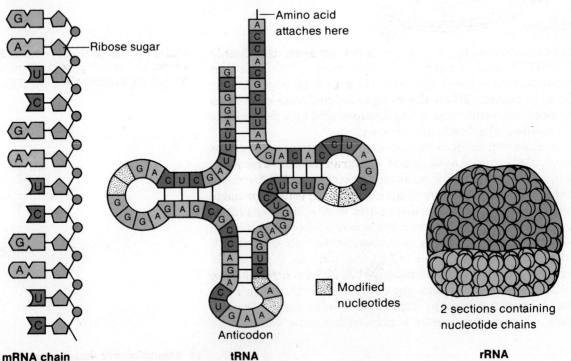

Ribose sugar

Amino acid attaches here

Modified nucleotides

2 sections containing nucleotide chains

Anticodon

mRNA chain

tRNA

rRNA

8–4 Transcription: DNA to RNA

Protein synthesis occurs at the ribosomes, which are located in the cytoplasm. DNA, with its set of directions for putting the amino acids together, is in the nucleus. The DNA never leaves the nucleus. Instead its directions are copied onto a strand of RNA called **messenger RNA**, or **m-RNA**. Messenger RNA then carries the DNA message from the nucleus to the ribosomes in the cytoplasm. The process by which the DNA code is copied onto a strand of messenger RNA is called **transcription**. Transcription is shown in Figure 8.5.

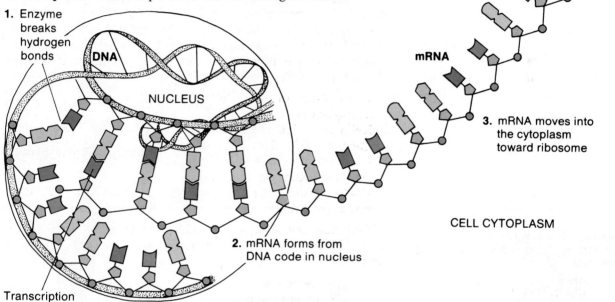

1. Enzyme breaks hydrogen bonds

DNA

NUCLEUS

Transcription

2. mRNA forms from DNA code in nucleus

mRNA

3. mRNA moves into the cytoplasm toward ribosome

CELL CYTOPLASM

Figure 8.5 Transcription occurs in the nucleus. The completed messenger RNA then travels to a ribosome.

When transcription begins, enzymes separate the double helix of DNA into two single-stranded pieces. The hydrogen bonds that hold the complementary bases together are weak and easily broken. When the hydrogen bonds break, it is as if the double strand were being unzipped. When the strands are separated, the bases are exposed.

Next, RNA nucleotides line up along the unzipped segment of DNA. Only one strand of DNA is transcribed. The RNA bases pair with the complementary bases on the DNA strand. Cytosine always pairs with guanine, adenine always pairs with uracil, and thymine always pairs with adenine. As more bases are added, the messenger RNA grows longer and longer.

A termination codon indicates when the enzyme should stop copying the DNA code. When the code for a protein is completely transcribed, the messenger RNA leaves the nucleus and goes to a ribosome in the cytoplasm. The messenger RNA carries with it all the information necessary for building a protein.

8–5   Translation: RNA to Protein

Once the messenger RNA reaches the ribosome, the cell can begin to build a protein. During **translation**, chains of amino acids are assembled according to the directions carried by the messenger RNA. The ribosome translates the messenger RNA's code into a particular protein.

The process of translation requires another kind of RNA called **transfer RNA (t-RNA)**. The cytoplasm contains all the amino acids necessary for building a protein. The task of transfer RNA is to bring the proper amino acids to the messenger RNA and to line them up in the correct order.

Transfer RNA is shown in Figure 8.6. At one end of the transfer RNA is a series of three nucleotide bases known as an **anticodon**. Anticodons are complementary to the codons of messenger RNA. Each anticodon codes for a specific amino acid. For example, a transfer RNA with the anticodon GCU codes for the amino acid arginine. Another portion of this transfer RNA will attach to a molecule of arginine.

Once the transfer RNA attaches to its specific amino acid, the combination moves toward a ribosome. The anticodon

Figure 8.6 In translation the messenger RNA code is used as a blueprint for a protein molecule.

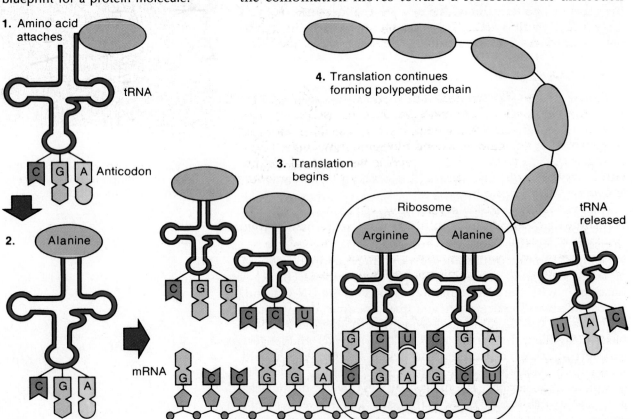

1. Amino acid attaches

tRNA

C G A Anticodon

2. Alanine

mRNA

4. Translation continues forming polypeptide chain

3. Translation begins

Ribosome

Arginine   Alanine

tRNA released

of the transfer RNA then lines up beside the messenger RNA, so that the bases of the anticodon complement those of the messenger RNA codon. For example, a transfer RNA with the anticodon GCU would attach to the RNA codon CGA.

The ribosomes bring together the incoming t-RNA-amino acid combinations and the messenger RNA. As the ribosome moves along the strand of messenger RNA, the amino acids fall into line as directed by the codons on the messenger RNA.

Once in place, the amino acids begin to form a chain. Enzymes in the ribosomes catalyze the formation of peptide bonds between the amino acids. After an amino acid attaches to another amino acid, it detaches from its transfer RNA. The detached transfer RNA is then free to leave the ribosome and pick up another amino acid.

As the ribosome moves along the messenger RNA, the proper amino acid is added for each codon. The amino-acid chain grows in length. Protein synthesis stops when the ribosome reaches a termination codon.

The completed protein leaves the ribosome and enters the cytoplasm. The function of the new protein depends upon its sequence of amino acids. For example, some proteins act as enzymes; others are important in the structure of the cell.

8–6   Polysomes

The messenger-RNA code can be read in only one direction. Once the beginning of the code has been translated by one ribosome, another ribosome can begin to translate the messenger-RNA code again. A second ribosome may begin translating even as one end of the strand is being translated by the first ribosome. The second ribosome will make another molecule of the same protein.

If the messenger RNA is very long, as many as 50 to 70 ribosomes can attach and build proteins at the same time. A group of several ribosomes attached to one strand of messenger RNA is called a **polysome**. Polysomes provide a quick way of making multiple copies of a given protein.

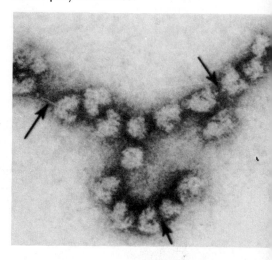

Figure 8.7 Polysomes are sometimes called polyribosomes.

Checkpoint

1. Where are the chromosomes of eukaryotes located?
2. Who proposed that DNA is a double helix?
3. How many nucleotides are in one codon?
4. What is produced during transcription?
5. Where is the anticodon located?
6. What is produced during translation?

Cell Reproduction

CONCEPTS

- DNA replication
- phases of mitosis
- cell division in plants and animals

As the cell theory states, all cells come from other cells. Organisms grow by cell division, followed by the enlargement of newly produced cells.

Some cells divide often. In an embryo, an organism just beginning its development, cell division is almost continuous. Naturally, cells in young, growing organisms divide more frequently than cells in older organisms. The function of a cell is also related to how often new cells will be produced. Skin cells, which rub off and must be replaced often, have a high rate of division. Some highly specialized cells, such as nerve cells, rarely if ever divide.

In the production of a new cell, three steps are necessary. First, the DNA must be copied, so that the new cell will contain a complete set of genetic instructions for its functions. Second, the nucleus must divide. Third, the cytoplasm must divide to form two new cells.

Figure 8.8 DNA is copied during the process of replication.

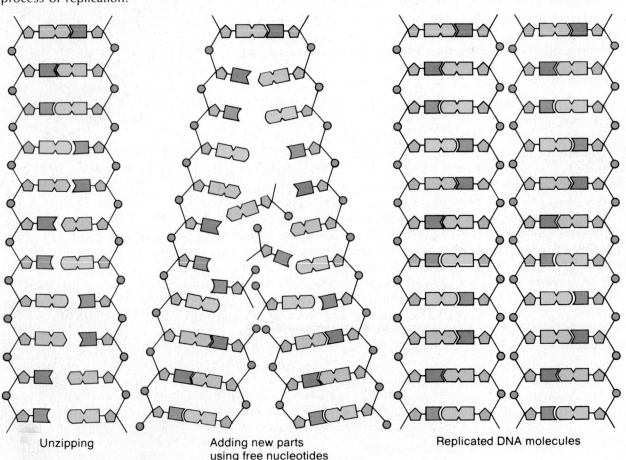

Unzipping   Adding new parts using free nucleotides   Replicated DNA molecules

8–7   Replication of DNA

A complete set of the DNA code is present in each of an organism's cells. The organism passes this information from cell to cell by forming exact copies of its DNA. The DNA code is copied by the process of **replication**.

Figure 8.8 shows how DNA replicates. New strands of DNA are built from a supply of nucleotides present in the nucleus. Replication begins when special enzymes separate, or unzip, the double-stranded DNA. Once the bases are exposed, enzymes catalyze the pairing of these bases with the free nucleotides in the nucleus.

Replication is an extremely precise process. As a result of replication, each single strand of DNA becomes part of a double strand identical to the original DNA molecule. Thus each new double helix of DNA receives one strand from the original DNA. Each strand serves as a mold for building a complementary strand.

8–8   Mitosis: Division of the Nucleus

Mitosis [my-TOH-sihs] is the process by which the nucleus of a cell divides into two identical nuclei. Every kind of living organism has a particular number of chromosomes per cell. In mitosis each new cell receives a complete set of chromosomes. While a nucleus is dividing, the chromosomes take up stain easily and are clearly visible with a light microscope.

Biologists have divided mitosis into four phases: prophase, metaphase, anaphase, and telophase. The period between mitotic divisions is called interphase. Actually, mitosis is a continuous process. Like the phases of the moon, each phase blends into the next.

Interphase   During most of its existence, a cell is in **interphase**. When scientists first observed cell division, they found that the chromosomes were not visible during interphase. They therefore assumed, wrongly, that the cell was resting. In fact, much occurs during interphase. The cell is growing. Most of the metabolic processes of the cell are taking place, including protein synthesis. DNA replicates during interphase.

Once the DNA replicates, the nucleus contains double the normal number of chromosomes. If you were to look at the cell under a microscope, the chromosomes would not be visible. At this time the chromosomes are long thin strands that are spread throughout the nucleus. The entire nucleus is enclosed by the nuclear membrane. The nucleolus is visible as a dark spot within the nucleus. Just outside the nuclear membrane of animals are a pair of **centrioles**, which are made of microtubules.

Figure 8.9 The structural features of a cell during interphase

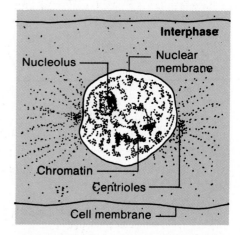

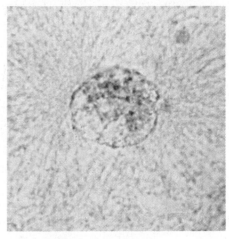

Prophase   When the chromosomes have doubled and the nucleus is ready to divide, the centrioles move to opposite ends of the nucleus, forming the **poles** of the cell. This event initiates **prophase**. As prophase progresses, **astral rays** form around each centriole. Additional microtubule fibers align themselves between the two poles, forming the mitotic **spindle**. Plant cells have no centrioles, but they do have spindles.

The chromosomes, which had been spread throughout the cell during interphase, become shorter and thicker. The two identical copies of each chromosome, called sister **chromatids** are attached by a protein structure called a **kinetochore** [kuh-NEH-tuh-kohr]. This attachment serves much the same function as attaching like-colored socks when sorting the laundry. It keeps one pair from getting mixed up with another.

In late prophase, the nucleolus disappears and the nuclear membrane disintegrates. The pairs of chromatids move toward an imaginary line that crosses the spindle fibers at points equal in distance from the two poles. This line is known as the **equator**.

Metaphase   In the next phase, **metaphase**, the chromatid pairs arrive at the equator. The chromatids seem to form a dark bushy line at the equator. After the chromatids arrive at the equator, the kinetochores split apart. This frees members of the pairs from one another. Immediately after the kinetochores split, the chromatids are called chromosomes. The kinetochore of each chromosome attaches to a spindle fiber on its side of the equator.

Anaphase   The two members of each pair of chromosomes begin to move away from one another. This is the start of **anaphase**. Led by the kinetochores that are attached to spindle fibers, the chromosomes move toward opposite poles of the cell. One member of each pair of chromosomes moves to each pole. Scientists are not certain how this movement occurs. Some think that the proteins in the spindle fibers contract, thus pulling the chromosomes along.

Telophase   When the matching chromosomes reach the opposite poles of the cell, anaphase ends and **telophase** begins. The chromosomes spread out and are no longer visible as thick, dark structures. The spindle fibers disappear. The nucleolus reappears. Protein and lipid molecules from the endoplasmic reticulum form two new nuclear membranes. A new interphase begins.

As a result of mitosis, each new nucleus contains an exact copy of the DNA from the original nucleus. Therefore, each new nucleus has the same DNA code as the original nucleus. All that remains is for the cell itself to divide.

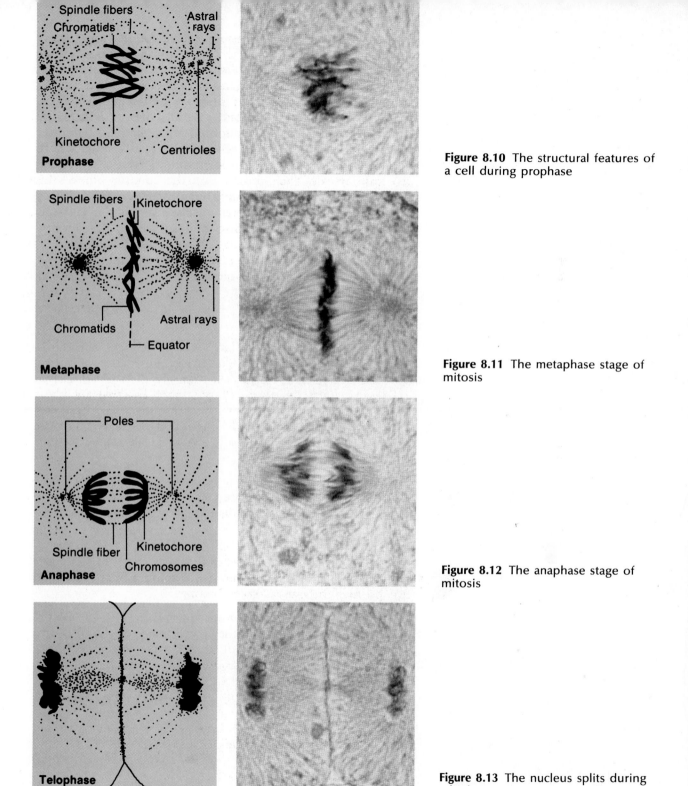

Prophase

Spindle fibers
Chromatids
Astral rays
Kinetochore
Centrioles

Figure 8.10 The structural features of a cell during prophase

Metaphase

Spindle fibers
Kinetochore
Chromatids
Astral rays
Equator

Figure 8.11 The metaphase stage of mitosis

Anaphase

Poles
Spindle fiber
Kinetochore
Chromosomes

Figure 8.12 The anaphase stage of mitosis

Telophase

Figure 8.13 The nucleus splits during telophase.

Cell Regulation and Reproduction   **121**

8–9 Cytokinesis: Division of the Cytoplasm

As the two new nuclei are forming in mitosis, the cytoplasm is also dividing. **Cytokinesis** [sy-toh-kih-NEE-sihs] is the division of the cell's cytoplasm and organelles into two cells. The cell that divides is the mother cell. When it divides, the mother cell becomes two daughter cells. The two daughter cells are identical to one another. They are also identical to the mother cell from which they came.

In animal cells the area around the equator pinches in, forming a **cleavage furrow**, as shown in Figure 8.14. Pieces of plasma membrane align themselves along the equator, dividing the cytoplasm in two. Finally there are two new daughter cells.

Figure 8.14 The cleavage furrow of an animal cell

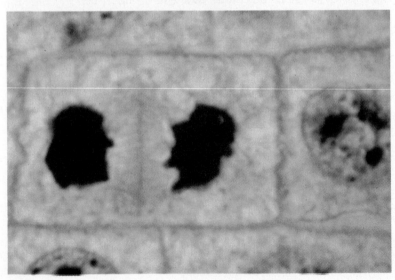

Figure 8.15 The formation of a cell plate in a plant cell

In the course of cytokinesis, the organelles of the mother cell are divided between the two daughter cells, although not equally. The Golgi apparatus comes apart during cell division. Some of it goes to each daughter cell, where it reorganizes and begins to function.

Cytokinesis of plant cells is slightly different from cytokinesis of animal cells. In plant cells the cytoplasm is divided by the formation of a **cell plate**. The cell plate is formed from tiny vesicles produced by the Golgi apparatus. When these vesicles fuse to become the cell plate, they create a boundary between the two daughter cells. Eventually each daughter cell constructs a new cell wall from molecules of cellulose.

8–10   Cell Growth and Differentiation

An organism increases its size by the growth of existing cells and by the addition of new cells. As an organism grows, some of the new cells may become specialized for particular functions. For example, in humans some cells develop into skin cells, while others become nerve cells or bone cells. The process by which cells become different from each other is called **differentiation**.

Since every cell receives an exact copy of the mother cell's DNA, every cell in the body of a multicellular organism has exactly the same DNA. If all your cells have exactly the same DNA, why do some of your cells become skin cells while others become bone cells? Although each of your cells contains the DNA necessary for manufacturing every protein in your body, no one cell makes all the proteins. In each type of cell, only certain types of proteins are produced. What controls the production of particular proteins in each cell?

The answers to these questions are not yet known. The means by which only certain portions of the DNA code are translated in each cell is currently being studied by many biologists. The process of differentiation is one of the most intriguing topics in biology today.

BIOLOGY INSIGHTS

The possession of a hereditary program coded on DNA or RNA is a unique characteristic of life. The only comparable system in the nonliving world is that of the information carried in a computer program.

Checkpoint

1. In what process does the DNA of a cell double?
2. In what process does a cell's nucleus divide into two new nuclei?
3. What structure connects the sister chromatids?
4. During which phase of mitosis are chromatids at the equator?
5. In what process does the cytoplasm of a cell divide to form two daughter cells?

CHAPTER REVIEW

Summary

- DNA contains the directions for making all the proteins necessary for the activities of the cell.
- DNA is composed of long chains of nucleotides. Each nucleotide contains a phosphate group, a deoxyribose sugar, and one of four different nitrogen bases. These bases are adenine, guanine, cytosine, and thymine.
- The structure of DNA was discovered by James Watson and Francis Crick. This structure is described as a double helix. Each molecule of DNA is composed of two coiled chains of nucleotides.
- The DNA code is copied in the process of replication. In replication, each original strand serves as a mold for a new double helix of DNA.
- In addition to DNA, cells contain other nucleic acids called RNA. The structure of RNA is similar to that of DNA, with three important differences. First, RNA contains the base uracil instead of thymine. Second, RNA contains the sugar ribose instead of deoxyribose. Third, RNA is usually a single strand rather than a double helix.
- The DNA code is carried in sequences of three nucleotides called codons. Each codon represents a particular amino acid.
- Protein synthesis begins when the DNA code for a particular sequence of amino acids is transcribed onto a strand of messenger RNA. The messenger RNA then leaves the nucleus and enters the cytoplasm.
- Amino acids are transported to the ribosome by molecules of transfer RNA.
- Translation of the messenger RNA occurs at a ribosome.

- The function of the DNA code can be summarized as shown below.

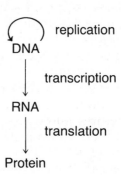

- In the formation of a new cell, three steps are necessary: replication of DNA; division of the nucleus; and division of the cytoplasm, or cytokinesis.
- The division of the nucleus is called mitosis. The stages of mitosis are prophase, metaphase, anaphase, and telophase.

Vocabulary

adenine	kinetochore
anaphase	messenger RNA
anticodon	(m-RNA)
astral rays	metaphase
base-pairing rule	mitosis
cell plate	poles
centriole	polysome
chromatid	prophase
cleavage furrow	replication
codon	ribonucleic acid
cytokinesis	(RNA)
cytosine	spindle
deoxyribonucleic	telophase
acid (DNA)	thymine
differentiation	transcription
double helix	transfer RNA
equator	(t-RNA)
guanine	translation
interphase	uracil

Review

1. Name two functions of proteins in the cell.
2. According to the base-pairing rule, which nucleotide pairs with guanine?
3. What nucleotides are found in RNA?
4. How many different DNA codons are there?
5. Which molecule carries the DNA code to the cytoplasm?
6. To which two molecules does transfer RNA attach?
7. In what organelle are messenger RNAs translated into proteins?
8. What structures allow several proteins to be manufactured from a single messenger RNA at one time?
9. Which phase of mitosis follows metaphase?
10. When does the replication of DNA occur? What is formed in replication?

Match the phase of mitosis with the proper description.

11. prophase
12. metaphase
13. anaphase
14. telophase

  a. Chromatids line up at the equator.
  b. Chromosomes reach opposite poles.
  c. Chromosomes begin to move toward opposite poles.
  d. The spindle forms.

Interpret and Apply

1. List three ways that the structure of RNA differs from that of DNA.
2. Compare replication and transcription. What is formed in each process?
3. What is the difference between mitosis and cytokinesis?
4. When are the sister chromatids formed?
5. In which phases of mitosis are chromosomes attached as chromatids?

6. Write the DNA codon, the messenger RNA codon, and the transfer RNA anticodon for the amino acid tryptophan.
7. For the DNA codon TAG, write the complementary messenger RNA codon and the transfer RNA anticodon. What amino acid does this codon represent?
8. In what ways does cell division of plants differ from that of animals?

Challenge

1. Why is m-RNA called a messenger?
2. The bases of the two DNA strands are held together by hydrogen bonds. What property of these bonds makes them well suited for the process of replication?
3. A protein has 250 amino acids. How many nucleotides are necessary to code for 250 amino acids?
4. The replication of DNA is usually very precise, resulting in new strands of DNA that are exactly the same as the original strand. What would happen if one of the strands were copied incorrectly? How would this affect the proteins manufactured by the cell?

Projects

1. Construct a model of DNA, using rope or flexible wire for the backbones and small pieces that can attach to the backbones and interlock with each other for the bases.
2. Protein synthesis in bacteria and other prokaryotes is different from that in the cells of humans. Do library research to find out some of the differences.
3. Antibiotics are drugs that prevent the spread of bacteria. Do research to find out how antibiotics affect the process of bacterial reproduction. Report your findings to your class.

Careers in Teaching Biology

Are you interested in the study of living things? Do you like helping others learn? Are you good at explaining how things work? If you enjoy these activities, consider a teaching career in biology. *Biology teachers* all share a fascination with living things and a desire to communicate their enthusiasm to others.

High school biology teachers do many things as part of their jobs. One day a biology teacher may make a difficult concept clear by discussing it and giving several examples of how it works. The next day might be spent supervising a laboratory investigation; the teacher helps students set up equipment, make observations, and evaluate data. Biology teachers also enrich and expand on the information presented in their students' textbooks. They may do this by showing films, working with computers, suggesting additional reading, and helping students with special projects. Teachers also help students relate what they are learning in biology to other subjects, such as math, chemistry, or even history.

College biology teachers usually specialize in one area of biology. Two such specialized subjects are botany (plant life) and anatomy (the structure of living things). In addition, college professors generally do research. They perform experiments in their areas of specialization.

A biology teacher needs to read magazines, books, and newspapers to learn about new scientific developments. Each year scientists learn a vast amount of new information about living things. Concepts that are taught this year may be changed or even replaced next year because of new experimental data. Teachers need to be able to answer students' questions about scientific discoveries.

Requirements: For high school biology teachers, requirements vary from state to state. In all cases, however, a person must prepare to teach biology by attending college. In addition to biology, courses in chemistry, mathematics, and physics are usually required. A future biology teacher may also study other sciences. These might include geology, anthropology, and psychology. Generally, a student teacher will also learn effective teaching methods and will do some practice teaching. College biology professors usually need a Ph.D. degree. This involves several years of study after college.

Well-trained science teachers are needed in many parts of the country. If you like biology, and if you enjoy working with people, maybe someday you'll be teaching a course like the one you are taking now.

UNIT REVIEW

Synthesis

1. You are told that a certain white powder is a pure enzyme that causes milk to curdle. (In curdled milk, the proteins and fats collect in large particles and settle to the bottom.) Describe a controlled experiment that would show whether the powder is, in fact, the milk-curdling enzyme. Also state the hypothesis you are testing.
2. Suppose you are the scientist in charge of examining rocks from Mars. On one of the rocks is a fuzzy green patch. How could you determine whether the fuzzy green material is alive?
3. Some detergents contain enzymes. These enzymes supposedly help to remove grass stains and blood stains better than detergents without enzymes. Why might enzymes take out some stains that ordinary detergents cannot?
4. a. What elements are in a phosphate group?
   b. Name two kinds of molecules that contain phosphate groups. How does the structure of these molecules affect their function in the cell?
   c. Living things share certain characteristics. Identify two of these characteristics that involve molecules with phosphate groups.
5. Many unicellular organisms that live in fresh water contain organelles called water vacuoles. Excess water from these organisms collects in the water vacuole and is then released from the cell. How does this organelle help these microorganisms maintain homeostasis? What would happen to these organisms if they did not have a water vacuole? Why is this organelle common in organisms that live in fresh water but not in those that live in salt water?
6. Membranes are found throughout all cells. Describe how membranes function in (a) maintaining homeostasis, (b) respiration, (c) secretion, and (d) cell division.

Additional Reading

Asimov, Isaac. *Asimov on Chemistry*. Garden City, NY: Doubleday, 1974.

Asimov, Isaac. *A Short History of Biology*. Westport, CT: Greenwood Press, 1980.

Asimov, Isaac. *The World of Carbon*. New York: Macmillan, 1962.

Biological Sciences Curriculum Study. *Research Problems in Biology: Investigations for Students*. (Series 1 through 4.) New York: Oxford University Press, 1976.

Brandwein, Paul F., and Hy Ruchlis. *Invitations to Investigate: An Introduction to Scientific Exploration*. New York: Harcourt Brace Jovanovich, 1970.

de Kruif, Paul. *The Microbe Hunters*. New York: Harcourt Brace Jovanovich, 1966.

Dubos, Rene. *Louis Pasteur, Free Lance of Science*. New York: Charles Scribner's Sons, 1976.

Goldstein, Thomas. *Dawn of Modern Science*. Boston: Houghton Mifflin, 1980.

Klein, Aaron. *The Complete Beginner's Guide to Microscopes and Telescopes*. Garden City, NY: Doubleday, 1980.

Marten, Michael, et al. *World Within Worlds: A Journey into the Unknown*. New York: Holt, Rinehart & Winston, 1977.

Pomasanoff, Alex. *Invisible World: Sights Beyond the Limits of the Naked Eye*. Boston: Houghton Mifflin, 1981.

Stehli, George. *The Microscope and How to Use It*. New York: Dover Publications, 1970.

Thomas, Lewis. *The Lives of a Cell: Notes of a Biology Watcher*. New York: Viking Press, 1974.

Trefil, James S. *From Atoms to Quarks: An Introduction to the Strange World of Particle Physics*. New York: Charles Scribner's Sons, 1980.

Watson, James D. *The Double Helix*. New York: Atheneum, 1968.

Unit Two

The Succession of Life

Tulip fields in Holland

9 The Basis of Heredity

American coot with young

"A chip off the old block." No doubt you've heard people say this about a child who reminds them of a parent. Everyone knows that offspring take after their parents. In fact, that's a characteristic of life.

Throughout history, people have wondered how offspring inherit their characteristics. Many people believed that inheritance was based on blood. They thought that the blood of parents blended and eventually poured into their children. This idea still remains in the language, as, for example, in the phrase *blood relatives*.

Because people did not understand the biological basis of heredity, they developed fanciful ideas about the origin of organisms. One author suggested that a giraffe was the result of a cross between a camel and a leopard. The camel contributed the long neck and the leopard contributed the spots!

Only during the last century has biology been able to explain the mechanisms of inheritance. Today scientists know that characteristics are not the result of blood but of the DNA in cells. Solving the puzzle of heredity has been one of the great achievements of modern science.

The Inheritance of Traits: Mendel's Discoveries

It has long been common knowledge that offspring resemble their parents. Yet there is so much variety among living things, it seemed impossible that inheritance could be governed by a simple set of principles.

The first scientist to discover basic rules that govern inheritance lived about 100 years ago. He was Gregor Johann Mendel, a monk who taught in a monastery school near what is now Brno, Czechoslovakia. Although Mendel's work was ignored during his lifetime, it ultimately provided the basis for the modern study of heredity.

9-1 Mendel's Hybrid Peas

Mendel studied patterns of inheritance by breeding pea plants in his monastery garden. His study took over seven years and required him to collect data from over 30,000 individual plants.

Mendel first took note of what he saw occurring naturally. He noticed that the tall pea plants in the garden always produced seeds that grew into tall plants. Likewise, short plants always produced seeds that grew into short plants. The tall and short pea plants were two distinct varieties, or **pure lines**. Offspring of pure lines have the same traits as their parents.

Mendel carefully selected pure lines of pea plants with contrasting pairs of characteristics. Each characteristic appeared in two contrasting forms. The texture of the seeds was either smooth or wrinkled. The color of the seeds was either yellow or green. The height of the plants was either tall or short. Mendel selected seven such contrasting characteristics. A complete list of these seven characteristics is shown in Figure 9.1.

Mendel first experimented with plants that varied in only one characteristic. By breeding one pure line of pea plants with another pure line, he produced hybrid peas. A **hybrid** is an offspring produced by breeding two pure lines.

To describe Mendel's results, it is helpful to give the generations of hybrids precise names. The purebred parents are called the **P_1 generation**. The first generation of offspring are called the **F_1 generation**. The second generation of offspring are called the **F_2 generation**. (*P* stands for *parental*. *F* stands for *filial*, which means "of an offspring.") Mendel used plants from pure lines for his P_1 generation.

CONCEPTS

- dominant and recessive genes
- genes as distinct units
- independent assortment of genes
- incomplete dominance
- genotype and phenotype
- Punnett squares for monohybrid and dihybrid crosses

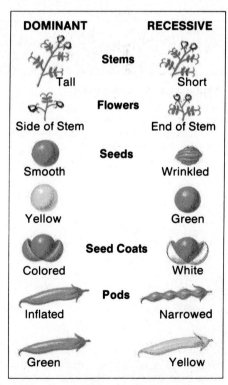

Figure 9.1 The seven pairs of characteristics Mendel studied

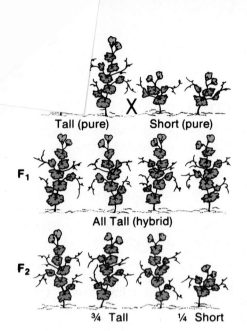

Tall (pure)   **Short (pure)**

F₁

All Tall (hybrid)

F₂

¾ Tall   ¼ Short

Figure 9.2 Crossbreeding tall and short pea plants

Mendel first crossed pure lines of tall plants with pure lines of short plants, as shown in Figure 9.2. You might expect the offspring from this cross to be a blend of their parents — in other words, to be of medium height. This was not the case. All the F_1 plants were tall. There were no short or medium-sized plants in the F_1 generation.

Had the F_1 plants lost the ability to produce short plants? To find out, Mendel crossed plants from the F_1 generation with each other. Surprisingly, not all of the F_2 offspring were tall. One out of every four of the F_2 offspring was short.

9–2   Dominant and Recessive Traits

From these results, Mendel hypothesized that there were two factors that controlled the height of pea plants. One factor produced tall plants and one produced short plants.

Mendel also hypothesized that the factor for shortness had not disappeared in the F_1 generation. Instead, it had been hidden by the presence of the tall factor. The short factor reappeared in the F_2 generation.

Mendel called the tall factor the **dominant** factor because it had masked the short factor. He called the short factor **recessive** because it had been hidden. The recessive factor seemed to recede into the background in the presence of the dominant factor.

Mendel tested his hypothesis by crossing pea plants that had the other six pairs of contrasting characteristics. For each of the pairs, he could identify one factor as dominant and the other as recessive. For example, round seeds were dominant and wrinkled seeds were recessive. In all of these crosses, only the dominant trait appeared in the F_1 generation. In all cases, too, the recessive trait reappeared in the F_2 generation.

Figure 9.3 A white tiger exhibits the recessive characteristic for coat color. In tigers, orange coat color is dominant.

9-3   The Law of Segregation

From his results, Mendel concluded that the factors governing dominant and recessive traits were distinct units. These factors were separate, or segregated, from each other. No matter how many times plants with round peas were crossed with plants with wrinkled peas, the round peas became no less round and the wrinkled peas became no less wrinkled.

Mendel's data showed another very important result. Not only did the recessive traits reappear in the F_2 generation, but they reappeared in a constant proportion. About three fourths of the plants showed the dominant trait. One fourth showed the recessive trait. In other words, the F_2 generation showed a ratio of about 3 to 1, or 3:1.

Because Mendel had been trained in mathematics, he recognized that these results could be explained in a very simple way. This explanation is called Mendel's first law, or the **law of segregation**. This law has three parts:

1. For each characteristic, an individual carries two factors.
2. Each parent contributes one of its two factors to each offspring. The chances of contributing either factor are equal.
3. If an offspring carries two dominant factors, or one dominant and one recessive factor, the offspring will appear to have the dominant trait. If the offspring carries two recessive factors, it will appear to have the recessive trait.

Since Mendel's time, numerous biologists have confirmed that the law of segregation holds true for most plants and animals. In fact, segregation of genes is a basic principle of inheritance.

Today biologists call the units of heredity that Mendel studied **genes**. Genes govern the characteristics of an organism. The two separate forms of a gene are called **alleles**. For example, a gene governs the seed color of peas. One allele of that gene produces green seeds and the other allele produces yellow seeds. (Mendel's "factors" were alleles.)

9-4   Genotype and Phenotype

Biologists represent alleles by symbols. Generally the symbol for a gene is the first letter of the dominant allele. So the symbol for tallness is a capital T. To represent the recessive allele, biologists use the same letter but in the lowercase form. Therefore, the allele for shortness is represented by a lowercase t.

Since each organism carries two alleles per characteristic, each characteristic can be represented by two letters. The two letters make up the organism's **genotype**, or set of alleles

Do You Know?
Mendel was so respected by his fellow monks that in 1868 he was unanimously elected abbot, head of the monastery.

for a characteristic. Thus a tall pea plant could have the genotype TT. A pea plant with the genotype tt would be short.

Notice that a pea plant with the genotype Tt would also be tall. Because tallness is dominant over shortness, plants with the genotypes Tt and TT appear identical. In other words, even though individual organisms have different genotypes, they may look alike.

The appearance of an organism is called its **phenotype** (FEE-nuh-teyep). A pea plant with the genotype TT has a tall phenotype. A plant with the genotype Tt also has a tall phenotype. What is the phenotype for the genotype tt?

An organism that carries two identical alleles is said to be **homozygous**. If the organism carries unlike alleles, it is said to be **heterozygous**. TT, ss, and YY are homozygous genotypes. Tt, Ss, and Yy are heterozygous genotypes. Notice that an organism with a heterozygous genotype has the same phenotype as an organism with a genotype that is homozygous for the dominant allele.

Genotype	GG	Gg	gg
Phenotype			
Pure or Hybrid?	Pure	Hybrid	Pure
Homozygous or Heterozygous?	Homozygous (dominant)	Heterozygous	Homozygous (recessive)

Figure 9.4 The allele for green pods (G) is dominant over the allele for yellow pods (g).

9–5 Using Punnett Squares

If you know the genotypes of the parents, it is possible to predict the likelihood of an offspring's inheriting a particular genotype. Consider a cross of parents who have the genotypes TT and tt. According to the law of segregation, each parent will contribute one allele to each offspring. Since both parents in this case are homozygous, all offspring of this cross will have the genotype Tt. Remember: One allele must come from each parent.

A helpful way to visualize crosses is by using a **Punnett square**. The Punnett square is a table devised by the British mathematician and biologist R. C. Punnett. The following

Punnett square shows the possible results of a cross between two pea plants, one of which is homozygous dominant and one of which is homozygous recessive. The two alleles that one parent can contribute are shown on the top line of the table. The two alleles that the other parent can contribute are listed on the left.

	T	T
t	Tt	Tt
t	Tt	Tt

Each of the four enclosed boxes in the table contains a possible combination of alleles for the offspring. Since there are four boxes in this Punnett square, four combinations of alleles are possible in the offspring. In this cross, however, all of the possible combinations result in the same genotype, Tt. The phenotype of all the offspring will be tall.

Recall that Mendel's first cross between pure lines resulted in an F_1 generation in which all the offspring were tall. As you can see from the Punnett square, all of Mendel's F_1 hybrids must have been heterozygous.

What happened when Mendel crossed the F_1 hybrids? Figure 9.5 is a Punnett square showing that cross. The Punnett square shows that each parent can contribute either a dominant or a recessive allele to each offspring. Each offspring could have one of three genotypes: TT, Tt, or tt.

The order in which the alleles are listed in the genotype has no meaning — the genotype Tt is the same as the genotype tT. Traditionally, however, the dominant allele is listed first in the genotype. An offspring's genotype does not depend upon which parent contributed which allele. The allele for tallness is the same whether it was contributed by the male or the female parent.

The Punnett square can also help calculate the probable ratios of genotypes in the offspring. Simply count the number of boxes occupied by each genotype. As you can see, there is 1 box with TT; 2 boxes with Tt; and 1 box with tt. This ratio can be written as 1 TT : 2 Tt : 1 tt, or simply 1 : 2 : 1. This means that each offpsring has a ¼ chance of having the homozygous dominant genotype, a 2/4 (½) chance of having the heterozygous genotype, and a ¼ chance of having the homozygous recessive genotype.

To calculate the possible phenotypes of the offspring from this cross, you would combine the heterozygous genotype

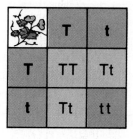

Figure 9.5 Mendel's F_1 hybrid cross

Do You Know?
R. C. Punnett did crosses to determine how the trait of size is inherited in poultry.

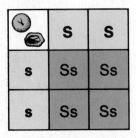

Figure 9.6 *Top:* Results of the test cross if the unknown plant is homozygous dominant. *Bottom:* Results of the test cross if the unknown plant is heterozygous.

with the homozygous dominant genotype. Remember that heterozygous individuals and individuals that are homozygous for the dominant allele exhibit the same phenotype. Therefore, the probable ratio of tall offspring to short offspring is 3:1. This is the Mendelian ratio found in Mendel's F_2 generation. When one hybrid fertilizes another, the offspring show the Mendelian ratio: ¾ have the dominant phenotype and ¼ have the recessive phenotype.

A Punnett square will help you predict the chance of occurrence of any genotype or phenotype in an offspring. If one parent is heterozygous tall and the other homozygous short, for example, each offspring will have a 50 percent chance of being heterozygous tall.

9–6   Test Cross

If you know the phenotype of an organism, is it possible to determine its genotype? Obviously, if the organism shows the recessive trait, you know that the genotype of that individual is homozygous recessive. A short pea plant must have a genotype of tt. But what if the phenotype is for the dominant trait? How can you tell whether the genotype is homozygous dominant or heterozygous?

To answer a similar question, Mendel developed the **test cross** shown in Figure 9.6. Mendel had a plant with smooth peas, but he did not know its genotype. The plant could have been SS or Ss. Mendel decided to cross this plant with a plant that was homozygous recessive. He reasoned this way:

1. If the unknown plants were SS, crossing them with plants that were ss would yield offspring that were all of the genotype Ss. These plants would have smooth peas.
2. If the unknown peas had the genotype Ss, ½ of the offspring would be Ss and ½ would be ss. Since these would have different phenotypes as well as different genotypes, they would be easy to distinguish. Half would have smooth peas and half would have wrinkled peas.

The test cross is important today to plant and animal breeders. They use the test cross to determine whether new varieties have established pure lines.

9–7   Incomplete Dominance

All of the characteristics that Mendel studied exhibited clear dominance of one allele over the other. His plants were either tall or short, and his peas were either wrinkled or smooth.

There are other cases, however, in which neither allele is dominant over the other. This situation is called **incomplete**

dominance. In incomplete dominance, heterozygous individuals express traits that are a blend of the phenotypes of two alleles. One example occurs in the Andalusian fowl, shown in Figure 9.7. In this bird the gene for feather color shows incomplete dominance. Birds that are homozygous are either black or white. Hybrids appear blue.

In writing genotypes for incomplete dominance, the lowercase initial letter of each allele is used. Thus the black fowl have the genotype bb and the white fowl have the genotype ww. The blue hybrids have the genotype bw. This indicates that both alleles have equal weight in determining the phenotype of the offspring.

Genes with incomplete dominance obey the law of segregation. If two blue fowl (bw) are crossed, their offspring yield the Mendelian ratio of 1 bb:2 bw:1 ww (1 black:2 blue:1 white). The only difference is that in cases of incomplete dominance, the phenotype of homozygous individuals is different from the phenotype of heterozygous individuals.

Incomplete dominance occurs in other organisms as well. The garden flowers called four-o'clocks show incomplete dominance in their color. Homozygous flowers are red or white, while heterozygous flowers are pink.

Incomplete dominance occurs even in pea plants, although not in any of the characteristics that Mendel selected for his investigations. For example, the flowering time of peas may be either early or late. Heterozygous plants have intermediate flowering times.

Figure 9.7 An Andalusian fowl

9-8   Law of Independent Assortment

So far in this chapter we have discussed crosses in which only one characteristic was considered. Crosses involving only one pair of alleles are called **monohybrid crosses**.

Of course, organisms possess many different genes. It is possible to study the inheritance of two characteristics, such as pea color and plant height, at the same time. Crosses involving two genes are called **dihybrid crosses**.

In addition to studying monohybrid crosses, Mendel carried out thousands of dihybrid crosses with his pea plants. These crosses led to his second important discovery, the law of independent asssortment.

The **law of independent assortment** states that the inheritance of alleles for one characteristic does not affect ·the inheritance of alleles for another characteristic. Whether a plant is short or tall, for example, has no effect upon whether its seeds are smooth or wrinkled. All of the genes separate independently.

Figure 9.8 Which of these four-o'clocks are heterozygous?

	TG	Tg	tG	tg
TG	TTGG	TTGg	TtGG	TtGg
Tg	TTGg	TTgg	TtGg	Ttgg
tG	TtGG	TtGg	ttGG	ttGg
tg	TtGg	Ttgg	ttGg	ttgg

☐ Tall, Green   ☐ Short, Green
☐ Tall, Yellow   ☐ Short, Yellow

Figure 9.9 A dihybrid cross

Do You Know?

The fractions ⁹⁄₁₆, ³⁄₁₆, ³⁄₁₆, and ¹⁄₁₆ can be expressed in the form of the ratio 9:3:3:1.

To test the law of independent assortment, Mendel crossed plants that were homozygous dominant for height and pod color (TTGG) with plants that were homozygous recessive for height and pod color (ttgg). As predicted, all of the F_1 generation were tall and had green pods. All of the F_1 generation were hybrids for both traits; their genotype was TtGg.

To explain the results of the F_2 generation, it is useful to use a Punnett square for a dihybrid cross. This Punnett square is similar to one for a monohybrid cross, but it is more complex. Both alleles for both genes must be entered for each parent.

Figure 9.9 shows the results of Mendel's F_2 dihybrid cross. As predicted by the law of independent assortment, individual plants may be dominant for one trait and recessive for another, dominant for both traits, or recessive for both traits. If you study this Punnett square, you will see that ⁹⁄₁₆ of the offspring are dominant for both characteristics. They are tall and have green pods. You will also see that ³⁄₁₆ of the plants are short and have green pods; ³⁄₁₆ are tall and have yellow pods. One out of 16 plants (¹⁄₁₆) is recessive for both characteristics. It is short and has yellow pods. Although there are only four combinations of phenotypes possible from this dihybrid cross, there are many more combinations of genotypes. How many can you find?

9–9   Mendel's Work Is Forgotten

Mendel presented his findings on inheritance to the Brno Society for the Study of Natural Science in 1865. His paper was published the next year and distributed to many countries. His extensive data demonstrated conclusively the laws of segregation and independent assortment, as well as the principle of dominance.

Despite his brilliant work, Mendel's conclusions were almost totally ignored until 1900, 16 years after his death. For many reasons, scientists were not ready before that time to accept Mendel's simple explanation of heredity.

Checkpoint

1. An organism's set of alleles for a gene is called its _____.
2. An organism's appearance is called its _____.
3. What word describes an organism that contains two like alleles?
4. What law states that the inheritance of one characteristic does not affect the inheritance of another characteristic?

Meiosis and the Cellular Basis of Heredity

One reason that Mendel's work was neglected for so long was that the cellular mechanisms that underlie heredity were not understood. Mendel referred to the "factors" controlling inheritance, but he had no idea what those factors might be. Mendel knew nothing about chromosomes or DNA. Not until the 1880s did biologists begin to realize that the cell nucleus plays an important role in inheritance. It was the study of the cellular process of sexual reproduction that finally linked Mendel's conclusions to the structure of the cell.

9–10 Chromosome Number

As you learned in Chapter 8, every type of living thing has a specific number of chromosomes per cell. The body cells, or **somatic cells**, of most organisms contain two complete sets of chromosomes, one set from each parent.

Because somatic cells possess double sets of chromosomes, they are described as being **diploid**. The number of chromosomes (n) in a diploid cell can also be written 2n. A single set of chromosomes (1n) is said to be **haploid**. In humans, the haploid number of chromosomes (1n) is 23 and the diploid number (2n) is 46. Fruit flies have four pairs of chromosomes, so their haploid number is 4 and their diploid number is 8.

The matching pairs of chromosomes in a diploid cell are said to be **homologous**. You could compare the chromosomes in a diploid cell to pairs of different-colored socks. The matching pairs of socks are like homologous chromosomes. A haploid set of socks would contain one sock of each color.

9–11 Asexual and Sexual Reproduction

Organisms can reproduce in two ways, either sexually or asexually. In **asexual reproduction** the offspring are genetically identical to the parent. In asexual reproduction new cells are produced by mitosis. As you learned in Chapter 8, during mitosis the number of chromosomes in the cells remains constant.

An example of asexual reproduction occurs in spider plants. The spider plant grows tiny plants along its stem. These new plants are produced by mitotic division, so the chromosomes of each tiny plant are exactly the same as those of the parent plant.

Figure 9.10 The new plants you see on this spider plant were produced asexually.

In **sexual reproduction** two haploid cells unite to form a new diploid cell. The haploid cells that unite are called **gametes**. In most organisms, males produce gametes called **sperm** and females produce gametes called **eggs**.

The union of two gametes is called **fertilization**. When an egg and sperm unite, they produce a **zygote**, or fertilized egg. The zygote carries the combined genetic material of both gametes, one set of chromosomes from each parent. After fertilization, the zygote grows and divides by mitosis to produce a new organism.

Note that the gametes carry a haploid number of chromosomes. If the gametes carried a diploid number of chromosomes, the resulting zygote would contain twice as many chromosomes as its parents, or 4n. If this doubling of chromosomes continued, the cell would be overloaded with chromosomes.

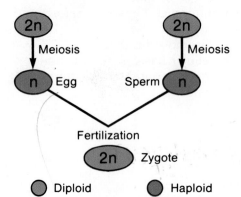

Figure 9.11 The formation of gametes and a zygote in sexual reproduction

9–12   Meiosis

The process by which a diploid cell produces haploid gametes is called **meiosis** (meye-OH-sis). Meiosis occurs in all sexually reproducing organisms. In higher plants and animals, meiosis occurs in specialized sex organs.

During meiosis, the chromosomes of a diploid cell replicate. The cell then divides into four haploid cells, or gametes. Because the process of meiosis results in haploid cells, it is also called reduction division.

The appearance of the chromosomes during meiosis is similar to the appearance of chromosomes during mitosis. Unlike mitosis, meiosis includes two cell divisions. These two divisions are distinguished by the Roman numerals *I* and *II*. The stages of meiosis are shown in Figure 9.12.

Interphase   Before meiosis begins, the chromosomes replicate, so the nucleus has a 4n set of chromosomes. The chromosomes at this time are uncoiled and not visible.

Prophase I   The chromosomes shorten, thicken, and become visible. Each chromosome is now double, consisting of two chromatids attached by a kinetochore.

Figure 9.12 Meiosis

Interphase

Prophase I

Metaphase I

Anaphase I

Then the pairs of homologous chromosomes line up next to each other. This pairing of chromosomes is called **synapsis** (sih-NAP-sis). In each synapsing group there are four chromatids — the replicated sets of homologous chromosomes. Each group of four is called a **tetrad**.

Metaphase I The tetrads align themselves along the equator of the nucleus and attach to the spindle fibers.

Anaphase I One pair of chromatids from each tetrad moves along the spindle fibers toward opposite poles of the cell. The paired chromatids themselves are still attached by their kinetochores. At this time the homologous chromosomes segregate. One complete set of chromosomes moves toward each pole.

Telophase I The cell divides into two smaller cells. Each new cell contains one of each pair of homologous chromosomes. Each chromosome consists of two chromatids, still attached by kinetochores. The new cells are not identical.

Interphase The chromatids uncoil and become invisible, but they do not replicate. Soon the two new cells begin the second stage of meiosis.

Prophase II The chromatids condense and become visible.

Metaphase II The paired chromatids, still attached by kinetochores, line up along the equator and attach to the spindle fibers.

Anaphase II The kinetochores divide. The separate chromatids, now called chromosomes, move along the spindle fibers to the opposite sides of the cell.

Telophase II The chromosomes reach their destinations, forming a total of four new haploid nuclei.

Each cell now divides into two smaller cells. These haploid cells will become the gametes. Each cell produces two sets of identical gametes.

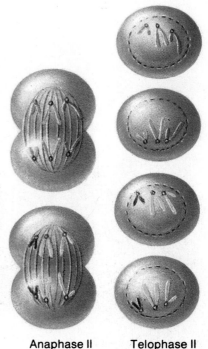

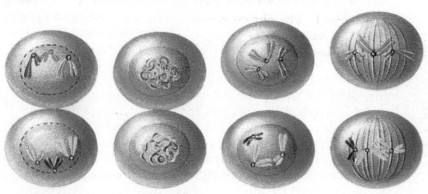

| Telophase I | Interphase | Prophase II | Metaphase II | Anaphase II | Telophase II |

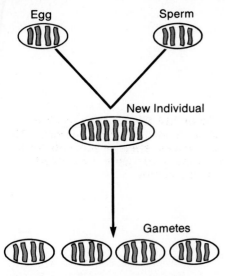

Figure 9.13 Some of the possible chromosome combinations in the gametes of an individual are shown. Notice that the chromosomes from the individual's parents assort independently.

Notice that every diploid cell contains one haploid set of chromosomes from each parent. During meiosis, the chromosomes from one parent will recombine with the chromosomes from the other parent. This reassortment, or segregation, is random. As Figure 9.13 shows, each gamete may have chromosomes derived from both parents.

9–13   Comparing Meiosis and Mitosis

If you compare meiosis with mitosis, as shown in Chapter 8, you will notice several important differences:

1. Mitosis involves a single replication of chromosomes, followed by a single division of the nucleus and cytoplasm. In meiosis a single replication is followed by two nuclear divisions and two cell divisions.
2. Mitosis results in two diploid cells. Meiosis results in four haploid cells.
3. In meiosis there is a pairing, or synapsis, of the homologous chromosomes. Synapsis does not occur in mitosis.
4. In meiosis there is segregation of chromosomes without division of the kinetochores. In mitosis, the kinetochores divide during metaphase.

By the beginning of this century, cell biologists had identified the stages of meiosis and mitosis just described. The groundwork was laid for understanding heredity.

9–14   The Chromosome Theory of Inheritance

It was in the spring of 1900 that a remarkable thing occurred. Three botanists working in three different countries simultaneously rediscovered Mendel's work. After lying unread for 34 years, Mendel's work was suddenly recognized to contain the basic principles of heredity!

In 1902, two scientists pointed out that Mendel's results could be related to the movement of chromosomes during meiosis. These two men were Walter Sutton, a graduate student at Columbia University in New York City, and Theodor Boveri, a German zoologist. Both Sutton and Boveri proposed that Mendel's "factors," were located on the chromosomes. One allele of each gene lay on one chromosome of each homologous pair. Different genes lay on different chromosomes. This explanation is called the **chromosome theory**.

The chromosome theory gives a cellular basis to Mendel's laws. According to the chromosome theory, genes occur in pairs because they are located on chromosomes, which also occur in pairs. One allele is derived from each parent because one chromosome comes from each parent.

Figure 9.14 Coat color in cocker spaniels involves two gene pairs. The chromosome theory accounts for the fact that those gene pairs assort independently.

The chromosome theory explains the law of segregation. Alleles segregate independently because they are located on homologous chromosomes. As you have learned, homologous chromosomes segregate during meiosis.

The law of independent assortment can also be explained by the chromosome theory. Genes on separate chromosomes assort independently because the chromosomes segregate randomly during meiosis. Not all genes assort independently, however. Genes on the same chromosome generally travel together, in a sort of package deal.

Mendel was very lucky to have discovered the law of independent assortment. Pea plants have only seven pairs of chromosomes. The seven traits that Mendel selected for study happened to be located on separate chromosomes. Had Mendel studied two genes located on the same chromosome, his data would not have revealed independent assortment.

With the announcement of the chromosome theory, the modern science of genetics was born. Today **genetics**, the study of heredity, is among the most exciting areas of biology. Modern geneticists can study and work with genes in ways that Mendel could never have imagined. But they owe the foundations of their work to his pioneering experiments in a monastery garden over a hundred years ago.

BIOLOGY INSIGHTS

The chromosome theory explains the results of many different experiments and has been confirmed by the work of many scientists. It is one of the unifying principles of cellular biology and genetics.

Checkpoint

1. The process in which two gametes fuse to form a zygote is called _____.
2. What is reduction division?
3. A cell that contains a matching pair of each type of chromosome contains a _____ number of chromosomes.
4. What is the name of the process in which homologous chromosomes line up next to each other?
5. During what stage of meiosis do the chromatids segregate?
6. What theory states that genes are located on chromosomes?

CHAPTER REVIEW

Summary

- Over one hundred years ago, Mendel observed the basic principles of genetics by carefully studying hybrid pea plants. His discoveries provided the foundations for modern genetics.

- Mendel established the concept that genes may have dominant and recessive alleles. Each generation inherits these alleles as distinct units rather than as blended traits.

- Genes reappear in hybrid crosses according to constant ratios. In an F_2 hybrid cross, this ratio is 3:1. The ratio is explained by Mendel's law of segregation.

- Genes on separate chromosomes are inherited independently of other genes. This is the law of independent assortment.

- Punnett squares can help predict the probable outcome of a cross between parents of known genotypes. The test cross can help to determine the genotype of an organism.

- Sexual reproduction occurs when two gametes unite to form a zygote. Sexual reproduction is characterized by fertilization and meiosis.

- Meiosis is reduction division, by which a diploid cell divides into four haploid gametes.

- The chromosome theory of inheritance states that genes are located on chromosomes. This theory relates Mendel's findings to the cellular processes of sexual reproduction.

Vocabulary

allele	F_2 generation
asexual reproduction	gamete
chromosome theory	gene
dihybrid cross	genetics
diploid	genotype
dominant	haploid
egg	heredity
fertilization	heterozygous
F_1 generation	homologous

homozygous	Punnett square
hybrid	pure line
incomplete	recessive
dominance	sexual reproduction
law of independent	somatic cell
assortment	sperm
law of segregation	synapsis
meiosis	test cross
monohybrid cross	tetrad
P_1 generation	zygote
phenotype	

Review

1. What is a hybrid?
2. What is meant by *recessive allele*?
3. A mother has two alleles for a particular characteristic. How many does she give to an offspring?
4. What is the genotype of a pea plant with wrinkled seeds?
5. Which kind of phenotype — dominant or recessive — can have more than one genotype? Give an example.
6. A white four-o'clock and a red four-o'clock produce offspring with pink flowers. This is an example of _____.
7. In which stage of meiosis does synapsis occur?
8. How many sperm form from a sperm-producing cell that undergoes meiosis?
9. What is the haploid chromosome number in humans? What is the diploid number?
10. Would cells in your bones be haploid or diploid? Explain.

Interpret and Apply

1. Is it possible to be heterozygous for a characteristic and show the recessive phenotype? Explain.
2. Does the height of a pea plant affect the color of the plant's flowers? Why or why not?

3. In a hybrid cross between homozygous dominant and homozygous recessive parents, there are 32 offspring in the F_2 generation. According to the Mendelian ratio, how many of the offspring should show the recessive trait?

4. The houseplant coleus has curves on the edge of its leaves. Deep curves (D) are dominant over shallow curves (d). Draw a Punnett square showing the possible offspring of a cross between a homozygous plant with deep-curved leaves and a plant with shallow-curved leaves. What are the possible phenotypes of the offspring?

5. In tomato plants, long vines (L) are dominant over short vines (l). The incomplete Punnett square below shows a cross between two tomato plants:

LL	LL
Ll	Ll

Copy the Punnett square on a separate sheet of paper. Complete it by filling in the alleles of both parents. Identify the phenotypes of the parents and offspring.

6. On the planet Tintopodium, the feet of the inhabitants are of different colors. You cross a yellow-footed Tintopodian with one who has blue feet. The results are shown in the Punnett square below:

	y	**y**
b	yb	yb
b	yb	yb

a. What is this an example of — complete dominance or incomplete dominance?

b. What color or colors do you think the feet of the offspring will be?

7. An organism has two pairs of chromosomes.
   a. One of its cells undergoes mitosis. How many cells result? How many chromosomes does each have?
   b. How many sperm cells result from the meiosis of one of the organism's cells? How many chromosomes are in each?

Challenge

1. In dogs, short hair is dominant over long and dark hair is dominant over light. One dog is heterozygous for hair length and shows the recessive trait for hair color. Another dog is homozygous dominant for hair length and heterozygous for hair color. Construct a Punnett square showing a cross between these two animals. Identify the phenotypes that might result.

2. Straight wings in fruit flies are dominant over curly wings. Describe a cross you could make to check whether a straight-winged fly is heterozygous or homozygous.

3. In guinea pigs, a black coat is dominant over a white coat. Can two white-coated parents produce an offspring with a black coat? Why or why not?

Projects

1. A trihybrid cross involves alleles for three different traits. Select any three pairs of traits that Mendel studied. On posterboard or a chalkboard, draw a Punnett square for the cross of two plants that are heterozygous for each of these characteristics.

2. Using pipe cleaners for chromosomes, make a model of a six-chromosome cell undergoing meiosis. Use one color of pipe cleaner to represent chromosomes inherited from the mother, and another color to represent those inherited from the father. Demonstrate the law of independent assortment by showing all the ways the chromosomes can be distributed.

10 Chromosomes, Genes, and Mutation

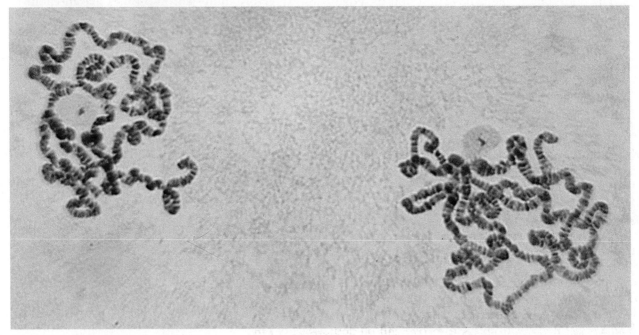

Giant chromosomes from salivary glands of *Drosophila melanogaster*

The study of genetics has been like the exploration of a new land. Like explorers, geneticists have searched for landmarks on the chromosomes of various organisms.

The photograph above shows a giant chromosome. Giant chromosomes like this are found in the salivary glands of fruit flies. Giant chromosomes are over 100 times larger than the chromosomes in other body cells. In these chromosomes the individual strands of DNA have replicated many times, until each chromosome is a thick bundle of chromatid strands. Because these chromosomes are so large, they are very useful in genetic research.

Notice the bands around the chromosomes. These bands are arranged in a distinctive pattern. The position and width of the bands varies from chromosome to chromosome, but most fruit flies have similar patterns on similar chromosomes.

By carefully comparing the bands on the giant chromosomes with the traits of fruit flies, geneticists have been able to chart the location of genes on the chromosomes. The bands are landmarks that allow geneticists to map the territory of their new found land.

Chromosomes and Inheritance

When Sutton and Boveri suggested the chromosome theory of inheritance in 1902, many biologists could see immediately that the behavior of genes and chromosomes is remarkably similar. But this similarity alone was not enough to prove the theory. Much more evidence was needed.

10–1 *Drosophila melanogaster*

Mendel was able to demonstrate the principles of heredity by breeding pea plants. But his experiments took seven years, and occupied rows and rows of his monastery garden. Instead of studying pea plants, many of the geneticists who worked during the first half of this century studied the common fruit fly, *Drosophila melanogaster. Drosophila* (droh-SAHF-uh-luh) is the tiny yellowish fly that often hovers around overripe apples and bananas. Even now, fruit flies are a favorite organism for genetic research.

Fruit flies are ideal organisms for genetic experiments. They reach maturity and reproduce within two weeks. Thus they have very short generations. They are easy and inexpensive to maintain — thousands can be grown in a few old milk bottles. They produce large numbers of offspring. It is easy to tell male flies from female flies. In fact, the principles that Mendel worked seven years to prove can be demonstrated in just two or three months with a few bottles of fruit flies.

10–2 Sex Determination

When geneticists examined *Drosophila* chromosomes, they found that each somatic cell had four pairs of chromosomes. As shown in Figure 10.1, three pairs of homologous chromosomes are the same in all of the flies. The fourth pair, however, appears different in the male and female flies. In the female, both members of the fourth pair are straight — like rods. In the male, one chromosome of the fourth pair is straight, but the other chromosome is hooked on the end — like a cane.

The rod-shaped chromosome is called the X chromosome. The cane-shaped chromosome is called the Y chromosome. Males have one X and one Y chromosome. Females have two X chromosomes.

The unmatched chromosomes are called **sex chromosomes**. The other chromosomes are called **autosomes**. The difference between male and female fruit flies can be explained by the

- advantages of using *Drosophila melanogaster* for genetic research
- chromosomal basis of sex determination
- linkage of genes
- relationship between incomplete linkage and crossing over

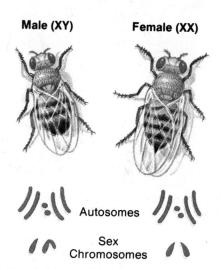

Male (XY)   **Female (XX)**

Autosomes

Sex Chromosomes

Figure 10.1 Male and female *Drosophila* and their chromosomes. Notice that the male *Drosophila* is smaller and has a darker posterior end.

Male Gametes

	X	Y
X	XX	XY
X	XX	XY

Female Gametes

Figure 10.2 Sex determination in *Drosophila*. Why is there no YY genotype?

presence of sex chromosomes. Sex, like other characteristics, is determined by two factors. Fruit flies that are homozygous for the X chromosome (XX) are females. Fruit flies that are heterozygous (XY) are males.

Figure 10.2 shows a Punnett square for sex determination. According to Mendel's laws, crossing a homozygous parent with a heterozygous parent should result in offspring of a constant ratio of 1:1. This is just the case in sex determination. The ratio of male to female fruit flies is 1:1. Half the offspring are male and half are female. When the chromosomes segregate during meiosis, each gamete receives one sex chromosome. Offspring have a 50 percent chance of being male and a 50 percent chance of being female.

Because all females are homozygous (XX), the egg always contributes an X chromosome to the zygote. Because males are heterozygous (XY), sperm can contain either an X or a Y chromosome. Thus the gamete contributed by the father determines the sex of the offspring.

The discovery of sex determination in *Drosophila* gave support to the chromosome theory. Geneticists were able to demonstrate that the phenotype of an organism — its sex — could be directly related to its chromosomes.

The determination of sex in many organisms is similar to that in *Drosophila*. In humans, each zygote has 23 pairs of chromosomes. Twenty-two pairs are autosomes and one pair is sex chromosomes. Women are XX and men are XY.

In certain organisms, such as butterflies and birds, sex determination is just the reverse of sex determination in *Drosophila*. In such organisms the male is homozygous and the female is heterozygous. Therefore, the gametes from the mother determine the sex of the offspring.

Figure 10.3 In butterflies, unlike in *Drosophila* and humans, gametes from the female determine the sex of the offspring.

10–3 Sex Linkage and Linkage Groups

Although the identification of the sex chromosomes supported the chromosome theory, it also raised another question. Did each characteristic have its own chromosome? Remember that *Drosophila* has only four pairs of chromosomes. But fruit flies have far more than just four characteristics. Surely there must be more than one gene on each chromosome.

Sutton had considered this problem when he proposed the chromosome theory. Sutton suggested that each chromosome carries many genes. The genes are linked together in a certain order on the chromosomes, like beads on a string. Genes on the same chromosome belong to the same **linkage group**.

Sutton further suggested that genes on a chromosome do not change position from generation to generation. In other words, the linkage groups are stable. Each gene occupies a specific position on a given chromosome. Different alleles for a gene occupy the same position on homologous chromosomes. For geneticists at the beginning of this century, one question stood out: Where are the genes located on the chromosomes?

The scientist who did the most to answer that question was the American geneticist Thomas Hunt Morgan. Like Sutton, Morgan and his research team worked at Columbia University. They worked in a laboratory called the fly room. During their years of research, Morgan and his team studied hundreds of thousands of fruit flies.

The first opportunity to locate a gene on a chromosome came in 1909, when Morgan discovered a white-eyed male in a colony of flies. This was odd. Drosophilas usually have red eyes.

To study this unusual trait, Morgan and his students crossed the white-eyed male with a normal red-eyed female. All the F_1 offspring had red eyes. From this, Morgan concluded that the allele for white eyes was recessive.

Do You Know?
Drosophila flies were not commonly seen in the United States until the 1870s. At that time, bananas began to be imported from Central America. The flies came along with this exotic new fruit.

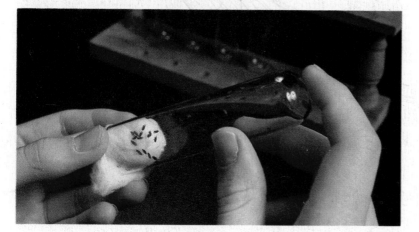

Figure 10.4 How do you keep track of fruit flies? What prevents them from flying all around? They are kept and nourished in test tubes or narrow-necked glass bottles stoppered with cotton. When researchers want to examine or separate flies, they apply enough ether to the cotton to put them to sleep but not to kill them.

Morgan and his students then crossed members of the F_1 generation. Again, the F_2 offspring conformed to the Mendelian ratio of phenotypes: 3/4 were dominant, with red eyes; and 1/4 were recessive, with white eyes. But there was something unexpected in the F_2 generation. All the white-eyed flies were males. None of the females had white eyes!

Morgan and his students interpreted this result according to the chromosome theory. They suggested that the gene for eye color in *Drosophila* must be on the same chromosome as the genes that determine sex. This gene for eye color is located on the X chromosome. In fact, the Y chromosome does not carry a gene for eye color.

Remember that a dominant allele masks a recessive allele. In most cases, an organism must have two recessive alleles to have a recessive phenotype. But in male fruit flies, there is only one chromosome with the gene for eye color. If that gene has the recessive allele, there will be no dominant allele to mask it. Thus one recessive allele is enough to make the male fly white-eyed. The female, of course, has two alleles for eye color because she has two X chromosomes. A female can have white eyes only if *both* her X chromosomes carry alleles for the recessive trait.

Genes that are located on, or linked to, the X chromosome, are called **sex-linked genes**. Traits determined by sex-linked genes are called **sex-linked traits**. White eye color in fruit flies is an example of a sex-linked trait.

Linkage of genes on the X chromosome is indicated by superscripts. A homozygous red-eyed female would be $X^R X^R$. A recessive male would be $X^r Y$. Because the Y chromosome carries no gene for eye color, it has no superscript.

Punnett squares showing Morgan's F_1 and F_2 crosses are given in Figure 10.5. As you can see, all the F_1 females have the genotype $X^R X^r$. They received X^R from their mother and X^r from their father. Study the Punnett square for the F_2 cross to determine the genotypes of the offspring.

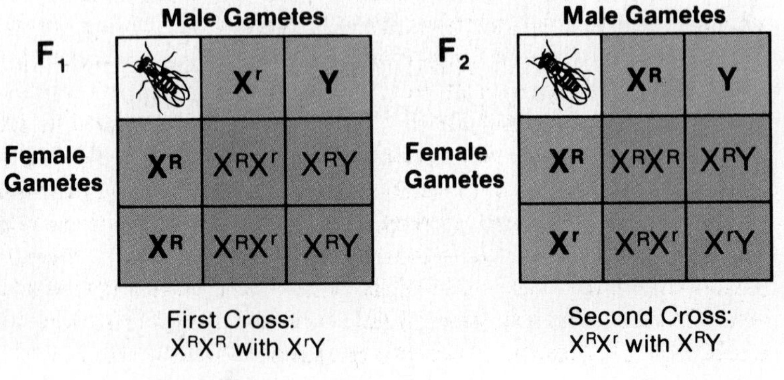

Figure 10.5 Sex-linked inheritance for red eyes in fruit flies

F₁

	Male Gametes	
	X^r	Y
Female Gametes X^R	$X^R X^r$	$X^R Y$
X^R	$X^R X^r$	$X^R Y$

First Cross:
$X^R X^R$ with $X^r Y$

F₂

	Male Gametes	
	X^R	Y
Female Gametes X^R	$X^R X^R$	$X^R Y$
X^r	$X^R X^r$	$X^r Y$

Second Cross:
$X^R X^r$ with $X^R Y$

White eyes were not the only sex-linked trait that Morgan and his students discovered in *Drosophila*. They found about 20 others, including unusual wing shape, body color, and bristle shape. Morgan and his students also demonstrated that the linkage of genes is not limited to genes located on the X chromosome. There are linkage groups on all of the chromosomes.

By 1915, Morgan and his group had investigated more than 100 genes. Each of these genes could be grouped into one of four linkage groups. Since *Drosophila* has four homologous chromosomes, each of these four linkage groups could be related to one chromosome. These results provided a strong confirmation of the chromosome theory.

10–4   Crossing Over

The linkage groups that Morgan demonstrated with *Drosophila* are an important exception to Mendel's law of independent assortment of genes. Genes that are located on the same chromosome, or in linkage groups, do not assort independently. If three genes are located on the same chromosome, they will be transmitted to the offspring as a group.

Traits that are linked together should follow the Mendelian ratio for a monohybrid cross. Imagine, for example, that a male *Drosophila* has three recessive alleles on its X chromosome — yellow body, white eyes, and miniature wings. If this male is bred with a female that is homozygous dominant for these genes, all of the F_1 offspring should display all three dominant traits. In the F_2 generation, half the males should display all three dominant traits and half the males should display all three recessive traits.

Morgan and his group carried out many crosses like the one just described. As they expected, in most cases the genes in a linkage group were inherited as a unit. Occasionally, though, Morgan found exceptions to these linkages. Sometimes males in the F_2 generation had yellow bodies and white eyes but normal wings. Other F_2 males had miniature wings and yellow bodies but normal red eyes. These results showed that sometimes the linkage groups break apart, or have **incomplete linkage**.

The cause of incomplete linkage can be found in meiosis. As you learned in Chapter 9, during prophase I the homologous chromosomes line up next to each other in synapsis. During synapsis, the pairs of chromatids twist around each other. As they twist, the chromatid strands often break and fuse. When this happens, the broken ends of the homologous chromatids may switch places, as shown in Figure 10.6. This exchange of genetic material is called **crossing over**.

Do You Know?
In *Drosophila*, crossing over rarely occurs in the male. In the silkworm moth, crossing over almost never happens in the female.

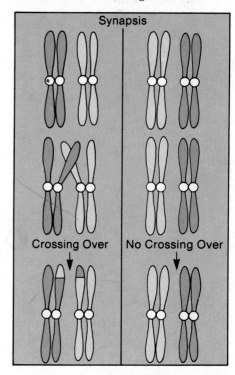

Figure 10.6 Crossing over produces new combinations of genes.

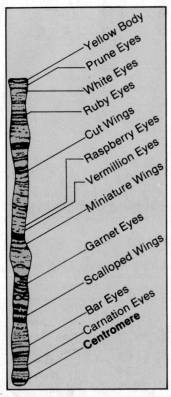

Figure 10.7 A gene map showing some of the genes that have been located on the X chromosome of *Drosophila*.

Crossing over is a very precise process. The genes on homologous chromosomes are lined up in the same order. When homologous chromatids cross over, they break and fuse at exactly the same points. Thus crossing over is an equal trade. Each chromatid ends up with a complete set of genes. As a result of crossing over, the new chromosomes have a combination of alleles not found in either parent.

Crossing over occurs often during meiosis. Sometimes homologous chromosomes cross over more than once.

Morgan noted an important fact about crossing over. Genes that are far apart on a chromosome will cross over more frequently than genes that are close together. Genes that are close together are unlikely to end up on separate chromosomes.

By carefully analyzing the gene combinations of offspring in hybrid crosses, geneticists can measure how often genes in a linkage group are separated by crossing over. Genes that cross over frequently must be farther apart than genes that rarely cross over. Using this information, geneticists can figure out the relative position of genes on the chromosome. This technique is called **chromosome mapping**. Chromosome mapping has allowed geneticists to map hundreds of genes on the chromosomes of *Drosophila*. Figure 10.7 shows a partial map of the genes on the *Drosophila* X chromosome. It has also been possible to map human chromosomes.

Although most genes have a specific location on the chromosomes, a few genes can move about. Evidence of such movement was gathered by the American geneticist Barbara McClintock. For over 40 years, McClintock studied the inheritance of kernel color in corn plants. Her results showed that certain genes could move from one position to another, or even from chromosome to chromosome. McClintock called these gene *jumping genes*. Recently jumping genes have been discovered in other organisms, including bacteria and *Drosophila*. In recognition of her discovery, McClintock was awarded the 1983 Nobel Prize.

Checkpoint

1. State three reasons why geneticists use fruit flies as experimental subjects.
2. How many chromosomes are found in each somatic cell of a *Drosophila*?
3. What chromosomes are characteristic of male fruit flies?
4. How many pairs of autosomes does a human somatic cell have?
5. What is the genotype of a white-eyed male fruit fly?
6. What causes incomplete linkage?

Mutations

The inheritance of genetic information is remarkably accurate. Most genes pass from generation to generation unchanged. Offspring differ from their parents because alleles are recombined through sexual reproduction, not because the genes have changed. Crossing over and the segregation of chromosomes reshuffle the genes each generation, but they do not alter the information in the genes.

Sometimes, though rarely, there is a change in the genetic information. Such a change is called a **mutation**. A mutation is an error in the replication of the genetic material.

CONCEPTS

- causes of mutation
- results of nondisjunction
- kinds of chromosomal rearrangements
- effects of gene mutations

10–5   Mutagens

Mutations are very rare. Geneticists estimate that an error in copying the genetic material occurs only once in every 100,000 replications. But there are certain substances and conditions that can increase the rate of mutation. These are called **mutagens**. Extremely high temperature, for example, is known to be a mutagen.

The best-known mutagen is radiation. Artificial radiation, such as that from X rays, and ultraviolet light have been shown to cause mutations. Certain chemicals are also mutagenic.

The first geneticist to demonstrate the effect of radiation on the rate of mutation was Hermann J. Muller. Muller studied with Morgan at Columbia University.

Muller showed that artificial radiation speeds up the rate at which genes mutate. The ability to increase the rate of mutation proved to be a very useful tool for geneticists. It allowed them to study the effects of various types of mutations. Because natural mutations occur so infrequently, geneticists had made little progress in the study of mutations until Muller's discovery. For his contribution, Muller received the Nobel Prize in Physiology and Medicine in 1946.

Today geneticists classify mutations in two groups: chromosomal mutations and gene mutations.

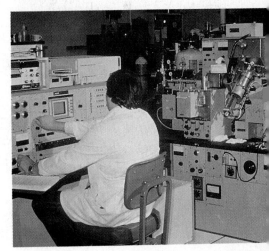

Figure 10.8 Some pesticides, food additives, and weed killers are possible mutagens. They are tested here at the National Center for Toxicological Research in Jefferson, Arkansas.

10–6   Chromosomal Mutations

Sometimes the movement of chromosomes during meiosis goes awry. When this happens, a gamete may end up with an unusual number of chromosomes. If this gamete then fuses with another gamete to become a zygote, the new organism will also carry an unusual number of chromosomes.

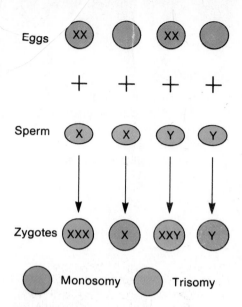

Figure 10.9 In this example nondisjunction has occurred in the formation of eggs.

Do You Know?

In honeybees, females have the diploid number of chromosomes. Males, however, are haploid. Females develop from fertilized eggs, while males come from unfertilized eggs.

Nondisjunction Recall that during the fir division of normal meiosis, the homologous chromosomes eparate from each other. During the second meiotic divisin, the chromatids separate from each other. Sometimes, thogh, the chromatids or homologous chromosomes stick togeter instead of separating. These chromosomes do not disjn, or come apart. When **nondisjunction** occurs, two gamets receive an extra chromosome and the other two gametesend up one chromosome short. An example of nondisjurction is shown in Figure 10.9.

If one of these abnormal gametes fertilize a normal gamete, the resulting zygote will also be abnorma. It will have one or three of the nondisjoined chromosom rather than the two found in a normal diploid cell. All the cells descended from the zygote by mitosis will also have anabnormal number of chromosomes.

If a cell has an extra chromosome, the ondition is called **trisomy**. If a cell is missing one chromosone, the condition is called **monosomy**. Either condition can be harmful. Organisms with either condition are often sterile, or unable to reproduce. Generally, monosomy is more harmful than trisomy. In the case of monosomy, an organismlacks the genetic information carried on the missing chromosome.

Polyploidy Sometimes a nucleus does not undergo the second meiotic division. When this happens, the gametes that result are diploid instead of haploid. The zygotes that result from such gametes have an extra set of chromosomes, so they are 3n. Occasionally diploid gametes will fuse, forming zygotes that have a 4n set of chromosomes. An organism with extra sets of chromosomes is said to be **polyploid**.

Polyploidy is lethal to most animals. But polyploidy is relatively common among plants. In fact, some polyploid plants are larger and healthier than their diploid relatives. Cultivated wheat and potatoes are polyploid.

Figure 10.10 Polyploidy, although lethal in most animals, is common in plants such as wheat.

Chromosomal Rearrangements Occasionally a piece of a chromosome will break off and be lost in the cytoplasm. When this occurs, the genetic information that the piece carried is lost. This kind of mutation is called a chromosomal **deletion**.

As you can see in Figure 10.11, a fragment from a chromosome may also become attached to another chromosome in the cell. This kind of rearrangement is called a **translocation**. In translocation, genes are transferred to a nonhomologous chromosome.

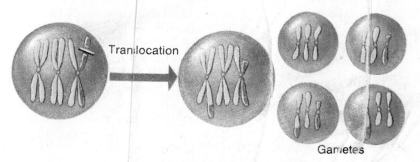

Translocation

Gametes

Figure 10.11 When translocation occurs in cells undergoing meiosis, the resulting gametes may carry too much or too little information. Some examples of gametes are shown.

If a deletion occurs in a cell undergoing meiosis, the resulting gametes will lack genetic information. If translocation occurs during meiosis, some of the gametes may also lack information. The effects of deletion and translocation are like those of trisomy and monosomy. The effects of chromosomal rearrangements are usually less severe than those of nondisjunction because fewer genes are involved.

10–7   Gene Mutations

The word *mutation* most often refers to a change within a gene. To understand gene mutation, it is important to remember the structure of the genetic material presented in Chapter 8.

As Watson and Crick stated in 1953, the chromosomes consist of long strands of DNA coiled in double helixes. The genetic program is carried in the sequence of the nucleotide bases. The codons are triplets, or groups of three nucleotide bases. Each triplet stands for a particular amino acid. One chromosome may carry the code for building thousands of proteins.

Many genes control the synthesis of specific proteins, usually enzymes. Each gene contains a portion of the DNA code.

Point Mutations You could think of each gene as a message written in words of three letters. A short message might read, "The old dog ran and the fox did too."

Sometimes one base replaces another in a base triplet. This kind of substitution is called a **point mutation**. Such a mutation changes only one nucleotide base in a gene. A substitution may change the meaning of the gene message slightly. (The old *h*og ran and the fox did too).

A point mutation may change the particular amino acid that the codon represents. Recall that the order of amino acids in a protein determines its three-dimensional shape. In most proteins, the shape of the molecule controls its function. Therefore, if the sequence of amino acids is changed, the function of the protein will also be changed.

A change in one amino acid may have little effect on an organism. Many of the alleles that Morgan identified in *Drosophila*, such as white eyes, were the result of point mutations.

Occasionally a point mutation may have serious consequences. For example, if the amino acid valine substitutes for the amino acid glutamic acid at one position on the protein hemoglobin, sickle-cell disease results. Sickle-cell disease is potentially fatal in humans.

Deletions and Insertions   Sometimes a nucleotide is lost from the DNA sequence. This kind of mutation is called a **base deletion**. As Figure 10.12 illustrates, when a deletion occurs, the chromosome may translate the entire message of the gene incorrectly. To understand why, consider what would happen if one letter was left out of the message about the dog and the fox — for example, the *a* in *ran*. If the triplet pattern was kept, the resulting message would be nonsense: "The old dog rna ndt hef oxd idt oo." In a similar way, base deletions often result in proteins that do not function in the cell. This may cause severe problems in cell metabolism.

The addition of an extra nucleotide base causes much the same problem as a deletion. Such a mutation is called a **base insertion**. It distorts the translation of the entire message. Deletions and insertions are called **frame-shift mutations** because the reference point is changed for the entire message.

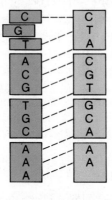

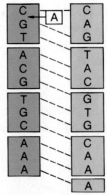

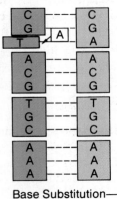

Base Deletion
(G deleted)

Base Insertion
(A inserted)

Base Substitution—
Point Mutation
(A substitutes for T)

Do You Know?
Many double-flowered plants are descendants of a single mutant plant that appeared spontaneously in someone's garden.

Figure 10.12 Which type of mutation changes the sequence least?

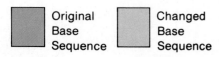

Original Base Sequence

Changed Base Sequence

Figure 10.13 A gene mutation causes albinism, a lack of pigmentation.

Gene mutations may occur in somatic or reproductive cells. If a mutation occurs in a somatic cell, the altered gene is passed to other cells in the organism through mitosis. Mutations in somatic cells cannot be passed on to offspring. Some cancers are caused by mutations in somatic cells.

If a mutation occurs in a reproductive cell, the altered gene may be passed to the gametes and to a zygote. Since all the cells of an organism descend from the zygote, every cell of the offspring will carry the mutation. A mutation in the reproductive cells may have far-reaching effects.

Each gene is usually represented twice in a diploid cell, once on each of the homologous chromosomes. If a mutation destroys or changes the function of one of the genes, the other gene may compensate for that loss. If, however, both genes of a pair are mutated, no such compensation is possible, and the organism loses that gene's function. If the mutated gene carried the code for making an enzyme, for example, the organism will lack that enzyme.

Although mutations may be harmful, even killing the organisms in which they occur, this is only one side of the coin. Most mutations have little effect, and may not even be noticeable. A few are beneficial. Mutations are very important to life on Earth. It is mutations that ultimately provide the diversity among living things.

Figure 10.14 Mutations provide diversity among living things.

Checkpoint

1. Who discovered that radiation increases the rate of mutation in cells?
2. What is the name of the condition in which a cell has one extra chromosome?
3. If one nucleotide is left out of a gene, what kind of mutation results?
4. What is a point mutation?

CHAPTER REVIEW

Summary

- The evidence collected by geneticists during the last century provides ample support for the chromosome theory of inheritance.

- *Drosophila melanogaster*, the common fruit fly, has been an important organism in genetics research. Drosophilas are small and inexpensive and have short reproductive cycles and many offspring.

- The sex of an organism is determined by its chromosomes. In most animals, males are heterozygous with the genotype XY, and females are homozygous with the genotype XX.

- Each gene has a particular location on a chromosome. Genes located on the same chromosome are said to be linked. Genes carried on the X chromosome are called sex-linked genes.

- Linkage groups can be broken by crossing over. In crossing over, homologous chromosomes exchange alleles.

- A sudden change in the genetic information is called mutation.

- Nondisjunction of the chromosomes results in cells with an abnormal number of chromosomes. In monosomy, each cell lacks one chromosome; in trisomy, each cell has an extra chromosome.

- Polyploid organisms have one or more extra sets of chromosomes.

- Gene mutations are the result of changes in the sequence of nucleotides on the DNA. Gene mutations include deletions, insertions, and substitutions (or point mutations).

- Mutation provides the ultimate source of variety among living things.

Vocabulary

autosome	monosomy
base deletion	mutagen
base insertion	mutation
chromosomal	nondisjunction
rearrangement	point mutation
chromosome mapping	polyploid
crossing over	sex chromosome
deletion	sex-linked genes
frame-shift mutation	sex-linked traits
incomplete linkage	translocation
linkage group	trisomy

Review

Choose the answer that best completes each of the following questions. Write the letters of your answers on a separate sheet of paper.

1. Which of the following is *not* a reason why Drosophilas are used in genetics experiments? (a) Males are easy to distinguish from females. (b) They have red eyes. (c) They are easy to raise. (d) They mature and reproduce rapidly.
2. In fruit flies and humans, females have (a) two Y chromosomes, (b) one X chromosome and one Y chromosome, (c) two X chromosomes, (d) only autosomes.
3. Genes located on the same chromosome are called (a) a linkage group, (b) alleles, (c) autosomes, (d) all of these.
4. *Drosophila* sperm cells can contain (a) only X chromosomes, (b) only Y chromosomes, (c) either X or Y chromosomes, (d) only autosomes.
5. In *Drosophila*, the allele for white eyes is (a) recessive, (b) sex-linked, (c) located on the X chromosome, (d) all of these.
6. A high frequency of crossing over between genes indicates that they are (a) far apart on the chromosome, (b) sex-linked, (c) dominant alleles, (d) mutations.

7. The condition in which a zygote has one chromosome less than the diploid number is known as (a) trisomy, (b) monosomy, (c) monoploidy, (d) polyploidy.
8. Frame-shift mutations are caused by (a) base insertions, (b) base deletions, (c) both *a* and *b*, (d) neither *a* nor *b*.
9. Which of these is a mutagen? (a) water (b) oxygen (c) ATP (d) radiation

Interpret and Apply

1. Why is *Drosophila melanogaster* better for genetics experiments than pea plants?
2. In what ways are sex chromosomes different from autosomes?
3. Compare the process of sex determination in fruit flies and butterflies. Identify which parent determines the sex of the offspring in each of these organisms.
4. An organism has 12 chromosomes. How many linkage groups should it have?
5. The illustration below shows a section of a chromosome. The letters *A*, *B*, and *C* indicate the location of genes.

  a. Between which two genes would crossing over occur most often?
  b. Which two of these genes are least likely to assort independently?
6. A white-eyed male *Drosophila* is crossed with a red-eyed female. The female is heterozygous for the trait of white eyes.
  a. Draw a Punnett square to show the genotypes possible in the offspring of this cross.
  b. What percentage of the offspring would you expect to be male?
  c. What percentage will probably be white-eyed females?

7. Explain the difference between crossing over and translocation.
8. Would a mutation in a skin cell on your hand affect your offspring? Explain.
9. How is a point mutation different from a frame-shift mutation?

Challenge

1. In examining a population of fruit flies, you notice that a certain trait appears much more often in males than in females. How can you account for this?
2. Three genes — *D*, *E*, and *F* — are located on the same chromosome. Crossovers occur between *D* and *E* 15% of the time. They occur between *E* and *F* 10% of the time. Between *D* and *F*, crossing over happens at a frequency of only 5%. Draw a chromosome showing the order in which these genes occur.
3. In general, a chromosomal mutation tends to affect the organism as a whole. A gene mutation, however, usually affects only one characteristic. Explain.
4. Part of a gene has the base sequence CAA CAT CTA GGG. Suppose the first adenine is deleted. Write the resulting triplet codons.

Projects

1. Use library resources such as books and magazines to find information about suspected mutagens. You may want to concentrate on the relationship between mutagens and cancer. Report your findings to the class.
2. Visit a college genetics department. Learn the kinds of research being done there. Observe the organisms that are being used for this research.

11 Human Heredity

Every person is unique.

Every human being is unique. Consider the great differences among your friends — in the color and texture of their hair, in the color and shape of their eyes, in the form of their noses and mouths. Notice the subtle shades of their skin. Compare the shapes of their hands and fingers, or even the sizes of their feet. Listen to the quality of their voices. You are probably already aware of most of these characteristics — you use them to recognize your friends. All of these characteristics are determined, at least to an extent, by genes.

A diploid human cell contains 46 chromosomes, each of which carries thousands of genes. The number of possible combinations of genes in any one person is enormous. Unless you have an identical twin, the probability of your sharing your set of genes with another human being is incredibly small.

Even twins who have identical genes interact with their environment so that each develops a distinct personality and differing skills. With the possibility of such variety, no wonder every person is unique.

Human Inheritance

Human genetics is governed by the same principles as the genetics of other organisms. Some human genes work in the same dominant-recessive fashion that Mendel described in his pea plants. A single pair of alleles determines a single trait. For example, the ability to roll the tongue into a U shape, as shown in Figure 11.1, is dominant over the inability to do so.

The study of humans has shown, though, that the inheritance of many traits cannot be explained by simple Mendelian genetics. Many traits cannot be classified as being simply dominant or recessive. All kinds of inheritance described in this chapter occur in other organisms, as well.

11–1   Traits Controlled by Multiple Alleles

In the examples considered so far, each gene could have only two different forms, or alleles. For example, fruit flies can carry alleles for either red or white eyes. It is possible, however, for a gene to occur in several different forms. A gene with more than two alleles is said to have **multiple alleles**.

Remember that each gene has a particular position on the chromosome. All of the alleles will occur in the same position. Thus in traits governed by multiple alleles, each individual can carry only two of the possible alleles, one on each homologous chromosome.

Human blood types are a good example of inheritance through multiple alleles. There is great variety in the chemistry of people's blood. As you may know, to carry out a blood transfusion, it is necessary to match the blood type of the donor with the blood type of the person receiving the blood. People belong to different blood groups because their genes code for different types of blood proteins.

The ABO group of blood proteins is the best known. Three different alleles determine blood type. These alleles are called A, B, and O. The A and B alleles are both dominant over the O allele. When the A and B alleles are present together, each shows its effect completely in the phenotype. Neither one masks, or even dilutes, the effects of the other. Thus there are four possible blood phenotypes: A, B, AB, and O. Figure 11.2 shows the combinations of alleles that produce the various blood types. (Notice that each person has only two alleles for these blood proteins, one on each homologous chromosome.)

CONCEPTS

- genes with multiple alleles
- traits controlled by more than one gene
- use of pedigrees to study human inheritance
- distinction between sex-linked, sex-limited, and sex-influenced traits
- influence of the environment on the phenotype

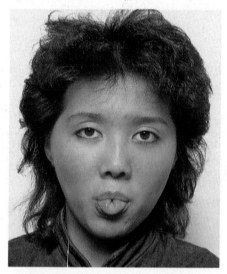

Figure 11.1 The allele for tongue rolling is dominant.

Genotype	Phenotype (Blood Type)
AA	A
BB	B
OO	O
AO	A
BO	B
AB	AB

Figure 11.2 Six blood genotypes produce four blood phenotypes.

Human Heredity   **161**

Female Gametes

+	O	O
A	AO	AO
B	BO	BO

Male Gametes

Figure 11.3 Would the result of this cross be any different if the father were type O and the mother were type AB?

The Punnett square in Figure 11.3 shows the possible offspring of a mother with type O blood and a father with type AB blood. What are the possible blood types of their children?

11–2 Traits Determined by Multiple Genes

Sometimes a characteristic is determined by more than one gene. Each of these genes has a different location on the chromosomes. Characteristics that are governed by more than one set of genes are said to have **polygenic inheritance**. Characteristics with polygenic inheritance tend to show a wide range of variation.

Human eye color is a good example of polygenic inheritance. Human eyes may range in color from light blue to almost black, as shown in Figure 11.4. Eye color is determined by the amount of the pigment **melanin** present in the eye. A small amount of melanin makes the eye color blue. More melanin makes the eyes look greenish, and still more makes them appear brown.

Figure 11.4 Which eyes have the most melanin?

Several different pairs of genes control the production of melanin in the eyes. Each pair of genes has a different location on the chromosomes. Some alleles of these genes produce large amounts of melanin, and some produce less. The more alleles for heavy melanin production a person has, the darker the eyes will be.

Skin color is also inherited through multiple pairs of genes. For this reason, there are many possible shades between the lightest and darkest skin colors.

As in eye color, the effects of different skin-color genes work together to produce the phenotype. Each gene directs the heavy or light production of melanin. If most of the alleles are for heavy melanin production, their effects will combine to produce dark skin. If most of the alleles are for light production of melanin, their effects will combine to produce light skin.

Many human characteristics, such as height and facial features, are the result of polygenic inheritance. Many of the genes involved in such traits also have multiple alleles. So it is not surprising that there is such variety in human appearance.

Figure 11.5 A person's skin color, although determined by multiple pairs of genes, is also affected by exposure to sunlight.

11–3 Sex-Linked Traits

As you learned in Chapter 10, females have two X chromosomes and males have one X chromosome and one Y chromosome. Sex-linked traits, those for which the genes are on the X chromosome, occur in humans. As you would expect from your knowledge of sex-linkage in *Drosophila*, the phenotype for a recessive sex-linked characteristic is more common in human males than females.

An example of sex-linkage in humans is red-green color vision. People who have the dominant allele for color vision can see all the colors in the visible spectrum. Some people have **red-green color blindness**, the inability to distinguish red from green. Red-green color blindness is a recessive condition. The gene for red-green color vision is on the X chromosome. For a woman to be color-blind, both alleles for red-green color vision must be recessive. In men, however, one recessive allele on the X chromosome will result in color blindness because the Y chromosome does not carry the gene.

There are five possible genotypes for red-green color vision:

1. $X^C X^C$ — a woman with normal vision
2. $X^C X^c$ — a woman with normal vision who carries the allele for color blindness
3. $X^c X^c$ — a color-blind woman
4. $X^C Y$ — a man with normal vision
5. $X^c Y$ — a color-blind man

A woman with the genotype $X^C X^c$ can pass a recessive gene on to her offspring, so she is said to be a carrier. A **carrier** is an individual who is heterozygous for a recessive trait. Although the trait does not appear in the phenotype, the heterozygous individual carries the allele.

As shown in Figure 11.6, a color-blind man can pass his recessive gene to his daughter. All of his daughters would carry that allele. Because the gene for red-green color vision is located on the X chromosome, a color-blind man cannot pass that allele on to his sons.

Gametes from Color-Blind Father

	X^c	Y
X^C	$X^C X^c$	$X^C Y$
X^C	$X^C X^c$	$X^C Y$

Gametes from Mother

Figure 11.6 Will any of the children from this cross be colorblind? Will any be carriers?

Figure 11.7 Queen Victoria (1819–1901) and Prince Albert (1819–1861)

Figure 11.8 The inheritance of hemophilia in the royal families of Europe. The current British royal family descends from Edward VII and Alexandra of Denmark. No genes for hemophilia are in that line.

Another sex-linked condition in humans is **hemophilia** [hee-muh-FIL-ee-uh], the inability of blood to clot. Hemophilia has consequences that are far more serious than those of red-green color blindness. In most hemophilia victims, the body is not able to manufacture a certain protein necessary for forming a blood clot. Hemophilia causes uncontrollable internal bleeding into the kidneys, brain, and other vital organs. Until recently, victims of hemophilia died at an early age.

Hemophilia is a recessive trait. The genes for the proteins necessary for blood clotting are located on the X chromosome. Therefore, a woman must have two recessive alleles to express hemophilia, whereas a man needs only one recessive gene to express hemophilia. A woman who is a carrier of hemophilia has a 50 percent chance of passing the recessive gene on to each child.

The most famous carrier of hemophilia was Queen Victoria. Queen Victoria unknowingly passed the gene on to one of her sons and two of her daughters. Fortunately the gene for hemophilia has not been passed on to any of the current European royalty.

To see how the gene for hemophilia was inherited in the royal families of Europe during the nineteenth century, refer to the pedigree in Figure 11.8. A **pedigree** is a diagram of

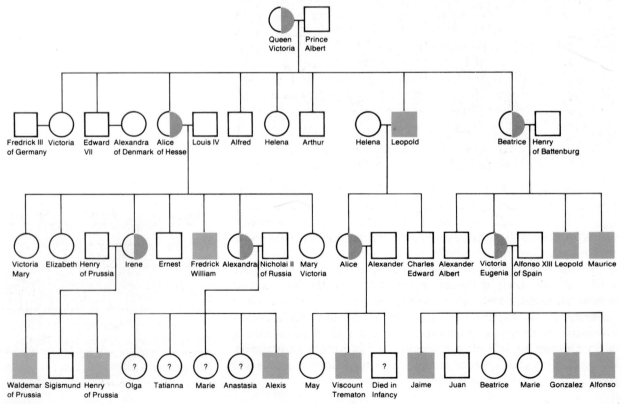

relationships in a family. In a pedigree, circles represent females, and squares represent males. The filled-in spaces represent people who are homozygous recessive for the hemophilia alleles. Half-filled spaces represent carriers, and empty spaces represent people who are homozygous dominant.

Not all sex-linked genes are located on the X chromosome. There is at least one condition of humans that is Y-linked. In India some men have long hair on their earlobes. The gene for hairy earlobes occurs on the Y chromosome. Hairy earlobes are passed on only from fathers to sons. This trait never appears in women.

11–4 Sex-Limited and Sex-Influenced Traits

Some genes are expressed only if they are carried by an individual of a particular sex. Such genes produce **sex-limited traits**. A sex-limited trait appears only in individuals of one sex. Genes for most sex-limited traits are located on the autosomes, although a few are located on the sex chromosomes.

Figure 11.9 Genes for a heavy beard can be carried by both males and females. However, the genes are expressed only in males.

The genes for a heavy beard are sex-limited. Their phenotype appears only in men. A woman may inherit genes for a heavy beard, but she will not exhibit this trait. She may, however, pass the genes for a heavy beard on to her son, who will express the trait.

Certain genes are dominant in one sex and recessive in the other. These genes produce **sex-influenced traits**. Baldness is a sex-influenced trait. It is dominant in men and recessive in women. As you can see in Figure 11.10, one allele causes baldness in a man. In a woman that same allele is recessive. A woman must inherit two alleles for baldness in order to be bald. For this reason, many more men than women are bald.

Genotype	Male	Female
BB	Bald	Very Thin Hair
Bb	Bald	Normal Hair
bb	Normal Hair	Normal Hair

Figure 11.10 Baldness is dominant in males and recessive in females.

11-5 Genes and the Environment

Genes provide the program for what an individual may become. But a particular gene will not produce the same features under all conditions. For example, an individual may inherit genes to be tall. Without enough food, however, this person will never grow to be tall. The development of the human phenotype is influenced by the environment. Factors such as diet, climate, and accidents all affect development.

One way to study the effects of the environment on humans is to compare identical twins. Identical twins are produced from a single zygote that splits soon after fertilization. For this reason, identical twins possess exactly the same genotype. This is why they look alike. Any differences between identical twins can be attributed to the effects of the environment. Among human twins, differences in intelligence, personality, and skills can be observed. Twins generally seem to become more dissimilar as they grow older.

Studies of identical twins indicate that genes provide the potential for development. But the phenotype is also the result of a wide range of other factors. All of these factors contribute to the great variety among humans.

Figure 11.11 Studies indicate that although twins may have identical genotypes, each twin develops as a unique individual.

Checkpoint

1. What are the three alleles that determine blood type?
2. What is the genotype of a color-blind man?
3. A diagram containing the genetic history of a family is called a _____.
4. Name a sex-influenced characteristic.

Human Genetic Disorders

Because human genetic disorders are of great concern to medicine, much has been learned about how they are inherited. Most genetic disorders are recessive, although a few are dominant. Often human genetic disorders are the result of a point mutation that changes a single kind of protein. Such a mutation often results in errors of metabolism. Other disorders are caused by chromosomal deletions or nondisjunction.

CONCEPTS

- human inheritance of dominant and recessive disorders
- effects of nondisjunction in human chromosomes

11–6 Sickle-Cell Disease

Sickle-cell disease is a condition that occurs among people whose ancestors lived in tropical regions. It is the result of a point mutation in the gene that codes for the protein **hemoglobin**.

Hemoglobin in the red blood cells carries oxygen from the lungs to all the other cells of the body. Normal red blood cells are shaped like disks. The sickle-cell allele produces hemoglobin molecules that cause red blood cells to be curved, or sickle-shaped. This shape is the result of one base substitution in the gene for hemoglobin. In the normal gene, this base triplet codes for the amino acid glutamic acid. In the sickle-cell gene, this triplet codes for valine. The presence of valine rather than glutamic acid in the hemoglobin protein changes the shape of the molecule, and also the blood cell. Sickled cells break easily.

Too many sickled cells may clog small blood vessels, causing damage and severe pain in the blocked areas. The body cannot produce new blood cells as fast as the defective ones break. Anemia, a shortage of red blood cells, results. People who are homozygous for the sickle-cell allele often die in childhood.

Although being homozygous for the sickle-cell allele is usually lethal, it may be an advantage to be heterozygous for the allele. In a person who is heterozygous for the allele, some of the hemoglobin is normal and some is abnormal. These people are said to have **sickle-cell trait**. Having sickle-cell trait lowers an individual's chances of developing malaria. In malaria-infested areas, such as tropical Africa, it is an advantage to carry the trait.

One out of ten children born to black families in North America is heterozygous for the sickle-cell gene. A blood test is available to identify people who have sickle-cell trait. If a husband and wife both have sickle-cell trait, they have a 25 percent chance of producing a child with sickle-cell disease.

Figure 11.12 *Top:* Normal red blood cells; *Bottom:* Red blood cells of a person with sickle-cell trait

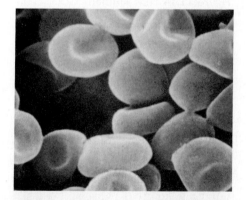

Male Gametes

	H	h
h	Hh	hh
h	Hh	hh

Female Gametes

Figure 11.13 In this example the male parent has Huntington's disease.

11–7 Huntington's Disease

Huntington's disease is an example of an autosomal disorder caused by a dominant gene. The gene produces a substance that interferes with the normal functioning of the brain. Loss of muscular coordination — and eventually mental deterioration and death — is the result of this condition.

Symptoms of the disease do not appear until the person is about 40. By this time, the person may have had children and unknowingly passed the gene on to the next generation. Because the gene is dominant, each of the offspring will have a 50 percent chance of inheriting the gene and having the disease, as shown in Figure 11.13. Fortunately Huntington's disease is quite rare, affecting only one in every 25,000 people.

11–8 Nondisjunction of Human Chromosomes

As you learned in Chapter 10, chromosomes occasionally fail to separate properly during meiosis. When this occurs, the resulting egg or sperm will carry an unusual number of chromosomes. The disorders caused by these abnormal chromosomes are often quite serious.

Geneticists can determine whether an individual has a normal set of chromosomes by making a karyotype. A **karyotype** [KAHR-ee-oh-teyep] is a photograph of the chromosomes of a cell, arranged in order from the largest to the smallest. To be prepared for a karyotype, a cell is chemically treated so that it will undergo mitosis. The cell is then stained and photographed through a microscope. The resulting photograph is cut apart, and the pictures of the paired chromatids are arranged on a sheet of paper. Figure 11.14 shows a normal human karyotype with 23 pairs of homologous chromosomes.

Figure 11.14 *Left:* Human chromosomes; *Right:* The 23 pairs arranged in order forming a karyotype

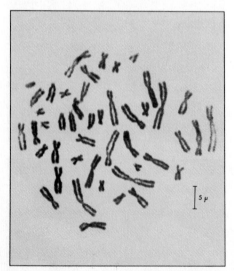

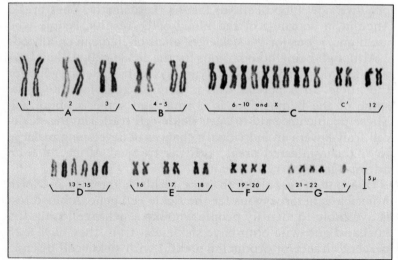

Carolina Biological Supply

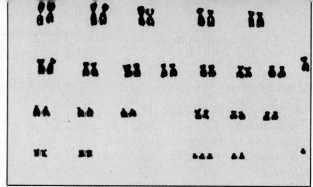

Study of human karyotypes has shown that nondisjunction may occur in any of the human chromosomes. Nondisjunction of a particular chromosome usually causes a particular group of symptoms called a **syndrome** [SIN-drohm]. A syndrome is a group of symptoms with a single underlying cause. Several of the syndromes caused by nondisjunction follow.

Down's syndrome is caused by nondisjunction of the 21st chromosome. Individuals with Down's syndrome have an extra copy of the 21st chromosome. Typically they have abnormal eyelids, noses with low bridges, large tongues, and hands that are short and broad. These persons are usually short in stature. Often they are mentally retarded. Many individuals with Down's syndrome have deformed hearts.

Klinefelter's syndrome is caused by nondisjunction of the sex chromosomes, resulting in a male with an extra X chromosome. These individuals have the genotype XXY instead of XY. Boys with Klinefelter's syndrome do not develop the physical traits typical of adult men. They may develop enlarged breasts and have high-pitched voices. Such men are sterile, and may have below normal intelligence.

Turner's syndrome is also caused by nondisjunction of the sex chromosomes. It results in a female who is missing one sex chromosome. Her genotype is XO instead of XX. These girls appear normal at birth, but throughout their lives they are shorter and stockier than other girls. Women with Turner's syndrome have large necks. Their sex organs and breasts do not develop to the adult stage, so they are sterile.

Figure 11.15 *Left:* A child with Down's syndrome in school; *Right:* A karyotype of a person with Down's syndrome.

Do You Know?

Many adults with Down's syndrome hold responsible, paid jobs in which they perform important work.

Checkpoint

1. Which protein is abnormal in people who have sickle-cell disease?
2. A photograph of a cell's chromosomes, arranged in order by size, is called a _____.
3. What is the name of the condition caused by trisomy of the 21st chromosome?
4. Write the genotype for Klinefelter's syndrome.

Treating Genetic Disorders

CONCEPTS

- treatment of errors in metabolism
- purpose of genetic counseling
- techniques of diagnosing birth defects
- methods of treating unborn children

Hereditary disorders have been recognized for centuries. But until the modern understanding of genetics was developed, there was little that could be done to help families who were at special risk of bearing a child with a disorder. Today the study of human genetics has shown how certain conditions can be treated. Biochemical tests and medical technology now provide help for individuals whose lives would once have been limited by their genes. Because of these advances in understanding, many children born with genetic problems can now lead normal lives.

11–9 Treating Errors in Metabolism

Phenylketonuria (PKU) is an autosomal recessive disease caused by an error in human metabolism. PKU occurs about once in every 10,000 North American births. Although PKU is a serious disorder, it can be successfully treated.

PKU results from the inability to break down phenylalanine, an amino acid that is common in many foods. Most people produce an enzyme that converts phenylalanine to another amino acid. The production of this enzyme is governed by a dominant allele. The recessive allele of this gene causes an error of metabolism because it does not produce the enzyme. Therefore, a child who is homozygous for the recessive allele will lack this important enzyme. Without the enzyme, the buildup of phenylalanine can poison the brain and cause severe retardation.

Figure 11.16 *Left:* Most babies are tested for PKU soon after birth. *Right:* The March of Dimes has provided millions of dollars for research into genetic defects. A March of Dimes research grantee developed the PKU test given to newborns.

Babies with PKU appear normal at birth. Damage to the brain begins when the baby begins to drink milk, which contains phenylalanine.

Most North American hospitals do a blood test for PKU within a week after birth. If a baby has PKU, a special diet lacking phenylalanine is started immediately. The baby must follow this diet for the first few years of life, while the brain is developing. The special diet restricts the amount of phenylalanine, thus preventing retardation. After the brain has developed, the child may follow a normal diet.

11–10   Genetic Counseling

In the last few years, the profession of genetic counseling has been established. Genetic counselors are trained geneticists who work in cooperation with doctors.

By studying the medical histories of couples and their families, genetic counselors help couples determine whether they have a higher-than-average risk of bearing a child with a genetic abnormality. Those at particular risk include parents who have already borne a child with a genetic defect, those who have genetic diseases in their families, and women who are over 35. Genetic counselors can recommend diagnostic tests for prospective parents and can help interpret the results of such tests. Based on this information, couples can make informed decisions about whether or not to have children.

Do You Know?

For best results, dietary treatment for PKU should begin before a baby is six weeks old. If it is begun after the child is three years old, it will have no effect.

NEWSBREAK

A decade ago, amniocentesis was one of the frontiers of modern medicine. But new techniques are being developed so rapidly that amniocentesis may soon be replaced. Its replacement could be a technique called chorionic villus biopsy.

In chorionic villus biopsy, cells are taken from the chorion, a membrane surrounding the fetus. Since the chorion develops from the same fertilized egg as the fetus, its cells have the same genes and chromosomes as the fetus.

Chorionic villus biopsy allows doctors to discover fetal disorders far earlier in pregnancy than does amniocentesis. Tissue can be taken from the chorion during the second month of pregnancy and analyzed within 24 hours. In contrast, the results of amniocentesis cannot be known until the woman is 5 months pregnant.

Medicine is rapidly finding ways of treating genetic problems in fetuses. These methods include surgery, drugs, blood transfusions, and modifications of the mother's diet. The sooner problems are discovered, the sooner they may be treated. Earlier treatment often means a healthier baby.

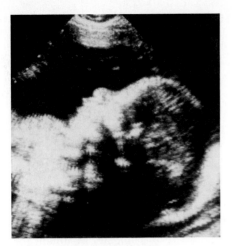

Figure 11.17 Head of a fetus as shown by an ultrasound

11–11 Diagnosing Birth Defects

During the past two decades medical science has developed techniques for examining an unborn child, or **fetus**. Using these techniques, doctors can determine whether a fetus has certain abnormal conditions.

A technique called **ultrasound** is used to locate the position of the fetus in the mother's womb. In ultrasound tests, high-frequency sound waves are transmitted through the mother's womb. The fetus reflects the waves. Special equipment translates these waves into a picture on a screen, as shown in Figure 11.17. In addition to the position and size of the fetus, an ultrasound picture may reveal structural abnormalities of the fetus.

The fetus develops in the mother's womb, a hollow, muscular organ. Inside the womb is a fluid-filled membrane called the **amnion**. The fetus floats in what is called the **amniotic fluid**.

Amniotic fluid contains cells that come from the fetus. To examine these cells, a doctor removes part of the fluid by carefully inserting a needle through the pregnant woman's abdomen. This is an almost painless procedure. The withdrawal of a small amount of amniotic fluid is called **amniocentesis**.

After the doctor has withdrawn the amniotic fluid, some of it is placed in a sterile container. The cells in the fluid grow and divide in the container for about a month. At that time, a karyotype of the cells is prepared. If the cells of the fetus contain any abnormal, missing, or extra chromosomes, they will appear in the karyotype. The karyotype also reveals the sex of the fetus.

The rest of the amniotic fluid withdrawn from the pregnant woman is used for biochemical tests called **assays**. Many genetic disorders are associated with the production of unusual kinds or amounts of proteins. Assays can detect some abnormal or missing proteins.

Figure 11.18 Amniocentesis

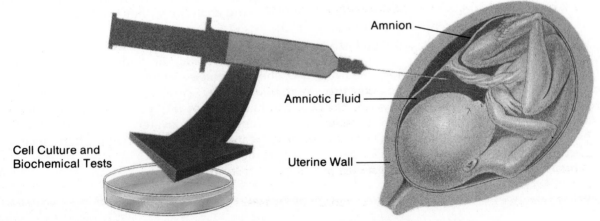

Amnion

Amniotic Fluid

Uterine Wall

Cell Culture and Biochemical Tests

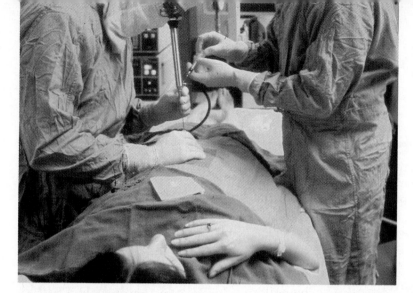

Figure 11.19 Doctors are now able to correct surgically some conditions before birth.

11–12   Treating the Unborn

Testing usually reveals that a fetus is normal and healthy. In about 2 to 3 percent of the cases, however, tests reveal that the fetus is abnormal. Recently doctors have been successful in treating certain conditions while the baby is still in the womb. Fetuses have even received blood transfusions before birth. A pregnant woman may sometimes be advised to take special drugs or to eat a restricted diet to help the fetus.

Unfortunately, only a small percentage of fetuses with disorders can benefit from existing techniques. Any treatment of the fetus is risky and demands great skill. Even usually harmless procedures, such as amniocentesis, can increase the chance of miscarriage.

Scientists are now working to develop tests and treatments for more disorders. Doctors hope too that current treatments will soon become more widely available. Then, although testing may reveal that a fetus has a genetic disorder, the baby may stand a better chance of being healthy when it is born.

Checkpoint

1. People who lack the enzyme that converts phenylalanine to another amino acid have a disease called _____.
2. The liquid in which a fetus floats is called _____.
3. The withdrawal of amniotic fluid for examination is called _____.
4. What technique is used to determine the position and size of the fetus?
5. What treatments have been given to abnormal fetuses?

CHAPTER REVIEW

Summary

- The principles of Mendelian genetics can be observed in humans. Much of human genetics, however, is governed by complex patterns of inheritance.
- Many human genes occur in more than two alleles. Such genes are said to have multiple alleles.
- Many human characteristics are governed by polygenic inheritance, in which several different genes combine to influence a single trait.
- A person's sex can influence the action of the genes. Recessive sex-linked characteristics are more common in men than in women. Sex-limited and sex-influenced genes act differently, depending upon sex.
- The environment may alter the expression of a gene in the phenotype.
- Human genetic disorders may be caused by genetic mutations or chromosomal nondisjunction.
- Some disorders are sex-linked, but most are caused by autosomal genes. Most disorders are recessive, requiring two alleles for a harmful effect. A few, such as Huntington's disease, are dominant.
- A person who is heterozygous for a recessive disorder is called a carrier.
- Nondisjunction of human chromosomes usually causes a set of symptoms called a syndrome. Some examples are Down's syndrome, Klinefelter's syndrome, and Turner's syndrome.
- Many genetic defects can be diagnosed before birth by the techniques of ultrasound, amniocentesis, and biochemical assays.
- In some instances, a fetus may be treated before birth.

Vocabulary

amniocentesis
amnion
amniotic fluid
assay
carrier
Down's syndrome
fetus
hemoglobin
hemophilia
Huntington's disease
karyotype
Klinefelter's
 syndrome
melanin
multiple alleles
multiple genes
nondisjunction
pedigree

phenylketonuria
 (PKU)
polygenic
 inheritance
red-green color
 blindness
sex-influenced trait
sex-limited trait
sex-linked
 characteristic
sickle-cell disease
sickle-cell trait
 syndrome
Turner's syndrome
ultrasound

Review

1. Explain what is meant by *multiple alleles*. Give an example of a trait that has multiple alleles.
2. What are two genotypes that produce blood type A?
3. How is skin color inherited in humans?
4. On which human chromosome is the gene for color vision located?
5. What is hemophilia? How is it inherited?
6. In a pedigree, what symbol represents a male and what symbol represents a female?
7. A _____ trait is one in which the gene will affect the phenotype of only one sex.
8. Identify two environmental factors that affect the development of the human phenotype.
9. Which type of mutation originally caused the sickle-cell allele to appear?

10. Name a genetic disease in humans that is inherited through a dominant gene.
11. How many chromosomes does a person with Down's syndrome have?
12. Why must babies who have PKU not eat foods containing phenylalanine?
13. What is amniocentesis? What can be learned from this procedure?
14. What is the purpose of genetic counseling?

Interpret and Apply

1. A man with blood type B (genotype BO) marries a woman with blood type A (genotype AA). What blood types could their children have? Draw a Punnett square to illustrate this.
2. Would you expect to find color blindness and hemophilia more frequently in men or in women? Explain.
3. Suppose two people who were heterozygous for PKU married and had a child. What is the probability that their child would have PKU?
4. A color-blind man marries a woman with normal red-green vision. They have two daughters and one son. The son is color-blind. One daughter is color-blind and the other has normal vision.
   a. Draw a pedigree showing the phenotypes of the parents and children. Shade in those symbols representing color-blind individuals. Symbols representing people with normal color vision should be left blank.
   b. What is the genotype of the father?
   c. What is the genotype of the mother?
5. Explain the difference between the way in which A-B-O blood groups are inherited and the way in which skin color is inherited.
6. What is the difference between a sex-limited and a sex-influenced trait? Give an example of each.
7. Expectant parents want to learn whether the fetus the woman is carrying has sickle-cell disease. Could a genetic counselor determine this by looking at the fetus's karyotype? Explain.

Challenge

1. Can an elderly person with a normal phenotype be a carrier of Huntington's disease? Explain.
2. Since any pair of chromatids can fail to separate during meiosis, there are theoretically 23 possible kinds of monosomy and trisomy. However, monosomies or trisomies for most of the 23 chromosome pairs are extremely rare — or unheard of — in live babies. Why do you think this is so?
3. A woman having blood type A marries a man having blood type B. They have five children. Two sons have blood type O. One daughter has blood type AB; another daughter, type A; and a third, type B.
   a. Draw a pedigree showing the blood types of the parents and offspring. Use letters in the pedigree symbols to represent the individuals' blood types.
   b. Figure out the genotypes of the parents and children.

Projects

1. Report to the class on a human genetic disease not mentioned in this chapter. Some possibilities are Tay-Sachs disease, Cooley's anemia, Edwards' syndrome, and cystic fibrosis. Include the following information in your report: how the disease is inherited; which group of people has the highest risk of producing a child with this disease; the characteristics of the genetic disorder; how often the disease occurs; whether it can be detected in the carrier; whether it can be detected in the fetus by amniocentesis or other tests; what treatment, if any, is available for the condition.
2. The son of Nicholas II and Alexandra, the last tsar and tsarina of Russia, had hemophilia. Alexandra was a granddaughter of Queen Victoria. Learn what effect this illness may have had on the course of Russian history.

12 Applications of Genetics

Squash for sale

A visit to an open-air market reveals a wonderful assortment of fruits and vegetables. Crates are filled with squashes of all kinds — crookneck and acorn, butternut and Hubbard, zucchini and pattypan. Watermelons and heads of lettuce are piled high next to fat tomatoes and dusty potatoes, not to mention cucumbers and cauliflowers and cabbages and corn.

On the ground are baskets of flowers — spectacular lilies and spicy carnations, and roses from white to deepest red. Cartons from a dairy are filled with beautifully matched eggs, laid by remarkable hens that are able to produce hundreds of eggs a year.

All of the foods on display are far larger and more abundant than any foods that grow wild. How did these marvels of agriculture come to be? All are the result of careful breeding over a period of many years. Breeding plants and animals to produce more and better food is the oldest form of applied genetics.

Controlled Breeding

Modern agriculture is the result of generations of controlled breeding of plants and animals. In **controlled breeding**, humans allow only those plants or animals with particular traits to reproduce. The purpose of controlled breeding is to produce offspring with traits that are desirable to humans. Often these traits make a plant or animal unfit to live in the wild.

People have practiced controlled breeding since ancient times. Drawings on stone from the ancient kingdom of Chaldea in the Middle East show that the Chaldeans bred horses over 6,000 years ago. Cattle, sheep, goats, and pigs were also domesticated in ancient times. Native Americans bred a type of wild grass to produce the ancestor of modern corn.

All of these successes in breeding occurred long before anyone had ever heard of genes or chromosomes. Many techniques of plant and animal breeding were developed thousands of years before Gregor Mendel was born. Today, however, plant and animal breeders are able to use their understanding of genetics to plan scientific breeding programs.

CONCEPTS

- use of inbreeding and selection to establish new breeds
- effects of inbreeding
- advantages and disadvantages of hybridization

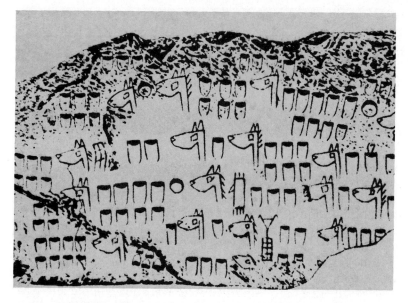

Figure 12.1 These ancient Chaldean drawings show that horse breeding was practiced over 6,000 years ago.

12–1 Selection

The first step in breeding new varieties of plants or animals is to select only those organisms that have a desired trait. In the process of **selection**, only a few organisms with desirable characteristics are allowed to reproduce. The offspring of these organisms stand a good chance of inheriting the desired characteristics.

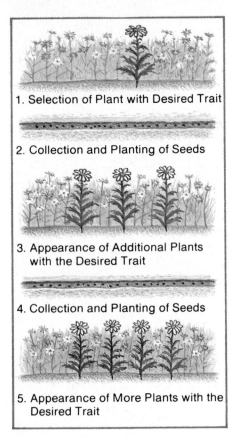

1. Selection of Plant with Desired Trait

2. Collection and Planting of Seeds

3. Appearance of Additional Plants with the Desired Trait

4. Collection and Planting of Seeds

5. Appearance of More Plants with the Desired Trait

Figure 12.2 Mass selection

Figure 12.3 Most live lobsters are dull brownish green. This blue lobster and others like it have been specially bred. Scientists study the behavior of these naturally-marked individuals in order to understand their species better.

Do You Know?
Luther Burbank developed many unusual fruits such as the white blackberry and the plumcot, a fruit derived from a Japanese plum and an apricot.

In early times, farmers did not have many plants or animals to choose from, so selection was carried out on a small scale. More recently, agriculture has been practiced with huge fields of crops and with enormous numbers of animals. Selection from a large number of organisms is called **mass selection**.

Luther Burbank was an American horticulturist who was known for his success in plant breeding during the last century. Burbank frequently used the technique of mass selection. Burbank planted huge fields of different flowers and vegetables. From these he would select plants that differed in certain ways. Some of his plants had unusually colored flowers, or slightly different fruit. Burbank collected and planted the seeds from these unusual plants. Often the offspring had the same characteristics found in the parent plants. Using mass selection, Burbank developed over 100 new varieties of fruits. Some of the potatoes, plums, and apples that you eat today were developed by Burbank.

Although mass selection can be used to develop a new variety of a plant or animal, it does not produce new characteristics. Selection can work only within the limits of the existing genotypes.

12–2 Inbreeding

Selection can be used to establish a new breed of plant or animal. New generations of this breed are produced by a controlled breeding method called **inbreeding**. Inbreeding is the crossing of two closely related individuals. In animals, inbreeding may be done with brothers and sisters. Since closely related individuals usually have a high percentage of genes in common, inbreeding makes it likely that the desired genes will be passed on to offspring. After many generations of inbreeding, most of the offspring will be homozygous for

Greyhound

Siberian Husky

Dachshund

Boxer

Figure 12.4 Each of these breeds was bred for a specific purpose. Can you guess what purpose?

the desired trait. When this occurs, breeders are said to have established pure lines. (Recall that Mendel worked with pure lines of pea plants in his experiments.)

Because pure lines are homozygous for the selected traits, all of the offspring will have those traits. Continued selection will not produce any new variation within a breed. Pure lines are said to "breed true." Selection and inbreeding have produced many distinct breeds. The breeds of dogs shown in Figure 12.4 are a good example. All dogs probably arose from wild wolves.

After many generations of inbreeding, a condition called **inbreeding depression** may result. Inbreeding depression is characterized by a decrease in the health or fertility of each succeeding generation. The cause of inbreeding depression is not fully known. Probably it is caused by harmful recessive alleles that were masked by dominant alleles in the original members of a breed. As the offspring in a pure line continue to be inbred, it becomes more and more likely that recombination will result in individuals that are homozygous for harmful alleles. Then the harmful traits will appear in the offspring.

The undesirable effects of inbreeding may be reduced by periodic **outcrossing**, or crossing an inbred organism with a less closely related individual. Dog breeders often use the technique of outcrossing to prevent inbreeding depression. A breeder may introduce new genes into a line by crossing a poodle of known ancestry with another, less closely related poodle.

Figure 12.5 Hybrid lilies

12–3 Hybridization

Selection and inbreeding preserve certain characteristics within a breed. But often organisms selected for one desirable trait will also carry other, less desirable traits. For example, corn plants that are selected for being hardy may not produce large kernels. Other breeds of corn may produce large kernels but not be hardy. If these two breeds were crossed, some of the offspring might carry both desirable traits.

When two breeds are crossed, the offspring are called hybrids. In **hybridization**, a breeder tries to combine the best qualities of different breeds.

Often the hybrids produced by crossing two inbred lines are larger and stronger than their parents. The increased growth of the F_1 hybrids is called **hybrid vigor**. The cause of hybrid vigor is not fully understood. It may be the result of combining favorable dominant alleles from one parent with unfavorable recessive alleles from another parent. Different pure lines probably do not carry the same unfavorable alleles.

Hybrids are not usually used as parents. One reason is that hybrids are usually heterozygous for many traits. As you know, heterozygous parents can produce offspring with many different phenotypes and genotypes. The offspring of hybrids tend to be extremely variable.

Occasionally breeders will cross two different pure lines to produce a new breed. Developing a new breed can be a painstaking, time-consuming process. Desirable traits are often linked on chromosomes with undesirable traits. With continued breeding, these traits may eventually recombine through crossing over, until some of the offspring have all the desirable characteristics of both pure lines. It may take generations to produce a new breed.

Figure 12.6 At least five different breeds contributed genes to the Rhode Island Red.

Figure 12.7 As new, more desirable breeds have been developed, many old breeds have been ignored and, as a result, have become endangered. These unusual-looking cattle are examples of such endangered breeds.

Often breeds of cattle and fowl result from more than one hybridization. Sometimes breeders make crosses from several different breeds to produce a line with all the desired traits. The Rhode Island Red hen contains genes from at least five different breeds: Red Malay, Shanghai, Chittagong, Brahma, and Leghorn.

The term *hybrid* may also refer to a cross between two totally different types, or species, of organisms. The best-known animal hybrid of this sort is the mule. A mule is a cross between a female horse and a male donkey. The horse and the donkey are closely related species. A mule combines the large size and strength of a horse with the hardiness of a donkey. Unfortunately, mules cannot reproduce.

Hybrids between different species are usually sterile, or unable to reproduce. Hybrid sterility is often caused by different numbers of chromosomes in the two parent species. The hybrid offspring, therefore, have unmatched sets of chromosomes. During meiosis, these unmatched chromosomes cannot form homologous pairs.

Do You Know?
The offspring of a male horse and a female donkey is called a hinny.

Checkpoint

1. What two techniques are used to preserve desirable traits in a breed?
2. What condition may result from generations of inbreeding?
3. Hybrid offspring that are larger or healthier than their parents have _____.
4. Hybrids between two species are usually _____.

- artificial production of polyploidy
- cloning as a form of asexual reproduction
- recombinant DNA and genetic engineering

Figure 12.8 *Left:* A diploid snapdragon; *Right:* A tetraploid snapdragon.

Do You Know?

More than one third of all species of domesticated plants are polyploid.

Artificial Methods of Genetic Control

In the past decade, genetics research has given breeders new tools with which to manipulate genes. It is now possible to cause certain desired changes in existing genes and chromosomes.

12–4 Polyploidy

As you learned in Chapter 10, polyploidy is a condition in which the cells of an organism contain more than two complete sets of chromosomes. Early in this century, biologists discovered a way to produce polyploid plants artificially. If the chemical **colchicine** [KOL-chuh-seen] is applied to growing buds, it will prevent spindle formation during mitosis. Without a spindle, the chromatids cannot separate. As a result, cells treated with colchicine have double the normal number of chromosomes. A cell with four sets of chromosomes (4n) rather than two sets (2n) is called a **tetraploid** cell. Treatment with colchicine may also produce cells with more than four sets of chromosomes.

Polyploid plants often produce larger fruits and flowers than normal diploid forms. Polyploid plants may also be hardier than diploid plants, or they may mature earlier in the growing season.

Many of the traits of polyploid plants are desirable to gardeners and farmers. Today gardening catalogs offer polyploid varieties of many plants, including lilies, blueberries, and snapdragons.

12–5 Cloning

Recently biologists have developed laboratory techniques for removing a single cell from an organism and stimulating it to develop into a complete, new organism. Offspring produced in this manner are called clones. A **clone** carries exactly the same genes as the somatic cells of its parent. Thus **cloning** is a form of asexual reproduction.

Geneticists have been able to clone carrots, mice, and frogs in the laboratory. Although it is not yet practical to do so, cloning may some day be useful for producing new breeds of livestock. Cloning may also allow breeders to produce organisms, such as hybrids, that are unable to reproduce sexually.

12–6 Recombinant DNA

Some of the most exciting genetic research today is being done with recombinant DNA. **Recombinant DNA** is produced when genes from one organism are transferred to another organism. Usually genes are transferred into the cells of bacteria or other quickly reproducing organisms.

Recombinant DNA has been made possible by the discovery of special enzymes called **restriction enzymes**. Each restriction enzyme can cut a chain of DNA between a particular sequence of nucleotides. For example, one restriction enzyme can cut a nucleotide sequence between two molecules of cytosine. This restriction enzyme would divide the nucleotide sequence ATGCCA into the pieces ATGC and CA. A scientist using a restriction enzyme to cut a piece of DNA knows exactly which nucleotides will be present after the cut is made. By using restriction enzymes, it is possible to remove a particular gene from a chromosome. This gene can then be transferred to the DNA of a bacterium.

Some of the DNA in bacteria is located in rings called **plasmids**. A plasmid can be cut open with a restriction enzyme. Then the gene from another organism can be inserted, and the plasmid can be reconnected. As shown in Figure 12.9, the reconnected plasmid ring carries the recombined gene.

When the plasmid replicates, it also copies the recombinant DNA. Thus all the offspring of the bacteria will also carry the recombinant DNA. The process of making extra copies of recombinant DNA is a form of cloning.

Figure 12.9 The altered plasmid contains recombinant DNA.

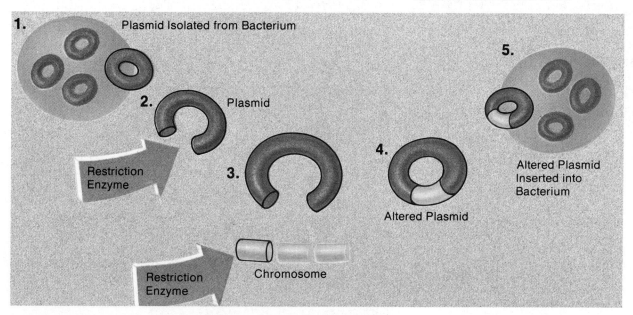

1. Plasmid Isolated from Bacterium
2. Plasmid
   Restriction Enzyme
3.
   Restriction Enzyme
   Chromosome
4. Altered Plasmid
5. Altered Plasmid Inserted into Bacterium

Bacteria containing recombinant DNA can be grown in huge vats. Because bacteria reproduce quickly, they produce many copies of themselves in a short time. If the recombinant DNA carries the code for a particular protein, these vats of bacteria will produce large amounts of that protein. This protein can then be harvested from the bacteria.

The use of recombinant DNA and cloning is popularly known as **genetic engineering**. Through genetic engineering, scientists have been able to produce large quantities of proteins that are useful in medicine. One such protein is used to protect cattle against foot-and-mouth disease. Foot-and-mouth disease kills large numbers of cattle in many countries.

Several drug companies have been working to clone the human gene for the production of insulin. **Insulin** [IN-sul-in] is a chemical that regulates the amount of sugar in the bloodstream. People who lack insulin have a disease called diabetes. A severe diabetic needs insulin to live. Currently insulin is expensive, and much of the insulin that is available causes unpleasant side effects. The production of human insulin through recombinant DNA and cloning could help solve these problems.

Scientists are also cloning the gene for interferon. **Interferon** is a blood protein that may be effective in protecting against disease-causing viruses. Interferon may be useful in fighting cancer.

If plants could be given genes for drought resistance or for higher yield, the worldwide production of food could be increased. Someday it may also be possible to use recombinant DNA to transfer to plants genes for the production of particular proteins.

Although genetic engineering offers great promise for medicine and agriculture, it is important for geneticists to take great care in their research. There is a slight danger that

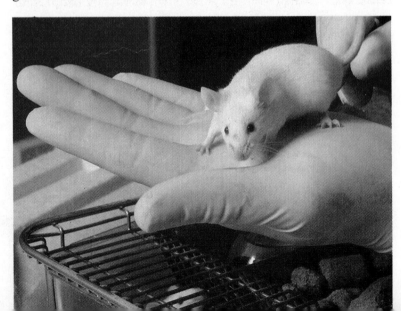

Figure 12.10 Genetic engineers have succeeded in cloning mammals. Researchers have extracted nuclei from mouse embryo cells and inserted the nuclei in fertilized mouse eggs from which all genetic material had been removed. The eggs developed normally.

scientists may accidentally create new forms of life that could be harmful to the environment or to people. For this reason, scientists should be careful in their research procedures. It is also important that citizens keep well informed about developments in this exciting new area.

12–7   Duplicating Nature

When news of the techniques of recombinant DNA and cloning first reached the public, many people were upset at what they considered tampering with nature. But all the techniques mentioned in this chapter occur naturally as well.

Polyploidy occurs naturally, although no one knows exactly why. Bread wheats, cotton, and sugarcane are a few of the many varieties of plants that have been changed through naturally occurring polyploidy.

Cloning is really only a form of asexual reproduction. Any time offspring have exactly the same genes as one parent, cloning has occurred. This happens regularly in yeasts. It also occurs in potatoes, grasses, strawberries, and any other plants that reproduce vegetatively.

Even recombinant DNA, as technological as it may seem, is not the original invention of humans. A certain type of bacteria called *Agrobacterium tumefaciens* invades many types of plants, including trees, tobacco, and many vegetables. It causes crown gall, a type of tumor. Although the tumor is part of the plant, it is not composed of true plant tissue. The bacterium inserts some of its DNA into that of the plant cells, so a recombinant type results.

From the dawn of agriculture about 10,000 years ago to the present, breeders and other scientists have made vast leaps in improving nature's yield. The potential for using modern genetic techniques to alleviate suffering due to genetic diseases and hunger is very great. For this reason, the present time is called the golden age of biology.

Checkpoint

1. What chemical do geneticists use to cause polyploidy artificially?
2. With which chemical do scientists cut chains of nucleotides to make recombinant DNA?
3. What are the rings of DNA in bacterial cells called?
4. DNA from one organism that is combined with DNA of another organism is called _____.
5. What two processes are involved in genetic engineering?

CHAPTER REVIEW

Summary

- For thousands of years, humans have used controlled breeding to produce plants and animals that are desirable for agriculture.
- Selection is the process by which only a few organisms with desirable characteristics are allowed to reproduce. Mass selection involves large numbers of organisms.
- Pure lines are established by inbreeding. Offspring of many generations of inbreeding may suffer from inbreeding depression.
- The offspring of a cross between two pure lines are called hybrids. Hybrids that are stronger or healthier than either parent have hybrid vigor.
- Hybrids between different species are usually sterile.
- Modern genetics has provided many techniques for manipulating genes and chromosomes.
- The chemical colchicine prevents spindle formation in mitosis, thus causing the formation of polyploid cells.
- The genes of a clone are identical to those of the parent organism.
- Restriction enzymes allow geneticists to splice genes from one organism onto the DNA of another organism. Such procedures result in recombinant DNA.
- Most of the techniques used by geneticists today also occur in some form in nature.

Vocabulary

clone
cloning
colchicine
controlled breeding
genetic engineering
hybridization
hybrid vigor
inbreeding
inbreeding
  depression

insulin
interferon
mass selection
outcrossing
plasmid
recombinant DNA
restriction enzyme
selection
tetraploid

Review

1. What is the purpose of controlled breeding?
2. What form of controlled breeding was practiced by Luther Burbank?
3. What is inbreeding?
4. What sometimes results from several generations of inbreeding? How can this result be avoided or reduced?
5. How is hybridization different from inbreeding?
6. Why are many hybrids sterile?
7. How many sets of chromosomes are in a tetraploid cell?
8. What chemical is used to produce polyploid plants artificially?
9. What is cloning?
10. What does a restriction enzyme do?
11. What name is given to the rings of DNA found in bacteria?
12. How might diabetics benefit from genetic engineering?

Interpret and Apply

1. You have two snapdragon plants. One is much larger than the other. You know that one of the plants is tetraploid. Which one?
2. What could a blueberry grower do to get a bigger and better crop of berries?

3. You are working in your garden and discover a beautiful yellow daisy among all the white ones. You would like to have more yellow daisies in the future. What method of controlled breeding would you employ to obtain more yellow daisies? How would you employ this method?

4. What reproductive or genetic technique is involved in each of the following?
   a. A cat has six kittens. Two of the kittens, a male and a female, are an unusually beautiful color. When the kittens mature, they are mated to each other in hopes of producing more cats of the same color.
   b. Bacteria are used to produce a human growth hormone.
   c. A horticulturist uses colchicine to produce large, juicy blackberries.
   d. A breeder of toy poodles crosses one of his females with an unrelated male in an effort to avoid inbreeding depression.
   e. You discover a four-leaf clover in a field of clover. You collect and plant seeds from that clover in hopes of one day having a whole field of four-leaf clover.
   f. A strawberry plant produces new plants by sending out stems that touch the ground and grow roots.

5. Hybrids are often large and strong. They exhibit hybrid vigor. You might think that crossing two hybrids would produce new individuals with even greater vigor and even more desirable traits. Why is this usually not the case?

Challenge

1. What is an advantage of hybridization over mass selection?
2. Why was the discovery of restriction enzymes necessary before scientists could produce recombinant DNA?

3. Why do you think scientists have focused much of their recombinant DNA research on bacterial cells rather than on other types of cells, such as mammalian cells?
4. What form of controlled breeding do you think was used to produce the dog known as the cockapoo?

Projects

1. Visit a nursery and observe the many varieties of roses, azaleas, tomatoes, and other plants that have been carefully bred over the years for particular, desirable traits. Research the history and value of these plants. Try to find out what the plants from which these were derived were like, and how the newer varieties are improvements over the older ones.
2. Research the history of several breeds of dogs. Identify which breeds are the working breeds. Try to determine which characteristics of each particular breed were selected in order to make the dog successful at its particular job. For example, a Labrador retriever, which was bred to retrieve ducks during hunting, must be a good swimmer. The skin between its paw pads forms webs.
3. Research the life and work of Luther Burbank. Make a list of the many varieties of plants that he developed.
4. Both inbreeding and outcrossing are practiced in the breeding of thoroughbred racehorses. Find out what horses won some of this year's big races (for example, the Kentucky Derby, the Preakness, the Belmont Stakes). What stables bred those horses? What specific breeding techniques were used? Are any of the horses related to other successful thoroughbreds?
5. Seedless grapes and oranges are plentiful. But there are no seeds to grow the orange trees or grapevines that produce them. How, then, are the groves of seedless orange trees and the fields of seedless grapevines produced? What reproductive technique is involved?

13 Population Genetics

Florida tree snails

In the Everglades of southern Florida, colorful tree snails similar to those shown above glide over the vegetation. Some of these snails have shells that are banded with yellow and brown. Other snails have shells mottled with brown and gold. The shells of yet other snails are almost entirely a beautiful creamy white.

If you were a shell collector, these snails would be confusing. Despite their great variety, all of them belong to the same species, *Liguus fascinatus*. Snails with any of these shell patterns can mate and produce fertile eggs. Within this species over 50 shell patterns have been found!

Although tree snails are an extreme example, almost all populations of organisms show variation among the members. Even organisms that appear identical to humans usually have differences in their genetic makeup. Biologists are very interested in the variations that occur in natural populations. These variations provide clues to how organisms become adapted to their environment.

Variation in Populations

No one would ever confuse a turtle with a turkey or a turnip. Organisms seem to be clearly separated into a number of distinct groups. From the time of Aristotle through most of the nineteenth century, biologists believed that living things occurred in a number of distinct, unchanging types, or species. People believed that any organism could be identified by comparing its physical appearance with other members of its species.

As scientists studied various kinds of plants and animals, though, they discovered that there is enormous variation among natural populations. Members of the same species may vary in size, color, or shape. Much of the variation in a population is the result of the genes of the individual organisms. But some variation within populations is caused by the environment. For example, a pine tree that grows near the top of a mountain will not be as tall as one that grows in a lush valley.

CONCEPTS

- definition of species
- distinction between clines and subspecies
- gene frequency and gene pools
- Hardy-Weinberg principle

13–1 Definition of Species

Today biologists realize that it is not always possible to recognize a species by its physical appearance alone. Members of the same species may be quite different. Biologists now define a **species** as a group of organisms that can mate among themselves and produce fertile offspring.

The snow goose and the blue goose were once believed to belong to separate species. As you can see in Figure 13.1, these birds look quite different. Careful observation of these birds in the wild, however, revealed that they represent merely two colors of the same species. Both white and blue forms may hatch from a single nest of eggs. Today the blue goose is classified as a member of the snow-goose species. Snow geese are often found with Canada geese. But Canada geese are a separate species. Snow geese and Canada geese cannot mate and produce fertile offspring.

Figure 13.1 *Left:* Blue geese; *Right:* Snow goose

When classifying species, many biologists work with collections of organisms that are no longer living. Botanists, for example, often study dried specimens of plants. When working with nonliving specimens, it is not always possible to determine whether or not the organisms can breed and produce fertile offspring. In such work, biologists must often depend upon physical characteristics to classify organisms. Such classifications must take into acount the great variation that occurs within some species.

The amount of variety in a species can be judged by comparing the characteristics present in a population of that species. A **population** is a community of interbreeding organisms that live in a particular location. All the catfish that live in a lake would be a population of catfish.

13–2 Clines and Subspecies

Variation in a species often follows a geographic pattern. Figure 13.2 shows how the height of individuals from a single species of a wild flower called yarrow varies gradually with the location of the plant. Plants growing at high altitudes are shorter than plants growing at low altitudes. When yarrow plants collected from different altitudes are grown under identical conditions in a greenhouse, the differences in height still persist. This experiment demonstrates that the height differences are hereditary. Gradual trends in the genotype of a population that correspond to differences in the environment are called **clines**.

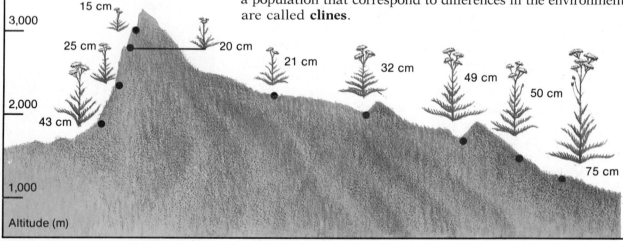

Figure 13.2 *Top:* Yarrow: *Bottom:* A cline in the height of yarrow plants growing at different altitudes.

Biologists have observed clines in many different species of plants and animals. Whitetail deer are found over most of North America. Whitetail deer that are found in the North are far larger than those in the South. Northern males may have masses up to 880 kilograms. On the Florida Keys a tiny form of this deer grows to only 110 kilograms.

Figure 13.3 *Left:* The western red-shafted flicker; *Right:* The eastern yellow-shafted flicker.

Variations in populations are not always gradual. Common flickers are woodpeckers that live in woodlots, forests, and towns. In the East, these birds have golden yellow feathers under the wings and tail, so they are called yellow-shafted flickers. In the West, these birds have red underwings, so they are called red-shafted flickers. Where these populations overlap in the central United States, they interbreed and produce fertile hybrid offspring. (Hybrids may have orange underwings.) Thus the two varieties belong to the same species. Distinct populations of a species are called **subspecies**, or **races**. Subspecies do not show the gradual transitions observed in clines. Yellow-shafted and red-shafted flickers are subspecies of the common flicker.

13–3   The Gene Pool

Much of the variation within a species is the result of heredity. Biologists often want to know how genetic variations are inherited within an entire population. **Population genetics** is the study of how Mendel's laws and other genetic principles apply to entire populations.

Population genetics often considers the frequency of a particular allele within a population. The frequency of an allele may be determined by sampling a population. In **population sampling**, data from part of the population are assumed to be true for the entire population. Thus, if a biologist studies 100 rabbits in an area and finds that half have dark hair and half have light hair, it can be assumed that in the entire population 50 percent have dark hair and 50 percent have light hair.

Do You Know?

Use of electronic sound-recording equipment has helped scientists to discriminate among species of birds and amphibians.

Figure 13.4 A gene pool. Brown marbles represent the dominant allele (B). White marbles represent the recessive allele (b).

The entire genetic content of a population is called the **gene pool**. The gene pool contains all the genes for all the characteristics of a population.

Figure 13.4 illustrates a way of imagining the gene pool for coat color in a population of rabbits. The dominant allele, B, produces brown fur. The recessive allele, b, produces white fur. Each allele in the rabbits can be represented by a marble in the barrel. A brown marble represents the allele for brown fur, and a white marble represents the allele for white fur. All the marbles in the barrel represent the gene pool for coat color. If all the rabbits in the original population were homozygous for the brown allele, then all the marbles in the barrel would be brown. If all the rabbits were white, then all the marbles would be white.

Figure 13.5 shows a mixture of brown and white marbles. The fraction of marbles that represents a particular allele is called the **gene frequency**. Gene frequency may be expressed as a decimal or as a percent. The sum of all the allele frequencies for a gene within a population is equal to 1.0, or 100 percent. In the illustration, 40 percent of the marbles are white, and 60 percent of the marbles are brown. These frequencies could also be expressed as 0.40 and 0.60.

13–4   The Hardy-Weinberg Principle

In 1908, Godfrey Hardy, a British mathematician, and Wilhelm Weinberg, a German physician, demonstrated how the frequency of alleles in the gene pool could be described by mathematical formulas. Using these formulas, it can be shown that under certain conditions the frequency of genes remains constant from generation to generation. The **Hardy-Weinberg principle** states that the frequency of dominant and recessive alleles remains the same from generation to generation.

This principle is very useful in population genetics. To show how this principle can be applied to a population, consider the rabbits shown in Figure 13.4. When these rabbits mate and produce offspring, each parent contributes one allele for coat color to each gamete. You can model the production of gametes in the rabbit population by reaching into the barrel and randomly withdrawing one marble at a time. Offspring are produced when two gametes fuse to form a zygote, so a pair of marbles represents the zygote formed when two gametes fuse.

The chance of choosing a particular color marble depends on the frequency of different marbles in the gene pool. Because 60 percent of the marbles are brown, you would choose a brown marble about 60 percent of the time and a white marble 40 percent of the time. In other words, on any draw the probability that you will select a particular color marble is equal to its frequency in the gene pool.

Each genotype is composed of two alleles. The probability of drawing a particular genotype is the product of the probabilities of the two alleles. Thus the chance of drawing the genotype BB is 60 percent times 60 percent, or 36 percent ($0.60 \times 0.60 = 0.36$).

The probabilities of drawing each genotype are shown in the table in Figure 13.6. This table, which looks like a Punnett square, is called a **cross-multiplication table**. The frequency of each allele for the males is listed across the top. Frequency of alleles for the females is listed on the left side. Frequencies are given as decimals rather than as percentages. As the cross-multiplication table shows, rabbits with the genotype BB make up 36 percent of the population and rabbits with the genotype bb make up 16 percent of the population. Two squares in the cross-multiplication table show the genotype Bb, so the percentage of heterozygous rabbits in the population would be the sum of these values, or 48 percent. Since the allele for brown coat is dominant over the allele for white coat, 84 percent of the rabbits will be brown, and 16 percent will be white.

Figure 13.5 The gene frequency for brown is 0.60. You have a 60-percent chance of drawing out a brown marble.

	Male Alleles	
	B 0.60	**b** 0.40
Female Alleles **B** 0.60	BB 0.36	Bb 0.24
b 0.40	Bb 0.24	bb 0.16

Figure 13.6 According to this cross-multiplication table, what is the total probability of producing a Bb offspring?

Figure 13.7 According to the Hardy-Weinberg principle, gene frequencies remain the same from generation to generation.

How common will the genotype bb be in the next generation? According to the Hardy-Weinberg principle, the gene frequencies will not change in the next generation. As long as any color rabbit is allowed to mate with any other color rabbit, the Hardy-Weinberg principle predicts that the probability of drawing each genotype will remain constant. After 15 or even 40 generations, there will still be 84 percent brown rabbits and 16 percent white rabbits.

In other words, a rare recessive gene will not be lost in a population over time. Rare genes will continue to appear in the phenotype of homozygous individuals. The frequency of homozygous individuals is the product of the frequencies of each allele. Since the alleles are the same, the frequencies will also be the same. Therefore, the frequency of a homozygous individual is the square of the gene frequency ($0.40^2 = 0.16$).

Population geneticists often calculate gene frequencies in a population by using the Hardy-Weinberg principle. For example, babies with the recessive disease PKU are born about once in every 10,000 births in the United States. Therefore, the frequency of the homozygous phenotype is about 0.01 percent (0.0001). To calculate the frequency of the gene causing PKU, a geneticist would take the square root of 0.01 percent ($\sqrt{0.0001} = 0.01$). According to these calculations, the gene for PKU has a gene frequency of 1 percent.

Checkpoint

1. Define the term *species*.
2. What term describes a population that shows a gradual trend in phenotype from one location to another?
3. What is the total genetic content of a population called?
4. What principle describes the tendency of gene frequencies to remain constant from one generation to the next?

Changes in Populations

The Hardy-Weinberg principle states that under certain conditions, gene frequencies will remain constant from generation to generation. A population in which there is no change in gene frequency over a long period is said to be in **genetic equilibrium**.

The Hardy-Weinberg principle makes five assumptions about any population that maintains genetic equilibrium. These assumptions are the following:

1. No mutations occur.
2. The population is large.
3. Mating between males and females is random.
4. Individuals do not leave the population or enter from outside.
5. No phenotype is more likely to survive and have offspring than any other phenotype.

In natural populations, these conditions are rarely met. The Hardy-Weinberg principle is used to compare natural populations with an ideal situation. When gene frequencies change from one generation to the next, the change is usually caused by a departure from one of these five assumptions.

13–5   The Effect of Mutation

Mutations are the original source of variation in populations. All genes are subject to mutation. Mutations change the frequency of alleles in a population. For example, mutations continually add genes for hemophilia to the human gene pool. Scientists have estimated that mutations for the hemophilia gene occur about 3 times in every 100,000 gametes. While this may not seem like a large number, in a population of hundreds of millions of people, a significant number can carry this gene.

Figure 13.8 Mutations are the original source of variation in populations.

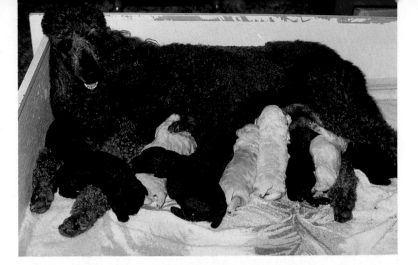

Figure 13.9 Which litter is probably closer to being 50-percent male and 50-percent female? The larger the litter (or population), the greater the chance that probabilities will be realized.

13–6   The Effect of Small Populations

When you flip a coin, your chances of getting either heads or tails is 50 percent. If you flip a coin 10 times, you would expect to get 5 heads and 5 tails. But in such a small number of tries, you might end up with all heads or all tails. Such a result is unlikely, but it is possible in such a small sample. If you flip a coin 1,000 times, you would probably end up with close to 50 percent heads and 50 percent tails.

In small samples, the results may deviate from the expected results. One of the assumptions of the Hardy-Weinberg principle is that populations are large enough so that changes in gene frequency will not be caused by random occurrences. About half of the human population is male, and half is female. But as you know, some human families have all girls or all boys. Such unlikely results are common in small samples.

A change in gene frequency due to random variations in small populations is called **genetic drift**. In small populations a rare allele may be lost or may become unusually common. Genetic drift occurs among humans. The Amish are a religious sect that live in small communities and tend to marry among themselves. These populations have a high frequency of a severe enzyme-deficiency disease. This high frequency is thought to be due to genetic drift.

13–7   The Effect of Nonrandom Mating

The Hardy-Weinberg principle assumes that any male in a population is equally likely to mate with any female. Most species, however, are distributed over large areas. An organism is most likely to mate with a member of its species that lives nearby. Because organisms are usually isolated in small groups, gene frequencies can vary from one local population to another.

Some organisms are more likely to mate with similar organisms than with dissimilar organisms. Such mating is called **assortative mating**. For example, white rabbits may be more likely to mate with white rabbits than with brown rabbits. In populations where this occurs, there will be an unusually high percentage of homozygous individuals and a low percentage of heterozygous individuals. In such populations, the frequency of a recessive allele will appear to be higher than it is. Assortative mating does not alter gene frequencies in a population, but it does change the frequency of phenotypes.

13–8   The Effect of Migration

Genetic equilibrium will be altered if organisms can move in or out of a particular breeding population. This kind of movement is called **migration**. During the last 400 years, migration has changed the gene frequencies of the human population in North America. Every ethnic group that has come to this continent has had a particular gene pool. The population today appears very different from the original population of American Indians.

Figure 13.10 Many people who migrated to the United States in the first half of the twentieth century arrived at Ellis Island in New York Harbor.

13–9   The Effect of Harmful Genes

The fifth assumption of the Hardy-Weinberg principle is that no genotype is more advantageous to an individual than any other genotype. But as you know, this is not always true. Genes for diseases such as hemophilia and PKU may be lethal. Organisms that are homozygous for harmful genes are less likely to survive and produce offspring than those that do not carry such genes. Over many generations harmful genes will become less frequent in the population.

In naturally occurring populations, one allele is often more advantageous to an organism than another allele. In fact this violation of the Hardy-Weinberg assumptions is so common that it is the basis of evolution.

Checkpoint

1. What are the five assumptions of the Hardy-Weinberg principle?
2. A population in which there is no change in gene frequency from generation to generation is said to be in _____.
3. What is the term for a change in gene frequency due to chance variations in a small population?
4. Movement of organisms into or out of a population is called _____.

CHAPTER REVIEW

Summary

- A species is a group of organisms that can interbreed and produce fertile offspring.
- All species show great variation. Some of this variation is caused by the environment, and some is caused by heredity.
- A population of organisms is an interbreeding community of a species that lives in a particular location.
- Clines occur when a species varies gradually along with a change in the environment.
- Subspecies or races are distinct groups within a species.
- Population genetics is the study of gene frequencies in populations.
- The gene pool is the total of all the genetic information in an interbreeding population.
- The Hardy-Weinberg principle states that under certain conditions the gene frequencies in a population will remain constant from one generation to the next. The five assumptions of the Hardy-Weinberg principle are these:
  1. no mutations;
  2. a large population;
  3. random mating;
  4. no migration;
  5. no phenotype favored over another.
- Changes in gene frequencies can usually be attributed to a violation of one of these assumptions.

Vocabulary

assortative mating
cline
cross-multiplication table
gene frequency
gene pool
genetic drift
genetic equilibrium

Hardy-Weinberg principle
migration
population
population genetics
population sampling
race
species
subspecies

Review

Choose the best answer for each of the following questions.

1. A group of organisms that can mate among themselves and produce fertile offspring is called a (a) cline, (b) species, (c) gene pool, (d) race.
2. The altitude-dependent variation in the height of yarrow plants is an example of a (a) mutation, (b) wild flower, (c) hybrid, (d) cline.
3. The Hardy-Weinberg principle assumes that (a) mating between males and females is random, (b) mating between males and females is restricted, (c) new individuals enter from outside the population, (d) mutations occur.
4. What remains constant in a population that is in genetic equilibrium? (a) genetic drift (b) gene frequencies (c) amount of available food (d) generations
5. Yellow-shafted flickers are an example of a (a) cline, (b) mutation, (c) subspecies, (d) species.
6. In what kind of population is genetic drift likely to occur? (a) small population (b) large population (c) hybrid population (d) plant population

7. The movement of individuals in or out of a particular breeding population is called (a) genetic drift, (b) gene frequency, (c) migration, (d) variation.
8. Random mating is rare in most natural populations because (a) most species are distributed over large areas and individuals become isolated in small groups, (b) genetic drift prevents it, (c) most populations are small.
9. Mutations (a) are rarely harmful, (b) can happen only to some genes, (c) rarely occur in subspecies, (d) are the original source of variation in a population.
10. Why aren't Canada geese members of the same species as snow geese? (a) They are found in different geographic areas (b) They cannot mate and produce fertile offspring. (c) They are subspecies. (d) They look very different.

Interpret and Apply

1. In the gene pool for a certain population of rabbits, the gene frequency for brown fur (B) is 63 percent. What is the gene frequency for white fur (b)?
2. A male donkey and a female horse can mate, producing a mule. Why, then, aren't donkeys and horses considered members of the same species?
3. Twenty-five homozygous brown rabbits are placed with 75 homozygous white rabbits. What are the gene frequencies for brown fur (B) and for white fur (b)?
4. You flip a coin 6 times. A friend flips a coin 60 times. Is it more likely that your results will be close to 50 percent heads and 50 percent tails, or that your friend's will be?
5. The gene frequency for the dominant allele for tongue rolling in a certain high school is 70 percent. Construct a cross-multiplication table for this gene.
   a. What percentage of the student population is heterozygous for this trait?
   b. What percentage of the population is homozygous recessive?

Challenge

1. Fifty heterozygous brown rabbits are placed with 100 homozygous white rabbits. What are the gene frequencies for brown fur (B) and for white fur (b)?
2. Why is the Hardy-Weinberg principle useful, even though its five conditions are almost never met in a real population?
3. Two plants of the same species but from two different locations are grown in the same greenhouse under the same conditions. A difference in height is apparent and persists. What conclusion can you draw from this experiment? What is the experimental variable in this experiment?
4. A small population of deer becomes geographically isolated from others of the same species. The isolated deer mate among themselves. If this situation persists for many years, harmful traits due to mutations may increase. What genetic principle may explain this?
5. Population geneticists have studied a human population in which 9 percent of the people are homozygous for a recessive gene that causes red hair. What is the frequency of this gene in the total population?

Projects

1. Find out about the gene that causes Tay-Sachs disease in humans. This gene is much more common in certain human populations than in others. Find out why scientists think such harmful genes have become common in human populations.
2. In a human-genetics text, find examples of genes that are more common in some groups of humans than in others. Report your findings to the class.

14 Evolution

The Grand Canyon near Yaki Point

Hiking from the rim of Arizona's Grand Canyon to the Colorado River far below retraces millions of years of Earth's history. As you descend you pass layers of different-colored rocks. The oldest rocks are in the bottom of the canyon. Newer rocks lie above them. The rocks in the canyon contain fossils, which are imprints of organisms that lived long ago.

There is a pattern to the way fossils occur in the Grand Canyon. Rocks near the top of the canyon contain imprints of lizardlike animals that lived on land. A quarter of the way down, all the fossils are of sea creatures, including fish. A little deeper into the canyon, the fish no longer appear, but there are fossils resembling clams and shrimp. About half way down, the rocks contain nothing but worm burrows. From there to the bottom of the canyon, there are no traces of life at all.

Almost any place in the world where fossils are found, organisms appear in the same order. The older the rocks, the more primitive the organisms that left their impressions. Scientists explain this pattern by the theory of evolution.

History of Life on Earth

Evidence indicates that Earth is about 4.6 billion years old. It is extremely difficult to imagine such an enormous span of time. It may help to think of the history of Earth as a piece of string that is the length of a football field (about 100 meters). Imagine that the beginning of Earth is at one end of the string and the present day is at the other end. On this string the entire 6,000 years of recorded human history would take up only 0.2 millimeter. A million years would be only 2 centimeters long!

Geologists, scientists who study rocks, divide the history of Earth into four **eras**. Geological time is further subdivided into **periods** and **epochs**. Pages 202 and 203 give a brief account of Earth's history.

Pages 202 and 203 give a brief account of Earth's history.

14–1   The Fossil Record

A **fossil** is a preserved remnant or trace of a once-living thing. The most common fossils are impressions left in sedimentary rocks. **Sedimentary rock** consists of layers of minerals and fragments of other rocks deposited over long periods of time. Sedimentary rocks are usually deposited at the bottom of bodies of water.

Fossils may be formed in other ways. An animal walking across mud or wet sand may leave footprints. If these prints are covered with mud that later hardens, the footprints may be preserved. Occasionally an entire animal is preserved as a fossil. As you can see in Figure 14.1, entire mammoths have been dug out of the ice of glaciers.

The position of a fossil in Earth's sediments indicates the fossil's relative age. In undisturbed deposits of sedimentary rocks, the layers that are at the bottom were formed before the layers above them. Because the lower layers of rocks are older than the upper layers, any fossil found in a lower layer must be older than the fossils found above it. Position, of course, gives only the relative age of fossils. It cannot tell the actual age in years.

A more accurate method for dating fossils is based on radioactive isotopes. As you read in Chapter 3, some elements are radioactive. All radioactive elements break down at a predictable rate called the half-life of the element. The **half-life** is the amount of time it takes for one half of the radioactive atoms to disintegrate. Every radioactive element has a characteristic half-life. The half-life of one form of uranium is longer than 700 million years. Radioactive uranium breaks

CONCEPTS

- how the age of fossils is determined
- the heterotroph hypothesis of the origin of life
- sequence of major events in the history of life

Figure 14.1 All fossils are not formed in rocks. This woolly mammoth was preserved by a glacier.

ERA	PERIOD	BEGINNING (millions of years ago)	HIGHLIGHTS
Cenozoic	Quaternary	1	Modern Humans, Glaciation
Cenozoic	Tertiary	64	Most Modern Mammals and Flowering Plants
Mesozoic	Cretaceous	136	Dinosaurs Dying Out, Many Small Mammals and Flowering Plants, Formation of Rockies
Mesozoic	Jurassic	195	First Mammals, First Birds, Many Dinosaurs
Mesozoic	Triassic	225	Many Reptiles and Gymnosperms, Desert Conditions
Paleozoic	Permian	280	First Gymnosperms, Modern Insects, Formation of Appalachians
Paleozoic	Carboniferous	345	First Reptiles, Winged Insects, Many Amphibians and Ferns, Origins of Fossil Fuels
Paleozoic	Devonian	410	First Amphibians, First Trees, Many Fish, Sharks, and Insects
Paleozoic	Silurian	440	First Land Plants, Giant Scorpions
Paleozoic	Ordovician	530	First Fish (first vertebrates)
Paleozoic	Cambrian	570	Many Invertebrates such as Clams, Coral, Snails, Sponges; Many Algae
Precambrian		4,500	Scant Fossil Evidence, Monerans, Fungi, Algae, Worms, Great Volcanic Activity

Organism group columns (shown graphically by column width): FLOWERING PLANTS, CONIFERS AND CYCADS, SEEDLESS LAND PLANTS, MOSSES, BACTERIA, ALGAE, LICHENS, and FUNGI, PROTISTS, SPONGES, COELENTERATES

Beginnings of periods and appearance of groups are approximations based on fossils and other forms of geologic evidence.

Column widths indicate comparative abundance of different groups.

Note: the widths of the periods do not reflect the actual time spans.

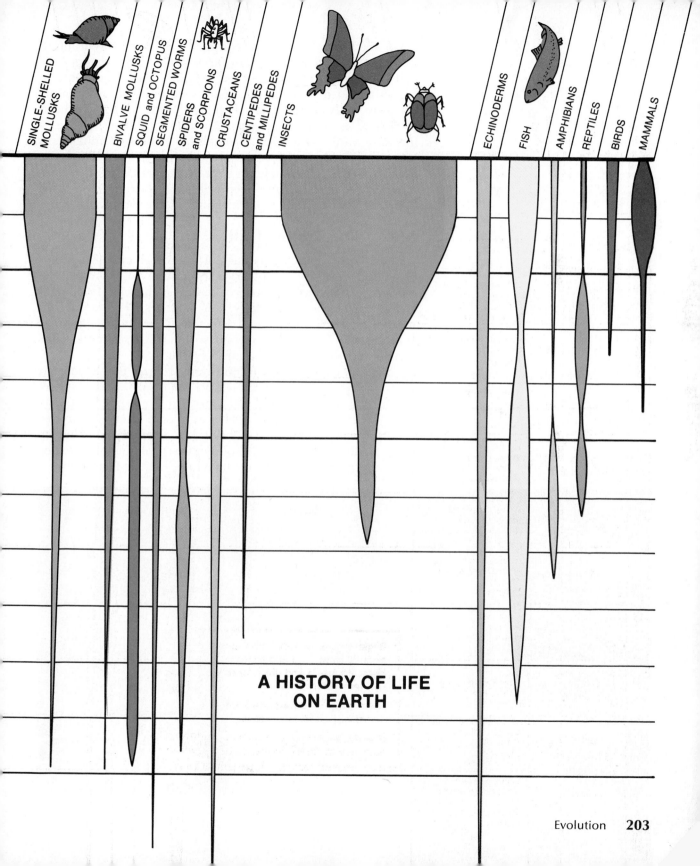

SINGLE-SHELLED MOLLUSKS
BIVALVE MOLLUSKS
SQUID and OCTOPUS
SEGMENTED WORMS
SPIDERS and SCORPIONS
CRUSTACEANS
CENTIPEDES and MILLIPEDES
INSECTS
ECHINODERMS
FISH
AMPHIBIANS
REPTILES
BIRDS
MAMMALS

**A HISTORY OF LIFE
ON EARTH**

down and forms lead. By measuring the proportion of uranium and lead in a rock, scientists can estimate its age.

By studying the fossil record, scientists have been able to construct an outline of the history of life on Earth. Unfortunately, only a small percentage of organisms have been preserved as fossils. One reason for this is that fossils usually form in water. Organisms that die on land are unlikely to leave fossil records. Because preservation is so unlikely, the fossil record is incomplete. In spite of gaps in the fossil record, however, scientists have been able to find similar patterns of evolution in fossils from all parts of the world.

14–2   The Origin of Life

In the late 1800s, Louis Pasteur and other biologists demonstrated that life cannot arise from nonliving sources. The concept of biogenesis is one of the most thoroughly demonstrated principles in biology. Yet biogenesis leaves one important question unanswered. Where did the first living things come from? Since it happened so long ago scientists once considered this question unanswerable.

Scientists agree that the conditions of early Earth were far different from those existing today. The primitive atmosphere was probably quite unlike the present atmosphere. It may have contained methane (CH_4), ammonia (NH_3), hydrogen (H_2), and water vapor (H_2O). Rains probably fell on the barren rock and formed oceans. The planet was probably bombarded with energy in the form of ultraviolet light and lightning.

Figure 14.2 An artist's conception of the primitive earth

In the 1930s, the Russian scientist A. I. Oparin presented a hypothesis to explain how the first living thing might have developed. Oparin suggested that although it is impossible for life to arise today, conditions on primitive Earth were so different that it was possible for life to arise then.

Oparin suggested that simple chemical processes in the early atmosphere created small organic molecules. Energy from the ultraviolet light and lightning rearranged the chemical bonds of molecules in the atmosphere. Over millions of years a large number of organic chemicals built up in the primitive oceans.

Given enough time, a random collection of organic molecules might begin to show some of the properties of a living thing. Any living thing that did develop could use the rest of the organic chemicals in the ocean as a food source. Thus Oparin proposed that the first living thing was a heterotroph. His idea was called the **heterotroph hypothesis**.

In the early 1950s, Oparin's hypothesis received support from an experiment performed by the American scientist Stanley Miller. Miller's experiment is illustrated in Figure 14.3. Miller put water in the bottom of a flask, then filled it with a mixture of gases similar to those that might have been found in the primitive atmosphere. The gases in his experiment were methane, ammonia, hydrogen, and water vapor. The water represented ocean water. Wires entering the top of the flask created electric sparks. The sparks represented lightning, a source of energy.

After several days the water in the flask changed color. Analysis of the water showed that several amino acids were present. As you have learned, amino acids are the building blocks of protein. Miller had not created life. He had, however, shown that nonliving conditions could produce at least some of the chemicals present in living things. The formation of amino acids in the ancient oceans could have been the first step in a long chain of events that resulted in a living cell.

Many similar experiments have been done since Miller's. These experiments have used different sources of energy and different gases. All the experiments have tried to recreate conditions that might have existed on early Earth. Such experiments have shown that under conditions resembling those of early Earth, amino acids can come together to form proteinlike molecules.

It is a long step from the formation of organic molecules in the laboratory to the formation of a living cell. Even the simplest cells alive today contain tens of thousands of complex macromolecules. The DNA of even these "simple" cells controls a complex series of biochemical reactions. Scientists have not yet been able to show how DNA came to control the cell.

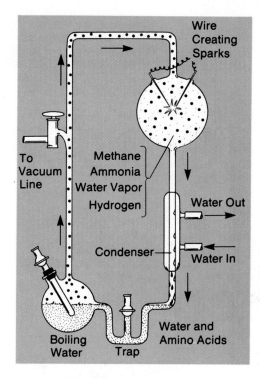

Figure 14.3 Miller's complete experimental setup

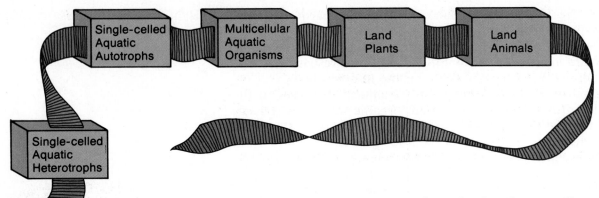

Figure 14.4 A probable order of the emergence of living things on Earth

Figure 14.5 Some of the oldest fossils known are these fossils of single-celled organisms. They were found in rocks estimated to be over a billion years old.

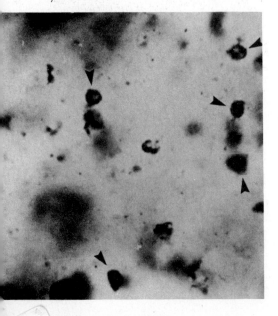

Scientists can never prove how the first living cell came into being. Experiments such as Miller's, however, do show a series of possible events that could have led to the formation of the first cell.

14–3   The Origin of Autotrophs

The first living cells probably depended upon the organic molecules dissolved in the primitive ocean for food. Because the early atmosphere contained no free oxygen, scientists assume that these organisms were anaerobic. They may have been similar to some modern bacteria.

As the first heterotrophs reproduced and spread throughout the ocean, the dissolved organic chemicals would have been used up. As food became scarce, organisms that could produce their own food from sunlight would have been favored. At this time, photosynthetic organisms could have arisen. These were the first autotrophs. As photosynthetic organisms increased in number, some heterotrophs may have begun to use them as a food source.

The photosynthetic organisms would have produced free oxygen. This changed the composition of the atmosphere. Once oxygen became available, some organisms could have developed aerobic respiration. As you learned in Chapter 7, aerobic respiration releases far more energy from food than does anaerobic respiration. Therefore organisms with aerobic respiration would have been favored and have increased in number.

14–4   Multicellular Organisms

The first autotrophs and heterotrophs were single-celled. Fossils of simple unicellular organisms have been found in rocks that are estimated to be 3.5 billion years old. Fossils in rocks that are more than 570 million years old are very rare. Rocks younger than 570 million years, however, show fossils from all the major groups of animals and many groups of plants that are alive today. These rocks contain fossils of worms, corals, shelled animals like clams, animals resembling lobsters and crabs, and relatives of today's starfish.

No one knows why fossils of multicellular organisms appear so suddenly in the fossil record. One hypothesis is that earlier organisms had soft bodies that did not fossilize easily.

The fossil record shows repeated evidence of groups of organisms that appeared, became very common, and then disappeared. Organisms that no longer exist on Earth are said to be **extinct**. The most famous disappearing act starred

Saber-Toothed Tiger

Dodo

Lepidodendron

Figure 14.6 Most of the species that have existed on Earth are now extinct. Three examples are the saber-toothed tiger, the dodo, and a *Lepidodendron* (an early tree).

the dinosaurs. Dinosaurs were reptiles related to modern lizards, turtles, snakes, and alligators. For millions of years, dinosaurs roamed on Earth. They are believed to have dominated most land environments for about 200 million years. About 60 million years ago, dinosaurs became extinct. Many reasons for their extinction have been proposed, but there is not yet convincing evidence for any of them.

Biologists estimate that there are about 5 million species of organisms living on Earth today. Although this is a huge number, the organisms living today represent only a small percentage of the total number of species that have existed during the history of life on Earth.

Checkpoint

1. What is the approximate age of Earth?
2. Who first proposed the heterotroph hypothesis?
3. Who first showed experimentally that organic molecules might have formed in the atmosphere of early Earth?

Theories of Evolution

Until the nineteenth century, scientists were puzzled by fossils of organisms that were no longer living on Earth. At that time, most scientists believed that species were distinct and unchanging. But unusual fossils, such as the bones of huge woolly mammoths and enormous dinosaurs, could not be explained by the theories of that time. In the 1800s, scientists developed new theories to explain the changes over time.

CONCEPTS

- Lamarck's theory of evolution through inheritance of acquired characteristics
- Darwin's theory of evolution through natural selection
- process of natural selection

14–5   Lamarck and Acquired Characteristics

One scientist intrigued by fossils was the French naturalist Jean Baptiste de Lamarck. Lamarck's observations of fossils and living organisms challenged the common idea that species were fixed types. Lamarck saw evidence that organisms had changed through time.

In 1809, Lamarck proposed that organisms evolved in response to their environment. To **evolve** means to change from one form to another. Lamarck was the first biologist to suggest that organisms undergo **evolution**.

Lamarck's theory explained two observed facts. The first was the fossil record, which showed that organisms in the past were different from those living today. Second, his theory explained why each organism was so well adapted to its environment. As Lamarck had observed, each organism has **adaptations** that suit its particular way of life. Elephants have long trunks for gathering food; lions have powerful claws and jaws for capturing prey; and antelope have long, swift legs for escaping predators.

Lamarck also suggested a mechanism to explain how evolution occurs. According to Lamarck, organisms develop specialized characteristics by the use or disuse of organs. For example, a deer that runs swiftly to escape wolves will develop strong running muscles. Traits that an organism develops during its lifetime are called **acquired characteristics**. 36

Lamarck believed that organisms are able to pass acquired characteristics on to their offspring. Thus a wading bird might develop long legs by stretching. The offspring of this bird would inherit these long legs. If these birds used their long legs to wade into deeper water, they would develop even longer legs. Over many generations, a short-legged bird could gradually evolve into another species.

Although the inheritance of acquired characteristics seems to be logical, no evidence has been found to support this concept. As you know, genetic material is contained in the

Figure 14.7 How would Lamarck explain the characteristic long legs of this heron?

chromosomes. Except for rare mutations, genetic information is passed on unchanged from generation to generation. If acquired characteristics could be inherited, then the children of concert pianists would be born already knowing how to play the piano. As you know, this is not the case. Acquired skills must be developed anew in each generation.

Lamarck's theory of evolution did not convince many scientists of his day. Most scientists were unwilling to accept the evidence that species have changed gradually through the ages. Since the development of the science of genetics, geneticists have searched for cases in which acquired characteristics are inherited. No such cases have been found. Geneticists today have been unable to find any evidence that acquired traits can be inherited.

14–6 Charles Darwin and Natural Selection

About 50 years after Lamarck proposed his theory of evolution, the British naturalist Charles Darwin revolutionized the thinking of most biologists. In 1859, Darwin published a book called *The Origin of Species by Means of Natural Selection.* Like Lamarck, Darwin stated that living things gradually evolve adaptations to the environment. But Darwin proposed an entirely different mechanism to account for the changes in species.

Unlike Lamarck, Darwin recognized the variations among members of a species. It is these variations, rather than acquired characteristics, that are inherited. Darwin observed how plant and animal breeders use selective breeding to develop different breeds. He then hypothesized that a similar type of selection takes place in the natural environment. Darwin named this process **natural selection.**

Natural selection results from the interaction of a population of organisms with its environment. Darwin realized that in nature, most organisms produce more offspring than can survive. For example, oak trees produce thousands of acorns and frogs lay hundreds of eggs. But only some of these offspring survive to produce offspring in the next generation.

Since not all offspring can survive, Darwin reasoned that there must be competition among the offspring. This competition results in the survival of only a few.

Darwin further reasoned that only those organisms most suited for the environment survive to produce offspring. This process is called the survival of the fittest. An example of survival of the fittest could be the wading birds described earlier. According to Darwin's theory of evolution, in each generation of birds, some would have longer legs than others. Only those birds with long legs would be able to capture fish

Figure 14.8 Charles Darwin

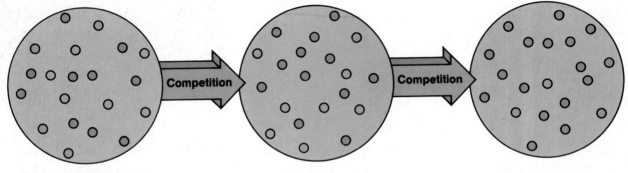

Variation in a
Population

Adapted Population
Fittest (◉) Dominate

Figure 14.9 According to Darwin, the members of a population that are best adapted to the environment are the fittest. The fittest survive to reproduce in greater numbers. After generations, individuals with the characteristics of the fittest dominate.

in deep water. These birds would get more food and be able to survive and produce offspring. The offspring of the long-legged birds would be likely to inherit long legs.

Darwin's theory of natural selection can be summarized as follows.

1. Species have the ability to produce a large number of offspring.
2. The resources of the natural world are limited.
3. Therefore, there must be competition for survival among the offspring in each generation.
4. There is great variability within populations of organisms. No two individuals are the same. Much of this variety is inherited.
5. The organisms that survive and produce offspring are those that have inherited the most beneficial traits for surviving in that particular environment.
6. As this process continues through many generations, the population gradually becomes better adapted to the environment.

Notice that variations in a population occur randomly. Variations do not arise in response to the environment. Natural selection "selects" from among those traits that already exist within the gene pool.

Darwin knew nothing of modern genetics. Since his time, however, research has shown that mutations arise independently of an organism's needs. These chance variations may be useful in an environment. Usually they are not. Only those variations that are useful will increase an organism's chance of survival.

Figure 14.10 Only those cheetahs that can run fast enough to capture prey are able to survive and produce offspring.

14–7 Comparing Darwin and Lamarck

Both Darwin's and Lamarck's theories state that the evolution of species occurs gradually from generation to generation. But the cause of the change is explained differently by the two theories.

Consider, for example, the evolution of a cheetah's speed. Cheetahs are the fastest land animals, able to run faster than 100 kilometers per hour. Both Darwin and Lamarck would explain the cheetahs' amazing speed as the result of evolution. Lamarck would have attributed their speed to the activity of early cheetahs. As early cheetahs ran after their prey, they developed strong legs. This acquired characteristic was then passed on to later generations.

In contrast, Darwin's theory would state that natural selection had acted upon variation in the cheetah population. Early populations of cheetahs would have included some individuals that could run more quickly than others. This variation would have been inherited randomly, as are variations in color, body size, and pattern of spots. In the cheetah's environment, being able to run fast is a strong advantage in capturing prey. The fastest cheetahs would be the most likely to catch food. They would survive and ultimately reproduce. Thus only the fastest cheetahs would survive to pass their traits on to the next generation.

An important difference between Darwin's and Lamarck's theories concerns when a variation occurs in a population. In Lamarck's explanation, the variations come about as a result of a change in the environment. As prey run faster, the cheetah evolves greater speed. In Darwin's theory, variations exist independently of the environment, not in response to environmental conditions.

As you know from your study of genetics, genes do not mutate in response to a need in the environment. Modern genetics research supports Darwin's theory, but no support has been found for Lamarck's explanations.

Figure 14.11 The tongue of the great anteater can be as much as 60 cm long. How would Lamarck explain this characteristic? How would Darwin explain the same characteristic?

Do You Know?

Darwin was not the only person to discover that natural selection is a mechanism of evolution. In 1858, Darwin received a letter from another British naturalist, Alfred Russel Wallace, that contained the ideas that Darwin had developed but not yet published. The two men presented their theory together.

Checkpoint

1. What theory explains how species become better adapted to their environment?
2. According to Lamarck, organisms can acquire characteristics throughout their life by _____.
3. What mechanism did Darwin propose to explain the process of evolution?
4. According to Darwin, when do variations arise in a population?

Evidence of Evolution

Darwin's book, *The Origin of Species*, contained a great deal of indirect evidence to show that evolution had occurred. For example, Darwin described evidence from the fossil record to show that different forms of life once existed on Earth. Because evolution occurs over long periods of time, it is very difficult to observe directly. Since Darwin's time, biologists have amassed a huge amount of information to support his theory of evolution.

14–8 Evidence from Structure

The physical structures of organisms provide clues to their ancestry. Darwin's theory of evolution proposed that one species could give rise to several others.

Figure 14.12 shows the bone structure of the front limbs of several different animals. The forelimbs of the bird have a different function from those of a horse or a dog, yet they all share a common internal bone structure. This similarity of structure is evidence that these animals have descended from a common ancestor. As different species evolved, natural selection resulted in modifications that were adapted to different types of environments. Structures with different functions but common ancestry are called **homologous** [hoh-MAHL-uh-guhs] structures.

Another kind of evidence of evolution is that of vestigial organs [veh-STIHJ-ee-ul]. **Vestigial organs** are small or incomplete organs that have no apparent function. According to evolutionary theory, vestigial organs are the remaining parts of once-functioning organs. Figure 14.13 shows the skeleton of a whale. The bones shown in red are vestigial.

CONCEPTS

- how vestigial organs and homologous structures support the theory of evolution
- evidence of evolution from embryology, biochemistry, genetics, and the fossil record
- evolution of the peppered moth

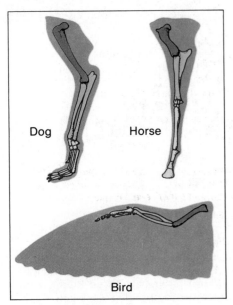

Figure 14.12 Homologous structures in the front limbs of different animals

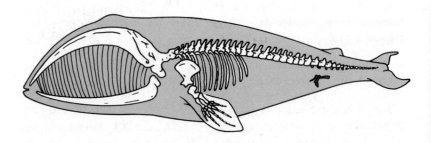

Figure 14.13 Vestigial bones in the skeleton of a whale

They do not seem to have a useful function in the whale. Biologists have evidence that whales evolved from four-legged animals that lived on land. When the whales entered the water, rear legs would have been a disadvantage. They would make the animal less streamlined. Through natural selection, whales with the smallest rear legs would have been able to survive and leave more offspring than whales with larger legs. This process of selection would have continued through million of years, until finally only the vestigial bones remained.

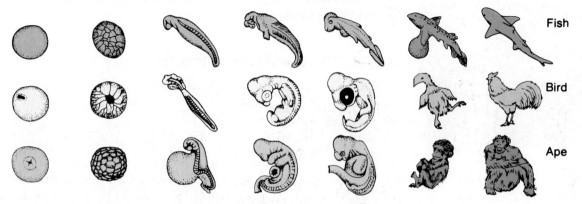

Figure 14.14 How can you explain the similarity in the early embryonic stages of these animals?

14–9 Evidence from Embryology

Evidence of evolution can also be found in the development of some organisms. A developing organism is called an **embryo**. The study of the development of an organism is called **embryology**.

When comparing the development of closely related organisms, it is often difficult to tell the early stages of one species from the early stages of another. As you can see in Figure 14.14, the early stages of a fish are quite similar to those of a bird or an ape. Since the adult organisms look quite different, it may seem strange that the earlier stages are so similar. The similarity of embryos is often used as evidence of evolution. If two organisms descended from a common ancestor, they may still have developmental stages that are very similar. As this explanation would predict, closely related organisms usually have more similar embryological patterns than organisms that are less closely related.

14–10 Evidence from Biochemistry and Genetics

Modern genetics also provides evidence of evolution. All organisms use the same genetic code to synthesize proteins. A universal genetic code is consistent with the idea that all organisms evolved from a single organism that used that code.

Figure 14.15 Light and dark peppered moths

Biochemists have compared the amino-acid sequences of proteins found in different organisms. Organisms that are closely related often have proteins with very similar amino-acid sequences. In dissimilar organisms, the amino-acid sequences of proteins show many more differences.

14–11 Natural Selection Observed

Evolution takes place over thousands or even millions of years. For this reason, it is difficult to observe natural selection in wild populations. One example, however, is very well documented. This case involves the evolution of wing color in a species of moth. Figure 14.15 shows two colors that are found in populations of the peppered moth. The peppered moth is common in the English countryside.

In the early 1850s, most of the peppered moths in the English countryside were light-colored. Collectors rarely found dark moths. When light-colored moths land on light tree trunks, they blend in with their background. Birds and other predators are unlikely to find such moths. In contrast, dark-colored moths are quite conspicuous on light tree trunks. Predators can readily find and eat dark moths.

By the early 1900s, industrial pollution had darkened the tree trunks. As the tree trunks became darker, light-colored moths stood out. The birds now noticed the lighter moths and ate a higher and higher proportion of light-colored moths. Dark-colored moths, once at a disadvantage, were now able to blend in with their background. So darker moths survived and reproduced. By natural selection, the gene frequency for dark color increased rapidly in the population, until dark moths became more common.

In recent years, pollution controls have resulted in trees once again having light-colored trunks. Natural selection now favors the light-colored moths. As predicted by Darwin's theory of evolution, light moths are once again more common in the English countryside.

Checkpoint

1. The front leg of a dog, the arm of a human, and the wing of a bird are examples of _____ .
2. The non-functioning remnant of a once functioning structure is called a _____ .
3. What is the branch of biology that studies the development of organisms?
4. When pollution changed the color of tree trunks in England, what kind of moths were favored by natural selection?

The Process of Evolution

In the 3.5 billion years since life arose on Earth, evolution has produced an enormous variety of living things. Millions of species have evolved successfully while others have become extinct. By studying the fossil record, biologists have observed patterns in the evolution and distribution of organisms in the world.

CONCEPTS

- causes of speciation
- adaptive radiation
- convergent evolution
- stabilizing selection

14–12 Speciation

Some environments remain the same for long periods. More frequently, however, environments change. Fossils from ancient oceans have been found in modern deserts. Forests have been covered by glaciers because of major climate changes. Organisms that are well adapted to one environment may not be as well adapted when the environment changes. In a changing environment, natural selection will alter gene frequencies.

Natural selection can lead to the formation of new species, or **speciation** [spee-see-AY-shuhn]. Speciation often occurs when part of a population becomes isolated from the rest. Since no two environments are identical, selective pressures that occur in one location may be different from the pressures in another location.

The most common way a population becomes divided is by **geographic isolation**. Geographic isolation occurs when a physical barrier develops between a segment of two populations. For example, two species of squirrels live on opposite sides of the Grand Canyon. Biologists assume that before the Colorado River took its present course a single population of squirrels lived over the entire area.

Figure 14.16 *Left:* The Abert squirrel; *Right:* The Kaibab squirrel. How do scientists explain the development of these two species?

About one million years ago, the Colorado River changed its course, splitting the population of squirrels in two. Since the environment on opposite sides of the canyon is different, different characteristics were favored on each side of the canyon. After many years of separation, the genetic differences between the populations became so large that the two squirrel populations became two separate species. They looked very different and could no longer interbreed.

Populations do not have to be physically isolated in order to diverge genetically. Many frog species live in the same area but breed at different times of the year. A population that breeds in May is effectively isolated from one that breeds in July. This kind of isolation is called **reproductive isolation**.

14–13   Adaptive Radiation

Sometimes many new species will evolve from a single ancestral species. This type of evolution is called **adaptive radiation**. All of the species share a common ancestor. Adaptive radiation often occurs when a species enters a new environment where there are few other competing species.

The finches that live on the Galápagos Islands are a classic example of adaptive radiation. The Galápagos Islands are volcanic islands that lie about 1,000 kilometers west of South America.

As a young man, Charles Darwin visited the Galápagos Islands and took particular interest in the different species of finches that lived there. These finches are similar in overall appearance. Yet each species has a distinctive shape of beak, a distinctive feeding habit, and distinctive behavior. The shapes of some of the finches' beaks are shown in Figure 14.17. In each species, the shape of the beak is well suited for what

Figure 14.17 The beaks of Galápagos finches are adapted to their diet.

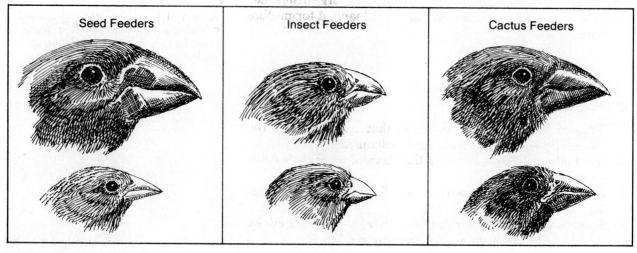

Seed Feeders   Insect Feeders   Cactus Feeders

the bird eats. Finches with large, heavy beaks eat nuts with hard shells. Finches with long, slender beaks reach for insects inside cracks and holes.

The Galápagos finches are all closely related. Evidence suggests that they are all descended from a species of finch that lived in South America. A single original population of this finch probably spread to all of the islands. Each of the populations was geographically isolated. Food sources on the islands varied enough so that different populations of the original finches could develop local characteristics. Over many years, these local populations became distinct species, each adapted to eat the local food.

14–14 Convergent Evolution

Sometimes natural selection favors adaptations that are quite similar in organisms that are not closely related. For example, Figure 14.18 shows several marine organisms that are adapted to swimming swiftly in the ocean. Despite their similarities, these organisms are not closely related. **Convergent evolution** occurs when the environment puts similar selective pressure on different species. Can you think of other examples of convergent evolution?

14–15 Stabilizing Selection

Natural selection does not necessarily change the gene frequencies in a population. In many cases, selection can stabilize the characteristics of a population. If a species is well adapted to a particular environment and the environment does not change, then new variations will be selected against.

Stabilizing selection maintains characteristics that are successful for an organism in its environment. Fossil evidence indicates that stabilizing selection has kept organisms such as sharks, turtles, and ferns virtually unchanged for millions of years.

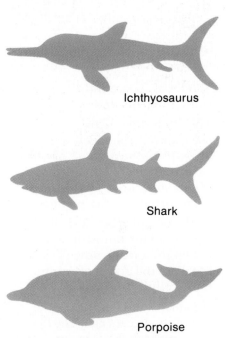

Ichthyosaurus

Shark

Porpoise

Figure 14.18 Notice the similarity in body shape of the shark (a fish), the porpoise (a mammal), and ichthyosaurus (an ancient reptile).

Do You Know?
Darwin died in 1882. He was buried in Westminster Abbey. Many dignitaries from England and abroad attended his funeral.

Checkpoint

1. What do scientists call selection that tends to keep the characteristics of a population unchanged?
2. What allowed the squirrels of the Grand Canyon to become separate species?
3. What process of evolution do the Galápagos finches demonstrate?
4. Species that appear similar but are not closely related are said to have undergone _____ evolution.

CHAPTER REVIEW

Summary

- The fossil record indicates that the first living thing developed about 3.5 billion years ago.
- The Russian scientist A. I. Oparin hypothesized that the first cell was a heterotroph that arose from the organic molecules in the early oceans. Experiments such as those by Stanley Miller show how organic molecules may have been formed in the primitive oceans.
- As the organic chemicals in the ancient oceans were used up, autotrophs could have evolved. Other important advances in the history of life were the origin of aerobic respiration and multicellular organisms.
- Organisms did not invade the land until about 400 million years ago. The first land organisms were plants; the first land animals were related to insects.
- Lamarck was the first biologist to develop a theory of evolution. He believed that evolution resulted from the use or disuse of organs and the inheritance of acquired characteristics. Although scientists have found ample evidence that organisms evolve, there is no evidence to support the inheritance of acquired characteristics.
- Darwin also proposed a mechanism for evolution, that of natural selection. Natural selection can be summarized as follows.

1. All organisms produce more offspring than can survive.
2. All species show variation.
3. Variations are inherited.
4. Natural selection favors survival of the fittest, or the best-adapted, offspring.
5. Offspring that survive pass their adaptations on to the next generation.

- There is considerable evidence to support evolution through natural selection. This evidence includes the fossil record, homologous structures, vestigial organs, a universal genetic code, and comparative embryology.
- Natural selection has been observed in the changing color of the peppered moths in Britain.
- Speciation occurs most frequently as a result of geographic isolation, although it can also occur as a result of reproductive isolation.
- Adaptive radiation occurs when a species evolves into several different species.
- Convergent evolution may result when organisms that live in similar environments are subjected to similar selection pressures.

Vocabulary

acquired characteristics	geographic isolation
adaptation	half-life
adaptive radiation	heterotroph
convergent evolution	hypothesis
embryo	homologous
embryology	natural selection
epoch	period
era	reproductive isolation
evolution	sedimentary rock
evolve	speciation
extinct	stabilizing selection
fossil	vestigial organ

Review

1. What was the source of food for the first living organism?
2. What parts of organisms most commonly form fossils?
3. Miller performed an experiment in which simple gases were exposed to electric sparks. What were the products in this experiment?
4. What is the approximate age of the oldest known fossil organism?

5. When does the fossil record show a sudden increase in the number of different types of fossils?
6. A structure that is well suited for a particular environment is called a _____ .
7. According to Darwin, what process causes the evolution of organisms?
8. When many different species evolve from a single ancestral species, what kind of evolution has occurred?

Interpret and Apply

1. What major question arises from the statement that all living things come from other living things?
2. Tell what each of the following parts of Miller's experiment was designed to duplicate about early Earth. (a) water (b) gases in the beaker (c) electric sparks
3. Explain why photosynthetic organisms are believed to have appeared after the first heterotrophs.
4. What are five types of evidence that evolution has occurred?
5. According to Lamarck, could a body builder pass highly developed muscles on to his or her children? What would scientists today say? Explain.
6. Compare and contrast homologous structures with structures that result from convergent evolution.
7. Which of the following statements support Lamarck's theory of evolution? Which support Darwin's theory? Some statements may support both theories.
   a. Species change gradually through time.
   b. Organisms tend to produce more offspring than can survive.
   c. Acquired characteristics are passed on to offspring.
   d. All natural populations show variation in inherited traits.
   e. The resources of the natural world are limited.
   f. Organs that are not used will become smaller and eventually disappear.
   g. Only those offspring that inherit favorable traits will survive and produce offspring.
   h. The fossil record contains evidence of organisms that are different from those living today.
8. Which of the statements listed in question 7 are false?

Challenge

1. Explain how adaptive radiation of the Galápagos finches might have occurred.
2. How has the development of modern genetics supported Darwin's theory of evolution?
3. Explain why the position of a fossil with respect to other fossils does not give any information about the actual age of the fossil.
4. How do you think Lamarck would have explained the origin of the vestigial bones of the whale?

Projects

1. Consider going fossil hunting. Your library has books that will tell you where to look and how to identify what you find. If you live in a city, you may be able to find fossils in the rock used in buildings. Limestone and sandstone often have fossils that are easily seen if you take the time to look.
2. Find out more about experiments concerning the development of the first living thing. What steps have been accomplished in the laboratory? What has not yet been demonstrated?
3. Learn what events and books influenced Darwin in the development of his theory of evolution. Compare his life to that of Alfred Russel Wallace. How were the experiences of these two men similar? How were they different?

15 The Classification of Life

Feather duster worms

If you were scuba diving near a coral reef, you might discover a colony of the organisms shown in the photograph above. Would you wonder if they were plants or animals? More than anything else, they look like beautiful underwater flowers. In fact, they are a kind of worm called a feather duster. These animals are more closely related to earthworms than to your garden flowers.

Feather dusters live in tubes that they build out of sand. Unlike many other animals, they do not move from place to place in search of food. Instead, these worms attach themselves to one spot and wait for food to drift by. Their "petals" are actually long feathery gills that they use for gas exchange. On their gills are eyespots. If you move your hand near the worms, they will quickly pull back into their tubes. Their rapid motion would tell you that they are animals.

As you can see, it is not always easy to classify organisms as either plants or animals. Not all organisms fit neatly into one category. Looking for order among the huge number of living things has been an activity of biologists for centuries.

Systems of Classification

Classifying is a way of organizing information. To **classify** is to put objects or ideas into groups on the basis of similarity. You classify many things in your everyday life. If you want to find a certain record, you must go to a record store that sells that kind of record. Then you look in a specific area of the store to find the artist's name alphabetically. Imagine how frustrating it would be if all the thousands of records in the store were piled up in no special order. By the time you found your record, it would be a "golden oldie."

The world contains an enormous number of living things. Some biologists estimate that there are about 5 million different species of organisms. Throughout history biologists have used various systems of classification to identify order among organisms.

The ancient Greek philosopher Aristotle made one of the first attempts at classifying living things. Aristotle classified all organisms as either plants or animals. He then classified each animal according to where it lived — on land, in water, or in the air. He classified each plant as an herb, a shrub, or a tree. Aristotle's system was a logical method of classification, but it is not very useful to modern biologists. Both bats and mosquitos fly, so under Aristotle's system they would both be air dwellers. Ants and mice live on the ground, so they would both be called ground dwellers. But scientists now know that a bat is really more closely related to a mouse than it is to a mosquito. An ant is more closely related to a mosquito than it is to a mouse.

CONCEPTS

- reasons for classifying living things
- binomial nomenclature as an international tool
- levels of classification
- modern techniques of classification
- distinction between prokaryotes and eukaryotes
- organization of the five-kingdom system

15–1 Binomial Nomenclature

When biologists study a particular organism, it is important to refer to that organism by a name that other scientists will understand. The use of local or common names for a species can be confusing. People who speak different languages give different names to the same species. Even within one country, one species may have many different names.

For example, what would you call the fruit shown in Figure 15.1? In some regions of the United States, this fruit is called a mango. In other regions of the country it is known as a bell pepper. In still other areas it is known as a sweet pepper or a green pepper. Scientists call this plant *Capsicum frutescens*. To make matters even more confusing, the fruit of the plant *Mangifera indica* is also called a mango, and the seeds of the plant *Piper nigrum* are called pepper.

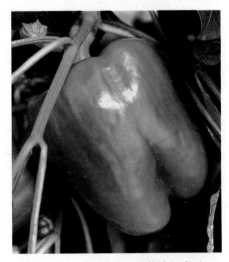

Figure 15.1 Scientists call this fruit *Capsicum frutescens*. What do you call it?

Figure 15.2 The common names for some organisms are very misleading. This fish is called a sea robin.

Do You Know?
The common names for many wild flowers are unusual. Have you ever seen mugwort, lambkill, dame's rocket, scuppernong, beard-tongue, or toadflax?

Figure 15.3 Linnaeus outfitted for collecting specimens

Because of the confusion of using common names, scientists have developed a system for naming and classifying organisms. The language used to give organisms scientific names is Latin. Latin is the universal language of scholars. Until recently, scientists of all countries were trained in Latin.

During the seventeenth century, naturalists began to group similar species into larger groups called **genera** (singular, **genus**). For example, dogs and wolves belong to the genus *Canis*. Each species was given a long name called a **polynomial**. The polynomial consisted of the name of the genus and several descriptive words following it. The descriptive words made it possible for an organism's name to describe the organism in detail. But such names were awkward to use. The plant catnip, for example, was called *Nepeta floribus interrupte spicatus pedunculatis*. That's quite a mouthful!

During the eighteenth century, a Swedish naturalist named Carl von Linné established a simpler method of naming organisms. In keeping with the custom of that time, von Linné called himself by the Latin form of his name, *Carolus Linnaeus*.

In Linnaeus's system of naming, each species is identified by two names — the name of the genus and a descriptive word that signifies the species. A wolf is known as *Canis lupus*, a dog as *Canis familiaris*, and a human as *Homo sapiens*. This two-part method of naming species is called **binomial nomenclature**. It is the system used by all scientists today.

Notice that in binomial nomenclature, the name of the genus appears first and is capitalized. The species name follows and is not capitalized. Both words should appear in italics. Italics may be indicated in handwritten or typed papers by underlining. Sometimes the genus name is abbreviated, so that *Drosophila melanogaster* may be written as *D. melanogaster*.

15–2   Levels of Classification

Suppose you were traveling in a foreign country and someone asked you where you live. If you simply said, "I live at 325 Spruce Street," without giving any more information, the stranger would have little idea of where you live. More likely you would first say what country you live in. Then you might mention your home state, your hometown, and maybe even your street address. In giving this information, starting with the general and then moving to the specific, you would be using a system of classification.

Linnaeus also used the technique of classifying generally, then more and more specifically, until he "zeroed in" on a particular species. He grouped together the organisms that most closely resembled each other. Like Aristotle, Linnaeus divided all living things into two vast groups, which he called the plant and animal **kingdoms**. He then divided each kingdom into many smaller **phyla** (singular, **phylum**). Organisms that he placed in the same phylum not only shared the characteristics of their kingdom, but they also had in common additional characteristics that members of other phyla did not share. Linnaeus divided each phylum into classes, each **class** into orders, each **order** into families, each **family** into genera, and each genus into **species**. Figure 15.4 illustrates the relationship between levels of classification. Each organism fits into one group at each level of classification. If two organisms belong to the same species, you may also assume that they are in the same genus, family, order, class, phylum, and kingdom. (In plant classification, the word **division** is used instead of *phylum*.)

Linnaeus published his first work, *Species Plantarum*, in 1753. Because Linnaeus lived about 100 years before Darwin, he had no idea that species could evolve from other species. He assumed that there were a fixed number of unchanging species that inhabited Earth. Linnaeus determined the closeness of relationship by the degree of physical similarity.

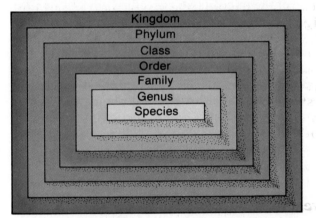 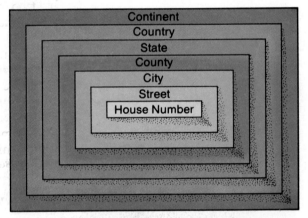

Figure 15.4 The relationship of different levels of classification can be compared to the relationship of geographic designations.

15–3 Modern Techniques of Classification

Since the time of Linnaeus, biologists have learned much more about the relationships between different organisms. Most **taxonomists**, the scientists who study classification, now accept the theory of evolution. This theory states that species arise from other species. Modern taxonomists attempt to classify organisms on the basis of their evolutionary relationships to each other. The evolutionary history of a species is called its **phylogeny** [feye-LOHJ-uh-nee].

Modern taxonomists have many techniques available to them to help in their task of determining phylogenetic relationships. Modern biochemical techniques provide new information that is helpful in classifying organisms.

Today it is possible to determine the amino-acid sequences of proteins. Differences in amino-acid sequences represent mutations. Taxonomists can compare the amino acids of proteins in different species. If two species have very similar sequences, scientists infer that the species are closely related. Human hemoglobin and baboon hemoglobin have more similar amino-acid sequences than human hemoglobin and horse hemoglobin. This observation confirms that humans and baboons are more closely related than humans and horses.

The theoretical basis of Linnaeus's scheme of classification was very different from that of modern taxonomy. Fortunately, though, Linnaeus's system was set up in such a way that scientists can still use it today. The information obtained from new techniques usually supports the relationships that taxonomists have hypothesized over the past several hundred years. The system of classification can change as new information becomes available.

15–4 The Three-Kingdom System

Before the use of the microscope, it seemed obvious to most people that living things were either plants or animals. The discovery of microorganisms, however, revealed many organisms that did not seem to fit neatly into either category. The euglena shown in Figure 15.5 is an example of one such troublesome organism. A euglena is a unicellular organism that contains chloroplasts and carries on photosynthesis. In this way, it resembles a plant. But it also swims by means of a flagellum and can ingest food. Both of these characteristics would seem to make *Euglena* an animal. So what is *Euglena* — plant or animal?

In 1866, Ernst Haeckel, a German scientist, proposed that a third kingdom be added to plants and animals. He called the third kingdom Protista. All one-celled organisms and others that were clearly neither plants nor animals were **protists**. Haeckel assumed that plants and animals had evolved from organisms in the protist kingdom. Haeckel's system was never widely accepted because, even within the protist kingdom, large differences existed between organisms.

15–5 Prokaryotes and Eukaryotes

Within Haeckel's protist kingdom were some organisms that had nuclei and some that did not. In 1937, a French marine biologist named Edouard Chatton suggested dividing living things into two major groups, those with nuclei and those without.

In most familiar organisms, DNA is located on chromosomes that lie within the nucleus of the cell. The nucleus is separated

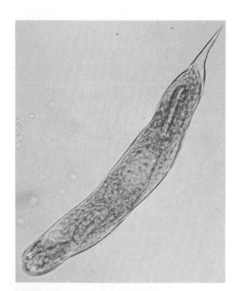

Figure 15.5 In what kingdom does *Euglena* belong?

from the rest of the cytoplasm by a membrane. Organisms with a membrane-bound nucleus are called **eukaryotes** [yew-KAHR-ee-ohts]. Eukaryotes also have other membrane-bound organelles such as chloroplasts and mitochondria.

Prokaryotes are organisms that lack a nuclear membrane. All prokaryotes are microscopic, and only a few are multicellular. Prokaryotes contain no mitochondria. Instead, their respiratory enzymes are located on their cell membranes. Some prokaryotes, such as the cyanophytes, are photosynthetic, but these organisms lack chloroplasts. Their photosynthetic pigments are located on their cell membrane.

15–6 The Five-Kingdom System

Throughout the twentieth century, the science of taxonomy has evolved to fit new ideas and new information. In 1969, Robert Whittaker, a biologist at Cornell University, proposed a system of classification that included five kingdoms. Whittaker's system is based on three criteria: the number of cells in an organism; the presence or absence of a nucleus; and the mode of nutrition. This book uses a five-kingdom system. Descriptions and examples of the kingdoms are on pages 226 and 227.

Any classification system is somewhat artificial. It is simply an attempt of humans to impose order on a vast, diverse group of organisms. So it is not surprising that a few organisms just do not fit neatly into one of the five kingdoms.

Some protists resemble plants more closely than they resemble other protists. That should not happen in a system of classification. Another problem is that most scientists believe that the various fungi evolved from different protist groups rather than from a single fungal ancestor. In a perfect system of classification, all members of a group should have descended from a common ancestor. The green algae, a group that includes unicellular and multicellular forms, are also a problem. Green algae are classified as plants, although many members of the green algae are unicellular.

Although the five-kingdom system is not perfect, it has gained wide acceptance. It is convenient to use, and it is more in keeping with current knowledge than any other classification scheme developed so far.

Figure 15.6 Coral is multicellular. Its cells have nuclei. Is coral a prokaryote or a eukaryote?

Checkpoint

1. List the levels of classification from species to kingdom.
2. Scientists who study classification are called _____.
3. What did Chatton call an organism that lacked a nucleus?
4. What criteria are used in Whittaker's classification system?

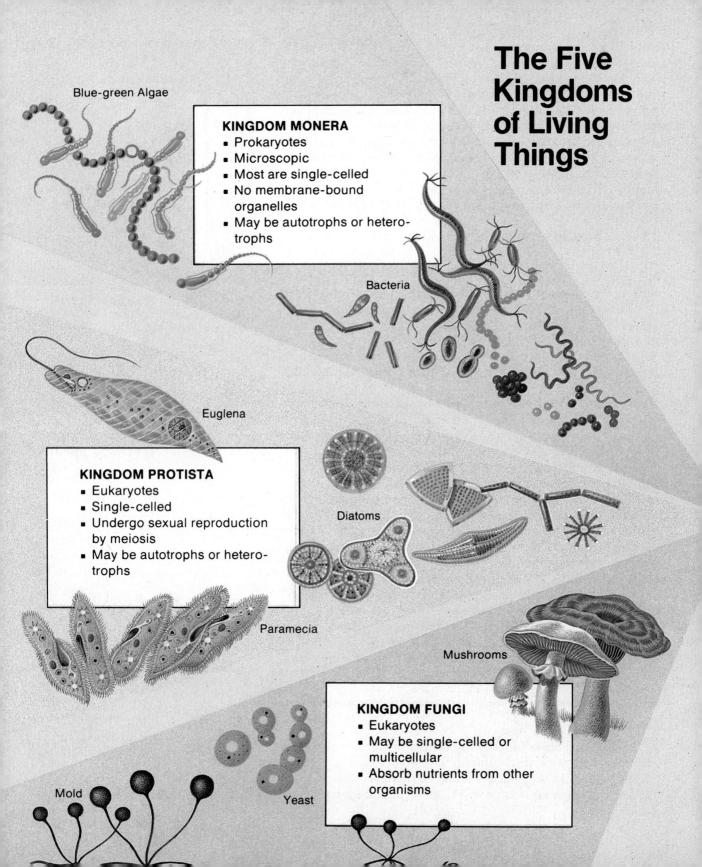

The Five Kingdoms of Living Things

Blue-green Algae

KINGDOM MONERA
- Prokaryotes
- Microscopic
- Most are single-celled
- No membrane-bound organelles
- May be autotrophs or heterotrophs

Bacteria

Euglena

KINGDOM PROTISTA
- Eukaryotes
- Single-celled
- Undergo sexual reproduction by meiosis
- May be autotrophs or heterotrophs

Diatoms

Paramecia

Mushrooms

KINGDOM FUNGI
- Eukaryotes
- May be single-celled or multicellular
- Absorb nutrients from other organisms

Mold

Yeast

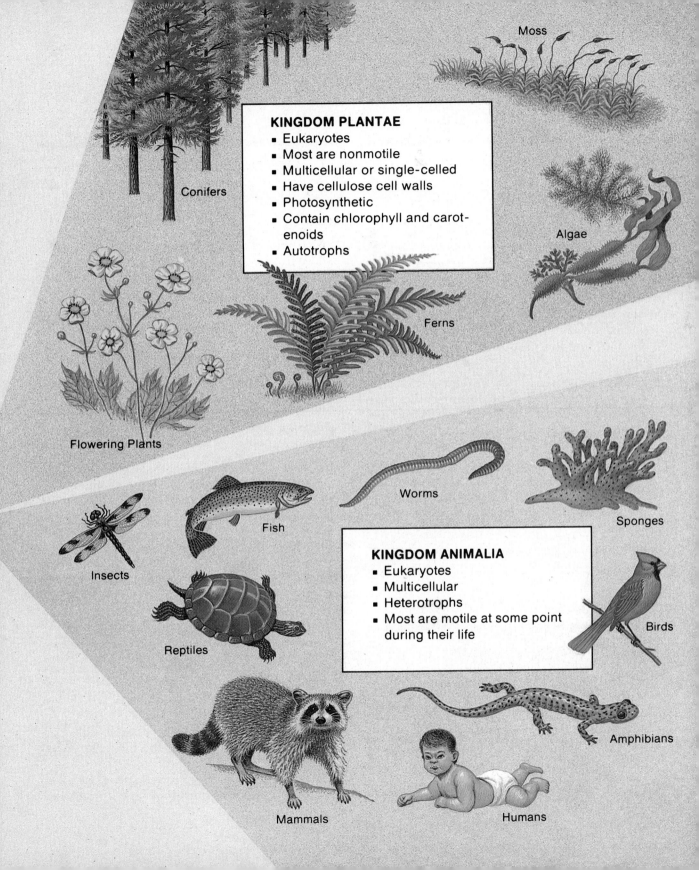

Moss

KINGDOM PLANTAE
- Eukaryotes
- Most are nonmotile
- Multicellular or single-celled
- Have cellulose cell walls
- Photosynthetic
- Contain chlorophyll and carotenoids
- Autotrophs

Conifers

Algae

Ferns

Flowering Plants

Insects

Fish

Worms

Sponges

KINGDOM ANIMALIA
- Eukaryotes
- Multicellular
- Heterotrophs
- Most are motile at some point during their life

Reptiles

Birds

Mammals

Humans

Amphibians

CHAPTER REVIEW

Summary

- For thousands of years, humans have tried to classify and determine relationships among living things. Aristotle developed a classification scheme that separated organisms into two groups — plants or animals.
- Linnaeus established a system of naming organisms called binomial nomenclature. Linnaeus also established the modern levels of classification.
- The levels of taxonomic groups are species, genus, family, order, class, phylum, and kingdom. Plants are grouped in divisions rather than phyla.
- Modern taxonomy tries to establish classification on the basis of phylogeny rather than physical similarity. Modern genetics and biochemistry provide evidence of phylogeny.
- Prokaryotes are organisms that lack nuclei and other membrane-bound organelles. Most multicellular organisms and all protists are eukaryotes, organisms with nuclear membranes.
- This textbook classifies organisms in five kingdoms. These kingdoms are animals, plants, protists, fungi, and monerans.

Vocabulary

binomial	moneran
nomenclature	order
class	phylogeny
classify	phylum
division	polynomial
eukaryote	prokaryote
family	protist
fungi	species
genus	taxonomist
kingdom	taxonomy

Review

1. How did Aristotle classify living things?
2. Why is binomial nomenclature preferable to the use of polynomials?
3. What language is used in binomial nomenclature?
4. *Homo* is to genus as *sapiens* is to _____.
5. Why don't scientists use regional or common names for species?
6. How are dogs and wolves related?
7. What are taxonomists?
8. What is the difference between prokaryotes and eukaryotes?
9. What are the five kingdoms recognized in this book?

For questions 10–14, determine whether the following descriptions refer to Linnaeus's classification system or to the modern classification system.

10. The evolutionary relationships of organisms are considered in classifying them.
11. The presence or absence of a nucleus is considered in the classification of organisms.
12. Two kingdoms are recognized.
13. This was the first system to use binomial nomenclature.
14. This system has a separate kingdom for fungi.

Interpret and Apply

1. Why were scientists uncertain about how to classify *Euglena?*
2. *Panthera leo* (lion), *Canis latrans* (coyote), *Panthera tigris* (tiger), and *Procyon lotor* (raccoon) are all members of the order Carnivora. Which two are the most closely related? Explain.
3. If two animals are in the same class, what other categories must they have in common?

	Human	Daffodil	Frog	Dog	 Wolf
Kingdom	Animalia	Plantae	Animalia	Animalia	Animalia
Phylum	Chordata	Tracheophyta	Chordata	Chordata	Chordata
Class	Mammalia	Angiospermae	Amphibia	Mammalia	Mammalia
Order	Primates	Liliales	Salientia	Carnivora	Carnivora
Family	Hominidae	Amaryllidacaea	Ranidae	Canidae	Canidae
Genus	Homo	Narcissus	Rana	Canis	Canis
Species	sapiens	pseudonarcissus	pipiens	familiaris	lupus

Use the table above to answer questions 4–6.

4. What organism is *Rana pipiens?*
5. The dog is least closely related to what other organism?
6. The dog is most closely related to what other organism?
7. To which of the five kingdoms does each of the following belong?
   a. rose
   b. *Euglena*
   c. bald eagle
   d. bacterium
   e. mushroom
   f. fern
8. Two species have similar amino acid sequences in many proteins. What does this tell you about the two species?

Challenge

1. You want to classify the hundreds of cars in a large parking lot. What are some of the characteristics you could use?
2. Arrange the following items in classification levels from general to specific.

cake pans   muffin tin
9-inch pie plate   baking equipment
kitchen equipment   angelfood cake pan
Bundt cake pan   pie plates
sheet cake pan   10-inch pie plate

3. Why is the classification of all the living things on Earth (a) a job that could never be done by one person alone and (b) a job that will never be finished?
4. You examine carefully two different organisms. What evidence might you find to indicate that the two organisms are closely related?

Projects

1. Choose 10 plants and 10 animals found in your neighborhood. Research the classification of all 20 organisms. List the kingdom, division or phylum, class, order, family, genus, and species of each. Which organisms are the most closely related?
2. Develop a four-level system of classification for all the students in your class.
3. In 1938, the American biologist Herbert Copeland developed a four-kingdom classification system. What was his system?

Careers in Genetics

Predicting the characteristics of offspring on the basis of genetic principles is an activity that fascinates many people. If you are one of these people, perhaps you should consider pursuing a career in genetics. Whether you enjoy working with test tubes, with plants and animals, or with people, there may be a career for you.

Genetic counselors combine detective work with a desire to help people understand their genes. A genetic counselor can help people who have genetic diseases in their families to determine the risk of bearing a child with a genetic disorder. Genetic counselors meet with couples to help explain the results of medical tests. Genetic counselors usually have had graduate training in human genetics. They often work for hospitals or clinics in cooperation with doctors.

Molecular genetics, or genetic engineering, is one of the most exciting areas of modern biology. *Molecular geneticists* move pieces of DNA from one organism to another, creating new combinations of genes that could be useful to society. Molecular geneticists will be in the forefront of many medical advances in the coming decades.

Today most genetics research is being done in laboratories with microorganisms, such as *Escherichia coli* and yeasts. In the future, though, many of these techniques may be applied to larger organisms, such as farm animals.

Most molecular geneticists are highly trained, usually holding either a master's degree or a doctorate. Universities employ geneticists, as do hospitals, pharmaceutical companies, and government agencies such as the National Institutes of Health. Recently many new companies in genetic engineering have been established, which may need skilled workers in the future.

If you enjoy working with plants and animals, a career in plant or animal breeding may interest you. *Plant and animal breeders* work to produce strains of plants and animals that yield more or better food, require less care, or are more attractive and healthy than existing breeds. This work requires much trial and error, and a great deal of patience.

Plant breeders often work for seed companies or in commercial greenhouses. Some of the work is done outside in fields or gardens. You may be able to receive on-the-job training for some positions.

There is a need for *technicians* in animal breeding. The technician may be asked to breed animals with specific traits for a research program. Technicians are also in charge of caring for the organisms and maintaining records about them. Guinea pigs, rabbits, mice, monkeys, and dogs are some of the animals used in genetics research.

To be qualified for a job as a technician, you will probably need at least two years of study in laboratory techniques. Technicians are needed by commercial laboratories, drug companies, medical schools, and research hospitals.

UNIT REVIEW

Synthesis

1. What do genetic and chromosomal mutations have in common with the process of hybridization? How are these processes important to evolution?
2. Most species of organisms reproduce sexually at some time during their life cycle. Why do you think this is an advantage?
3. A particular strain of roses has been inbred to produce large yellow blooms. These plants remain healthy only if fertilized properly, watered often, and protected chemically from insects and fungi. Wild roses, with their smaller, red blossoms, are able to thrive without any of these artificial aids. Explain why this is so.
4. How has modern science allowed harmful genes to remain in the human gene pool?
5. Although modern taxonomists attempt to classify organisms on the basis of their evolutionary relationships, in practice organisms are more often classified on the basis of their morphology. Why do you think this is true?
6. When Charles Darwin developed his theory of evolution, Mendel's principles of inheritance were unknown. How do the findings of modern genetics support the theory of evolution?
7. In a certain village, the population consists only of people descended from a small group that settled there several hundred years ago. No new people have moved into the village since then. What characteristics would you expect to find in the population?
8. It has been said that natural selection does not act on genes but on phenotypes. Give an example that supports this statement.

Additional Reading

Apgar, Virginia, and Joan Beck. *Is My Baby All Right?* Trident, 1980.

Bornstein, Jerry, and Sandy Bornstein. *What Is Genetics?* New York: Messner Publications, 1979.

Darwin, Charles, with R.E. Leakey. *The Illustrated Origin of Species.* New York: Hill and Wang, 1979.

Dawkins, Richard. *The Selfish Gene.* New York: Oxford University Press, 1976.

Gamon, Linda. "A New Recipe for Primordial Soup," *Science News,* January 31, 1981.

Gilbert, Lawrence E. "The Coevolution of a Butterfly and a Vine," *Scientific American,* August, 1982.

Gould, Stephen Jay. *The Panda's Thumb.* New York: W.W. Norton and Company, 1980.

Hamilton, W.R., A.R. Woolley, and A.C. Bishop. *The Larousse Guide to Minerals, Rocks, and Fossils.* New York: Larousse and Company, Inc., 1977.

Hitching, Francis. *The Neck of the Giraffe.* New Haven: Ticknor and Fields, 1982.

McKinnell, R.G. *Cloning: A Biologist Reports.* Minneapolis: University of Minnesota Press, 1979.

Silverstein, Alvin, and Virginia Silverstein. *The Genetics Explosion.* New York: Four Winds Press, 1980.

Singer, Sam. *Human Genetics.* San Francisco: W.H. Freeman and Co., 1978.

Valentine, James W. "The Evolution of Multicellular Plants and Animals," *Scientific American,* September, 1978.

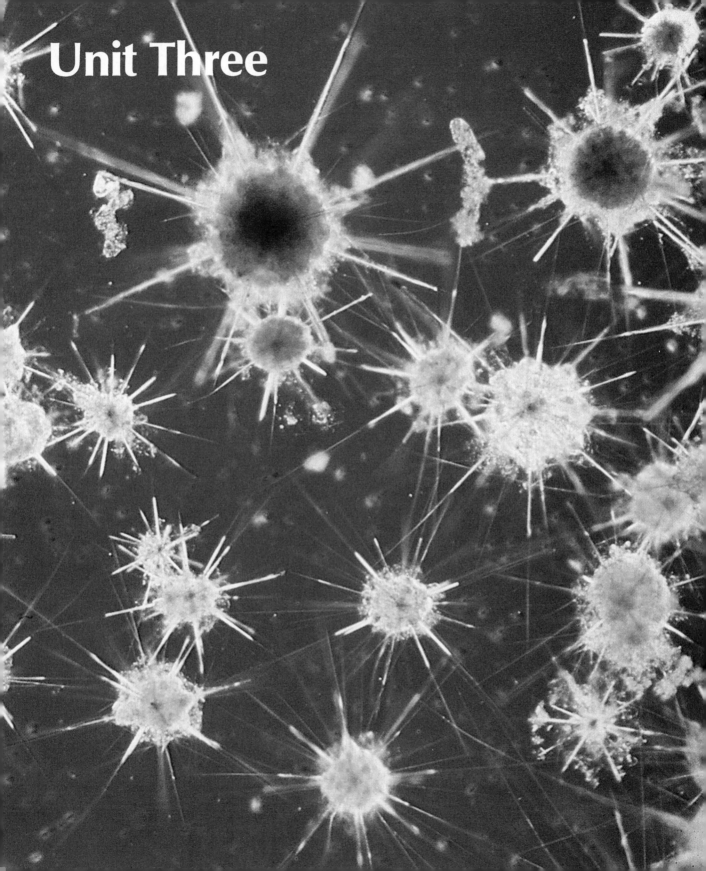

Unit Three

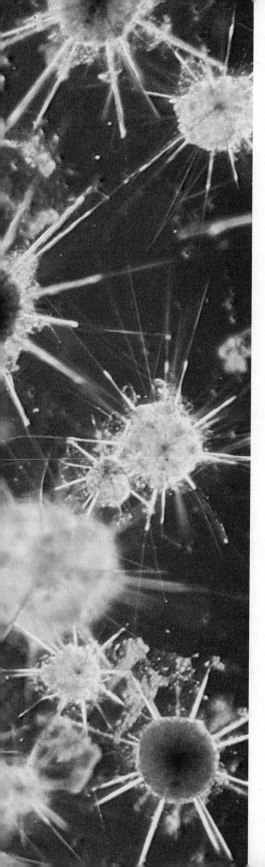

Monerans, Protists, and Fungi

Heliozoans, freshwater protists

16 Monerans and Viruses

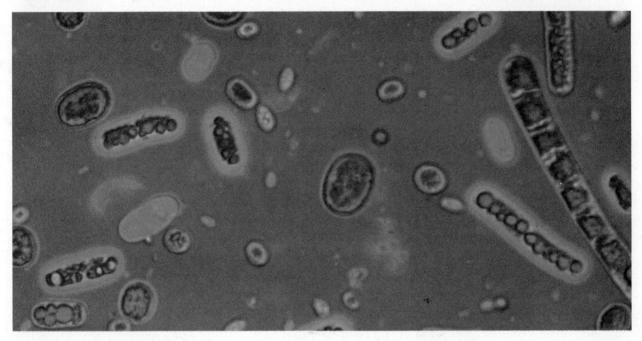

Unicellular and filamentous
cyanophytes in a drop of pond water

The organisms shown above are cyanophytes. Cyanophytes are also called blue-green algae. You may have seen mats of cyanophytes growing at the bottom of ponds. Often such mats are covered with silvery bubbles of oxygen.

Some of the oldest-known fossils may be remnants of early cyanophytes. Fossils as much as 3.5 billion years old contain traces of organic compounds similar to chlorophyll. This evidence indicates that the early cyanophytes were among the first photosynthetic organisms. Like autotrophs today, they probably used the energy of sunlight to transform carbon dioxide and water into sugar and oxygen.

The early atmosphere of Earth lacked oxygen. Cyanophytes may have been the first oxygen-producing organisms. After millions of years, the photosynthesis of cyanophytes allowed oxygen to accumulate in the atmosphere. This oxygen permitted the evolution of aerobic cells. Thus, silvery bubbles like those in ponds today may have set the stage for the evolution of all aerobic life.

Characteristics of Monerans

The smallest independently living things are prokaryotic organisms that belong to the kingdom Monera. Most monerans are far smaller than eukaryotes. A typical bacterium, for example, is about 2 micrometers long, whereas the average eukaryotic cell is about 50 to 200 micrometers long. Many monerans are single-celled organisms that are so small that between 5,000 and 10,000 could lie end to end across your thumbnail. Yet each of those monerans is a complete organism. Each one metabolizes food, produces wastes, grows, and reproduces. Packaged into each of these tiny organisms are all the nucleic acids, enzymes, and other substances necessary to carry out life processes.

CONCEPTS

- structure of moneran cells
- modes of moneran nutrition
- photosynthesis in cyanophytes and bacteria
- nitrogen fixation
- binary fission
- conjugation and transformation
- disease-causing bacteria

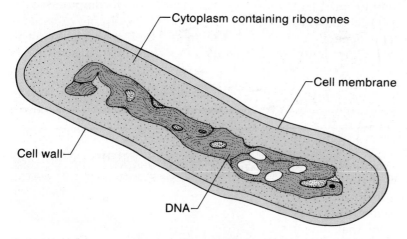

Cytoplasm containing ribosomes

Cell membrane

Cell wall

DNA

Figure 16.1 *Left*: Moneran. *Below*: Some differences between prokaryotes and eukaryotes

Prokaryotes

- no nuclear membranes
- no mitochondria
- no chloroplasts
- cell walls contain murein
- some contain chlorophyll
- some are motionless, others move by gliding or use of flagella
- most are unicellular

Eukaryotes

- have nuclei and nuclear membranes
- have mitochondria
- some have chloroplasts that contain chlorophyll
- cell walls, if present, lack murein
- movement can occur by means of flagella, contractile fibrils, cilia, and amoeboid movement; some are motionless
- many are multicellular

16–1 Moneran Cells

All monerans are prokaryotes. The cells of prokaryotes are so different from those of eukaryotes that biologists classify them in completely separate kingdoms. The major differences between prokaryotes and eukaryotes are listed in Figure 16.1.

Almost all monerans have a cell wall. Unlike the cellulose cell wall of plants, however, the cell wall of monerans is made of a nitrogen-containing polysaccharide called **murein** [MYOOR-ee-uhn]. Murein is not found in the cells of organisms from any other kingdom.

16–2 Nutrition in Monerans

Though the cell structure of prokaryotes differs from that of eukaryotes, the metabolic processes are remarkably similar in the two types of organisms.

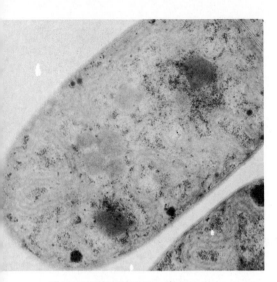

Figure 16.2 A cyanophyte photosynthesizes using chlorophyll located on its cytoplasmic membranes.

There are two major groups of monerans, the **bacteria** and the **cyanophytes** [sy-AHN-uh-fyts]. All of the cyanophytes are autotrophic. Cyanophytes contain chlorophyll, but they do not have chloroplasts. Instead, their chlorophyll is located on cytoplasmic membranes. The process of photosynthesis in cyanophytes is similar to that in eukaryotes.

Most members of the second group of monerans, the bacteria, are heterotrophs that feed by secreting enzymes into their environment. These enzymes break down large molecules of food. The resulting smaller molecules are absorbed through the cell membrane.

Many bacteria live independently in soil or water. These species are usually **saprobes** [SAP-rohbz], organisms that feed on dead plants or animals. Saprobes convert this organic matter into simple chemicals. Because they break down decaying material, saprobes are also called **decomposers**.

Other bacteria live on or in the bodies of living organisms and depend on their host for food. Often bacteria living in other organisms have little effect on their host. In some cases

NEWSBREAK

Until very recently, scientists thought that all communities of living things were dependent upon the sun for energy. But marine scientists have discovered a new group of monerans that are independent of sunlight. They live deep in the ocean around cracks in the ocean floor. Heat from Earth's interior heats up the water around the cracks to several hundred degrees. The hot water combines with chemicals in the rock of Earth's crust to produce hydrogen sulfide (H_2S). Bacteria break down the H_2S bonds to synthesize carbohydrates, just as plants use energy from the sun to synthesize carbohydrates.

These bacteria are called chemoautotrophs. Clams, mussels, crabs and other organisms depend on the chemosynthetic bacteria for food. The giant tube worms shown here live at depths of 2.5 kilometers, where they feed on chemosynthetic bacteria. Such organisms represent a rare exception to the general rule that organisms depend upon the sun for energy.

they may even be beneficial. For example, bacteria live in the digestive tract of many large grazing animals. Without these bacteria, sheep and cows would not be able to digest the cellulose of grass. These bacteria have a warm, moist environment and absorb food from the animal's intestine. Thus both organisms benefit from the association.

Sometimes bacteria harm their host. Organisms that harm their host are called **parasites**. Bacteria that cause diseases in humans are examples of parasites.

Many heterotrophic bacteria are anaerobes. They break down food in the absence of oxygen. As you read in Chapter 7, this process produces only two ATP molecules for every glucose molecule. Yet these bacteria can live in environments where aerobic organisms cannot survive, such as mud at the bottom of still ponds. Anaerobes are classified by their metabolic wastes. For example, some anaerobes produce acetic acid. Others produce lactic acid.

Certain bacteria are poisoned by oxygen. These are called **obligate anaerobes**. **Facultative anaerobes** are organisms that do not use oxygen but are not harmed when it is present.

Aerobic bacteria are also common. Aerobes require oxygen for cellular respiration. While the chemistry of aerobic respiration in bacteria is similar to that in eukaryotes, prokaryotes do not have mitochondria. Instead, the electron transport proteins of respiration are built into the cell membrane.

Some bacteria are autotrophic. These bacteria do not have chlorophyll, however. The photosynthetic pigment in these species, which is either purple or green, is chemically very different from chlorophyll. Instead of using water as a source of electrons, autotrophic bacteria use the compound hydrogen sulfide (H_2S). Instead of oxygen, this reaction gives off sulfur. This is the chemical equation for bacterial photosynthesis.

$$12H_2S + 6CO_2 \longrightarrow C_6H_{12}O_6 + 12S + 6H_2O$$

16–3 Nitrogen-Fixing Monerans

All living things require nitrogen for the synthesis of proteins and nucleic acids. Air is about 80 percent nitrogen gas (N_2), but most organisms cannot use nitrogen in this form. Some monerans, however, can capture the nitrogen in the atmosphere. This process is called **nitrogen fixation**. Nitrogen fixers have an enzyme that converts nitrogen gas into nitrates (NO_3^-), a form of nitrogen that monerans and other organisms can use.

Nitrogen-fixing cyanophytes and bacteria supply nitrogen to eukaryotic organisms in a usable form. Plants like clover, beans, and alfalfa have large populations of nitrogen-fixing bacteria growing in swollen areas of their roots. In this re-

Figure 16.3 The swollen areas of these roots contain nitrogen-fixing bacteria.

Monerans and Viruses **237**

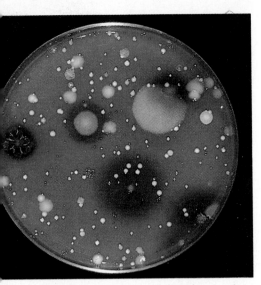

Figure 16.4 Agar contains the nutrient medium for the growth and reproduction of bacteria.

lationship the bacteria receive food from the plant, while the bacteria permit the plant to grow in nitrogen-poor soils.

16–4   Growing Bacteria in Laboratories

In addition to food, all organisms must take other substances from the environment for the maintenance of cell structure. Understanding the nutritional requirements of bacteria allows scientists to cultivate these organisms in the laboratory. A **growth medium** is a substance that allows the growth and reproduction of an organism. For heterotrophic bacteria, the growth medium usually contains water, food molecules such as sugars, a source of nitrogen, and minerals.

Bacteria can be grown in flasks containing such a medium. The medium often contains **agar**. Agar is a liquid when heated, but at room temperature it solidifies like gelatin. Bacteria can grow on the agar surface and absorb food molecules from the medium by diffusion.

A single bacterium that settles on an agar dish will grow and reproduce. Millions of descendants of the original cell will soon form a visible colony on the surface of the agar. Some monerans require a very simple growth medium. For example, some bacteria will grow on a medium with only glucose, nitrate ions, and a few minerals. Other bacteria require a complex medium containing amino acids, vitamins, and other substances the cell cannot make for itself.

16–5   Reproduction in Monerans

Moneran cells do not divide by mitosis. Yet monerans do have several methods of copying their genetic material and passing copies on to new generations. By far the most common method of moneran reproduction is simple cell division. Bacteria reproduce by **binary fission**. Binary fission is different from the process of mitosis in eukaryotic cells. There is no condensing of chromosomes and no formation of spindle fibers. Bacteria have only one chromosome, a single, circular molecule of DNA. During binary fission the molecule copies itself, and

Figure 16.5 This electron micrograph shows the single chromosome of a bacterium.

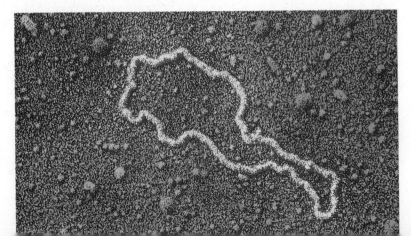

one copy goes to each end of the cell. The cytoplasm pinches in half to form two new cells.

Many cyanophytes and some bacteria can form **spores**. Spores are reproductive cells that originate from asexual division. Spores contain extra nutrients and can survive long dry periods.

16–6   Exchange of Genetic Material

Monerans do not reproduce sexually. They do not undergo meiosis, nor do they form gametes that fuse to form a zygote. There are, however, several ways in which the genetic material of monerans can be recombined. Two of these methods are conjugation and transformation.

The process of **conjugation** is shown in Figure 16.6. In addition to a large chromosome, some bacteria contain additional genetic information in the form of small circular molecules of DNA. These molecules are called **plasmids**. The plasmids of some bacteria carry a sex factor. Bacteria that carry the sex factor can conjugate with cells that do not carry the factor.

In conjugation, a bridge of cytoplasm forms between the two cells. The cell that carries the sex factor makes a copy of its chromosome. The DNA copy begins to move across the bridge into the second cell. The bridge usually breaks before

Figure 16.6 The conjugation of *Escherichia coli* produces bacteria with new gene combinations.

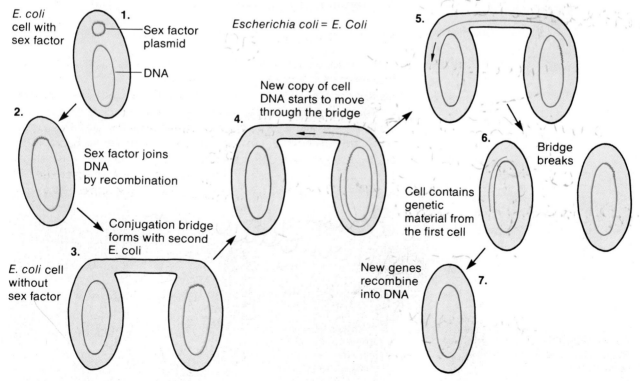

E. coli cell with sex factor
1.
Sex factor plasmid
DNA

Escherichia coli = E. Coli

2.
Sex factor joins DNA by recombination

Conjugation bridge forms with second E. coli

3.
E. coli cell without sex factor

4.
New copy of cell DNA starts to move through the bridge

5.

6.
Bridge breaks

Cell contains genetic material from the first cell

New genes recombine into DNA

7.

the entire chromosome is transferred, so the recipient cell receives only part of the genes of the donor cell. The recipient cell may then incorporate the new genes into its chromosomes. Like the sexual reproduction of eukaryotes, conjugation results in cells with new combinations of genes. But in conjugation there is no meiosis or fusion of gametes.

Another process by which bacteria can obtain new genes, called **transformation**, has been observed in laboratory experiments. In transformation, bacteria absorb DNA molecules from their surrounding medium. Transformation of *Escherichia coli* cells is shown in Figure 16.7. Most *E. coli* cells can make all the necessary amino acids from simple chemicals in the medium. Some mutant *E. coli* cells lack the ability to make certain amino acids. For example, one mutant form cannot make the amino acid lysine. This bacterium will not grow unless the agar contains lysine.

If DNA from *E. coli* that can make lysine is added to a culture of cells that cannot make it, then some of the cells will be transformed. These cells incorporate the lysine-manufacturing genes into their genome by recombination. Transformed cells can grow on a medium without lysine. The processes of conjugation and transformation are used frequently in the study of bacterial genetics. Recombinant DNA, which is described in Chapter 12, uses these processes to develop new strains of bacteria.

Figure 16.7 This experimental procedure shows how transformation can give mutant *E. coli* the genetic material for making lysine.

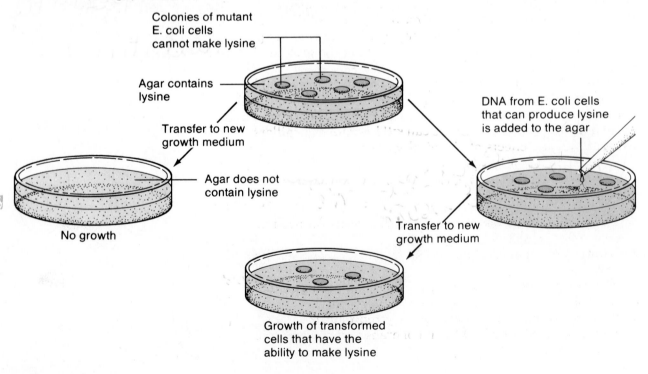

Colonies of mutant
E. coli cells
cannot make lysine

Agar contains
lysine

Transfer to new
growth medium

Agar does not
contain lysine

No growth

DNA from E. coli cells
that can produce lysine
is added to the agar

Transfer to new
growth medium

Growth of transformed
cells that have the
ability to make lysine

Figure 16.8 Bacteria convert the enormous numbers of leaves that fall each year into simple chemicals that enrich the soil.

Figure 16.9 Deer rely on bacteria in their digestive systems to break down the cellulose in the grass they eat.

16–7   Bacteria and Disease

Parasitic bacteria cause many human diseases. Food poisoning, tuberculosis, and strep throat are just a few examples. Farm animals and plants are also susceptible to a number of bacterial diseases. Still other bacteria are responsible for the spoilage of food. Humans spend billions of dollars each year trying to preserve food. Heating, salting, refrigerating, and adding chemicals are all ways of slowing the growth of bacteria on foods.

Only a small percentage of bacterial species are harmful to humans. A significant number of bacteria are very helpful. For example, some bacteria cause diseases of pest organisms. Spraying these bacteria on crops can kill harmful caterpillars without the side effects of chemical sprays.

Checkpoint

1. What term describes an organism that feeds on dead or decaying materials?
2. What terms describe an organism that is poisoned by oxygen?
3. In what process do monerans convert nitrogen gas into compounds that are useful to other organisms?
4. By what process do bacteria usually reproduce?
5. Name two processes by which monerans exchange genetic information.

Diversity of Monerans

Inconspicuous as they are, monerans are a diverse and wide-ranging group of organisms. It is difficult to find a place where these organisms do not live. They are found in the hottest deserts and the coldest, driest parts of the Antarctic. One species has even been found growing in the fuel tanks of jet airplanes.

Monerans are classified into two subkingdoms, the subkingdom Schizophyta and the subkingdom Cyanophyta.

CONCEPTS

- characteristics of schizophytes and cyanophytes
- typical forms of eubacteria
- major phyla of schizophytes
- cell specialization in monerans

16–8   Subkingdom Schizophyta

The **schizophytes** [SKIHZ-uh-fyts] include the bacteria and related forms. There are about 15,000 species in this subkingdom. Taxonomists base classification within subkingdoms on features such as cell shape, energy source, and the chemistry of the cell wall.

Phylum Eubacteria   Most schizophytes are **eubacteria** [yew-bak-TIHR-ee-uh]. Several typical shapes of eubacteria are shown in Figure 16.10. Spherical eubacteria are called **cocci** [KAHK-seye]. Rod-shaped eubacteria are called **bacilli** [buh-SIHL-eye]. Spiral-shaped eubacteria are called **spirilla** [speye-RIHL-uh].

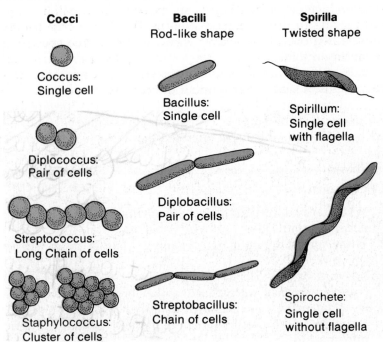

Cocci

Coccus:
Single cell

Diplococcus:
Pair of cells

Streptococcus:
Long Chain of cells

Staphylococcus:
Cluster of cells

Bacilli
Rod-like shape

Bacillus:
Single cell

Diplobacillus:
Pair of cells

Streptobacillus:
Chain of cells

Spirilla
Twisted shape

Spirillum:
Single cell
with flagella

Spirochete:
Single cell
without flagella

Figure 16.10 Many bacteria can be classified by their distinctive shapes.

Some eubacteria have distinctively colored pigments. Other bacteria have **flagella** [fluh-JEHL-uh], whiplike structures that move the cells.

A characteristic of many eubacteria is their ability to form thick-walled cells called **endospores** [EHN-doh-spawrz]. An endospore is a resting stage that allows the bacteria to withstand extremes of temperature and drought. If the environment becomes too dry or too hot, a thick wall forms inside the cell. This wall encloses the nuclear material and some cytoplasm. Endospores can withstand boiling water and have been known to survive dry conditions for as long as 50 years.

Eubacteria live in a wide variety of habitats, including some extremely harsh environments that are uninhabitable by most organisms. A few eubacteria live in the Great Salt Lake in Utah, which has almost four times the salt concentration of sea water. Other species occupy hot springs, where temperatures can reach 90°C and the water is strongly acidic.

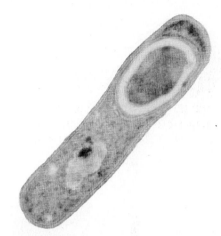

Figure 16.11 An endospore can withstand extreme changes in the environment.

Phylum Myxobacteria **Myxobacteria** [mix-oh-bak-TIHR-ee-uh] are the closest thing to multicellular organisms in the moneran kingdom. The cells of a species live in colonies that glide along the forest floor. The means by which the entire colony moves as a unit is not well understood. Most myxobacteria absorb food from decaying leaves or wood.

When conditions become unfavorable for movement and feeding, the colony stops moving. Cells pile on top of one another, forming a stalk. At the top of the stalk is a swollen structure called a **fruiting body**. Within the fruiting body, individual cells form resistant spores. Wind blows the spores to new locations. Under favorable conditions each spore can reproduce and form a new colony. Movement and the formation of fruiting bodies require cell specialization and communication, traits that are not found in other schizophytes.

Figure 16.12 Scanning electron micrograph showing a myxobacterium with fruiting bodies

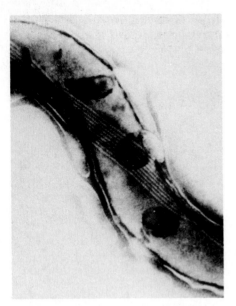

Figure 16.13 Electron micrograph of spirochetes showing axial filaments.

Phylum Chlamydobacteria Most **chlamydobacteria** [klah-muh-duh-bak-TIHR-ee-uh] are soil organisms. Most are harmless, but two species in the genus *Mycobacterium* cause severe human diseases — tuberculosis and leprosy. These bacteria have a tendency to form interconnecting filaments.

The genus *Streptomyces* contains species that are the source of some of the most useful **antibiotics**. Antibiotics kill or slow the growth of other bacteria. Humans have learned to isolate these antibiotics and use them to kill many disease-causing bacteria.

Phylum Spirochaetes Many **spirochetes** [SPY-ruh-keets] are anaerobes that live in mud or water. A few species are parasitic. One parasitic spirochete is *Treponema pallidum*, which causes syphilis in humans.

Spirochetes have a spiral shape much like the eubacterial spirilla. Unlike the spirilla, they possess an **axial filament**. The axial filament is a series of fibers located between the cell membrane and the cell wall. By twisting and coiling rapidly, the axial filament helps the organism move.

Phylum Rickettsia Rickettsiae [rih-KEHT-see-ee] are very small parasitic bacteria that live and reproduce within eukaryotic host cells. Rickettsiae cause several human diseases, including epidemic typhus.

Phylum Mycoplasma Mycoplasmas [my-koh-PLAZ-muhz] are parasites that live inside cells. They are even smaller than rickettsiae, and they have no cell wall. Absence of a cell wall makes the mycoplasmas unique among the monerans. Biologists believe these cells are at the lower limit of size for a living thing. Anything smaller could not hold the number of molecules necessary for metabolism.

Some mycoplasmas cause diseases in animals and humans. One type causes a rather mild form of pneumonia in children and young adults.

16–9 Subkingdom Cyanophyta

The subkingdom Cyanophyta has only about 1,500 species. Because they are photosynthetic, members of this subkingdom were once classified as plants and called blue-green algae. Their prokaryotic cell structure, however, indicates that the cyanophytes are much more closely related to the bacteria than to plants or protists.

Cyanophytes occur in a wide variety of locations. Many live in fresh water or moist soils. Only a few species are marine. Some cyanophytes are able to live in the acidic water of hot springs.

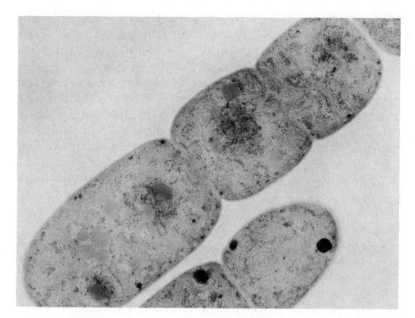

Cyanophytes also have two photosynthetic pigments not found in eukaryotic plants. **Phycocyanin** [fy-coh-SY-ahn-uhn] is a blue pigment that gives many of the species a characteristic blue-green color. Some species contain **phycoerythrin** [fy-coh-EHR-uh-thrihn], a red pigment that makes the cells red or brown.

Some cyanophytes are single-celled; others form small colonies. Most species secrete a gelatin sheath or capsule outside of the cell wall.

Many cyanophytes are multicellular, with cells joined end to end in long green filaments. To reproduce, the chains of cells simply break into pieces. Cells at the broken ends divide, thus increasing the length of the new filament.

Some filamentous cyanophytes, such as the *Nostoc* shown in Figure 16.15, contain thick-walled cells called **heterocysts**. Heterocysts contain the enzymes for nitrogen fixation, but do not contain chlorophyll. Heterocysts supply the other cells of the filament with nitrogen compounds. The other cells, in turn, supply the heterocysts with food from photosynthesis. Thus these cyanophytes exhibit some cell specialization.

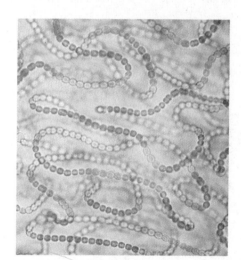

Figure 16.15 *Nostoc* has a filamentous structure.

Checkpoint

1. What shape are the cells of cocci? Of bacilli? Of spirilla?
2. What is the drought-resistant resting stage of a bacterium called?
3. How do spirochetes move?
4. What specialized function do heterocysts perform?

- structure of viruses and viroids
- reproduction of lytic and lyso-genic viruses
- process of transduction

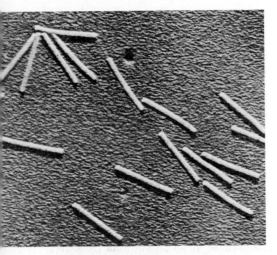

Figure 16.16 Electron micrograph of a tobacco mosaic virus

Figure 16.17 Adenoviruses have a geometric packing arrangement.

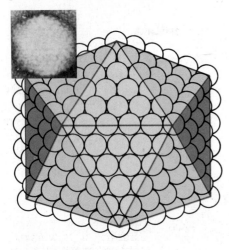

Viruses

In 1892, a Russian biologist, Dmitri Iwanowski, made an unexpected discovery. Iwanowski was studying a disease of tobacco plants called mosaic disease, which makes the leaves appear spotted. When Iwanowski rubbed juice from the leaves of an infected plant on the leaves of a healthy plant, the healthy plant developed the disease. Iwanowski assumed that bacteria caused the disease. To isolate the cause of the disease, he poured juice from an infected plant through a filter with pores so small that no bacteria could get through. He was very surprised when the clear, filtered fluid continued to transmit the disease.

The cause of mosaic disease was too small to be seen with a light microscope. Over the next 50 years, scientists discovered a number of diseases of plants and animals caused by particles that were invisible under a light microscope. The electron microscope finally showed the structure of these particles, which are called **viruses**. Viruses are particles that consist of a single molecule of nucleic acid surrounded by a coat of protein molecules.

16–10   Structure of Viruses

The most obvious characteristic of viruses is their incredibly small size. They range in diameter from 0.03 to 0.30 micrometers. The largest virus has about one tenth the volume of the smallest eubacterium.

The nucleic acid molecule of a virus may be a double or a single stranded molecule of DNA. A few kinds of viruses have a molecule of single or double stranded RNA. The amount of nucleic acid in a virus is much smaller than the amount in any cell. The smallest eubacteria have enough DNA for about 2,000 genes. Many viruses have only 10 genes; even the largest viruses have only about 100 genes.

The protein coat surrounding the nucleic-acid core is usually made of several hundred protein molecules packed together in a geometric pattern. Some larger viruses, such as the human influenza virus, also have a very complex capsule surrounding the protein coat.

Viral genes carry instructions for the production of new virus particles, yet the virus has no ribosomes or other cytoplasmic structures to carry out the genetic instructions. Viruses cannot live independently. They are all parasites of living cells. Viruses use the energy and protein-producing machinery of cells to make new virus particles.

Each type of virus infects a particular kind of cell in a host organism. The tobacco mosaic virus infects the cells of tobacco plants. The common cold in humans is caused by a virus that infects cells lining the respiratory tract.

Some viruses infect bacteria. Such viruses are called **bacteriophage** [bak-TIHR-ee-uh-fayj], or phage for short. Some bacteriophages have an unusual appearance. The phage that infects *E. coli*, for example, has a tail attached to the protein coat. At the base of the tail there are several long fibers that look like spider legs.

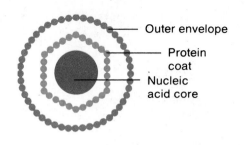

16–11   Reproduction of Viruses

The reproductive cycle of the *E. coli* phage shown in Figure 16.19 is typical of many viruses. The tail fibers are made of proteins with a shape that matches molecules in the cell membrane of *E. coli*. This molecular matching process explains why most viruses recognize and infect only one kind of host cell.

Once attached to its host cell, the phage acts like a syringe and injects its DNA into the host. Inside the cell the phage DNA takes over the cytoplasmic machinery of the host cell. Host cell enzymes and nucleotides make many duplicate copies of phage DNA. Host cell ribosomes make coat and tail fiber protein according to the instructions of the phage genes.

The newly synthesized phage protein and nucleic acids come together in the cell and form as many as several hundred new phage particles. The final step is for the phage DNA to instruct the host cell to self-destruct. The host cell makes an enzyme that **lyses** [LEYE-sehz], or digests, the bacterial cell wall, thus releasing the new phage particles. Each new phage can repeat the reproductive cycle if it comes in contact with an uninfected *E. coli*. A reproductive cycle like that of the *E. coli* phage is called a **lytic** [LIHT-ihk] **cycle**.

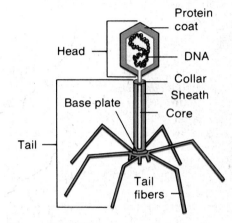

Figure 16.18 The structural features of a common virus and bacteriophage

Figure 16.19 Reproductive cycle of an *E. coli* phage

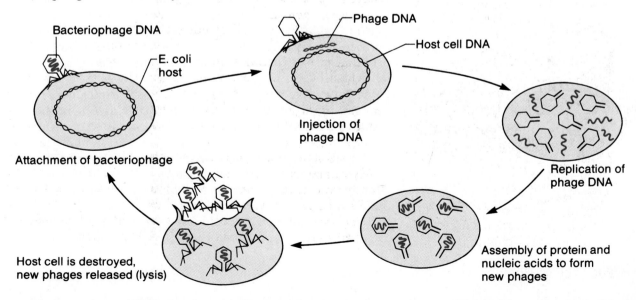

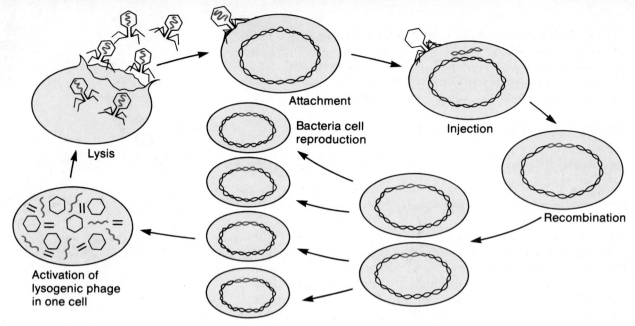

Figure 16.20 Reproductive cycle of a lysogenic virus

Some viruses have a modified lytic cycle. The human influenza virus, for example, does not lyse the host cell. It exits the host cell by pushing out through the cell membrane. Such viruses have capsules that consist partly of host cell membrane and partly of viral protein embedded in the membrane.

Some viruses have a very different reproductive cycle, which is shown in Figure 16.20. After entering a cell, the viral DNA inserts itself into the host cell DNA by recombination. That is, the virus DNA becomes part of the host cell DNA. Although it becomes part of the host DNA, the viral DNA does not take over the host cell. When the host cell reproduces its genetic content, the viral genes are also duplicated. For many generations of the host cell, there may be no active viral particles produced. Occasionally, however, the virus DNA will become active in a host cell and trigger reproduction. Viruses that reproduce in this way are called **lysogenic viruses**.

When lysogenic phage DNA becomes active in a host cell, it breaks out of the host DNA. As it breaks loose, the phage may take several bacterial genes with it. In the next infection cycle, the phage can carry bacterial genes from the previous host cell to the new host. Carrying genes from one bacterium to another in a lysogenic phage is a process called **transduction** [trans-DUK-shuhn]. In addition to conjugation and transformation, transduction is a way in which bacteria increase genetic variety. Scientists use lysogenic phages in recombinant DNA research. These phages can transfer a desired gene into the chromosome of a bacterium.

Lysogenic viruses cause cold sores. Certain lysogenic viruses are also under suspicion in the study of human cancer. For over 50 years scientists have known that viruses cause some cancers in animals. Proof that viruses cause human cancers has been elusive. There is strong evidence, however, that some lysogenic viruses can transform human DNA. Such transformations might result in the host cell's becoming cancerous.

16–12   Are Viruses Alive?

Like all living things, viruses contain nucleic acids and proteins. The presence of these molecules might indicate that viruses are also living things. Recall, though, that viruses by themselves can neither make nor use food, nor can they grow or reproduce. The host cell performs these functions for the virus. So is the virus a living thing?

It might be easier to answer this question if scientists knew the origin of viruses. Some scientists hypothesize that viruses are descendants of structures that developed in the early oceans before the first cells appeared. These structures then became parasites of the first living cells. According to this hypothesis, viruses were never independently living organisms.

A second hypothesis states that viruses evolved from bacteria similar to the mycoplasmas or rickettsiae. Through natural selection, these cells lost all structures except those necessary to transfer genes from one host to another. If this hypothesis is correct, viruses could be considered living things.

A third hypothesis is that viruses are simply genes that have escaped from the genomes of living cells. Unfortunately there is little evidence to support any of these ideas. The question of whether viruses are alive now, or ever were alive, is one that scientists today cannot answer.

The question has been further complicated by the recent discovery of **viroids**. Viroids are short pieces of RNA with no protein coat. They cause several plant diseases. Little is known about them except that they have a reproductive cycle similar to that of viruses. Viroids make viruses look large and complex. The shortest nucleic acid in any known virus is about 5000 bases long. Viroids are only about 350 bases long.

 BIOLOGY INSIGHTS

All viruses of a particular type are identical in size. Each is assembled from the same number of small pieces. Thus viruses lack one of the important characteristics of life — the ability to grow.

Checkpoint

1. What kind of viruses infect bacteria?
2. What two substances do all viruses contain?
3. What kind of viruses insert their DNA into the chromosome of a host cell?
4. By what process do viruses carry bacterial genes from one bacterium to another?
5. What is a viroid?

CHAPTER REVIEW

Summary

- Monerans are prokaryotic organisms. Most monerans have cell walls containing murein.
- Schizophytes are primarily heterotrophic, bacterialike organisms. Cyanophytes are autotrophic prokaryotes that contain chlorophyll.
- There are both anaerobic and aerobic monerans. Anaerobes occupy habitats where there is little or no oxygen. Obligate anaerobes are poisoned by oxygen.
- Nitrogen-fixing cyanophytes and bacteria are able to transform the nitrogen in the atmosphere into compounds that are usable by other organisms.
- Cyanophytes reproduce asexually by the fragmentation of filaments or by spore formation. Bacteria reproduce asexually by binary fission.
- Bacteria have several ways of achieving genetic variability. Conjugation, transformation, and transduction are all mechanisms by which genes can be transferred from one bacterium to another.
- Bacteria affect humans in a number of ways. Some cause disease or spoil foods. Many bacteria, however, are useful. Some bacteria maintain soil fertility by decomposing dead organisms. Certain species fix nitrogen. Other bacteria produce antibiotics, which doctors can use to control disease-causing species.
- Monerans are classified according to their physical appearance, nutritional requirements, and cell chemistry.
- Some monerans are multicellular. Myxobacteria form moving colonies and reproduce by developing fruiting bodies. Some filamentous cyanophytes have nitrogen-fixing cells called heterocysts.
- Viruses are made of a nucleic-acid core surrounded by a protein capsule. All viruses re-

produce inside living cells and use the cells' machinery to make new virus particles.
- Some viruses reproduce through a lytic cycle; others are lysogenic.
- Scientists are unsure of the evolutionary origin of viruses.

Vocabulary

agar	lysogenic virus
antibiotic	lytic cycle
axial filament	murein
bacilli	mycoplasma
bacteriophage	myxobacteria
bacterium	nitrogen fixation
binary fission	obligate anaerobe
chlamydobacteria	parasite
cocci	phycocyanin
conjugation	phycoerythrin
cyanophyte	plasmid
decomposers	rickettsia
endospore	saprobe
eubacteria	schizophyte
facultative	spirilli
anaerobe	spirochete
flagella	spore
fruiting body	transduction
growth medium	transformation
heterocyst	viroid
lyse	virus

Review

1. Name two kinds of parasitic schizophytes that live inside cells of host organisms.
2. What pigment makes some cyanophytes appear red?
3. Name two waste products of anaerobic breakdown of glucose by bacteria.
4. What do autotrophic bacteria use as a source of electrons?
5. What substance is used to solidify bacterial growth mediums?

6. What structure carries the sex factor of certain bacteria?
7. What are the asexual reproductive cells of cyanophytes called?
8. In what process are genes transferred between cells through a cytoplasmic bridge?
9. Give an example of an organism that depends on bacteria to digest cellulose.
10. Name the two moneran subkingdoms.
11. What is the basic food of myxobacteria?
12. Name a human disease caused by a spirochete.
13. From what kind of bacteria are antibiotics produced?
14. What are the products of bacterial photosynthesis?
15. Name two types of viral life cycles.

In the following list, match the moneran with the appropriate characteristic.

16. eubacteria
17. chlamydobacteria
18. cyanophyte
19. myxobacteria
20. rickettsia
21. mycoplasma
22. spirochete

a. no murein cell wall
b. phycocyanin
c. spiral, rod, or sphere
d. source of antibiotics
e. one species causes syphilis
f. cell parasite with cell wall
g. develop fruiting body

Interpret and Apply

1. How many average-sized bacteria cells would fit across the diameter of a typical eukaryotic cell?
2. List three ways in which prokaryotes differ from eukaryotes.
3. How do most bacteria feed?
4. Describe the difference between facultative and obligate anaerobes.
5. What is the difference between autotrophic cyanophytes and autotrophic bacteria?
6. How does bacterial conjugation differ from transformation?

7. How are rickettsiae and mycoplasmas different from other bacterial parasites?
8. What kinds of organisms can fix nitrogen?
9. List some of the principal habitats of cyanophytes.
10. Give an example of cell specialization in monerans.
11. Describe how the first virus was discovered.
12. What kinds of nucleic acids occur in viruses?

Challenge

1. You are given an agar plate with a colony of bacteria growing on it. If this colony is made up of a species that cannot synthesize guanine, what conclusion can you draw about the composition of the growth medium?
2. What characteristics of myxobacteria make these organisms a little like multicellular organisms?
3. Why is the evolution of cyanophytes believed to have occurred before the evolution of eukaryotes?
4. In what ways are viruses different from rickettsiae?
5. Explain why viruses must be parasites.

Projects

1. Bacteria and viruses can sometimes be used to control organisms that are pests to humans. Find out in the library how bacteria are being used to control gypsy moths, Dutch elm disease, or some other pest organism.
2. Collect some water from a nearby pond or lake and examine it with a microscope for cyanophytes. Be sure to collect some of the stringy green material that you see around the edges of the shore. Use a field guide to identify some of the species you collect.
3. Find out how a modern sewage-treatment facility works and what role bacteria play in the operation of such a plant.
4. Find out how yogurt, sourdough bread, or cheese is made. Yogurt is easy to make — you might want to give it a try.

17 Protists

Diatoms

Floating near the surface of the seas are billions of tiny organisms called plankton. The word *plankton* comes from a Greek word meaning "wanderer." Planktonic organisms are not attached anywhere. Instead they simply drift with the ocean currents.

The diatoms shown in the photograph above are among the most common kinds of photosynthetic plankton. Diatoms are tiny unicellular organisms with cell walls composed of two parts. The two pieces of the cell wall fit together like the top and bottom of a shoe box. Diatoms occur in a fantastic variety of geometric shapes. Some are round, some are triangular, and some are long and narrow like needles. Their cell walls are sculptured with delicate patterns.

Despite their small size, diatoms are food for countless other organisms. They are so abundant that they are the major photosynthetic organisms in much of the sea, as well as in many lakes and ponds. Creatures ranging in size from the tiniest protists to the biggest whales rely on plankton as their ultimate source of food.

Plantlike Protists

The single-celled organism shown in Figure 17.1 is a member of the genus *Euglena*. Its bright green color indicates that it is photosynthetic. Unlike the cyanophytes, however, this organism is eukaryotic. Its chlorophyll is confined to chloroplasts and it has a nuclear membrane. At one end of the euglena is a whiplike structure that propels it through the water.

When biologists tried to classify all organisms as either plants or animals, organisms like the euglena presented a serious problem. Euglena's chloroplasts identify it as a plant. Yet its lack of a cell wall and its ability to swim are more like an animal. To resolve this issue, taxonomists created the kingdom Protista. Protists are those organisms that cannot be classified as monerans, fungi, plants, or animals.

Unlike monerans, protists are eukaryotic. They have nuclei with a surrounding membrane, mitochondria, and other organelles. Almost all the protists are single-celled organisms, though a few are colonies of nearly identical cells. All protists reproduce by mitosis and cell division. Many forms also reproduce sexually.

The protists are a diverse group. Some protist groups are primarily autotrophic and are classified as plantlike protists. Others are primarily heterotrophic and are classified as animal-like protists. There are about 10,000 species in the three phyla of autotrophic, or plantlike, protists.

CONCEPTS

- distinction between protists and monerans
- characteristics of the three phyla of plantlike protists
- structure and function of flagella
- anatomy of a typical euglena, dinoflagellate, and diatom
- function of the contractile vacuole

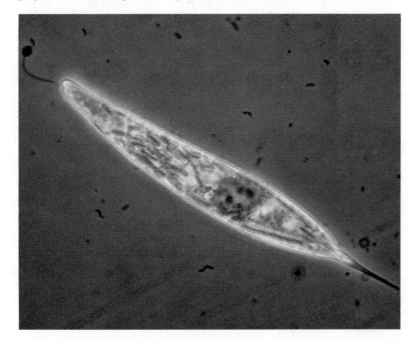

Figure 17.1 A euglena is a single-celled protist.

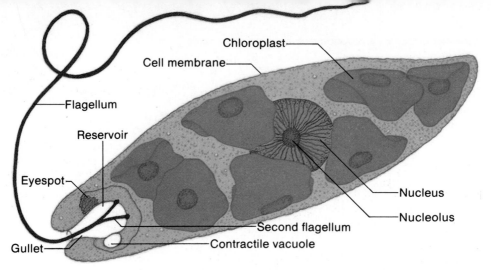

Figure 17.2 The structural features of a euglena

Labels: Chloroplast, Cell membrane, Flagellum, Reservoir, Eyespot, Gullet, Nucleus, Nucleolus, Second flagellum, Contractile vacuole

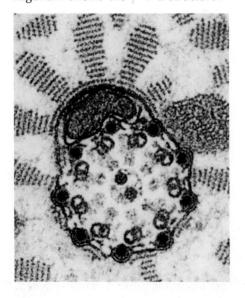

Figure 17.3 This cross-section of a flagellum shows the 9 + 2 structure.

17–1 Phylum Euglenophyta

Like *Euglena*, most members of the phylum **Euglenophyta** [yoo-GLEE-nuh-fy-tuh] have chloroplasts and are autotrophic. Some euglenoids are heterotrophic and do not have chloroplasts. A few species are parasitic.

The internal structure of *Euglena*, a typical euglenoid, is shown in Figure 17.2. Each cell contains a large nucleus and nucleolus.

Usually bright green chloroplasts are distributed throughout the cytoplasm. If a euglena grows in the dark for several days, its chloroplasts disappear. Without chloroplasts, the cell survives by absorbing nutrients through the cell membrane. When the euglena is exposed to light again, chloroplasts reappear and photosynthesis resumes.

Euglenas move by means of whiplike structures called **flagella** [fluh-JEHL-uh]. Flagella (singular, *flagellum*) are common in many eukaryotes. All eukaryotic flagella have the same structure. Each flagellum is an extension of the cell membrane with 11 microtubules inside. As shown in Figure 17.3, the 9 outer tubules are double and the 2 inner tubules are single. This organization is referred to as the 9 + 2 structure.

Each euglena has two flagella — one long and one short. The long flagellum propels the cell through the water. Scientists are unsure of the function of the smaller flagellum. Both flagella are attached at the **reservoir**, a depression at the front end of the cell. The long flagellum emerges through the **gullet**, a canal that opens into the reservoir.

Near the reservoir is a mass of red pigment called the **eyespot**. The eyespot is sensitive to light. When the euglena senses light, its flagellum allows it to swim toward the light source. This ability is a useful adaptation in a photosynthetic organism.

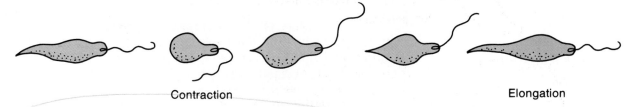

Contraction   Elongation

Euglena does not have a cell wall. On the outer surface of its cell are spiral strips of protein. The protein forms a **pellicle** [PEHL-ih-kuhl], which gives the cell its shape. The pellicle is flexible. Euglenas crawl by changing shape, as shown in Figure 17.4. This motion is called **euglenoid movement**.

Euglenas live in fresh water. The cytoplasm of their cells is always more concentrated than fresh water. As a result, water tends to diffuse into the cell by osmosis. To control the water balance of the cell, euglenas and other freshwater protists have a **contractile vacuole**. Figure 17.5 shows how water entering the cell collects in the contractile vacuole. The vacuole expands until the membrane of the vacuole fuses with the cell membrane of the reservoir, thus releasing excess water through the gullet. The empty vacuole then begins to swell again as water continues to diffuse into the cell. The filling and emptying cycle of the contractile vacuole usually takes less than a minute.

Euglena reproduces asexually. The nucleus undergoes mitosis and the cell splits lengthwise to form two daughter cells. Sexual reproduction has never been observed in this phylum.

Figure 17.4 All euglenas assume a set of characteristic shapes in moving through their environment.

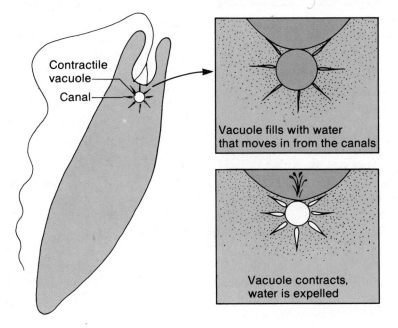

Contractile
vacuole
Canal

Vacuole fills with water
that moves in from the canals

Vacuole contracts,
water is expelled

Figure 17.5 A contractile vacuole maintains the water balance of a cell.

17–2   Phylum Pyrrophyta

Most members of the phylum **Pyrrophyta** [pih-ruh-FYT-uh] are marine. The most common pyrrophytes are **dinoflagellates** [dy-noh-FLAJ-uh-layts]. Many of the enormous number of **plankton**, or small organisms that float near the surface of the ocean, are dinoflagellates.

The chloroplasts of dinoflagellates contain chlorophyll. However, abundant red and yellow pigments mask the green chlorophyll, giving the dinoflagellates a characteristic red or brown color. Most dinoflagellates have a cellulose cell wall made of many segments. The segments fit together like the pieces of a suit of armor.

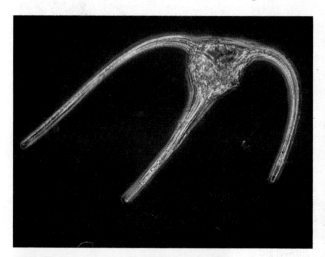

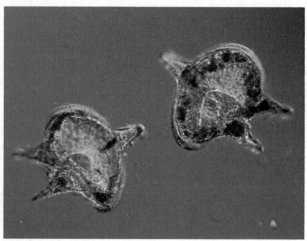

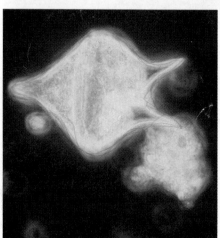

Figure 17.6 Dinoflagellates contain chlorophyll and other pigments that give them a red or brown color.

Most dinoflagellates have two flagella. One flagellum extends backward from the middle of the cell. This flagellum propels the organism forward. The second flagellum wraps around the middle of the cell in a groove. When this flagellum vibrates, the cell spins. For this reason, dinoflagellates spin as they move through the water.

Some dinoflagellates do not have chloroplasts. These heterotrophic dinoflagellates feed on smaller protists and monerans. They are classified as dinoflagellates because of their similarity to the photosynthetic forms. Biologists assume that the heterotrophic dinoflagellates evolved from autotrophic forms.

The nucleus of dinoflagellates is unusual. Recall that in most eukaryotes, chromosomes are visible only during mitosis. In dinoflagellates, though, the chromosomes are always compact and visible. Because mitosis in dinoflagellates shows some similarities to prokaryotic cell division, some biologists think of dinoflagellates as being intermediate between prokaryotes and eukaryotes.

Occasionally the population of some dinoflagellates increases dramatically. Large numbers of dinoflagellates may turn the water red, an event called a red tide. Species that cause red tides produce powerful nerve poisons. High concentrations of these poisons may kill fish. Shellfish such as clams and oysters are not affected by the poison, but they do collect the poison in their bodies. Humans who eat these shellfish may be paralyzed or even killed.

Many dinoflagellates can produce light. The ability to produce light is called **bioluminescence** [by-oh-loo-muh-NEHS-uhns]. When boats, fish, or waves disturb such dinoflagellates at night, the water may glow with an eerie blue or green light.

17–3   Phylum Chrysophyta

Most members of the phylum **Chrysophyta** [KRIHS-uh-fy-tuh] are photosynthetic. Their characteristic gold or brown color comes from the predominance of pigments other than chlorophyll. Most chrysophytes do not have flagella.

Most of the 6,500 species of chrysophytes are **diatoms** [DY-uh-tahmz]. Diatoms, such as those shown on page 252, live in both fresh and salt water.

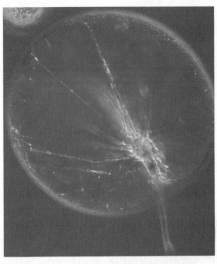

Figure 17.7 *Noctiluca* is a bioluminescent pyrrophyte.

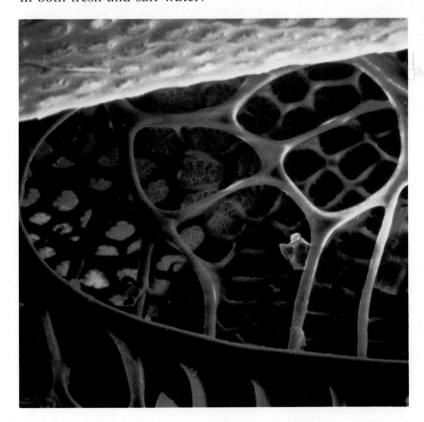

Figure 17.8 This scanning electron micrograph of a diatom shell shows the silica structure of its cell wall.

Do You Know?

In some places, thick deposits of fossil diatom skeletons are mined as diatomaceous earth. Diatomaceous earth is used as a fine abrasive in metal polishes and toothpaste.

Diatoms are characterized by cell walls with two overlapping halves. Instead of cellulose, the cell wall is composed of a gelatinous material called **pectin** [PEHK-tihn]. In most diatoms there is also **silica** [SIHL-ih-kuh] in the cell wall. Silica is a glassy material rich in the element silicon.

Diatoms usually reproduce asexually. After mitosis the cytoplasm divides so that each daughter cell gets half of the old cell wall. The new daughter cells then produce a new half cell wall.

Phylum	Example	Method of Locomotion	Cell Wall Composition	Photosynthetic Pigments	Habitat	Mode of Nutrition
Euglenophyta	*Euglena*	Two flagella (1 long, 1 short)	No cell wall, protein pellicle	Chlorophyll a, Chlorophyll b, other yellow and red pigments	Mostly fresh water	Autotroph (few heterotrophs)
Pyrrophyta	Dinoflagellates	Two flagella (equal lengths)	Cellulose	Chlorophyll a, Chlorophyll c, other yellow and red pigments	Fresh and salt water	Autotroph (few heterotrophs)
Chrysophyta	Diatoms	Most lack flagella, some can glide	Pectin, silica	Chlorophyll a, Chlorophyll c, other yellow and red pigments	Fresh and salt water	Autotroph (few heterotrophs)

Figure 17.9 Characteristics of three phyla of plantlike protists

Occasionally diatoms reproduce sexually. The parent cell undergoes meiosis. Only one haploid nucleus survives meiosis; the other three degenerate. A flagellated gamete breaks out of the old cell wall and swims until it encounters another gamete of the same species. The cells fuse to form a diploid zygote. The zygote then develops an entirely new shell.

The important characteristics of the three phyla of plantlike protists are compared in Figure 17.9.

Checkpoint

1. What are the most common types of pyrrophytes?
2. How are the microtubules arranged in a flagellum?
3. What structure covers the cells of euglenoids?
4. What structures allow euglenas to swim toward light?
5. What substance gives the cell walls of diatoms a glassy appearance?

Animal-like Protists

The animal-like protists are single-celled eukaryotes with no obvious relationship to photosynthetic protists. The classification of animal-like protists is based largely on the way they move and feed. Figure 17.10 summarizes some of the principal characteristics of the animal-like protists.

17–4   Phylum Mastigophora: The Flagellates

The phylum **Mastigophora** [mas-tih-GAHF-uh-ruh] contains the animal-like protists that move by flagella. Species may have one, two, or many flagella. A few species live in fresh or salt water, but most live in the bodies of larger organisms.

One of the best-known flagellates is *Trypanosoma*, a human parasite that causes African sleeping sickness. *Trypanosoma* inhabits the blood of wild and domestic animals throughout much of Africa. This parasite is transmitted from one animal to another through the bite of the bloodsucking tsetse [SEHT-see] fly. An animal such as the tsetse fly that carries a disease from one host to another is called a **vector**.

CONCEPTS

- characteristics of the four phyla of animal-like protists
- anatomy of an amoeba and a paramecium
- function of pseudopods
- structure and function of cilia
- life cycle of *Plasmodium*

Figure 17.10 Characteristics of four phyla of animal-like protists

Phylum	Example	Method of Locomotion	Skeleton or Shell	Feeding	Life Style	Reproduction
Mastigophora	*Trypanosoma* *Trychonympha* *Codosiga*	Flagella, one, two, or many	None	Absorption, phagocytosis	Some free-living, some in bodies of other animals	Asexual, sexual
Sarcodina	*Amoeba* *Arcella* *Difflugia* Heliozoans Radiolarians Foraminiferans	Pseudopods	None, some silica, some calcium carbonate	Phagocytosis	Some free-living in marine and fresh water, some parasites	Asexual, and sexual (only asexual in *Amoeba*)
Sporozoa	*Plasmodium*	None	None	Absorption	All parasites	Asexual and sexual
Ciliophora	*Paramecium*	Cilia	Pellicle	Food vacuole at end of gullet	Most free-living, some parasites	Asexual and sexual by conjugation

Not all flagellates living in animals are parasites. *Try-chonympha* is a flagellate that lives in the intestines of termites. The termite itself is incapable of digesting the wood that it eats. *Trychonympha* makes an enzyme that digests the cellulose in the wood particles. Without the flagellates in its intestine, the termite would continue to eat wood but would die of starvation.

17–5   Phylum Sarcodina

The phylum **Sarcodina** [SAHR-koh-dy-nuh] contains protists that move and take in food by **pseudopods** [SOO-duh-pahdz]. Pseudopods, or "false feet," are temporary extensions of cytoplasm. When a sarcodine moves, some of its cytoplasm flows forward, thus extending the cell membrane.

All sarcodines feed by **phagocytosis** [fag-oh-sy-TOH-sis]. In phagocytosis, an organism surrounds its prey with pseudopods, then forms a **food vacuole**. Digestive enzymes released into the food vacuole break down the prey. Food molecules are then absorbed by the cell.

Many sarcodines have an external shell or an internal framework that gives them a distinctive shape. Other sarcodines, however, have no such structure and are basically shapeless blobs of cytoplasm.

Probably the best-known sarcodine is *Amoeba proteus*. This organism lives in ponds, where it crawls along the bottom

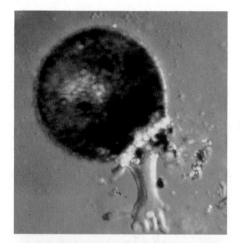

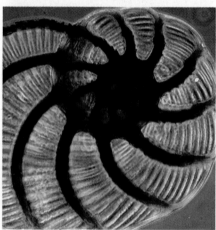

Figure 17.11 Sarcodines exhibit a variety of shapes but all feed by phagocytosis. *Top: Difflugia; Bottom: a foraminiferan*

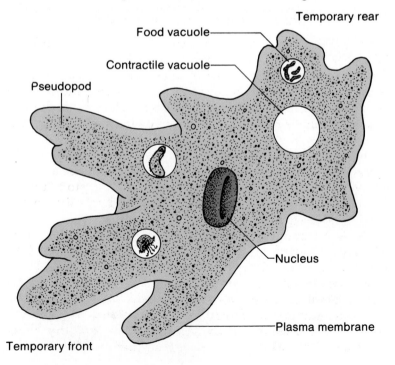

Figure 17.12 The structural features of *Amoeba proteus*

or over plants. Figure 17.12 shows the general structure of an amoeba. Pseudopods can extend in any direction at any time, so the cell has no permanent front or rear. Within the cytoplasm there are usually several food vacuoles, each containing food in various stages of digestion. Like other freshwater protists, amoebas have contractile vacuoles that remove excess water.

Amoebas reproduce asexually by mitosis and cell division. No one has ever observed sexual reproduction in an amoeba.

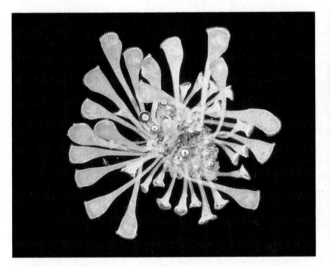 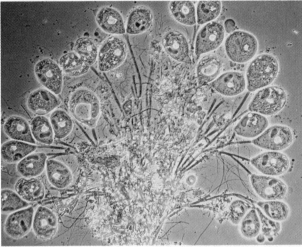

Figure 17.13 Ciliates are characterized by the presence of cilia. *Left: Stentor; Right: Vorticella*

17–6   Phylum Ciliophora: The Ciliates

Protists in the phylum **Ciliophora** [sihl-ee-AHF-ur-uh] use **cilia** [SIHL-ee-uh] to move and capture food. Cilia are short flagella with the 9 + 2 microtubule arrangement. Flagella usually occur in small numbers, but cilia are much more numerous. Cilia often cover the entire surface of a ciliate.

Like the euglenoids, the ciliates have a pellicle. This protein coating determines the characteristic form of each species, yet permits temporary changes in shape. Figure 17.13 shows some of the variety in this large group. Most ciliates are free-living in fresh or salt water. A few species attach to a surface by a stalk and stay in one place. Other ciliates live in the bodies of host animals.

The most commonly studied ciliate is *Paramecium* [par-uh-MEE-see-uhm]. This slipper-shaped ciliate lives in ponds. Along the surface of the cell are parallel rows of cilia. These cilia function like the arms of a swimmer. When a cilium moves in one direction, it remains rigid. This movement has the same function as a swimmer's arm pulling through the water. On the return stroke the cilia relax and slip along the side of the cell. For a paramecium to move, all the cilia

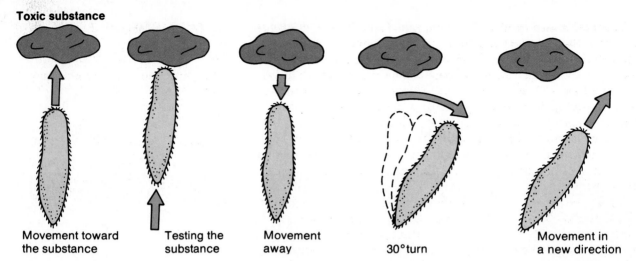

Toxic substance

Movement toward
the substance

Testing the
substance

Movement
away

30° turn

Movement in
a new direction

Figure 17.14 When a paramecium encounters a toxic substance it backs up, turns, then proceeds forward.

must move in a coordinated pattern. In a row of cilia, the strokes occur in waves that travel along each row.

A paramecium can respond to stimuli. It swims toward food by detecting the presence of chemicals in the water. It can swim away from harmful chemicals such as acids. Figure 17.14 shows how a paramecium can avoid obstacles in its path. Such directed movement requires complex coordination of beating cilia. Just how this coordination is accomplished is not known, but it involves a network of fibers under the cell membrane.

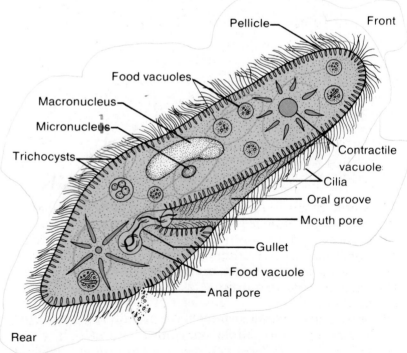

Pellicle

Front

Food vacuoles

Macronucleus

Micronucleus

Trichocysts

Contractile
vacuole

Cilia

Oral groove

Mouth pore

Gullet

Food vacuole

Anal pore

Rear

Figure 17.15 The structural features of a paramecium

Paramecia use their cilia to capture food. The cilia create currents that sweep food into an **oral groove** on the side of the cell. The oral groove leads to a narrow gullet. Cilia sweep food organisms down to the base of the gullet where a food vacuole forms. The food vacuole then pinches off and moves into the cytoplasm. Food in the food vacuoles is digested by enzymes and absorbed into the cytoplasm. Undigested food is removed from the cell when the food vacuole fuses with the cell membrane at the **anal pore**. As in other freshwater protists, a contractile vacuole removes excess water from the cytoplasm of the cell.

Under the pellicle are flask-shaped capsules called **trichocysts** [TRIHK-uh-sihsts]. Trichocysts can suddenly release a threadlike structure with a barb at the end. When approached by larger organisms, a paramecium releases its trichocysts, which seem to have a defensive function. In other ciliates, trichocysts may be used to capture prey or to anchor the organism in place.

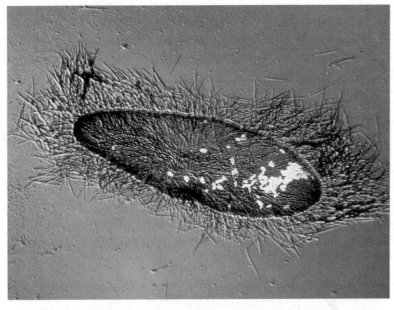

Figure 17.16 A paramecium with barb-like structures released from trichocysts

Paramecium has one other characteristic common to ciliates but not present in other protists: It has two kinds of nuclei. Both kinds of nuclei contain DNA, but they differ in function. The **macronucleus** is similar in function to the nucleolus. RNA is manufactured in the macronucleus. The smaller nucleus, called the **micronucleus**, becomes active only during reproduction.

Paramecia reproduce asexually by mitosis and cell division. In addition, these organisms undergo a kind of sexual reproduction called **conjugation**. Conjugation, which is shown

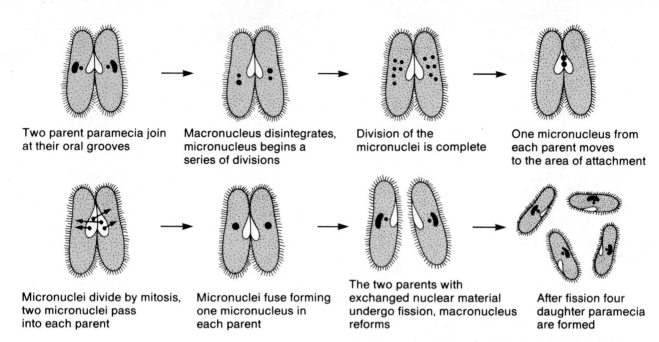

Two parent paramecia join at their oral grooves

Macronucleus disintegrates, micronucleus begins a series of divisions

Division of the micronuclei is complete

One micronucleus from each parent moves to the area of attachment

Micronuclei divide by mitosis, two micronuclei pass into each parent

Micronuclei fuse forming one micronucleus in each parent

The two parents with exchanged nuclear material undergo fission, macronucleus reforms

After fission four daughter paramecia are formed

Figure 17.17 The conjugation process is a form of sexual reproduction.

in Figure 17.17, is a mechanism by which two individuals combine genetic information. Notice that the macronucleus disintegrates. Only the micronuclei are involved in conjugation. Each of the daughter cells receives a new combination of genetic material from the two original parent cells.

17–7 Phylum Sporozoa

All members of the phylum **Sporozoa** [spawr-uh-ZOH-uh] are parasitic, absorbing food from the fluids of their host. Sporozoans have no means of locomotion.

Sporozoans have complex life cycles that include reproduction by the formation of spores. In spore formation, the nucleus of the parent cell undergoes mitosis many times. The parent cell later bursts, thus releasing the spores.

The best-known sporozoans are those that cause malaria in humans. Malaria-causing sporozoans belong to the genus *Plasmodium*. The life cycle of *Plasmodium vivax* is shown in Figure 17.18. Malaria is transmitted by an insect vector, the *Anopheles* mosquito. *Plasmodium* spores enter the blood stream of a human through the bite of an infected mosquito. The spores travel through the blood to the liver, where they reproduce asexually. The new cells return to the blood where they enter red blood cells and, again, divide asexually.

When red cells fill up with the parasites, the red cells burst open, releasing new parasites that infect other red cells. Usually the red blood cells burst open simultaneously. When this happens the patient's temperature soars for a few hours, then

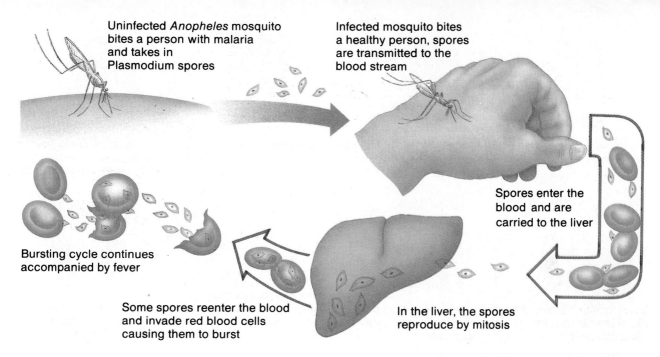

Uninfected *Anopheles* mosquito bites a person with malaria and takes in *Plasmodium* spores

Infected mosquito bites a healthy person, spores are transmitted to the blood stream

Spores enter the blood and are carried to the liver

In the liver, the spores reproduce by mitosis

Some spores reenter the blood and invade red blood cells causing them to burst

Bursting cycle continues accompanied by fever

Figure 17.18 Life cycle of *Plasmodium vivax*

drops rapidly. The fever cycles coincide with the reproductive cycle of the parasite.

After several cycles of asexual reproduction in red cells, some of the *Plasmodium* parasites undergo meiosis and produce gametes. When a mosquito bites an infected human and takes *Plasmodium* gametes into its intestine, the gametes unite to form a zygote. The zygote divides by mitosis to form spores. The spores travel to the mouth of the mosquito, where they can enter another human and start the cycle again.

In tropical countries where malaria is common, one method of control is to kill the mosquitoes that transmit the disease. In the 1950s and 1960s widespread spraying of insecticides reduced the incidence of malaria in many countries. Unfortunately, in the last decade the *Anopheles* mosquito has developed partial resistance to pesticides. Today malaria continues to be a major human disease.

Checkpoint

1. How do members of the phylum Mastigophora move?
2. How do sarcodines move?
3. What disease do sporozoans of the genus *Plasmodium* cause?
4. Name two functions of cilia in a paramecium.
5. How does undigested food leave the cytoplasm of a paramecium?
6. What organism is the vector of malaria?

CHAPTER REVIEW

Summary

- The kingdom Protista is composed of organisms that cannot be classified as monerans, fungi, animals, or plants. All protists are eukaryotic and can divide by mitosis. Most are single-celled. The kingdom is divided into plantlike protists and animal-like protists.
- The three phyla of plantlike protists are distinguished by their photosynthetic pigments, cell wall structure, and means of locomotion. These phyla are Euglenophyta, Pyrrophyta, and Chrysophyta.
- The dinoflagellates are the largest group of pyrrophytes. Dinoflagellates have cellulose cell walls composed of separate plates. Some dinoflagellates are heterotrophic. Dinoflagellates usually reproduce asexually.
- Members of the phylum Euglenophyta have two flagella, one long and one very short. Many, such as *Euglena*, have eyespots and are able to swim toward light. Their cell membrane is protected by a flexible pellicle. Sexual reproduction has never been observed in these organisms.
- Diatoms are the most common of the members of the phylum Chrysophyta. The silica cell walls of diatoms are divided into two parts. Diatoms reproduce asexually and sexually. In sexual reproduction, flagellated gametes are produced.
- The animal-like protists are distinguished primarily by their means of locomotion. There are four phyla of animal-like protists: Mastigophora, Sarcodina, Sporozoa, and Ciliophora.
- The phylum Mastigophora contains heterotrophic organisms that move by means of flagella. Although some are free-living, most live in the bodies of other organisms. *Trypanosoma*, which causes African sleeping sickness, and *Trychonympha*, which lives in the intestines of termites, are flagellates.
- Members of the phylum Sarcodina move and feed by extensions of the cytoplasm called pseudopods. Some sarcodines, such as *Amoeba*, are essentially shapeless. Others contain structures of silica or calcium carbonate that give them a definite shape.
- All members of the phylum Sporozoa are parasitic and have complex life cycles that include the formation of spores. During most of their life cycle these organisms have no means of locomotion. *Plasmodium*, which causes malaria, is a well-known sporozoan.
- Members of the phylum Ciliophora move by means of cilia. Cilia are also used to capture prey. Ciliates reproduce sexually by conjugation. *Paramecium* is the best-known ciliate.

Vocabulary

anal pore	Mastigophora
bioluminescence	micronucleus
Chrysophyta	oral groove
cilia	pectin
Ciliophora	pellicle
conjugation	phagocytosis
contractile vacuole	plankton
diatom	pseudopod
dinoflagellate	Pyrrophyta
euglenoid movement	reservoir
Euglenophyta	Sarcodina
eyespot	silica
flagellum	Sporozoa
food vacuole	trichocyst
gullet	vector
macronucleus	

Review

1. What two traits do all protists have in common?
2. How are plantlike protists distinguished from animal-like protists?
3. What term describes small organisms that

float near the surface of the oceans or other bodies of water?

4. Name two methods by which a euglena moves.

5. What organelle allows freshwater protists to maintain their water balance?

6. What is the vector of African sleeping sickness?

7. How does *Trychonympha* help the organism in which it lives?

8. By what method do sarcodines feed?

9. Where does the formation of sex cells by *Plasmodium* take place? Where does fertilization occur?

10. What structure in ciliates controls the day-to-day chemical activities of the cell?

In the following list, match the phylum of protists with the proper description.

11. Pyrrophyta
12. Sarcodina
13. Chrysophyta
14. Ciliophora
15. Mastigophora
16. Sporozoa

a. have cilia
b. all are parasites
c. have pseudopods
d. includes organisms that cause red tides
e. heterotrophs with flagella
f. diatoms most common group

Interpret and Apply

1. Describe the characteristic arrangement of flagella in the dinoflagellates.

2. Which phyla of plantlike protists have heterotrophic forms?

3. Why are red tides considered dangerous to humans?

4. Under what conditions can a euglena be totally heterotrophic?

5. What two protist phyla are characterized by a pellicle?

6. Explain the function of the contractile vacuole in some protists.

7. What characteristic is shared by the mastigophorans and the euglenoids?

8. How are the methods of reproduction in a euglena and in an amoeba similar?

9. What are the similarities in the life cycle of *Trypanosoma* and *Plasmodium*?

10. In what ways are cilia and flagella similar? In what ways are they different?

11. List two functions of trichocysts in ciliates.

12. Compare feeding in an amoeba and a paramecium.

Challenge

1. Why are the dinoflagellates considered intermediate between prokaryotes and eukaryotes?

2. What were the characteristics of organisms such as *Euglena* that led taxonomists to develop a separate kingdom for them?

3. Why are some heterotrophic protists placed in the plantlike phyla while others are placed in the animal-like phyla?

Projects

1. Collect samples of water from a nearby pond, lake, or stream and examine them under a microscope. Draw pictures of the protists you see and keep a record of how common each type is. Compare the protists found in different bodies of water. You can also examine the same jar of water over several weeks or even months. Are those protists you observed at the beginning the same as the kinds you observe later?

2. Find out about the various kinds of malaria. What kinds are common in what locations? How are the different forms treated by doctors? Report your findings to the class.

3. Look up some recent articles on outbreaks of red tide. What hypotheses are there about the cause of the blooms? What are some of the economic effects of red tides? Report on your findings to your class.

18 Fungi

Mushrooms of the genus *Cortinarius*

After it rains, colorful mushrooms may suddenly appear on the forest floor. White and brown mushrooms are common, but there are purple, yellow, and red varieties as well. Although you have not seen them, these mushrooms have been growing for a long time. What you recognize as a mushroom is only the reproductive structure. The rest of the mushroom is composed of a network of tiny threads that grow through the decaying matter on the forest floor. Mushrooms are fungi. Some fungi contain deadly poisons, but others are among the most prized delicacies.

Perhaps the most flavorful of all edible fungi are truffles. Truffles grow underground near the roots of trees. Only in parts of France and Italy are truffles numerous enough for harvesting to be practical. Finding truffles would be exceptionally difficult without the help of pigs. Pigs can smell the buried truffles easily. Each fall truffle hunters lead trained pigs on leashes to sniff out the treasure. The search is well worth the effort. A single pound of truffles may sell for as much as $400.

Characteristics of Fungi

For many years, **fungi** [FUHN-jy] were classified as plants. Like plants, most fungi have a cell wall surrounding the cell membrane. Also like plants, most fungi do not move actively about.

But there are important differences between plants and fungi. Unlike plants, fungi lack chlorophyll and cannot make their own food. Nor do fungi contain the specialized tissues found in most plants. Today most biologists classify fungi in a kingdom of their own.

18–1 Fungi Structure

All fungi are eukaryotes. As fungi grow, their cytoplasm forms long tubelike extensions called **hyphae** [HY-fee]. The hyphae are surrounded by cell walls. In several groups of fungi the cell wall is made of a complex carbohydrate called **chitin** [KY-tihn].

As a hypha (singular of *hyphae*) grows longer, nuclei in the cytoplasm divide. Typically cell walls do not form between nuclei. The cytoplasm, therefore, becomes **multinucleate**. Hyphae branch to form a tangled network called a **mycelium** [my-SEE-lee-uhm].

CONCEPTS

- food sources of fungi
- structure of hyphae and mycelia
- reproduction of fungi

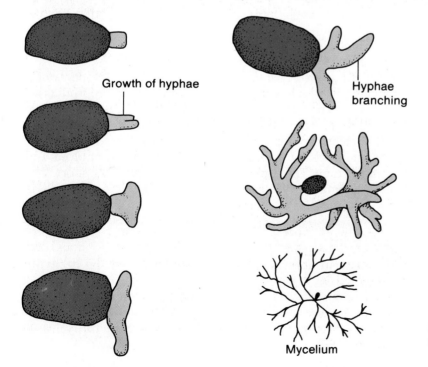

Growth of hyphae

Hyphae branching

Mycelium

Figure 18.1 The formation of a mycelium from a germinating spore

Figure 18.2 Fruiting bodies of different fungi

18-2   Fungi Nutrition

All fungi are heterotrophs. Most fungi feed by secreting enzymes into their surroundings. The enzymes break food into small molecules. The cells of the fungi then absorb these molecules. This mode of nutrition is called **absorption**.

Most fungi are **saprophytes** [SAHP-roh-fyts]. A saprophyte is an organism that absorbs its food from dead or decaying organic matter. Fungi are commonly found growing on rotting leaves, wood, or animal wastes. The enzymes that fungi secrete help break down these organic materials. For this reason, fungi are very important in the decomposition of plants and animals.

Some fungi are parasites. Most parasitic fungi grow on plants. Parasitic fungi extend their hyphae between the cell walls of their host plant and then absorb food from its cells. Some parasitic fungi attack important crops such as corn, wheat, or potatoes. A few fungi are parasites of animals. Fungal parasites of humans include athlete's foot and ringworm.

18-3   Reproduction in Fungi

Most fungi can reproduce asexually. In some cases simple fragmentation of the mycelium results in the growth of another individual. Many fungi produce asexual reproductive cells called **spores**. Each spore has a tough cell wall that retains moisture. Spores can be carried through the air or water. If a spore lands in a suitable environment with food and moisture, it can grow into a new mycelium.

Most fungi also reproduce sexually. In fact, the parts of a fungus with which you are most familiar are reproductive structures. The caps of mushrooms and bracket fungi are reproductive structures called **fruiting bodies**. The fruiting bodies release spores produced by sexual reproduction.

The life cycle of a fungus usually involves a haploid and a diploid stage. The diploid stage is generally very short. The nuclei of fungal mycelia are almost always haploid.

Checkpoint

1. What term describes an organism that feeds on decaying materials?
2. Of what is the mycelium of a fungus composed?
3. What are the asexual reproductive cells of fungi called?
4. In sexual reproduction of most fungi, what structure releases the spores?

Variety of Fungi

Fungi are classified into three subkingdoms. The subkingdom **Gymnomycota** [JIHM-nuh-my-koh-tuh] is composed of the slime molds. The second subkingdom, **Dimastigomycota** [dy-MAS-tih-goh-my-coh-tah], contains a group of fungi commonly called water molds. There are only a few thousand species in these two subkingdoms.

Most fungi belong to the subkingdom **Eumycota** [yoo-my-COH-tuh], which contains tens of thousands of species. Mushrooms and yeasts are familiar members of this subkingdom.

CONCEPTS

- life cycle of slime molds
- characteristics of water molds
- structure and reproduction of zygomycetes, ascomycetes, and basidiomycetes
- classification of the deutero-mycetes
- symbiosis in lichens

18–4   Subkingdom Gymnomycota

Sometimes the most interesting organisms are the least familiar. You have probably never noticed a slime mold. Slime molds live in moist, decaying leaves or rotting logs. All slime molds have an amoebalike stage during their life cycle. This amoebalike stage feeds by creeping over the forest floor and engulfing bacteria or decaying matter by phagocytosis. During this stage slime molds seem to be more like animals than fungi. At other stages in their life cycles, slime molds form fruiting bodies and produce spores, a characteristic that is more like fungi. Because of their unusual characteristics, biologists have had trouble classifying the slime molds.

Figure 18.3 shows the life cycle of a **cellular slime mold**. Notice that at one stage the organism consists of independent single cells. Periodically the free-living cells move together, forming a large coordinated mass of cells. This group of cells is able to crawl along, a bit like a garden slug.

Figure 18.3 The life cycle of a cellular slime mold. Note that all stages are haploid.

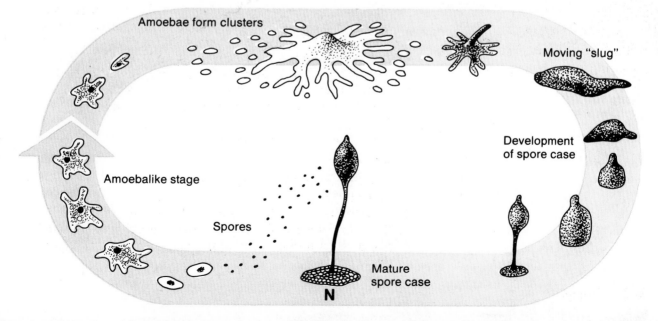

Amoebae form clusters

Moving "slug"

Development of spore case

Amoebalike stage

Spores

Mature spore case

N

When the slime mold stops moving, the individual cells form a mound. Some cells then form a stalk that extends from the mound. The cells in the stalk have cellulose cell walls. The stalk develops a spore case at its tip. When the spore case is mature, it ruptures, releasing spores into the air. Each spore then develops into an amoebalike cell and begins the life cycle again. The spores are a form of asexual reproduction. Cellular slime molds rarely reproduce sexually.

In **acellular slime molds** the feeding stage of the life cycle is composed of a large mass of multinucleate cytoplasm called a **plasmodium** [plahz-MOH-dee-uhm]. After a nucleus divides, the cytoplasm does not divide into separate cells by forming new plasma membranes. For this reason, these slime molds are described as being acellular.

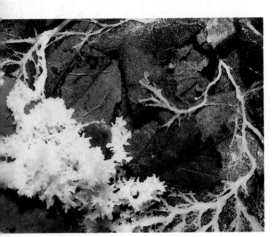

Figure 18.4 A portion of the plasmodium of the acellular slime mold *Physarium*

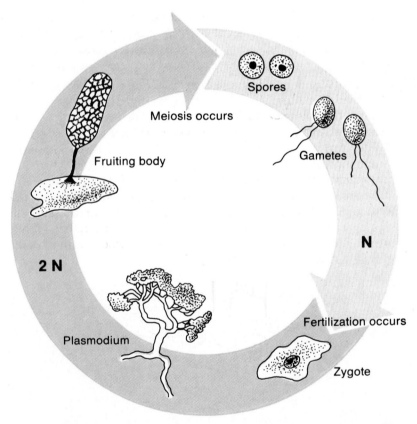

Figure 18.5 The life cycle of an acellular slime mold. Note how it differs from the life cycle of a cellular slime mold.

As the plasmodium crawls over the forest floor, it engulfs pieces of leaves and decaying material. When it encounters unfavorable conditions, the plasmodium forms fruiting bodies that produce spores. The spores form flagellated gametes. When two gametes meet, they fuse, forming a zygote. The zygote grows into a new plasmodium. Thus acellular slime molds undergo sexual reproduction.

18–5 Subkingdom Dimastigomycota

Since many members of the subkingdom Dimastigomycota are aquatic, this group is often called the water molds. Unlike most fungi, during asexual reproduction the water molds produce flagellated spores.

Not all members of this subkingdom live in water. Several species are parasites of land plants. One species causes a disease of potatoes called late blight. From 1846 to 1847, the entire potato crop of Ireland became infected with this disease. Over one million people starved to death. Many others left Ireland for other countries at this time. Most of these people came to Canada and the United States.

18–6 True Fungi

Members of the subkingdom Eumycota are also called the true fungi. Most true fungi have hyphae that form a mycelium. They all have a cell wall, which is usually made of chitin. With the exception of one group, true fungi do not have flagella. The division of the subkingdom into phyla is based on the kind of reproductive structures present.

Phylum Zygomycetes Most **zygomycetes** [zy-goh-MY-seets] are terrestrial saprophytes. A few live in water, and some are parasites.

The common bread mold, *Rhizopus* [RY-zoh-puhs], is the best-known zygomycete. Despite its name, *Rhizopus* can grow on many different foods. Its mycelium has several specialized types of hyphae. Horizontal hyphae grow across the surface of the food. Where they contact the surface, a branching network of hyphae grows into the food. These rootlike fibers are called **rhizoids** [RY-zoids].

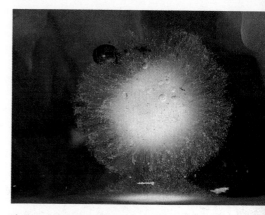

Figure 18.6 *Saprolegnia* is a mold found commonly in aquariums. It infects injured fish and grows on dead fish in the tank.

Do You Know?
The distinctive flavors of many cheeses are caused by fungi. Some of these cheeses are Roquefort, Brie, Stilton, and Camembert.

Figure 18.7 *Rhizopus* gets its name from its fibrous structure.

Figure 18.8 *Rhizopus* reproduces both sexually and asexually.

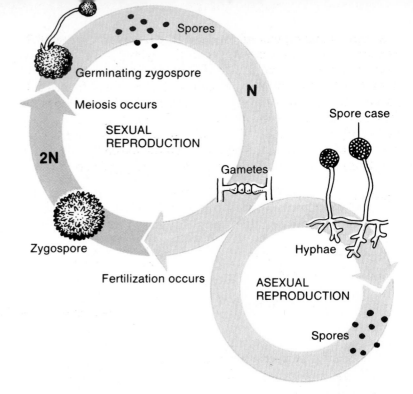

BIOLOGY INSIGHTS

Many organisms can reproduce both sexually and asexually. Such organisms tend to reproduce asexually when conditions are favorable and sexually when conditions become unfavorable.

Rhizopus reproduces asexually by growing vertical hyphae. On top of these stalks, black spore cases form. Inside each spore case are individual spores with one or more nuclei. The spores may be carried long distances by air currents. If one lands on suitable food, it will form a new mycelium.

Sexual reproduction generally occurs when conditions become unfavorable for growth. Sexual reproduction in *Rhizopus* involves two genetically different mycelia. The two types of mycelia are called plus and minus mating types. The two mating types appear to be identical, but have slight chemical differences. When hyphae from plus and minus types touch, their nuclei fuse. This fusion results in a diploid **zygospore** [ZY-goh-spawr]. The zygospore gives the phylum its name.

The zygospore remains dormant until conditions become favorable again. At that time the diploid zygote undergoes meiosis. A hypha with haploid nuclei grows from the zygospore, thus beginning a new generation.

Phylum Ascomycetes All members of the **ascomycetes** [as-koh-MY-seets], have a saclike reproductive structure called an **ascus** [AS-kuhs]. For this reason, the ascomycetes are also called sac-fungi.

Like the other true fungi, these organisms have a mycelium made of hyphae with chitin walls. The hyphae have partial cross walls. Each cross wall has a large hole that permits nuclei to move from one cell to another.

A typical sac-fungus life cycle is illustrated in Figure 18.9. Sexual reproduction begins as in the zygomycetes. Hyphae from two mating types fuse. After fusion a mycelium forms with two haploid nuclei per cell — one nucleus from each parent. In certain cells the haploid nuclei fuse to form a diploid nucleus. The diploid stage is very short, with meiosis taking place soon after the nuclei fuse. The haploid reproductive cells line up in an ascus. When the haploid cells break free from the ascus, they can develop into new mycelia.

Figure 18.9 *Top*: *Peziza* is a cup fungus that is classified as a sac-fungus. *Left*: The life cycle of a sac-fungus involves the formation of an ascus that releases spores to form new hyphae.

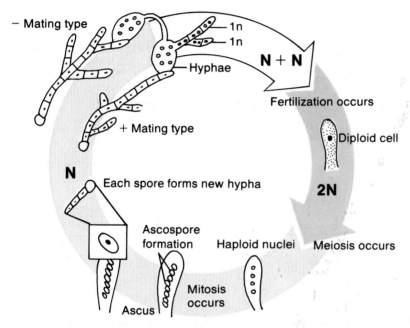

Many of the sac-fungi are important to humans. *Neurospora* is a species used in many laboratories for genetic research. Truffles and morels are prized edible ascomycetes. Yeasts are ascomycetes. Normally yeasts are single-celled organisms that reproduce asexually. Only occasionally do they reproduce sexually and form an ascus. For thousands of years humans have used yeasts to produce bread and alcoholic beverages.

Some sac-fungi grow around or within the roots of plants. These fungi help the plants absorb minerals from the soil. In return, the fungi probably use products made by the plant. As many as 90 percent of all land plants may have ascomycetes associated with their roots.

Not all the sac-fungi are beneficial to humans. Many are parasitic and cause considerable damage. American elm trees are parasitized by a sac-fungus that causes Dutch elm disease. This disease is carried by beetles and enters the elms through wounds in the bark. Biologists are working on a way to halt the spread of this disease.

Figure 18.10 The morel is an edible ascomycete.

Phylum Basidiomycetes

Mushrooms are the most familiar **basidiomycetes** [buh-sihd-ee-oh-MY-seets]. The mushrooms that appear suddenly after rainstorms are actually only the fruiting bodies of spreading networks of underground mycelia. These mycelia may live for many years. Each mycelium consists of cells with two haploid nuclei. As in the ascomycetes, the haploid nuclei arise from the fusion of plus and minus mating types.

Figure 18.11 The life cycle of a mushroom. A mushroom is the fruiting body of an underground mycelium.

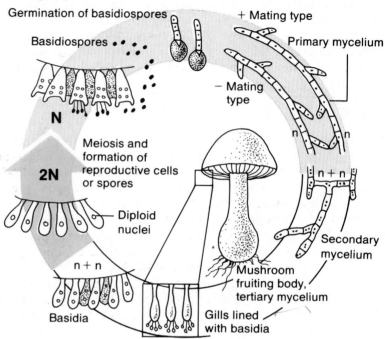

Figure 18.12 A hollow puffball contains millions of spores that are released when the puffball is disturbed.

The mushroom fruiting body is a mass of hyphae. Beneath its cap are numerous thin gills. Lining the **gills** are special cells called **basidia**. A basidium is a club-shaped reproductive hypha. When the two nuclei in the basidium fuse to form a diploid nucleus, meiosis occurs immediately. The haploid nuclei move into four reproductive cells at the end of stalks on the basidium. These haploid cells are spores. Each mushroom can release millions of spores into the air.

Bracket fungi, which commonly grow on decaying trees, are also basidiomycetes, as are puffballs. When a mature puffball is disturbed, it sends clouds of spores through an opening in the top.

An important group of basidiomycetes are the parasitic **rusts**. Different rust species damage such valuable crops as wheat, corn, oats, and barley. Rusts have very complex life cycles. For example, part of the wheat rust life cycle is in the wheat plant, and part is in the barberry bush. Destruction of the barberry bush is the best way to control wheat rust.

18–7 Phylum Deuteromycete: Imperfect Fungi

Occasionally certain organisms defy classification in other groups. The **deuteromycetes** [doo-tuh-roh-MY-seets] are such a group. This group contains the fungi in which sexual reproduction has never been observed. Although some species never reproduce sexually, others belong to this phylum only temporarily. Any of these species will be placed in another phylum when a sexual stage is observed. In fact, many species are moved out of this phylum each year.

Penicillium and *Aspergillis* are well-known deuteromycetes. These are among the common blue and green molds you may have seen growing on food. *Penicillium* is the genus that produces the antibiotic penicillin.

18–8 Lichens

A **lichen** [LY-kuhn] is not a single organism but a combination of two. Two organisms that live in close association with one another are said to be **symbiotic** [sihm-by-AHT-ihk]. Each lichen is a symbiotic association of a fungus species and a photosynthetic organism. The photosynthetic partner is usually a cyanophyte. Both the fungus and the autotroph benefit from their association. The cyanophyte supplies the lichen with food. The fungus keeps the lichen from drying out and attaches the organism to a surface.

Because the fungus and autotroph complement each other, lichens can grow in places where few other organisms can live. For example, they can grow on the surface of bare rocks or the bark of trees.

Do You Know?
One deuteromycete feeds by capturing small roundworms that live in the soil. Its hyphae form tiny nooses, which tighten around the worms. The roundworm is then digested and absorbed by the fungus.

Figure 18.13 Lichens can grow in places where few other organisms can live.

Checkpoint

1. What are the rootlike structures in the zygomycetes called?
2. What is the principal characteristic of the deuteromycetes?
3. What two kinds of organisms make up a lichen?

CHAPTER REVIEW

Summary

- Kingdom Fungi is made up of organisms that are plantlike in some respects but lack chlorophyll. All fungi are heterotrophs — some are saprophytic and others are parasitic. Most fungi feed by absorption of material from their surroundings.
- Most fungi have bodies made of hyphae that grow in a network called a mycelium. The cell walls of many fungi contain the carbohydrate chitin.
- Fungi show both sexual and asexual reproduction. The sexual reproductive structures of fungi are an important characteristic in classification.
- The life cycles of most fungi include a haploid and a diploid stage. The nuclei of the mycelium are usually haploid.
- Gymnomycotes have unusual life cycles that involve both one-celled and many-celled stages. Some are cellular slime molds, and others are acellular slime molds.
- Dimastigomycotes, or water molds, have flagellated cells at one point in their life cycle.
- The true fungi belong to the subkingdom Eumycophyta. True fungi have a mycelial body plan and generally have complex life cycles with sexual reproduction.
- Zygomycetes are true fungi that reproduce by forming zygospores.
- Ascomycetes are true fungi that are characterized by saclike reproductive structures, or asci.
- The deuteromycetes are fungi in which sexual reproduction has never been observed.
- Lichens are composed of two symbiotic organisms — a photosynthetic organism and a fungus.

Vocabulary

absorption	Gymnomycota
acellular slime mold	hyphae
ascomycete	lichen
ascus	multinucleate
basidiomycete	mycelium
basidium	plasmodium
cellular slime mold	rhizoid
chitin	rust
deuteromycete	saprophyte
Dimastigomycota	spore
Eumycota	symbiotic
fruiting body	zygomycete
fungi	zygospore
gills	

Review

1. By what process do most fungi obtain food?
2. Name the three subkingdoms of the fungi.
3. What is the large multinucleate mass of cytoplasm in the acellular slime molds called?
4. What is a network of hyphae called?
5. What material is found in the cell walls of most of the true fungi?
6. What is the common name for the dimastigomycotes?
7. What structure is formed as a result of sexual reproduction in *Rhizopus*?
8. Are the hyphal nuclei in true fungi haploid or diploid?
9. What is the structure that holds the reproductive cells of the sac-fungi? Of the mushrooms?
10. What group of basidiomycetes are parasites of plants and have very complex life cycles?

In the following list, match the group of fungi with the proper description.

11. Gymnomycota
12. Dimastigomycota
13. zygomycetes
14. ascomycetes
15. basidiomycetes
16. lichens
17. deuteromycetes

a. have a mycelium and flagellated reproductive cells
b. form a zygospore
c. composed of a symbiotic fungus and an autotroph
d. have flagellated reproductive cells but no mycelium
e. have reproductive cells in saclike structures
f. sexual stage unknown
g. have club-shaped reproductive cells

Interpret and Apply

1. List two ways in which fungi are similar to plants. List two ways in which they are different.
2. List two characteristics seen in most true fungi that are generally not present in the other subkingdoms.
3. What is the difference between a saprophyte and a parasite?
4. What is the difference between absorption and phagocytosis?
5. In what ways are slime molds more like protists than fungi?
6. Under what conditions does *Rhizopus* reproduce sexually?
7. What is unusual about the cells of ascomycetes?
8. In which fungal groups is the fusion of plus and minus mating groups a regular part of the reproductive cycle?

9. How do the two organisms in a lichen aid one another?
10. Which groups of true fungi commonly have two nuclei in each cell of the mycelium?

Challenge

1. Describe some of the ways fungi are harmful to humans or other organisms. What are some of the ways they are beneficial?
2. In what way is sexual reproduction in ascomycetes different from sexual reproduction in zygomycetes?
3. Describe the symbiotic relationship that exists between the fungi and many land plants.
4. Why is the phylum deuteromycetes considered to be a temporary classification?

Projects

1. Find out how fungi are used to provide food for humans. Possible topics include methods of cultivating mushrooms, the use of yeasts in making bread, and the use of molds in making various kinds of cheese.
2. Find a book on the classification of lichens in your library. See how many different kinds you can identify in your area.
3. See how easy it is to collect molds from your environment by leaving pieces of moist bread in the open for several days. See if you can get *Rhizopus* to grow. If possible, use bread that does not have preservatives. Design an experiment testing whether breads that have preservatives keep longer than breads that do not have preservatives.
4. Research one of the following fungal diseases and report to your class: the late blight fungus that caused the Irish potato famine of 1846; the chestnut tree fungus that has killed most of the chestnut trees in North America; the fungus that causes Dutch elm disease.

Careers in Pharmaceuticals

Antibiotics are substances produced largely by molds, yeasts, and bacteria. These substances can either destroy or inhibit the growth of disease-causing microorganisms.

Before an antibiotic is put on the market, much research is necessary to determine whether it is safe and effective. Initial tests are performed on animals such as mice, guinea pigs, and monkeys. In the final stages of research, the antibiotic is administered to humans.

Most of the tests for antibiotic activity in animals are performed by *lab technicians*. They measure the animals' physiological responses before, during, and after the antibiotic is given. They then record such information as behavior patterns, blood pressure, heart action, and respiration. Lab technicians are often required to have a college degree in biology.

A *biochemist* analyzes the changes that have occurred in tissues and body fluids due to the presence of an antibiotic. *Pharmacologists* analyze how the antibiotic acts in the body. Both of these careers requires additional education after a college degree.

After extensive testing has been completed, the antibiotic moves on to the development stage. Developing the product requires determining a suitable dosage, the stability, and the potential side effects of the antibiotic. These tests are often performed by lab technicians. The results are analyzed by both biochemists and pharmacologists. A new antibiotic is ready for marketing when sufficient data have been accumulated.

Pharmaceutical companies produce millions of tons of antibiotics annually. A variety of different jobs are required for the production process. In one production process, a large quantity of microbial broth is allowed to ferment in a large tank. While in the tank, the liquid is stirred, aerated, and provided with growth nutrients. The antibiotic broth must be purified by filtration and further cleansed by the use of solvents. This process must be carefully monitored by *workers* who have a knowledge of the life-sustaining requirements of microorganisms.

Quality control of medicines is vital. Many different types of analytical procedures are used to ensure the stability and uniformity of antibiotic preparations. Lab technicians perform many of these tasks. The size of particles and their crystalline structure are checked using a microscope to assure product uniformity. Each tablet and ointment batch must be uniform in shape, color, weight, taste, odor, stability, and purity.

There are many positions in a pharmaceutical company that require only a few weeks of on-the-job training. For example, workers are needed to perform inventory management, manufacturing, and packaging of products.

UNIT REVIEW

Synthesis

1. How does the reproduction of monerans differ from the reproduction of protists?

2. In what ways are fungi similar to plants? How do fungi differ from plants? What characteristics of fungi are not found in the members of other kingdoms?

3. Scientists do not classify viruses in any of the five kingdoms. State two reasons why this is so.

4. Of the moneran, protist, and fungus kingdoms, which have members that are autotrophic? Give an example of an autotroph in each kingdom you name.

5. Of the moneran, protist, and fungus kingdoms, which have members that are anaerobic?

6. What is the fundamental distinction between monerans and all other living things?

7. Describe the structure of a lichen. What is unusual about lichens?

8. Name a plant or animal disease that is caused by a moneran, a protist, and a fungus.

9. Give an example of one organism that is beneficial to humans from each of the three kingdoms covered in this unit.

10. Some biologists classify the slime molds as protists rather than as fungi. State two reasons why slime molds could be called protists.

11. Chapter 2 describes the characteristics that distinguish living things from nonliving things. State which of these characteristics apply to viruses. Based on your analysis, do you think that viruses are alive? Explain.

12. In unicellular organisms each cell must carry out all of the functions necessary for life. In multicellular organisms cells may be specialized for particular functions. Describe one example of cell specialization in monerans and four examples in fungi.

Additional Reading

Anderson, Dean A. *Introduction to Microbiology.* St. Louis, MO: Mosby, C.V., 1980.

Anderson, Lucia. *The Smallest Life around Us.* New York: Crown Pubs., Inc., 1978.

Aylesworth, Thomas. *The World of Microbes.* New York: Franklin Watts, Inc., 1975.

Boettcher, Helmuth. *Wonder Drugs: A History of Antibiotics.* Philadelphia: J.B. Lippincott Co., 1963.

Christensen, Clyde M. *Molds, Mushrooms, and Mycotoxins.* Minneapolis, MN: University of Minnesota Press, 1975.

Dixon, Bernard. *Magnificent Microbes.* New York: Atheneum Pubs., 1979.

Ford, Brian J. *Microbe Power.* New York: Stein & Day, 1976.

Kavaler, Lucy. *Mushrooms, Molds, and Miracles.* New York: John Day Co., Inc., 1965.

Kavaler, Lucy. *The Wonders of Fungi.* New York: John Day Co., Inc., 1964.

Patent, Dorothy H. *Bacteria: How They Affect Other Living Things.* New York: Holiday House, Inc., 1980.

Prescott, Gerald W. *The Diatoms.* New York: Coward, McCann, & Geoghegan, Inc., 1977.

Rossmoore, Harold W. *Microbes, Our Unseen Friends.* Detroit, MI: Wayne State University Press, 1976.

Silverstein, Alvin and Virginia. *Cancer.* New York: Harper-Row Pubs., Inc., 1976.

Volk, Wesley A., and Margaret F. Wheeler. *Basic Microbiology.* New York: Harper-Row Pubs., Inc., 1983.

Walter, William B., et al. *Introduction to Microbiology.* New York: Van Nostrand Reinhold Co., 1973.

Unit Four

Plants

Ferns from the Elwha River Forest,
Olympic National Park, Washington

283

19 Nonvascular Plants

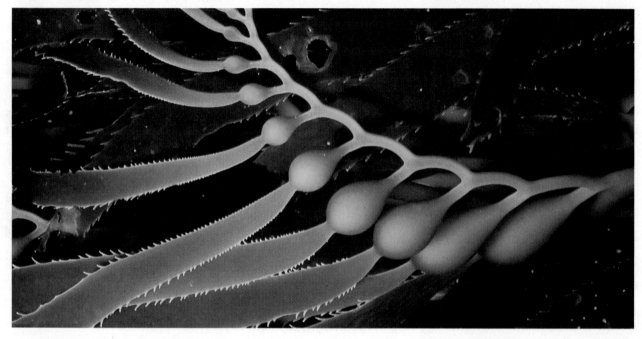

Blades of kelp with air bladders

The graceful kelp floating in the photograph above probably doesn't remind you much of an oak tree in a forest. An oak tree stands tall and solid, while kelp bends and sways in the ocean currents. Yet the oak and the kelp have many similarities. Both are large multicellular plants. Both have chlorophyll and produce their own food by photosynthesis. Therefore, both require adequate sunlight to survive.

The floor of the forest is shady and dim. The tall trunks and sturdy branches of oak trees hold their photosynthetic organs — the leaves — above the other plants. Like the forest floor, the bottom of the ocean is dark. The vegetation of kelp is held afloat by bubble-shaped air bladders, thus reaching the sunlight near the surface.

As you know, an oak tree is anchored in the ground by an underground system of roots. In a similar way, kelp is anchored to rocks on the bottom of the ocean by structures called holdfasts. Some giant kelp plants grow to be over 50 meters long. Kelps like these form undersea kelp forests through which colorful fish swim, just as birds soar through the forests on land.

The Plant Kingdom

Plants are eukaryotic organisms that manufacture their own food by photosynthesis. The plant kingdom includes a vast array of organisms. They range in size from single-celled algae to the enormous redwood trees of the Pacific Coast forests. All plants contain chlorophyll in chloroplasts. All plants also have cell walls composed of cellulose. Cellulose cell walls are stiff, which prevents plant cells from taking in too much water and bursting. Stiff cell walls also provide some protection against being eaten by animals.

Most plants are multicellular. A few unicellular algae are classified as plants because of their close evolutionary relationship to multicellular plants.

The plant kingdom is composed of five divisions: red algae, brown algae, green algae, mosses and their relatives, and vascular plants. **Vascular plants** contain specialized tissues for conducting food and water. The organs that you probably associate with plants — leaves, stems, roots, and flowers — are found only in vascular plants. **Nonvascular plants** lack vascular tissues. The multicellular body of nonvascular plants is called a **thallus** (plural, *thalli*).

Unlike animals, most plants are nonmotile. Instead of moving around to search for food, plants have developed structures that bring together the materials and energy necessary for photosynthesis. In addition to being unable to seek food, plants' lack of motility presents another problem — that of uniting gametes in sexual reproduction. Plants have solved this problem in many different ways. Some use water to transport male gametes to female gametes. Others use wind or even animals to bring about fertilization.

Figure 19.1 Nonvascular plants, such as the moss in this photograph, make up four out of the five divisions in the plant kingdom.

19–1 Asexual Reproduction

Many plants can reproduce both sexually and asexually. **Vegetative reproduction** involves cell division by mitosis. No specialized cells are formed in vegetative reproduction. **Fission**, in which one cell divides in two, is a common form of vegetative reproduction among unicellular plants. **Fragmentation** is a form of vegetative reproduction common in multicellular algae. In fragmentation, pieces of plants that are torn apart by animals or ocean currents can grow into complete new plants.

Some plants reproduce asexually by the formation of spores. Spores that are able to swim by means of flagella are called **zoospores**.

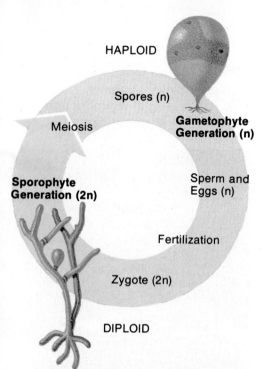

HAPLOID

Spores (n)

Meiosis

**Gametophyte
Generation (n)**

**Sporophyte
Generation (2n)**

Sperm and
Eggs (n)

Fertilization

Zygote (2n)

DIPLOID

Figure 19.2 Alternation of generations. Notice that the haploid (n) part of the cycle is yellow and the diploid (2n) part is blue. Color will be used in the same way in other life cycles in this and other chapters.

19–2   Alternation of Generations

Most plants reproduce sexually. As you learned in Chapter 9, sexual reproduction involves two processes: meiosis and fertilization. In meiosis, diploid cells divide to produce haploid gametes. In fertilization, two haploid gametes fuse to form a diploid zygote. In humans and most animals, the adult organism is diploid; gametes exist only as single-celled eggs or sperm.

Although it may seem normal for multicellular organisms to be diploid, among plants this is not necessarily the case. In many plants, the cells produced by meiosis do not immediately undergo fertilization. Instead, a haploid spore may grow into a multicellular plant body. This haploid organism may then produce gametes, which fuse with other gametes to form a zygote. In this situation, meiosis and fertilization are separated by a generation. A life cycle with an orderly sequence of haploid and diploid generations is said to have **alternation of generations**. A generalized diagram of alternation of generations is shown in Figure 19.2.

In alternation of generations, the diploid phase is called a **sporophyte.** The word *sporophyte* means "spore-producing." The sporophyte undergoes meiosis to produce haploid spores. Spores develop into haploid plants. Multicellular haploid plants are called **gametophytes**. As you can guess from the name, a gametophyte produces gametes.

Not all plants follow precisely the sequence of events shown in the diagram. In some species, the sporophyte and gametophyte look very much alike. In other plants, the sporophyte and gametophyte are so dissimilar that at one time they were mistaken for different species! Such a mistake was made with the green alga *Valonia*. The sporophyte and gametophyte generations of *Valonia* are illustrated in Figure 19.2. Because the two thalli are so different, the gametophyte was once called *Halicystis* while the sporophyte, assumed to be a different organism, was named *Derbesia*.

Checkpoint

1. What division includes plants with specialized tissues for conducting food and water?
2. A motile spore is called a _____ .
3. A life cycle in which a diploid generation is followed by a haploid generation is called _____ .
4. Which generation is haploid?
5. Which generation produces a haploid spore? Which produces a haploid gamete?

Algae

All three divisions of algae included in the plant kingdom have at least some multicellular species. The three divisions are believed to have evolved at separate times from three different groups of unicellular organisms. Multicellular algae have relatively unspecialized thalli.

All algae contain chlorophyll. Algae also contain other pigments. These pigments are able to capture light at various wavelengths and pass its energy on to chlorophyll. Algae in different divisions contain different types of pigments. In fact, these pigments give the divisions characteristic colors that are the basis of their common names: red algae, brown algae, and green algae. Algae are also classified according to their mode of reproduction and their biochemistry.

19–3   Division Chlorophyta: Green Algae

Division **Chlorophyta** [klohr-AH-fuh-tuh], or the green algae, is the most diverse group of algae. Some green algae are single-celled, some are colonial, and some are multicellular. The major pigment in green algae is chlorophyll, but green algae also contain yellow carotenes. High concentrations of carotenes make some green algae appear yellow-green. Green algae are common in lakes and ponds. Some are marine.

Chlorella, shown in Figure 19.3, is an example of a unicellular green alga. Each cell contains a cell wall, a chloroplast, and a nucleus. *Chlorella* does not reproduce sexually. Asexual reproduction occurs by the formation of many nonmotile spores within the parent cell. When the cell wall disintegrates, the spores are released.

Some green algae have flagella and are motile. *Chlamydomonas*, shown in Figure 19.4, is a unicellular, flagellated alga that lives in fresh water. Each cell has a light-sensitive eyespot. The eyespot allows a *Chlamydomonas* cell to move in the direction of light, thus aiding in photosynthesis.

CONCEPTS

- characteristics of red, brown, and green algae
- definition of unicellular, colonial, and multicellular organization
- distinction between isogamy and oogamy
- process of conjugation
- structure of *Fucus*

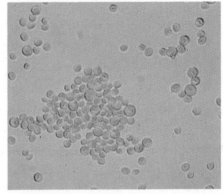

Figure 19.3 *Chlorella,* a unicellular green alga

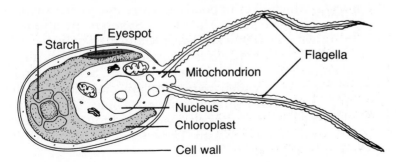

Figure 19.4 *Chlamydomonas,* a motile green alga

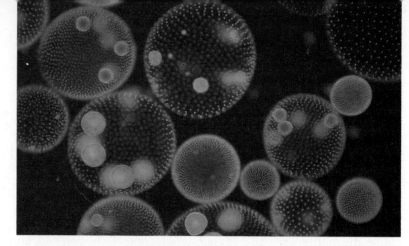

Figure 19.5 *Volvox,* a colonial green alga

Although *Chlamydomonas* reproduces sexually, it does not produce eggs or sperm. Instead, the gametes appear identical. Such gametes are called **isogametes**. **Isogamy,** or reproduction by isogametes, is the simplest form of sexual reproduction.

Volvox is an example of a colonial green alga. A **colonial** organism is multicellular, but the individual cells are similar in structure. In colonial organisms there is no specialization of cells or division of labor. *Volvox* colonies contain from 200–20,000 cells. Several colonies of *Volvox* are shown in Figure 19.5. Each *Volvox* colony is shaped like a hollow ball. Individual cells are enclosed in gelatin but are connected to each other by strands of cytoplasm. Each cell has two flagella and looks like a *Chlamydomonas* cell.

Sexual reproduction in *Volvox* is oogamous. In **oogamy,** two types of gametes are formed. Some cells produce large, nonmotile eggs. The eggs store food that can be used by the zygote for germination and growth. Other cells produce many small, motile sperm. The egg and sperm fuse in the center of the colony to form a zygote. When the parent colony disintegrates, it releases the zygote. The zygote undergoes a dormant period, then it begins to grow. Meiosis occurs, forming meiospores. A **meiospore** is a haploid spore that results from meiosis. Only one meiospore survives. This meiospore eventually produces a new colony. Notice that in the life cycle of *Volvox,* the only diploid cell is the zygote.

Spirogyra, which lives in ponds and streams, is an example of a filamentous green alga. The cells of *Spirogyra* are arranged in long threads, or **filaments**. Each filament is only one cell thick. Each cell of *Spirogyra* is a transparent cylinder. A ribbonlike chloroplast spirals through each cell. Several starch-forming structures called **pyrenoids** are embedded in the chloroplast. The cell contains a large vacuole. The nucleus, located in the center of the cell, is attached to the cell membrane by strands of cytoplasm. The cells of the filaments are haploid gametophytes.

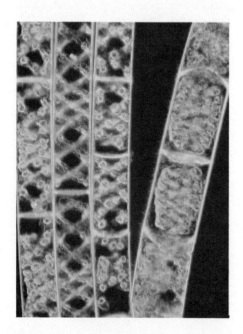

Figure 19.6 *Spirogyra,* a filamentous green alga

Spirogyra can reproduce sexually by a process called **conjugation**, which is illustrated in Figure 19.7. In conjugation, two filaments line up so that they touch each other. Small bumps grow out from each cell, forming bridges between each pair of cells. The cell walls dividing the bridges then dissolve, leaving passageways between the pairs of cells. The contents of the cells in one filament then enter the cells of the other filament. The transfer of gametes from one strand to the other results in one filament of empty cells and one filament containing zygotes.

The zygotes separate from each other, develop thick cell walls, and become zygospores. A **zygospore** is a diploid spore. When conditions are favorable, each zygospore undergoes meiosis. The resulting haploid cells eventually grow into new filaments of *Spirogyra*.

Oedogonium is a filamentous freshwater alga that is somewhat more complex than *Spirogyra*. *Oedogonium* shows some specialization of cells. Cells called **holdfasts** attach the filaments to rocks or other objects. *Oedogonium* reproduces sexually or asexually. In asexual reproduction, any cell except the holdfasts can produce a zoospore. The zoospores swim away from the parent filament. If a zoospore finds a suitable place, it will attach itself and grow into a new filament by cell division.

Sexual reproduction in *Oedogonium* involves two kinds of specialized reproductive cells, the oogonium and the antheridium. An **oogonium** [oh-uh-GOH-nee-uhm] is a cell that produces an egg. An **antheridium** [an-thur-RID-ee-uhm] is a cell that produces a sperm. Sperm swim to the oogonium and enter through a small pore. Once inside the oogonium, a sperm fertilizes the egg, thus forming a zygote.

When the zygote is released from the oogonium, it forms a thick wall and becomes a zygospore. The zygospore enters a period of dormancy that may last several months. It then undergoes meiosis, producing four zoospores, each of which can start a new filament.

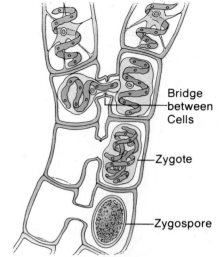

Figure 19.7 Conjugation in *Spirogyra*

Figure 19.8 Asexual and sexual reproduction in *Oedogonium*. Both kinds of reproduction may occur on the same filament.

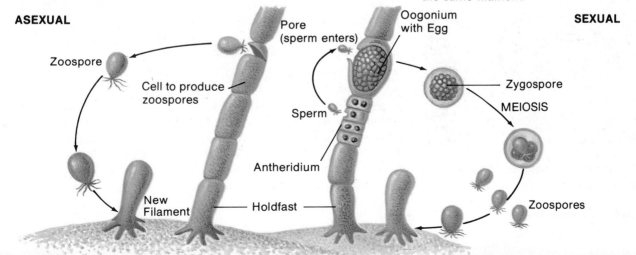

ASEXUAL

SEXUAL

Figure 19.9 *Top: Polysiphonia,* a red alga; *Bottom:* The red alga *Chondrus crispus,* or Irish moss. People who live on the coasts of Europe and North America eat Irish moss.

 BIOLOGY INSIGHTS

Sexual reproduction promotes genetic variability. As the algae show, there are many different variations on the basic theme of meiosis and fertilization. The nearly universal occurrence of sexual reproduction among eukaryotes is strong evidence that it is an evolutionary advantage.

19–4 Division Rhodophyta: Red Algae

Division **Rhodophyta** [roh-DAH-fuh-tuh] contains the red algae. Almost all red algae are marine. Most live in tropical waters, although they are also common along rocky coasts in colder waters. Red algae seldom exceed one meter in length. The thalli may be threadlike, but often they have a more complex, branched structure, such as those shown in Figure 19.9. All red algae grow attached to rocks, shells, or other surfaces. Larger forms are attached by holdfasts. A few red algae are unicellular.

All red algae contain the reddish pigment **phycoerythrin** [fy-koh-ur-ITH-ruhn], although not all red algae appear red. The presence of phycoerythrin allows some red algae to live in very deep water. Phycoerythrin is able to capture the energy of blue light, the only wavelength of light that can penetrate deep water. Phycoerythrin then transfers this energy to chlorophyll. Some red algae are able to live more than 100 meters below the surface.

Many species of red algae withdraw calcium from ocean water, depositing it in their cell walls. When the cells die, they leave behind beds of calcium salts. In some cases, deposits from red algae have formed a layer of limestone that is as much as 300 meters thick.

All red algae reproduce sexually. Many have very complex life cycles. The multicellular gametophytes produce two types of gametes — large eggs and smaller sperm. Thus reproduction is oogamous. Each egg is formed in a special flask-shaped oogonium. Sperm are produced in antheridia (plural of *antheridium*). Sperm lack flagella. Ocean currents carry the sperm to the egg.

In some species, the zygote remains attached to the oogonium and develops into a sporophyte. The sporophyte produces nonmotile spores. Currents carry the spores to new locations, where they begin a new gametophyte generation.

Some red algae are important food plants in parts of Asia. Some red algae contain a substance called carrageenin. Carrageenin is used in puddings, preserves, and ice cream. Red algae are also used to manufacture **agar**, a material used in laboratories for growing bacteria and fungi.

19–5 Division Phaeophyta: Brown Algae

Division **Phaeophyta** [fee-AH-fuh-tuh] contains about 1,000 species of brown algae. Most brown algae are marine. They are common in coastal areas, especially in cold water. Brown algae are the largest algae, sometimes reaching lengths of 50 meters. Brown algae contain a brown pigment called **fucoxanthin** [fyew-koh-ZAN-thin].

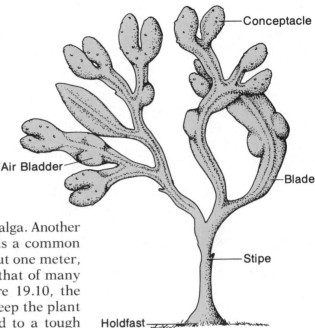

Figure 19.10 *Left:* Harvesting kelp, a brown alga; *Right:* The brown alga *Fucus*, or rockweed

The kelp shown on page 284 is a type of brown alga. Another brown algae, rockweed or *Fucus* [FYEW-kus], is a common seaweed in rocky areas. Rockweed grows to about one meter, and has a structure that is more complex than that of many other types of algae. As you can see in Figure 19.10, the branched thallus contains **air bladders**, which keep the plant afloat. The broad, leaflike **blades** are connected to a tough stalk called a **stipe**. Multicellular holdfasts anchor the plant in place.

As in red algae, sexual reproduction is oogamous. Reproductive organs called **conceptacles** are located at the ends of the blades. Each conceptacle contains a pore that opens to the outside. In gametophytes, a conceptacle may contain oogonia or antheridia. Eggs are large and nonmotile. Sperm are small and swim by means of two flagella.

Mature gametes are expelled from the conceptacle. Fertilization occurs in the water. The resulting zygote then develops into a multicellular sporophyte. The sporophyte reproduces by forming motile spores. These spores, in turn, grow into multicellular gametophytes. *Fucus* may also reproduce asexually by fragmentation.

Humans use brown algae in many ways. In Asia kelp and other brown algae are often eaten. In northern Europe brown algae are used as animal feed and fertilizer. Algin, a chemical contained in brown algae, is often used in the manufacture of latex, ceramic glazes, cosmetics, and ice cream.

Do You Know?

The brown algae *Sargassum natans* reproduces by fragmentation, creating masses of algae that cover millions of square kilometers in the Atlantic Ocean. It grows in the Sargasso Sea, an area between the Bahamas and the Azores.

Checkpoint

1. What criteria are used to classify algae?
2. What structure attaches an alga's thallus to a rock?
3. What is the function of air bladders in *Fucus*?
4. Name an alga that reproduces by conjugation.

Division Bryophyta

Bryophytes [BRY-uh-fyts] are small land plants that do not contain vascular tissue. Mosses and liverworts are bryophytes. Evidence indicates that bryophytes evolved from green algae about 400 million years ago.

Bryophytes have a few specializations that allow them to live on land. A protective outer layer of cells called the **epidermis** and a waxy covering called the **cuticle** prevent the thallus from drying out. Tiny pores in the epidermis allow exchange of gases between the cells and the air. Bryophytes are anchored in the ground by rootlike structures called **rhizoids.** Rhizoids lack chloroplasts.

Although bryophytes can grow on land, they are still restricted to moist areas. Because bryophytes lack specialized conductive tissues, they cannot transport food or water over distances of more than a few centimeters. Water moves by osmosis. All movement of materials within the thallus is by diffusion. Bryophytes also lack supportive tissue, so they never grow more than a few centimeters tall. Bryophytes require water for sexual reproduction.

19–6 Mosses

There are about 14,000 species of mosses. Mosses grow in moist, shady places such as rocky ledges, on the sides of trees, or along the banks of streams. They tend to grow in large carpets composed of many plants.

The conspicuous generation of mosses is the gametophyte. Each gametophyte has a slender stalk and many tiny, leaflike structures. Each leaflet is only one cell thick, and can absorb water directly from rain or dew. The hairlike rhizoids absorb water and minerals.

The life cycle of a moss plant begins when a haploid spore germinates. The spore grows into a filament that resembles a green alga. This stage is called a **protonema**. The protonema develops into a small gametophyte. Multicellular sex organs develop. The **archegonium** produces eggs and the antheridium produces sperm. When the sperm are mature, they swim to the eggs through a thin film of water. The fertilized egg develops into an **embryo,** or immature diploid organism. The embryo grows a stalk that remains attached to the archegonium. The upper end of the stalk develops a **capsule** that produces spores. The stalk and capsule are the sporophyte generation.

CONCEPTS

- how bryophytes are adapted to life on land
- why bryophytes are restricted to moist areas
- life cycle of a moss
- asexual reproduction in liverworts

Do You Know?

The name liverwort comes from the appearance of the plant. People once thought that the thallus resembled a piece of liver. *Wort* is an English word meaning "plant."

Figure 19.11 In moss plants the sporophyte generation grows on the gametophyte thallus.

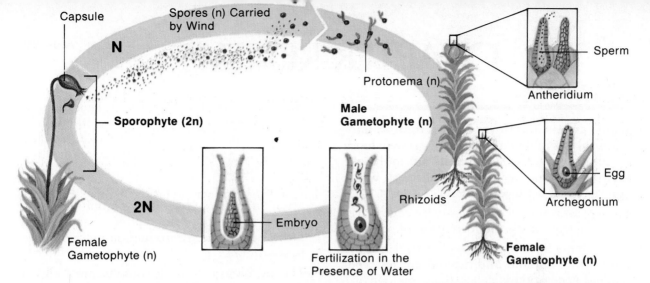

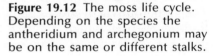

Figure 19.12 The moss life cycle. Depending on the species the antheridium and archegonium may be on the same or different stalks.

Mosses are beneficial in the formation of soil. Since mosses need only a thin layer of soil, they can grow in places where other plants cannot, such as in the cracks between rocks. When mosses die, they add their organic material to the soil. This builds up the soil so that larger plants may eventually grow there. Mosses also prevent the soil from drying out and blowing away. *Sphagnum* is a type of moss that grows in bogs. *Sphagnum* decays to form peat. Gardeners use peat to improve the texture of soil.

19–7 Liverworts

Liverworts are often found along streambanks. The thallus of the gametophyte is flattened. Like mosses, liverworts reproduce vegetatively to form carpets of tiny plants. Rhizoids anchor them to the ground. Their antheridia and archegonia grow on stalks that project above the thallus.

Some liverworts have an unusual means of asexual reproduction. These liverworts send up short stalks with little cups on the ends. In the cups are tiny flat structures called **gemmae**. When the gemmae are mature, raindrops can splash them out of the cups. If a gemma lands on a suitably moist spot, it develops rhizoids and grows into a new gametophyte that is genetically identical to the parent plant.

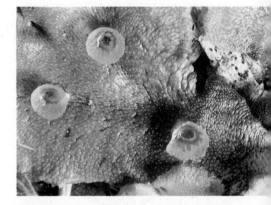

Figure 19.13 The liverwort *Marchantia* with gemmae cups

Checkpoint

1. Is the protonema part of the sporophyte or gametophyte generation?
2. Name two adaptations that allow bryophytes to live on land.
3. By what structures do liverworts reproduce asexually?

CHAPTER REVIEW

Summary

- Plants are eukaryotic organisms that contain chloroplasts and manufacture their own food by photosynthesis. Most plants are multicellular and nonmotile. All plants have cell walls composed of cellulose.

- Plants can reproduce asexually by vegetative reproduction or by the formation of spores.

- Most plants have life cycles characterized by alternating haploid and diploid phases. The haploid generation is called the gametophyte. The gametophyte produces gametes. The diploid generation, which undergoes meiosis to produce spores, is called the sporophyte.

- Three divisions of algae are included in the plant kingdom. Algae are classified according to their biochemistry, mode of reproduction, and the type of pigments present. Algae lack vascular tissue.

- Green algae may be unicellular, colonial, or multicellular. In addition to chlorophyll, green algae contain carotenes. Some unicellular species are motile. *Chlorella*, *Chlamydomonas*, *Volvox*, *Spirogyra*, and *Oedogonium* are green algae.

- Green algae may reproduce asexually by cell division or the formation of zoospores. Sexual reproduction may be isogamous or oogamous. Sperm are usually flagellated.

- Most red algae are multicellular. The presence of the pigment phycoerythrin allows some species to live at very great depths. Sexual reproduction is oogamous. Sperm lack flagella. Asexual reproduction occurs by the formation of nonmotile spores.

- Brown algae contain the pigment fucoxanthin. Some species show differentiation of the thallus into blades, stipes, holdfasts, and air bladders. Sexual reproduction may be oogamous. Reproductive organs called conceptacles may contain oogonia or antheridia. Rockweed and kelp are common brown algae.

- Bryophytes are land plants that lack vascular tissue. Mosses and liverworts are bryophytes. Although they live on land, they require water for sexual reproduction. Bryophytes are limited in size because they lack vascular tissues.

- The gametophyte is the conspicuous generation in bryophytes. The sporophyte is dependent upon the gametophyte for water and nutrients. Sexual reproduction in bryophytes is oogamous.

- The development of bryophytes includes a diploid embryo. The gametophyte of mosses has a developmental stage that is called the protonema.

- Liverworts may reproduce asexually by the formation of gemmae.

Vocabulary

agar	holdfast
air bladders	isogamete
alternation of	isogamy
generations	liverwort
antheridium	meiospore
archegonium	nonvascular plant
blade	oogamy
bryophyte	oogonium
capsule	Phaeophyta
Chlorophyta	phycoerythrin
colonial	protonema
conceptacles	pyrenoid
conjugation	rhizoid
cuticle	Rhodophyta
embryo	sporophyte
epidermis	stipe
filament	thallus
fission	vascular plant
fragmentation	vegetative
fucoxanthin	reproduction
gametophyte	zoospore
gemma	zygospore

Review

1. A spore that can swim is called a _____ .
2. What pigments are characteristic of (a) green algae, (b) red algae, (c) brown algae?
3. The body of a multicellular algae is called a _____ .
4. From which division of algae did bryophytes evolve?
5. What factors limit the size of a moss plant?

For questions 6–10, choose the descriptions in the right-hand column that apply to the green algae listed in the left-hand column. More than one description may fit a particular plant.

6. *Chlorella*
7. *Chlamydomonas*
8. *Volvox*
9. *Spirogyra*
10. *Oedogonium*

a. nonmotile and unicellular
b. no sexual reproduction
c. spherical colony
d. filamentous
e. motile and unicellular
f. sexual reproduction by conjugation
g. isogamous sexual reproduction
h. antheridia and oogonia present

Interpret and Apply

1. What are the functions of rhizoids?
2. How is sexual reproduction in *Oedogonium* more complex than sexual reproduction in *Spirogyra*?
3. How are the zoospores of *Oedogonium* like the gemmae of liverworts?
4. What is the difference between isogamy and oogamy?
5. Why are red algae able to live at depths of water that exclude other plant life?
6. What is the difference between a gamete and a meiospore?
7. In what way are land-living mosses still dependent upon water?

8. Is a moss embryo haploid or diploid? Is the protonema haploid or diploid?
9. What is the difference between a colonial organism and a multicellular organism?

Choose the answer that best completes each of the following questions. Write your answers on a separate sheet of paper. Do not write in this book.

10. Which of the following is *not* a form of asexual reproduction? (a) isogamy (b) gemmae (c) fission (d) fragmentation
11. Which of the following is *not* found in the brown algae *Fucus*? (a) stipe (b) archegonia (c) conceptacle (d) air bladders
12. Which of the following is diploid? (a) a meiospore (b) a gametophyte (c) a zygospore (d) a protonema
13. Which of the following is *not* found in bryophytes? (a) cuticle (b) pores (c) roots (d) archegonium
14. Which of the following is found in red algae? (a) motile sperm (b) protonema (c) air bladders (d) phycoerythrin

Challenge

1. Why are pores necessary in land plants but not in algae?
2. Which part of a kelp plant has the same function as a rhizoid?
3. Compare the mechanisms of dispersal in green algae, red algae, and bryophytes. How are offspring transported to new locations?

Projects

1. Explore moist areas near your home to find mosses or liverworts. Gather some moss capsules. Open the capsules and examine the spores under a microscope.
2. If you live near the ocean, make a trip to a rocky area and gather algae such as *Fucus*. Identify the structures described in the text.
3. Find out how the Sargasso Sea affects ships that sail through it. How did this influence the early exploration of the New World?

20 Vascular Plants

Cycad with cones growing in a New Zealand forest

Do you recognize the plant in the picture above? You may have seen one like it in a greenhouse. But unless you live in southern Florida, chances are that you have never seen one growing in the wild.

The plant is a cycad. Some people think it looks like a palm tree. In fact, its common name is sago palm. Other people think its leaves resemble those of a fern. Actually, the cycad is more closely related to a pine tree than either a fern or a palm. Its reproductive organs are the cones that you can see in the picture.

Although cycads are rare today, they were abundant 230 million years ago, when dinosaurs first appeared on Earth. The palmlike trees in the background of dinosaur illustrations are often cycads.

When flowering plants began to dominate the landscape about 135 million years ago, the cycads became less plentiful. Only about 100 species of cycads are living today. Most are found in Australia, Asia, and South Africa. A few grow in the American tropics.

Division Tracheophyta

Although mosses and other bryophytes live on land, they are restricted to growing in extremely moist areas. The plants that have truly conquered dry land are vascular plants. Vascular plants belong to the division Tracheophyta. Vascular plants are also called **tracheophytes** [TRAYK-ee-oh-fyts].

20–1 Adaptations to Life on Land

Life on land is very different from life in the oceans. For plants to be successful on land, they must have adaptations that are different from those of plants that are successful in the oceans.

The most obvious difference between life in the oceans and life on land is the availability of water. Algae can absorb water and nutrients from their surroundings. It is more difficult for land plants to obtain water. Unlike bryophytes, vascular plants have developed structures that obtain water and dissolved nutrients from deep in the ground.

Land plants also lose water to the air by evaporation. For this reason, land plants need some type of waterproof covering to reduce the rate of evaporation. Like bryophytes, vascular plants are protected by a layer of cuticle.

Water provides physical support to algae, allowing some algae to reach large sizes. Air is less dense than water and cannot support the tissues of large plants. To grow to large sizes, land plants must have strong supportive tissues.

Aquatic plants rely on water for the transport of gametes. Without water, sperm cannot swim to eggs. Most vascular plants have adaptations that allow fertilization to take place without water. Land plants must also rely on agents other than water for the dispersal of spores or seeds.

CONCEPTS

- adaptations necessary for success on land
- tissues of vascular plants
- organs of vascular plants
- trends in the evolution of vascular plants

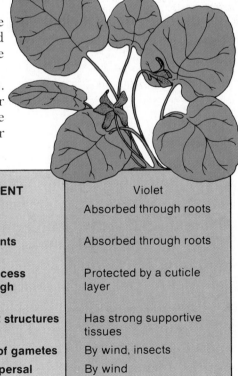

Figure 20.1 Comparing kelp (nonvascular plant) and a violet (vascular plant)

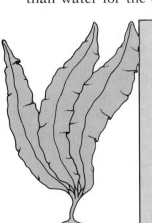

Kelp	REQUIREMENT	Violet
Absorbed directly from surroundings	**Water**	Absorbed through roots
Absorbed directly from surroundings	**Dissolved nutrients**	Absorbed through roots
No evaporation	**Prevention of excess water loss through evaporation**	Protected by a cuticle layer
Supported by water	**Support of plant structures**	Has strong supportive tissues
By water	**Transportation of gametes**	By wind, insects
By water	**Seed/spore dispersal**	By wind

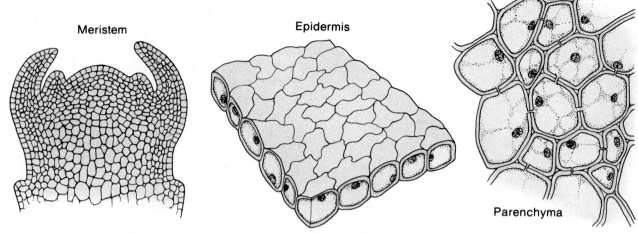

Meristem

Epidermis

Parenchyma

Figure 20.2 Tissues found in vascular plants

20–2   Tissues in Vascular Plants

Many of the adaptations of vascular plants result from the development of specialized tissues. The major types of tissues found in vascular plants are shown in Figure 20.2.

Meristematic Tissue   **Meristem** is a tissue that contains unspecialized cells that are continually dividing and producing new cells. The cells in the meristem have thin walls and dense cytoplasm.

Meristematic tissue found at the tip (or apex) of a root or stem is called **apical meristem**. A single layer of meristematic cells is also found between the bark and wood of a tree. This type of meristem is called **vascular cambium**.

Cells produced by meristematic tissues eventually differentiate into other tissues. The walls of some cells become thickened. Other cells elongate. Each cell becomes specialized for another function, such as absorption, transport, reproduction, or storage. All of the following tissues develop from meristematic tissue.

Epidermis   Surrounding the organs is a tissue that is specialized to reduce the loss of water. This tissue is the **epidermis** [ehp-uh-DUR-mihs]. The epidermis is usually one cell thick and is covered by a waxy cuticle. The cuticle keeps water in the cells.

Parenchyma   **Parenchyma** [puh-REN-kuh-muh] is tissue that is specialized for the storage of sugars and starches. The cells of parenchyma are more or less spherical. They have thin walls and large vacuoles. **Chlorenchyma** [kloh-REN-kuh-muh] is a kind of parenchyma that is specialized for photosynthesis. Chlorenchyma cells contain chloroplasts.

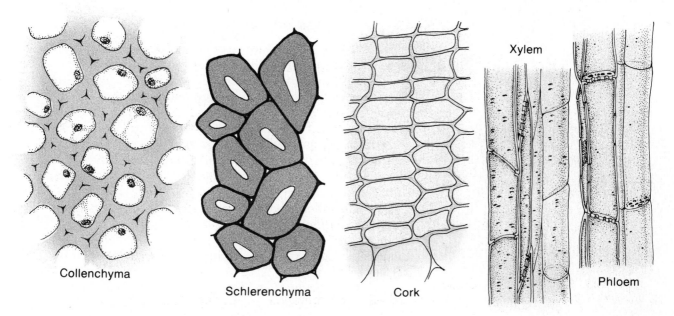

Collenchyma

Schlerenchyma

Cork

Xylem

Phloem

Supportive Tissue **Collenchyma** [kol-EHNK-uh-muh] is strengthening and supporting tissue. The cells of collenchyma are long and somewhat thickened near the corners. Collenchyma is often found in young stems and may be associated with vascular tissues. Long **sclerenchyma** [skluh-REN-kuh-muh] fibers give plants strength, mechanical support, and protection. Sclerenchyma cells have very thick secondary cell walls. Mature sclerenchyma cells often lack cytoplasm.

Cork Cork cells are specialized for conserving water and protecting the plant. Cork cells are dead at maturity. The dead cork cells form a waterproof layer around many stems.

Vascular Tissue All tracheophytes contain **vascular tissues**, which perform two important functions. Vascular tissues can support the weight of a large plant, and they can conduct food, water, and dissolved minerals from one part of the plant to another. Vascular tissues allow plants to grow to enormous sizes. In fact, the giant sequoias of the West Coast, the largest living things, are vascular plants.

In general, the cells of vascular tissues are quite long and have thick cell walls. There are two major types of vascular tissues. **Phloem** [FLOW-uhm] is the tissue that transports sugars and starches from one part of a plant to another. Phloem cells are living. **Xylem** [ZY-luhm] is specialized for the transport of water and dissolved minerals. The cells of xylem are hollow and no longer living at maturity. Vascular tissue often occurs in strands composed of xylem and phloem. The strands of conducting and supporting tissue are called **vascular bundles**.

Leaves (food making)

Flower (reproduction)

Stem (conduction of water, minerals, food)

Roots (support, collects water and dissolved minerals)

Figure 20.3 The organs of vascular plants

20–3 Organs of Vascular Plants

As you know, organs are composed of several types of tissues grouped together to perform a particular function. Most vascular plants have roots, leaves, stems, and reproductive organs. These organs are connected by continuous pipelines of vascular tissues. Figure 20.3 shows a generalized diagram of a vascular plant.

Roots are organs that are specialized to collect water and dissolved minerals from the soil. Roots also hold plants in place. Unlike the rhizoids of mosses, roots may extend far into the ground.

A **stem** is an organ that conducts water and minerals from the roots to other parts of the plant. Stems also conduct food from leaves to the rest of the plant. Many stems can store food. Some stems carry on photosynthesis. Tree trunks are actually stems.

Leaves are the main photosynthetic organs of vascular plants. Leaves are usually somewhat flattened, which greatly increases the amount of surface area exposed to the sun for photosynthesis. This allows maximum collection of light energy. Leaves produce food that is used by the rest of the plant.

Vascular plants have developed several kinds of reproductive organs. Spores are produced in multicellular organs called **sporangia** (singular, *sporangium*). Seed-bearing plants may bear either **cones** or **flowers**.

Checkpoint

1. What are the two types of vascular tissues?
2. What organ connects the leaves and the roots?
3. Name three kinds of tissues that are specialized for supporting vascular plants.
4. What is the function of meristematic tissue?

Spore-Bearing Vascular Plants

Early vascular plants appeared on land over 400 million years ago. Some of them, the club mosses and the horsetails, were giant trees, with stems as much as two meters in diameter. The remains of these early trees form some of the coal used today.

Like the mosses, the early vascular plants reproduced by means of spores. A spore is a simple structure that contains a single haploid cell.

There are four subdivisions of spore-bearing vascular plants alive today. They are the whiskferns, the horsetails, the club mosses, and the ferns. In all of these groups, spores germinate to produce a gametophyte. The gametophyte lives independently of the sporophyte but is much smaller. All spore-bearing vascular plants alive today require water for fertilization. Because the gametophyte is small and grows close to the ground, the sperm usually can use dew and other temporary sources of water for fertilization.

20–4   Whiskferns

The simplest living vascular plants are members of the subdivision Psilopsida [seye-LAHP-sih-duh]. Only a few members of this subdivision are still in existence. The only **whiskferns** in North America grow in Florida.

Whiskferns are small plants, rarely more than a meter tall. Whiskferns have no leaves or true roots. Their lack of leaves and roots indicates that they are the most primitive of vascular plants. Their erect branches look like bundles of green, forked sticks.

At the intersection of some branches are sporangia. Each sporangium releases numerous small spores that are spread by the wind. A spore that falls on suitable land develops into a small, algaelike gametophyte called a **prothallus**. The prothallus grows underground, where it sends out long brown rhizoids that penetrate the soil. Each prothallus is only a few millimeters in diameter. Many antheridia (sperm-producing organs) and archegonia (egg-producing organs) cover its surface. Sperm swim through moisture in the soil to reach the eggs of other prothalli. After fertilization, a simple embryo develops and eventually grows into a mature sporophyte.

Because the prothallus grows underground, it is not able to photosynthesize. Instead, it relies for food on fungi that grow near it. The hyphae of the fungi in the soil penetrate the tissue of the prothallus.

CONCEPTS

- characteristics of whiskferns, horsetails, club mosses, and ferns
- life cycle of a fern

Figure 20.4 A whiskfern

Figure 20.5 Club moss

Figure 20.6 Horsetails

Figure 20.7 Fiddleheads

20–5 Club Mosses

Despite their name, **club mosses** are not bryophytes. Instead, they are simple vascular plants that belong to the subdivision Lycopsida. Club mosses are common in the tropics and on the forest floor in cooler climates.

The club moss sporophyte has tiny, scalelike leaves. Sporecases grow at the base of some branches. As in whiskferns, the club moss gametophyte is a prothallus that grows underground and obtains its food from fungi.

20–6 Horsetails

Horsetails usually grow in swampy areas. They are the only living representatives of a once common subdivision, the Sphenopsida. The only living genus is *Equisetum*, which means "horsetail" in Latin. The stems and leaves of *Equisetum* are bushy like a horse's tail. At each joint, small leaves encircle the stem. The jointed stems are woody and contain the element silicon.

Cones develop at the tips of some stems. Inside the cones are sporangia. Spores germinate on the surface of wet soil. The gametophyte prothallus that grows from the spore is green and either branched or lobed.

20–7 Ferns

The **ferns** are among the oldest groups of vascular plants. Their 9,000 species are widely distributed from the tropics to the Arctic. Ferns range in size from tiny water ferns to tropical tree ferns, which may reach heights of 25 meters. Most North American species do not exceed one meter.

Ferns have true leaves, roots, and stems. The stems usually grow horizontally underground and are called **rhizomes**. Roots arise from the rhizomes and branch into the soil. Fern leaves called **fronds** grow up from the rhizomes. Although the fronds of the sporophyte may die each fall, the rhizomes may live for many years. When young, fronds are tightly coiled into **fiddleheads**. In many places, the gracefully unfurling fiddleheads are a sure sign of spring. The fiddleheads of some ferns are considered a delicacy and are eaten by many people.

The lower surfaces of some fronds have brown spots called sori (singular, *sorus*). Each **sorus** is a cluster of sporangia containing many spores.

Ferns show a clear alternation of generations, as illustrated in Figure 20.8. As in all vascular plants, the sporophyte is far larger than the gametophyte.

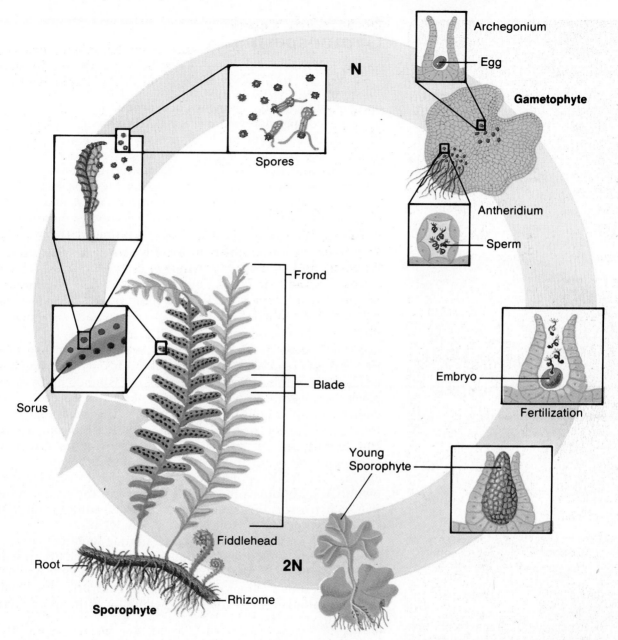

N

Archegonium

Egg

Gametophyte

Antheridium

Sperm

Spores

Frond

Embryo

Fertilization

Blade

Sorus

Young
Sporophyte

Fiddlehead

2N

Root

Rhizome

Sporophyte

Figure 20.8 The life cycle of a fern

Checkpoint

1. Why are whiskferns considered the most primitive tracheophytes?
2. How does the club moss prothallus obtain its food?
3. What is a rhizome?
4. Where are the spores of ferns produced?

- characteristics of gymnosperms
- advantages of reproduction by seeds
- life cycle of a pine

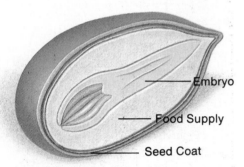

Figure 20.9 The three parts of a seed

Spore	Seed
One cell	Many cells
One part	Three parts
Haploid — becomes a gametophyte	Diploid — embryo of sporophyte
Delicate	Hardy
Produced by mosses, ferns, clubmosses, whiskferns, and horsetails	Produced by gymnosperms and angiosperms

Figure 20.10 Comparing spores and seeds

Gymnosperms

By far the largest subdivision of the vascular plants is the subdivision Spermatophyta, or the seed plants. The development of the seed as a means of reproduction and dispersal has allowed **spermatophytes** [spur-MAHT-uh-fyts] to dominate the forests and grasslands of the world. Scientists divide modern spermatophytes into two major classes: the gymnosperms and the angiosperms, or flowering plants.

Gymnosperms are an ancient group, having appeared during the Carboniferous period some 300 million years ago. Today there are about 700 species of gymnosperms. Gymnosperms make up about one third of the vegetation of the world's forests. Modern gymnosperms include cycads, ginkgoes, gnetophytes, and conifers.

20–8   The Seed

One characteristic common to all gymnosperms is the production of **seeds**. Seeds are much better adapted for dispersal than are spores. Whereas spores contain only one haploid cell, seeds contain many cells. Each seed is made up of three parts — an embryo, a food supply, and a seed coat. The **embryo** is an immature diploid plant. The **seed coat** is a tough, waterproof covering. Protected by the seed coat, a seed can lie dormant for many years without losing its ability to **germinate**, or begin to grow. When the seed germinates, it can use the food supply until it is capable of producing its own food by photosynthesis. The embryo in the seed is a bit like an astronaut in a spaceship — the seed contains all that the embryo needs for survival in a new location.

Although spores and seeds serve similar functions, a seed is not simply a modified spore. Spores and seeds represent different stages in the life cycle of a plant. A spore is haploid and grows into a gametophyte plant. In contrast, a seed contains a diploid embryo and is the beginning of the sporophyte generation.

20–9   Alternation of Generations in Gymnosperms

As in all vascular plants, the sporophyte of the gymnosperms is far larger than the gametophyte. But the gametophytes of gymnosperms are much smaller than the gametophytes of ferns. In fact, the gametophyte develops within the body of the gymnosperm sporophyte. The gametophyte generation does not live independently of the sporophyte generation.

The sporophytes of gymnosperms produce two kinds of spores. Small **microspores** give rise to the male gametophytes. Larger **megaspores** give rise to female gametophytes.

Unlike ferns and mosses, most gymnosperms do not require water for fertilization. Instead, the microspores give rise to male reproductive structures called **pollen**, which are transported to the eggs by wind. Pollen grains are immature male gametophytes. When they reach a female gametophyte, they complete their development.

20–10 Ginkgoes and Gnetophytes

The **ginkgo**, or maidenhair tree, is the only surviving species of a once-large group. Ginkgoes are natives of China. Today they are often planted along city streets. Ginkgoes grow to be tall trees, often reaching over 30 meters. Their leaves are shaped like fans. The veins in the leaves are parallel. Ginkgoes are deciduous, losing their leaves in the winter.

Ginkgoes bear their pollen and ovules on separate trees. Wind transfers pollen from male trees to female trees. Ginkgo seeds resemble yellow cherries, but have an unpleasant odor.

The **gnetophytes** [NEE-toh-fyts] are also gymnosperms. This small group includes a shrub called *Ephedra*, which is common in the southwestern deserts. *Ephedra* is also called Mormon tea. The leaves of *Ephedra* plants are very tiny. Their green stems carry on photosynthesis.

20–11 Cycads

Cycads, such as the one shown on page 296, have unbranched stems that are crowned by long, leathery leaves. Like ginkgoes, cycads produce pollen and ovules on separate plants. The wind aids in pollination.

Cycads have a method of fertilization that represents, in abbreviated form, the process found in lower plants. The pollen grains produce large sperm. Each sperm is covered with cilia. The cycad egg is surrounded by a drop of water. The sperm must swim through the drop of water before it can unite with the egg. So in a very small way, the cycads, like their ancestors, depend on water for fertilization.

Figure 20.11 *Left: Ephedra; Right:* A ginkgo. Ginkgoes are able to tolerate high levels of air pollution. This is one reason why they are often planted along city streets.

20–12　Conifers

Because they are so widespread, **conifers** are familiar to everyone. Conifers are able to grow in many different environments. They thrive in cool climates, poor or sandy soil, the salt air of the seashore, and the harsh conditions of mountains. Conifers form vast forests in northern Europe and North America. Among the 600 species of conifers are pines, firs, spruces, cedars, hemlocks, and sequoias.

The leaves of most conifers are modified into **needles**. Needles have a small amount of surface area compared to the broad leaves of other types of trees. This shape reduces water loss during dry seasons and also reduces their chance of freezing. Most conifers are evergreen, keeping their needles all year.

Conifers have woody stems, allowing them to grow to huge sizes. California redwoods may grow taller than 30-story buildings. Because of their fast growth, conifers are a major source of lumber and of pulp for paper. Pines are an important source of turpentine. The seeds of conifers are important food for many birds and rodents. The seeds of some pines, called pine nuts, are used in Middle Eastern cooking. They are also eaten by the Indians of the Southwest.

20–13　The Life Cycle of a Pine

The life cycle of a typical conifer, a pine, is shown in Figure 20.13. Male **pollen cones** and female **seed cones** are produced on the same tree, although usually on separate branches.

Inside the seed cones are **megasporangia**. Cells in the megasporangia undergo meiosis, thus producing megaspores. The megaspores develop into female gametophytes inside the cone. The female gametophytes are protected and nourished by the sporophyte.

At the same time, **microsporangia** in the pollen cones produce microspores. Microspores begin to develop into male gametophytes. Before they reach maturity, however, they are released as pollen grains. Each pollen grain contains a few haploid nuclei.

Pollen grains, carried by the wind, drift down between the scales of the female cones. **Pollination** occurs when the pollen grains land near the female gametophytes inside the seed cones. Once inside the seed cones, each pollen grain sends out a tiny **pollen tube**. The pollen tube is the mature gametophyte.

Each female gametophyte produces eggs. Fertilization occurs when sperm from the pollen tube unite with the eggs. The fertilized egg is the first cell of the sporophyte, or diploid generation. As long as a year may pass between pollination and fertilization.

Figure 20.12 The needles of conifers are well adapted to cold, dry climates.

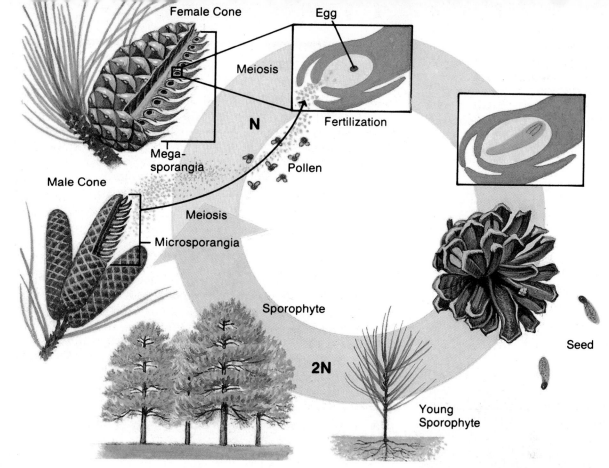

Female Cone
Egg
Meiosis
Fertilization
N
Mega-sporangia
Pollen
Male Cone
Meiosis
Microsporangia
Sporophyte
Seed
2N
Young Sporophyte

The young seed grows inside the seed cone. The female gametophyte absorbs food from the sporophyte and develops into the food supply for the seed. The seed coat forms around the zygote and food supply. When the seeds are ripe, the woody cone opens. Each seed has papery wings, which allow the wind to carry it away.

If a seed lands in a good location, it will germinate. An embryonic root pushes into the soil, and the young stem and leaves push up through the soil. The young plant absorbs the food stored in the seed until it is able to manufacture its own food by photosynthesis. Eventually it grows into the familiar evergreen tree. Pine trees may live for several hundred years.

Figure 20.13 The life cycle of a conifer

Do You Know?
Not all conifers are evergreens. The larch tree, or tamarack, loses its needles in winter. This is also true of the bald-cypress.

Checkpoint

1. Name four major groups of gymnosperms.
2. What are the three parts of a seed?
3. To what generation does pollen belong? The cones of pine trees?

The most plentiful kinds of plants living today are **angiosperms** [AN-jee-oh-sperms], or flowering plants. Angiosperms arose about 135 million years ago. Angiosperm fossils appear rather suddenly in the geological record, so botanists are not sure from which group they arose. Once they arose, they spread rapidly and diversified into many forms. Today there are over 250,000 species of angiosperms. They take the form of trees, shrubs, herbs, grasses, vines, and floating plants.

20–14 Characteristics of Angiosperms

All angiosperms possess two characteristics not found in gymnosperms: all have flowers, and all have seeds that develop within fruit. In fact, the name *angiosperm* means "covered seed," referring to the surrounding fruit. In contrast, *gymnosperm* means "naked seed."

The development of the flower was a great advantage to seed plants. Before flowers appeared, seed-bearing plants depended upon the transfer of pollen by wind for the union of egg and sperm. Wind was powerful, but not very precise. Only a tiny percentage of pollen actually reached eggs of the same species.

In contrast, the early flowers relied on insects to transfer pollen from one plant to another. Insects flew directly from flower to flower, making pollination much more precise. Far less pollen was wasted.

As is true of all vascular plants, the sporophyte generation of angiosperms is dominant over the gametophyte. As in gymnosperms, the gametophyte is small and contained within the sporophyte. Reproduction of angiosperms is similar to that of gymnosperms. It is covered in detail in Chapter 23.

Figure 20.14 Examples of angiosperms

Water lily

Orchid

Oak

Grass

Dicot

- Two embryonic leaves
- Branched veins on leaves
- About 170,000 species

- Seed structure:

Rose

Monocot

- One embryonic leaf
- Parallel veins on leaves
- About 65,000 species

- Seed structure:

Lily

Figure 20.15 Comparing monocots and dicots

20–15 Monocots and Dicots

Inside the seeds of angiosperms are tiny embryonic leaves. The leaves of the embryo are called **cotyledons** [kaht-uh-LEED-uhnz]. Cotyledons usually provide food for the young plant. In some angiosperms, the embryo has two cotyledons. These angiosperms are called **dicotyledons** or dicots. Other angiosperms have one cotyledon. These plants are called **monocotyledons** or monocots.

In addition to a single embryonic leaf, monocots have parallel veins in their leaves. Some common monocots are grasses, sedges, lilies, and palm trees. There are about 65,000 species of monocots.

The leaves of dicots have branched veins. Among the 170,000 species of dicots are buttercups, peas, roses, sunflowers, and maple trees.

20–16 Use by Humans

Angiosperms produce the majority of human food. You can be quite sure that any fruit or vegetable in your refrigerator is part of an angiosperm. The chicken or beef you eat came from an animal that once fed on angiosperms, probably grain. Angiosperms are the basis of modern agriculture. They provide people with wood and cotton, oils, medicines, spices, and many other products. In addition, they provide much of the beauty of the natural world. In short, it is difficult to imagine living in a world without angiosperms.

Do You Know?

Duckweed is a common plant in ponds. This tiny angiosperm floats on the surface of the water. The entire plant is smaller than a dime.

Checkpoint

1. What are the two major differences between angiosperms and gymnosperms?
2. Why was the flower an advantage to early angiosperms?
3. What is the difference between a dicot and a monocot?

CHAPTER REVIEW

Summary

- The evolution of vascular plants has followed several major trends. These trends include
  1. the differentiation of cells into tissues and the grouping of tissues into organs;
  2. the development of vascular tissues for conducting water, dissolved minerals, and food;
  3. the reduction of the gametophyte;
  4. the replacement of spores by seeds as the method of dispersal;
  5. the development of flowers and fruit.

- Vascular plants have several well-developed organs, each with a specific function. They are roots, stems, leaves, and reproductive organs.

- The earliest vascular plants were spore-bearers. Modern representatives of these plants include whiskferns, club mosses, horsetails, and ferns.

- The most successful vascular plants are the spermatophytes, or seed plants. The seed plants include the gymnosperms and the angiosperms.

- A seed is composed of an immature plant and its temporary food supply, surrounded by a tough seed coat. Seeds can remain dormant until conditions for their growth are favorable.

- Gymnosperms bear seeds that are naked, not enclosed within a fruit. Gymnosperms produce two kinds of spores — microspores and megaspores. Ginkgoes, gnetophytes, cycads, and conifers are gymnosperms.

- The angiosperms have seeds that are surrounded by fruit. Angiosperms also have flowers, which provide an extremely efficient means of pollination. Angiosperms are the most successful plants on Earth.

Vocabulary

angiosperm
apical meristem
chlorenchyma
club moss
collenchyma
cone
conifer
cork
cotyledon
cycad
dicotyledon
embryo
epidermis
fern
fiddlehead
flower
frond
germinate
ginkgo
gnetophyte
gymnosperm
horsetail
leaf
megasporangium
megaspore
meristem
microsporangium

microspore
monocotyledon
needle
parenchyma
phloem
pollen
pollen cone
pollen tube
pollination
prothallus
rhizome
root
sclerenchyma
seed
seed coat
seed cone
sorus
spermatophyte
sporangium
stem
tracheophyte
vascular bundle
vascular cambium
vascular tissue
whiskfern
xylem

Review

1. What is another word for *vascular plants*?
2. What is the function of vascular tissue?

In the following list, match the tissue type to its function. Each tissue may have more than one function.

3. xylem
4. phloem
5. epidermis
6. cork
7. parenchyma
8. chlorenchyma
9. root
10. meristem

a. protection
b. photosynthesis
c. conduction of food
d. conduction of water
e. support
f. storage
g. growth
h. not a tissue

Interpret and Apply

1. The following structures are found in vascular plants. For each structure, identify whether it is a part of the gametophyte generation or of the sporophyte generation. (a) prothallus (b) spore (c) seed (d) pollen (e) fern frond (f) egg
2. What two characteristics are present in angiosperms, but not in gymnosperms?
3. What are two differences between ginkgoes and conifers?
4. Name one gymnosperm and one angiosperm that gives us wood.
5. Name one characteristic present in ferns, but not in mosses.
6. Name one characteristic present in gymnosperms, but not in ferns.
7. Compare the pollen of a gymnosperm with the spores of a fern. How are they similar? How are they different?
8. Ferns are to spores as conifers are to ____ .
9. Conifers are to cones as angiosperms are to ____ .
10. Which of the following characteristics represent earlier plants (E), and which represent more recently evolved plants (R)? (a) spores (b) seeds (c) gametophyte dominant (d) organs well developed (e) flowers (f) no vascular tissue

Choose the best answer for each of the following questions. Write the letters of your answers on a separate piece of paper.

11. Which of the following is *not* an organ?
    (a) root (b) stem (c) xylem (d) leaf
12. Which of the following does *not* need water to reproduce?
    (a) fern (b) cycad (c) whiskfern (d) conifer

Challenge

1. You live in an insect-free house. You are growing tomato plants in pots on the windowsills. Although the plants produce plenty of flowers, they never develop their fruits, tomatoes. Why is this so? How can you make the plants produce fruit indoors?
2. You have a brown bag lunch consisting of a cheese sandwich, an apple, and a can of tomato juice. Tell which plant, directly or indirectly, was the source of (a) the bag, (b) the bread, (c) the cheese, (d) the apple, and (e) the juice.

Projects

1. Using a field guide, try to determine which species of conifers are present in your area.
2. Visit a conservatory or university greenhouse. Ask to see cycads, if they have any growing there.
3. Make a collection of different types of cones and of different types of angiosperm seeds. Your collection of angiosperm seeds will almost certainly be much larger. Why?
4. Try some "supermarket gardening." Attempt to grow plants from the seeds of fruits and vegetables you buy at the market. Many people have had success in growing plants from avocado seeds, or pits.

21 Leaves

Young leaves of a horse chestnut,
Aesculus hippocastanum

It is spring, and a new growing season has begun. Unfolding buds reveal new leaves, tiny but perfectly formed. As spring progresses, the cells in these tiny leaves will expand by taking in water and nutrients.

The branches of the tree hold the young leaves in position so that they catch the sunlight falling on them. As sunlight strikes them, they capture its energy, making food for their own growth and that of the rest of the plant. Leaves like these, and countless others in years past, have provided all the organic matter of which the entire tree is composed.

Leaves are not only beautiful to look at, but they are also a tasty meal for many insects. Caterpillars and many other insects nibble on the tender leaves. These insects, in turn, become food for larger animals such as birds. The leaves of plants are the basic source of food for all animals on land. When you eat a crispy salad, much of what you enjoy is the leaves of various plants. Cabbage, lettuce, watercress, and chives are all leaves that people eat. The leaves of some plants — including peppermint, parsley, sage, and basil — are used as herbs for cooking.

Leaf Structure and Function

Although roots and stems have multiple functions, the leaf in its usual form has few. Leaves are the main organs of photosynthesis. Leaves use carbon dioxide and water, in the presence of light and chlorophyll, to produce sugar.

Leaves vary greatly in shape and size. Some leaves are so tiny that they are barely visible to the unaided eye. Some, like those of the banana tree, are huge. Banana leaves may be four meters long. Some are heart-shaped, some egg-shaped, and some spear-shaped. The leaf margin, or edge, may be smooth, lobed, or toothed, as illustrated in Figure 21.1. Yet certain features are common to the structure of all leaves. This is not surprising, since structure determines function.

CONCEPTS

- external structure of a leaf
- cross section of a typical leaf
- difference between leaves of dicots and monocots
- how leaf structure favors efficient photosynthesis
- function of guard cells and stomata

21–1 Leaf Shape and Arrangement

Leaves grow out of meristematic tissue in the stem. The region of the stem where the leaf is attached is called the **node**. Each leaf is usually composed of two parts, the blade and the petiole. The **blade** is the flattened portion of the leaf. The **petiole** is the stemlike structure that connects the leaf to the stem. At the base of each petiole is a bud.

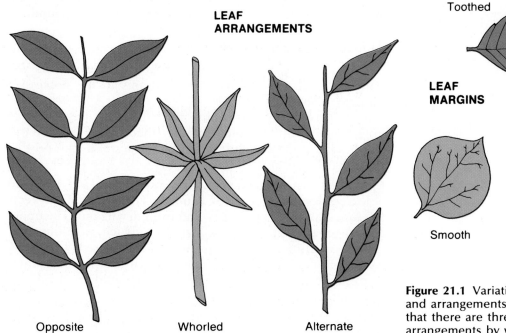

LEAF ARRANGEMENTS

Opposite   Whorled   Alternate

Toothed

LEAF MARGINS

Smooth   Lobed

Figure 21.1 Variations in the margins and arrangements of leaves. Notice that there are three possible arrangements by which leaves can be attached to a stem.

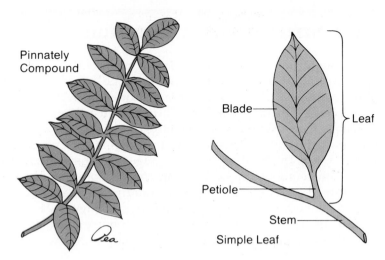

Figure 21.2 Simple and compound leaves

If a petiole is attached to only one blade, the entire structure is called a **simple leaf**. Sometimes, though, many small blades, or **leaflets**, are attached to one petiole. The leaflets all arise from one bud. The entire structure is then called a **compound leaf**. Figure 21.2 shows several types of compound leaves.

In the leaf of the horse chestnut, the leaflets come together at a central point. This is like the arrangement of your fingers, which all join at your palm. Therefore, this leaf type is said to be **palmately compound**. In other plants, such as the pea, the leaflets attach to the petiole in a pattern resembling a feather. Such leaves are said to be **pinnately compound**.

21–2 Leaf Cross Section

Several types of tissue are present in all leaves. As you will see, each type of tissue contributes to the process of photosynthesis.

Most leaves are quite thin, much like this page. But an amazing amount of photosynthetic "machinery" fits into this small space. As you read about the tissues of a leaf, refer to the diagram in Figure 21.3.

Epidermis The top and bottom layers of the leaf are composed of the **epidermis** [ehp-uh-DUR-mihs]. The epidermis protects the inner tissues from injury and from drying out. The upper and lower epidermis form a sort of sandwich, with the inner tissues as filling. Cells within the epidermis secrete a waxy substance that forms the **cuticle**. The cuticle prevents water from escaping from the leaf. Most of the epidermal cells do not contain chloroplasts.

The leaves of many plants are covered by fine hairs. These hairs are extensions of the epidermal cells. **Epidermal hairs** slow the rate at which water evaporates from the leaf.

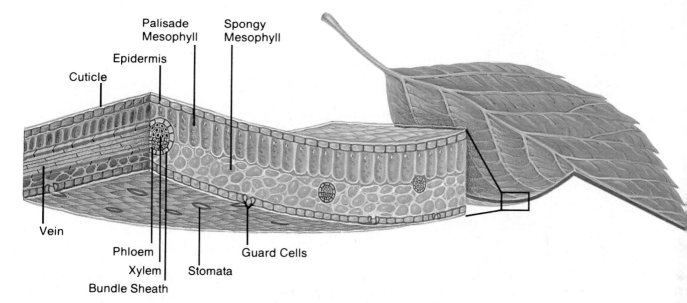

Cuticle
Epidermis
Palisade Mesophyll
Spongy Mesophyll
Vein
Phloem
Xylem
Bundle Sheath
Stomata
Guard Cells

Figure 21.3 Inside a leaf

Guard Cells and Stomata Embedded in the epidermis, especially the lower epidermis, are crescent-shaped cells called **guard cells**. Unlike other cells of the epidermis, guard cells contain chloroplasts and carry out photosynthesis. Each pair of guard cells surrounds an opening called a **stoma** [STOH-muh]. The stoma (plural, *stomata*) is a pore that opens and closes, depending on the shape of the two guard cells around it. When the stomata are open, gases can move in and out of the leaf.

Mesophyll Inside the epidermis are two layers of chlorenchyma cells called **mesophyll** [MEHZ-oh-fil]. Most of the photosynthetic action takes place in the mesophyll. Mesophyll cells near the upper epidermis are long and narrow. Because they resemble the palisades, or stakes, of a fence, these cells are called **palisade mesophyll**.

Below the palisade mesophyll are loosely packed cells with many air spaces between them. The air spaces give these cells the name **spongy mesophyll**. The cells of the spongy mesophyll contain fewer chloroplasts than those of the palisade mesophyll.

Leaf Veins Throughout the mesophyll are vascular bundles containing xylem and phloem. Vascular bundles that are located in the leaf are called **veins**. These vascular bundles continue through the petiole and into the stem, connecting the leaf to the stem. Xylem cells deliver water and minerals to other cells in the leaf. Phloem cells carry newly made food away from the mesophyll to other parts of the plant. Besides conducting materials to, from, and within the leaf, the veins help support the leaf blade.

The veins are surrounded by tightly packed cells that form the **bundle sheath**. The bundle sheath is usually composed of parenchyma cells, although sometimes sclerenchyma cells are present.

Several vascular bundles enter the leaf blade through the petiole. Within the leaf blade, each bundle branches and rebranches into smaller and smaller groups of vessels. The branching becomes so fine that it is often difficult to see with the unaided eye. Thus no mesophyll cell is more than a few cells away from vascular tissue. The location of vascular bundles in the leaf ensures a rapid exchange of materials within the leaf.

21–3 Leaf Venation

The arrangement of veins in a leaf is called its **venation**. Like the leaflets of a compound leaf, the veins of a leaf may be arranged pinnately or palmately, as shown in Figure 21.4. In some plants, the leaf veins are nearly parallel. Monocots, such as grasses and lilies, have parallel veins.

In dicots, the veins of the leaves are branched in a network pattern. A leaf that has one main vein from which other veins branch off is said to have **pinnate venation**. A leaf in which several veins radiate from a single point is said to have **palmate venation**.

21–4 Photosynthesis in the Leaf

As you read in Chapter 7, chloroplasts require water, carbon dioxide, and light energy in order to carry on photosynthesis. The major product of photosynthesis is glucose. Oxygen is given off during photosynthesis.

Leaves are well adapted for carrying out photosynthesis. The water and carbon dioxide necessary for photosynthesis are readily available within the mesophyll. The flattened leaf blade allows for maximum exposure of the leaf surface to sunlight. In addition, the arrangement of leaves on a plant gives maximum exposure to the sun.

Water travels through the vascular bundles to the mesophyll cells. Since the branching of the xylem is so fine, no mesophyll cell is more than a short distance from the water supply. Water can easily diffuse the distance of a few cells.

The spongy mesophyll is composed of loosely packed cells and much air space. The air spaces are close to the stomata, through which carbon dioxide enters the leaf. From the air spaces, the carbon dioxide diffuses into the mesophyll cells.

Phloem, like xylem, branches out in the leaf so that no mesophyll cell is far from phloem. Glucose produced during photosynthesis is quickly removed by the phloem. Some of

Palmate
Venation

Parallel
Venation

Pinnate
Venation

Figure 21.4 *Top:* Variations in the venation of leaves; *Bottom:* The soft tissue and smaller veins of this leaf have been eaten by an insect. The larger veins are protected by tough, fibrous sheaths.

the glucose is converted to starch, which may be stored in the mesophyll cells. It is difficult to imagine a leaf structure that would be more efficient for the process of photosynthesis than the one that exists.

21-5 Gas Exchange

The guard cells and the stomata regulate the exchange of gases between the leaf and the atmosphere. Special adaptations of the guard cells allow them to control the rate at which water vapor leaves the leaf.

Because the guard cells contain chloroplasts, they are able to carry out photosynthesis. During photosynthesis, the guard cells become swollen with water, or **turgid**.

The walls of the guard cells next to the stomata are thick and relatively inflexible. The outer walls of the guard cells, the ones next to the epidermis, are thinner and more elastic. As the guard cells become turgid, the thinner, outer walls of the cells push outward into the epidermal cells. This change in shape pulls the thicker inner walls away from each other, opening the stomata.

On sunny days when photosynthesis is proceeding rapidly, the cells in the leaf require carbon dioxide. At that time the stomata are usually open. When it is dark, of course, photosynthesis cannot occur. Then the guard cells lose water. The loss of water causes the guard cells to become limp, closing the stomata. When the stomata are closed, carbon dioxide does not enter the leaf, and water vapor does not leave. Since photosynthesis does not occur at night, there is no need for carbon dioxide. The closed stomata conserve water.

Like all aerobic organisms, the tissues of the leaf carry out cellular respiration. In respiration, sugars are broken down to provide energy for the processes occurring in the plant. Leaves use the food they produce during photosynthesis for respiration. In respiration, oxygen is used to break down the sugar, and carbon dioxide is given off. The cells of the leaf use some of the oxygen produced in photosynthesis for respiration. Whereas photosynthesis occurs only while it is light, respiration continues throughout the night.

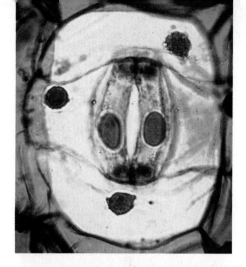

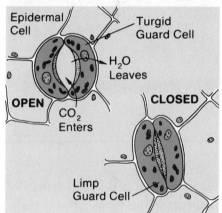

Figure 21.5 When guard cells are turgid, the stomata open. When guard cells are limp, the stomata close.

Checkpoint

1. What tissue protects the leaf from injury or drying out?
2. What are the two types of mesophyll?
3. What two conductive tissues do the vascular bundles contain?
4. What structures control the exchange of gases between the leaf and the atmosphere?

Leaf Modifications

CONCEPTS
- examples of leaf modifications
- adaptations of insectivorous plants

The leaves of some plants are so modified that you may not even recognize them as being leaves. In some plants, leaves perform a variety of unusual functions, including storing food or water, providing support for climbing plants, or even capturing insects!

21-6 Specialized Leaves

The leaves of conifers are often modified into **needles**. In comparison to the leaves of angiosperms, needles have a very small surface area. They are covered with a thick, water-resistant cuticle. Needles are also very resistant to freezing. For these reasons, needles are able to remain on conifers during the cold winter months.

Some leaves, such as those of the grape in Figure 21.6, are modified into tendrils. **Tendrils** are long, slender, curling structures that wrap around branches or other objects. Tendrils support the plant as it climbs.

Some leaves are modified into sharp structures called **spines**. If you have ever grasped the stem of a plant with spines, you know that they serve as protection. The spines of a cactus are actually modified leaves. (Cacti can be confusing. The fleshy pads of some cacti are not leaves, but actually modified stems.)

Some leaves also have hairs that serve as protection. Nettle leaves, for example, have cells that are modified into hairs. Each hair has a tiny vessel on its tip. When you brush against it, it releases an irritating substance that stings for several minutes after it contacts your skin. Once you have touched one nettle, you are unlikely to touch another.

Sometimes leaves become thickened and may store food in their blades or petioles. Succulents, like the familiar houseplant in Figure 21.7, store water in their thick, fleshy leaves. **Succulents** are plants with fleshy tissues that conserve water. In what climate might this ability be useful?

Figure 21.6 The tendrils of a grapevine are really modified leaves.

Figure 21.7 The jade plant, a succulent, stores water in its leaves.

NEWSBREAK

Since plants are stationary, people usually think of them as being defenseless against hungry predators. Recently, however, scientists have discovered that many plants are quite effective at waging chemical warfare against their predators. The weapons of this battle are a variety of naturally occurring pesticides.

Marigolds, for example, contain chemicals that become poisonous when exposed to light. When an insect bites into a leaf, it liberates some of the chemical, which then kills the insect.

Oak trees also produce chemical deterrents. During the spring, the tender leaves of oak trees are an excellent source of food for insects —

about 200 species of caterpillars are known to feed on them. As the leaves mature, however, they become tougher and begin to produce chemicals called tannins. The tannins and the change in texture make the older leaves indigestible to most caterpillars.

You are probably already aware of the chemicals defenses of poison ivy. The nicotine in tobacco plants and the oils found in mints are other plant defenses. Scientists are very interested in all such natural pesticides. Research on them may lead to the development of new pesticides. Such pesticides may be less harmful to the environment than those now available.

21–7   Insectivorous Plants

Insectivorous, or insect-eating, plants have highly modified leaves. Insectivorous plants usually grow in bogs or other areas where there is little nitrogen in the soil. These plants capture and digest insects to obtain nitrogen and other nutrients.

The pitcher plant is an example of an insectivorous plant. In pitcher plants, the leaf is modified into a tube with an overhanging hood and hairs that point downward. This arrangement traps insects unfortunate enough to enter the leaf. Another insectivorous plant is the sundew. In the sundew, glands on the leaf margin secrete a gluey substance that traps insects that land on the leaf. In both cases, enzymes in the leaves digest the captured insects. The leaves of insectivorous plants are able to carry out photosynthesis, so they do not actually eat the insects. They use insects only as a source of nitrogen.

Figure 21.8 A sundew

Checkpoint

1. Modified leaves that curl around other objects for support are called _____.
2. The pitcher plant is an example of a _____ plant.
3. What kind of leaf modification do most conifers have?
4. What kind of plants store water in their thick, fleshy leaves?

CHAPTER REVIEW

Summary

- Leaves are organs that are specialized for carrying out photosynthesis.
- Leaves grow from meristematic tissues in the stem. A leaf is usually composed of a blade and a petiole. The petiole is attached to the stem at a node.
- A cross section of a leaf reveals the internal tissues — epidermis, mesophyll, and veins.
- The epidermis surrounds the leaf. The epidermis is covered by the waxy cuticle. Some leaves have epidermal hairs. The epidermis prevents the loss of water from the leaf and protects the internal tissues.
- Guard cells and stomata are located in the epidermis. Most guard cells are located on the underside of the leaf. Unlike other cells in the epidermis, the guard cells contain chloroplasts.
- The stomata are pores that lie between the guard cells. When the stomata are open, they allow the exchange of gases between the atmosphere and the tissues inside the leaf. Stomata also allow water vapor to escape from the leaf. The shape of the guard cells controls the opening of the stomata.
- The mesophyll is composed of two layers — the palisade layer and the spongy mesophyll. The mesophyll is the site of most photosynthetic activity in the leaf. Mesophyll tissues may also store sugar and starch that the leaf uses in respiration.
- Throughout the leaf are veins composed of vascular bundles. The veins of monocots are parallel. The veins of dicots occur in a network pattern.
- The vascular bundles contain xylem and phloem, as well as strengthening tissues such as sclerenchyma.
- Xylem supplies the leaf with water and dissolved nutrients from the roots of the plant.
- The sugar and dissolved starches that the leaf manufactures are transported to the rest of the plant by phloem.
- Some types of leaves are modified to perform functions other than photosynthesis. The leaves of some plants serve as storage organs. Tendrils are modified leaves that support climbing plants. Spines are modified leaves that protect plants. Insectivorous plants have leaves that trap insects.

Vocabulary

blade	palmately compound
bundle sheath	petiole
compound leaf	pinnate venation
cuticle	pinnately compound
epidermal hairs	simple leaf
epidermis	spine
guard cells	spongy mesophyll
insectivorous	stoma
leaflet	succulent
mesophyll	tendril
needle	turgid
node	vein
palisade mesophyll	venation
palmate venation	

Review

1. Which two plant parts does the petiole connect?
2. State two functions of leaf veins.
3. Name two leaf modifications that protect leaves.
4. Name in order, from lower surface to upper, the tissues found in a leaf.
5. Where are the guard cells located?
6. In which tissues are the chloroplasts located?
7. What is a succulent?

8. A leaf in which many leaflets are attached to one petiole is called a ____ leaf.
9. A leaf in which the veins come together at one point has ____ venation.
10. What nutrient do insectivorous plants obtain from insects?

In the following list, match the leaf part with its function.

11. cuticle
12. epidermis
13. mesophyll
14. stomata
15. veins

a. conduction of food and water
b. protection
c. waterproofing
d. exchange of gases
e. photosynthesis

In the following list, match the leaf modification with its function.

16. fleshy leaves
17. tendril
18. spine
19. insect trap
20. needle

a. protection
b. water storage
c. prevention of water loss
d. obtaining nitrogen
e. climbing

Interpret and Apply

1. How are spongy and palisade mesophyll alike? How are they different?
2. How does the flat shape of many leaves aid in photosynthesis?
3. How do guard cells control the size of the stomata?

Choose the best answer for each of the following questions. Write your answers on a separate sheet of paper.

4. Which of the following is *not* contained in a vascular bundle?
   (a) xylem (b) phloem (c) parenchyma (d) mesophyll
5. Which of the following does *not* belong with the others?
   (a) pinnate (b) palmate (c) petiole (d) parallel
6. Which of the following is *not* a leaf tissue?
   (a) cork (b) epidermis (c) mesophyll (d) phloem
7. Which cell type does *not* contain chlorophyll?
   (a) guard cell (b) spongy mesophyll (c) xylem (d) palisade mesophyll
8. Which of the following does *not* belong with the others?
   (a) spine (b) stomate (c) tendril (d) needle

Challenge

1. Could a broad-leaved plant, such as a banana plant, live in the desert? Explain.
2. How are the veins in a leaf like the veins in your body?
3. What would happen to the rate of photosynthesis if leaves were spherical instead of flat? Explain.
4. If the stomata were closed during the day, how would the rate of photosynthesis be affected? Explain.

Projects

1. Do some library research on irrigation. Consider the various forms used, the locations in which different forms are used, and the plants that can be grown in those locations as a result.
2. Make a collection of leaves from your area. Using a leaf-identification book, try to identify each one. If possible, find out the Latin name as well as the common name.
3. The leaves of certain plants contain chemicals that prevent insects from eating them. The production of these chemicals evolved with the appetites of insects. This is an example of coevolution. Do research to find some specific instances in which this occurs.

22 Roots and Stems

Collecting sap

All summer long the leaves of maple trees manufacture sugar. This sugar is transported to the rest of the plant, where it provides energy for all the plant's activities. When autumn comes, the leaves fall, and the tree becomes dormant. Special cells in the wood of the tree trunk store sugar throughout the winter.

Toward the end of winter the days begin to turn warm. Then sap containing the sugar stored in the trunk starts to move upward. As the sap moves upward, buds on the twigs begin to swell, ready to produce flowers and new leaves.

At that time, metal tubes can be driven into the wood of the tree trunk. From these tubes drips the clear, faintly sweet-tasting sap, which is collected in buckets. From the buckets the sap is poured into long, shallow pans. Then it is boiled until most of the water evaporates. The sap that drips from the wood is very dilute. But when it is boiled down, it yields a wonderful-tasting golden syrup. You know this liquid as maple syrup.

Roots

A highway serves as a route for transporting materials from one point to another. The roots and stems of plants serve much the same function. Water and dissolved minerals are absorbed by the roots and carried up through the stem to the leaves. Food molecules produced in the leaves are carried to the rest of the plant by the stems.

CONCEPTS

- taproots and fibrous root systems
- longitudinal section of a root
- cross section of a mature root
- primary and secondary growth of roots
- adventitious roots

22–1 Root Systems

In many plants, more of the plant is located under the ground than above it. The plant shown in Figure 22.1 is about as tall as an umbrella. Underground, however, the plant has millions of branching roots. If you placed all the roots end to end, they would reach from Memphis, Tennessee, to Atlanta, Georgia.

Root systems tend to be large because roots are the anchoring and absorbing organs of the plant. Plants obtain necessary water and minerals through their roots. Roots also hold the plants in place and keep the soil around them from washing away.

The roots of some plants are greatly branched. This type of root system is called a **fibrous root system**. Grasses have fibrous root systems. In other plants, a single large **taproot** extends deep into the soil with other smaller roots branching off it. Dandelions have taproots.

In some plants, taproots store food for the future growth of the plant. Without this stored food, many plants could not survive through the winter or during dry seasons. Carrots, parsnips, beets, turnips, and radishes all store food in fleshy taproots.

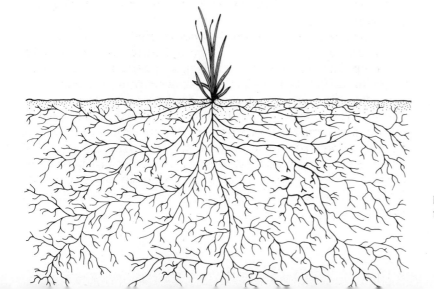

Figure 22.1 This rye plant has a fibrous root system.

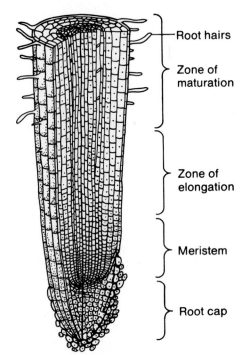

Figure 22.2 A longitudinal section of a typical root tip

- Root hairs
- Zone of maturation
- Zone of elongation
- Meristem
- Root cap

22–2 Primary Growth in Roots: Growth in Length

If you cut a root down the middle, you make a longitudinal section, as shown in Figure 22.2. When examined with a microscope, a longitudinal section of a root tip has four different areas. They are, from bottom to top, the root cap, the meristematic region, the zone of elongation, and the zone of maturation.

The **root cap** is a thimble-shaped group of cells covering the tip of the root. It protects the meristematic cells behind it from injury. As the root grows down into the soil, the cells of the root cap are constantly rubbed off. These cells are replaced by new cells that form in the meristematic region. The shed cells make soil particles slippery, easing the growth of the root through the soil.

The **meristem** is located just behind the root cap. It contains small, rapidly dividing cells. All of the tissues that arise from the meristem are called **primary tissues**.

About 1 to 3 millimeters above the meristem is the **zone of elongation**. In this region, the cells have ceased to divide. Rather, the cell walls of the existing cells expand and the vacuoles increase in size, making the cells longer. This growth has the effect of pushing the root deeper into the soil.

The growth of cells in the zone of elongation is responsible for increasing the length of the root. More than a century ago, the German botanist Julius Sachs showed that root growth is concentrated in the zone of elongation. He marked the root tip of a pea plant, as shown in Figure 22.3, and observed the plant for several hours. He found that the distance between the marks increased only in the zone of elongation.

The **zone of maturation** is above the zone of elongation. Most of the cells in the zone of elongation are uniform in structure. In the zone of maturation, though, the cells begin to differentiate, or develop, into other kinds of tissues.

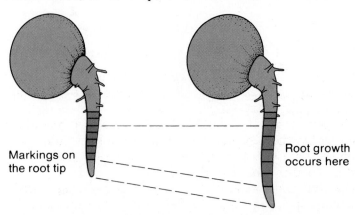

Markings on the root tip

Root growth occurs here

Figure 22.3 By marking the root tip of a pea plant, Sachs was able to determine that root growth occurs in the zone of elongation.

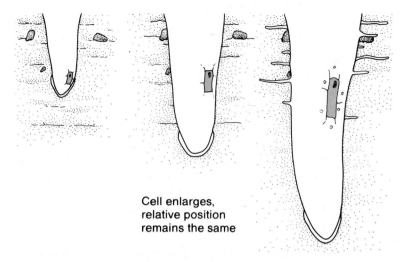

Cell enlarges,
relative position
remains the same

Figure 22.4 Growing cells do not change position relative to the soil.

As the cells formed in the meristem enlarge and differentiate, the root cap and meristem are pushed deeper into the soil. As you can see in Figure 22.4, although individual cells enlarge and mature, they do not change position in relation to the soil.

The outermost tissue in the zone of maturation becomes the epidermis. Projecting into the soil from the epidermis are tiny fingerlike structures called **root hairs**. Each root hair grows from a single epidermal cell. A single plant may have millions of root hairs, which greatly increase the surface area of the root. The increased surface area enables the root to absorb water and dissolved minerals from the soil.

As the root pushes deeper into the soil, the uppermost root hairs are worn off. These hairs are replaced by new root hairs that form at the lower end of the zone of maturation. Because they lack root hairs, the older parts of the root cannot absorb water.

22–3   Cross Section of Primary Root Tissues

A cross section through the zone of maturation reveals the primary tissues of the root. As you read about the structure of the primary root, refer to Figure 22.5.

The outermost tissue of the young root is the epidermis, from which the root hairs extend. Inside the epidermis is a wide section of loosely packed parenchyma cells called the **cortex**. Food is stored in the cortex.

The innermost cells of the cortex form a ring called the **endodermis** [en-doh-DUR-muhs]. The cells in the endodermis

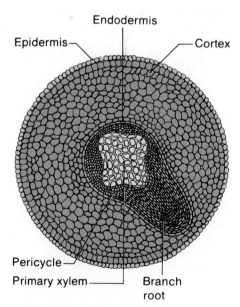

Figure 22.5 Cross section of a primary root

have a waxy layer in their cell walls that limits the movement of water and other materials. The endodermis is important in controlling the movement of substances between the cortex and the interior tissues of the root.

Between the endodermis and the vascular tissues is a ring of parenchyma cells called the **pericycle**. Branch roots grow from the pericycle, as shown in Figure 22.5. As branch roots grow outward, they push aside the surrounding tissues, until finally they reach the soil.

Inside the pericycle is the central cylinder of vascular tissues. In dicots, the primary xylem is a star-shaped structure with arms that reach outward from the center of the root. Between the arms of the primary xylem are strands of primary phloem.

22–4 Secondary Growth in Roots: Growth in Width

After the primary tissues are mature, the root begins to grow in width. This widening of the root is called **secondary growth**. Secondary growth does not increase the length of the roots. In trees and shrubs that live for many years, most root cells are formed by secondary growth.

Secondary tissues arise from the cambium. Late in primary growth, the **vascular cambium** develops between the primary xylem and the primary phloem. The vascular cambium is a thin layer of cells that never loses its ability to divide. The cells that form on the inside of the vascular cambium tissue become secondary xylem. The secondary xylem eventually fills in the spaces between the arms of the star-shaped primary xylem, forming a cylinder of xylem.

Cells formed on the outside of the vascular cambium become secondary phloem. As the secondary phloem develops, it pushes against the older phloem to its outside, crushing the outer cells. Therefore, the secondary phloem does not build up year after year as the secondary xylem does.

Figure 22.6 Phases in the secondary growth of a root

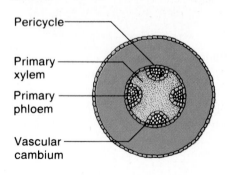

Pericycle
Primary xylem
Primary phloem
Vascular cambium

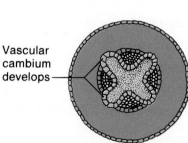

Vascular cambium develops

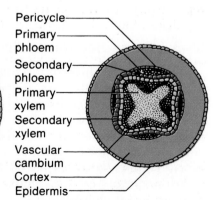

Pericycle
Primary phloem
Secondary phloem
Primary xylem
Secondary xylem
Vascular cambium
Cortex
Epidermis

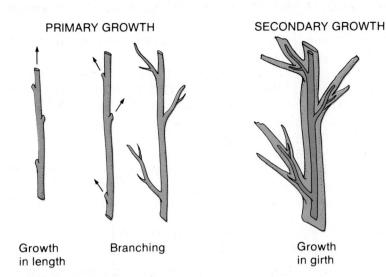

PRIMARY GROWTH   SECONDARY GROWTH

Growth   Branching   Growth
in length   in girth

Figure 22.7 A comparison of the primary and secondary growth of stems

Another meristematic tissue called **cork cambium** develops in the pericycle. The cork cambium produces a layer of tough, water-resistant **cork** cells. After cork forms, the cortex and epidermis of the root die and are rubbed off. The cork then serves as the protective covering of the root. Older roots that are covered by cork can no longer absorb water.

22–5   Adventitious Roots

Most roots grow out of other roots. In some plants, however, roots can arise from stems or leaves. Roots that grow from an unusual place are called **adventitious roots**. At the lower part of a corn stem are roots that grow down into the soil and help support the plant. These adventitious roots are called **prop roots**.

Adventitious roots often arise from the stems or leaves of climbing plants. These roots help to support the vine. Adventitious roots are also found in many plants that reproduce vegetatively. If you place the leaf of an African violet in water, it will produce adventitious roots.

Figure 22.8 The adventitious roots of a corn plant support the stalk.

Checkpoint

1. Cells in a root tip that divide very rapidly are called ___ cells.
2. In what region of the root tip do cells become different from each other?
3. From what tissue do branch roots arise?
4. What tissue transports food in the root?
5. What tissue produces secondary growth in the root?

Stems

CONCEPTS

- comparison of herbaceous dicot and monocot stems
- anatomy of a winter twig
- primary and secondary growth of stems
- stem adaptations

The most obvious function of a stem is that it physically connects the roots with the leaves. Vascular tissues in the stem transport molecules of food, water, and minerals between the leaves and the roots. In addition to transporting materials, stems have several other functions. Stems support the leaves. They also store food. Some stems make their own food by photosynthesis.

Plants that do not contain woody tissue are called herbs. **Herbaceous** [hur-BAY-shus] plants usually do not live for more than one year. Their size is limited because their soft stem tissues cannot support much weight.

Vascular plants that live for more than one year often have woody stems. The roots and stems of these plants increase in diameter each growing season. Woody tissues allow some plants to reach great heights. In the case of large trees, for example, the stem may support many tons.

22–6 Herbaceous Stems

Like the root tip, the stem contains a meristem, a zone of elongation, and a zone of maturation. Unlike the root, however, there is no root cap, so the meristem is at the end of the stem. Why do you think there is no need for a covering like the root cap?

The stems of herbaceous dicots and monocots are somewhat different in structure. Cross sections of typical dicot and monocot stems are shown in Figure 22.9.

Figure 22.9 Cross sections of herbaceous monocot and dicot stems

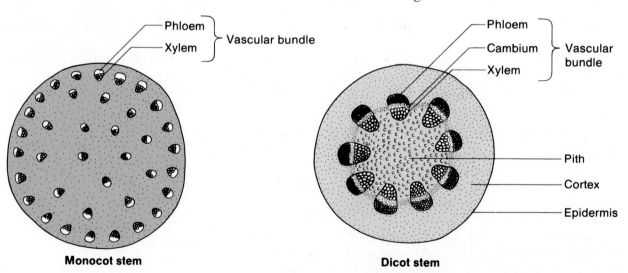

Monocot stem   **Dicot stem**

In the middle of the dicot stem is a region of parenchyma cells called the **pith**. A ring of vascular bundles surrounds the pith. Each vascular bundle consists of phloem cells on the outside, xylem cells on the inside, and cambium in the middle. The cambium cells divide so that they eventually produce an uninterrupted ring around the pith. The xylem and phloem bundles remain separate from each other. Outside the vascular bundles is the cortex. The cortex contains chloroplasts and carries on photosynthesis. There is a thin epidermis outside the cortex.

In the stem of a monocot, the vascular bundles are scattered rather than arranged in a ring. This arrangement makes it impossible to tell the pith from the cortex. The xylem is always on the inside of the vascular bundles and the phloem is always on the outside. A band of sclerenchyma fibers often surrounds the entire bundle. In most monocots there is no vascular cambium and therefore no secondary growth.

22–7   Structure of a Winter Twig

A good way to understand the structure of a woody stem is to study a winter twig, such as the one shown in Figure 22.10. The winter twig contains all of the tissues necessary for the next growing season.

At the tip of the twig is the **terminal bud**. In the spring the bud may develop into leaves or flowers. Thick **bud scales** protect the tissues within the bud. The terminal bud also contains meristematic tissue, which will add cells to the length of the stem during the growing season. When the bud scales fall off, they leave bud-scale scars, which look like rings around the stem. These scars mark the location of past terminal buds. Since a new terminal bud forms each year, the distance between bud-scale scars shows how much the twig grew during each season.

In past seasons leaves grew from the stem. When the leaves fell off, they left **leaf scars**. The tiny dotlike marks on the leaf scars are scars left by the vascular bundles. Directly above each leaf scar are tiny side buds called **lateral buds**. New branches develop from lateral buds.

Along the length of the stem are many raised areas that look like dots or blisters. These are groups of loosely spaced cells called **lenticels**. Lenticels allow the exchange of gases between the atmosphere and the inner tissues of the twig.

22–8   Primary Tissues of a Woody Stem

A cross section of a young woody stem is shown in Figure 22.11. Many of the tissues found in stems are similar to those in roots, but stems do not have a pericycle or an endodermis.

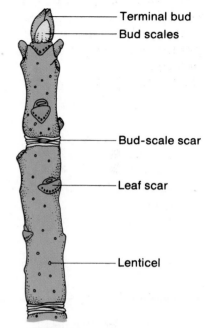

Figure 22.10 The structural features of a winter twig

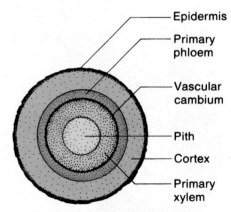

Figure 22.11 Cross section of a young woody stem

Roots and Stems   **329**

The inner tissues of the young stem are protected by a single layer of epidermal tissues. Just inside the epidermis is a layer of cortex. Most of the cells of the cortex have thin walls and large vacuoles. They store food for the twig. Some of the cortex cells may have thick cell walls and serve to support the stem. In young woody stems, the cortex may contain chlorophyll and carry on photosynthesis.

Inside the cortex is the primary phloem. Directly inside the primary phloem is a ring of vascular cambium. Within the vascular cambium is a narrow ring of primary xylem. In the center of the stem are parenchyma cells that make up the pith. These are large, thin-walled cells that store food.

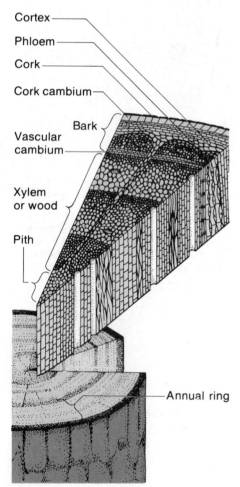

Figure 22.12 Cross section of a tree trunk

Cortex
Phloem
Cork
Cork cambium
Bark
Vascular cambium
Xylem or wood
Pith
Annual ring

22–9   Secondary Growth of a Woody Stem

All of the primary growth of a stem occurs directly below the meristem, in the zone of elongation. For the stem to grow in width, meristematic tissues in the cambium must produce new tissues. As in the root, secondary tissues of the stem are produced by cambium tissues. Cells that form on the inside of the vascular cambium become part of the wood. Those that form on the outside become part of the bark.

The main trunk of a woody dicot such as an oak tree is a stem, as is each branch of the tree. The cross section of a trunk in Figure 22.12 shows the tissues of a woody dicot stem.

Wood   *Xylem* is the Greek word for "wood." Every year the vascular cambium produces new xylem cells, which you would recognize as the wood of the tree. If you examine a piece of wood, you will see alternating bands of dark and light xylem, one inside the other. Because the conditions for growth are usually more favorable in the spring than in the summer, wood cells that form in the spring are usually larger than those that form in the summer. The light xylem bands are composed of cells that formed in the spring. The dark xylem bands are composed of smaller cells that formed in the summer. The tree adds one light and one dark band each year. By counting the number of bands, called **growth rings**, you can determine the age of the tree.

As the years pass, new xylem forms, increasing the width of the trunk. At the same time, the pith and the older wood, which are closer to the center of the trunk, gradually become filled with resin and other materials. This prevents the passage of water through these cells. The clogged inner wood, called **heartwood**, appears darker than the newer **sapwood**.

Bark All tissues outside the vascular cambium are part of the bark. The phloem is the innermost of the bark tissues. Phloem formed by the cambium does not increase the width of the tree. Instead, the new phloem pushes the existing phloem against the outer tissues, crushing the older phloem cells.

The cork cambium lies outside the cortex. When this meristematic tissue divides, it produces cork. The cork cells produce a waxy, water-resistant substance that separates the epidermis from its food and water supplies. This causes the epidermis to die and peel off. Eventually, the cork cells die too and become filled with air. The inner living tissues exchange gases with the air through lenticels in the cork layer.

Figure 22.13 *Left:* The bark of the slash pine is rough. *Middle:* Smooth bark is characteristic of beech trees. *Right:* Most birch trees are identified by peeling bark.

Cork has several important functions. It prevents water loss from the other stem tissues. Cork quickly forms over tree wounds, preventing fungi from entering the stem. The cork of some trees gives the bark a distinctive appearance. Often you can identify a tree by its bark. Several kinds of bark are shown in Figure 22.13.

22–10 Modified Stems

Not all stems grow above the ground. A familiar example of an underground stem is the white potato. A swollen underground stem such as the potato is called a **tuber**. The

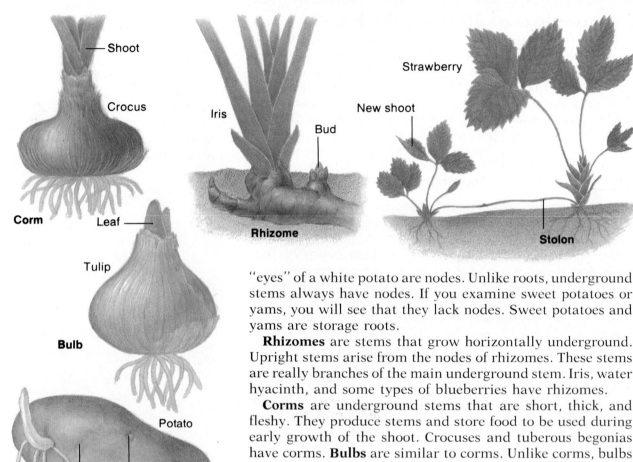

Figure 22.14 Five types of modified stems

"eyes" of a white potato are nodes. Unlike roots, underground stems always have nodes. If you examine sweet potatoes or yams, you will see that they lack nodes. Sweet potatoes and yams are storage roots.

Rhizomes are stems that grow horizontally underground. Upright stems arise from the nodes of rhizomes. These stems are really branches of the main underground stem. Iris, water hyacinth, and some types of blueberries have rhizomes.

Corms are underground stems that are short, thick, and fleshy. They produce stems and store food to be used during early growth of the shoot. Crocuses and tuberous begonias have corms. **Bulbs** are similar to corms. Unlike corms, bulbs are composed of a short stem surrounded by numerous fleshy leaves. The leaves, which are full of food, store energy for the plant to use in spring growth. Onions and daffodils develop from bulbs.

Stolons are horizontal stems that grow along the surface of the ground. New leaves and roots develop where a node touches the ground. When the stolon dies, the roots and stems become independent plants. Strawberries reproduce asexually by stolons. You may call these stolons runners.

Checkpoint

1. From what tissue does the primary growth of the stem arise?
2. What is the innermost region of a dicot stem?
3. In a winter twig, what structures protect the developing leaves and flowers?
4. What type of underground stem is a white potato?

Conduction of Water and Food

As you know, all vascular plants contain xylem and phloem. Xylem conducts water from the roots to the leaves. Phloem transports sap containing dissolved sugars from the leaves or storage organs to the rest of the plant. How are plants able to move fluids within their tissues against the force of gravity?

22–11 Uptake of Water and Nutrients

Water from the soil enters a plant through its root hairs, which extend into the particles of the soil. Many of the particles of soil are surrounded by a thin layer of water. This long-lasting water supply, called **capillary water**, provides the roots with water during periods when there is no rain.

As you learned in Chapter 6, molecules move from an area of high concentration to an area of lower concentration. The cytoplasm of the root hairs contains a high concentration of organic chemicals. Therefore, the concentration of water molecules in the plant is lower than the concentration of water in the capillary water. For this reason, water molecules in the soil tend to move through the cell membrane and into the root hair. When water molecules move across a selectively permeable membrane, the process is called osmosis. Thus water flows into the root hair by osmosis.

After water enters the root hair, it passes by osmosis through the cells of the cortex, and eventually into the xylem and upward to the rest of the plant. The concentration of water

CONCEPTS

- structure and function of xylem and phloem
- uptake of water and minerals
- transpiration-cohesion theory
- function of the stomata
- pressure-flow hypothesis

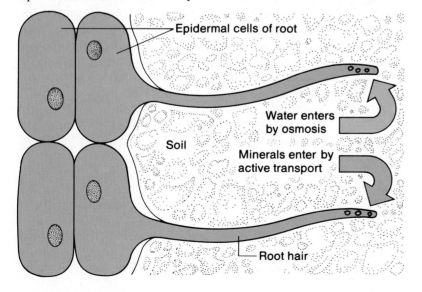

Figure 22.15 Water moves through the root hairs and into the plant by osmosis.

outside the root is always greater than that inside the root. Therefore, osmosis occurs continuously. The difference in water concentration between the root tissues and soil has the effect of pushing water into the root. The water in the root exerts a pressure called **root pressure**. Root pressure pushes water up the stem.

Plants also obtain mineral nutrients from the soil. Nutrients such as nitrogen, calcium, and potassium are taken into the root in the form of ions. Unlike water, minerals are more highly concentrated within the cells than in the soil. Therefore, the root cells must rely upon active transport to take in minerals. This means that they must expend energy in the form of ATP.

22–12 Conduction through the Xylem

Water and dissolved minerals are conducted to the rest of the plant through the xylem. The two major types of conducting cells in the xylem are tracheids and vessel elements. **Tracheids** [TRAY-kee-udz] are long, thick-walled cells with tapering ends. Tracheids are dead at maturity, so they are hollow. The ends of the tracheids overlap, allowing water to pass from one cell to the next.

Vessel elements are much larger in diameter than tracheids. Like tracheids, vessel elements are dead at maturity and contain no cytoplasm. Individual vessel elements are arranged end to end, much like barrels piled on top of each other. The vessel elements form long tubes through the plant called **xylem vessels**. Each xylem vessel may be as much as a meter long.

Once inside the xylem, water molecules travel upward toward the leaf. There are many hypotheses to explain this movement. One explanation that fits most of the available evidence is the **transpiration-cohesion theory**. According to this theory, water is pulled up the xylem in a continuous column that stretches from the roots to the leaves.

Cohesion is the attraction between molecules of the same type. Water molecules are polar. Each water molecule has an end that is positively charged and one that is negatively charged. The positively charged end of one water molecule attracts the negatively charged end of another, forming a long chain of water molecules. Water molecules high in the column of xylem vessels are attached to those behind them by cohesion.

Water molecules also stick to the sides of their container, in this case a xylem vessel or tracheid. This attraction of unlike molecules is called **adhesion**. The water molecules

Xylem

Phloem

Figure 22.16 This scanning electron micrograph of a grass stem shows the vascular bundles.

adhere to the surfaces of the xylem vessels. The forces of adhesion and cohesion make the thin column of water in the xylem behave like a dense, tightly-pulled wire.

22–13 Transpiration

Water eventually enters the leaf, where it is used in photosynthesis and other kinds of cell metabolism. When the stomata of a leaf are open, water can evaporate through them into the atmosphere. The evaporation of water from leaves is called **transpiration**.

As water evaporates from the stomata, cells close to the stomata absorb water from neighboring cells by osmosis. Those cells, in turn, absorb water from more distant cells, until eventually water is absorbed from the xylem in the veins of the leaf.

Transpiration pulls water up the xylem. When water molecules leave the leaf by transpiration, they pull other water molecules after them. In an unbroken chain, the molecules of water move upward through the xylem. The water column extends from the root, through the stem and leaf, to the stomata. This column is held together by adhesion and cohesion. Water molecules in the soil replace those that leave the plant through its leaves. Therefore, the xylem vessels are never empty.

Figure 22.17 Scientists estimate that the woody stems of huge trees contain hundreds of liters of water.

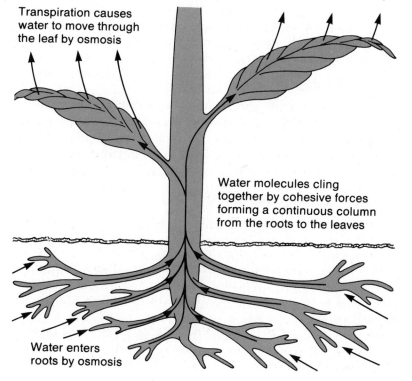

Transpiration causes water to move through the leaf by osmosis

Water molecules cling together by cohesive forces forming a continuous column from the roots to the leaves

Water enters roots by osmosis

Figure 22.18 Water transport in plants involves osmosis, cohesive forces, and transpiration.

Figure 22.19 Wilting occurs when the loss of water in a plant reduces the turgor pressure.

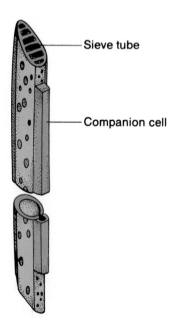

Sieve tube

Companion cell

Figure 22.20 Movement of dissolved sugars occurs through sievelike structures in the phloem.

22–14   Wilting

When a plant cell is full of water, its cytoplasm presses outward against the cell wall. As you learned in Chapter 6, a cell in this condition is said to be turgid. Turgor pressure provides the support that keeps the stems of herbaceous plants erect.

When a plant cell lacks water, its cytoplasm shrinks away from its cell wall, resulting in plasmolysis. If a plant's rate of water loss by transpiration is greater than its rate of water absorption, its cells suffer plasmolysis. This causes **wilting**, or loss of turgor, as shown in Figure 22.19.

When plants wilt, the stomata close. With the stomata closed, the rate of transpiration decreases. Closed stomata conserve water. When more water becomes available, the stomata open again. Thus wilting is a response that allows plants to regulate their water balance.

22–15   Translocation of Food

Sap containing dissolved sugars is transported through the plant by the phloem. The movement of food from one part of a plant to another is called **translocation**.

Like the xylem vessels, the cells of phloem form a continuous pipeline through the plant. In phloem the pipelines are called **sieve tubes**. The cells of the sieve tubes, called **sieve tube elements**, are long and thick-walled. Their sloping ends contain many tiny holes, giving them the appearance of sieves. The sieve tube elements are arranged end to end through the length of the plant.

Unlike the vessels of xylem, the sieve tubes are made up of living cells. Although sieve tube elements contain cytoplasm, as they mature they lose their nuclei. Sieve tube elements are connected to nearby cells, called **companion cells**, by thin strands of cytoplasm. The nuclei of the companion cells probably control the activities of the sieve tube elements.

Although phloem has been studied for many years, botanists have not been able to determine exactly how translocation occurs. The hypothesis that has the most experimental support is called the **pressure-flow hypothesis**. According to this hypothesis, food is transported through the phloem as a result of differences in pressure.

When sugar molecules produced in a leaf enter a particular sieve tube element, the concentration of water in that element is lowered. Therefore, water enters from neighboring cells by osmosis. As water enters the sieve tube element, it increases the pressure in the cell. Eventually the contents of the element are pushed out through the sieve at the end and into the next element. Evidence indicates that translocation is an energy-requiring process.

Usually dissolved food moves downward from its point of manufacture in the leaf to other parts of the plant. There it may nourish stem and root tissues or it may be stored. In late winter, just before the growing season begins, food stored in the roots travels upward. The food provides energy for the upper parts of the plant until the new leaves are able to manufacture food.

If you peel a ring of bark from a tree, a process called **girdling**, the phloem peels off with the cork. Without phloem, the tissues below the girdled area are cut off from their supply of food. Without food, the root tissues starve. Eventually the entire tree dies. Early American settlers used girdling as a method of clearing land.

 BIOLOGY INSIGHTS

Wilting is one way in which plants maintain homeostasis. Plants respond to a lack of water by wilting, thus slowing the rate at which water is lost by transpiration.

Checkpoint

1. What process causes water to enter root hairs?
2. What is the attraction between like molecules called?
3. What theory explains the conduction of water through the xylem?
4. What is the pressure of water against a plant's cell wall called? What occurs when plant cells lose water?
5. What type of cell conducts sap through the phloem?
6. What hypothesis explains the movement of sap through the phloem?

CHAPTER REVIEW

Summary

- Roots and stems conduct materials within the plant. Roots also anchor plants in place and absorb water. Stems hold up the leaves and may manufacture food. Both roots and stems may act as storage organs.
- Primary growth occurs in the meristem. New cells grow longer in the zone of elongation and differentiate in the zone of maturation.
- Plants increase in width through secondary growth. Vascular cambium produces secondary xylem and phloem.
- The inner tissues of the root and stem include pith and cortex, which store food; xylem and phloem, which transport materials; epidermis and cork, which protect the inner tissues; and cambium, which produces new cells.
- Roots and stems may form branches. Branch roots grow from the pericycle. Branches of the stem develop from lateral buds.
- Herbaceous monocots and dicots have different arrangements of vascular tissues.
- Some stems, such as rhizomes, tubers, and corms, grow underground. Underground stems have nodes.
- Vascular tissues transport water, dissolved minerals, and food throughout the plant. Xylem is composed of hollow vessels and tracheids. Phloem contains sieve tubes.
- Water enters the root hairs by the process of osmosis. Once inside the root, water travels upward through the vessels of the xylem. Water leaves the plant through the stomata by the process of transpiration. The best explanation for the conduction of water through the stem is the transpiration-cohesion theory.
- Phloem conducts sap containing dissolved sugars throughout the plant. The best explanation for this process is the pressure-flow hypothesis.

Vocabulary

adhesion	primary tissue
adventitious root	prop root
bud scale	rhizome
bulb	root cap
capillary water	root hair
cohesion	root pressure
companion cell	sapwood
cork	secondary growth
cork cambium	sieve tube
corm	sieve tube element
cortex	stolon
endodermis	taproot
fibrous root system	terminal bud
girdling	tracheid
growth ring	translocation
heartwood	transpiration
herbaceous	transpiration-
lateral bud	cohesion theory
leaf scar	tuber
lenticel	vascular cambium
meristem	vessel element
pericycle	wilting
pith	xylem vessel
pressure-flow	zone of elongation
hypothesis	zone of maturation

Review

1. Name three functions of roots.
2. What is the function of the root cap?
3. What tissue is found in the center of a mature dicot root? In the center of a mature dicot stem?
4. Place the following tissues of a dicot root in the correct order, beginning with the innermost tissue. (a) cork (b) cork cambium (c) cortex (d) endodermis (e) epidermis (f) pericycle (g) phloem (h) primary xylem (i) secondary xylem

In the following list, match the stem tissue with its function.

5. cork
6. cork cambium
7. cortex
8. phloem
9. pith
10. vascular cambium
11. xylem

a. stores food in young plant
b. carries water
c. produces secondary xylem and phloem
d. absorbs water from soil
e. carries food
f. reduces water loss from stem
g. produces cork cells

12. What tissues are found in the bark? What tissues are found in the wood?
13. Where in the stem does growth in length occur?
14. Indicate which of the following types of cells are found in xylem and which are found in phloem. (a) companion cell (b) vessel element (c) sieve tube element (d) tracheid
15. What hypothesis explains the translocation of food in vascular plants?

Interpret and Apply

1. The epidermis of the root lacks the water-proof cuticle found on the epidermis of most stems and leaves. Why is this important to the function of the root?
2. Compare the formation of branch roots with the formation of branches in the stem.
3. Name two ways in which tracheids are different from xylem vessels.
4. Name two tissues found in the root that are not found in the stem.
5. Which of the following tissues are composed of cells that are dead at maturity? (a) vascular cambium (b) cork (c) xylem (d) epidermis (e) phloem
6. Place the following in the correct order to show the path of water through a plant. (a) xylem (b) stomata (c) root hair (d) endodermis (e) root cortex (f) capillary water (g) atmosphere

7. For which of the following processes must the plant expend energy? (a) absorption of water (b) translocation of sugars (c) uptake of minerals (d) transpiration
8. Why does girdling kill a tree?

Challenge

1. You have twigs from two different trees of the same species. On one twig the bud scale scars are much closer together than on the other. Explain.
2. When houseplants are transplanted, many of the root hairs are accidentally broken off. For this reason, it is important to water transplanted houseplants frequently. Explain why this is necessary.
3. You are given a branch of a tree. Describe two methods you could use to determine the age of the branch.
4. A five-year-old boy carved his initials on the trunk of a tree. Forty years later he returned to see if he could find his initials. Will he have to stoop down to find his initials or should he bring a ladder? Explain.

Projects

1. Do some library research on lumber-producing trees. Find out which characteristics make a tree desirable for lumber, how lumber is graded, and how the different types of lumber are used. Visit a lumberyard and see what types of wood are sold.
2. If your community has a soil-testing service, invite a representative from it to talk to your class. Determine what type of soil is found in your area.
3. Find out how maple syrup is obtained from trees and how it is processed.
4. In the science of dendrochronology the growth rings of trees are used to determine and date past events. Do library research on dendrochronology. Report to the class on your findings.

23 Reproduction in Flowering Plants

A tomato is classified as a fruit.

If you are like many people, you might say that your favorite vegetable is a juicy, garden-ripe tomato. A vegetable is any edible part of a plant. The vegetables that people eat come from many parts of plants. The leaves of lettuce and cabbage are vegetables. The roots of carrots and beets are vegetables. Vegetables may also be the flowers of a plant, as in cauliflower, and even the buds of a plant, as in artichokes.

You may be surprised to learn that botanists classify tomatoes as fruits. A fruit is a structure that develops from the female part of a flower. According to this definition, strawberries, cherries, oranges, apples, and bananas are all fruits. But so are squashes, green beans, chili peppers, and even corn on the cob!

Not only are tomatoes fruits; they are a special kind of fruit known as a berry. Grapes and oranges are also berries. Berries are fleshy fruits that develop from the ovary of a flower. The terms *fruit* and *berry* have specific meanings in the study of plants. Although the term *vegetable* is useful in food preparation, it has little meaning to a botanist.

Flowers

During sexual reproduction, gametes from one organism fuse with gametes from another organism. Since plants cannot move, they have evolved special mechanisms to allow the gametes of one plant to reach those of another. **Flowers** are reproductive structures that take advantage of outside agents such as wind and animals to carry pollen between plants. Fertilization within the flower results in the production of seeds, which, in turn, are capable of germinating into new plants.

CONCEPTS

- structure of a typical flower
- formation of ovules and pollen
- flower adaptations that aid in pollination
- process of double fertilization

23–1 Flower Anatomy

Figure 23.1 shows a typical flower. The enlarged tip of the stem that supports the flower is called the **receptacle**. Extending from the receptacle is an outer circle of modified leaves called **sepals**. Sepals protect the developing flower bud. Often sepals are green and leaflike. All the sepals together form the **calyx** [KAY-lihks]. Just inside of the calyx is another circle of modified leaves called **petals**. The petals form the **corolla** [kuh-ROHL-uh] of the flower.

Inside the corolla is a circle of stamens. **Stamens** are the male parts of the flower. Each stamen has a slender stalk, or **filament**, that supports a knoblike **anther**. Pollen grains form inside the anther.

The innermost structure of the flower is the **pistil** [PIHS-tihl]. The pistil is the female part of the flower. The pistil is composed of the **stigma**, the **style**, and the **ovary**. At the tip of the pistil is the stigma, which generally has a sticky surface to which pollen grains can adhere. The stigma is attached to the ovary by a long, slender style. The large, swollen ovary rests on the receptacle. Inside the ovary is one or more ovules. Each **ovule** [OH-vyool] is covered by two tissue layers and is attached to the ovary wall by a stalk. Between the two covering tissue layers is a small opening called the **micropyle** [MY-cruh-pyl]. A **carpel** is a single ovary, style, and stigma. In many flowers, several carpels fuse together to form a pistil. A pistil may have one or many carpels.

Each angiosperm has a distinctive flower. Flowers vary in the number, color, shape, and arrangement of the floral parts. Not all flowers contain all of the floral parts. A **complete flower** is one that has sepals, petals, stamens, and a pistil. The sepals and petals are not essential to reproduction. A flower that lacks sepals or petals is an **incomplete flower**.

Flowers that contain both stamens and pistils are called **perfect flowers**. **Imperfect flowers** are missing one of two

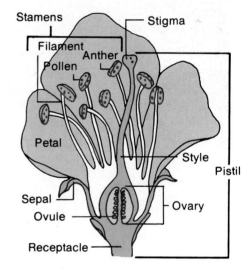

Figure 23.1 The parts of a flower

reproductive structures. Corn, for example, has male flowers on the top of the plant. The corn tassel is composed of many imperfect flowers that have only stamens. Imperfect female flowers grow farther down on the stalk of the same plant. These female flowers eventually form the ear of corn.

The characteristics of flowers are very useful in classification. Dicotyledons and monocotyledons can be distinguished easily by differences in flower structure. In monocots, the sepals, petals, and stamens occur in multiples of 3. In dicots, the floral parts occur in multiples of 4 or 5. Examples of the flowers of dicots and monocots are shown in Figure 23.2.

Figure 23.2 What differences do you notice between these monocot and dicot flowers?

Lily-Monocot

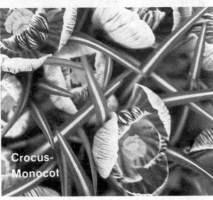

Crocus-Monocot

Tulip-Monocot

Anemone-Dicot

Rose-Dicot

Saguaro-Dicot

The arrangement of flowers on a stem also varies from species to species. Some flowers occur singly, others occur in a group, or **inflorescence**. The most compact grouping occurs in the group of dicots called **composites**. Daisies are composites, as are sunflowers and dandelions. What you may call the flower of a daisy is really an inflorescence composed of many tiny individual flowers. If you examine a daisy closely, you will see that each "petal" is actually a perfect flower.

23–2   Ovule and Pollen Formation

Whatever the specialization of the flowers, the formation of ovules and pollen is basically the same in all angiosperms. Each flower produces an egg in each ovule and many thousands of pollen grains in each anther.

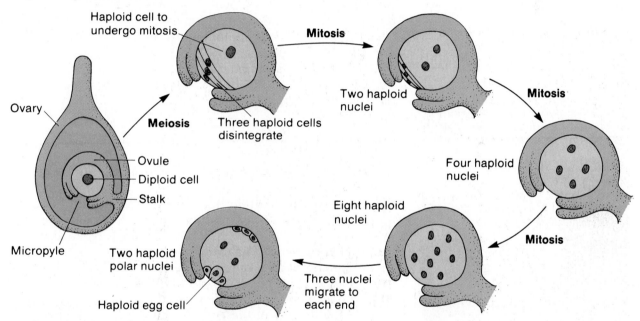

The formation of eggs is shown in Figure 23.3. Within each newly formed ovule is a diploid cell that undergoes meiosis to form 4 haploid **megaspores**. Of these 4 cells, 3 degenerate. The 4th cell undergoes 3 mitotic divisions to form 8 haploid nuclei. Three nuclei migrate to one end of the ovule, and 3 others migrate to the opposite end. These 6 nuclei are then surrounded by cell membranes and become cells. The middle cell of the 3 cells near the micropyle is the egg cell. The 2 nuclei in the middle of the ovule are called **polar nuclei**.

The mature ovule is a female gametophyte. Thus compared to other groups of plants, the haploid generation of the angiosperms is greatly reduced. At maturity the gametophyte consists of only the two polar nuclei and the egg.

Figure 23.3 The process by which eggs form in the ovule involves both meiosis and mitosis.

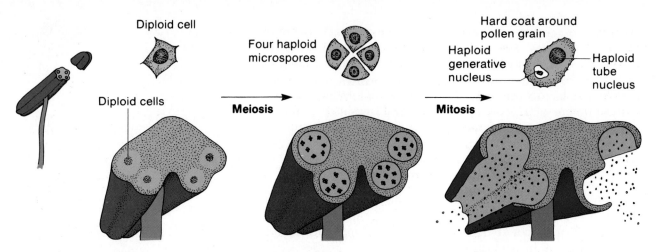

Diploid cell

Diploid cells

Four haploid
microspores

Meiosis

Hard coat around
pollen grain

Haploid
generative
nucleus

Haploid
tube
nucleus

Mitosis

Figure 23.4 The formation of pollen in the anther involves both meiosis and mitosis.

Do You Know?

The peas that Gregor Mendel studied were self-pollinating. This was one reason that he could be sure that he was working with pure lines.

Figure 23.5 The honey possum transports pollen among flowers in the process of obtaining nectar from flowers for food.

Pollen formation is shown in Figure 23.4. In each anther there are large numbers of diploid cells, each of which undergoes meiosis to form 4 haploid **microspores**. Each microspore then undergoes mitosis. A pollen grain forms when a hard coat is deposited around the 2 haploid cells. Each pollen grain contains 2 nuclei, the **tube nucleus** and the **generative nucleus**. Pollen grains are released when the anther dries and splits open.

23–3   Pollination

Pollination is the transfer of pollen from the anther of one flower to the stigma of another flower. In some kinds of plants, pollen from an anther can fertilize eggs in the same flower. Yet cases of **self-pollination** are relatively rare. In many plants, pollen grains and ovules mature at different times, making self-pollination impossible.

Like gymnosperms, many angiosperms depend on wind to carry pollen from one plant to another. Grasses and trees such as oak, maple, and birch are examples of wind-pollinated plants. The flowers of these plants usually have small sepals and petals. Wind is a random pollinator. There is no way to predict the direction or distance a pollen grain will travel. To ensure that pollen reaches another plant, wind-pollinated plants produce enormous amounts of pollen.

Animals are much more efficient than wind as carriers of pollen. The angiosperms that depend on particular animals to carry pollen provide food for those animals. Many animals eat pollen. As animals travel from flower to flower seeking pollen, some of the pollen from one flower is accidentally transferred to the stigma of another flower. Animal-pollinated plants do not produce as much pollen as wind-pollinated species, since the pollen is carried directly by the animal and not randomly distributed.

Plants that depend on insects or other animals to carry pollen often have large and brightly colored petals that advertise the pollen to insects. But color and size are not the only attractions. Many flowers produce a sugary food, called **nectar**, which animals eat. Nectar is not necessary for the formation of seeds, but it does attract pollinators to flowers.

The most common animal pollinators are insects, though birds and bats pollinate a few species. Many flowers have evolved structures that allow only certain insects to pollinate them. These insects, in turn, have evolved feeding structures adapted for particular plants.

Different animals are attracted to different flower colors. Honeybees, for example, cannot see the color red and are rarely found at red flowers. Bees more commonly pollinate blue or yellow flowers. Many flowers have patterns of stripes that direct the bees to the nectar in the center of the flower. Such markings are called **honey guides**.

Unlike bees, hummingbirds can see red quite well. Flowers that are pollinated by hummingbirds are often bright red. Hummingbirds hover while drinking nectar, and the flowers they pollinate often have long tubes that fit the bird's beak. Pollen is deposited on the bird's feathers, then carried to the next flower.

Many flowers produce sweet-smelling scents that advertise their pollen and nectar. But not all insects are attracted to sweet-smelling flowers. Flies are attracted to flowers that smell like decaying meat, such as those of the skunk cabbage.

Moths are common pollinators. They are drawn to white flowers that open at dusk when moths are most active. Moth-pollinated flowers often have heavy scents that help attract

Figure 23.6 Some insects pollinate accidentally by transferring pollen picked up by the body.

Figure 23.7 *Left:* The spots on the rhododendron act as lights on an airport runway in directing insects to the center of the flower. *Right:* The flower of the skunk cabbage releases an odor like that of decayed meat to attract flies as pollinators.

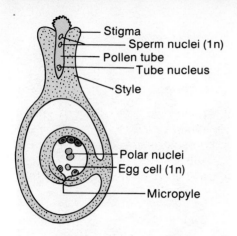

Stigma
Sperm nuclei (1n)
Pollen tube
Tube nucleus
Style

Polar nuclei
Egg cell (1n)

Micropyle

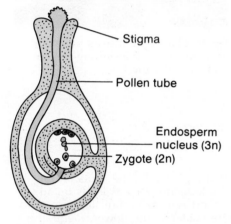

Stigma

Pollen tube

Endosperm
nucleus (3n)
Zygote (2n)

Figure 23.8 Double fertilization. *Top:* As the pollen tube grows through the style, the generative nucleus divides to form two sperm nuclei. *Bottom:* When the pollen tube reaches the ovule, one sperm cell fuses with the egg cell to form the zygote (2n). The other sperm cell fuses with the two polar nuclei to form the endosperm nucleus (3n).

the moths. Flowers pollinated by moths often have petals that form a tube with nectar at the base. Moths feed by inserting their long feeding tubes into the flowers.

Charles Darwin once observed a flower that had nectar at the base of a tube that was over 30 centimeters long. He hypothesized that this flower was pollinated by a moth with a feeding tube that could reach that deep, although no such moth had ever been seen. Many years later, the pollinator of this flower was discovered. As Darwin had predicted, the feeding tube of this moth matched the length of the flower.

23–4 Fertilization

Pollination is complete when a pollen grain lands on the stigma of a flower of the same species. Chemicals in the stigma cause an extension of cytoplasm to grow out of the pollen grain. As shown in Figure 23.8, the **pollen tube** pushes through the cells of the style and grows toward the ovary.

The tube nucleus is located at the front of the growing tube. The generative nucleus undergoes mitosis, forming two haploid **sperm nuclei**. When the pollen tube reaches the micropyle, the end of the pollen tube pushes through the ovule wall and breaks open. The tube nucleus disintegrates, but the two sperm nuclei will fertilize the nuclei in the ovule.

One sperm nucleus fertilizes the egg cell. The resulting diploid zygote divides by mitosis and forms an embryo. The second sperm nucleus joins with both polar nuclei to form a single triploid (3n) nucleus. The new triploid cell divides, forming a tissue called **endosperm**, which surrounds the embryo. The cells of the endosperm are rich in food — usually oil or starch — that nourishes the embryo. The embryo and its triploid endosperm along with the covering layers of the ovule will mature to form the seed.

As you know, fertilization occurs when haploid gametes fuse, thus forming a new cell. In flowering plants, fertilization involves the fusion of two pairs of nuclei. One sperm nucleus fertilizes the egg and the other fertilizes the polar nuclei. This type of fertilization is called **double fertilization**. Double fertilization occurs only in angiosperms.

Checkpoint

1. What part of the stem supports the flower?
2. To what part of the pistil does the pollen adhere?
3. What term describes a flower that has both stamens and pistils?

Fruits and Seeds

After fertilization, the seeds of a plant begin to develop. This process is not unlike the development of seeds in gymnosperms. But in angiosperms, a fruit develops around the seed. A **fruit** is a structure that develops from the ovary of a plant and surrounds the seeds. Some fruits also contain tissues from other parts of the flower. Fruits aid in dispersing seeds. As with flowers and pollination, fruits depend on wind, animals, and other factors to achieve dispersal.

23–5 Seed Structure

A seed is a mature ovule. As in the gymnosperms, the seeds of angiosperms contain an embryo, a food supply, and a seed coat. Figure 23.9 shows the seed of a typical dicotyledon, a bean. The layers of tissue surrounding the ovule harden and thicken to form a tough seed coat. A scar called the **hilum** shows where the seed was once attached to the ovary by a stalk.

Just inside the seed coat and above the hilum is the bean embryo. The embryo is a many-celled structure. The tip of the embryo is called the **epicotyl** [EHP-ih-kaht-uhl]. The epicotyl becomes the meristem of the shoot. On the other end of the embryo is the **radicle**, which will develop into the root of the young plant. The epicotyl and radicle are connected by tissue called the **hypocotyl** [HY-puh-kaht-uhl].

Connected to the embryo are two leaflike structures called cotyledons. **Cotyledons** [kaht-uh-LEED-uhnz] digest and absorb food molecules from the surrounding endosperm and transport the food to the embryo. In the bean seed, the cotyledons have absorbed the entire endosperm so that each half of the bean consists primarily of a large cotyledon.

As you read in Chapter 20, the seeds of dicotyledons have two cotyledons and those of monocots have one. Since the bean has two cotyledons, it is obviously a dicot. Figure 23.9 shows the structure of a corn seed, a typical monocot. Corn seeds have only one cotyledon. This cotyledon does not digest all of the endosperm, so much of it remains in the seed.

23–6 Fruit Development and Structure

While seeds mature within the ovary, the ovary walls themselves become modified to form the fruit. Fruits that develop from a single ovary in a single flower are called **simple fruits**. Tomatoes, plums, and pears are simple fruits. **Aggregate fruits**, such as raspberries, develop from many different ovaries in

CONCEPTS

- structure of typical dicot and monocot seeds
- characteristics of major types of fruits
- mechanisms of seed dispersal

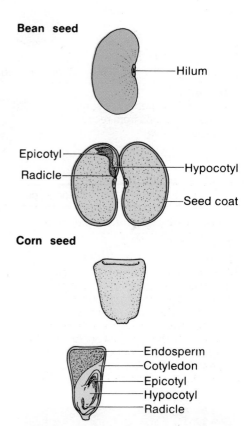

Figure 23.9 *Top:* The structural parts of a bean seed. *Bottom:* The structural parts of a corn seed.

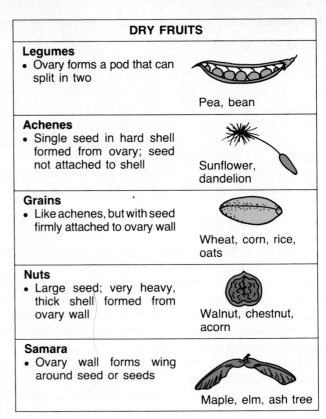

FLESHY FRUITS	DRY FRUITS

FLESHY FRUITS

Berries
- Seed enclosed in soft flesh that develops from ovary wall

Grape, tomato, orange

Drupes
- Seed enclosed in hard pit; pit and soft flesh both derived from ovary wall

Cherry, peach, olive

Pomes
- Seeds in papery ovary; flesh develops from receptacle of flower

Apple, pear

DRY FRUITS

Legumes
- Ovary forms a pod that can split in two

Pea, bean

Achenes
- Single seed in hard shell formed from ovary; seed not attached to shell

Sunflower, dandelion

Grains
- Like achenes, but with seed firmly attached to ovary wall

Wheat, corn, rice, oats

Nuts
- Large seed; very heavy, thick shell formed from ovary wall

Walnut, chestnut, acorn

Samara
- Ovary wall forms wing around seed or seeds

Maple, elm, ash tree

Figure 23.10 Types of simple fruits

a single flower. **Multiple fruits**, such as pineapples, develop from single ovaries of each flower in a cluster.

Several categories of dry and fleshy simple fruits are shown in Figure 23.10. In fleshy fruits, the ovary wall thickens into a soft pulp, often with a high sugar content.

Dry fruits are often mistaken for seeds. **Achenes** [ah-KEENZ] are dry fruits with a seed enclosed in a thin, hard layer formed from the ovary wall. Birds crack open the hard shell of the sunflower fruit (an achene) to get at the seed inside. The seed coats of **grains** are attached to the ovary wall. Wheat, corn, rice, oats, and other grasses form grains.

Aggregate and multiple fruits can fit in the classifications described for simple fruits. Strawberries, for example, are aggregate fruits with achenes on the outside surface.

23–7 Dispersal

Many plants depend on wind to disperse seeds. Dandelion and milkweed are perhaps the best-known plants with wind-dispersed seeds. These plants produce fruits with a "parachute" of fibers that are so fine that even a slight draft bears them aloft. Maple trees have winged fruits called **samaras** [SAM-uh-ruhz] that also aid in wind dispersal. Tumbleweeds of the

American Southwest show yet another interesting adaptation. In these species the entire adult plant breaks loose from its roots and is blown across the landscape. Seeds are jarred free as the plant rolls.

The seeds of some plants are dispersed by water. The coconut is the most impressive example. The coconut fruit has an extremely hard outer shell that can float for long periods. It is not uncommon for coconuts to drift thousands of kilometers before washing up on a beach and germinating.

Many fruits rely on animals for dispersal. The soft, sweet, and fleshy fruits appeal to animals as much as they do to humans. Animals often carry fruits to a safe place to eat them. Sometimes they drop seeds as they eat the fruit. Squirrels are known for hiding large numbers of acorns for winter feeding. More often than not, squirrels forget where they hid the acorns. Many an oak tree has sprouted from misplaced squirrel supplies.

Many times animals eat seeds that pass unharmed through their digestive tracts. These seeds are deposited in the animals' droppings, often a long way from the parent plant. Not only are the seeds dispersed, but they are left with a supply of fertilizer, thus increasing their chance for survival.

Other seeds are transported on the hair or feathers of animals. Many dry fruits are covered with tiny hooks. These seeds get caught in the fur of passing animals and can be carried for long distances.

Figure 23.11 *Top left:* Wind disperses the seeds of the milkweed. *Top right:* Birds transport berries over long distances. *Bottom:* Water is the medium for the dispersal of these seeds.

Checkpoint

1. What part of the plant embryo will eventually develop into the roots of the plant?
2. From what part of a flower are most fruits derived?
3. In addition to protecting the seeds, what is the major function of fruits?
4. How are samaras dispersed?

Reproduction in Flowering Plants   **349**

Vegetative Propagation

In addition to reproducing sexually with flowers, many angiosperms can reproduce asexually as well. Asexual reproduction, the development of new plants from only one parent, is also called **vegetative propagation**.

New plants may arise from many different parts of the parent plant. Roots, stems, and occasionally leaves give rise to new plants. Since a plant that arises through vegetative propagation has only one parent, its genetic makeup will be identical to that of its parent.

23–8   Natural Vegetative Propagation

The strawberry is an example of a plant that reproduces asexually by means of its stems. The parent plant sends out stems called stolons, which grow along the ground. Roots grow downward from the stolon's tip and into the soil. Shoots grow upward into the air. The root and shoot form a new plant that is independent of the parent plant.

Sometimes horizontal roots form shoots that become independent plants. Milkweed, sumac, beech, elderberry, and lilac are examples of plants that reproduce by means of their roots. In a few cases, the leaves produce offspring. *Bryophyllum*, shown in Figure 23.12, is the best-known example of propagation by leaves.

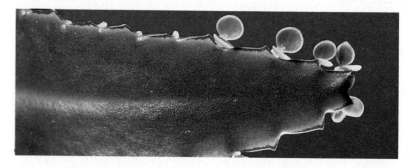

Figure 23.12 *Bryophyllum* with tiny plants forming on its leaves

23–9   Artificial Vegetative Propagation

People involved in the production of agricultural and ornamental plants have developed many ways of using vegetative propagation. Plants produced by vegetative propagation often reach maturity more quickly than plants grown by seeds. Vegetative propagation allows the production of plants that are genetically identical to desirable plants, such as hybrids. As you know, the offspring of hybrids often do not resemble their parents.

Do You Know?

Grafting is an ancient practice. It was known to the Chinese over 3,500 years ago. Aristotle mentioned grafting in his writings.

Have you ever wondered how seedless fruits, such as navel oranges, reproduce? The original navel orange developed from a mutation in the bud of an orange tree that contained seeds. When this fruit was discovered, it was recognized as a desirable food. The branch of the tree containing the seedless oranges was propagated vegetatively to produce more seedless oranges. All navel oranges are descended from this single bud mutation.

One common method of vegetative propagation is to take **cuttings**. In this method, a leaf or stem is cut from a plant and placed in water or soil. The part of the stem in contact with the soil or water develops roots. Once a cutting establishes roots, it becomes an independent plant.

Other methods of vegetative propagation are shown in Figure 23.13. In the process of **layering**, roots are induced to grow from a stem that is still attached to the parent plant. In one method of layering, a branch of the plant is bent down to the ground and covered with soil except at the tip. Roots will grow from the buried part of the plant, and a shoot will arise from the tip. Eventually the new plant can be cut away from the parent plant. Layering is used with blackberries, raspberries, and roses.

In the technique of **grafting**, a part of one plant is attached to a healthy, rooted part of another plant. The rooted plant is called the **stock**. The part of the plant that is attached to the stock is called the **scion**. The scion does not form new organs, as in other forms of asexual reproduction. Rather, it becomes a part of the stock plant. When grafting a branch onto another tree, the vascular cambiums of the stock and scion must be placed carefully so that they touch. Thus the newly formed vascular tissue will form a continuous pipeline between the two branches.

The technique of **budding** is similar to that of grafting, but in budding the scion is a bud instead of a branch. A bud from one tree is slipped into a T-shaped slit in the bark of another tree. The year after the bud graft is made, the bud grows into a shoot. The part of the tree above the graft is cut off so that the budded portion becomes the apical meristem of the tree. Pears, plums, peaches, citrus fruits, and apples are produced by budding.

Checkpoint

1. Strawberries reproduce asexually by means of horizontal stems called _____.
2. A piece of a plant that is cut and put in water or soil is called a _____.
3. What two plant parts are joined in grafting?

Layering

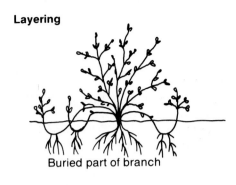

Buried part of branch

Grafting

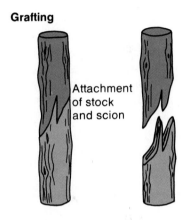

Attachment of stock and scion

Budding

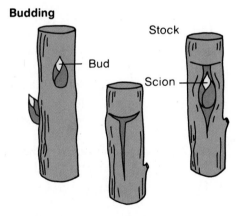

Bud

Stock

Scion

Figure 23.13 Layering, grafting, and budding are artificial methods of plant propagation.

CHAPTER REVIEW

Summary

- Flowers are the reproductive organs of angiosperms. A complete flower is composed of a pistil and rings of sepals, petals, and stamens. The male stamen consists of a filament and an anther. The female pistil is composed of the stigma, style, and ovary.

- Ovules are the female gametophytes of angiosperms. Each ovule contains 8 haploid nuclei, 1 of which belongs to the egg cell. Pollen grains are the male gametophytes. Each pollen grain contains 2 haploid sperm nuclei.

- Pollination occurs when the pollen grains are transferred from the anther to the stigma of another flower. Some flowers are self-pollinated.

- The structure of a flower often indicates the kind of pollinator. Shape, petal color, odor, and location of nectar ensure pollination by a particular animal.

- When the pollen grain lands on the stigma, it develops a pollen tube, which grows through the style to the ovule. One of the sperm nuclei fertilizes the egg; the other fertilizes the polar nuclei to form a triploid (3n) nucleus. Double fertilization occurs only in angiosperms.

- After fertilization, the ovule develops into a seed. The seed coat develops from layers of tissue covering the ovule. Endosperm forms from the triploid nucleus. The diploid zygote develops into the plant embryo.

- The embryo is composed of the epicotyl, which will develop into the shoot of the young plant; the radicle, which will develop into the roots; and the hypocotyl.

- Dicotyledons and monocotyledons may be distinguished on the basis of flower structure and seed structure. Monocots have 1 embryonic leaf, or cotyledon; the floral parts of monocots occur in multiples of 3. Dicots have 2 cotyledons; their floral parts occur in multiples of 4 or 5.

- A fruit is a mature ovary or group of ovaries surrounding the seeds. Some fruits are thick-walled and fleshy, others are hard and dry. Fruits are classified by the number of ovaries and flowers from which they form.

- Fruits have many adaptations that aid in the dispersal of seeds. Agents of seed dispersal include wind, water, and animals.

- Many angiosperms can reproduce vegetatively as well as sexually. Naturally occurring forms of vegetative reproduction include stolons, roots, and leaves. Artificial methods of vegetative propagation include cuttings, layering, grafting, and budding.

Vocabulary

achene	hypocotyl
aggregate fruit	imperfect flower
anther	incomplete flower
budding	inflorescence
calyx	layering
carpel	megaspore
complete flower	micropyle
composite	microspore
corolla	multiple fruit
cotyledon	nectar
cutting	ovary
double fertilization	ovule
endosperm	perfect flower
epicotyl	petal
filament	pistil
flower	polar nuclei
fruit	pollen tube
generative nucleus	pollination
grafting	radicle
grain	receptacle
hilum	samara
honey guide	scion

self-pollination
sepal
simple fruit
sperm nuclei
stamen
stigma

stock
style
tube nucleus
vegetative
   propagation

Review

1. What is the female part of a flower?
2. What are all the sepals of a flower called?
3. What are the two parts of the stamen?
4. What term describes a flower without petals? A flower without stamens?
5. How many nuclei does the pollen tube have just prior to entering the micropyle?
6. What is the female gametophyte of an angiosperm?
7. In double fertilization, which two nuclei fuse to form a diploid nucleus? Which two fuse to form a triploid nucleus?
8. What tissue stores food in the seed?
9. What is the name of the scar where the seed was once attached to the ovary?
10. What part of the embryo will develop into the stem of the new plant?
11. What kind of fruit forms from many ovaries in a single flower?
12. What are two advantages of vegetative propagation over sexual reproduction?
13. Place the following events in the correct order.
    a. Fertilization occurs.
    b. Sepals cover the flower bud.
    c. Seeds and fruit mature.
    d. Pollen forms in the anther.
    e. The zygote develops into an embryo.
    f. Pollen lands on the stigma.
    g. The pollen grain has three nuclei.

Interpret and Apply

1. Why do wind-pollinated plants produce more pollen than animal-pollinated plants?
2. People sometimes use the terms *pollination* and *fertilization* as though they mean the same thing. Why is this incorrect?

3. What is a honey guide?
4. What is meant by *double fertilization?*
5. What tissue produces the seed coat?
6. What is the function of the cotyledon?
7. You find a flower that has three petals and three sepals. Is it a dicot or a monocot?
8. List three different ways seeds can be dispersed and give an example of each.
9. Which artificial method of vegetative propagation is similar to the natural vegetative propagation by stolons?

Challenge

1. Self-pollination is rare in plants. What adaptations of plants prevent self-pollination from occurring?
2. How does the biological meaning of the terms *fruit, berry,* and *nut* differ from the way these terms are commonly used?
3. Why is seed dispersal important to plants?
4. What do all fruits have in common?
5. Your garden contains a healthy apple tree, but the apples do not taste good. Your neighbor has a tree with good-tasting apples. How can you improve the taste of the apples that your tree produces?

Projects

1. Learn to identify some of the common wild flowers. Make a chart showing the characteristics of some of the major families of wild flowers.
2. Dissect several common garden flowers. You may need a hand lens for some of the smaller flowers. Make drawings of each kind of flower you dissect and identify the parts. Compare the variations in structure that you observe in the different kinds of flowers.
3. Find out what laws protect the wild flowers in your state and report to your class.
4. Collect as many different kinds of seeds as you can find. Cut some open and identify the various parts.

24 Plant Growth and Response

Autumn in New England

Plants respond to changes in their environment. Here you see autumn leaves setting the countryside ablaze with color. This dazzling display is the result of the trees' preparation for winter.

During the growing season, leaves contain a large amount of chlorophyll, which makes them appear green. But leaves also contain other pigments, such as xanthophylls and carotenes, that are yellow or orange. As winter approaches, the chlorophyll in the leaves begins to break down. As the chlorophyll disappears, the other pigments become apparent. This accounts for the golden color of some autumn leaves.

Weather can affect the color of the fall foliage. If the nights are cold and the days sunny, another pigment, anthocyanin, develops. This pigment gives the leaves of plants such as maples and sumacs a brilliant blue-red color. The climate of northeastern North America is ideal for autumn foliage. In Europe, falls are usually cloudy and warm. Maples transplanted there do not produce the burning reds that set the autumns of the Northeast aflame with color.

Germination of Seeds

The life cycle of an angiosperm begins with a seed. Seeds that land in favorable locations will eventually **germinate**, or begin to grow. How quickly a seed germinates depends upon the type of plant and the external conditions.

24–1 Seed Dormancy

Some seeds, such as those of certain willow trees, germinate within 24 hours of landing in a favorable place. In damp weather, peas may germinate while still attached to the vine. The seeds of most plants, however, must undergo a period of inactivity, or **dormancy**, before germination. During dormancy the cellular respiration of the embryo proceeds very slowly. The period of dormancy may last from a few weeks to many years.

Dormancy is an adaptation that ensures that seeds do not germinate at inappropriate times. Many seeds that mature in the fall, for example, must be frozen before they can germinate. This ensures seeds will not germinate during a warm period in the fall, only to be killed during the cold winter that follows.

CONCEPTS

- conditions producing dormancy
- process of germination in dicots and monocots

Figure 24.1 Seeds come in a variety of shapes and sizes. Some of the seeds shown here are beginning to sprout.

Seeds cannot germinate until water has seeped through their coat. The seed coats of some seeds are impermeable to water. Over time, freezing and thawing weaken the seed coat, allowing water to enter.

The seeds of plants that live in deserts often have adaptations to ensure that they do not germinate until there is enough water available. Some seeds contain chemicals that **inhibit**, or discourage, germination. Such seeds cannot germinate until rains have washed all the inhibitory chemicals away. Figure 24.2 shows a desert in bloom after a rare, heavy rainfall. The seeds of these plants may have lain dormant for many years, until proper conditions allowed them to germinate.

If a seed does not encounter the proper conditions for germination, eventually it will die. Then it will not germinate even under favorable conditions. A seed that has the capability of germinating is said to be **viable** [VY-uh-buhl]. Seeds maintain their viability best under cool, dry conditions.

Figure 24.2 Some desert plants bloom only after a heavy rainfall.

24–2 Germination of Dicots and Monocots

Viable seeds that have undergone a period of dormancy and have favorable growth conditions will germinate. Several factors influence germination. There must be sufficient moisture and oxygen in the soil, and the temperature must be favorable.

Before germination, the seed begins to absorb water. As water enters the seed, its enzymes become active. Digestive enzymes break down food stored in the endosperm or cotyledons. The embryo begins to grow. The swelling tissues of the seed break open the seed coat.

Refer to Figure 24.3 as you read about the germination of a bean seed. The radicle, or embryonic root, usually emerges from the seed first. Root hairs quickly develop, enabling the plant to obtain water from the soil.

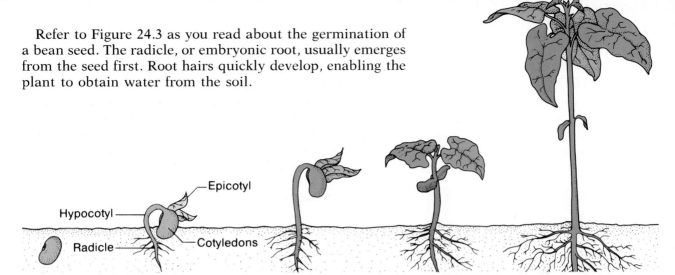

Hypocotyl

Epicotyl

Radicle

Cotyledons

Figure 24.3 Stages in the germination of a bean seed

After the radicle appears, the hypocotyl begins to grow. The curved hypocotyl is the first part of the seedling to appear above the soil. As the hypocotyl grows longer, it begins to straighten out. The growing hypocotyl pulls the cotyledons and epicotyl out of the soil. Eventually the epicotyl develops into the shoot, or stem and leaves, of the seedling.

Until it is able to make its own food by photosynthesis, the bean seedling obtains nutrients from its cotyledons. As the food in the cotyledons is digested and transported to the growing parts of the seedling, the cotyledons shrivel and fall off.

The germination of a monocot seed, such as the corn seed shown in Figure 24.4, is somewhat different from that of a dicot. The root that arises from the radicle in the corn seedling is a temporary structure. Branch roots soon arise from the primary root. Later, adventitious roots develop from the stem.

In monocots, the seedling's source of food is the endosperm. Unlike the cotyledons of the bean seed, the endosperm does not emerge from the soil. Instead, it remains buried throughout germination.

In grasses such as corn, the epicotyl is covered by a sheathlike structure called the **coleoptile** [koh-lee-AHP-tihl]. The coleoptile protects the shoot as it pushes upward through the soil.

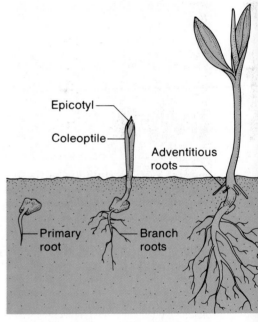

Epicotyl

Coleoptile

Adventitious roots

Primary root

Branch roots

Figure 24.4 Stages in the germination of a corn seed

Checkpoint

1. What is the inactive period between seed formation and germination called?
2. What is the food source of dicot seedlings? Of monocot seedlings?
3. What structure protects the shoot of the corn seedling?

Plant Movements

Like all living things, plants respond to stimuli. You may never have noticed the movements of vascular plants. Because they are rooted in one place, their responses are not obvious. If you observe plants carefully, however, you will discover many ways in which plants respond to their environment.

24–3 Tropisms

If you place a houseplant on a sunny windowsill, during the day its leaves will move so that they are facing the sun. The plant is responding to the stimulus of the light. Unlike the movement of your arm or leg, the plant's movement is not caused by muscles. Rather, it is the result of growth of the stem. The growth of a plant in response to a stimulus is called a **tropism** [TROH-pihzm].

Tropisms result from unequal stimulation on opposite sides of the plant. In tropisms, the movement of the plant is dependent upon the direction from which the stimulus comes. Movement toward a stimulus is called **positive tropism**. Movement away from a stimulus is **negative tropism**.

The growth of the plant toward a source of light is positive **phototropism**. One of the first scientists to study phototropism was Charles Darwin. In the 1890s, Darwin demonstrated that when seedlings are exposed to a light source, the coleoptile grows in that direction. When Darwin removed the tips of the coleoptiles, the shoots did not bend toward the light. From this experiment, Darwin concluded that a substance produced at the tip of the shoot influenced the growth of the stem. Since Darwin's time, scientists have identified this substance, which is called an **auxin** [AWK-suhn].

To understand how auxins cause phototropism, study the oat seedlings shown in Figure 24.6. When light is more intense on one side of a plant than on the other, auxins in the stem

Figure 24.5 The orientation of these plant leaves toward the light is the result of positive phototropism.

Figure 24.6 Auxins in the stem tip can pass through an agar barrier, allowing the seedling to show phototropism.

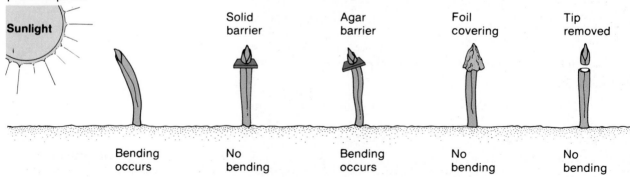

migrate toward the darker side of the plant. This causes the side of the stem farther from the light to grow more quickly. The uneven growth causes the stem to curve toward the light. Because tropisms result from the growth of cells, they are permanent.

In addition to light, plants respond to other stimuli, such as gravity and touch. **Geotropism** is the growth of a plant in response to gravity. Positive geotropism, or movement toward gravity, occurs in roots. Negative geotropism, or movement away from gravity, occurs in the stem and leaves.

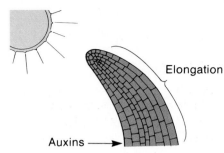

Figure 24.7 Elongation of the cells on the dark side of the plant causes uneven growth.

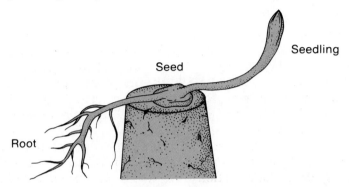

Figure 24.8 The accumulation of auxins on the lower side of the plant results in uneven growth. The stem curves upward.

Like phototropism, negative geotropism results from an unequal distribution of auxins in the stem. If you place a growing plant in a horizontal position, as shown in Figure 24.8, most of the auxin accumulates in the lower side of the plant. The shoot, responding to the presence of auxins, elongates more on its lower side than on its upper side. The uneven growth causes the shoot to curve upward. The tissues of roots display positive geotropism.

Thigmotropism is growth in response to touch. The tendrils of climbing plants show thigmotropism. When a tendril contacts a solid object, the side of the tendril away from the object grows faster than the side touching the object. The unequal rates of growth cause the tendril to curl around the object.

Figure 24.9 The growth pattern of tendrils is caused by thigmotropism.

24–4 Nastic Movements

Morning glories, as their name implies, open in the morning and close again at night. What causes the petals to move? As the temperature of the air rises, changes in turgor pressure cause the morning glories to open their petals. The falling temperature of the evening causes their petals to close. Other kinds of flowers open and close in response to light.

This kind of response is called a **nastic movement**. Unlike tropisms, nastic movements are independent of the direction from which the stimulus comes. Nastic movements usually occur as a result of changes in turgor pressure and are reversible.

Figure 24.10 The opening of a morning glory is a nastic movement.

Probably the best-known example of a nastic movement in response to contact is found in the mimosa, or sensitive plant. If you touch the leaflets of this plant, they fold upward and the petiole droops. The response is immediate. As is true of all nastic movements, the reaction is reversible, and the leaflets soon assume their original, open position. The response of the mimosa leaf is the same if you touch the top or the bottom of the leaf. Unlike thigmotropism, nastic movement in response to touch is independent of the direction of contact.

The insect-trapping action of the Venus's-flytrap is another example of a nastic movement. Hairs in the center of the leaves are stimulated when an insect lands on them. This stimulation causes the two sides of the leaf to snap together, trapping the insect between them.

Checkpoint

1. What term describes the growth of leaves toward the sun?
2. What substance causes leaves to grow toward light?
3. What plant organ has positive geotropism?
4. List three ways in which nastic movements are unlike tropisms.

Plant Growth and Development

Once a seed germinates, it begins to grow into an adult plant. A plant's growth and final form are determined by many factors. External factors can cause two plants with the same genetic makeup to turn out quite differently. External factors that influence plant growth include temperature, intensity of light, and amount of rainfall.

For example, plants grown in darkness look very different from plants grown in sunlight. Compare the two plants shown in Figure 24.11. Dark-grown plants are pale and spindly, with their leaves unopened. Without light, leaves cannot form chlorophyll.

Figure 24.11 A comparison of plants grown in sunlight and darkness. Darkness inhibits the formation of chlorophyll.

24–5 Life Span

Different plants live for different lengths of time. The potential life span of a plant is genetically determined. An **annual** is a plant that lives only one growing season. The seeds produced at the end of one growing season germinate, grow, flower, and produce seeds by the end of the season. Most annuals are herbaceous rather than woody. Tomatoes, beans, peas, and marigolds are all annuals.

A **biennial** is a plant that lives for two growing seasons. During the first season it germinates and produces leaves and roots. During the second season it flowers and produces seeds. Biennials may be either herbaceous or woody. Often biennials store food from one growing season to the next in fleshy stems or roots. Carrots, beets, celery, and cabbage are biennials.

Figure 24.12 A climbing rose is a perennial that blooms year after year.

A **perennial** is a plant that lives for more than two growing seasons. Perennials may be either woody or herbaceous. Herbaceous perennials often grow from bulbs or rhizomes. Some garden perennials are peonies, iris, and roses. Trees, woody shrubs, and vines are also perennials.

24–6 Hormones

Plants grow as the cells in the meristem divide, enlarge, and differentiate. How is this process controlled? All parts of a plant's life cycle — germination, growth, flowering, and production of seeds — are governed by the interaction of internal and external factors.

The external environment of a plant often stimulates the production of growth-regulating chemicals called hormones. **Hormones** are chemicals that are produced in one part of a plant, then transported to another part of the plant where they cause a response. The first plant hormones to be discovered were auxins. As you know, auxins produced in the meristem cause phototropism and geotropism.

Some hormones stimulate cell growth and division. Others inhibit growth and cause dormancy. Sometimes the actions of several hormones combine to cause a particular plant response. The function of plant hormones is not fully understood. The study of hormones is one of the most exciting areas of plant research today.

Figure 24.13 The excessive growth of the mung bean plants *(right)* is due to the plant hormone gibberellic acid.

24–7 Apical Dominance

The presence of auxins can inhibit growth of the stem. As you learned in Chapter 22, growth at the terminal bud makes a stem longer. Growth of lateral buds makes the stem branch and become bushy. The terminal bud produces auxins. When these auxins are transported through the stem, they inhibit the growth of the lateral buds. Since the terminal bud is at the apex of the stem, the dominant growth of the terminal bud is called **apical dominance**.

In many conifers, such as fir or spruce trees, the main trunk shows complete dominance over the lateral branches. Such plants are cone-shaped. In other plants, such as maple trees, one main trunk does not dominate. Instead, the trunk divides into several branches, making the tree appear rounded.

Figure 24.14 *Left:* Many deciduous trees exhibit dominant growth of lateral buds, which gives them a bushy appearance. *Above:* The typical cone shape of many conifers is a result of apical dominance.

24–8 Gibberellins and Cytokinins

Gibberellins are hormones that are produced in young leaves and affect cell enlargement. The action of gibberellins was first observed in a disease of rice plants. In this disease the fungus *Gibberella* produces a gibberellin that causes seedlings to grow unusually tall. The Japanese researchers who studied this disease called the plants *bakanae*, which means "foolish seedlings."

Gibberellins are important in the elongation of stems. Dwarf varieties of plants are often caused by mutations that result in an unusually low production of gibberellins. If gibberellins are applied to dwarf plants, the plants often grow to normal heights.

Figure 24.15 Poinsettias are short-day plants.

Figure 24.16 The abscission layer forms at the base of the petiole.

Another class of growth hormones are the **cytokinins**. Cytokinins stimulate cell division rather than cell elongation. Cytokinins may be important in regulating the transport and storage of food in plant tissues. Cytokinins are produced in the meristems of the roots.

24–9 Control of Flowering

Many plants flower only when the day is a certain length. Flowering of plants in relation to the length of day is called **photoperiodism**. You have probably noticed that certain plants flower in the spring, others in the summer, and still others in the autumn.

The conditions that cause flowering vary from species to species. **Long-day plants** flower only when the photoperiod is longer than a certain critical amount. The critical period varies from plant to plant. In some plants the critical period is 13 hours; in others, as much as 17 hours. Long-day plants include spinach, iris, and clover.

Short-day plants flower only when the period of light is shorter than a certain critical amount. Poinsettias, ragweed, goldenrod, and chrysanthemums are short-day plants. **Day-neutral plants** appear to be unaffected by the period of daylight. Plants such as tomatoes, beans, and roses flower over a wide range of photoperiods.

Early research indicated that the length of daylight determined the time of flowering. More recent studies, however, have shown that flowering is actually the result of the period of darkness. Thus short-day plants might better be called long-night plants, and long-day plants are actually short-night plants.

The mechanism by which photoperiod controls flowering is not fully understood. Evidence indicates that pigments in the leaves are sensitive to the amount of daylight. Proper photoperiod causes the leaves to produce a hormone that travels through the phloem to the flower buds. There it stimulates flowering. The hormone that controls flowering has not yet been isolated.

24–10 Abscission

Toward the end of the growing season, the decreasing photoperiod causes some plants to produce the hormone **ethylene**. Unlike the other plant hormones, ethylene is normally a gas.

The presence of ethylene causes a layer of parenchyma cells to form at the base of the petiole, as shown in Figure 24.16. This layer is called the **abscission layer**. Later, enzymes destroy the walls of the cells in the abscission layer. When the cell walls are destroyed, only the vascular bundles remain to connect the leaf and the stem. Each leaf is thus hanging by only threads. Leaves in this condition are easily knocked from the plant by wind or rain. The separation of leaves from the stem is called **abscission**. After abscission, a layer of cork forms over the leaf scar. This cork protects the tissues of the stem.

Figure 24.17 Leaves are separated from stems by the process of abscission.

Ethylene also stimulates the formation of an abscission layer in the stems of fruit. Abscission allows ripe fruit, such as apples, to fall from trees. The presence of ethylene also promotes the ripening of fruit.

Studies have shown that other hormones besides ethylene may be involved in the process of abscission. For example, the presence of cytokinins can delay the formation of an abscission layer in older leaves and fruits.

Do You Know?

The expression "one rotten apple can spoil the whole barrel" is quite true. An apple that is overripe produces ethylene, which causes the other apples near it to become overripe too.

Checkpoint

1. For how many growing seasons do biennial plants live?
2. What class of plant hormones stimulate cell division? What hormones stimulate cell elongation?
3. How does the production of auxins in the apical meristem influence the growth of lateral buds?
4. What hormone stimulates the abscission of leaves?

CHAPTER REVIEW

Summary

- Many types of seeds require a period of dormancy before they can germinate. Impermeability of the seed coat to water and germination-inhibiting chemicals in the seed are possible causes of dormancy.
- As the tissues of the seed absorb water, enzymes begin to digest food stored in the seed. Germination occurs when the embryo starts to grow.
- The first organ to develop in the seedling is the young root, which grows from the radicle.
- The epicotyl develops into the shoot of the seedling. In dicots such as the bean, the growing hypocotyl pulls the shoot and cotyledons above the surface of the soil.
- In monocots, the endosperm stays beneath the surface of the soil. The shoot is protected by a sheath called the coleoptile.
- Like all living things, plants respond to stimuli. Tropisms are responses to directional stimuli. Growth toward a stimulus is positive tropism; growth away from a stimulus is negative tropism. Gravity, light, and contact can cause tropic movements.
- Nastic movements are responses that are independent of the direction of the stimulus. Most nastic movements are caused by changes in turgor pressure and are reversible. Temperature, light, and touch can cause nastic movements.
- The potential life span of each plant species is genetically determined. Annuals live for one season. Biennials live for two seasons. Perennials live for many years.
- The growth and development of plants is coordinated by the production of plant hormones. Hormones are chemicals that are produced in one part of the plant, then transported to another part of the plant, where they cause a response.
- Auxins, cytokinins, and gibberellins are classes of hormones that are important in cell growth and division.
- The hormone that controls flowering in plants has not yet been isolated.
- Ethylene promotes the ripening of fruit and stimulates the abscission of fruits and leaves.

Vocabulary

abscission	hormone
abscission layer	inhibit
annual	long-day plant
apical dominance	nastic movement
auxin	negative tropism
biennial	perennial
coleoptile	photoperiodism
cytokinin	phototropism
day-neutral plant	positive tropism
dormancy	short-day plant
ethylene	thigmotropism
geotropism	tropism
germinate	viable
gibberellin	

Review

1. If a seed is not viable, what happens when it is planted under favorable conditions?
2. Name four factors that influence germination.
3. What part of the seedling emerges from the bean seed first?
4. What organ provides nutrients for dicot seedlings? For monocot seedlings?
5. Describe the physical appearance of a plant grown in near darkness.
6. What hormone is produced by the coleoptile in oat seedlings?

7. What stimulus produces thigmotropism?
8. What is the difference between phototropism and photoperiodism?
9. Which of the following statements refer to tropisms and which refer to nastic movements? Some statements may refer to both.
   a. The movement is not reversible.
   b. The movement is due to changes in turgor.
   c. The response is independent of the direction of stimulation.
   d. It can be a response to gravity.
   e. It can be a response to touch.
   f. It is caused by unequal distribution of auxins within the plant.
   g. It is reversible.

In the following list, match the hormone or class of hormones with the plant response or process that it controls. One hormone may control more than one process.

10. auxins	a. leaf abscission
11. gibberellins	b. flowering
12. ethylene	c. cell elongation
13. cytokinins	d. cell division
14. unknown hormone	e. phototropism
	f. fruit ripening
	g. apical dominance

Interpret and Apply

1. Compare the germination of a bean seed with that of a corn seed.
2. Why is it important for root hairs to develop soon after germination?
3. Leaves grown in full sunlight often have thicker cuticles than those grown in shade. Why is this an advantage?
4. A seed lacks cotyledons. What will happen to it after it germinates? Explain.
5. Why is a plant tropism considered to be irreversible?
6. The roots of plants usually grow toward water. Is this a positive or negative tropism?
7. Most oak trees flower in the spring. Do you think they are long-day or short-day plants? Explain.

Challenge

1. Most plants of a species in a particular area flower at about the same time. Why is this an important adaptation?
2. Why can't there be nastic movement in response to gravity?
3. You live in a temperate climate. Each year you collect and plant the seeds from one species of garden plant. Each year they germinate and grow. When you move to the tropics, though, your seeds will not germinate. Explain why not.

Projects

1. Design an experiment to test whether a flower is responding to light intensity or to temperature when it closes its petals at night.
2. Obtain a packet of seeds and divide them into two equal groups. Soak one group of seeds in water for 24 hours before planting. Do not soak the other group. Plant both groups of seeds under identical conditions and observe the time necessary for the seeds in each group to germinate.
3. Do library research or speak to people at your county extension service to find several commercial uses for auxins.
4. Investigate hydroponics. Find out the ways in which it is superior to traditional methods of agriculture. What are the limitations of this form of agriculture? Find out also if any foods you eat are grown hydroponically.
5. Investigate how commercial nurseries induce flowering in their plants.

Careers in Botany

Humans could not exist without plants. Our food comes directly or indirectly from plants. Plants also provide us with such products as furniture, drugs, paper, and clothing. There are many career opportunities in the field of botany.

Florists sell cut flowers and potted plants. They help customers choose the appropriate flower or plant for various occasions. In many cases, they prepare ornamental flower arrangements. Some florists grow many of the flowers and plants sold in their shops. There are no specific requirements for this job. Many florists offer apprenticeships to interested workers. There are schools, however, that offer courses in floriculture, the science of growing and caring for ornamental plants.

A nursery is a place where plants are grown and maintained. *Nursery workers* fertilize, feed, and water young plants. They must have a knowledge of plant germination, the growth habits of plants, and plant nutrition. In addition, they must know how to control diseases caused by insects and weeds. Nurseries sell trees, shrubs, flowers, and seedlings. These plants are transplanted in fields, orchards, homes, gardens, and landscaped areas. Federal and state nurseries provide saplings to reforest public lands. Commercial nurseries sell to the public. Many high schools offer vocational training programs in plant management.

Landscape architects plan the use of land for conservation and human enjoyment. They study soil composition, water supply, and local vegetation to plan appropriate land development. They recommend designs for parks and gardens. Landscape architects are responsible for the trees, shrubs, and flowers lining city streets. They work with planners on highway development to conserve farmland and forested areas. A college degree

in landscape architecture is required for this profession.

Agronomy is an agricultural science dealing with food and fiber crops, and the soil in which they grow. *Agronomists* conduct research on crop rotation, irrigation, drainage, plant breeding, and soil fertility. They also develop ways to control weeds, diseases, and insect pests. The results of their work often lead to more efficient crop production, higher yields, and an improvement in the quality of the crop. A college degree is required for this profession.

Plant pathologists study the causes and methods of controlling plant diseases. After isolating disease-causing agents, these scientists find ways to destroy the agent. Then they perform studies on healthy and diseased plants to test their findings. They also study the spread of the disease under different environmental conditions. Plant pathologists have often completed degree programs beyond the college level.

UNIT REVIEW

Synthesis

1. Each of the following is a major advance in the evolution of land plants. List these adaptations in their order of occurrence, beginning with the first. Name the group of plants in which these adaptations first appeared. (a) cuticle (b) vascular tissue (c) flowers (d) seeds (e) roots
2. In a mature tree, many of the cells no longer contain living cytoplasm, although they continue to function as part of the living plant. Name two tissues of a mature tree that are composed of nonliving cells. What is the function of these tissues?
3. Describe briefly the gametophytes of bryophytes, ferns, conifers, and angiosperms. How would you describe the evolutionary trend in the alternation of generations among land plants?
4. Since plants are stationary, they must rely on other agents for the fertilization of gametes. Describe the ways in which egg and sperm are brought together in red algae, brown algae, conifers, and angiosperms.
5. Describe one means of asexual reproduction found in each of the following: brown algae, bryophytes, and angiosperms.
6. Angiosperms are classified as either monocotyledons or dicotyledons. Copy the following table onto a piece of paper and fill in the information.

	Monocots	Dicots
Number of cotyledons in a seed		
Pattern of leaf venation		
Arrangement of vascular bundles in herbaceous stems		
Number of petals and other floral parts		

Additional Reading

Bold, Harold C., and C.L. Hundell. *The Plant Kingdom*. Englewood Cliffs, NJ: Prentice-Hall, Inc., 1977.

Cronquist, Arthur. *How to Know the Seed Plants*. Dubuque, IA: William C. Brown, Co., Pubs., 1979.

Cuthbert, Mabel, and Susan Verhoek. *How to Know the Spring Flowers*. Dubuque, IA: William C. Brown, Co., Pubs., 1982.

Eshleman, Alan. *Poison Plants*. Boston: Houghton Mifflin, 1977.

Huxley, Anthony. *Plant and Planet*. New York: Viking Press, Inc., 1975.

Kapp, Ronald O. *How to Know the Pollen and Spores*. Dubuque, IA: William C. Brown, Co., Pubs., 1969.

Line, Les, and Walter H. Hodge. *The Audubon Society Book of Wildflowers*. New York: Harry N. Abrams, Inc., 1978.

Milne, Lorus and Margery. *Because of a Flower*. New York: Atheneum Pubs., 1975.

Neiring, William, and Nancy Olmstead. *The Audubon Society Field Guide to North American Wildflowers*. New York: Alfred A. Knopf, Inc., 1979.

Newcombe, Lawrence, *Newcombe's Wildflower Guide*. Boston: Little, Brown & Co., 1977.

Pohl, Richard W. *How to Know the Grasses*. Dubuque, IA: William C. Brown, Co., Pubs., 1978.

Poling, James. *Leaves: Their Amazing Lives and Strange Behavior*. New York: Holt, Rinehart & Winston, 1971.

Slack, Adrian. *Carnivorous Plants*. Cambridge, MA: MIT Press, 1980.

Wohlrabe, Raymond A. *Exploring the World of Leaves*. New York: Thomas Y. Crowell, Co., 1976.

Unit Five

Invertebrates

Coral polyps from the Red Sea

25 Sponges and Coelenterates

Asymmetrical sponges

Sponges are the simplest animals. Sponges have several types of cells that are specialized for different functions within the animal. Yet each cell is also quite independent.

In 1907, the American embryologist H. V. Wilson performed an experiment with a sponge. Wilson pushed a living sponge through the fibers of a fine silk mesh cloth. This caused the cells of the sponge to break apart. Wilson then left the cells of the sponge in water. Within a few hours, the cells began to crawl together. After three weeks, a complete functional sponge had formed from the cells that were broken apart.

Since Wilson's time, biologists have tried similar experiments with sponges. If several sponges of different species are forced through a mesh, the individual cells will sort themselves out. Each cell will recombine only with cells of the same species.

The ability of sponge cells to recombine into a complete adult organism is quite unlike other animals. Imagine the results if you tried such an experiment with an elephant!

Characteristics of Animals

Animals are multicellular heterotrophs. All animals ingest their food. Some animals eat plants; others eat animals or other kinds of heterotrophs.

Most animals are motile, moving from place to place to capture their food. Other animals, such as sponges, are attached to a single spot and feed by capturing food that passes close to them. Animals that are attached to a single spot are said to be **sessile**. Animals that are sessile as adults usually have a stage during their development when they are motile.

CONCEPTS
- cell specialization and interdependence
- stages of animal development
- types of symmetry in animals

25–1 Cell Specialization

Imagine yourself abandoned in a forest far from civilization. You would have to find food, make tools, build a shelter, treat injuries, and do everything else necessary to survive. You probably do not have the skills to do all of these things. In modern society, each person has a specialized job. Specialists such as farmers, mechanics, architects, and doctors are very good at doing one kind of job, yet each depends on the other members of society to survive.

Protists are totally independent organisms. Each cell can carry out every life function. In contrast, animals contain many different kinds of cells, each performing a particular function. Animal cells usually cannot survive apart from the organism. A reproductive cell, for example, cannot digest food.

Specialization of cells is a characteristic of the plant and animal kingdoms. Figure 25.1 shows some of the specialized animal cells that perform functions such as movement, support, digestion, and communication. Like the specialists in human societies, animal cells depend upon each other. For example, nerve cells that send messages depend on other cells to supply their food.

There are about 30 phyla of animals, which are divided into 2 subkingdoms. This division is based partly on the degree of interdependence among an animal's cells. One subkingdom, the **Parazoa**, contains only the sponges. Sponges have specialized cell types, but as the mesh experiment shows, the cells are not so interdependent that they die when separated. Sponge cells are not permanently specialized. Cells that perform one function can change to another cell type.

The second subkingdom, called the **Metazoa**, includes all animals except the sponges. In metazoans, cells are more highly specialized and have little flexibility in function.

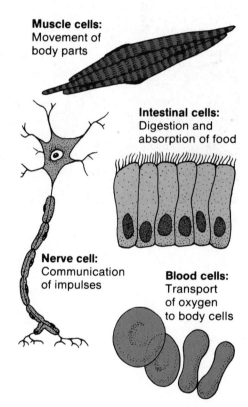

Muscle cells: Movement of body parts

Intestinal cells: Digestion and absorption of food

Nerve cell: Communication of impulses

Blood cells: Transport of oxygen to body cells

Figure 25.1 Some specialized animal cells and their functions

Most animals have tissues and organs that are more highly differentiated than the tissues of plants. In almost all animals, tissues and organs are held together by a tough, stretchy, fibrous protein called **collagen** [KAHL-uh-juhn].

Most animals are far more responsive to stimuli than are plants or fungi. With few exceptions, animals have nerve and muscle cells that allow rapid responses.

25–2 Animal Development

All members of the animal kingdom reproduce sexually, though many reproduce asexually as well. All animal cells develop from one original cell, the zygote. The development of an animal is different from the development of plants or fungi. Figure 25.2 shows the first stages in the development of most animals.

Figure 25.2 In most animals the first stages of development follow a similar pattern. The gastrula is the same size as the zygote. Little cell growth occurs during this stage of development.

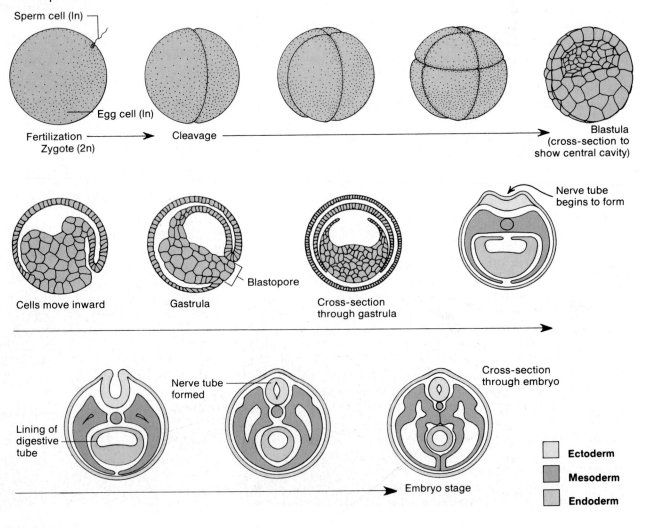

The first cell divisions of the zygote are called **cleavages**. Several cleavages result in the production of a small, hollow ball of cells called a **blastula** [BLAS-choo-luh]. As the cells continue to divide, they push into the interior, so the developing animal looks almost as though someone had pushed a thumb into the ball of cells.

The developing organism becomes a **gastrula** [GAS-troo-luh]. Because each cleavage results in smaller and smaller cells, the gastrula is usually about the same size as the original zygote. At the gastrula stage, cells begin to differentiate. Through the center of the gastrula is a tube that will eventually become the animal's digestive tube. The opening into the gastrula is called the **blastopore** [BLAS-tuh-pawr]. In some animals, the blastopore will ultimately become the entrance to the digestive tube, or the mouth. In other animals, the blastopore will become the exit from the digestive tube, or the **anus**.

During the later development of the gastrula the cells begin to differentiate. The single layer of cells lining the digestive tract is called the **endoderm** [EHN-doh-durm]. The outer layer of cells, called the **ectoderm** [EHK-toh-durm], becomes the epidermis of the animal. In most animals the ectoderm also forms the nervous system. Many animals form a third, middle layer of cells called the **mesoderm** [MEHZ-uh-durm]. All of the organs in an animal can be traced back to one of the three original cell layers: the ectoderm, the mesoderm, or the endoderm. These three layers are called the **germ layers** of the developing organism.

By the time these germ layers form, the developing animal is called an embryo. In some animals the embryo develops until it is a miniature version of the adult. In others, the embryo develops into an independent form that looks very different from the adult. This young stage is called a **larva** [LAHR-vuh].

Figure 25.3 The larva of an organism may look quite different from the adult. *Left:* Starfish larva; *Right:* Adult starfish.

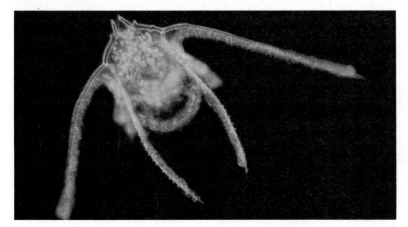

The developmental sequence shown in Figure 25.3 is typical of many animals, but the different groups of animals show variations. In fact, classification of animals depends in part on the details of their development.

25–3   Body Symmetry

The bodies of most animals show some type of symmetry. Figure 25.4 shows three kinds of symmetry. Organisms that lack symmetry are **asymmetrical**.

Figure 25.4 *Top left:* A sponge is asymmetrical. *Top right:* A radiolarian shows spherical symmetry. *Bottom left:* A sea anemone shows radial symmetry. *Bottom right:* Humans show bilateral symmetry.

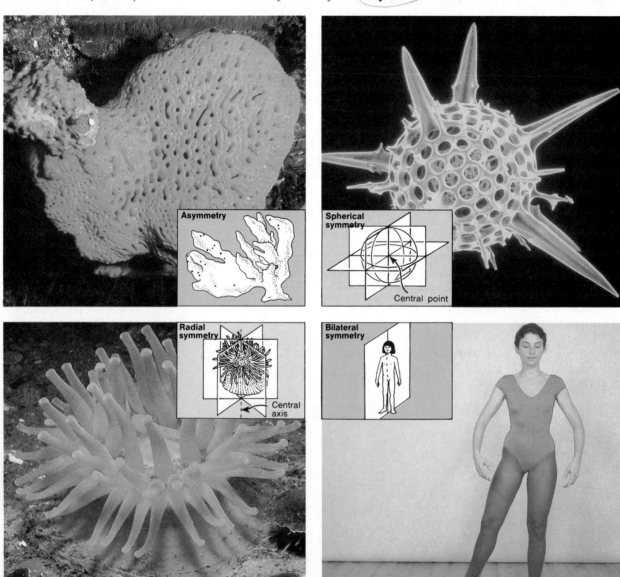

An organism with **spherical symmetry** can be divided into equal halves by passing a plane in any direction through a central point. All of the organisms with this type of symmetry are either protists or plants such as the colonial *Volvox*. **Radial symmetry** occurs in several animal phyla. An animal with radial symmetry can be divided into equal halves by passing a plane through the central axis of the animal in any direction. Animals with **bilateral symmetry** can be divided into equal halves only along a single plane.

Figure 25.5 shows several terms that are used to describe the body of an organism that has bilateral symmetry. The front of the animal is the **anterior**; the back of the animal is the **posterior**. The top of the animal is the **dorsal** surface; the **ventral** surface is underneath. **Lateral** structures are near the side of the animal. Notice that these terms can be applied to a vertically standing human in the same way that they are applied to a horizontal animal.

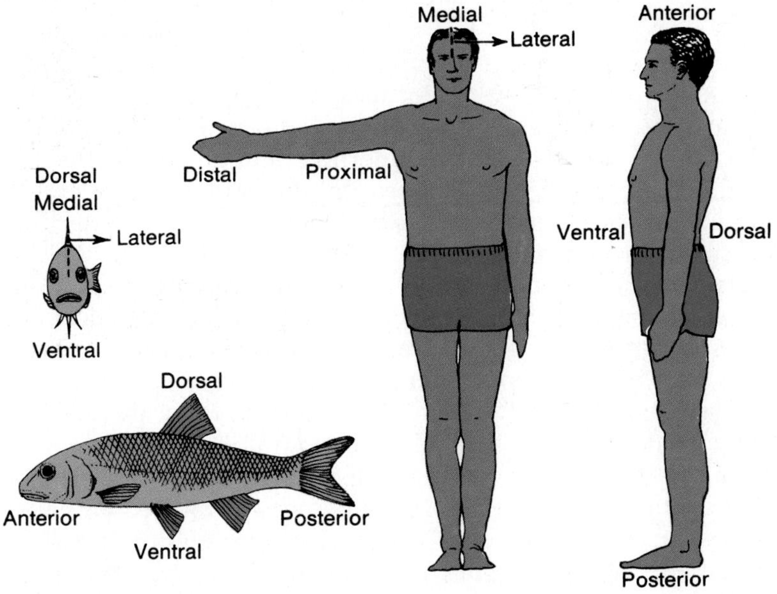

Figure 25.5 Different spatial positions on an organism that has bilateral symmetry

---

Checkpoint

1. What are the two subkingdoms of the animal kingdom?
2. What is the name of the hollow ball of cells that develops from a zygote?
3. What is the middle germ layer of the gastrula?
4. What are the two major types of symmetry in the animal kingdom?
5. On which end of the fish is the mouth located? On which end is the tail fin located?

CONCEPTS

- structure of sponges
- asexual and sexual reproduction in sponges
- variety of sponges

Figure 25.6 Structural features of a typical sponge

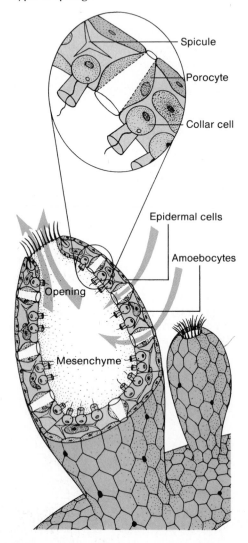

Spicule

Porocyte

Collar cell

Epidermal cells

Amoebocytes

Opening

Mesenchyme

Phylum Porifera

Sponges are not readily recognized as animals. They do not have heads or limbs, characteristics that most people associate with animals. Because sponges are sessile, they seem more like plants than animals. In fact, the ancient Greeks believed that sponges were plants.

The body of a sponge is riddled with interconnecting channels. The channels open to the outside through many tiny pores. These pores give the phylum **Porifera** its name. Porifera is the only phylum in the subkingdom Parazoa. While a few simple sponges show radial symmetry, most are asymmetrical. Sponges have very primitive tissue development and no organs. They never develop a mesoderm.

25–4 A Typical Sponge

The typical sponge has four basic types of specialized cells organized into two layers. Because these layers are composed of various types of cells, they are not considered to be tissues. The outer layer, called the **epidermis** [ehp-uh-DUR-mihs], is made of flattened cells. Penetrating the epidermis are cylindrical cells called **porocytes**, which permit water to enter the central cavity of the sponge.

Just below the epidermis is a jelly-like material called the **mesenchyme** [MEHS-uhn-kym]. Embedded in the mesenchyme are structures called **spicules**. Spicules have two functions. First, they provide support for the cells, thus giving the sponge a distinctive shape. Second, they help protect the sponge from predators. Few fish relish a mouthful of needles.

Lining the interior cavity of the sponge is a layer of tissue that contains a number of flagellated cells called **collar cells**. A close-up view of a collar cell is shown in Figure 25.6. The collar cells create currents that draw water through the pores and out the opening at the top of the sponge. The collar cells then withdraw food particles, such as algae or organic debris, from the water. In this way the collar cells supply not only themselves but also the rest of the cells with food.

A fourth type of cell found in sponges is a wandering cell that looks something like *Amoeba*. These cells, which are called **amoebocytes**, move through the mesenchyme by means of pseudopods. Amoebocytes have several functions. They carry food particles from collar cells to epidermal cells and porocytes. Amoebocytes also make spicules in the mesenchyme. Amoebocytes are the least specialized cells in the sponge and sometimes differentiate into other kinds of cells.

25–5 Reproduction of Sponges

Sponges reproduce both sexually and asexually. **Budding** is one form of asexual reproduction. In budding, small groups of cells grow from the body wall of the adult. Eventually the bud breaks off and attaches elsewhere.

Another type of asexual reproduction occurs in many fresh-water sponges. In late fall these sponges produce masses of amoebocytes that are surrounded by a tough wall. These structures are called **gemmules**. Gemmules can withstand winter freezing. In the spring the wall dissolves and the amoebocytes differentiate into a new sponge.

Most sponges are **hermaphroditic**. A hermaphrodite [hur-MAF-ruh-dyt] is an organism that produces both eggs and sperm. Egg and sperm cells are produced either by amoe-bocytes or by collar cells that undergo meiosis. Sperm are released into the water, where they may enter a pore of another sponge of the same species. Once inside the other sponge, the sperm cell is surrounded by an amoebocyte and carried to an egg cell, where fertilization takes place.

The zygote undergoes cleavage to form a flagellated larva. When the larva settles on a surface, it grows into a sessile adult.

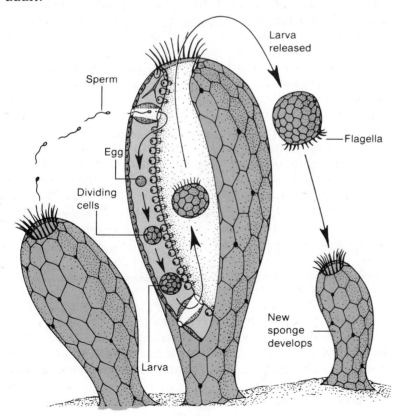

Figure 25.7 The reproductive process of a sponge

Figure 25.8 *Left:* A vertical tube sponge; *Right:* A vase sponge

25–6 Sponge Diversity

There are about 10,000 species of sponges, most living in salt water. They show a remarkable variety of shapes, sizes, and colors. Figure 25.8 shows some of the variety of sponge shapes. The internal structure of some sponges shows a complicated pattern of interconnected channels.

Sponges are classified according to the kind of material found in the skeleton. The most common sponges have mats of flexible fibers in the mesenchyme. The fibers are made of a protein called **spongin** [SPUHN-jihn]. Spongin is chemically related to collagen, the protein that holds tissues together in all other kinds of animals.

Sponges that are commercially marketed contain spongin. Sponges harvested from the ocean floor must be dried and pounded to remove the cell material and spicules. What remains is the spongin skeleton.

Some sponges have spicules made of calcium carbonate. Glass sponges have spicules made of silica. Other sponges have spicules of both calcium carbonate and silica.

Because their mineral skeletons are easily preserved in rocks, fossil sponges are quite common. They appear continuously in rocks dating as far back as 500 million years. Because the structure of sponges is so unlike that of other kinds of animals, it is unlikely that sponges gave rise to any of the metazoans.

Checkpoint

1. To what phylum do sponges belong?
2. What is the outer layer of cells in sponges?
3. What is the name of the flagellated cells in sponges?
4. What word describes an animal that produces both egg and sperm?
5. What two materials make up the spicules of sponges?

Phylum Coelenterata

Some of the most beautiful animals on Earth belong to the metazoan phylum Coelenterata. The transparent jellyfish, flowerlike sea anemones, and lustrous corals all belong to this phylum.

All **coelenterates** [sih-LEHN-tuh-rayts] are radially symmetrical and have two distinct cell layers. The cells of coelenterates are more highly specialized than those of sponges. As in sponges, the cell layers are not true tissues, since each layer is embedded with many different types of cells. Coelenterates have no mesoderm.

Most coelenterates are marine. Only a small percentage of the 10,000 species live in fresh water. Most coelenterates are carnivorous but do not actively chase prey. Instead, they trap food organisms that accidentally collide with their special stinging cells.

25–7 Polyps and Medusae

Coelenterates exist in one of two body forms, shown in Figure 25.9. One form is known as a **polyp** [PAHL-ihp]. Polyps are vase-shaped, sessile animals that attach to a surface with their mouth facing up. The other body form of coelenterates, the bell-shaped **medusa** [muh-DOO-suh], is a free-swimming form. A medusa is a bit like an upside-down polyp.

Many coelenterates have a life cycle that alternates between a medusa and a polyp stage. The life cycle of the jellyfish *Aurelia* is shown in Figure 25.10. Medusae reproduce sexually, producing egg and sperm. After fertilization, the zygote develops into a blastula, which elongates to form a ciliated larva called a **planula** [PLAN-yoo-lah].

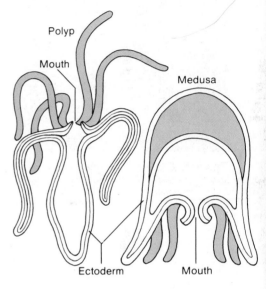

Figure 25.9 The structural differences between a polyp and a medusa are shown in these cross-sectional diagrams.

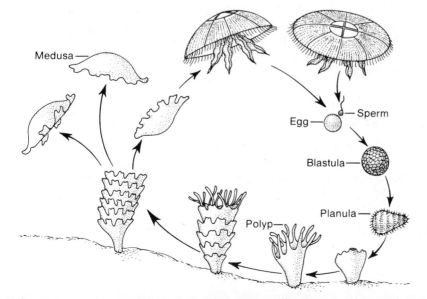

Figure 25.10 The life cycle of *Aurelia*

Sponges and Coelenterates **381**

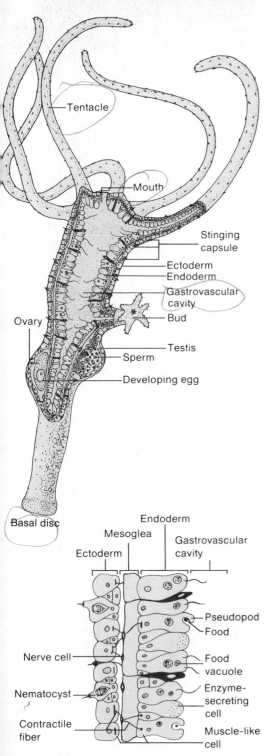

Figure 25.11 The structural features of a hydra

The planula eventually attaches itself to the bottom, where it grows into a polyp. The polyp reproduces asexually by forming medusae, which form one on top of another. When the medusae form egg and sperm, the cycle is complete.

The alternation of sexual and asexual stages in coelenterates may appear to be similar to the alternation of generations found in plants. In the coelenterates, however, there is no haploid generation. Both the medusa and the polyp are diploid.

25–8   The Hydra: A Typical Coelenterate

The hydra is a common freshwater coelenterate. The structure of the hydra is typical of coelenterate polyps. Hydras have no medusa stage.

Hydras are small, only about 0.5 centimeter long. The hydra's body is a cylinder with two layers of cells. The inner layer is endoderm, and the outer layer is ectoderm. Between the two layers is a jelly-like material called **mesoglea** [meh-soh-GLEE-uh]. The cylindrical body attaches to surfaces by a **basal disk**. Projecting from the top are a number of **tentacles**, which trap food organisms that float or swim within reach.

The interior space of the hydra is called the **gastrovascular** [gas-troh-VAS-kyuh-lur] **cavity**. Food organisms are pushed into the cavity through a single opening. Enzymes released by specialized cells in the endoderm digest the food. Food molecules move within the gastrovascular cavity to all parts of the organism. Notice that the gastrovascular cavity extends into the tentacles. The opening of the cavity serves as both an entrance for food organisms and an opening from which indigestible wastes are expelled.

Organisms that come near a hydra's tentacles are stung by poisonous barbs called **nematocysts** [NEHM-uh-tuh-sihsts]. These stinging cells can paralyze relatively large organisms. Once the prey is slowed by the poison, the tentacles push it into the gastrovascular cavity. Nematocysts are found in all coelenterates.

Figure 25.11 shows a section of the body wall of a hydra. In the ectoderm are cells that function like muscle cells. Some of these cells encircle the body. When these cells contract, they make the body and tentacles longer. Contraction of other muscle-like cells along the length of the body shorten the animal.

The coordinated movement of tentacles during feeding requires communication among muscle cells. Nerve cells found in the mesoglea carry messages from one part of the animal to another. The nerve cells coordinate the hydra's movements.

During most of the year, hydras reproduce asexually by budding. But when winter approaches, hydras reproduce sexually. Some *Hydra* species are hermaphrodites, but most have two separate sexes. Male reproductive glands called **testes** and female reproductive glands called **ovaries** develop from ectodermal cells. Sperm released from the testes of one hydra swim to the ovaries of another, where fertilization occurs.

The developing zygote remains attached to the wall of the parent. A gastrula forms and is surrounded by a hard, protective coat. The encapsulated gastrula drops from the parent and survives winter. The following spring the coat dissolves, and the young hydra emerges.

25–9 Jellyfish, Sea Anemones, and Corals

All of the 200 or so species of jellyfish are marine. They spend most of their life cycle as medusae. Jellyfish swim with a gentle pulsing motion. A ring of muscles around the edge of the medusa contracts and pushes against the water. Such contractions move the jellyfish upward. When the muscles relax, the jellyfish slowly sinks. Jellyfish do not actively pursue prey. Food organisms that accidentally brush against the tentacles are paralyzed and pushed into the mouth. Jellyfish feed on anything from plankton to small fish.

The polyps of sea anemones have a more complex internal structure than that of the hydras. Figure 25.13 shows a sea anemone. The gastrovascular cavity of sea anemones is divided into a number of compartments. Stinging cells line the inner walls of these compartments as well as the tentacles. Sea anemones feed on a variety of small animals, including fish.

The polyps of coral secrete a wall of calcium carbonate around themselves. Most corals are small, colonial animals, and their skeletons grow together into large masses. New generations of polyps build skeletons on top of old generations. Coral "houses" grow in a wide variety of colors and shapes.

In many coral species, dinoflagellates live with the polyps. Corals grow only in clear shallow water where there is sufficient light for the photosynthetic dinoflagellates. Coral animals sometimes occur in such large numbers that they form ridges, called coral reefs, around islands and near coastlines. The Great Barrier Reef off the coast of northeastern Australia is almost 2,000 kilometers long.

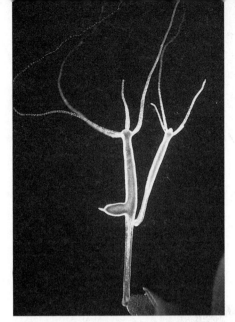

Figure 25.12 Hydras most frequently reproduce by budding.

Figure 25.13 Cross section of a sea anemone

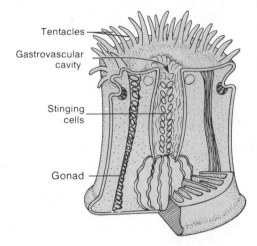

Tentacles

Gastrovascular cavity

Stinging cells

Gonad

Checkpoint

1. What is the material between the endoderm and the ectoderm of coelenterates?
2. What is a nematocyst?
3. What are the two basic body forms of coelenterates?
4. What is the larval form of coelenterates called?

Sponges and Coelenterates **383**

CHAPTER REVIEW

Summary

- Animals are multicellular heterotrophs that show specialization of cells. Many animals have tissues organized into organs.

- Most animals develop through the stages of zygote, blastula, and gastrula. Some animals have a larval form.

- Some sponges are asymmetric, but all other animals show either radial or bilateral symmetry.

- Sponges are placed in their own subkingdom, the Parazoa, since they do not have organs and their bodies are usually asymmetric. Sponges are not believed to have given rise to any other animal phyla.

- Sponge cells are less dependent on each other than the cells of other animals. Water circulates freely through channels in the body of the sponge.

- The outer surface of sponges is composed of epidermal cells. Cylindrical cells called porocytes allow water to enter the central cavity. Flagellated collar cells create currents and capture food. Amoebocytes are the least specialized sponge cells; among other functions, they transport food to other cells.

- Coelenterates belong to the subkingdom Metazoa. Coelenterates have a body with just two layers of cells surrounding a central digestive cavity. Between the endoderm and the ectoderm is the jelly-like mesoglea. Coelenterates also contain stinging structures called nematocysts.

- Coelenterates occur in two forms — sessile polyps and free-swimming medusae. Some have a life cycle with both forms. The larva of the coelenterates is called a planula.

- The hydra is a common freshwater coelenterate. Hydras attach to surfaces by a basal disk. They capture their food by means of tentacles. Nerve cells coordinate the hydra's movements.

- Sea anemones, jellyfish, and corals are coelenterates. The polyps of corals secrete a hard outer skeleton of calcium carbonate; large colonies of corals growing together may form reefs.

Vocabulary

amoebocyte	larva
anterior	lateral
anus	medusa
asymmetrical	mesenchyme
basal disk	mesoderm
bilateral symmetry	mesoglea
blastopore	Metazoa
blastula	nematocyst
budding	ovary
cleavage	Parazoa
coelenterate	planula
collagen	polyp
collar cell	Porifera
dorsal	porocyte
ectoderm	posterior
endoderm	radial symmetry
epidermis	sessile
gastrovascular	spherical symmetry
cavity	spicule
gastrula	spongin
gemmule	tentacles
germ layer	testes
hermaphroditic	ventral

Review

1. What is the basic function of nerve cells?
2. Cell divisions of the zygote are called _____.
3. Put the following stages of development in the correct sequence.
   a. cleavage
   b. embryo
   c. zygote
   d. blastula
   e. meiosis
   f. fertilization
   g. three germ layers
   h. gastrula
4. Name the three germ layers of animals.
5. Which of the three germ layers is lacking in coelenterates?
6. On the surface of the gastrula is an opening into the developing digestive tube. What is it called?
7. What fibrous protein holds the tissues and organs of most animals together?
8. To what subkingdom do humans and fishes belong?
9. What sponge cells allow water to move from the outside through the epidermis?
10. What is the flexible protein material found in the mesenchyme of some sponges?
11. What is the only phylum in the subkingdom Parazoa?
12. What type of symmetry do all coelenterates have?
13. Through what opening do wastes leave the gastrovascular cavity of coelenterates?
14. Which of the coelenterate body forms is sessile?
15. What type of protist often lives with the polyps of corals?

Interpret and Apply

1. As the cells of organisms become more specialized, what abilities are lost by these cells?
2. Name a major characteristic other than food source that distinguishes plants from animals.
3. Is your head anterior or posterior to your arms? Describe the location of your arms in relation to your shoulders.
4. What evidence can you give that sponge cells retain considerable independence?
5. What kinds of symmetry occur in the sponges?
6. Why are the cell layers of sponges and coelenterates not considered true tissues?
7. Describe the two major functions of the gastrovascular cavity of coelenterates.
8. Why are sponges considered to be simpler organisms than coelenterates?
9. What is the function of a gemmule?
10. How are the functions of nematocysts and spicules similar?

Challenge

1. Describe the anatomical position of your backbone.
2. An entire fossilized coral reef has been discovered extending from Ontario, Canada, into Ohio. This reef is thought to have formed over 400 million years ago. What inferences about the environment 400 million years ago can you draw from this discovery?
3. How does the life cycle of *Aurelia* compare to the alternation of generations in plants? In what ways are they similar? In what ways are they different?

Projects

1. Find out the difference between an atoll, a fringing reef, and a barrier reef. How do scientists think these various reefs have formed?
2. Make a chart with drawings that compare the early development of a frog and a chicken. Your diagrams should go as far as showing the development of the three germ layers.

26 Worms

The earthworm, a typical annelid

Have you ever started a garden early in the spring? Before you can plant anything, you have to get the soil ready. You dig in the garden, loosening large clumps of earth. What is the first sign of animal life you see? Earthworms — maybe hundreds of them.

Earthworms help make soil suitable for plant growth. They are busy beneath the surface of backyard gardens and huge farms. Earthworms feed on dead plant and animal material. They consume sand particles along with food. As the worms eat, they dig tunnels through the earth. These tunnels provide pathways for air and water to get to plant roots.

Earthworms eliminate undigested food as wastes. Plants use these wastes for fertilizer. An earthworm may eliminate sand and plant material far from where the material was eaten. This movement of material renews and rotates the soil.

Charles Darwin understood the importance of earthworms. He wrote, "It may be doubted whether there are many other animals which have played so important a part in the history of the world as have these lowly organized creatures."

Phylum Platyhelminthes: The Flatworms

The three major phyla of worms are commonly known as flatworms, roundworms, and annelids. These three groups are quite different from one another. However, all worms share certain characteristics. Unlike sponges and coelenterates, worms have bilateral symmetry. In addition, they have organs and organ systems for carrying on life functions. These organs and organ systems are in sharp contrast to the simpler specialization of cells in sponges and coelenterates. Worms' organs and tissues develop from three germ layers — ectoderm, endoderm, and mesoderm. (Recall that sponges and coelenterates have no mesoderm.)

Members of phylum **Platyhelminthes** [plat-ih-hehl-MIHNTH-eez] — the flatworms — have no spaces between these tissue layers. Because of the flat shape of the flatworm's body, all its cells are close to the worm's environment. Oxygen diffuses directly from the environment into these cells. Similarly, carbon dioxide diffuses from the body cells directly into the environment.

Flatworms are the most primitive animals to have a definite head. This is a characteristic of animals with bilateral symmetry. Most bilaterally symmetrical animals actively move through their environment. The anterior end is the first part of the animal to come in contact with its surroundings. Animals with senses concentrated at the anterior end can respond to their environment quickly. For example, with the sense of sight and smell located in the head, the animal can sense food and move toward it.

Nerve cells are concentrated near the sense organs. Nerve cells receive information from the sense organs and send information to other parts of the body. The **brain**, a collection of nerve cells located in the anterior end, acts as a control center. The tendency in animal evolution toward larger brains and more complex senses in the head is called **cephalization** [sehf-uh-luh-ZAY-shuhn].

26–1 Class Turbellaria: Free-Living Flatworms

Planarians [pluh-NAIR-ee-uhns] are representative **turbellarian** [tur-buh-LAIR-ee-uhn] worms. Planarians, such as the one in Figure 26.1, are usually less than 1 or 2 centimeters long. While most turbellarians live in salt water, planarians live in fresh water. They crawl along the bottom of ponds and streams. Planarians, like most other turbellarians, are

CONCEPTS

- organ systems of turbellarians
- structure and habits of parasitic flatworms

Figure 26.1 Planarians live in lakes and streams. Food enters and wastes exit from the same opening.

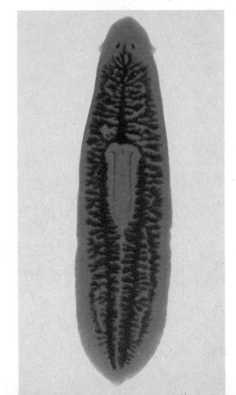

free-living; that is, they are not parasites.

To pick up signals from the environment and coordinate response, planarians have a nervous system. This nervous system, shown in Figure 26.2, is much more complex than the nerve network of coelenterates. The brain is a large collection of nerve cells that coordinates information coming from the sense organs and directs the body's responses. Signals to and from the brain are carried along nerve cells that form a ladderlike system.

A planarian's head has two light-sensitive spots that resemble eyes. They sense the difference between light and dark. Planarians move away from light. The projections at the side of the planarian's head contain many cells that are sensitive to touch and to water currents. These cells are probably also sensitive to chemicals in the water.

The digestive system of planarians is shown in Figure 26.2. Like the digestive cavity of coelenterates, it has only a single opening. This opening, called the mouth, is on the ventral surface near the middle of the animal. The worm feeds by extending a muscular tube called the **pharynx** [FAR-ihngks] from its mouth. The pharynx connects to the digestive cavity, or **gut**. The gut has two posterior branches and a single anterior branch. Each major branch has many small side branches that increase the surface area and bring the gut cavity close to many body cells.

Figure 26.2 The digestive system of a planarian has only one opening. The nervous system has a ladderlike structure. Water is eliminated through the flame cells.

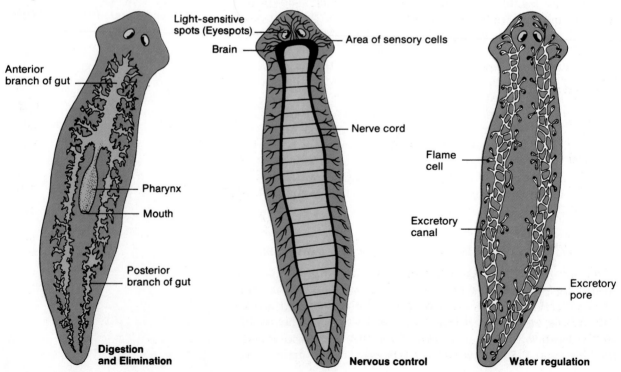

Planarians eat protists and small animals. The pharynx breaks food organisms into small pieces and pushes them into the gut. Cells lining the gut enclose food particles in vacuoles. Food is then digested in these vacuoles, and the resulting molecules diffuse directly from gut cells to other body cells. Any undigested food is expelled through the pharynx and the mouth. Notice that food enters and wastes exit through the same opening.

A water-regulating system like the one in Figure 26.2 is found in planarians. The primary function of this system is similar to that of contractile vacuoles in protists. Freshwater turbellarians take in excess water by osmosis. Special ciliated **flame cells** help move excess water out of the body.

Planarians have two methods of moving. The cells of the epidermis produce mucus. In addition, the ventral epidermal cells have cilia. As the cilia beat, the planarian glides over the mucus. The second form of movement involves three layers of muscle cells in the mesoderm. With these muscles, the worm can stretch or shorten its length. It can wrap itself around food and push material in and out of its gut.

Planarians are hermaphrodites—each planarian produces both male and female gametes. During sexual reproduction, two planarians exchange sperm. Cross-fertilization occurs — that is, sperm from one worm fertilize the other worm's eggs. (Self-fertilization, in contrast, involves the union of male and female gametes produced by the same organism. Planarians are not normally self-fertilizing.)

Fertilized eggs are released from the worm's body in capsules. Each capsule contains one or more eggs. In a few weeks, the young worms emerge.

Figure 26.3 Asexual reproduction and regeneration of a planarian

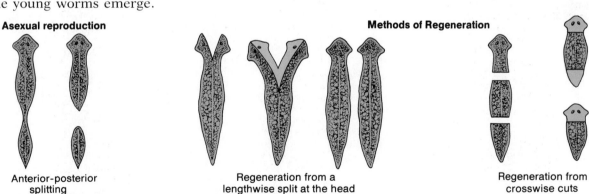

Asexual reproduction

Anterior-posterior splitting

Methods of Regeneration

Regeneration from a lengthwise split at the head

Regeneration from crosswise cuts

Sometimes planarians reproduce asexually. They can actually pull themselves apart to make two pieces, splitting into an anterior half and a posterior half. Each half grows into a complete worm. Planarians have a remarkable ability to regenerate. When a planarian is cut into pieces, each piece usually becomes a complete individual.

26–2   Class Trematoda: The Flukes

Trematodes [TREHM-uh-tohdz], also known as flukes, are parasitic flatworms. Flukes have organs and organ systems similar to those of planarians.

Many of a fluke's characteristics are typical adaptations to a parasitic way of life. For example, the surface of a fluke consists of a nonliving material called a **cuticle** [KYOO-tih-kuhl]. The cuticle is produced by underlying cells. It protects the fluke from digestive enzymes of the host organism. In addition, most flukes have two suckerlike disks. One is on the worm's ventral surface, and the other surrounds the mouth. The suckers attach the worm to the host, generally in the host's digestive tract. The fluke absorbs digested food from the host's intestine.

Parasitic worms often have more than one host during their life cycle. Usually each stage in the life cycle will take place in only one kind of host organism. For a parasite to survive, it must encounter the right host at the right time. Most eggs produced by parasites do not survive long, because they have not been picked up by the right host. Parasitic worms usually produce a huge number of eggs. Large numbers of eggs make it likely that a few, at least, will find the right host. A single fluke commonly produces hundreds of thousands of eggs during its lifetime.

The life cycle of the sheep liver fluke is shown in Figure 26.4. Flukes are hermaphroditic, and cross-fertilization is the rule. Adult worms in an infected sheep reproduce sexually.

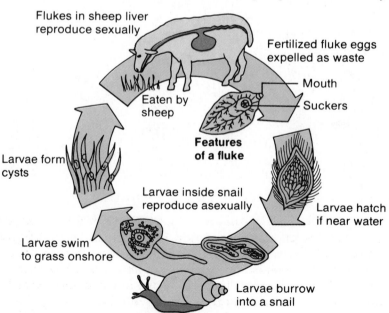

Flukes in sheep liver reproduce sexually

Fertilized fluke eggs expelled as waste

— Mouth

— Suckers

Eaten by sheep

Features of a fluke

Larvae form cysts

Larvae inside snail reproduce asexually

Larvae hatch if near water

Larvae swim to grass onshore

Larvae burrow into a snail

Figure 26.4 The life cycle of a sheep liver fluke involves two host organisms. Different developmental stages occur in each host.

Fertilized eggs are released in solid wastes from the sheep's intestine. If the eggs are deposited near a marsh or pond, they hatch into larvae. To survive, a larva must encounter a particular species of snail within eight hours. The larva then burrows into the snail.

Within the snail, the larva reproduces asexually. The resulting larvae are different in form from the original larva. After several weeks, these new larvae leave the snail. They swim until they reach a blade of grass near the edge of the water. On the grass, each larva forms a hard, protective covering, or **cyst** [sihst], around itself. The larva can last for months in this form.

If a sheep eats the grass, the larva breaks out of its protective cyst. The fluke is carried to the intestine of the sheep. From there, it burrows into the liver, where it grows to full size and produces a new generation of eggs.

The blood fluke, schistosoma [shihs-tuh-SOHM-uh], is another important flatworm parasite. The larvae of this worm live in several species of snail. The adults live in the blood vessels of humans and other animals. While there, the parasites damage internal organs. In many parts of the world, millions of humans suffer long illness and even death from this parasite.

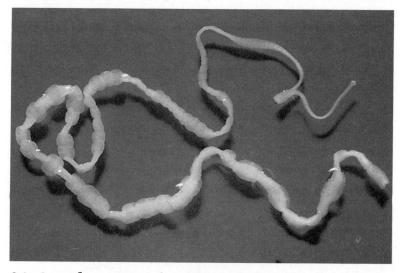

Figure 26.5 A tapeworm similar to those found in a human intestine

26–3 Class Cestoda: The Tapeworms

The **cestodes** [SEHS-tohdz], or tapeworms, are all parasitic flatworms. Tapeworms are even more specialized than flukes. Figure 26.5 shows a typical tapeworm. The head of the tapeworm has hooks that attach to the intestine of the host. Unlike other flatworms, the tapeworm has a body divided into many sections, or **proglottids** [proh-GLAHT-ihdz]. The tapeworm continually makes new proglottids just behind the

Do You Know?
Some tapeworms are 20 meters long.

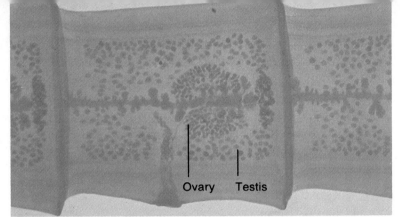
Ovary   Testis

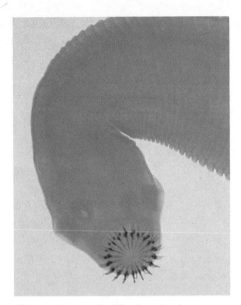

Figure 26.6 *Left:* The head of a tapeworm may contain suckers or hooks that attach the parasite to the host. *Right:* Each proglottid contains both male and female reproductive organs.

 BIOLOGY INSIGHTS

Many parasitic organisms show a reduction or loss of structures that are not essential for feeding, reproduction, or finding a new host. The loss of the digestive system in the tapeworm is a good example. This trend is sometimes called degenerative evolution. Despite the negative sound of the term, the resulting simplified organisms are often extremely successful at being parasites.

head. As each proglottid is pushed away from the head, it grows in size. Species vary in length and number of proglottids. Some tapeworms have thousands of proglottids.

Figure 26.6 shows a typical tapeworm proglottid. There is no digestive system. Food is absorbed directly from the intestine of the host into the cells of the tapeworm. Nerves run through each section. Each section also has a flame-cell system for removing water from the body.

Most of each section is filled with reproductive organs. Eggs are produced in ovaries and sperm in testes. Self-fertilization is possible. Cross-fertilization between different worms in the same host also occurs. Proglottids distant from the head are swollen with thousands of fertilized eggs. These proglottids break off and are excreted in the solid waste of the host. To survive, these eggs must reach the host for the next stage in their life cycle.

The life cycle of tapeworms is similar to that of flukes. It may involve one, two, or three different host organisms. Several human tapeworms are transmitted by infected pork, beef, or wild game that has not been thoroughly cooked. The meat contains a larva of the tapeworm in a cyst. Government meat inspection prevents most infected meat from reaching the market. However, it is still important to cook meat, especially pork and wild game, thoroughly.

Checkpoint

1. To what phylum do flatworms belong?
2. Identify two organ systems that planarians have.
3. Which cells found in flatworms help remove excess water from the body?
4. Of the two classes of parasitic flatworms, which is more like the planarians in structure?
5. What organ system found in other flatworms is missing in tapeworms?

Phylum Aschelminthes:
The Roundworms and Rotifers

Two major features characterize the phylum **Aschelminthes** [ask-hehl-MIHNTH-eez]: a one-way digestive tract and a body cavity. All of the organisms you have read about so far have only one opening to the digestive system. This opening serves both as an entryway for food and an exit for wastes. Material passes through this opening in two directions. Aschelminthes, however, have a complete digestive tract. Food enters at the mouth. Undigested wastes are expelled through a second opening, the **anus**. Food travels in one direction through the digestive tube. This one-way digestive tube is characteristic of more complex animals.

Members of phylum Aschelminthes have a body cavity. The fluid that fills the body cavity gives the organism rigidity, much like air in a tire. The fluid also circulates materials throughout the body.

This phylum includes microscopic, aquatic organisms called **rotifers**. It also includes roundworms.

CONCEPTS
- characteristics of roundworms
- parasitic roundworms

26-4 Class Nematoda: The Roundworms

Instead of the flat turbellarian body shape, **nematodes** [NEHM-uh-tohdz] have a round, tubelike shape. In fact, they are often called roundworms. You have probably never seen a roundworm, yet they are extremely common. There are over 10,000 species in the class. Most roundworms are small, usually less than a few millimeters in length. They live in the soil and in most bodies of water. Most roundworms are harmless. However, some parasitic species do great damage to plants, animals, and humans.

Figure 26.7 shows a typical roundworm. Beneath the cuticle is the epidermis, the outermost layer of cells. Roundworms

Figure 26.7 Roundworms are considered to have a tube-within-a-tube structure.

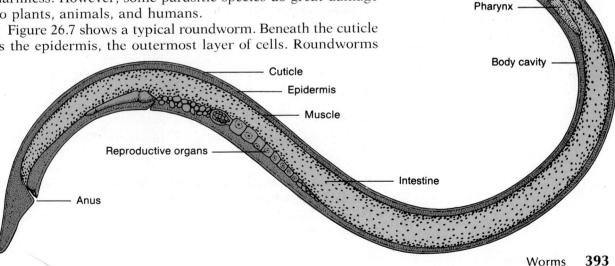

obtain oxygen and release carbon dioxide by diffusion through the epidermis. Under the epidermis is a single layer of muscle running the length of the body. Below the muscle layer is the fluid-filled body cavity.

Within the body cavity is the digestive tract. Just posterior to the mouth is a muscular pharynx, which sucks food into the mouth. The pharynx joins the long **intestine**, where food is digested and absorbed. Undigested food is expelled at the anus.

The body cavity also houses the male or female sex organs. Most nematodes are not hermaphroditic. Males and females are separate individuals.

26–5   Parasitic Nematodes

Hookworm is a well-known roundworm parasite of humans. It occurs in areas where sanitation is poor and where human wastes are used as fertilizer. Human wastes from an infected person contain hookworm eggs. If these eggs get into the soil, they develop into larval worms. If the larval worms come in contact with human skin, they burrow into the body. The worms then travel in the blood to various body parts. They burrow through tissues and cause severe damage. The adult worms settle in the intestine. They attach to the intestinal wall, feeding on blood and tissue fluids. The adult worms reproduce. Eggs pass out of the body with wastes, and the life cycle begins again.

Hookworm is found in many millions of humans. Hookworm, schistosoma, and the malaria protist *Plasmodium* are the three most common human parasites in the world today.

Trichina [trih-KY-nuh] is another important roundworm parasite. At one stage in their life cycle, trichina worms may form cysts in the muscles of pigs and other mammals. If humans eat undercooked pork containing trichina cysts, the larvae will emerge. These larvae then infect human muscles. The disease trichinosis may result. Its symptoms include muscular aches and breathing difficulties.

Because of meat inspection, trichina infection is rare in meat sold in the United States. However, for safety's sake, pork products and game meats should be thoroughly cooked.

Checkpoint

1. What two major characteristics distinguish the phylum Aschelminthes from the phylum Platyhelminthes?
2. By what common name are nematodes known?
3. Identify two nematode parasites of humans.

Phylum Annelida: The Segmented Worms

Two major characteristics make members of phylum **Annelida** [uh-NEHL-ih-duh] different from other worm phyla: presence of a coelom and segmentation. A **coelom** [SEE-luhm] is a fluid-filled body cavity that is surrounded by mesoderm. The **peritoneum** [pehr-uh-tuh-NEE-uhm], a membrane that originates from the inner mesoderm, suspends the internal organs in the coelom.

You will recall that roundworms have a body cavity. The roundworm's body cavity is not a coelom, however, because it is not surrounded by mesoderm. Instead, it lies between the mesoderm and endoderm. In addition, the internal organs in the roundworm's body cavity are not held in place by a membrane. Figure 26.8 diagrams the cross-sectional differences between flatworms, roundworms, and annelids, including the development of a body cavity.

The coelom is an important structural development. It provides room for complex internal organs. The peritoneum provides support for these organs. A coelom is found in the more complex phyla, from annelids through chordates.

Animals with a coelom have muscle tissue around the body wall and also around the digestive tract. These two sets of muscles operate independently. Body-wall muscles move the

CONCEPTS

- coelom and segmentation as annelid adaptations
- characteristics of earthworms

Figure 26.8 Cross-sectional comparisons of a flatworm, roundworm, and segmented worm. Note that no space exists between the body wall and digestive tube of flatworms.

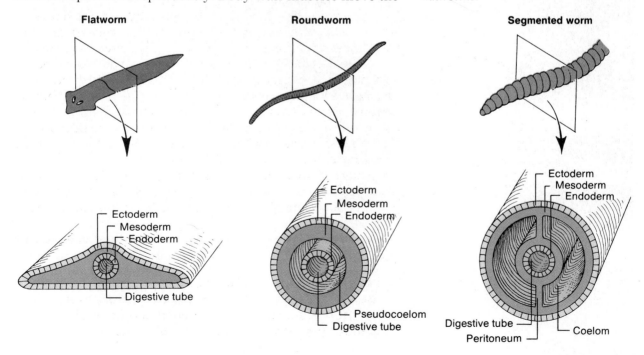

Flatworm   Roundworm   Segmented worm

Ectoderm, Mesoderm, Endoderm, Digestive tube

Ectoderm, Mesoderm, Endoderm, Pseudocoelom, Digestive tube

Ectoderm, Mesoderm, Endoderm, Digestive tube, Peritoneum, Coelom

organism. Muscles around the digestive tract move food through the digestive system. By comparison, in roundworms the body-wall muscles must carry out both functions.

The second major characteristic of annelids is **segmentation**, the division of the body into sections. The coelom itself is divided by cross walls of tissue. Segmentation is important for two reasons. First, an animal can increase in size by adding more identical segments. Second, different segments can adapt to carry out special functions. Annelids are often referred to as segmented worms.

26–6   Class Oligochaeta: The Earthworms

The earthworm is the most familiar of about 2,500 species of **oligochaete** [AHL-ih-goh-keet] worms. Figure 26.9 shows the internal structure of an earthworm. The following sections describe how the earthworm carries out various life functions.

Gas Exchange and Circulation   In flatworms and round-worms, gas exchange occurs by diffusion through the epidermis. Few flatworms or roundworms are large, because oxygen cannot penetrate many layers of cells.

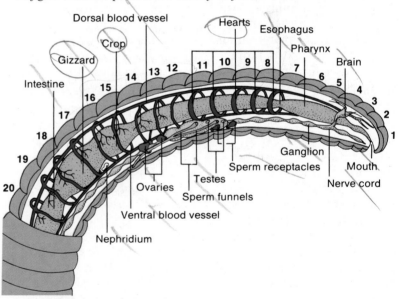

Figure 26.9 Some internal features of an earthworm

Earthworms have many more cell layers than flatworms or roundworms. In earthworms, a watery fluid called **blood** carries gases to and from body tissues. Gases are exchanged with the environment at the epidermis. Oxygen diffuses through the epidermis and into nearby blood vessels. Oxygen is carried by the blood to cells deep in the body of the worm. Similarly, carbon dioxide is carried from body cells to the epidermis, where it diffuses into the surroundings.

Besides carrying gas molecules, blood also carries molecules of digested food to the body cells. The movement of blood through the body is called **circulation**. Earthworms have a circulatory system of blood vessels passing to all parts of the body.

The blood of earthworms contains a red protein called **hemoglobin** [HEE-muh-gloh-buhn]. Hemoglobin attracts oxygen molecules. Blood with hemoglobin carries 50 times more oxygen than blood without hemoglobin.

Near the anterior end of the worm, five pairs of muscle-lined vessels alternately squeeze and relax to move blood through the body. Blood moves from these simple pumps, or **hearts**, into a ventral vessel. This vessel takes blood toward the body cells. Blood returns to the hearts by a dorsal vessel. Between the ventral and dorsal vessels, blood travels through microscopic branches. Gases, food, wastes, and other molecules enter and leave the blood by diffusion.

Digestion and Excretion   The digestive system of earthworms is more complex than those of other worm phyla. As earthworms tunnel, they consume dirt, which contains both food and sand particles. The food consists of material from plants and animals that have died and partly decomposed.

The earthworm takes food and sand in through its mouth. The mouth leads to a muscular pharynx. As shown in Figure 26.9, a short tube called the **esophagus** [ih-SAHF-uh-guhs] carries food from the mouth to a large storage organ called the **crop**. The food and sand are stored in the crop before moving on to the gizzard. The **gizzard** is a muscular organ that grinds food. Sand particles in the dirt break organic material into small pieces. These pieces move on to the intestine. In the intestine, food is digested and absorbed into the blood.

Sand particles and undigested food move on to the end of the intestine. They are expelled through the anus. The expelled material, called castings, fertilizes the soil.

In addition to undigested food wastes, all animals produce small molecules as waste products of metabolism. Burning protein as a fuel, for example, produces poisonous nitrogen-containing molecules. **Excretion** is the process of removing these poisonous wastes from the body. In flatworms and roundworms, poisonous wastes diffuse into the digestive cavity and are expelled. Earthworms, however, have an excretory system that gets rid of nitrogen wastes. Each segment, except the first three and the last one, has a pair of structures called **nephridia** [nuh-FRIHD-ee-uh]. A nephridium is shown in Figure 26.9 Nitrogen wastes from the blood diffuse into the nephridium. The wastes are excreted through an opening in the body wall.

Movement Earthworms move by using large muscle groups in each segment. Just beneath the epidermis is a layer of circular muscle. Below the circular muscle is a muscle layer extending the length of each segment. The earthworm moves by coordinated contraction and relaxation of the two layers. This process is shown in Figure 26.10.

Aiding movement are bristles called **setae** [SEE-tee]. Except for the first and last segments, each segment has four pairs of setae. They anchor each segment in the soil.

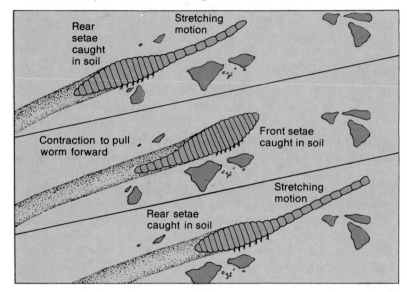

Rear setae caught in soil

Stretching motion

Contraction to pull worm forward

Front setae caught in soil

Rear setae caught in soil

Stretching motion

Figure 26.10 An earthworm moves by the contraction and stretching of its body segments. Motion is aided by the setae, which anchor in the soil.

BIOLOGY INSIGHTS

In organisms with more complex nervous systems, the ability to regenerate becomes more and more limited. If a planarian is cut in half, both pieces can grow into a complete individual. If an earthworm is cut in half, the front end will grow a tail, but the tail will not grow a head. Mammals and birds have almost no ability to regenerate.

Coordination and Senses The complex motion of the earthworm requires coordination from a well-developed nervous system. The brain is near the anterior end of the animal. The two brain halves send a nerve cord around each side of the pharynx. The two cords join to form one cord, which extends along the length of the worm.

The nerve cord is swollen in each segment. Each swelling, or **ganglion** [GANG-glee-uhn], is a grouping of nerve cells. These cells send messages up and down the nerve cord and along nerves that branch into each segment.

Nerves in the epidermis detect touch and chemicals. Some also detect light. Earthworms avoid light whenever possible. In their dark burrows, they are safer from animals that might catch and eat them.

Reproduction Earthworms reproduce sexually. Like many other worms, they are hermaphrodites. Eggs are produced in the ovaries, which are located in the thirteenth segment. The testes, which produce sperm, are found in the tenth and eleventh segments. During mating, two earthworms line up side by side. Sperm move from each earthworm to openings

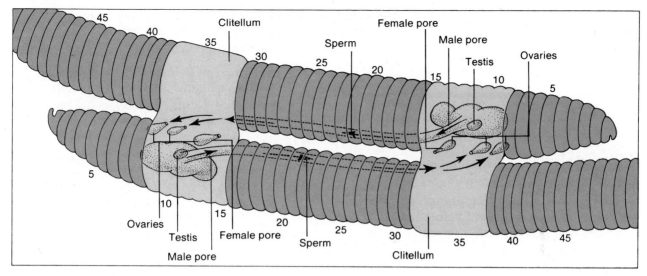

in the other's body, as shown in Figure 26.11. The sperm are stored temporarily. After the worms part, each worm secretes a capsule. The capsule is secreted by the **clitellum** [kly-TEHL-uhm], an enlarged area of the earthworm's body. The capsule stays around the clitellum. Eggs move out of the worm's body into this capsule. The stored sperm are also released into the capsule. The gametes unite, and fertilization occurs. The capsule slips off the worm and is left in the soil. The eggs develop into small worms.

Figure 26.11 Mating earthworms exchange sperm, which travel from the male pore of one worm to the female pore of the other worm. Fertilization occurs later, within the capsule.

26–7 Class Hirudinea: The Leeches

Hirudineans [hihr-uh-duhn-EE-uhns], or leeches, are best-known as bloodsucking parasites. Many of the 300 or so species, however, are free-living. Nonparasitic leeches feed on worms, snails, and soft-bodied insect larvae. Parasitic leeches attach to the outer surface of animals such as fish. The leech sucks the host's blood, secreting a substance that keeps the blood from clotting. During a single feeding, parasitic leeches take in many times their own weight in blood.

Do You Know?
Before the days of modern medicine, people believed that diseases could be cured by removing "bad blood" from the patient. Doctors carried leeches with them for this purpose.

Checkpoint

1. What two major structural characteristics make annelids different from other worms?
2. What organ systems are present in earthworms but not in flatworms or roundworms?
3. What molecule carries oxygen in the blood of annelids?
4. What structure in earthworms grinds food into tiny particles?
5. What is the food of parasitic leeches?

CHAPTER REVIEW

Summary

- Platyhelminthes are flat-bodied worms with three cell layers and simple organ systems. The digestive system of flatworms has only one opening. Flatworms have simple nervous and reproductive systems.
- Turbellarians, including planarians, are flatworms that are generally free-living. Planarians can regenerate lost parts.
- Trematodes are parasitic flatworms. In the life cycle of the sheep liver fluke, eggs are produced by adult worms in a sheep. The eggs, released in solid wastes, hatch into larvae, which enter the body of a snail. Structurally different larvae leave the snail and form cysts. When a sheep eats grass containing these cysts, the worm's life cycle begins again.
- The tapeworm, a cestode, is an important flatworm parasite. Its body includes a head and sections called proglottids.
- Members of the phylum Aschelminthes have a body cavity and a complete digestive tract through which food moves in only one direction. This phylum includes roundworms, or nematodes, and rotifers.
- Roundworms have long, tubelike bodies. Hookworm and trichina are two important roundworm parasites of humans. Hookworm eggs are produced in human intestines and expelled with solid wastes. The eggs develop into larvae that can burrow into humans. The adult worms reach the intestine, and the life cycle begins again. Trichina worms infect humans via contaminated meat.
- Annelids are segmented worms. They have a coelom, which allows for the development and support of complex internal organs.
- Earthworms have a circulatory system in which blood transports materials between the body cells and the environment. An excretory system removes nitrogen-containing wastes.

The earthworm's digestive, nervous, and reproductive systems are more complex than those of flatworms. Earthworms move by means of muscles and setae.

- Leeches are annelids. Some are blood-sucking parasites, while others are free-living.

Vocabulary

Annelida	gut
anus	heart
Aschelminthes	hemoglobin
blood	hirudinean
brain	intestine
cephalization	nematode
cestodes	nephridium
circulation	oligochaete
clitellum	peritoneum
coelom	pharynx
crop	Platyhelminthes
cuticle	proglottid
cyst	rotifer
esophagus	segmentation
excretion	setae
flame cell	turbellarian
ganglion	trematode
gizzard	

Review

Choose the answer that best completes each of the following questions. Write the letters of the answers on a separate sheet of paper.

1. The body cavity of earthworms is called a (a) coelom, (b) gastrovascular cavity, (c) gut, (d) peritoneum.
2. The layer of cells found in flatworms but not in sponges or coelenterates is the (a) ectoderm, (b) mesoderm, (c) endoderm, (d) epidermis.
3. The nonliving protective covering of flukes is called the (a) epidermis, (b) ectoderm, (c) cuticle, (d) skin.

4. Which of these human parasites is a flatworm? (a) plasmodium (b) schistosoma (c) hookworm
5. In earthworms, the function of the nephridia is to (a) excrete nitrogen wastes from the body, (b) excrete undigested food from the body, (c) absorb water from the surroundings, (d) sense light.
6. The swollen areas of the nerve cord in each segment of the earthworm are called (a) brains, (b) nerve branches, (c) sensory knobs, (d) ganglia.
7. Which of the following does *not* have a digestive system in which food travels in only one direction? (a) flatworm (b) roundworm (c) annelid
8. Which of the following has a circulatory system? (a) flatworm (b) roundworm (c) annelid
9. Which of the following does *not* have a body cavity of any kind? (a) flatworm (b) roundworm (c) annelid
10. Which of the following is *not* an adaptation to parasitism? (a) production of a large number of eggs (b) suckers (c) setae (d) cuticle
11. Worms exhibit which type of symmetry? (a) radial (b) spherical (c) bilateral

Interpret and Apply

1. Put the following structures of the earthworm's digestive system in the correct sequence, beginning with the most anterior structure.

   a. pharynx   e. esophagus
   b. crop   f. mouth
   c. intestine   g. gizzard
   d. anus

2. List the major features that distinguish the worms from sponges and coelenterates.
3. How do members of the phylum Platyhelminthes obtain oxygen?
4. Give an explanation for the absence of a digestive system in tapeworms.
5. How is the flatworm gut different from the digestive tube of a roundworm?

6. Briefly describe the life cycle of the sheep liver fluke.
7. What are the differences in structure between flukes and tapeworms?
8. Why are flukes and hookworms placed in different phyla?
9. What are two functions of a coelom?
10. In roundworms, why isn't the space between the digestive tract and the body wall considered a true coelom?
11. Why is a circulatory system a useful adaptation in annelids?
12. Explain the advantage of cephalization in bilateral animals.

Challenge

1. What might be a method to get rid of the sheep liver fluke from a given area?
2. Explain the adaptations of flukes and tapeworms to a parasitic way of life.
3. Flatworms and roundworms do not have special structures for exchanging gases. Explain.
4. How is a cyst a protective adaptation for a parasite?
5. Why might hermaphroditism be a useful adaptation for a parasite?

Projects

1. Take a sample of moist soil or water from the bottom of a pond. Look at it with a hand lens or the low-power lens of a microscope. Try to find nematodes. Make drawings of the organisms that you think might belong to this group.
2. Look up the life cycle of any of the tapeworm species. Make a chart showing this life cycle.
3. Learn more about one of the parasites listed below. Find out where it is found in the world, how common it is, how infection can be prevented, and what, if any, medical treatment is appropriate:

   schistosoma   Guinea worm
   Chinese liver fluke   hookworm
   trichina

27 Mollusks and Echinoderms

Starfish eating a sea urchin; both organisms are echinoderms.

Spiny sea urchins are strange and sometimes beautiful animals. They are also food for starfish. The sea urchin's spines protect it from most enemies. The starfish, however, does not give up easily. It pushes its stomach out of its mouth and into an opening in the sea urchin's shell. Secretions from the starfish's stomach will digest the unlucky sea urchin.

Starfish also feed on oysters. The starfish wraps around the oyster and pulls the shells apart. The oyster fights to keep closed but usually fails. A starfish can slide its stomach through a very narrow crack no thicker than a piece of cardboard. One starfish can eat ten oysters each day.

Starfish and sea urchins are members of a small but important phylum of marine animals. This phylum and the phylum to which humans belong may have descended from the same ancestor.

Oysters, on the other hand, belong to a very large phylum with over 50,000 species. Organisms as different as the garden slug and the octopus are in the same phylum as oysters.

Phylum Mollusca

Oysters, snails, and squid belong to the phylum Mollusca. Among the **mollusks**, there is an incredible variety of forms. While most are marine, there are many freshwater species. Still other mollusks are **terrestrial** — that is, they live on land. How can such varied organisms all belong to the same phylum? Mollusk species that are quite different as adults resemble each other in the larval stage. In addition, varied though they are, adult mollusks share certain structural characteristics.

CONCEPTS

• development of mollusks
• common characteristics of mollusks
• diversity of mollusk body forms
• classification of mollusks

Figure 27.1 The colorful Triton's trumpet is an example of a marine mollusk.

27–1 Development of Mollusks

After fertilization of the egg, most mollusk species develop into a distinctive kind of larva called a **trochophore** [TROHK-uh-fawr]. As shown in Figure 27.2, a trochophore larva has its own digestive system. Tufts of cilia are located at each end. There is a ring of cilia around the middle. In many aquatic mollusks, the trochophore larva is free-swimming and feeds on plankton.

Some annelids also go through a trochophore larval stage. Because of this, many biologists conclude that mollusks and annelids share a common ancestor. There is no evidence in the fossil record of what this common ancestor might have looked like.

Figure 27.2 Most mollusks have a trochophore larva.

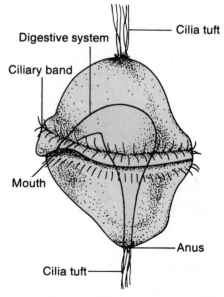

Cilia tuft

Digestive system

Ciliary band

Mouth

Anus

Cilia tuft

Mollusks and Echinoderms **403**

27–2 Mollusk Structure

The easiest way to see the common structures of mollusks is to create an imaginary organism like the one in Figure 27.3. Such an organism does not exist, but it possesses all the characteristics found in most mollusks. The ancestral organism from which all other mollusks evolved may have looked something like this imaginary creature.

General Body Structure The imaginary mollusk has a soft body without a skeleton. It is bilaterally symmetrical. A coelom is present. Covering the body is a layer of cells called the **mantle**. The mantle secretes a hard material that forms a shell on the outside of the organism. The mantle and the shell extend out farther than the body. This overhang is only slight for the most part. At the posterior end, however, the overhang is so great that it forms a protected space called the **mantle cavity**. Water from the outside environment usually flows through the mantle cavity.

Do You Know?

If a particle of foreign material gets trapped in the mantle of a bivalve, the shell secretes a smooth, shiny covering around the particle. That is how pearls form in oysters.

Figure 27.3 This representation of a typical mollusk shows an organism that does not actually exist. However, it illustrates the characteristic structures found in organisms of this phylum.

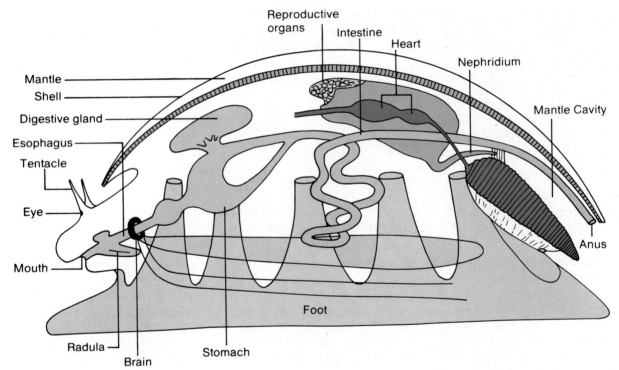

Another feature of this organism is its large muscular **foot** used for locomotion. The foot secretes mucus, which helps it glide along.

This imaginary mollusk has distinct cephalization. Associated with the head are many specialized sensory organs that pick up information from the mollusk's environment.

Digestive System The digestive system begins at the mouth. The **radula** [RAJ-oo-luh] is a feeding device found only in mollusks. It is a muscular structure with hard, toothlike projections. Like a file, the radula scrapes food from surfaces. Food travels to the **stomach** through the esophagus. Most digestion and absorption take place in the stomach and a nearby digestive gland. The intestine forms waste pellets for excretion through the anus. The wastes pass from the anus into the mantle cavity. From the mantle cavity, they pass out of the body on water currents.

Respiratory System The imaginary mollusk has a pair of **gills**, specialized structures that water animals have for gas exchange. Gills are thin, folded tissues with microscopic blood vessels running through them. The gills are located within the mantle cavity. Water flows into the mantle cavity. The gills are in direct contact with this water. They provide a large surface for gas exchange. The gills absorb oxygen from the water and release carbon dioxide into it.

Circulatory System Blood circulation in mollusks is different from circulation in annelids. Recall that in annelids, blood constantly stays in vessels as it travels around the body. Such a system is called a **closed circulatory system**. Most mollusks, however, have an **open circulatory system** in which blood is not confined to vessels after leaving the heart. A two-chambered heart pumps blood around the coelom and between internal organs. The blood travels through spaces between tissues and organs. Mollusk blood has an oxygen-carrying molecule called **hemocyanin** [hee-mu-SY-uh-nuhn]. Unlike red hemoglobin, hemocyanin is blue.

Excretory System Paired nephridia are found in the coelom. As in annelids, nephridia remove nitrogen-containing wastes. Wastes are removed from the fluid in the coelom and excreted into the mantle cavity.

Reproductive System Mollusks reproduce sexually. The sexes are separate in most mollusks. Some of these animals, however, are hermaphroditic.

Groups of living mollusks have modified the basic structural features just described. For example, clams have paired shells that protect soft body parts. The snails, on the other hand, have a single shell into which they can retract their body. The squid shell is a supporting rod inside the body.

27–3 Class Gastropoda: Snails and Slugs

Gastropods [GAS-truh-pahdz] are the largest mollusk group, with over 35,000 species. They show a wider variety of forms and live in more different environments than any other mollusk group. Many live in water: some are marine and others live in fresh water. Gastropods also include the only mollusks that live on land. The most common gastropods are snails and slugs. In some gastropods, such as the garden slug and the marine nudibranchs [NYOOD-uh-branks], the shell is reduced or absent.

A snail is a representative gastropod. The garden snail is a **herbivore** — that is, it eats plants. Land snails and slugs do extensive crop damage. However, not all gastropods are herbivores. Some are **carnivores**; that is, they eat meat. Some are **scavengers**, feeding on dead organisms. A few gastropods are parasites.

The snail scrapes up food material with its radula. In its search for food, the snail travels slowly on its foot. Glands in the foot secrete mucus, which helps the snail slide along. Cephalization helps the snail sense where food is. Two eyes are located on stalks in the head region.

Gastropods that live on land do not have gills. Instead, land snails have evolved a simple **lung**, an organ for gas exchange in air-breathing animals. Lungs are infoldings of the body wall with only a single, narrow opening to the outside. The small size of the opening prevents air from drying out the lung tissue. In the lung, gases diffuse between the air and the blood.

Many aquatic gastropods have separate sexes. Some species release eggs and sperm directly into the water. Fertilization occurs in water, not in the female's body. In other species the two sexes mate, and fertilization occurs in the female's body. In a few species, development of the fertilized eggs also takes place within the female.

In most gastropods, a trochophore larva develops within the egg. However, the trochophore never leaves the egg. Inside the egg, the trochophore of some species develops into another form of larva. In other species, the trochophore becomes a tiny adult snail within the egg.

BIOLOGY INSIGHTS

In all animals, gas exchange occurs across moist surfaces. The respiratory systems of land animals are structured in a way that helps prevent respiratory surfaces from drying out.

Figure 27.4 The structural features of a garden snail, a gastropod

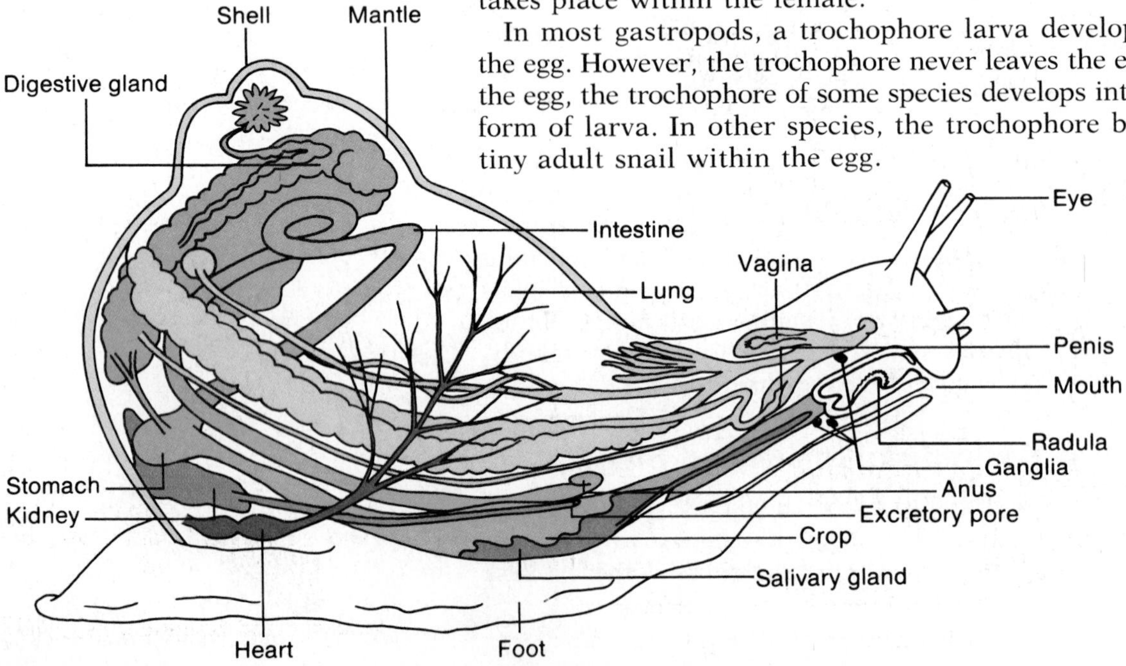

Shell　Mantle
Digestive gland
Intestine
Vagina
Lung
Eye
Penis
Mouth
Radula
Ganglia
Stomach
Kidney
Anus
Excretory pore
Crop
Salivary gland
Heart　Foot

27-4 Class Pelecypoda: The Bivalves

The **pelecypods** [puh-LIH-suh-pahds] are mollusks with two shells, or valves. Pelecypods are therefore called **bivalves**. The two valves are hinged so they open or close through the action of several large muscles. When closed, the valves protect the animal from predators. Oysters, clams, scallops, and mussels are all bivalves.

The foot of most bivalves is specialized for burrowing in soft mud or sand. The foot extends out from between the valves and pushes into the sand. The leading edge of the foot fans into an anchor. Contraction of the foot then pulls the clam body deeper into the sand.

Figure 27.5 shows the internal structure of the clam, a representative bivalve. Bivalves do not have a radula. Most bivalves use their gills for feeding as well as for respiration. The bivalve keeps its shells partly opened. Water, which carries food and oxygen, flows into the clam. Cilia on the gills create water currents in the mantle cavity. Mucus on the gills traps plankton from the water. Cilia sweep the mucus and food particles toward the mouth. In addition, oxygen from the water diffuses into the blood. Carbon dioxide diffuses from the blood into the water. Bivalves have an open circulatory system. Nephridia function in excretion, removing nitrogenous wastes and excess water.

Clams and oysters certainly don't *look* as if they have a head. Cephalization is not well developed in bivalves. The nervous system is bilaterally symmetrical, with two pairs of long nerve cords and three ganglia. The edge of the mantle contains sense organs that respond to light, chemicals, and touch.

The sexes are separate in most bivalves. Sperm and eggs are shed into the water, and fertilization occurs outside the body. The trochophore larva swims freely for a time. Then it settles to the bottom and develops into an adult.

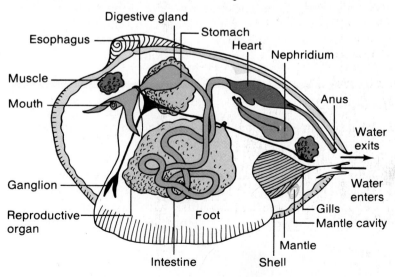

Figure 27.5 The internal anatomy of a clam shows the structural features of bivalves.

Do You Know?

The nautilus is free-swimming. Its shell has many chambers filled with gas. The nautilus adjusts its depth in the water by adding or removing gas from the chambers.

Do You Know?

When a predator threatens, a squid releases a dark fluid from an ink gland. The ink cloud confuses predators and helps the squid escape. At one time people used squid ink for writing and drawing.

The **cephalopods** [SEHF-uhh-luh-pahds] are the most highly specialized mollusks. Squids and octopuses are typical cephalopods. Fossil cephalopods have a large shell protecting the body, but only one type of living cephalopod, the nautilus, has retained an external shell. In the squid the shell is an internal rod secreted by the mantle. The octopus has no shell at all.

In the cephalopods the foot has evolved into long arms that project from the head. The squid has ten arms, while the octopus has eight. The arms are equipped with suction disks. The cephalopod uses its arms to grasp prey and pull the food toward its mouth. All cephalopods are carnivorous. The mouth of cephalopods has a pair of hard, beaklike teeth used for biting and tearing its prey.

Unlike most mollusks, cephalopods have a closed circulatory system. Closed circulation is usually an adaptation of rapidly moving animals. Of all the mollusks, the cephalopods are the most active movers. Such animals have greater metabolic requirements because they need energy for rapid swimming. With closed circulation, blood carrying oxygen and food is delivered efficiently to all parts of the body.

Movement in squids is unusual. They normally swim with graceful wavelike motions. In times of danger, they use a nozzlelike **siphon** on the ventral surface to move more rapidly. Rapid muscle contractions force water out of the mantle cavity through the siphon. Like a jet, the force of water moving out of the siphon propels the squid. This helps the squid escape.

Cephalopods have a highly developed nervous system with a large brain. Cephalopods also have complex sensory organs. The eyes of the squid and the octopus are remarkably similar in structure and function to your eyes. Complex eyes had not evolved at the time a common ancestor of humans and mollusks existed. Therefore, mollusk eyes and human eyes must have evolved independently. Scientists consider the eyes to be an example of convergent evolution.

Checkpoint

1. What is the layer of cells that produces the mollusk shell?
2. What is the mollusk feeding structure that has toothlike projections?
3. What are the respiratory structures of aquatic mollusks?
4. In which mollusk class do some members have lungs?
5. What is the term for a mollusk with two shells?
6. Mollusks in which class have tentacles and a beaked mouth?

Phylum Echinodermata

All **echinoderms** [ih-KY-nuh-durmz] are marine organisms. There are over 5,000 species in the phylum. Starfish, sea urchins, sand dollars, and sea cucumbers are some members. Echinoderms, like mollusks, have a coelom and a one-way digestive system.

27–6 Characteristics of Echinoderms

Most echinoderms exhibit **pentamerous** [pehn-TAM-ur-uhs] **radial symmetry**. An animal with this kind of symmetry can be divided into five equal parts from a central axis.

Radial symmetry has adaptive value in sessile and slow-moving animals. In such animals there is no real advantage for one part of the body to contact the environment sooner than another. Recall that in bilateral animals cephalization occurs at the end that moves first into the environment. The radially symmetrical echinoderms do not show cephalization.

During development echinoderms go through a **bipinnaria** [by-puh-NA-ree-uh] larval stage. The bipinnaria is bilaterally symmetrical. This suggests that echinoderms evolved from an ancestor with bilateral symmetry. The bipinnaria larva differs structurally from the trochophore larva of mollusks.

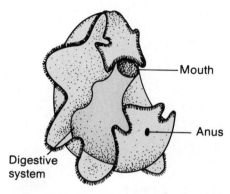

Mouth

Anus

Digestive system

Figure 27.6 The bipinnaria larva of an echinoderm

Figure 27.7 *Left:* A starfish; *Right:* A sea urchin. Both exhibit radial symmetry.

Besides the bipinnaria, two other features are unique to echinoderms. One is their system of **tube feet**, a series of suction disks that are used in locomotion and food getting. Tube feet are powered by a unique system of water-pumping tubes. The other is the **endoskeleton** [ehn-doh-SKEHL-uh-tuhn], or internal skeleton. The endoskeleton protects and supports the organism's soft tissues. It also provides a place to which muscles can attach. The endoskeleton is made of calcium compounds that form plates just below the epidermis. A number of spiny projections extend from these plates through the epidermis. Different spines are modified for different functions in the various classes of echinoderms. The name *echinoderm* means "spiny skin."

27–7 Class Asteroidea: The Starfish

The starfish, also called seastars, are members of the class **Asteroidea** [as-tuh-ROID-ee-uh]. These organisms demonstrate many features of echinoderms in general. A starfish has five arms, or rays, projecting from a central disk. The outermost surface of a typical starfish consists of a layer of ciliated epidermal cells. A network of nerve cells lies just below the epidermis. Beneath this outer skin is the endoskeleton. The plates of the skeleton are flexible at their joints. A variety of spinelike projections emerge from the skeleton.

Figure 27.8 A sea cucumber exhibits the spiny skin that is characteristic of echinoderms.

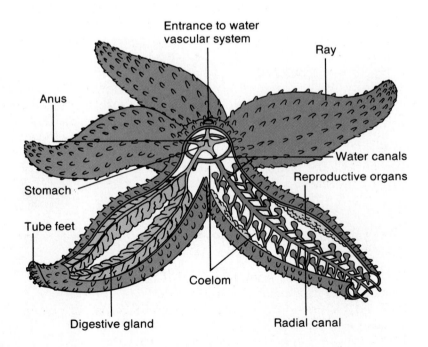

Figure 27.9 The internal anatomy of a starfish

Starfish are generally bottom dwellers. They usually move by using tube feet. The tube feet are located on the lower side of each of the five rays. The tube feet are part of a unique system called the **water vascular system**. Seawater enters the system through a pore in the center of the starfish's upper surface. The water moves through a series of canals out into the tube feet. Each tube foot moves by a continuous filling and emptying of water. The mechanism of filling and emptying is not well understood.

Most starfish are carnivores. Food is taken into the mouth, located on the starfish's lower surface. From the mouth, food goes through the esophagus to the stomach, where digestion takes place. Many starfish can push the stomach outside of their body to surround a food organism. Digestive enzymes are produced by digestive glands in each arm. Undigested wastes are eliminated through the anus on the starfish's upper surface.

Digested food molecules move to the cells of the animal through the coelomic fluid. (This fluid is not the same as the water in the water vascular system.) The coelom is lined with ciliated cells that circulate the fluid. In fact, the coelomic-fluid circulation functions as a circulatory system.

Starfish have no excretory system. Wastes diffuse from cells into the coelomic fluid. They then diffuse out of the body through the tube feet. Specialized spines function as gills. Gases are exchanged between the coelomic fluid and the exterior through these spines and the tube feet.

Starfish have no obvious head. Their nervous system is a simple ring of nerve cells. It has branches into the arms.

Reproduction in starfish is usually sexual. Males and females generally shed egg and sperm cells into the water. The eggs are fertilized in the water. Starfish also have remarkable powers of regeneration. If a starfish is broken into pieces, many of the pieces will regenerate. For example, a severed arm will regenerate into an entire animal as long as the arm has part of the central disk attached to it. A few species of starfish reproduce asexually by shedding arms.

Do You Know?

People who fished for oysters formerly tried to destroy starfish by cutting them into pieces. However, because of starfish regeneration, this actually increased the number of starfish.

Checkpoint

1. The name of the echinoderm phylum is based on what structural feature of the group?
2. Tube feet are part of what system that is unique to echinoderms?
3. Where is the mouth of starfish located?
4. What is a term for a skeleton located within an organism?

CHAPTER REVIEW

Summary

- Mollusks include such varied organisms as oysters, snails, and squid. Most mollusks go through a trochophore larval stage. Structural characteristics shared by most mollusks include a shell, a mantle, a mantle cavity, gills, and an open circulatory system. Most mollusks also have a muscular foot used for movement and a radula used in feeding.

- The gastropod class, the largest group of mollusks, includes snails, slugs, and nudibranchs. Most gastropods live in water, but some are terrestrial. Terrestrial gastropods have developed a lung for respiration. Gastropods reproduce sexually. Some species are hermaphroditic, while in others the sexes are separate. The shell is absent in some gastropods.

- The pelecypods include mollusks having two shells. The foot of most bivalves is specialized for burrowing in mud. Most bivalves use gills for both feeding and respiration. The sexes are separate in most bivalves, and fertilization occurs outside the body.

- Most cephalopods do not have external shells. The foot has evolved into tentacles. Cephalopods, unlike most mollusks, have a closed circulatory system. Cephalopods have a well-developed brain and sense organs.

- Echinoderms are marine animals. Most exhibit pentamerous radial symmetry. The phylum includes animals such as starfish, sea urchins, sand dollars, and sea cucumbers. Echinoderms go through a bipinnaria larval stage. Echinoderms have tube feet and an endoskeleton with spiny projections extending through the epidermis.

- Starfish are members of the Asteroidea class. Most have five rays. They move by means of tube feet, which are part of a water vascular system. Many starfish can push their stomach out of their body to surround food, which is digested by enzymes. The coelomic fluid transports materials to and from cells. Starfish usually reproduce sexually. Starfish also regenerate lost parts.

Vocabulary

Asteroidea	mantle cavity
bipinnaria	mollusk
bivalve	open circulatory
carnivore	system
cephalopod	pelecypod
closed circulatory	pentamerous radial
system	symmetry
echinoderm	radula
endoskeleton	scavenger
foot	siphon
gastropod	stomach
gill	terrestrial
hemocyanin	trochophore
herbivore	tube feet
lung	water vascular
mantle	system

Review

Choose the answer that best completes each of the following questions. Write the letters of the answers on a separate sheet of paper.

1. The larva that is characteristic of most mollusks and of some segmented worms is the (a) tornaria larva, (b) bipinnaria larva, (c) bilateral larva, (d) trochophore larva.
2. The kind of symmetry shown by all mollusks is (a) radial symmetry, (b) bilateral symmetry, (c) pentamerous radial symmetry, (d) spherical symmetry.
3. Digestion and absorption of food in mollusks takes place in the (a) stomach and digestive glands, (b) crop, (c) intestine, (d) radula.
4. The foot of most bivalves is specialized for (a) burrowing, (b) crawling over surfaces, (c) swimming, (d) feeding.

5. For rapid escapes, cephalopods direct a jet of water through the (a) mantle cavity, (b) siphon, (c) mouth, (d) tentacles.
6. Echinoderms are all (a) terrestrial, (b) freshwater, (c) marine, (d) marine and freshwater.
7. The larva of echinoderms shows (a) pentamerous radial symmetry, (b) radial symmetry, (c) asymmetry, (d) bilateral symmetry.

Answer each of the following questions.

8. What term means "living on land"?
9. What kind of circulatory system do most mollusks have?
10. What is the oxygen-carrying molecule in the blood of mollusks?
11. What is the respiratory structure of land animals?
12. In bivalves, where does fertilization occur?

Interpret and Apply

1. Copy the following chart. Put an X in the boxes where the characteristic is present in most members of the group.

Group	Mantle	External Shell	Cephalization
Gastropods			
Pelecypods			
Cephalopods			

2. Why is the existence of a trochophore larva in a species not enough to classify the species as a mollusk?
3. How is the shell of a snail different from that of an oyster?
4. What is unusual about the trochophore larva of land snails?
5. What are the two functions of clam gills?
6. What is the advantage of a closed circulatory system to cephalopods?
7. Describe the escape behavior of a squid.
8. Explain why cephalization would not be as advantageous to echinoderms as it is to animals such as annelids.
9. Where does the fluid in the water vascular system of a starfish come from?
10. What performs the function of a circulatory system in echinoderms?
11. What is the evidence that echinoderms evolved from an animal with bilateral symmetry?
12. What evidence indicates that annelids and mollusks may have had a common ancestor?
13. A starfish is cut into two pieces. One piece consists of four arms attached to the central disk. The other piece is the fifth arm without any of the central disk. Will either — or both — of these pieces regenerate? Explain.
14. Bivalves have a shell that can open and close. How is this type of shell a useful adaptation?

Challenge

1. Most aquatic snails have separate sexes and shed their eggs and sperm into the surrounding water. Can you explain why the mating of land snails is a useful adaptation to land life?
2. Explain how the distinct modifications of the foot in pelecypods, gastropods, and cephalopods are adaptations for different kinds of motion.
3. Explain how the eyes of humans and octopuses are an example of convergent evolution.
4. Slow-moving species, such as sea urchins, often go through a highly motile larval stage. How might a fast-moving larva be an advantage to such species?

Projects

1. Find out about the destructive habits of the garden slug and garden snail. What do they eat, what time of day are they active, and what can be done to control them?
2. Learn about the methods used to farm oysters for food and for pearls. Write a report.

28 Arthropods

A scorpion

If you had a contest for the most lovable animal, the scorpion might well finish last. Scorpions are sinister. But they are survivors. They have been around for a long, long time. Fossils indicate that scorpions were among the first animals to adapt to the terrestrial environment.

Most people associate scorpions with deserts. Indeed, many species live there, but others inhabit humid forests. In North America, scorpions are most common in the southern United States and Mexico.

Most scorpions hunt at night. During the day they remain hidden under stones or logs. All scorpions have a venomous sting on the tip of the tail. In a few species the venom is very poisonous. Where scorpions are common, people shake out their shoes each morning as a precaution.

The phylum to which scorpions belong is an evolutionary success story. There are far more species in this phylum than in any other. Some are sessile, some swim, some crawl, and some fly. These animals occupy oceans, fresh water, deserts, and Antarctic snows. It is difficult to find an environment they do not inhabit.

Subphylum Chelicerata

The phylum Arthropoda contains about 800,000 species. **Arthropods** [AHR-thruh-pahdz] make up about 80 percent of the known animal species. Lobsters, spiders, insects, and centipedes are all present-day arthropods. The phylum also includes extinct organisms such as trilobites. You may have seen trilobite fossils in pictures or at a museum.

Taxonomists divide the arthropods into two subphyla, the chelicerates and the mandibulates. The **chelicerates** [kih-LIHS-ur-ayts] include horseshoe crabs, spiders, and other related animals. The **mandibulates** [man-DIHB-yuh-layts] include organisms such as crabs, centipedes, millipedes, and insects. Before considering the distinctive traits of these two groups, you should be familiar with some characteristics shared by all arthropods.

28–1 General Arthropod Characteristics

In comparison to humans, arthropods almost seem to be built backward. Your main nerve cord is dorsal; the arthropod nerve cord is ventral. Your circulatory system is closed; the arthropod circulatory system is open. Your heart is ventrally located in your chest; the arthropod heart is dorsal and in the posterior half of the body. Your skeleton is inside your body; the arthropod skeleton is outside.

The most prominent characteristic of arthropods is their outside skeleton, or **exoskeleton** [ehk-soh-SKEHL-uh-tuhn]. An exoskeleton, like any skeleton, gives soft tissues support and protection. It also provides an anchoring place for muscles. The arthropod exoskeleton is made of chitin, a strong, flexible polysaccharide.

If an animal is surrounded by a hard exoskeleton, how can it grow? All arthropods **molt**, or shed, their exoskeleton periodically. After an arthropod molts, there is a short time before the new exoskeleton hardens. During this time, the animal grows significantly. However, an exoskeleton limits the maximum size to which the animal can grow.

A skeleton that surrounds all parts of the body must have flexible joints to allow movement. All arthropods have joints between body sections. In addition, arthropods have jointed appendages. An **appendage** is a structure such as a leg that grows out from the main part of the body. In fact, the name *arthropod* means "jointed foot."

To move the joints, arthropods have pairs of muscles. When one muscle contracts, the joint bends. When the other muscle contracts, the joint straightens.

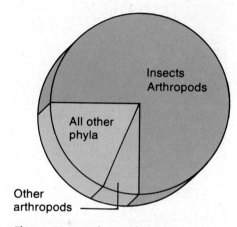

Figure 28.1 Arthropods make up a large majority of the animal species. Insects are the most common arthropods.

Figure 28.2 Arthropods periodically molt their exoskeletons.

Like annelids, all arthropods have segmented bodies. In arthropods, however, the segments are more highly specialized. Many arthropods have segments with appendages that function as jaws. Segments just behind the head are often adapted for locomotion with paired limbs attached.

The nervous system of arthropods is highly developed. Cephalization is more prominent than in annelids, with the brain and complex sense organs in the head region. Special organs sense touch, vibration, and chemicals. The eyes of many arthropods are particularly specialized.

All arthropods have an open circulatory system. The dorsal heart pumps blood from the posterior end of the animal to the anterior end.

28–2   Characteristics of Chelicerates

The scorpion shown in the opening photograph is a chelicerate. The chelicerate body has two major parts. It has a **cephalothorax** [sehf-uh-loh-THAWR-aks], a fused section composed of the head and any body segments that have legs attached. The posterior segments that contain most of the internal organs comprise the **abdomen** [AB-duh-muhn]. Within each of these parts, there may or may not be signs of segmentation.

Most chelicerates have six pairs of appendages. The four posterior pairs are walking legs. The two anterior pairs are highly specialized. The first pair, called **chelicerae** [kih-LIHS-ur-ee], are modified to aid in feeding. They have the same function as the jaws of other animals. The second pair of appendages are called **pedipalps** [PEHD-uh-palps]. Pedipalps are modified in different chelicerates for a variety of functions. They are often sensory receptors, picking up sensations of touch, taste, and smell. They perform basically the same functions as the antennae of other arthropods.

28–3   Class Arachnida: Spiders

Arachnids are a major class of chelicerates. The largest order of arachnids is the spiders. Spiders have a two-part body consisting of a cephalothorax and an abdomen. The abdomen is segmented, but the segmentation is not conspicuous. One pair of chelicerae, one pair of pedipalps, and four pairs of walking legs arise from the cephalothorax. All arachnids have eight legs.

Spiders' chelicerae are not modified for chewing. Rather they have piercing fangs with poison sacs used to kill prey. While all spiders have poison, only a few species are dangerous to humans. The black widow and the brown recluse are the most dangerous spiders in North America.

Digestion With no jaws to chew food, spiders digest food externally. They pump liquid from their digestive tract onto their prey. Enzymes digest the food. The food is then pulled into the esophagus by muscular contractions of the pharynx. A series of tubes branching from the stomach absorb food into the blood. The digestive system and other internal organs of a spider are shown in Figure 28.3.

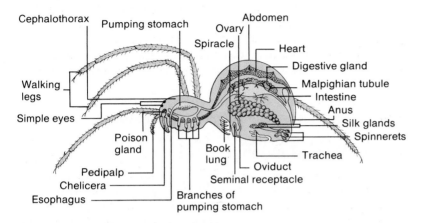

Figure 28.3 The internal structure of a female spider

Cephalothorax — Pumping stomach — Abdomen — Ovary — Spiracle — Heart — Digestive gland — Malpighian tubule — Intestine — Anus — Silk glands — Spinnerets — Walking legs — Simple eyes — Poison gland — Book lung — Trachea — Oviduct — Seminal receptacle — Pedipalp — Chelicera — Esophagus — Branches of pumping stomach

Silk Production All spiders have silk glands in the abdomen. Silk is released from the body through nozzlelike openings called **spinnerets** [spihn-uh-REHTS]. Many spiders use their silk to make webs. Small animals, usually insects, become trapped in the sticky web. Not all spiders build webs, but they all make silk. Some spiders wrap excess food organisms in a silk cocoon. Females often wrap eggs in a protective silk case. Trap-door spiders line their hiding places with silk walls.

Respiration All spiders are terrestrial. Instead of gills, spiders have **book lungs** for gas exchange. Book lungs consist of folded membranes arranged in stacks, much like the pages in a book. This arrangement exposes a large surface area of lung tissue to the air. Book lungs only open to the environment through a single small passage to the outside. Recall that such a single opening helps to keep the respiratory surfaces from drying out. The opening to the book lungs in the exoskeleton is called a **spiracle** [SPY-ruh-kuhl].

In addition to book lungs, some spiders have tracheae. **Tracheae** [TRAY-kee-ee] are tubes that bring air close to the spider's cells and to the circulating blood. Air gets into tracheae through openings in the abdomen. The tracheae branch through the inner spaces of the spider.

Circulation and Excretion In the spider's circulatory system, blood leaves the heart and moves through vessels to various parts of the body. Blood then leaves the vessels. It passes into open spaces around tissues and organs.

Malpighian [mal-PIHG-ee-uhn] **tubules** are the spider's major excretory organs. These tubules branch from the intestine and extend into the abdominal spaces. Nitrogen wastes from the blood pass through these tubes. The wastes then move into the intestine and out of the body.

Nervous System and Senses   The nervous system of spiders consists of a rather large brain and a ventral nerve cord. Sensory organs are well developed in many spiders. Most spiders have eight simple eyes. A **simple eye** is a small light-sensitive organ. These eyes are arranged in two rows of four.

Web-building spiders have a sensory organ in their legs that detects vibrations. A trapped insect will struggle to get free from the web, causing the web to vibrate. From the vibrations a spider can distinguish among its own young, another spider crawling on the web, and trapped prey.

28–4   Reproduction in Spiders

The ovary of the female spider produces eggs. The female's body has a small chamber called the **seminal receptacle**. After a female mates with a male, the seminal receptacle holds the sperm cells within the female. Later, when eggs are released from the female's body, they are fertilized by sperm stored in the receptacle.

The male spider produces sperm in testes. The sperm are released from the body through an opening in the abdomen. Male spiders have modified pedipalps that carry sperm. Each pedipalp has a suctionlike device that draws sperm into it. During mating, the male releases sperm from the pedipalp into the female's seminal receptacle.

The reproductive behavior of spiders is often very complex. In many species the male is much smaller than the female. Female spiders are often more interested in devouring males than in mating with them. In fact, this rather bizarre behavior has given the black widow spider its name.

To avoid being devoured, and to insure successful mating, males must approach females very carefully. In many species, the male offers the female an insect wrapped in silk. While the female busies herself with this gift, the male mates with her and then makes a hasty retreat. In other species the male strums the web in a special way. The female recognizes these vibrations as special and allows the male to approach her. In species that do not spin webs, the male often performs an elaborate mating dance.

After the eggs are fertilized, the female usually wraps them in a silk cocoon until they develop into young spiders. If you are familiar with E. B. White's classic story *Charlotte's Web*, you may remember another unusual spider behavior. The

Do You Know?

Eyes are larger in spiders that stalk prey than in those that trap prey in webs.

Figure 28.4 The female black widow often devours its mate.

young of some species spin a small bit of webbing that acts like a parachute. Winds can lift the young spiders and carry them for kilometers. Such dispersal takes each spider far from its several hundred brothers and sisters. There is less competition for food that way.

28–5 Other Arachnids

Scorpions are considered among the most primitive living arachnids because the segments in their abdomen are distinct, not fused together the way a spider's are. The scorpions of today may be most like the original arachnids.

Scorpions differ from spiders in a number of other ways. The chelicerae of scorpions are small chewing structures. The chelicerae have no fangs or poison glands. The sting and poison gland of scorpions is located in the last segment of the abdomen. The pedipalps of scorpions are not sensory. Rather they are enlarged into pincers that grasp prey.

The daddy longlegs, or harvestman, belongs to another arachnid order. Daddy longlegs differ from spiders in significant ways. The cephalothorax and abdomen of these animals are fused into a single rounded body. They do not have poison glands or silk glands. Unlike spiders, which are carnivores, daddy longlegs eat both plant and animal material. They do not digest food externally.

Mites are the most widespread of the arachnids. Most are less than a millimeter in length and are very hard to see. The exoskeleton of mites shows few signs of segmentation. Mites are parasites of plants and animals, including humans.

Ticks are larger than mites but have a similar body form. They are parasites of many terrestrial animals. Like leeches, ticks attach to their host to feed on blood and then drop off. Ticks carry a number of human diseases, such as Rocky Mountain spotted fever. People are more afraid of spiders and scorpions than mites and ticks, yet the latter do far greater damage.

A survey of the arachnids illustrates one very important trend of arthropod evolution: the reduction of body segmentation. The primitive scorpions show clear body segmentation. Segmentation is reduced in spiders. It is nearly absent in mites and ticks.

Do You Know?
Young scorpions often ride on their mother's back until their first molting.

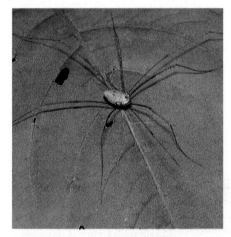

Figure 28.5 The daddy longlegs, or harvestman, is a common relative of spiders.

Do You Know?
Some mites are so small that they weigh less than the nuclei of large cells.

Checkpoint

1. Name the two body divisions of chelicerates.
2. What is the function of the chelicerae of spiders?
3. Name the two structures that spiders use for respiration.
4. On what do ticks feed?

Subphylum Mandibulata

The second subphylum of the arthropods is the mandibulates. Unlike chelicerates, mandibulates have **mandibles** [MAN-duh-buhlz], or jaws, for chewing food. They also have **maxillae** [mak-SIHL-ee] for holding food and passing it to the mandibles and mouth. All mandibulates have **antennae** — segmented sense organs on the head. Mandibulates also have three or more pairs of walking legs.

Insects are the largest class of mandibulates; they are the subject of the next chapter. There are three other major classes of mandibulates. The **crustaceans** [kruh-STAY-shuhnz] include such organisms as crabs, lobsters, and shrimp. The **diplopods** [DIHP-luh-pahdz] are better known as millipedes. The **chilopods** [KY-luh-pahdz] are the centipedes.

28–6 Class Crustacea: Crayfish, Lobsters, and Shrimp

With over 20,000 species, the crustaceans show a tremendous diversity. Crustaceans include many animals used by humans for food, such as crayfish, lobsters, crabs, and shrimp. Barnacles and *Daphnia*, the water flea, are also crustaceans. Most crustaceans are marine, although some live in fresh water. Sow bugs are among the few terrestrial crustaceans.

Figure 28.6 The external and internal features of a crayfish

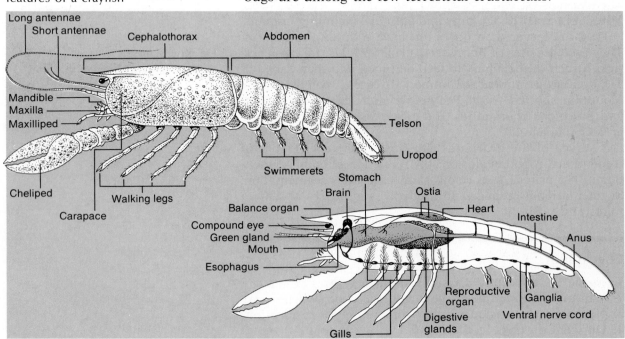

The crayfish is a typical crustacean. Its body is divided into a cephalothorax and an abdomen. The cephalothorax is covered by a single piece of exoskeleton called the **carapace** [KAR-uh-pays]. The crustacean exoskeleton contains calcium and other minerals in addition to chitin. The minerals make the shell particularly hard and inflexible.

Appendages   Crustaceans have paired appendages attached to each segment. The most anterior appendages are two pairs of antennae. Just behind the antennae are the mandibles, or jaws. They crush, tear, and chew food before it enters the mouth. Following the mandibles are two pairs of maxillae. Behind the maxillae are three pairs of **maxillipeds** [mak-SIHL-uh-pehds], which serve as sense organs. They also help pass food toward the mouth.

The next appendages are the large, pincer-bearing **chelipeds** [KEE-luh-pehds]. The crayfish uses its chelipeds to get food and protect itself from enemies. Behind the chelipeds are four pairs of walking legs. The abdominal segments bear appendages called **swimmerets**, which aid in swimming. In females the swimmerets hold fertilized eggs. At the posterior end, there are several flattened appendages called **uropods** [YOOR-uh-pahds]. They lie on both sides of the flattened tail, or **telson**, and are used for swimming.

Feeding and Digestion   Crayfish are scavengers; they also feed on small animals, such as snails. The mandibles shred food into small pieces. The esophagus, which leads to the stomach, has teethlike structures made of chitin that grind food into fine particles. Final digestion and absorption of food take place in the large digestive glands located on both sides of the stomach.

Circulation, Respiration, and Excretion   Gills are located at the base of many appendages. The largest gills are attached to the walking legs and extend up under the carapace. As the crayfish moves, water flows over the gills. In the thin-walled gills, gases diffuse between the water and the blood.

Like all arthropods, crayfish have open circulation. Vessels carry blood from the heart to the various organs of the body. Blood leaves these vessels and flows into spaces between the body organs. Blood returns from the organs and travels through the gills. Gases are then exchanged in the gills. From the gills, blood moves to a space around the heart. Blood re-enters the heart through slits called **ostia** [AHS-tee-uh].

Crayfish excrete nitrogen wastes from the two **green glands** located in the head. These two glands filter wastes from blood in the body cavities. Filtered wastes pass through pores to the outside.

 BIOLOGY INSIGHTS

Before an organism can use food for energy and growth, the food must be digested, or broken down into small molecules. Physical tearing and grinding is usually the first part of this process. Later, food particles are split into small molecules by chemical means.

Senses The nervous system of the crayfish is quite complex. The brain receives stimuli from a variety of sense organs. The antennae are sensitive to touch and to chemicals in the water. The entire body of the crayfish is covered with fine, hairlike projections. These are also sensitive to touch and to vibrations in the water.

The crayfish has two large compound eyes. A **compound eye** is composed of many individual light-sensitive units. The crayfish's compound eyes can sense motion and can probably see crude images.

Crayfish also have a pair of balance organs near the base of the antennae. These balance organs are small spherical cavities lined with nerve endings. The crayfish inserts a grain of sand into each balance organ. The sand is pulled down by gravity. The crayfish receives information about its body position from the nerve endings touched by the sand grain.

Reproduction Crayfish always reproduce sexually, and the sexes are separate. During mating, the male deposits sperm in the female's body. Sperm stay in the female until the eggs leave the ovary. Each egg is then fertilized as it leaves the female's body. The eggs stick to swimmerets and stay there until they hatch. In the spring, females can be seen carrying large egg masses under their abdomens.

28–7 Class Diplopoda: Millipedes

Turn over a pile of leaves and you are likely to see diplopods scurrying around. The diplopods are commonly known as the millipedes. Literally, millipede means "thousand feet." In fact, no millipede has anywhere near a thousand legs. However, some have several hundred.

A millipede's head has two groups of simple eyes, a pair of antennae, mandibles, and maxillae. The first four segments behind the head each have a single pair of legs. The abdominal segments are unique, however, since each external segment is actually two segments fused together. The most obvious result of fusion is that each segment has two pairs of legs.

Millipedes range in length from 2 millimeters to 30 centimeters. The number of segments varies from about 10 to over 100. Millipedes are among the vegetarians of the animal kingdom — they are strictly herbivorous.

28–8 Class Chilopoda: Centipedes

The chilopods are more commonly called centipedes, a name meaning "hundred feet." Centipedes vary in size. They may have between 15 and 150 pairs of legs and are usually only a few centimeters long. Some tropical species, however, reach a length of 30 centimeters.

Figure 28.7 *Top:* A millipede; *Bottom:* A centipede

The principal difference between millipedes and centipedes is that centipedes have simple, unfused body segments. Each segment has only one pair of legs.

Like millipedes, centipedes live under leaves and stones, where they hunt prey. Unlike millipedes, centipedes are all carnivores. A pair of anterior appendages are modified into poison claws. Centipedes use these claws to capture prey.

Centipedes have a reputation for being dangerous. But only the very largest of the tropical centipedes can seriously harm humans. North American centipedes are generally harmless and quite shy.

Figure 28.8 A summary of the characteristics of four major classes of arthropods

PHYLUM ARTHROPODA	SEGMEN-TATION	APPENDAGES	RESPIRATION	HABITAT	EXAMPLES
Subphylum Chelicerata Arachnida	2 body segments; fused to single body in some	Poison chelicerae in some; chewing in others	Book lungs, tracheae	Terrestrial	Scorpions, spiders, harvestmen, mites, ticks
Subphylum Mandibulata Crustacea	2 body segments	2 pairs antennae; number of walking legs varies	Gills	Most marine; some terrestrial	Shrimp, crab, lobster, pill bugs
Diplopoda	Numerous body segments	2 pairs of legs on each body segment	Tracheae	All terrestrial	Millipedes
Chilopoda	Numerous body segments	1 pair of legs on most body segments	Tracheae	All terrestrial	Centipedes

Checkpoint

1. What is the term for the appendages that function as jaws in crustaceans?
2. What appendages are located directly behind the jaws of a crayfish?
3. What are the excretory organs of the crayfish called?
4. Name three kinds of sensations the crayfish can detect with its sensory organs.
5. Through what structures does a crayfish's blood return to the heart?
6. How many legs are on each segment of a centipede's abdomen?

CHAPTER REVIEW

Summary

- Arthropods have an exoskeleton, jointed legs, and segmented bodies. In order to grow, all arthropods molt. Many arthropods have jaws for tearing food. Biologists divide arthropods into two major subphyla, the chelicerates and the mandibulates.

- Chelicerates do not have jaws. They usually have only two body divisions and six pairs of appendages. Two anterior pairs of appendages are modified for feeding and sensory functions. The four posterior pairs of appendages function as walking legs.

- The arachnids are a major class of chelicerates. They include the spiders, scorpions, daddy longlegs, mites, and ticks.

- Spiders digest food externally with enzymes. All spiders produce silk. Spiders have book lungs and tracheae for gas exchange. Excretion is carried out by Malpighian tubules. Sensory organs include eight simple eyes and an organ that detects vibrations.

- Spiders reproduce sexually. After mating occurs, sperm are stored in the female's body. Eggs are fertilized when they are released.

- Because the segments in their abdomen are distinct rather than fused, scorpions are considered to be more primitive than spiders. Daddy longlegs resemble spiders but do not have poison or silk glands. Their cephalothorax and abdomen are fused. Ticks and mites are parasitic arachnids.

- Mandibulates have mandibles, antennae, and three or more pairs of walking legs. Insects, crustaceans, chilopods, and diplopods are the major classes of mandibulate arthropods.

- Crustaceans are the crayfish, crabs, shrimp, and others. Specialized paired appendages function in feeding, motion, sense perception, protection, and reproduction. Crayfish have compound eyes with which they see motion and probably images.

- Diplopods have many body segments, with two pairs of legs on each of the abdominal segments. Chilopods have only one pair of legs on each segment.

Vocabulary

abdomen	Malpighian tubule
antenna	mandible
appendage	mandibulate
arachnid	maxilla
arthropod	maxilliped
book lung	molt
carapace	ostia
cephalothorax	pedipalp
chelicera	seminal receptacle
chelicerate	simple eye
cheliped	spinneret
chilopod	spiracle
compound eye	swimmeret
crustacean	telson
diplopod	trachea
exoskeleton	uropod
green gland	

Review

1. What substance is an arthropod's exoskeleton made of?
2. What is the name for the process in which arthropods shed their exoskeletons?
3. What are the two arthropod subphyla?
4. What is the function of spinnerets?
5. Identify the structures spiders have for gas exchange.
6. What class do shrimp belong to?
7. What types of organisms have pedipalps? Where are these structures located?
8. Why are scorpions considered more primitive than spiders?
9. What two things do crayfish sense through hairs on the body surface?

For questions 10 through 13, match the organism with the class.

10. chilopods   a. crab
11. arachnids   b. millipede
12. crustaceans   c. tick
13. diplopods   d. centipede

Choose the answer that best completes each of the following questions.

14. The anterior body section of chelicerates is called the (a) head, (b) cephalothorax, (c) thorax, (d) abdomen.
15. Spiders digest their prey (a) outside the body, (b) in the pumping stomach, (c) in the intestine, (d) in Malpighian tubules.
16. Millipedes are unusual because they have (a) no abdominal segments, (b) no legs on their abdominal segments, (c) two pairs of legs on each abdominal segment, (d) a separate heart in each abdominal segment.
17. The arachnids that transmit disease to humans are the (a) black widow spiders, (b) ticks, (c) daddy longlegs, (d) scorpions.
18. Web-building spiders have special sense organs in their legs that detect (a) vibrations, (b) chemicals, (c) smell, (d) light.
19. Which of the following is *not* an arthropod characteristic? (a) segmented body (b) exoskeleton (c) closed circulatory system (d) cephalization
20. Which of the following is *not* a characteristic of chelicerates? (a) mandibles (b) cephalothorax (c) abdomen (d) pedipalps
21. Female spiders store sperm from males in a structure called the (a) pedipalp, (b) spinneret, (c) ovary, (d) seminal receptacle.

Interpret and Apply

1. In what ways is the basic body plan of arthropods different from your own body?
2. List several functions of the silk produced by spiders.
3. Explain the difference between simple and compound eyes.
4. Why do arthropods grow larger only after they molt?

5. The young of some spiders spin parachute-like webs. How are these tiny parachutes adaptations that help the young spiders survive?
6. List three differences between daddy longlegs and spiders.
7. What function do the modified pedipalps of scorpions perform?
8. What is the function of calcium and other minerals in the crustacean exoskeleton?
9. What is the difference in function between mandibles and maxillae?
10. Compare the ways that spiders and crayfish get rid of nitrogenous wastes.
11. What is the role of sand grains in the crayfish's sense of balance?
12. In male crayfish, swimmerets have only one function, but in females, these structures perform two jobs. Explain.

Challenge

1. What is the major difference between the exoskeleton of arthropods and the various protective coverings of animals described in earlier chapters?
2. You discover a fossil organism with the following structures: exoskeleton, mandibles, maxillae, antennae, abdominal segments with four legs each. Into which phylum, subphylum, and class would you put the fossil?
3. Explain how the structure of each of the following organs is related to its function.
   a. antenna   c. spider chelicerae
   b. book lung   d. chelipeds

Projects

1. Collect millipedes from under rocks, leaves, or fallen and decaying trees. Do some simple experiments to test their reaction to touch, light, or humidity (dampness).
2. Use a microscope to examine pond water for crustaceans. Make drawings of those that you find. Try to identify them.

29 Insects

Bark beetle

There are more kinds of insects than all other animals combined. Almost 700,000 species have been identified. Some biologists estimate that there may be another million yet undiscovered.

Beetles, such as the bark beetle in this photograph, are the largest order of insects. Beetles display enormous diversity. The biggest, for example, are the goliath beetles of Africa, which can be over 11 centimeters long — about as long as a typical teaspoon. In contrast, the smallest beetles are less than a millimeter long.

One type of beetle, the scarab, was sacred to the ancient Egyptians. They believed that the scarab represented the sun on Earth. Jewelry and ornaments were carved in the shape of scarabs. Today these are valuable relics of ancient Egyptian civilization.

Members of the weevil family of beetles destroy many farm crops. On the other hand, the familiar red ladybird with black spots is a welcome sight in any garden. Ladybird beetles eat aphids and other pests. In fact, gardeners sometimes buy these beetles to use for pest control.

Characteristics of Insects

Insects live in almost every habitat imaginable. They live in and on the soil. They live under and on top of fresh water. Insects are found in, on, and around plants and animals. Oddly enough for such an enormous group of animals, however, almost none live in the ocean.

29–1   The Insect Body

Insects are typical arthropods. They have an exoskeleton made of chitin. They also have jointed legs. The insect body is segmented like that of other arthropods. However, while most arthropods have two major body sections, insects have three. These are the anterior head, middle thorax, and posterior abdomen.

The head of every insect has mouthparts, one pair of antennae, and eyes. There are usually a number of simple eyes as well as a pair of compound eyes.

The **thorax** [THAWR-ahks], or middle section, is specialized for locomotion. Every insect has three pairs of legs; these are attached to the thorax. In addition, there are usually two pairs of wings attached to the thorax. The thorax contains muscles that operate the legs and wings. Insects are the only arthropods with wings.

The abdomen is the third body section. The insect abdomen, like that of other arthropods, contains many internal organs, including those of reproduction. All insects show distinct male and female sexes. Segmentation of the thorax and abdomen is obvious in most insects.

CONCEPTS

- general characteristics of insects
- the typical insect body
- insect development

Do You Know?
The larvae of different insect species may be known by different names. For example, the larvae of moths and butterflies are called caterpillars, while fly larvae are known as maggots.

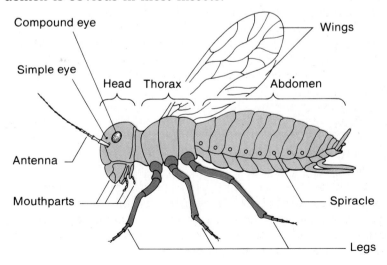

Figure 29.1 The structural features of a typical insect

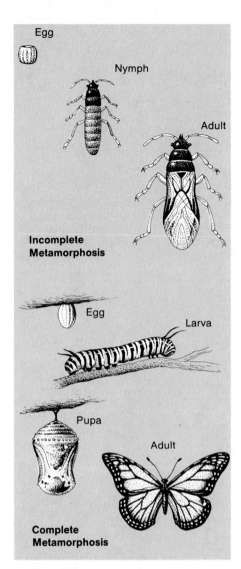

Egg

Nymph

Adult

**Incomplete
Metamorphosis**

Egg

Larva

Pupa

Adult

**Complete
Metamorphosis**

Figure 29.2 *Top:* The nymph stage of incomplete metamorphosis resembles the adult but does not have wings or reproductive organs. *Bottom:* The larva and pupa of complete metamorphosis do not resemble the adult.

An insect's thorax and abdomen also contain spiracles. Insects breathe air, and air enters the insect's body through spiracles. Oxygen gets to the insect's cells by means of tracheae.

29–2 Insect Development

Like all arthropods, insects must molt in order to grow. Insects generally go through several distinct stages during their development. **Metamorphosis** [meht-uh-MOR-fuh-sihs] is the process in which an animal develops into an adult by progressing through different structural stages.

Some species of insects, such as dragonflies, grasshoppers, and aphids, go through gradual, or incomplete, metamorphosis. **Incomplete metamorphosis** has three stages — egg, nymph, and adult. The immature form called a **nymph** [nihmf] hatches from the egg. Nymphs look much like small adults. However, they do not have wings or reproductive organs. After a series of molts, the nymph finally reaches adult form and size.

Other insects, such as butterflies, beetles, and ants, undergo complete metamorphosis. There are four stages to **complete metamorphosis** — egg, larva, pupa, and adult. A larva hatches from the egg. Insect larvae are segmented and look like worms. They are specialized for eating, and they eat greedily. They do not have wings or reproductive organs.

After several molts, the larva becomes a **pupa** [PYOO-puh]. During the pupal stage the insect appears to be resting. In fact, though, the body of the larva is being broken down and transformed into the complex body of the adult. By the time the adult insect emerges, it has complete reproductive organs and wings.

Complete metamorphosis gives an insect adaptive advantages. Many insects go through their larval stage during the spring and summer, a time when much food is available. The larvae eat enough to carry them through the pupal stage.

Often, adults and larvae of the same species have different diets. Also adults eat far less than larvae. Thus competition for food between adults and larvae is reduced or eliminated. In many insect species the adult does not eat at all. Its sole function is reproduction.

Checkpoint

1. Name the three major divisions of an insect's body.
2. How many legs do insects have?
3. What is the thorax of insects specialized for?
4. What part of an insect's body contains the reproductive organs?
5. In which type of metamorphosis is there a pupal stage?

The Grasshopper

No single species of insect is typical of the entire group. Each species has adaptations for its specific way of life. The grasshopper, however, has characteristics common to many insects.

29–3   An Introduction to the Grasshopper

Grasshoppers, crickets, and locusts all belong to the same order, which includes some 10,000 species. These insects have enlarged rear legs specialized for jumping.

Figure 29.3 shows the external structure of a grasshopper. The head contains the brain and many sensory organs, including a single pair of antennae, three simple eyes, and one pair of compound eyes. Also located on the head are the specialized chewing mouthparts.

The thorax is divided into three segments. A pair of legs is attached to each thoracic segment. Two pairs of wings are attached to the thorax. The first pair of wings is somewhat thickened. These wings protect the more delicate second set of wings underneath.

The abdomen of most grasshoppers is divided into ten segments. On the first abdominal segment is a round membrane called the **tympanum** [TIHM-puh-nuhm], or hearing organ. Each abdominal segment has a pair of spiracles, as do the two posterior segments of the thorax. The spiracles open into the tracheae.

CONCEPTS

- external structure of the grasshopper
- internal anatomy of the grasshopper
- reproduction in the grasshopper

Figure 29.3 *Left:* The external anatomy of a grasshopper *Right:* The structural features of a grasshopper's mouth

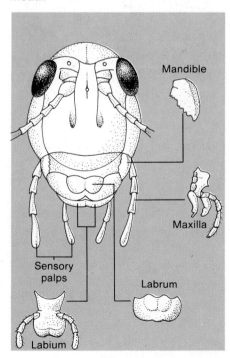

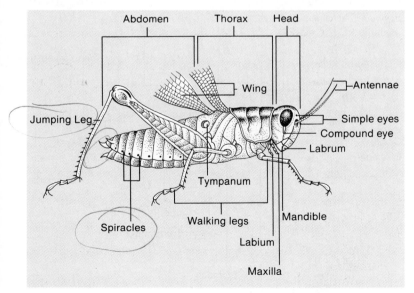

29–4 Feeding, Digestion, and Excretion

The mouthparts of insects, like those of crustaceans, are modified appendages. The grasshopper eats grass, and its mouthparts are adapted to that diet. The **labrum** [LAY-bruhm] is a flap of exoskeleton covering the other mouthparts. It helps to hold food between the biting and chewing mandibles. Behind the mandibles are a pair of maxillae that hold food for chewing. The **labium** [LAY-bee-uhm], located behind the maxillae, also holds and manipulates food. The maxillae and labium also contain **sensory palps**, organs that taste food.

The grasshopper has a complete, one-way digestive tract. Chewed food travels from the mouth through the esophagus and into the crop, where it is stored temporarily. Just behind the crop is a gizzard, where hard, chitinous teeth grind the food further. Food passes from the gizzard to the stomach, or **midgut**. A number of blind pouches called **caeca** [SEE-kuh] (singular, *caecum*) branch from the stomach and extend into the body space. The function of caeca in grasshoppers is not certain. In many insects, however, bacteria live in these pouches. The bacteria supply the insect with vitamins.

In the midgut, food is broken down by enzymes. Molecules of digested food move through the stomach lining and into the bloodstream. Solid wastes form in the intestine.

Grasshoppers have Malpighian tubules, which remove nitrogen wastes. The tubes extend into the abdominal cavity. Nitrogen wastes leave the blood and enter the tubules. The wastes are excreted into the intestine. They are expelled with the solid wastes through the anus.

Figure 29.4 The internal anatomy of a female grasshopper

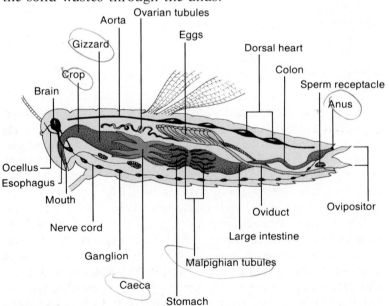

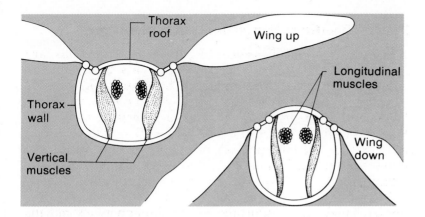

Figure 29.5 When the vertical flight muscles contract, the roof of the thorax comes down and the wings are pushed up. When the longitudinal muscles contract, the roof of the thorax is pushed up and the wings beat downward.

29–5 Senses, Nervous System, and Muscles

The large compound eyes of the grasshopper record crude images. These eyes can detect shapes and movement. The smaller simple eyes probably detect changes in brightness.

The exoskeleton of the grasshopper is covered with tiny sensory hairs; they are particularly numerous on the antennae. These hairs are sensitive to the slightest touch. The antennae also have nerve cells that detect odors.

As in other arthropods, the nervous system of the grasshopper consists of a brain and a double nerve cord extending ventrally. Nerves branch to all parts of the body from the brain and from ganglia in each body segment. Nerves carry messages to various parts of the body, including muscles.

Pairs of muscles bend joints of the exoskeleton in either direction. When one muscle contracts, the other relaxes. The wings are like levers that move up and down. The flight muscles move the wings by changing the shape of the thorax; the muscles do not actually attach to the wings themselves.

29–6 Circulation and Respiration

The grasshopper's circulatory system is open. The heart is on the dorsal side of the abdomen. A vessel called the **aorta** [ay-AWR-tuh] extends forward from the heart to the head. The heart pumps blood through the aorta. Blood flows out of the aorta and into the body cavity. The blood moves back toward the posterior end of the grasshopper and finally back into the heart. The grasshopper's blood is a clear, watery fluid that transports food, waste molecules, and some gases.

Like spiders, insects obtain oxygen by means of a tracheal system that opens to the outside through spiracles. The tracheae of the grasshopper and many other insects, unlike those of spiders, open into large, balloonlike **air sacs**. Air sacs allow the grasshopper to move larger amounts of air through the tracheal system than would otherwise be possible. Increased

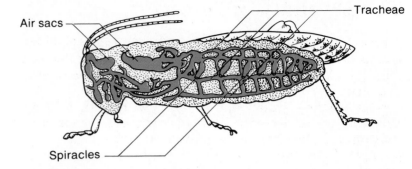

Air sacs · Tracheae

Spiracles

Figure 29.6 The respiratory system of a grasshopper

BIOLOGY INSIGHTS

The fertilization of insect eggs occurs inside the female's body. This process ensures that the sperm will not dry out before reaching the eggs. Internal fertilization is found in all the major classes of land animals, including reptiles, birds, and mammals.

Do You Know?

Insects have lived on Earth at least 300 million years.

gas exchange is an important adaptation in actively moving insects.

The grasshopper breathes by moving its abdomen as well as by opening and closing its spiracles. The grasshopper expands its abdomen, opens the anterior four pairs of spiracles, and closes the posterior pairs. Then the anterior pairs close, the posterior pairs open, and muscles contract the abdomen. All these movements force fresh air through the air sacs and the tracheal system.

29–7 Reproduction and Development

In males, sperm are produced in paired testes. During mating, sperm cells travel through tubes to the **penis**, with which the male deposits sperm in the female's reproductive tract. The female stores sperm in seminal receptacles. In the female, eggs develop in the ovaries. The eggs travel from the ovaries through tubes called **oviducts** [OH-vuh-duhktz]. Before the eggs leave the body, they are fertilized by sperm cells from the seminal receptacles. Female grasshoppers have an external ovipositor. The **ovipositor** [oh-vuh-PAHZ-uh-tur] is a structure through which fertilized eggs travel to the outside.

Most grasshoppers mate in the fall. The females deposit their eggs in a hole dug with the ovipositor. The following spring, the nymphs emerge from the eggs.

Checkpoint

1. What structure does food enter after leaving the mouth of the grasshopper?
2. What removes nitrogen wastes from the grasshopper's body?
3. What senses are located in the antennae of the grasshopper?
4. What structures allow the grasshopper to move large amounts of air through its tracheae?
5. Identify the structure that female insects use for laying their eggs.

The Diversity of Insects

From large, brightly colored butterflies to tiny brown fleas, insects exhibit a variety of characteristics. Some differences among insects have to do with body structure. The number and structure of wings and the type of mouthparts are important anatomical characteristics. Another difference, as you have learned, involves the kind of metamorphosis an insect goes through. Insects also vary in the way they behave. For example, some insects live in groups, while others live as individuals. These and other characteristics are used to classify insects. Not all taxonomists agree on how insects should be divided into orders. Most classifications show between 20 and 26 orders.

Different characteristics allow insects to live under widely varying conditions. Some adaptations protect insects from predators. Others help predatory insects catch their prey. Specialized mouthparts and digestive systems enable different insects to eat everything from wool to other insects. Reproductive adaptations help account for the large numbers of insects that exist.

29–8 Feeding Adaptations

Insect mouthparts are adapted to widely different functions. Mosquito mouthparts are modified into a pair of hollow tubes. These tubes puncture the skin of an animal and suck blood. Similar piercing and sucking mouthparts are found in aphids, which suck juices from plant stems. In some butterflies the mouthparts are coiled into a very long tube. This tube unrolls to reach nectar deep within certain flowers.

Predatory insects use a variety of structures to help capture prey. In the dragonfly nymph the labium is modified into a hinged structure. The labium unfolds to capture prey and then pulls the victim back toward the mouth. The praying mantis has modified forelegs that reach out and capture insects. Wasps use poison glands and stingers in the abdomen to paralyze prey.

29–9 Adaptations in Appearance

Sometimes an animal has an advantage if it is not recognized for what it is. An animal can escape predators if it cannot be seen easily or if it resembles another animal. Similarly a predator, if it goes unnoticed, can take its victims by surprise. The appearances of many insects aid in concealment.

CONCEPTS

- feeding adaptations of insects
- adaptations of insects' appearance
- reproductive adaptations of insects
- insect societies
- effects of insects on humans

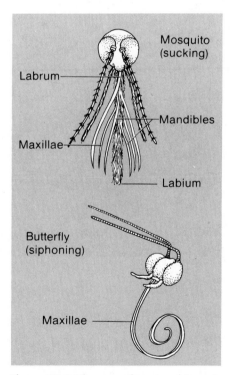

Figure 29.7 The mouthparts of insects are specialized for certain methods of food-getting.

Figure 29.8 The bright colors of this caterpillar act as a warning to predators.

Figure 29.9 *Left:* The monarch butterfly is distasteful to birds. *Right:* Birds avoid the viceroy butterfly since it resembles the monarch.

Camouflage [KAM-uh-flahzh] is a method by which an organism blends into its environment so that it cannot easily be seen. For example, an insect may be the same color as its background. The praying mantis is about the same shade of green as the plants on which it stays. The praying mantis is thus concealed from the insects it feeds on.

In some cases an insect benefits by attracting attention. Insects that are brightly colored are often poisonous or otherwise harmful to predators. After one taste of such an insect, predators learn to avoid the insect. Such body coloring is called **warning coloration**. Ladybird beetles, for example, are inedible. They are usually brightly colored and spotted.

A number of harmless insects have evolved bright coloration similar to that of poisonous or stinging species. Many nonstinging insects, such as the buprestid beetle, have coloring similar to bees and wasps. **Mimicry** is an adaptation in which one organism closely resembles another organism or an object in its natural environment. Predators avoid mimics because the mimics closely resemble harmful species.

29–10 Reproductive Adaptations

The enormous number of insects on this planet reflects their ability to reproduce successfully. Insects generally have a short life span, usually less than a year. During this short time, most species produce large numbers of offspring.

Insects have a number of adaptations that allow males and females of the same species to recognize and attract each other. Many female insects release a specific chemical into the air to attract males. A **pheromone** [FEHR-uh-mohn] is a chemical released by an animal that affects the behavior of others of the same species.

In some insects fertilization of eggs is not always necessary. During most of the year aphids reproduce asexually by laying eggs that are not fertilized. These eggs develop into adult aphids. The development of eggs without fertilization is called **parthenogenesis** [pahr-thuh-noh-JEHN-uh-sihs].

Reproduction is the primary function of adult insects. In the case of mayflies, the adult insect lives for only one day. During a few days in spring, adults emerge in large numbers. They mate, lay eggs, and die within a twenty-four-hour period. Adult mayflies do not even have a digestive system.

29–11   Social Insects

The behavior of social insects is a particularly interesting adaptation. Termites, ants, most bees, and some wasp species live in societies. A **society** is a group of animals that live together and show division of labor. That is, different individuals within the colony perform different jobs. Some jobs of social insects include nest building, caring for the young, getting food, defending the colony, and reproducing. While humans live in societies by choice, social behavior in insects is inborn.

Honeybees are probably the best known social insects. A typical honeybee colony has from 40,000 to 80,000 individuals. Each colony has three types of bees: the queen bee, the worker bees, and the drones. The **queen bee** is the only egg-laying female in the hive. Each hive has only one queen bee. **Worker bees** are nonreproducing females. They care for the young, gather food, and maintain the hive. The male bees, called **drones**, exist only to mate with a queen bee.

A honeybee colony starts when a queen bee leaves the hive and mates with a drone during flight. The sperm she receives during this single mating will fertilize all the eggs she lays during her lifetime. After her mating flight the queen bee returns to the hive and begins laying eggs. Eventually all the members of the hive will be the offspring of this queen.

Figure 29.10 Bees use the cells of the comb to store honey and to raise young.

Do You Know?
A queen bee may lay as many as
200,000 eggs each day.

The hive contains a comb made of six-sided chambers called cells. The queen lays a single egg in each cell. Each egg develops into a larva. After the pupal stage the new bee emerges from the cell and joins the colony.

The sex of a bee is determined by fertilization. Drones develop from unfertilized eggs. Females come from fertilized eggs. A queen bee develops from a female larva that is fed a substance called royal jelly, a food secreted by the workers' bodies. Female larvae not fed royal jelly become workers.

Some worker bees specialize in caring for the queen, making new hive cells, and feeding larvae. Others find and gather flower pollen and nectar. Bees communicate the location of food sources through special body movements. These movements, called a dance, are discussed in Chapter 46.

29–12   Insects and Humans

Humans generally consider insects to be harmful, and it is true that many insects damage valuable plants. Butterflies have been long appreciated for their beauty, but the caterpillars from which they develop can harm plants. The potato beetle, the European corn borer, and the boll weevil do extensive damage to agricultural crops each year.

Some destructive insect species have been accidentally brought to new locations where they have no natural enemies. The gypsy moth, for example, was accidentally released in the United States. Population explosions of gypsy moths periodically occur in various parts of North America. The insects strip leaves from thousands of square kilometers of forest each year.

Figure 29.11 *Left:* The ladybird beetle eats insects that are harmful to plants. *Right:* Gypsy moth caterpillars do extensive damage to forests.

However, many insects are beneficial. For example, humans raise bees for the honey they produce. Honeybees and certain other insects also pollinate flowers. Many important agricultural crops are pollinated by insects. Without insects these crops would not grow.

Other beneficial insects eat harmful insects. The praying mantis, the ladybird beetle, and many parasitic wasps fall into this group.

NEWSBREAK

Pheromones are beginning to be used to control many insect pests. For example, certain insects can be captured and killed in traps containing a sex-attractant pheromone. Unlike toxic insecticides, a pheromone usually affects one species and does not damage the environment.

Scientists are experimenting with pheromones as a method of controlling fire ants. These aggressive ants have invaded large areas of the southern United States. Fire ants inflict painful stings on humans and animals.

The queen of a fire-ant colony produces a specific pheromone that keeps other female ants from becoming fertile queens. As long as the queen is alive, other queens will not be produced in the colony. When the queen dies, numerous females become fertile queens. Each new queen releases the pheromone. When all the queen ants together produce an excess of pheromone, worker ants kill queens until only one queen is left.

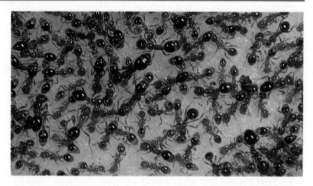

When scientists isolate this particular pheromone, they will spray large amounts of it on a fire-ant colony. The hope is that the worker ants, in response to the excess pheromone, will kill the queen. This action would ensure the elimination of the colony.

Other researchers have isolated the pheromone that fire ants use to establish trails between the colony and food supplies. In test situations, ants will follow trails of the pheromone into poisoned bait traps. Such experimentation with pheromones may lead to a solution to the fire-ant problem.

Checkpoint

1. What function are a mosquito's mouthparts adapted for?
2. What is the term for the adaptation in which one species closely resembles another?
3. Name the process in which certain insects reproduce without fertilization.
4. Identify one kind of social insect.
5. How are insects important in the reproduction of certain plants?

CHAPTER REVIEW

Summary

- Insects are the largest class of arthropods. Insects have three body parts — a head, thorax, and abdomen. Attached to the thorax are three pairs of legs. Most insects have two pairs of wings attached to the thorax.

- During the development from egg to adult, insects go through a series of structural changes called metamorphosis. Some go through a gradual, or incomplete, metamorphosis consisting of three stages. Others go through complete metamorphosis, which has four stages.

- A grasshopper grinds food in its gizzard. Food is digested and absorbed in the midgut. Solid wastes and nitrogen wastes from the Malphigian tubules are eliminated via the anus.

- The nervous system of the grasshopper includes a brain and a typical arthropod ventral nerve cord. Sensory organs detect light, touch, smell, taste, and sound.

- The grasshopper has an open circulatory system and obtains oxygen through tracheae.

- The female grasshopper lays eggs with its ovipositor. Grasshoppers undergo incomplete metamorphosis.

- Insects show many adaptations to particular conditions. Structural, behavioral, and developmental characteristics are used to classify insects. Insect mouthparts are adapted to different functions. Camouflage, warning coloration, and mimicry are adaptations in insects' appearance.

- Insects generally produce large numbers of offspring. Pheromones and parthenogenesis are both reproductive adaptations of insects.

- Insect societies, such as those of honeybees, exhibit division of labor. The queen bee's sole function is reproduction. The workers care for the hive and the larvae. The drones mate with the queen bee.

- Beneficial insects pollinate plants and destroy other insect pests. However, some insects do extensive damage by eating food crops.

Vocabulary

air sac	nymph
aorta	oviduct
caeca	ovipositor
camouflage	parthenogenesis
complete	penis
metamorphosis	pheromone
drone	pupa
incomplete	queen bee
metamorphosis	sensory palp
labium	society
labrum	thorax
metamorphosis	tympanum
midgut	warning coloration
mimicry	worker bee

Review

1. What is the exoskeleton of insects made of?
2. How many pairs of wings do most insects have?
3. The reproductive organs of insects are found in what body section?
4. Which type of metamorphosis has an immature stage that resembles the adult? What is this stage called?
5. Which type of metamorphosis has a stage that is highly specialized for eating?
6. What function are the rear legs of grasshoppers specialized for?
7. Name the four mouthparts of the grasshopper. To what type of diet are they adapted?
8. What is the specialized part of the grasshopper's digestive system that grinds food?

9. Is the grasshopper's circulatory system open or closed? Describe the overall pattern of circulation.
10. What is the male honeybee called? What is its sole function?
11. What is a pheromone?
12. How does camouflage coloring help a prey organism? How does it help a predator?

For questions 13 through 19, match the function or description with the appropriate structure.

13. organ of hearing
14. sense of taste
15. opening to trachea
16. dead-end pouches
17. covers mouthparts
18. digestion and absorption
19. sense of touch

a. caeca
b. labrum
c. midgut
d. palps on labium
e. spiracle
f. hairs on exoskeleton
g. tympanum

Interpret and Apply

1. Describe how a grasshopper's body shows cephalization.
2. Name, in order, the structures that break food into small pieces before it reaches a grasshopper's midgut.
3. The flight muscles of a grasshopper are not attached to the wings themselves. Explain how they can move the wings.
4. What is the primary function of the air sacs in a grasshopper?
5. What are some characteristics of insects that taxonomists use to divide the class into orders?
6. Give an example of how the mouthparts of a specific insect are adapted for a particular kind of feeding.
7. Explain the difference between mimicry and camouflage. Give examples of each.
8. What determines the sex of a honeybee?
9. Explain how division of labor works in the honeybee society.
10. What is unusual about the life stages of mayflies? What is the adaptive function of

this unusual characteristic?
11. Compare complete and incomplete metamorphosis.

Challenge

1. Compare the body plan of insects with the body plan of spiders. In what ways are they similar and in what ways are they different?
2. Why might a flying insect need a more efficient respiratory system than one that does not fly?
3. The monarch butterfly and viceroy butterfly closely resemble each other. Both are brightly colored. The monarch butterfly tastes unpleasant to birds, but the viceroy can be eaten by birds.
   a. How is the monarch butterfly's appearance advantageous to the insect?
   b. How does a viceroy's appearance help it survive?
   c. Suppose that in one meadow there were many viceroys but very few monarchs. In that situation, would the viceroy's coloring greatly improve its chance of survival? Explain.
4. Explain how complete insect metamorphosis is different from the process in which a human baby grows to become an adult.

Projects

1. In a glass container, raise a moth or butterfly caterpillar to maturity. Use caterpillars that you find in your area. Alternatively, your teacher may order eggs of the painted-lady butterfly, which is an easy species to care for in captivity.
2. Do library research to learn how some scientists think it may be possible to use juvenile hormone as a method of insect control. Also find out the drawbacks to this method.

Careers in Invertebrate Biology

Commercial beekeeping, or apiculture, is a highly developed industry in the United States, Canada, and Australia. Each year in the United States, 93 million kilograms of honey and 1.8 million kilograms of beeswax are sold. *Apiculturists* study the social structure and breeding of bees. They conduct research on the causes and treatment of disease within the bee colony. Apiculturists also investigate factors affecting the yield of nectar and pollen on various plants favored by bees. Their goal is to improve bee strains and increase honey and beeswax yields. Experience is often the only requirement for this industry.

Although bees are beneficial insects, many insects and arachnids are major pests of humans. Some insects transmit serious and often fatal diseases. Mosquitoes, fleas, ticks,

lice, and mites can transmit diseases including malaria, African sleeping sickness, typhoid fever, and bubonic plague. Food can be contaminated by houseflies that transmit typhoid fever, cholera, and dysentery.

Pest-control services have contributed enormously to the control of disease. Certified *pest controllers* can exterminate roaches, carpenter ants, and termites from a building. Pest controllers often supervise aerial spraying of crops and mosquito-infested areas. They can even inject livestock with a specialized insecticide that kills bloodsucking insects.

The job of pest controller requires a knowledge of the structural composition of pesticides. Some pesticides are pest specific and do little or no harm to other organisms. Other pesticides persist in the environment and become concentrated and deadly as they move up the food chain. A certified exterminator must pass a state examination.

Entomologists have a Ph.D. in the study of insects and their relationship to plants and animals. They do research to develop new and improved pesticides. They also study biological methods of pest control that use the pests' natural enemies. They examine insect dispersal and habitat preferences. Using this information, they can prevent the dispersal and the subsequent spread of insect pests. *Parasitologists* do the same type of work as entomologists, but they specialize in the study of animal and human parasites such as arachnids and nematodes. They too must have a Ph.D.

The vast majority of insects and arachnids are harmless. To kill them indiscriminately can damage entire industries and individual food chains. A knowledge of the biology and behavior of pest species is necessary before pests can be controlled.

UNIT REVIEW

Synthesis

1. Two invertebrate phyla have only two tissue layers; the members of these phyla also lack organs and organ systems. What are these two phyla? How are these animals able to live without circulatory or excretory systems?
2. Most large organisms have a digestive system with two openings. Why is a one-way digestive system considered to be more advanced than a digestive system with only one opening?
3. Most motile animals with well-developed muscular systems are bilaterally symmetrical and show a degree of cephalization. How is cephalization an advantage for a motile animal? How are cephalization and bilateral symmetry related?
4. Name three phyla that show radial symmetry. How is radial symmetry related to the way in which these animals live?
5. What are the principal characteristics shared by the members of the mollusk phylum? List the major groups within this phylum.
6. How do arthropods differ from the members of all other phyla? List the major classes in this phylum.
7. What characteristics of insects allow them to live on land so successfully?
8. Compare briefly the manner in which gas exchange occurs in the coelenterates, the annelids, the crustaceans, and the terrestrial insects.
9. Which of the invertebrate phyla have a circulatory system? What is the function of a circulatory system?
10. Most freshwater invertebrates have lost the larval stage that is found in the life history of their marine relatives. How may this adaptation be an advantage to a freshwater animal?

Additional Reading

Buchsbaum, Ralph. *Animals without Backbones.* Chicago: University of Chicago Press, 1975.

Caras, Roger. *Venemous Animals of the World.* Englewood Cliffs, NJ: Prentice-Hall, Inc., 1974.

Cousteau, Jacques-Yves, and Philippe Diole. *Octopus and Squid: The Soft Intelligence.* Garden City, NJ: Doubleday, 1973.

Dance, S. Peter. *The World's Shells.* New York: McGraw-Hill Book Co., 1976.

Emerson, William K., and Morris K. Jacobson. *The American Museum of Natural History Guide to Shells.* New York: Alfred A. Knopf, Inc., 1976.

Faulkner, Douglas. *This Living Reef.* New York: Times Books, 1974.

Gosner, Kenneth L. *A Field Guide to the Atlantic Seashore.* (The Peterson Field Guide Series) Boston: Houghton Mifflin, 1979.

Grzimek, Bernard. *Grzimek's Animal Life Encyclopedia.* New York: Van Nostrand Reinhold Co., 1974.

Howe, William H. *The Butterflies of North America.* Garden City, NJ: Doubleday, 1976.

Kaston, B.J. *How to Know the Spiders.* Dubuque, IA: William C. Brown, Co., Pubs., 1978.

Line, Les. *The Audubon Society Book of Marine Wildlife.* New York: Harry N. Abrams, Inc., 1980.

Morris, Percy A. *A Field Guide to Pacific Coast Shells, Including Shells of Hawaii and the Gulf of California.* (The Peterson Field Guide Series) Boston: Houghton Mifflin, 1974.

Patent, Dorothy H. *The World of Worms.* New York: Holiday House, Inc., 1978.

Schisgall, Oscar. *That Remarkable Creature, the Snail.* New York: Julian Messner, 1970.

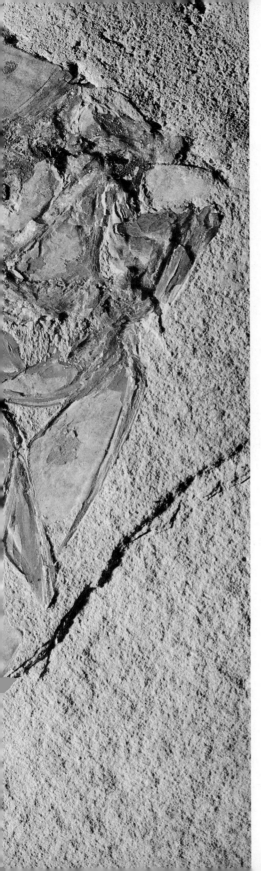

Chordates

Gasteronemus, an ancient fish, preserved as a fossil

443

30 Vertebrates

Urochordates, such as these sea squirts, are close relatives of the vertebrates. These are also called sea peaches.

If you have ever been to a zoo, think about the variety of animals you have seen there. Some are huge, some are small, some have feathers, some have fur, some fly, and some slither. But they all share one important physical characteristic. Each of them has a backbone. Animals without a backbone far outnumber animals with one. Yet animals without backbones are rarely displayed in zoos. Why is this so?

Likewise, the animals you see on a farm also have backbones. Cows, pigs, horses, and chickens all have backbones. The animals people choose as pets generally have backbones. All animals with backbones, including humans, share common characteristics. People tend to be most interested in the animals most closely related to them.

So where does the peculiar-looking organism in this photograph fit in? You are unlikely to see a sea squirt in a zoo. It does not have a backbone. Yet the sea squirt has more in common with a human than with any animal without a backbone.

The Lower Chordates

To see how one animal is related to others, it is important to consider the animal's entire life cycle. Early development often reveals relationships that would be missed by looking only at the adults. Some of the organisms discussed in this chapter would be classified differently if the early stages in their life cycles were not noted.

30–1   What Is a Chordate?

Three basic characteristics distinguish Phylum **Chordata** [kawr–DAH–tah] from all other animal phyla.

1. All chordates have a strong, flexible, rodlike structure called a **notochord** [NOH–tuh–kawrd] at some time in their lives. The notochord runs the length of the organism near the dorsal surface. All chordate embryos have a notochord. However, in most chordate adults the notochord is replaced by a backbone.
2. The second characteristic structure of all chordates is the hollow **dorsal nerve cord**. It lies just above the notochord. The dorsal nerve cord becomes the brain and spinal cord of the adult. The dorsal nerve cord begins to form in the embryo. The outer layer, the ectoderm, folds over to form a hollow tube. In time this tube forms the brain and spinal cord of the adult.
3. Thirdly, all chordates have **gill slits** at some time in their development. Gill slits are paired openings in the wall of the **pharynx** [FAR–ingks]. The pharynx is the throat area just behind the mouth. Perhaps you are familiar with gill slits in fish. Water entering the mouth can pass through the gill slits and out of the body without going through the entire digestive system.

CONCEPTS
- characteristics of chordates
- classification of chordates

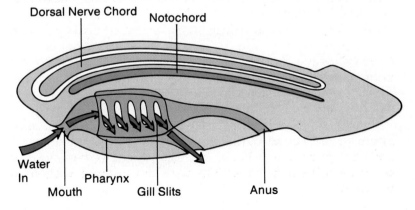

Dorsal Nerve Chord   Notochord

Water In   Mouth   Pharynx   Gill Slits   Anus

Figure 30.1 A generalized chordate diagram

All chordate embryos have a notochord, a dorsal nerve cord, and gill slits. Most chordates, however, lose or modify one or more of these structures as they mature into adults.

Chordates also have many characteristics that are not unique to the group. They all have bilateral symmetry. Their muscle and nerve tissues show definite segmentation. This segmentation is most obvious in embryos. All the chordates have a true coelom.

30–2 The Chordate Subphyla

The chordates are divided into three major subphyla: urochordates, cephalochordates, and vertebrates.

Subphylum Urochordata Of the approximately 2,000 species in the subphylum **urochordates** [yur-uh-KAWR-dayts], all are marine and most are stationary, or sessile. Probably the most common members of this group are the sea squirts.

The chordate characteristics of the urochordates are apparent only in the larva. Figure 30.2 shows a typical sea squirt and its larva. The larva has all three of the typical chordate characteristics. The notochord and the dorsal nerve cord have disappeared in the adult.

The adult urochordate is so simple it even lacks a definite head. It also retains gill slits throughout its life. The gill slits are used in both respiration and feeding. Ciliated cells lining the pharynx sweep water into the mouth and out the gill slits. Here gases are exchanged between the water and the blood. At the same time, small organisms stick to the mucus on the pharynx wall. The ciliated cells sweep the food particles into the digestive tube. Straining water through gill slits in this way is called **filter feeding**.

Urochordates develop as free-swimming larvae. Most urochordate larvae attach to a surface and become sessile adults. Others, however, remain free swimming throughout their lives. Some species of sessile urochordates live as individuals.

Figure 30.2 What chordate characteristics present in the larva of this sea squirt are absent in the adult?

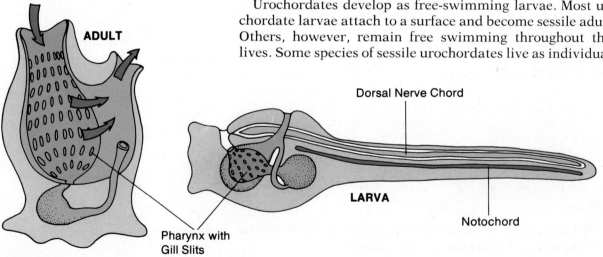

ADULT

Dorsal Nerve Chord

LARVA

Notochord

Pharynx with Gill Slits

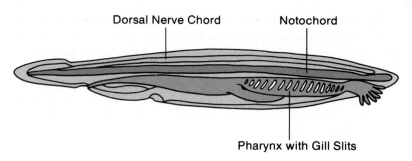

Dorsal Nerve Chord   Notochord

Pharynx with Gill Slits

Others live in colonies, where many individuals share a common outer covering.

Subphylum Cephalochordata   The **cephalochordates** [sehf–uh–loh–KAWR–dayts] are a small group of about 200 species. They live in shallow water near seacoasts. The name *cephalochordate* means "chordate with a head." These animals retain all three of the chordate characteristics throughout their life.

Amphioxus is a typical cephalochordate. It has a notochord, which it retains as an adult. A hollow nerve cord runs the entire length of its body. As in urochordates, the gill slits of *Amphioxus* function in both respiration and filter feeding.

Unlike urochordates, *Amphioxus* has a definite head with sensory organs. It has sensitive "feelers" near the mouth opening. *Amphioxus* also shows clearly segmented muscles. In some ways the cephalochordates are intermediate between the urochordates and the third subphylum, vertebrates [VUR–tuh–brayts].

Subphylum Vertebrata   **Vertebrates** derive their name from the large number of bones that surround and protect the nerve cord. These bones are called **vertebrae**. Vertebrae develop from and replace the notochord.

Vertebrates are by far the largest subphylum of chordates with over 40,000 species. Since humans fall into this category, people tend to divide animals into vertebrates and invertebrates. The division is not particularly logical. You have already seen that the animals are divided into many phyla. The vertebrates are a subphylum of the Phylum Chordata. Look at Figure 30.4. As you can see, vertebrates represent a small segment of the animal kingdom. Dividing the animal kingdom into vertebrates and invertebrates certainly presents the human bias.

Figure 30.3 *Left:* A diagram of *Amphioxus; Right:* This lancelet belongs to the genus *Amphioxus*.

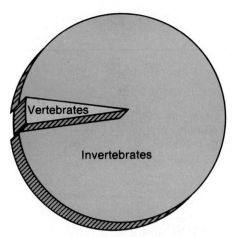

Vertebrates

Invertebrates

Figure 30.4 Species in the animal kingdom

Do You Know?

There are only about 42,000 species of living vertebrates compared to over 1,150,000 species of living invertebrates.

Checkpoint

1. What are the three characteristics common to all chordates?
2. Name the three subphyla of chordates.

- characteristics of vertebrates
- classification of vertebrates
- evolutionary trends in vertebrate classes

Figure 30.5 The endoskeleton of a salamander

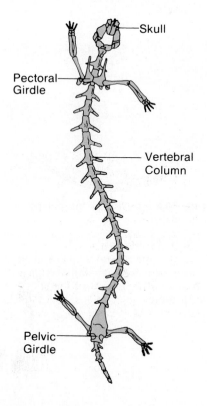

Skull

Pectoral Girdle

Vertebral Column

Pelvic Girdle

The Vertebrates

Vertebrates are called "animals with backbones." They are the most complex organisms in the animal kingdom.

30–3 What Is a Vertebrate?

Vertebrates have unique characteristics in the animal kingdom. Vertebrates have an internal framework known as an **endoskeleton**. The endoskeleton may be made up of cartilage or bone. **Cartilage** is a tough, flexible material. **Bone** is a harder, inflexible material. The vertebrate endoskeleton has many of the same functions as the arthropod exoskeleton. It provides support and protection for soft internal organs. Muscles attach to the skeleton and move the body. But an endoskeleton can grow with the organism. Remember that arthropods must molt, or shed, their exoskeletons in order to grow.

All vertebrate skeletons are built on a similar plan. The **skull** is a group of fused bones protecting the brain. The vertebrae protect the spinal cord. Ribs extend from some of the vertebrae and form the **rib cage**. The rib cage protects many internal organs. The skull, vertebral column, and rib cage form the **axial skeleton**.

In addition to the axial skeleton, most vertebrates have two pairs of limbs. The bones of the anterior limbs are attached to the axial skeleton by bones called the **pectoral** [PEHK-toh-ral] **girdle**. The bones of the posterior limbs attach to the skeleton at the **pelvic girdle**. The two girdles and the limb bones form the **appendicular skeleton**. See Figure 30.5.

In addition to skeletal differences, invertebrates and vertebrates are different in many ways. The vertebrate's circulatory system is more developed than the invertebrate's. Vertebrates have a closed circulatory system; arthropods have an open circulatory system. The heart of a vertebrate is ventral and has specialized chambers; the heart of an arthropod is dorsal. Vertebrates have a dorsal nerve cord and highly developed brain; arthropods have a ventral nerve cord.

30–4 Vertebrate Classification

Most taxonomists divide vertebrates that are now living on Earth into seven classes.

These vertebrate classes are listed in order of their appearance in the fossil record. Jawless fish are the most primitive vertebrates. Birds and mammals appeared most recently.

Class Agnatha

Class Chondrichthyes

Class Amphibia

Class Aves

Class Osteichthyes

Class Mammalia

Class Reptilia

Figure 30.6 The seven classes of vertebrates

1. Class **Agnatha** [AG–nah–thuh]: the jawless fish. There are only a few living species, such as the lamprey and the hagfish. These fish retain the notochord and have a minimal skeleton consisting of only a few cartilage plates in the skull.

2. Class **Chondrichthyes** [kahn-DRICK-thee-eez]: the cartilage fish. Sharks, skates, and rays belong to this group. These fish have a movable jaw attached to the skull. Their skeleton is made entirely of cartilage.

3. Class **Osteichthyes** [ah-stee-IHK-thee-eez]: the bony fish. Most fish belong to this group. Their skeleton is made largely of bone.

4. Class **Amphibia** [am–FIHB–ee–uh]: the first terrestrial animals. Frogs, toads, and salamanders are amphibians. Most go through an aquatic larval stage and have gills. As adults, they have lungs and limbs adapted for life on land.

5. Class **Reptilia** [rehp–TIHL–ee–uh]: the reptiles. Snakes, lizards, turtles, and alligators belong to this group. They reproduce on land by laying eggs.

6. Class **Aves** [AH–vez]: the birds. Birds have feathers and bodies adapted for flight. They reproduce by laying eggs.

7. Class **Mammalia** [mah–MAY–lee–uh]: the mammals. Most mammal young develop internally and after birth are nursed on milk. A few hatch from eggs. Mammals have fur at some time during their lives.

BIOLOGY INSIGHTS

Biologists often arrange groups of organisms to show evolutionary trends toward greater specialization and complexity. Yet every animal living today has specializations that suit its way of life. It is misleading to think of fish as incomplete amphibians, or of reptiles as unformed mammals.

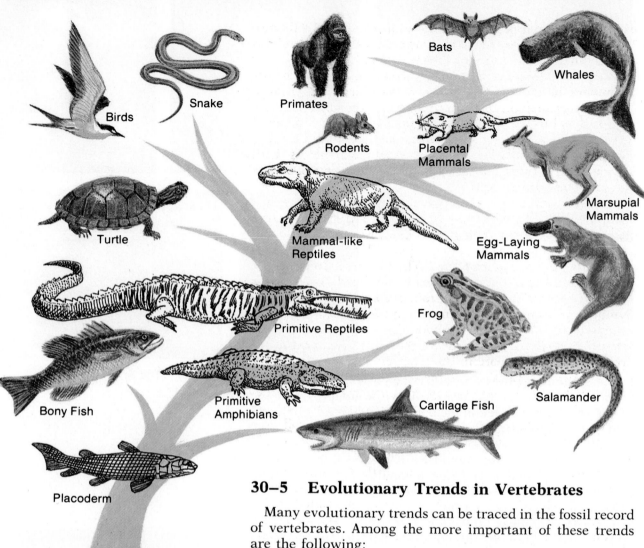

Figure 30.7 A brief summary of vertebrate evolution showing representative examples of the seven vertebrate classes

Birds

Snake

Primates

Bats

Whales

Rodents

Placental Mammals

Marsupial Mammals

Turtle

Mammal-like Reptiles

Egg-Laying Mammals

Primitive Reptiles

Frog

Bony Fish

Primitive Amphibians

Cartilage Fish

Salamander

Placoderm

Jawless Fish

30–5 Evolutionary Trends in Vertebrates

Many evolutionary trends can be traced in the fossil record of vertebrates. Among the more important of these trends are the following:

1. adaptations leading from total dependence on water to survival on land;
2. development of a more complex heart structure;
3. increase in cephalization;
4. increase in the size and complexity of the cerebrum.

One obvious trend in vertebrate history is the evolution of animals that can live on land. The agnathans and the cartilage and bony fish are aquatic. Amphibians are adapted to both water and land. The other classes are primarily terrestrial.

One example of adaptation to life on land is the evolution of varied methods of locomotion. Some vertebrates swim in water, some move on land, and some fly in the air. Adaptations of the basic vertebrate body structure have allowed vertebrates to be successful in each of these environments. Recall the examples of homologous structures in Chapter 14 (Figure 14.12). In each case, the same basic bones of the forelimb are modified to function in different ways.

As the complexity of vertebrates increases, so does the development of the heart. Fish have two-chambered hearts. One chamber receives blood from the body. The other chamber pumps blood to the gills. Amphibians have three-chambered hearts. These hearts are slightly more efficient than a fish's. Birds and mammals have even more efficient hearts, with four chambers. This trend allows for better transport of oxygen and nutrients to the body's cells.

Another evolutionary trend among vertebrates is increasing **cephalization**. Cephalization is the concentration of nerve tissue in the anterior region of an organism. This trend can be traced through the chordate subphyla. Urochordate adults usually do not have a head at all. The cephalochordates have a brain and some sensory organs in the head. In the more recent vertebrate classes, the brain becomes larger. Also the number and complexity of sense organs in the head increase.

Another trend in vertebrate evolution is the increasing development of the anterior part of the brain. This part of the brain is called the **cerebrum**. The cerebrum has many functions, but primary among them is the control of learning and of complex behaviors. Most vertebrates can learn from experience. They can store events in their memory and use past experience to modify behavior. A dog can learn to roll over on command if it has been rewarded for this behavior in the past.

The invertebrates show relatively little learning ability. Among the vertebrates, on the other hand, learning is highly developed. The ability to learn seems to be related to the size of the cerebrum. Scientists compare the size of the cerebrum to total body size. Mammals have the largest cerebrum. Mammals also have the greatest learning capacity.

Among the mammals, human beings are capable of the most complex kinds of learning. The ability to solve problems never before encountered is considered the most complex behavior. Human beings are unequaled in problem solving.

Checkpoint

1. List three functions of an endoskeleton.
2. What are the two major parts of a vertebrate framework?
3. Name the seven classes of vertebrates.
4. Describe four evolutionary trends shown in the vertebrate fossil record.

CHAPTER REVIEW

Summary

- Chordates are animals that have a notochord, a hollow dorsal nerve cord, and gill slits — at least during their early development. There are three subphyla of chordates.
- The urochordates are marine organisms that become sessile and lose the notochord and dorsal nerve cord as adults. They are filter feeders.
- The cephalochordates retain the three chordate characteristics throughout life. These organisms, such as *Amphioxus*, are free–swimming filter feeders.
- Members of the third subphylum, vertebrates, replace the notochord during early development with bones called vertebrae. They have an endoskeleton and are by far the largest group of chordates.
- The vertebrate endoskeleton consists of a central axial skeleton and an appendicular skeleton. The axial skeleton includes the skull, spine, and ribs. The pectoral girdle, pelvic girdle, and limb bones make up the appendicular skeleton.
- All vertebrates have a closed circulatory system and a ventral heart.
- The vertebrates are divided into seven classes: jawless fish, cartilage fish, bony fish, amphibians, reptiles, birds, and mammals.
- Vertebrates have shown evolutionary trends that include adaption to life on land and increasing complexity of the heart and brain.

Vocabulary

Agnatha	filter feeding
Amphibia	gill slits
appendicular	Mammalia
skeleton	notochord
Aves	Osteichthyes
axial skeleton	pectoral girdle
bone	pelvic girdle
cartilage	pharynx
cephalization	Reptilia
cephalochordate	rib cage
cerebrum	skull
Chondrichthyes	urochordate
Chordata	vertebra
dorsal nerve cord	vertebrate
endoskeleton	

Review

For each of the following, select the best answer.

1. Which of the following is a characteristic found *only* in chordates? (a) bilateral symmetry (b) notochord (c) specialized organs (d) the ability to fly
2. In the embryo, the chordate nervous system forms from (a) endoderm, (b) mesoderm, (c) ectoderm, (d) the blastopore.
3. What chordate characteristic is retained in adult urochordates? (a) gill slits (b) nerve cord (c) notochord (d) none of the above
4. The subphylum of chordates containing many sessile and colonial species is (a) urochordates, (b) cephalochordates, (c) vertebrates, (d) all of the above.
5. During development, what structure develops into vertebrae? (a) the dorsal nerve cord (b) the gill slits (c) the ventral nerve cord (d) the notochord

6. The skeleton of most vertebrates is made from (a) cartilage, (b) bone, (c) both a and b, (d) neither a nor b.
7. In vertebrate skeletons, the pelvic girdle is (a) posterior to the pectoral girdle, (b) anterior to the pectoral girdle, (c) dorsal to the pectoral girdle, (d) ventral to the pectoral girdle.
8. Fish without a jaw belong to the vertebrate class (a) Amphibia, (b) Reptilia, (c) Agnatha, (d) Chondrichthyes.
9. Osteichthyes have a skeleton made primarily from (a) cartilage, (b) cellulose, (c) pectin, (d) bone.

Each of the following questions requires a short answer.

10. All chordates have _____ symmetry.
11. Segmentation of nerves and muscles is most obvious during what part of the life cycle of vertebrates?
12. The chordate subphylum with the fewest species is _____.
13. Water is swept into the mouth of most urochordates by the action of _____.
14. Cephalochordates get their name from what structure?
15. Vertebrae support and protect the _____ of vertebrates.
16. What bones make up the appendicular skeleton?
17. All vertebrates have a _____ circulatory system.

Interpret and Apply

1. In what ways are vertebrates and arthropods different in structure?
2. Why are cephalochordates considered intermediate between urochordates and vertebrates?

3. Fill in the chart.

Subphylum	Chordate Characteristics in Embryo	Chordate Characteristics in Adult
Urochordates		
Cephalochordates		
Vertebrates		

Challenge

1. Scientists sometimes refer to the invertebrate chordates. What animals are these?
2. What are some of the major trends in the evolution of vertebrates?
3. Elephants and whales have much larger brains than humans. Yet humans are more intelligent than either of these animals. What accounts for human intelligence?
4. Explain the importance of studying the development of embryos in classifying chordates.

Projects

1. What makes some scientists think chordates evolved from echinoderms? Research the evidence and present your findings to the class.
2. Research the brain sizes and body sizes of various vertebrates. Make a graph that compares the brain sizes of various vertebrates to their body size. What conclusions can you make from your graph? Present your results to the class.
3. If you live near a freshwater pond, find some tadpoles and set them up in a classroom aquarium. Watch the process of change from tadpole to adult frog. (Check with local laws first. In some states it is illegal to collect tadpoles.)

31 Fish

A school of parrot fish

As water dwellers, fish are uniquely and extraordinarily well adapted to their environment. Fish live in a medium more dense than air. If you have ever tried to run in water, you understand how much more dense it is. Yet fish move easily and rapidly through water. Their design is an adaptation to life in water. The smooth lines of their body allow them to "slide" through the water. Instead of legs for walking, fish are equipped with fins, which push or pull them through their water environment.

Even fish behavior is adapted to water existence. Fish generally move *within* their medium rather than *on* it. They are vulnerable to attack from all sides. Many types of fish — including the parrot fish in the picture — swim in groups called schools. Schooling behavior provides many protections. If one fish in the school is wounded, the school can sense this and avoid the danger. Schools also present larger, but more intimidating targets for other fish.

Fish are the oldest vertebrates in the fossil record. Hundreds of millions of years of natural selection may have served to strengthen these adaptations.

Class Agnatha: The Jawless Fish

Fish are not only the most common vertebrates; they also have the longest history. Fossil fish have been found in rocks as old as 480 million years. This is more than 100 million years before the first evidence of land-living vertebrates. The oldest fossil fish were unmistakably fish. Their bodies were fish-shaped, and they had scales and fins. Yet they were different from anything swimming in the oceans today. They were heavily armored animals with no moving jaw.

31–1   Primitive Fish

The earliest fish in the fossil record were members of the class **Agnatha** [ag-NATH-uh]. *Agnatha* means "jawless." The most primitive of these jawless fish were the **ostracoderms**. Ostracoderms had a true endoskeleton with vertebrae surrounding their spinal cord. They were filter feeders that had no moving jaw. They used their pharyx and gill slits to strain food from the water. It is probable that these fish also used their gill slits to get oxygen from the water. In most modern fish, the gill slits are used entirely for gas exchange. Use of the gills for feeding has been abandoned.

CONCEPTS

• first vertebrates in the fossil record — jawless fish

Do You Know?

Ostracoderms became widely distributed over Earth's oceans before they all died out about 350 million years ago. Their extinction was speeded by the evolution of predatory jawed fish called placoderms, which took over the seas until they were, in turn, replaced by other forms.

Figure 31.1 This fossil shows an ostracoderm, the earliest known fish.

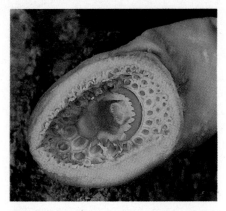

Figure 31.2 The circular shape of the lamprey's mouth identifies it as a jawless fish.

Today there are only a few species of jawless fish remaining. They are called **cyclostomes** [SY-kluh-stohmz] and are quite different from the early ostracoderms. The jawless fish living today, like the lamprey and the hagfish, are parasites and scavengers. The lamprey shown in Figure 31.2 is a typical cyclostome. The lamprey's circular mouth is modified and serves as a suckerlike device. The lamprey attaches to the bodies of other fish. Its filelike tongue then cuts through the skin of the host fish. This allows the lamprey to feed on blood and tissues.

In addition to lacking a jaw, the lamprey has several other features that biologists consider primitive. The lamprey, for example, does not have paired fins like those found in all other fish. Swimming is accomplished by snakelike movements of the body. Another primitive feature is the presence of multiple gill slits. Gill slits allow water that passes over the gills to leave the body.

The lamprey skeleton is also very primitive. The notochord remains in the adult. The internal skeleton consists of the skull, which is made of **cartilage** [KAHR-tuh-lihj]. Cartilage is a strong, flexible material that makes up some of the endoskeleton of all vertebrates. You have some cartilage in the tip of your nose and in your ears.

Lampreys are a serious nuisance to the fishing industry in the Great Lakes. Lampreys have moved into the Great Lakes and caused enormous damage to the trout-fishing industry. Hagfish are scavengers rather than parasites but they attack fish trapped in fishing nets.

Checkpoint

1. The jawless fish belong to the _____ class.
2. Name two examples of jawless fish.

Class Chondrichthyes: The Cartilage Fish

A fish with a movable jaw can grasp, chew, and crush; it can be a predator. The **placoderms** were an early group of fish with jaws. Now extinct, the placoderms were replaced by other fish. One group with placoderm ancestors is the cartilage fish.

Chondrichthyes [kahn-DRIHK-thee-eez] are jawed fish that have an endoskeleton made of cartilage. Sharks, skates, and rays are the best-known members of this group.

Sharks are typical cartilage fish. Yet they are perhaps the most dramatic. In this section, the characteristics of the shark will represent the typical cartilage fish.

31–2 Skeleton and Movement of the Shark

Every vertebrate has an endoskeleton made of cartilage at the beginning of its life. As most vertebrates mature into adults, the cartilage skeleton is replaced by bone. Adult Chondrichthyes, however, retain a cartilage skeleton all of their lives.

Sharks have a skeleton made entirely of cartilage. This type of skeleton provides flexibility. Sharks have two sets of paired fins. The front pair is called the **pectoral** [PEHK-tur-uhl] **fins**. The rear pair is called **pelvic fins**. These paired fins are found in most fish except the Agnatha. The paired fins allow the shark to turn or move up and down in the water. The large tail fin of the shark pushes from side to side and propels the fish forward. If a shark stops swimming, it will sink to the bottom. The body of a shark is denser than water.

CONCEPTS

- characteristics of cartilage fish
- respiration and reproduction of sharks
- diversity of cartilage fish

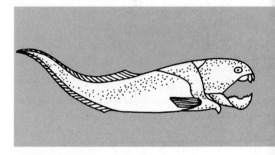

Figure 31.3 Placoderms were an ancient group of fish with powerful jaws.

Do You Know?

It was once thought that sharks had to keep swimming all of their lives in order to breathe. However, the discovery of sleeping sharks, lying stationary on the sea floor, has dispelled this theory for some species.

Figure 31.4 The front pair of fins on the shark are pectoral fins; the rear pair are pelvic fins.

Figure 31.5 Notice the shape and angle of teeth in the shark's jaw. Why do the teeth slant backward?

31–3 Shark Skin and Teeth

Shark skin feels like sandpaper. It is covered with small, spiny projections called **placoid [PLAK-oid] scales**. Placoid scales are made of the same material as your teeth. In fact, the teeth of the shark appear to be large versions of these scales. Biologists hypothesize that the teeth of the shark evolved from scales surrounding the jaw. Fish possessing these special "scales" near the mouth might have been favored by selection. Shark teeth are triangular in shape and very sharp. The teeth tend to slant backward in the mouth. This helps to prevent food from slipping out once the shark bites into it. The teeth grow in rows. As new teeth grow, the teeth in the front row fall out and are replaced by others growing in from behind.

31–4 Gas Exchange in the Shark

Sharks, like all cartilage fish, have **gills**. The gills remove oxygen from the surrounding water and release waste carbon dioxide into the water. Gills are composed of many folded tissues containing blood vessels. The folded structure of the gills provides a large surface area for the exchange of gases. Water enters the mouth of the shark and passes across the gills. Oxygen from the water passes into the blood in the gills. Carbon dioxide passes from the blood into the surrounding water. Each gill opens to the outside through a gill slit.

31–5 Temperature Regulation in Fish

Sharks, like most fish, are **cold-blooded**. This term has nothing to do with the shark's disposition. Cold-blooded animals do not maintain a constant body temperature. Therefore, as their surroundings get colder, their body temperature drops. Likewise, as their surroundings get warmer, their body temperature increases. Water does not change temperature as quickly as air does. Thus, fish are able to survive without the ability to maintain their body temperature. They simply must stay in water that provides the temperature their bodies need to function.

Figure 31.6 The gills of a shark provide the surface for the exchange of oxygen and carbon dioxide.

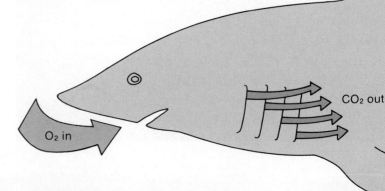

CO_2 out

O_2 in

31–6 Shark Reproduction

The method of reproduction in sharks is somewhat unusual for fish. Sharks have internal fertilization. That is, sperm are deposited in the body of the female by the male. In some shark species, the fertilized eggs are enclosed by a leathery egg case. The female deposits these in the water. The young sharks then develop on their own. In many shark species, however, the female retains the eggs inside her body until the embryos have developed. The eggs hatch, and the young are born live. Newly born sharks are independent, and they receive no care from their mothers.

Figure 31.7 Newborn sharks develop on their own; they receive no care from their mother.

31–7 Rays and Skates

Rays — and their close relatives the skates — are also Chondrichthyes. They have the same general characteristics as sharks, but their bodies are greatly flattened. The pectoral fins are expanded and merge along the length of the body. As you can see in Figure 31.8, most rays and skates are adapted to living on the ocean bottom.

Figure 31.8 *Left:* A ray has a flattened body that is an adaptation for life at the ocean bottom. *Right:* Skates are closely related to rays.

Bottom-dwelling rays have their mouths on the ventral surface, which is often buried in the sand. This makes it impossible to take water into the mouth for gas exchange at the gills. In these rays, water enters through two openings on the top of the head. It passes through the gills and out the gill slits on the bottom. Although most skates and rays are bottom dwellers, some, like the manta ray, swim freely in the ocean.

Checkpoint

1. The shark skeleton is made of _____ .
2. What kinds of animals belong to the class Chondrichthyes?
3. The paired front fins of the shark are called the _____ fins.
4. Shark skin is covered with _____ .

Class Osteichthyes: The Bony Fish

Bony fish show a variety of sizes and structures that do not occur in the cartilage fish. The bony fish are adapted to a wide range of environments and patterns of life. They range in size from the tiny guppy to the 400-kilogram tuna. In shape, they range from the sleek barracuda to the elegant sea horse.

Over 90 percent of the fish belong to the class **Osteichthyes** [ah-stee-IHK-thee-eez], the bony fish. Like all vertebrates, bony fish begin development by forming a skeleton of cartilage. While sharks retain cartilage throughout their life, bony fish and other vertebrates grow bone to replace the cartilage. Bone is a tissue made of mineral deposits produced by specialized bone cells.

While there is enormous variety within bony fish, the perch is a typical member of the class. A description of the internal and external structure of the perch applies in general to the other members of the class.

31–8   External Anatomy of the Perch

The external covering of the perch is different from that of the shark. The perch has overlapping scales arranged like shingles on a roof. The scales of different bony fish vary in size and shape. The primary functions of all scales are to protect the fish and to prevent water from entering or leaving the body.

A fish will have the same number of scales its entire life. Adult fish do not grow new scales. The scales' rate of growth varies with the seasons. As a result, annual lines form in the scales. You can judge a fish's age by the number of dark, concentric lines on one of its scales.

Have you ever held a live fish? You probably noticed how slimy it felt. The perch has glands that secrete a slippery mucus, which covers the scales. The mucus protects against microorganisms. It also gives the fish a smooth surface, which eases movement through the water.

The perch has several types of fins. The fins are made of thin membranes. Within the membranes are supporting cartilage rays. The perch has a pair of **dorsal fins** along the back, a **caudal fin** on the tail, and a ventral **anal fin**. These fins are all located on the midline of the fish. Just as feathers on an arrow keep the arrow traveling in a straight line, these fins help the fish swim in a straight line.

In addition to the midline fins, there are two sets of lateral,

Figure 31.9 The annual lines on the scales of an adult fish can be used to determine its age.

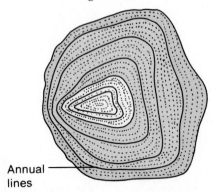

Annual lines

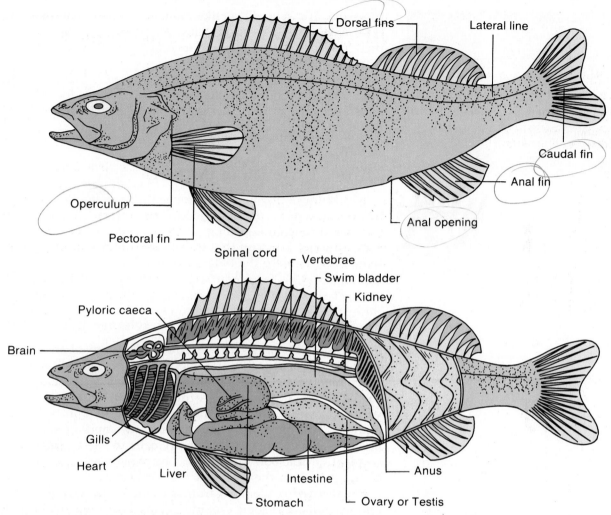

Figure 31.10 *Top:* The external structure of the perch
Bottom: The internal structure of the perch

paired fins. On the sides near the gill openings are two pectoral fins, and just below these are the two pelvic fins. The tail fin moves the fish forward through the water. The other fins help the fish maintain balance and change direction. In some bony fish, the pectoral and pelvic fins aid the tail fin in producing forward motion.

31–9   Digestion in the Perch

The perch is carnivorous. Small, sharp teeth help it grasp and hold prey. The mouth leads into a short tube called the **esophagus**. The esophagus leads to the stomach, where food is broken down into a soupy consistency. From the stomach, food enters the **intestine**. In the intestine, enzymes reduce the food to small molecules that can be absorbed into the blood. Also, located near the junction of the stomach and

intestine are several saclike pouches called **pyloric caeca** [py-LAWR-ihk-SEE-kuh]. Digestion and absorption occur in these pouches as well. Food that cannot be digested is expelled from the body through the anus.

The **liver** is an organ with many functions. Several of its functions are related to digestion. The liver produces **bile**, a substance that helps enzymes in the digestive system break down fats. The liver also stores sugar for future energy needs.

31–10 Excretion in the Perch

The **kidneys** are a pair of long, thin organs that remove nitrogen wastes from the blood. The wastes leave the body as **urine** through an opening just behind the anus. The kidneys serve another function that is especially important to marine fish. They regulate the balance of water and salt in the fish's tissues.

31–11 Circulation and Gas Exchange in the Perch

Figure 31.11 shows the circulatory system of the perch. Three kinds of vessels carry blood through the fish. **Arteries** carry blood away from the heart, and **veins** carry blood back to the heart. **Capillaries** are microscopic vessels that have very thin walls. Because their walls are so thin, nutrients and oxygen diffuse from the blood in the capillaries into the body cells. This fuel enables body cells to carry out cellular respiration. Carbon dioxide and nitrogen wastes diffuse out of the cells into the blood in the capillaries.

Blood entering the heart from the body is depleted of oxygen and is rich in carbon dioxide. Veins returning blood from the body empty into a sac just behind the heart. This sac is called the **sinus venosus**. From here blood enters the heart itself.

The fish's heart is a muscular pump with two separate chambers. The first chamber of the heart is called the **atrium** [AY-tree-uhm]. Blood is pushed by contractions of the atrium into the second chamber, called the **ventricle** [VEHN-trih-kuhl]. This ventricle, in turn, pushes blood through a large blood vessel, the **ventral aorta**, to the gills. In the gill capillaries, blood picks up oxygen from the water and releases carbon dioxide. The blood then enters the **dorsal aorta** and travels to all parts of the body. As it passes through the various organs, the blood gives up its oxygen and nutrients to the body cells. It then carries off the carbon dioxide and wastes. As in the earthworm, the circulatory system of fish and all other vertebrates is closed.

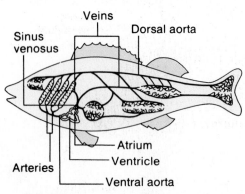

Figure 31.11 Circulatory system of a perch

As in the shark, respiration occurs at the perch's gills. The perch takes water in through its mouth. Then, by raising the floor of its mouth, the perch forces water over its gills. The water leaves through a single slit on each side of the head. This single opening for gills is typical of bony fish, whereas the cyclostomes and Chondrichthyes have several gill slits. The **operculum** [oh-PUR-kyuh-luhm] is a semicircular covering on the side of the head that protects the delicate gill tissue from damage. You can see the operculum move on a live fish as water moves over its gills.

Figure 31.12 shows the detailed structure of the perch gills. There are four **gill arches** on each side of the head. Each arch is supported by a piece of cartilage. On the front of each arch are folded tissues called **gill rakers**, which keep food particles from passing through the gills and damaging delicate tissue. The gills themselves have capillaries, which exchange gases with the water passing over each gill.

Gases also enter and leave the blood in another organ called the **swim bladder**. The swim bladder has no respiratory function. It acts as a gas bag, which functions to control the fish's depth. Changing the volume of gas in the bladder allows the fish to change its depth in the water.

31–12   The Perch's Nervous System

Perch have a well-developed brain and spinal cord. The brain, as shown in Figure 31.13, has five major parts.

1. The **olfactory** [ohl-FAK-tur-ee] **bulb** brings information about smell from the nostrils to the brain via the olfactory nerve.
2. The **cerebrum** [suh-REE-bruhm] consists of the swollen areas and is primarily involved in the interpretation of smell.
3. Behind the cerebrum are the **optic lobes**, which process visual information. These lobes also send impulses to muscles, so the fish responds to what it sees.
4. Located behind the optic lobes is the **cerebellum** [sehr-uh-BEHL-uhm], a structure that coordinates complex muscle movements.
5. Under the cerebellum is the **medulla**, which controls the internal organs of the fish.

The spinal cord continues from the medulla down the vertebral column. The spinal cord is the major pathway for information passing between the body and brain. Nerves branch from the brain and spinal cord. **Cranial nerves** branch from the brain itself, and **spinal nerves** branch from the spinal cord.

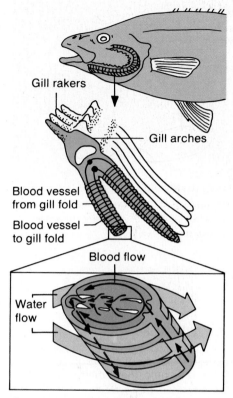

Figure 31.12 The gills of a perch

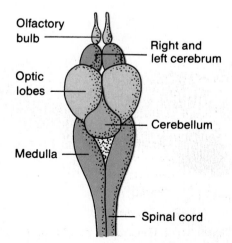

Figure 31.13 The brain of a perch

Lateral line

Figure 31.14 The lateral line of a fish is used to sense changes in water pressure.

Do You Know?

There is evidence that fish can smell different kinds of plants in the water. This may help them maintain location or seek out likely spots for food. The ability of the salmon to find the precise stream where it hatched has been shown to be due to the sense of smell.

31–13   The Perch's Senses

The sense of smell is very important to the perch. Two olfactory sacs located internally near the mouth contain nerve endings. These endings are very sensitive to chemicals dissolved in the water. Cells sensitive to taste are also located in and around the mouth.

Despite its large eyes and large optic lobes, the perch does not see very well. Most fish see only things that are quite close to them. However, most fish can visually detect movement at limited distances.

Near the back of the brain, the fish has a pair of **semicircular canals,** which are involved in the fish's sense of balance and hearing. The perch does not have external ears. But it probably hears sounds transmitted through the body and the skull bones to the semicircular canals.

All fish, including cyclostomes and sharks, have a sense organ called the **lateral line,** which functions very differently from any human sense organ. The lateral line runs along each side of the fish's body. It is sensitive to pressure changes in the water. Fish use this sense to detect nearby movement. Fish that form schools use the lateral line to locate others in the school and to synchronize changes in direction.

31–14   Reproduction in the Perch

The female perch produces eggs in **ovaries**. The male produces sperm cells in **testes**. In either case, the reproductive cells leave the body through an opening just behind the anus. Fertilization in the perch, unlike the shark, is external. The female lays several hundred eggs in the water. The male swims near the eggs and releases **milt** into the water. Milt is a fluid containing the sperm cells. Fertilization occurs in the open water, and the parents swim away without protecting the young.

This seems to be an inefficient way of reproducing. Many eggs are never fertilized. Those that are left are unprotected and eaten by predators. If it were not for the large number of eggs that are fertilized, survival of enough perch to continue the species would be doubtful.

31–15   Adaptations of the Bony Fish

Fish are adapted to their specialized environments in many ways. At the beginning of this chapter, you read about some of these adaptations to life in water. Some more specific adaptations are discussed in this section.

Saltwater Fish   Some bony fish are adapted to fresh water while others are adapted to salt water. Saltwater and freshwater fish have opposite problems with maintaining the salt balance in their bodies. Salt water has a higher concentration of salts than is found in blood. Thus saltwater bony fish tend to lose water from their cells by osmosis. Scales, which are impermeable to water, help prevent the loss. Also, the gills of saltwater fish actively transport salt *out* of the body. Their kidneys excrete only small amounts of highly concentrated urine. This helps them to conserve water in their bodies.

Freshwater Fish Freshwater fish have the opposite problem. They tend to absorb water from their surroundings by osmosis. The scales of freshwater fish, therefore, keep water out of the body. In addition, the gills of these fish actively transport what little salt there is in the surroundings *into* the body. Kidneys help by excreting large volumes of excess water. Only a few bony fish, such as the salmon, can go from fresh to salt water and back. The gills and kidneys of these fish can reverse their water and salt transport functions.

Life Cycles Salmon have an extraordinary life cycle. They hatch in freshwater streams, then swim to the sea. They live out most of their adult lives in the ocean. When they are mature, they exhibit a very strong homing instinct. Adult salmon leave the open ocean and return to the same freshwater stream of their birth. Here they reproduce and die. The new generation spawned here will return to this same stream to reproduce and die.

Feeding Other adaptations of bony fish are related to feeding. The sharp teeth of the barracuda are characteristic of predators. The barracuda's streamlined shape is an adaptation for swift pursuit of its prey. The hard, beaked tooth of the parrot fish is used to scrape algae from rocks. The strange wormlike appendage on the head of the anglerfish attracts prey in the same way that a worm on a fishhook attracts fish.

Figure 31.15 Salmon swim from the ocean back to the freshwater stream of their birth to spawn.

Figure 31.16 The parrot fish uses a hard beak-like tooth to scrape algae from rocks.

Fish   **465**

NEWSBREAK

Humans learned thousands of years ago how to farm the land. Many research programs are now underway to learn how to farm lakes and oceans, a technique called *aquaculture*. The Chinese produce millions of metric tons of carp each year in freshwater aquaculture ponds. The Chinese produce more fish in this way than is caught each year by the entire United States fishing industry. Aquaculture programs in the United States currently produce catfish. Just as farmers have cultivated genetically superior wheat and corn, artificial selection of salmon and trout has produced fish that grow faster and larger than their wild counterparts. What advances in the field of aquaculture have made the news in recent years?

Figure 31.17 Color is used by some fish as a means of recognition or defense against predators.

Coloration Some bony fish have brilliant colors. The distinctive coloring allows males and females of the same species to recognize one another. Distinctive coloration can also be a defensive adaptation. Potential enemies of the lion-fish have learned to recognize its bright colors and, therefore, to avoid its poisonous spines. The flounder uses its ability to change color for camouflage.

Deep-Ocean Fish Some remarkable adaptations are seen in the bony fish of very deep seas. Very little light reaches depths below 150 meters. At these depths some fish generate their own light. In some cases deep-sea fish have lights that attract mates; others have lights that lure prey.

Reproductive Behavior The bony fish show many variations in reproductive structures and behavior. While most bony fish carry out external fertilization, some fertilize internally and bear live young. A number of these live-bearing fish, such as guppies, are popular in home aquariums. Some fish are mouthbreeders. In these fish, eggs are fertilized externally. The female (or the male in some species) then takes the eggs into its mouth and holds them there until they hatch. A few fish even build nests for their eggs and guard them carefully until their eggs hatch.

Lungfish There are several fish that have special adaptations for breathing air. The African lungfish lives in ponds that dry up completely for one season of the year. In the pond, the lungfish uses gills for respiration. Before the pond dries, the lungfish buries itself in the mud. It leaves a small passageway for air to enter the hole. The fish draws this air into a structure called a **lung**. A lung is an organ that is used to exchange oxygen and carbon dioxide with the atmosphere. The lungfish can survive in its mudhole until the next rainy season fills the pond.

31–16 Fossil Osteichthyes

The fossil record shows that ancestral Chondrichthyes and Osteichthyes evolved from placoderms about 380 million years ago. Soon after their appearance, the bony fish divided into three distinct groups. One group, quite common at that time, was the lungfish. The lungfish are represented today by only three genera. The second group successfully radiated into the many thousands of species that now occupy the waters of the world.

A third group, called the lobe-finned fish, also appears early in the fossil record. Scientists thought that these fish had become extinct about 70 million years ago. But in 1938, a fishing boat in the Indian Ocean found a strange-looking fish in its nets. The fish was a **coelacanth** [SEE-luh-kanth], a lobe-finned fish.

Scientists think of this fish as a "living fossil." They are especially interested in it for another reason. Notice in Figure 31.18 that the pectoral and pelvic fins of this fish are on the ends of fleshy stalks. Many scientists think that this fish is descended from a common ancestor of the first vertebrates that walked on land with four legs.

Figure 31.18 The coelacanth is the only known lobe-finned fish alive today.

Checkpoint

1. What is the major difference between the Chondrichthyes and the Osteichthyes?
2. The saclike pouches in the perch's digestive system are called _____ .
3. The protective covering of the gills in bony fish is called a(n) _____ .
4. The two muscular chambers of the perch's heart are the _____ and the _____ .
5. The largest part of the perch brain, where visual information is interpreted, is the _____ .
6. Schools of fish depend on which sense organ?
7. In most bony fish, where does fertilization take place?
8. Give two functions of bright coloration in fish.
9. Coelacanths are examples of what kind of bony fish?

CHAPTER REVIEW

Summary

- The first vertebrates to appear in the fossil record were the jawless fish. Only a few organisms alive today, such as the lamprey and the hagfish, represent the class Agnatha. Without a movable jaw, these fish are parasites or scavengers.

- The placoderms evolved from the Agnatha but they had a movable jaw. The Chondrichthyes with cartilage skeletons and the Osteichthyes with bony skeletons evolved from the placoderms.

- In all fish, gills are used for respiration. Another major characteristic of fish is the presence of paired pectoral and pelvic fins. Sharks, skates, and rays are the major living members of the Chondrichthyes.

- There are more species of bony fish than any other vertebrate group. The anatomy of the perch is typical of the group. The following systems are present in the perch:
  1. a digestive system to break down food into small molecules that can travel to body cells through the blood;
  2. a two-chambered heart that pumps blood in a closed loop, from the heart to the gills to the body cells and back to the heart;
  3. four pairs of gills that take oxygen from the water and deposit carbon dioxide in the water;
  4. a reproductive system that produces egg or sperm cells for external fertilization.

- Within the many species of bony fish, there are various adaptations for specific environments.

- The bony fish have a long history in the fossil record. One of the most unusual fish is the coelocanth, which is a lobe-finned fish. It is thought to be a descendant of the fish that gave rise to the first land-living vertebrates.

Vocabulary

Agnatha	liver
anal fin	lung
arteries	medulla
atrium	milt
bile	olfactory bulb
capillaries	operculum
cartilage	optic lobe
caudal fin	Osteichthyes
cerebellum	ostracoderms
cerebrum	ovary
Chondrichthyes	pectoral fins
coelacanth	pelvic fins
cold-blooded	placoderm
cranial nerves	placoid scales
cyclostomes	pyloric caeca
dorsal aorta	semicircular canals
dorsal fins	sinus venosus
esophagus	spinal nerves
gill arches	swim bladder
gill rakers	testes
gills	urine
intestine	veins
kidney	ventral aorta
lateral line	ventricle

Review

1. The first fish in the fossil record are ____ .
2. ____ is the most distinguishing characteristic of the lamprey.
3. Ostracoderms obtained food through the process called ____ .
4. The lamprey and hagfish are classified as ____ , a group which does not include the ostracoderms.
5. Give one example of a lamprey characteristic that is considered primitive.
6. What structure does the lamprey retain in adulthood that other fish do not?
7. The posterior paired fins of fish are called ____ fins.

8. Biologists think that shark teeth evolved from _____ .

9. Fertilization in sharks is _____ .

10. The largest class of fish is _____ .

11. The _____ is the tube that carries food from the mouth to the stomach.

12. Nitrogen wastes are removed from fish by _____ .

13. Vessels which carry blood to the heart are called _____ .

14. The vessel in perch that carries blood away from the gills is called the _____ .

15. Information about smell goes to the _____ of the brain.

16. Coordination of the muscle movements of the perch is under the control of the _____ .

17. What organs in the perch produce eggs? Sperm?

18. _____ and _____ are two organs of bony fish involved in maintaining salt balance.

19. Saltwater fish lose water from their body cells by _____ .

20. _____ is a country that produces more fish per year by cultivation than are caught by the entire United States fishing fleet.

For questions 21–25, match the organ with the system. You may use an answer more than once.

21. liver	**a.** nervous system
22. capillaries	**b.** digestive system
23. sinus venosus	**c.** circulatory system
24. spinal cord	**d.** reproductive system
25. ovaries	

For questions 26–30, match the characteristic with the group. You may use an answer more than once.

26. first jawed fish	**a.** chondrichthyes
27. no paired fins	**b.** placoderms
28. cartilage skeleton as adult	**c.** ostracoderms
29. swim bladder	**d.** Osteichthyes
30. round mouth used as sucker	**e.** cyclostomes
	f. Agnatha

Interpret and Apply

1. What fish groups possess a jaw? Paired fins? Gills for respiration? Cartilage skeleton? Individual gill slits for each gill arch?

2. Explain the function of paired fins in the fish that have them.

3. What is the basic difference between sharks and rays?

4. Why do gills have a large surface area?

5. What is unique about the way water enters the gills of a ray?

6. What are two functions of fish scales?

7. Explain the function of the swim bladder.

8. What are two functions of the liver?

9. Compare reproduction in sharks and in bony fish.

10. Describe one specific adaptation of deep-sea fish and explain the function.

11. Why were scientists particularly interested in the coelacanth?

Challenge

1. Why are there no predators among the Agnatha?

2. Give an explanation of how shark teeth might have evolved by natural selection.

3. Describe the path of a single blood cell on one trip around the circulatory system of a perch.

4. In what ways is the world sensed by fish similar to your own? In what ways is it different?

Projects

1. Find out about some of the adaptations shown by different species of sharks. Report your findings to the entire class.

2. If there is a local fish hatchery or fish-stocking program, try to arrange a visit to see firsthand how people are involved in conservation programs for fish.

32 Amphibians

South American tree frog of the genus *Dendrobates*

Some people think that if you touch a toad, warts will grow on your skin. While there is absolutely no truth to this belief, you would be wise never to touch a frog like the one shown here. This colorful frog lives in South America. Although it is beautiful to look at, touching it would be very dangerous. Its skin secretes a powerful poison. Local natives use this substance to make poison-tipped arrows.

Poisonous frogs are relatively rare. If you live in North America, you will probably never encounter such a dangerous frog. The frogs you are familiar with live near ponds. You may also have seen brown toads on your lawn or in a garden. Around ponds or on moist forest floors, you are also likely to find salamanders that frequent these areas.

Frogs, toads, and salamanders represent a group of related vertebrates whose lives are closely dependent on the moisture of their environments. In many ways, these animals are intermediates between the fishes that live in water and the vertebrates that live entirely on land.

Characteristics of Amphibians

Biologists divide amphibians into three orders. The order **Anura** [ah-NUR-uh] includes the frogs and toads. The order **Urodela** [yuro-DE-la] contains the salamanders — sometimes called newts. The order **Apoda** [AY-pod-uh] is an uncommon group of legless amphibians that live in tropical regions. All modern amphibians live in or near fresh water.

32–1   From Water to Land

Amphibian [am-FIHB-ee-uhn] means "dual life." Amphibians hatch from eggs as fishlike larvae. These larvae have fins for swimming, gills for gas exchange, and a circulatory system similar to that of a fish. At some point in their lives, however, most amphibians undergo metamorphosis, changing into an adult form that will live on land. Adult amphibians generally have four legs for movement on land and lungs for gas exchange in the air. They also have a more complex circulatory system than that of the larvae.

All amphibians have smooth skin without scales. Their skin is often covered with mucus and must be kept moist. For all amphibians, the skin is an important respiratory surface.

Like fish, all amphibians are cold-blooded. Since they cannot control their internal body temperature, most species of amphibians live in areas where the temperature shows little variation. Species that do live where it is very hot or very cold have special adaptations that allow them to survive.

CONCEPTS
- orders of amphibians
- adaptations to life on land

Do You Know?
The animal commonly called the horned toad is not a toad at all. It is not even an amphibian. It is a lizard (a reptile).

Figure 32.1 A salamander shows characteristics typical of amphibians. Notice that it has smooth skin.

Checkpoint

1. What does the word *amphibian* mean?
2. Name the three orders of amphibians.

A Typical Amphibian: The Frog

CONCEPTS
- external anatomy of the frog
- internal anatomy of the frog

Frogs and toads do not have tails. This characteristic distinguishes the order Anura from other amphibians. The bodies of frogs and toads are broad and flat with no distinct neck. Anurans all have very large hind legs specialized for jumping. All adult frogs and toads are carnivorous. They eat worms, insects, insect larvae, and other small animals. Larvae of frogs are called **tadpoles** or polliwogs. Tadpoles have a tail but no legs. They have gills, and they eat plants.

32–2 External Anatomy of the Frog

The skin of a frog is smooth and unlike the scaly skin of a fish. Frog skin is very permeable to water. Frogs do not drink water because they absorb all the water they need through their skin. Because their skin is permeable, however, frogs can dry out when exposed to air. Frogs cannot stay in direct sun for long periods without moistening their skin.

Do You Know?

Some toads have glands in their skin that secrete poison. The poison is bad-tasting and causes enough irritation that most animals will leave them alone. Toads often burrow under moist soil to avoid long exposure to direct sunlight.

Glands secrete mucus onto the skin. Mucus slows the evaporation of water and also makes the frog slippery to predators. The frog's skin is only loosely attached, making it difficult for predators to hold onto frogs. Although frogs and toads are very similar, there are some differences. Toads live farther from water than frogs. Toads have drier skin, but they must stay in humid places.

Figure 32.2 shows the external characteristics of a frog. All anurans lack an obvious neck connecting the head and the body. At the front of the head, two nostrils open into nasal passages. These nasal passages connect to the mouth cavity. In most fish, the nostrils do not open into the mouth cavity. Fish nostrils serve only as organs of smell. Frog nostrils, though, function not only as organs of smell but also as air passages. The frog can be submerged in water and breathe by exposing only the nostrils. Behind the nostrils are two very large eyes that stick up above the head. When the frog is submerged in water, its eyes can be above the surface. Frogs have eyelids that protect their eyes. Their eyes also have another covering called a **nictitating** [NIHK-tuh-tay-tihng] **membrane**. The nictitating membrane covers the eye, protecting it from water and keeping it moist when the frog is out of water.

Behind each eye is a round, flat membrane called the **tympanic** [tihm-PAN-ihk] **membrane**. These are the ears of the frog. Males emit sounds to attract females. If you live near an area inhabited by frogs, you may have heard this sound

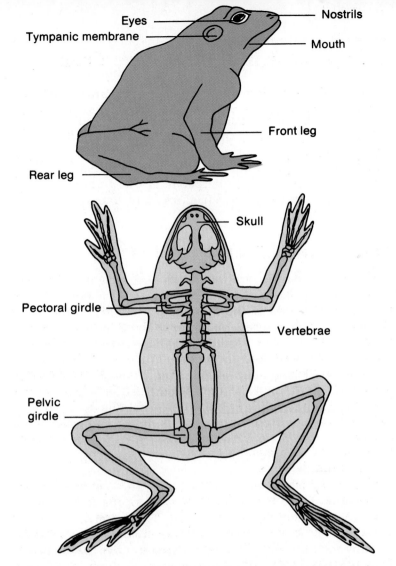

Eyes

Tympanic membrane

Nostrils

Mouth

Front leg

Rear leg

Skull

Pectoral girdle

Vertebrae

Pelvic girdle

Figure 32.2 The external and skeletal features of a frog

in the spring or summer. In many frog species, the male frog pushes air from its mouth into vocal sacs under the chin. These vocal sacs help to amplify the sound.

The front legs of the frog are smaller than the rear legs. The "thumb" of the male frog often has an additional pad. This thumb pad helps to push eggs out of the female's body during mating. The rear legs of the frog are large and well adapted for leaping.

32–3   The Frog Skeleton

Look at the skeleton of a frog in Figure 32.2. In some ways, this skeleton has features in common with those of a fish. Yet it is a skeleton that shows adaptations for living on land. The skull consists of a lower jawbone and a number of bones that surround the brain. Vertebrae surround the spinal cord, as in fish. In frogs the number of vertebrae is small, and there are no ribs. Adult frogs have no tail, but there is a long bone running from the end of the spine to the most posterior point of the body.

The frog skeleton is most different from the fish skeleton in the bones that support the front and rear limbs. The **pectoral girdle** is a group of bones that almost surround the thorax and attach the front limbs to the body. The rear limbs are attached to the body by the **pelvic girdle**. In later chapters you will see that similar structures are found in all four-limbed vertebrates.

32–4   Digestion in Frogs

Several structures are visible in the open mouth of the frog. The frog has a number of very small **maxillary teeth** lining the margins of the upper jaw. Just inside the upper mouth, near the internal openings of the nasal passages, are two additional small **vomerine** [VOHM-er-een] **teeth**. Frogs use their teeth to hold their prey. Frogs do not chew with their teeth. The tongue of the frog is unusual. Instead of attaching at the back of the mouth, like your tongue, the frog's tongue attaches at the front. This allows the frog to flick its tongue far out in front of its mouth and grasp flying insects or other prey. A frog can flick out its tongue and have it back in its mouth in less than a second.

Food organisms are immediately pushed to the back of the mouth toward the **gullet** [GUHL-iht], the beginning of the esophagus. Trace the digestive system of the frog in Figure 32.4 as you read this explanation. The esophagus leads to the stomach. In the stomach, acid secretions reduce food to a soupy mixture. From the stomach, food enters the **duodenum** [doo-uh-DEE-nuhm], the first part of the small intestine.

The liver is a large organ near the stomach. It has many functions, and several are related to the use of food. The liver produces a substance called **bile**, which aids in the digestion of fats. Bile is stored in a small sac called the **gallbladder**. Bile is transported to the duodenum through a tube called the **bile duct**. In the duodenum bile breaks down fats into very tiny droplets, allowing fat-digesting enzymes to hydrolyze the fats more easily.

While the small intestine produces some digestive enzymes, many are produced in a gland near the stomach called the **pancreas** [PAN-kree-uhs]. Enzymes from the pancreas are transported to the duodenum through a tube called the **pancreatic duct**.

Food molecules are absorbed into the bloodstream through

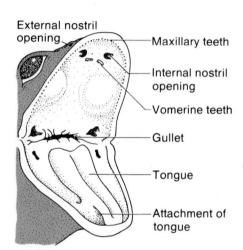

External nostril opening — Maxillary teeth

Internal nostril opening

Vomerine teeth

Gullet

Tongue

Attachment of tongue

Figure 32.3 The anatomy of a frog's mouth

Do You Know?
Frogs will eat only food that is alive and moving.

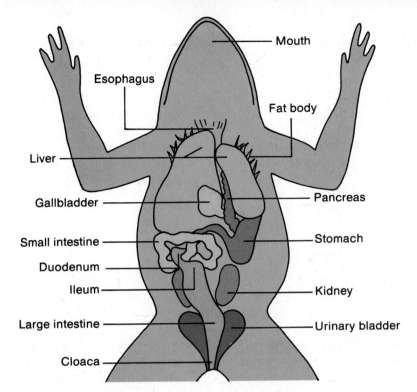

Figure 32.4 The digestive and excretory organs of a frog

Mouth

Esophagus

Fat body

Liver

Gallbladder — Pancreas

Small intestine — Stomach

Duodenum

Ileum — Kidney

Large intestine — Urinary bladder

Cloaca

the walls of the small intestine. Blood carries food molecules directly from the small intestine to the liver. In the liver, glucose is converted to glycogen and stored. Between meals, the liver hydrolyzes glycogen to release glucose into the blood. The blood transports glucose to the other cells of the body. Like other vertebrates, frogs store excess food in the form of fat. The fat is stored in **fat bodies** located near the kidneys.

Food that is not absorbed in the small intestine is passed on to the large intestine. The large intestine removes excess water from the waste material. The last part of the digestive system is the **cloaca** [kloh-AY-kuh]. The cloaca is a common opening, through which solid wastes, liquid wastes from the kidneys, and reproductive cells are expelled from the body.

32–5 Excretion in Frogs

As in other vertebrates, the frog's major organs of excretion are the kidneys. The two kidneys are located on either side of the vertebral column near the dorsal body wall. Blood enters the kidneys from the **renal** [REE-nuhl] **arteries**. The kidneys remove nitrogenous wastes from the blood. The cleansed blood returns to the circulation through the **renal veins**. The nitrogen-containing wastes dissolved in water form urine. Urine leaves the kidneys through a tube called the **ureter** [yu-REE-tur]. Urine can be held in the saclike **urinary bladder** before it is expelled through the cloaca.

32–6   The Frog's Circulatory System

Frog blood is similar in function and composition to fish blood. The most common cells in frog blood are **red blood cells**. These cells have nuclei. The cytoplasm contains oxygen-carrying hemoglobin. Red blood cells transport oxygen from the respiratory surfaces of the frog to the cells of the body. The **white blood cells** in frog blood have nuclei and colorless cytoplasm. Their function is to defend the frog against diseases. The liquid portion of frog blood carries food molecules, the waste products of cell metabolism, and proteins.

Like all vertebrates, frogs have a closed circulatory system. The circulation of blood in the adult frog is more complex than circulation in fish.

In fish, blood circulates from the heart to the respiratory surface (the gills), to the cells of the body, and back to the heart. This is a simple loop. In frogs, blood makes two separate loops. Blood that leaves the heart travels to the lungs, becomes oxygenated, and returns to the heart. The circulation between the heart and the lungs is called the **pulmonary** [PUL-muh-nehr-ee] **loop**. Blood leaves the heart again and travels to the rest of the body, where it loses oxygen and then returns to the heart. The circulation between the heart and the rest of the body is called the **systemic** [sih-STEHM-ihk] **loop**.

Figure 32.5 shows the frog's heart in more detail. The frog's

Figure 32.5 The heart and circulatory system of a frog

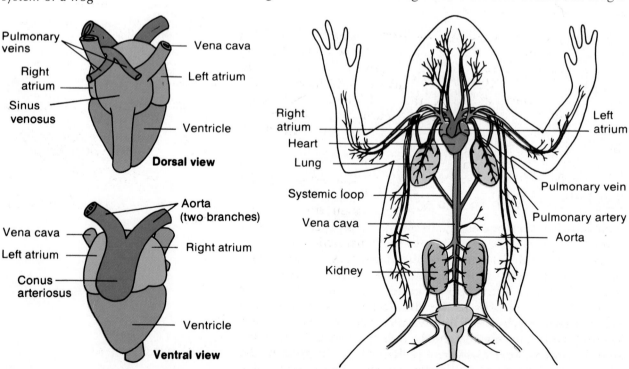

heart has three chambers. Deoxygenated blood from the body cells returns to the heart through the **venae cavae**. These veins empty into a large collecting area in back of the heart, which is called the **sinus venosus**. Blood then enters the **right atrium** of the heart. The right atrium pumps blood into the ventricle. The ventricle pushes blood upward. Some of the blood enters the **pulmonary artery**, which takes blood toward the lungs. In the lungs, blood is oxygenated and returns by the **pulmonary veins** to the **left atrium**. Oxygenated blood from the left atrium is pumped into the ventricle. Blood leaving the ventricle passes through the **conus arteriosus** and can enter either the pulmonary artery and go to the lungs; or it can enter the **aorta** and travel to the body cells.

Because a frog's heart has a single ventricle, deoxygenated blood from the right atrium and oxygenated blood from the left atrium mix together. Some deoxygenated blood goes into the aorta and out to the body cells. Sending some deoxygenated blood to body cells does not harm the frog. Since frogs are cold-blooded animals, their body temperature is close to the temperature of their surroundings. As a result, frog cells do not use as much oxygen for respiration as cells of animals that maintain a higher body temperature. Blood leaving a frog's heart does not have to be fully oxygenated.

32–7 Frog Respiration

The respiratory system of the frog is very different from that of the fish. As shown in Figure 32.6, the lungs of a frog are air sacs that branch off from the gullet. The two sacs are slightly folded on the interior surface. This increases the amount of surface area in contact with blood vessels. Capillaries cover the outer surface of each lung. Oxygen and carbon dioxide are exchanged between the air in the lungs and the blood in the capillaries.

In addition to the lung surface, all frogs depend on two other surfaces for gas exchange. One of these surfaces is the moist skin, which is richly supplied with blood capillaries. Deoxygenated blood that gets into the systemic loop can be oxygenated when the blood passes near the surface of the skin.

Most frogs also use the moist membranes lining the inside of their mouth as a respiratory surface. Gases are exchanged both in the lungs and through the lining of the mouth when a frog gulps air. A frog pulls air into its mouth and lungs by lowering the floor of the mouth. Notice that frogs have a **larynx** [LAR-ihngks] between the mouth cavity and the lungs. Within the larynx are the **vocal cords** used by frogs to make sounds. Many male frogs use additional air trapped in the skin below the lower jaw to magnify the sounds they make.

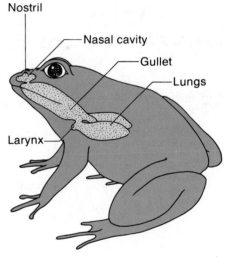

Figure 32.6 The respiratory system of a frog

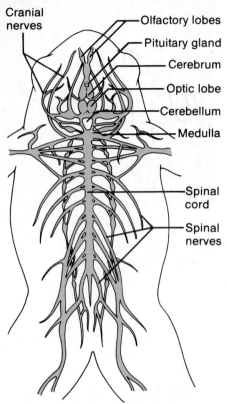

Cranial nerves

Olfactory lobes

Pituitary gland

Cerebrum

Optic lobe

Cerebellum

Medulla

Spinal cord

Spinal nerves

Figure 32.7 The nervous system of a frog

32–8   The Nervous System of the Frog

The frog's **central nervous system** consists of the brain and the spinal cord. The most anterior parts of the brain are the **olfactory** [ohl-FAK-tur-ee] **lobes**. The olfactory lobes receive input from the nose for the sense of smell. Behind each olfactory lobe is an area called the cerebrum. In frogs, this part of the brain is associated with memory and the initiation of body movements. Behind the cerebrum is a pair of optic lobes, which are associated with vision. Behind the optic lobes are the cerebellum and the medulla. The cerebellum of frogs is associated with the control of muscle movement. The medulla controls basic body functions such as heart rate and breathing. Attached to a stalk of nerves at the base of the brain is a small piece of tissue called the **pituitary** [pih-TOO-uh-tehr-ee] **gland**. This small gland secretes many chemicals that control a variety of body processes.

This basic brain structure is found in all vertebrates. You will see, however, that the size of a brain is directly related to the importance of that part in the life of the animal. In frogs the sense of vision is very important, and the optic lobes are large and well developed.

The rest of the frog's nervous system is made up of the nerves that branch off the central nervous system and into the body. These nerves make up the **peripheral nervous system**. Ten pairs of **cranial** [KRAY-nee-uhl] **nerves** branch from the brain itself. A number of **spinal nerves** branch from the spinal cord.

32–9   The Frog's Senses

The frog's brain receives information from a variety of sense organs. Frogs have senses of taste and smell. They will accept or reject food based on information from these senses. Frogs depend on a good sense of vision to see flying insects and capture them with the tongue. The frog's ear is similar in structure to the ear of other vertebrates. The tympanic membrane transmits sound to the inner ear. The inner ear then sends information about sound to the brain. The **Eustachian** [yoo-STAY-shuhn] **tube** connects the space behind the tympanic membrane to the mouth. The Eustachian tube allows air pressure on both sides of the tympanic membrane to be the same. An organ that senses balance is also located in the region of the inner ear.

Frogs use their eyes to help them swallow. When a frog swallows food, it closes its eyes and pushes them down against the roof of its mouth. This pressure helps to push food back into the gullet.

32–10   Reproduction and Development of Frogs

The male frog produces sperm cells in a pair of testes located near the kidneys. Sperm cells then travel through several fine tubes called **vasa efferentia**. These tubes merge with the urinary ducts in the kidneys. From the kidneys, sperm cells travel through the ureter to the cloaca. During mating, sperm cells are expelled from the body through the cloaca.

The female produces eggs in the ovaries. The eggs develop there and burst from the ovary into the abdominal cavity. From there, they are swept into funnellike tubes called **oviducts** [OH-vuh-duhkts]. Each oviduct has cilia lining its inner surface, which move the eggs toward an enlarged sac called the **uterus** [YOO-tur-uhs]. During the trip through the oviduct, each egg cell is surrounded by a capsule of gelatinlike material. This material protects the eggs. The eggs accumulate in the uterus until mating. During mating the eggs are expelled from the female's body through the cloaca.

Each species of frog has a definite mating season, usually sometime in early spring. Males attract females by croaking specific mating calls. A female enters the water and is mounted by a male. The male grasps the female around the abdomen and helps squeeze eggs out of her body. As the eggs are expelled, the male releases sperm on top of the eggs. External fertilization of the eggs takes place in the water. Development of fertilized eggs begins immediately, and tadpoles emerge from the eggs within a few days.

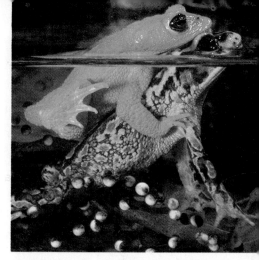

Figure 32.8 Fertilization of frog eggs occurs in water. The male releases sperm on the eggs expelled from the female's body.

Figure 32.9 The life cycle of a frog involves the metamorphosis from tadpole to adult.

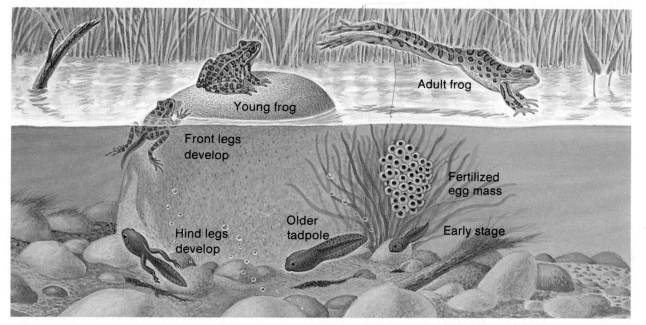

Young frog

Adult frog

Front legs develop

Hind legs develop

Older tadpole

Fertilized egg mass

Early stage

The tadpole stage of the frog's life cycle may last as little as a few months or as long as two years, depending on the species. Tadpoles are more like fish than like frogs. They hatch with a tail and no legs. They have gills for a respiratory surface. Tadpoles eat only plants. Their mouth structure is suited to eating algae. Tadpoles have a very long, coiled small intestine which is typical of plant-eating animals. The circulatory system of the tadpole is like that of the fish. A two-chambered heart pumps blood to the gills, and from the gills directly to the rest of the body.

When the frog undergoes metamorphosis, its fishlike features gradually change into those of an adult frog. The appearance of hind legs is one of the first changes to show. Gills are replaced by lungs, and the three-chambered heart develops. The tail disappears. The mouth changes to the adult form, and the intestine becomes much shorter, which is typical of carnivorous animals. The metamorphosis of a frog takes one or two months.

In terms of maintaining body temperature, frogs are at the mercy of the surrounding environment. Frogs, like fish and reptiles, are cold-blooded animals. For many frogs that live in tropical regions, temperature is not a major problem. But a number of frog species live in climates that become extremely cold in the winter or extremely hot in the summer. Frogs that live through cold winter climates **hibernate**. They dig into the mud at the bottom of a pond. All of their metabolic activity slows down greatly. In this condition they require very little oxygen. During hibernation, frogs live on the stored food in the fat bodies of the abdomen. Frogs that live in hot areas where ponds dry up burrow in the mud and **aestivate** [EHS-tuh-vayt]. Like hibernation, aestivation is a resting period, during which the frog awaits the return of more suitable environmental conditions.

Checkpoint

1. To what order of amphibians do frogs belong?
2. What term describes animals that cannot regulate their body temperature?
3. What hearing structure is visible on an adult frog?
4. What internal organ produces bile and stores glycogen?
5. How many chambers are in the heart of an adult frog? A tadpole?
6. What surfaces are used by adult frogs to exchange gases?
7. What organs make up the central nervous system of a frog?
8. What structure do tadpoles have for the exchange of gases?

Other Amphibians

While frogs and toads are probably the most familiar amphibians, they are not the only group. Anyone who has spent time in the woods or around ponds has probably encountered members of the order Urodela. These are the salamanders. Some salamanders are only a few centimeters in length. But one variety of giant Japanese salamander reaches a length of 1.5 meters! This species is the largest type of amphibian alive today. While amphibians are more common in tropical climates, a number of salamanders are found in the colder regions of the world.

The third group of amphibians is the order Apoda. The apods, or legless amphibians, are a much rarer group. They are not found at all in North America.

32–11   Order Urodela: Salamanders

Salamanders have a different body plan from frogs. A salamander is long and slender. It has a neck between the head and body and a long tail. Its body resembles that of a lizard. However, lizards are reptiles, as you will learn in the next chapter. Unlike lizards, salamanders have smooth, moist skin like other amphibians.

Salamanders show more variation in body form and function than do frogs and toads. Some salamanders, for example, remain totally aquatic during their entire life. Other woodland species rarely return to the water. In fact, some woodland salamanders even lay eggs out of the water, in the humid areas of forests. The eggs of these species are surrounded by a gelatin capsule that prevents them from drying out. The young of these salamanders undergo complete development to the adult, legged form within the egg capsules.

One species of Mexican salamander, shown in Figure 32.10, can remain in the larval form all its life. These larval sala-

Figure 32.10 *Left:* An axolotl *Right:* A salamander's body differs in structure from that of a frog.

Figure 32.11 A mud puppy. Notice the gills.

Figure 32.12 A mud siren

Figure 32.13 A typical apod

manders are called **axolotls** [ack-suh-LOT-uhlz]. Axolotls may never develop lungs, yet they can still lay eggs. If, however, the ponds where this species lives dry up, axolotls can metamorphose into land-living adults. They will find a new pond and reproduce. Axolotls were once thought to be a separate species. However, recent studies have shown them to be larval stages of the tiger salamander. It seems that the ponds where axolotls are found lack iodine. Most amphibians need iodine in their diet in order to undergo metamorphosis. Since axolotls lack iodine in their diet, they never change into adult tiger salamanders.

Some species of salamanders retain external gills throughout their life. The mud puppy is an example. This large salamander, up to 60 centimeters long, is found in streams in the midwestern United States. It has dark red, bushy gills on either side of its neck.

One species of salamander has lost both lungs and gills and depends on skin respiration for all its gas exchange needs. Several species of salamanders that are totally aquatic have very small limbs. The mud siren shown in Figure 32.12 has no hind limbs at all.

32–12   Order Apoda

The apods are the most unusual of the amphibians. These legless creatures live only in the tropical regions of Asia, Africa, Central America, and South America. There are only about 50 known species of this rare group of animals. These legless amphibians can be found burrowing under moist soils. As you can see in Figure 32.13, an apod could easily be mistaken for an earthworm. Yet these amphibians are carnivorous and hunt for earthworms, insects, and insect larvae.

Apods lay eggs in batches of 20 to 30 in the soil near water. In some species, the animal develops within the egg. In others, a swimming larval stage precedes the adult.

32–13 Fossil Amphibians

In many ways amphibians appear to be intermediate between fish and land-living animals. The amphibian body structure and life cycle support this idea. In fact, the fossil record also supports the hypothesis that amphibians were the first vertebrates to venture onto land. It shows also that other land-living vertebrates evolved from amphibians.

The oldest fossils of amphibians have been dated at about 350 million years. These animals looked much like those shown in Figure 32.14. They had four legs and looked much like modern salamanders. These legs possibly evolved from the stumplike fins of fish like the coelocanth, shown in Chapter 31.

Figure 32.14 *Diplovertebron* was an ancient form of amphibian.

Evidence found in rocks indicates that the period when the amphibians appeared was a time of worldwide droughts. As temperatures increased, many small bodies of water evaporated. This often happened as the seasons changed. In some cases, these conditions might have favored the selection of animals with amphibian characteristics. For example, any fish that had respiratory surfaces other than gills would have had an advantage.

The amphibians represent a group that was very successful for about 100 million years. Yet like modern amphibians, early amphibians had to live close to a source of water. They had to return to water to reproduce. They were not truly land creatures like the reptiles that soon appeared. Many amphibians became extinct as the reptiles became more successful. The amphibians that survived were the ancestors of today's amphibian forms.

Checkpoint

1. What are the two most obvious structural differences between salamanders and frogs?
2. What larval structure is maintained in axolotls?
3. What structural feature most clearly distinguishes the apods from other amphibians?
4. What two major structures did the first amphibians possess that allowed them to occupy a land habitat?

CHAPTER REVIEW

Summary

- Amphibians are usually terrestrial vertebrates, with an aquatic stage at one point of their life. The larva that hatches in water has gills, fins, a fishlike heart, fishlike circulation, and no legs. This stage develops into an adult with lungs, no fins, a more complex circulation, and four legs.

- The anatomy of the frog is typical of most amphibians and serves as an introduction to the anatomy of other land vertebrates.

- Frogs have short bodies with no neck and no tail. The skin of a frog is usually moist. The front legs are small, and the rear legs large and modified for jumping.

- The skeleton of a frog is similar to that of other four-legged vertebrates. The pectoral and pelvic girdles are the bones that support the front and rear legs.

- Frogs are carnivores that eat only live, moving food. The digestive tract of a frog is divided into specialized organs, which have specific functions in the digestion and absorption of the frog's food.

- Frogs have a three-chambered heart and two circulatory loops for the blood. Respiration takes place on the lung surfaces, the skin, and the inner lining of the mouth.

- The brain of the frog is divided into a number of specific areas with specific functions. As in other vertebrates, the nervous system of the frog can be divided into the central and peripheral nervous systems.

- Reproduction of frogs takes place in water. Eggs hatch into tadpoles, which are fishlike organisms. The tadpoles then undergo metamorphosis and become adult frogs.

- Salamanders belong to the order Urodela. They are amphibians with a long body and tail. Some retain gills throughout life, while others have lungs.

- The order Apoda includes some rare species of legless amphibians.

- The fossil record indicates that the amphibians were the first land vertebrates, as their body structure suggests. The first amphibians appeared about 350 million years ago.

Vocabulary

aestivate	pancreatic duct
amphibian	pectoral girdle
Anura	pelvic girdle
aorta	peripheral nervous
Apoda	system
axolotl	pituitary gland
bile	pulmonary artery
bile duct	pulmonary loop
central nervous	pulmonary vein
system	red blood cell
cloaca	renal arteries
conus arteriosus	renal vein
cranial nerves	right atrium
duodenum	sinus venosus
Eustachian tube	spinal nerves
fat bodies	systemic loop
gallbladder	tadpoles
gullet	tympanic membrane
hibernation	ureter
larynx	urinary bladder
left atrium	Urodela
maxillary teeth	uterus
nictitating	vasa efferentia
membrane	vena cava
olfactory lobes	vocal cords
oviduct	vomerine teeth
pancreas	white blood cell

Review

1. In what way does the skin of amphibians differ from the skin of other vertebrates?
2. Where are the eggs of most amphibians laid?
3. What is the covering that protects the frog's eyes from drying out?
4. Name one type of bone found in a fish skeleton but not in a frog skeleton.
5. Name some bones that could be found in a frog skeleton but not in a fish skeleton.
6. What organs in the digestive system of a frog produce digestive enzymes?
7. What part of the frog's brain receives information from the eyes?
8. What blood vessel carries blood from the ventricle of the frog heart to the cells of the body?
9. What vessels carry blood to and from the lungs of the frog?
10. What is the function of the cerebrum in a frog's brain?
11. What organ produces egg cells in the female frog? Sperm cells in the male frog?
12. Salamanders belong to what order of amphibians?
13. Where would be the best place to look for a legless amphibian?
14. Which group of modern amphibians most closely resembles the first fossil amphibians?

Interpret and Apply

1. Why must amphibians live near water?
2. What is the role of the mucous glands in the skin of a frog?
3. What is the difference between frogs and toads?
4. What bones in their skeletons do the frog and the fish have in common?
5. What are two functions of the frog's liver?
6. Name the three chambers of a frog's heart.
7. What part of the frog's brain receives information from the eyes?
8. In what major ways is a tadpole more like a fish than a frog?
9. In what way is the reproduction of apods similar to the reproduction of other amphibians?

Challenge

1. Explain in what ways amphibians are intermediate between fish and land-living animals.
2. What are the major differences in the external body shape of the three orders of amphibians?
3. Suppose you are riding on a red blood cell in the vena cava of a frog. Describe the structures you would pass as you travel around the circulatory system, ending up back in the vena cava again.
4. Explain how using the skin as a respiratory surface is both an advantage and a disadvantage to the frog.
5. What is unusual about the life cycle of the Mexican axolotl?

Projects

1. Use an identification guide to find out what kinds of amphibians live in your community or nearby environment. Plan a field trip to find and observe amphibians that live in your area.
2. If it is legal in your state, collect some frog or salamander eggs from a local pond. Return them to your home or classroom and place them in a freshwater aquarium. Observe the development of these animals.
3. Draw a poster-sized chart comparing the blood circulation pattern in a fish and in an amphibian. Display the chart in your classroom.
4. Find out why the fossil amphibian *Eusthenopteron* is considered by many scientists to be one of the earliest amphibians. Learn how it is closely related to the ancestral fish from which it is thought to have evolved.

33 Reptiles

A Ridley sea turtle

The turtle in this photograph is carrying out a ritual that may have occurred on this same beach each year for millions of years. Climbing onto the beach, the female sea turtle digs a hole in the sand. There she lays several dozen eggs. When the eggs hatch in two or three months, the young turtles will scramble to the sea. If they avoid predators, they will swim hundreds or even thousands of kilometers out into the open ocean, where they will live and grow to adulthood. When mature, the turtles will mate, and the females will find their way back to the same stretch of beach to continue the cycle.

The turtle is just one kind of reptile. The first reptiles appeared in the fossil record over 300 million years ago. During the next 100 million years they occupied most of the major land areas of Earth. Then many reptiles, including the sea turtle, returned to the seas. Others took to the air. Reptiles were the dominant animals on Earth for over 200 million years.

Characteristics of Reptiles

When reptiles first appeared, the only other vertebrates on land were amphibians. What characteristics of reptiles allowed them to move onto land and radiate into so many species? The answer lies in the reptiles' independence from water. Amphibians must stay close to water to keep their skins moist and to reproduce. Reptiles do not have to stay near water.

33–1 Adaptations to Land

The skin of reptiles is thick, tough, and dry. It is covered with overlapping scales or flat plates made of a protein called **keratin** [KEHR-uh-tihn]. Human fingernails are also made of keratin. Reptile skin is impermeable to water, thus preventing the bodies of reptiles from drying out.

Reptiles are better adapted to movement on land than amphibians. Figure 33.1 compares the limb position of amphibians and reptiles. The legs of most reptiles are directed downward, unlike those of amphibians. This position keeps the reptile's body off the ground and makes rapid movement over land much easier. A further distinguishing feature of reptile limbs is the presence of keratin claws on each toe.

Like fish and amphibians, reptiles are cold-blooded. Reptiles

Figure 33.1 Compared to the limbs of amphibians, the limbs of reptiles are better able to support the body on land.

are not able to regulate their body temperature by their metabolism. Life on land, however, exposes reptiles to greater variations in temperature than does life in water. Many reptiles are adapted to these extremes by specialized behaviors. One such behavior is **basking**. Lizards and snakes often bask in the morning sun. By basking, these reptiles are using the sun's energy to increase their body temperature.

A further adaptation to life on land is the reptile's method of reproduction. When amphibians mate, they must release eggs and sperm into water, where fertilization takes place. Eggs and sperm dry out if exposed to the air. Reptile reproduction is characterized by **internal fertilization**. When reptiles mate, the sperm cells of the male are deposited inside the body of the female, where the sperm fertilize the eggs.

33–2   Reptile Eggs

Reptiles lay very large eggs with leathery shells. The shell protects the contents of the egg and provides a barrier against drying out.

Four membranes within the shell aid the developing reptile embryo. Figure 33.2 shows the internal structure of a typical reptile egg. Just inside the shell is a thin membrane called the **chorion** [KAWR-ee-ahn]. The chorion holds the contents of the egg. Yet the chorion is permeable to gases. Oxygen and carbon dioxide are exchanged between the egg and its surroundings. The **amnion** [AM-nee-uhn] is a sac that surrounds the embryo. Fluid within the sac acts like a shock absorber and protects the embryo.

The **allantois** [uh-LAN-toh-ihs] is a membrane that contains many blood vessels. It is a respiratory surface for the embryo. Oxygen and carbon dioxide are exchanged between the blood vessels and the surrounding fluid. Nitrogen wastes accumulate within the allantois as the embryo increases in size. The last of the four membranes is the **yolk sac**. The yolk sac surrounds the yellow yolk, which serves as food for the developing embryo. Blood vessels in the yolk sac carry the food from the yolk to the growing embryo.

When reptiles hatch, they are able to survive on land. Unlike amphibians, reptiles do not have an aquatic larval stage.

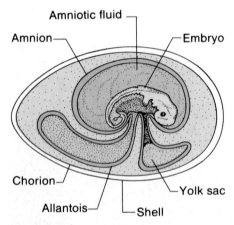

Figure 33.2 The embryonic membranes of a reptile egg

Checkpoint

1. How is the skin of reptiles different from the skin of amphibians?
2. What are the four membranes in a reptile egg?

Living Reptiles

There are four orders of living reptiles. The **Squamata** [skwa-MAH-tuh] are lizards and snakes. The **Chelonia** [kee-LOH-nee-uh] are tortoises and turtles. The **Crocodilia** [krah-ko-DIHL-ee-ah] include alligators and crocodiles. The **Rhynchocephalia** [ring-koh-suh-FAYL-yuh] consist of a single species called the **tuatara** [too-uh-TAHR-uh]. There are about 6,000 species in the four orders.

CONCEPTS
• snake anatomy
• variety of living reptiles

33–3 The Anatomy of the Snake

The anatomy of the snake shows many features that are characteristic of all reptiles. It also shows many adaptations unique to this particular group of reptiles.

External Anatomy The most obvious feature of snakes is the absence of limbs. The entire body is covered with overlapping scales. It is a common misconception that the skin of a snake is wet and slimy. In fact, the scales are dry. The scales on the ventral surface help the snake gain a hold on the ground and push itself forward.

The head of the snake has nostrils at the anterior end above the mouth. Snake eyes have no lids. Instead, the eyes are covered by a transparent, protective membrane. No snake has external ears, though it does have internal ears in the skull, where you would expect them to be. The anus marks the boundary between the abdomen and the tail.

Skeleton The most unusual feature of the skull of a snake is the way the jaws are hinged to the head. Figure 33.3 shows how the snake opens its jaws to swallow very large prey. Such jaws are typical of snakes. The entire snake skeleton is also shown in Figure 33.3. The skeleton consists mostly of vertebrae and ribs. There are often more than 100 vertebrae with ribs attached to most of them. In most snakes there is nothing resembling a pectoral or pelvic girdle.

Figure 33.3 *Top*: The jaws of a snake can open wide, thus allowing the snake to swallow large prey. *Bottom*: The skeleton of a snake is mostly vertebrae and ribs.

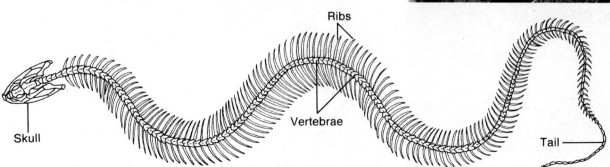

Ribs

Vertebrae

Skull

Tail

Digestion and Excretion Many of the internal structures of snakes reflect their unusual feeding behavior. All snakes are carnivores and eat very infrequently. When they do eat, they eat extremely large meals and swallow their prey whole. Some of the largest snakes of Africa and South America eat only once every few months. Some can live as long as a year between meals. Just as the jaws unhinge to swallow large organisms, the ribs can also separate. Without pectoral or pelvic girdles in the way, large food organisms can pass along the digestive tract.

Snake teeth are adapted for grasping and holding prey, rather than for chewing or biting. The teeth point backward, thus making it difficult for prey organisms to escape.

Figure 33.4 shows the internal anatomy of the snake. The liver is elongated. The digestive organs of the snake have the same function as similar organs in other vertebrates.

Figure 33.4 The internal anatomy of a snake

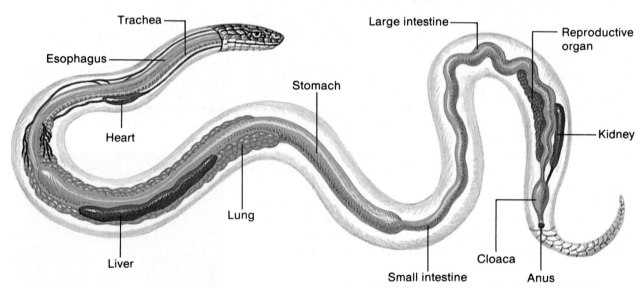

The excretory system of the snake contains a pair of long kidneys. One kidney is found on each side of the body. Instead of being located opposite each other, the kidneys are staggered, so that one is in front of the other. As in amphibians, the ureter drains urine from the kidneys into the cloaca.

Circulation and Respiration Recall that in amphibians, oxygenated and deoxygenated blood mix in the single ventricle of the three-chambered heart. This is not a critical problem, since amphibians add further oxygen to the blood by gas exchange through the skin. Reptile skin is impermeable to water and also to gases. Reptiles cannot use their skin as a respiratory surface. A three-chambered heart would be a problem for reptiles.

BIOLOGY INSIGHTS

The internal walls of the lungs are subdivided into many tiny chambers. These chambers greatly increase the surface area of the lung, thus increasing the rate of gas exchange. This is an example of how an increase in the surface-to-volume ratio affects the function of an organ.

Most reptiles, including snakes, have a heart like the one shown in Figure 33.5. Notice the wall that separates the right side of the ventricle from the left side. While a small amount of blood can mix, mixing is minimal. The reptile heart keeps oxygenated and deoxygenated blood largely separate.

Without the skin as a respiratory surface, reptile lungs have to be more efficient gas-exchange structures than amphibian lungs. The interior surfaces of reptile lungs are more highly folded and have a much greater surface area for gas exchange.

Snakes generally have only a single lung. The right lung is very long but the left lung is tiny or completely absent. In snakes and other reptiles air enters the lungs through a long tube called the **trachea** [TRAY-kee-uh].

The Nervous System and Sense Organs   The structure of the brain and nervous system in snakes, and in reptiles in general, is much the same as that of the frog. The snake shows a number of specific adaptations of sense organs, however. Most snakes depend on the sense of smell to find prey. As an aid to the sense of smell, many snakes continually sample the surrounding air with flicks of their forked tongues. The tongue brings molecules from the air into the mouth. These are sensed by the **Jacobson's organs** in the roof of the mouth.

Snakes do not have external ears, but have sensory organs in the skull that are similar in structure to the ears of other vertebrates. Although snakes are deaf to sounds, scientists think that snakes use their "ears" to detect vibrations of the ground, thus obtaining information about animals moving near them.

Pit vipers are snakes that have a small pair of pitlike structures located between the nostrils and the eyes. These pits are heat sensors. Pit vipers use them to detect and locate the warm bodies of nearby birds and mammals that are potential prey.

Reproduction   The major difference between the reproductive organs of reptiles and those of amphibians is the adaptation related to internal fertilization and the manufacturing of eggs in the female reptile. Male reptiles have a structure that transfers sperm cells into the cloaca of the female during mating.

Many snakes lay shelled eggs and leave them on their own to hatch. Other snakes hold the eggs internally until they hatch. In some of these species, the eggs never have shells. Reptiles that lay eggs are called **oviparous** [oh-VIHP-uh-ruhs]. Reptiles that hold eggs internally and then bear live young are **ovoviviparous** [oh-voh-vih-VIHP-uh-ruhs].

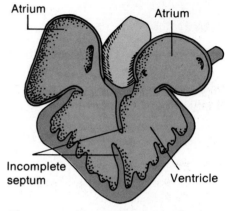

Figure 33.5 The heart of a snake

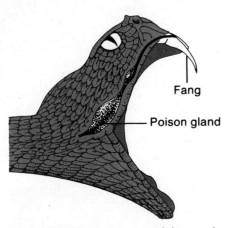

Fang

Poison gland

Figure 33.6 Poison sacs and fangs of a rattlesnake

Figure 33.7 Snakes vary greatly in coloring.

33–4   The Variety of Snakes

A number of snake species are poisonous. In North America the best-known poisonous snakes are the 13 species of rattlesnakes. Rattlesnakes are pit vipers. Notice the poison glands and fangs of the rattlesnake in Figure 33.6. The fangs are hinged and swing forward only when the snake is about to strike. The hollow fangs inject poison into a prey organism, which dies quickly and is then swallowed.

Rattlesnakes strike from a coiled position with incredible speed. The rattle at the end of the tail serves as a warning for any large animal to stay away. The venom not only kills prey but also makes the rattlesnake an unlikely prey for larger organisms.

Most snakes are nonpoisonous and subdue their prey in other ways. Some snakes are **constrictors.** Constrictors wrap quickly around their prey and squeeze. The prey cannot breathe and soon die. The large boa constrictors and pythons of South America and Africa are best known for this method of killing their prey, but many small common snakes use it as well. The large pythons, which reach a length of six or eight meters, can kill small antelopes or pigs and swallow them whole. Snakes can eat meals that weigh as much as one fourth of their own weight.

33–5   Lizards

Lizards and snakes belong to the order Squamata. Typically, lizards are four-legged terrestrial animals. The skeleton and internal anatomy of the lizard do not show the specializations of the snakes. The limbs are supported by a pectoral and pelvic girdle. The legs are arranged to keep the body off the ground, and lizards can move rapidly. Both lungs are well developed. Lizards also have external ears and eyelids, which snakes do not.

Figure 33.8 shows some members of the lizard family. Geckos are small lizards with special pads on the ends of their toes that allow them to climb vertically or upside down on very smooth surfaces. While most lizards are relatively small, the monitor lizards of Sumatra can reach a length of over three meters. The Galápagos iguana is a marine lizard. Although most lizards are carnivorous, the Galápagos iguana is an herbivore, feeding exclusively on marine algae. The Gila monster is one of only two species of poisonous lizards. Even though its poison is dangerous, the animal is generally considered rather shy.

A few species of lizards are confused with snakes because they are legless. While this makes them appear outwardly like snakes, they have few of the internal specializations of snakes. Legless lizards live on forest floors and feed on insects and worms.

33–6 Order Chelonia: Turtles

While there are only about 200 living species of chelonians, they are a group with an ancient fossil history. Forms clearly related to modern turtles have been found in rocks over 200 million years old.

As shown in Figure 33.9, the skeleton of the turtle is highly modified. The vertebrae are fused to the shell. The ribs are widened and flattened against the shell. The dorsal shell of the turtle is called the **carapace** [KAR-uh-pays]. The flattened ventral shell is the **plastron** [PLAS-truhn]. The vertebrae bend the neck into an S-shape when the head is withdrawn into the shell.

A land-living chelonian is called a **tortoise**. Although most tortoises are rather small, the Galápagos tortoise can have a mass of almost 200 kilograms. Chelonians do not have teeth, and most are herbivores. Many turtles are aquatic. Freshwater turtles, or **terrapins**, are common inhabitants of ponds and lakes. Snapping turtles are carnivorous, with very powerful jaws. Marine turtles, or sea turtles, can be very large. They spend their adult lives at sea and only come to land to lay eggs.

33–7 Order Crocodilia

Like turtles, the fossil history of this group of reptiles is ancient. Forms that look much like modern crocodiles and alligators are found in rocks 225 million years old. All members are adapted to living in shallow water. They use their powerful tails to propel themselves in the water. The eyes and nostrils, which are positioned on top of the head, are often the only things visible above the surface of the water.

Figure 33.8 Lizards are a diverse group. *Top*: Gecko; *Bottom*: Galápagos iguana

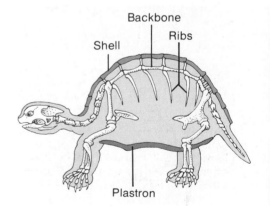

Figure 33.9 The skeleton of a turtle shows that the shell is supported by bone.

Figure 33.10 *Top:* The snout of a crocodile is long and tapered. *Bottom:* That of an alligator is more rounded.

Figure 33.11 The tuatara is the only surviving species of the order Rhynchocephalia.

The heart of crocodilians has four chambers. The right and left ventricles are fully separated. All members of this order lay their eggs on land.

There are only about 25 living species of this order, some of which are shown in Figure 33.10. Alligators have a much broader and more rounded snout than crocodiles. Alligator teeth are hidden when the mouth is closed, but the teeth of crocodiles are visible. The Asian **gavial** [GAY-vee-uhl] and the tropical American **caiman** [KAY-muhn] are other crocidilians. They differ in the shape of the snout and the arrangement of scales on the skin.

33–8   Order Rhynchocephalia: Tuataras

Living on a few remote islands near New Zealand is the tuatara, the only surviving species of an ancient order of reptiles. Though the tuatara shown in Figure 33.11 looks like a lizard, its anatomy is more closely related to that of a group of reptiles called rhynchocephalians. They appeared in the fossil record 225 million years ago—at about the same time as the earliest crocodilians and chelonians.

The bony skull plates of this reptile are different from those of any other living group. The tuatara has a third "eye" in the middle of its forehead, called a **pineal** [PIHN-ee-uhl] **eye**. This small eye is covered by scales and cannot form images. Its function is unknown, but scientists think it is somehow involved in the animal's temperature control. The pineal eye was much better developed in some fossil ancestors of the tuatara and may have once been used for vision.

Checkpoint

1. What is special about the lungs of the snake?
2. What is the function of the sensory pit of a pit viper?
3. How does the heart of crocodiles differ from that of other reptiles?

Reptile History

Reptiles have a long history. The first reptiles probably looked something like a large, heavy lizard. The earliest reptiles were sharp-toothed carnivores. These reptiles belonged to a group called the **cotylosaurs** [KAHT-uhl-oh-sawrz].

About 100 million years after the appearance of the first cotylosaurs, reptiles radiated into many different orders. At that time there were far more species of reptiles than there are today. In fact, there were 15 orders of reptiles, compared to only 4 today. For this reason, the Mesozoic Era is often called the Age of Reptiles.

The anatomy of living animals and the fossil record give scientists clues about how reptiles took over the land from the amphibians. Evidence also shows that reptiles were the ancestors of modern birds and mammals.

CONCEPTS
- variety of fossil reptiles
- orders of extinct reptiles

33–9 Dinosaurs

The size and appearance of the extinct reptiles called dinosaurs have made them a source of fascination for many people. Yet a number of misconceptions surround these reptiles. While some dinosaurs were the largest land animals ever to walk on Earth, many were little larger than a dog. While some were ferocious carnivores, most were harmless plant eaters.

The first real dinosaurs appear in the fossil record about 200 million years ago. They fall into two distinct groups based on differences in the pelvic girdle, as shown in Figure 33.12. The **saurischians** [sahw-REE-shee-uhnz] had hip bones

Figure 33.12 A comparison of the hip bones of two groups of dinosaurs. *Left: Brontosaurus,* a saurischian; *Right: Iguanodon,* an ornithischian

much like modern lizards. The **ornithischians** [ohr-nih-THEE-shee-uhnz] were dinosaurs that had hip bones similar to those of modern birds. Some members of both dinosaur groups walked on two legs, while others walked on four.

For many years, scientists assumed that dinosaurs were cold-blooded like modern reptiles. Recent evidence indicates that many, if not all, of the dinosaurs may have been warm-blooded. However, not all scientists accept the evidence.

The last dinosaurs disappeared more than 50 million years before the first humans walked on Earth. Many controversies still surround this group of animals, especially how and why they disappeared.

33–10   Other Extinct Reptiles

Not all early reptiles were dinosaurs. Many of the creatures people assume were dinosaurs actually belonged to completely different reptilian orders.

Soon after the evolution of the first reptiles, some returned to water. Thus while the dinosaurs were the dominant land reptiles, a group of marine reptiles dominated the oceans.

Two groups of marine reptiles appear in the fossil record about 225 million years ago. They are the **plesiosaurs** [PLEE-zee-oh-sawrz] and the **ichthyosaurs** [IHK-thee-oh-sawrz]. Plesiosaurs were carnivores that became extinct about the same time as the dinosaurs. Ichthyosaurs, like the one in Figure 33.13, show a remarkable physical resemblance to modern-day porpoises. Still, ichthyosaurs became extinct many millions of years before the plesiosaurs.

Figure 33.13 Not all ancient reptiles were dinosaurs. *Left:* An ichthyosaur; *Right:* A plesiosaur

Appearing about the same time as the dinosaurs were a group of flying reptiles or **pterosaurs** [TEHR-uh-sawrz]. These bizarre creatures are in no way related to modern-day birds. Figure 33.14 shows a typical member of this group called a *Pteranodon*.

Scientists who have studied these animals have concluded that they must have been gliders. Pterosaurs probably did not have strong enough muscles to beat their wings and take off from the ground. Like ichthyosaurs, the pterosaurs became extinct before the dinosaurs disappeared.

Another group of early reptiles, the **therapsids** [thuh-RAP-suhdz], is of considerable interest to scientists. The fossil record seems to show that they gave rise to modern-day mammals. Figure 33.14 shows a drawing of just such an animal, called *Moschops*. Soon after the appearance of the dinosaurs, most of the therapsids became extinct. Some therapsid descendents survived and appear in the fossil record as bones of very small mammals that looked something like rats. With the unexplained disappearance of the dinosaurs, these small mammals suddenly took over and became the dominant animals on Earth.

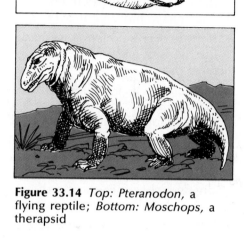

Figure 33.14 *Top: Pteranodon*, a flying reptile; *Bottom: Moschops*, a therapsid

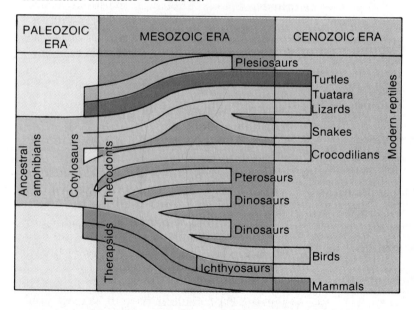

Figure 33.15 The evolutionary relationships of reptiles

Checkpoint

1. What is the name of the first reptiles to appear in the fossil record?
2. What group of marine reptiles resembled modern-day porpoises?
3. How did the pterosaurs fly?

CHAPTER REVIEW

Summary

- Reptiles are well adapted to living on land. They have impermeable skin, which keeps the animal from drying out. The position of their limbs keeps their body off the ground and makes movement over land easier.
- Reptile reproduction is well adapted to land life, with internal fertilization and eggs that have protective shells.
- The reptile egg is characterized by four membranes. These membranes are the chorion, the amnion, the allantois, and the yolk sac.
- Reptile lungs are highly folded internally and are therefore more efficient than amphibian lungs. The ventricle of the heart is partially divided, thus minimizing the mixing of oxygenated and deoxygenated blood.
- The four orders of living reptiles are Squamata, which include the snakes and lizards; Chelonia, which include the turtles and tortoises; Crocodilia, which include the alligators and crocodiles; and Rhynchocephalia, which contain only the tuatara.
- Snakes show a number of special adaptations that reflect their unusual body shape and feeding habits.
- Scientists think that all present and extinct reptiles descended from a group of reptiles called cotylosaurs.
- Dinosaurs can be classified into two groups by their pelvic structures.
- Extinct flying reptiles moved by gliding and were not related to modern birds.
- From 65 to 80 million years ago the dinosaurs all became extinct. Yet some reptiles survived, as did the mammals, which had existed in the shadow of the dinosaurs for many millions of years.

Vocabulary

allantois	oviparous
amnion	ovoviviparous
basking	pineal eye
caiman	plastron
carapace	plesiosaur
Chelonia	pterosaur
chorion	Rhynchocephalia
constrictor	saurischians
cotylosaur	Squamata
Crocodilia	terrapin
gavial	therapsid
ichthyosaur	tortoise
internal fertilization	trachea
Jacobson's organ	tuatara
keratin	yolk sac
ornithischians	

Review

1. Of what material are reptilian scales and claws made?
2. What is the function of the chorion in the reptilian egg?
3. Name a form of behavior that allows reptiles to regulate their body temperature.
4. What two adaptations of the snake skeleton make it easy for these reptiles to swallow large food organisms?
5. What organ in the mouth of the snake aids the sense of smell?
6. What are two anatomic features of lizards that are not found in snakes?
7. What is the major difference between the vertebrae of chelonians and that of other reptiles?
8. What two groups of reptiles belong to the order Squamata?

9. What kinds of organisms are in the order Crocodilia?
10. What is the major difference between the reptile heart and the amphibian heart?
11. What primitive reptile group is ancestral to the tuataras?
12. What characteristic separates the saurischian dinosaurs from the ornithischian dinosaurs?
13. Where did plesiosaurs and icthyosaurs live?
14. What group of reptiles is probably the ancestor of the mammals?
15. Name two ways in which snakes reproduce.

Interpret and Apply

1. Describe four adaptations of reptiles that make them better adapted to life on land than amphibians.
2. Describe the feeding habits of snakes and state how they are different from the feeding habits of other animals.
3. Why are legless lizards classified with lizards and not with snakes, which they seem to resemble so closely?
4. What features distinguish alligators from crocodiles?
5. Why are tuataras classified in a different order than the lizards?
6. Name three groups of reptiles that lived on Earth at the same time as the dinosaurs.

Challenge

1. Why is internal fertilization an important adaptation for terrestrial animals like reptiles?
2. Snakes and lizards are quite different in many ways. Why do scientists consider them enough alike to place them in the same order?

3. Describe how snake teeth are adapted to the habits of snakes.
4. What is the adaptive value of reptiles having partially or completely separated ventricles in the heart?
5. Describe an example of convergent evolution in the bodies of reptiles and modern mammals.

Projects

1. From a field guide to reptiles, find out what kinds of reptiles live in your local environment. Report your findings to the class.
2. Indicate on a map of North America the inclusive habitat of each of the following poisonous snakes: copperhead, water moccasin, coral snake, and any species of rattlesnake. Investigate what is considered good first aid in case of a poisonous snakebite and report your findings to the class.
3. Find out what is known about the ability of sea turtles to navigate across vast expanses of open ocean to locate the particular beach on which they will lay their eggs.
4. Find the evidence that supports the idea that dinosaurs were warm-blooded. What evidence does not support the idea?
5. Explain the theory of Walter and Luis Alvarez that states that the extinction of the dinosaurs resulted from the effects of a collision of a large asteroid with Earth. What evidence supports the theory? What evidence does not support the theory?

34 Birds

A tern

The animal in the photograph above is obviously a bird. Only birds can soar on feathered wings. Birds are widely distributed on Earth. They have reached the most remote land masses and, because of their versatile ways, have been able to live in a great variety of locations.

One of the most distinctive features of birds is the ability to fly. Flight can take a bird away from predators and harsh climates. It can also take a bird to a new food source when the old source threatens to run out.

The ability to fly is, in turn, due to the many structural and functional changes that are present in birds, but not in other vertebrates. Birds are the most specialized class of vertebrates. In fact, you could think of the bird as a beautifully designed flying machine. All of the parts of a bird coordinate to help it fly.

Humans have tried for thousands of years to devise ways of doing what birds have been able to do for the past 135 million years: to fly.

Characteristics of Birds

Feathers alone can identify an animal as a bird. No adult bird is without feathers and only birds have feathers. Egg laying is another characteristic present in all birds. Although there are some fish, amphibians, reptiles, and mammals that bring forth live young, no bird uses this method of reproduction.

34–1   The Origin of Birds

In 1861, scientists in Germany found a fossil that resembled a reptile with feathers. They named this creature **Archaeopteryx**, which means "ancient bird." Closer examination revealed that *Archaeopteryx* was similar to reptiles in many ways. Its forelimbs had claws, which may have been used for climbing and walking. Its bones were solid. Its breast bone was too small to permit the attachment of flight muscles. Its heavy beak contained teeth. It had a heavy, bony tail. Most of these characteristics indicate that it could not fly by flapping its wings. It was probably able to use its outstretched wings to glide from branch to branch. But it did have feathers. A reconstruction of *Archaeopteryx* is shown in Figure 34.1.

Archaeopteryx seems to represent a transition in the history of life between reptiles and birds. The *Archaeopteryx* fossils were found in the rock of the Jurassic Period, which began 180 million years ago. Modern birds did not appear until the Cretaceous Period, which began 135 million years ago.

CONCEPTS

- features of an ancient bird
- external features of modern birds
- the importance of feathers
- adaptations of beaks, wings, and feet

Do You Know?

The hoatzin is a modern bird that has clawed wings very early in life, but the claws do not persist until adulthood.

Figure 34.1 *Left:* Fossils of *Archaeopteryx* were first discovered in the 1860s. *Right:* The reconstruction of this animal shows that it has characteristics of both birds and reptiles.

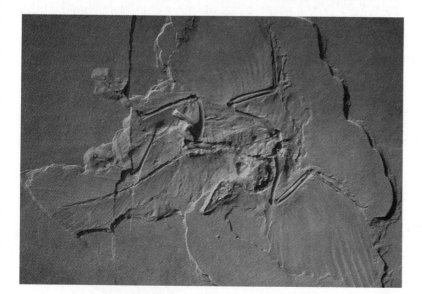

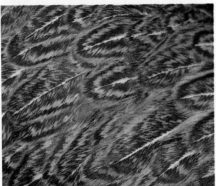

Figure 34.2 *Top:* Down feathers; *Middle:* Contour feathers; *Bottom:* Quill feathers. Each has a different function.

Figure 34.3 The structural features of a quill feather

34–2 Feathers

Except for their feet and beaks, feathers cover the entire body of most birds. Like the scales of reptiles, feathers are made of keratin. The structure of feathers, however, is very different from that of the scales of reptiles.

Feathers are light yet very strong. This strength is due to the structure of a feather. Rather than having a flat shape as in the scales of reptiles, the keratin of a feather forms a hollow tube called the **shaft**. A hundred or more **barbs** attach to each side of the shaft. Each barb has a fringe of **barbules**. The barbules of one barb connect to those of another barb by means of tiny hooks. There are about 4 million hooks on a single feather, strengthening the structure.

There are three main types of feathers: down feathers, contour feathers, and quill feathers. The feathers closest to the body are called **down feathers**. Down feathers are most obvious in newly hatched birds and in water birds. They insulate the body against heat loss. Birds burn energy quickly. They have body temperatures as high as 45°C, much higher than the surrounding air or water.

Covering the down feathers are **contour feathers**. As their name implies, they give shape to the bird's body, making it streamlined for flight. They also give the bird its coloration. Brown or gray contour feathers may help the bird to blend with its surroundings.

Colored feathers may act as a signaling device to other birds. The bird uses color to establish its territory and to attract a mate during mating season. Color, along with a bird's song, identifies a bird to other birds as a member of a particular species.

In species in which the male does not sit on the nest or care for the young, the male is apt to be much more brightly

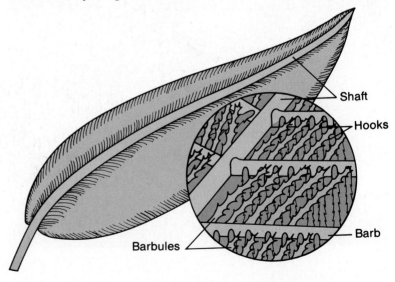

Shaft

Hooks

Barb

Barbules

colored than the female. In species in which both parents help to rear the young, the male and female are apt to have a similar dull coloring. Signaling his location by color would be dangerous if a male were protecting young birds.

The third group of feathers, **quill feathers**, grow on the wings and tail. Like the wings and tail of an airplane, the quill feathers help the bird to lift, balance, and steer while in the air.

Most birds have oil glands at the base of the tail. With its beak, a bird takes oil from its gland and spreads the oil over its feathers to waterproof them. This is especially important in water birds.

Many birds periodically lose feathers. The loss is gradual, with new feathers replacing those that are lost. This replacement of feathers is called **molting**.

34–3 Structures of the Head

The bird's beak is also made of keratin. Two **nares** [NAYR-eez], or nostrils, located on the beak function in breathing. The beak, unlike the reptilian mouth, is toothless. Birds use their beaks for scratching, cleaning, repairing feathers, kissing other birds, collecting nesting materials, and as weapons against enemies. Most importantly, birds use their beaks to obtain food.

The size and shape of a bird's beak are adaptations to the type of food it eats. For example, the beak of a sword-billed hummingbird is four times longer than the body of the bird. The hummingbird's food source is nectar that lies deep within flowers. A shorter beak would not allow the hummingbird to reach the nectar. The large, hooked beak of a parrot allows it to crack the shells of nuts, no small task. A flamingo's beak contains a sieve that strains tiny crustaceans out of the water.

Birds have keen vision. They are able to see colors and are

Figure 34.4 The size and shape of a bird's beak are adaptations to the type of food it eats.

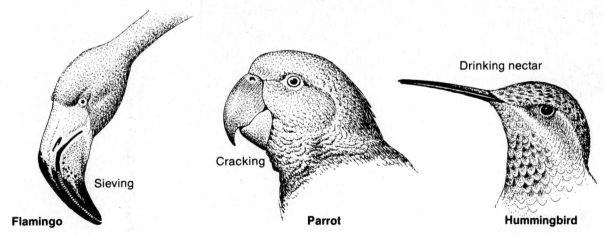

Sieving

Flamingo

Cracking

Parrot

Drinking nectar

Hummingbird

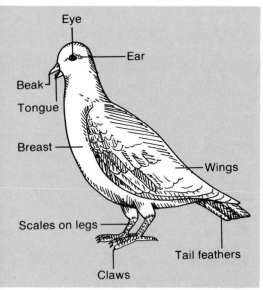

Figure 34.5 The external features of a bird

Eye
Ear
Beak
Tongue
Breast
Wings
Scales on legs
Tail feathers
Claws

Figure 34.6 The structure of a bird's foot reflects its way of life.

able to discern objects at great distances. Such keen vision is useful to predatory birds, such as hawks, in searching for mice or other prey. It also allows birds to watch for predators.

The eyes of most birds are located on the sides of the head. As a result, both eyes cannot look in the same direction at once. A few birds, such as owls, have eyes located at the front of the head. This position allows owls to focus both eyes on a single object and to judge distances accurately.

The ears of a bird are located directly behind the eyes. They are not obvious because feathers cover and protect them. A bird's sense of hearing is acute. Canals starting at the outer ears lead to eardrums, or tympanic membranes, within the head. Eustachian tubes connect the mouth cavity with the eardrums and keep the pressure on both sides of the eardrum equal.

The senses of smell and taste are not well developed in birds. Birds rely instead upon their senses of hearing and sight. The bird's tongue is used merely as a means of picking up food.

The bird's neck is quite flexible. A bird can turn its head 180 degrees, so that it can look directly behind itself. This movement is possible because there are many more vertebrae in the neck of a bird than in the necks of other vertebrates.

34–4   Other External Features

Unlike most vertebrates, birds stand on two legs. A bird's forelimbs are wings, rather than arms or fins. Its tail consists only of feathers, not of bones like the reptilian tail. Bones would be too heavy for efficient flight.

Like reptiles, birds' feet are clawed and covered with keratin scales. The feet vary with a bird's life-style. A typical bird's

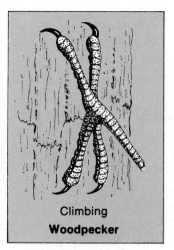

Climbing
Woodpecker

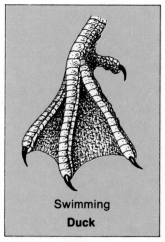

Swimming
Duck

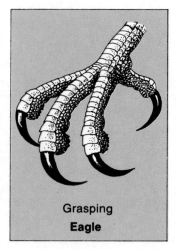

Grasping
Eagle

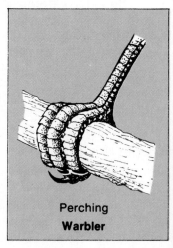

Perching
Warbler

foot has four toes, three pointing forward and one pointing backward. This arrangement permits easy perching. Some birds, such as ducks, have webbed feet that allow them to swim. Others, such as hawks and eagles, have pointed talons that they use to kill their prey. Swifts spend most of their lives in flight. Their feet are reduced to tiny structures.

Wings vary greatly in size and shape. Birds with long wings, including swifts, swallows, falcons, and many sea birds, are long-distance fliers. They require wide-open spaces to accelerate, turn, glide, and brake. They rely upon their speed in escaping from enemies.

Short-distance fliers live in woods, bushes, and reeds. Their short, wide wings do not permit long, swift flight but do allow them to turn easily in crowded areas. Blackbirds are examples of short-distance fliers. Compare the wings of an albatross, a sea bird, with those of a woodcock, a bird of the woods, shown in Figure 34.7.

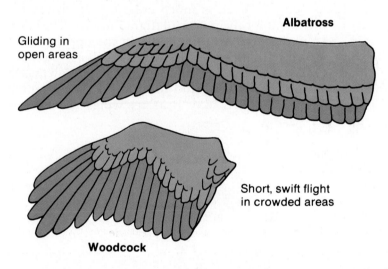

Figure 34.7 The structure of a bird's wings is an adaptation to its flight requirements.

Some birds, such as ostriches, penguins, and cassowaries, have lost the ability to fly. Many flightless birds have other protective adaptations. A cassowary, for example, can kick a large animal hard enough to rip its body open.

Checkpoint

1. What are two functions of the beak?
2. What structural adaptation is found in the feet of most swimming birds?
3. Name a flightless bird.
4. What fossil is considered to represent the earliest bird?

Internal Features of Birds

CONCEPTS

- skeletal adaptations for flight
- energy requirements of warm-bloodedness
- structure and function of internal organs

Much of a bird's anatomy differs markedly from that of a reptile. Most of the differences serve to enhance the flying ability of a bird. For example, the internal organs within a bird's trunk are packed close together, forming a compact center of gravity. This arrangement ensures stability in flight.

34–5   Skeleton

A bird's skeleton is the heaviest part of its body. Compared to the skeletons of other vertebrates, though, it is very light. The bones are hollow. Their strength is provided by cross struts, which add little weight. The bird skeleton is composed of the pectoral and pelvic girdles, the cranium, the backbone, and the limbs. Can you find the wishbone?

The breastbone, or **keel**, is much enlarged. It provides a point of attachment for the powerful flight muscles. The other end of the muscles attach to the bones in the upper part of the wing. A bird in flight moves its wings much as you move your arms when you row a boat. The wings go downward and backward, then upward and forward to their original position. A hummingbird may beat its wings as often as 80 times per second.

Figure 34.8 The skeletal features of a bird

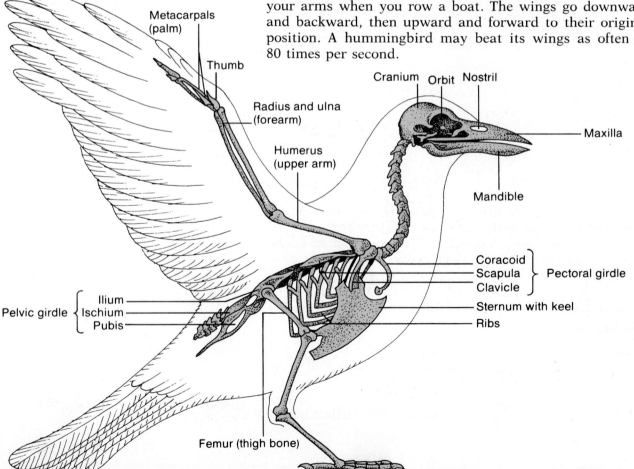

34–6   Feeding and Digestion

Flying requires an enormous amount of energy. A bird's body has many adaptations that help to provide the necessary energy. One is the maintenance of a high body temperature. To maintain high body temperatures, birds require large quantities of food. The foods of most birds, such as fish, nuts, fruit, nectar, and insects, are high in calories.

Because a bird has no teeth, it cannot chew its food. Rather, it usually swallows its food whole. After a bird takes food into its beak, the food passes through the pharynx and down the esophagus. The **crop**, an enlargement at the base of the esophagus, stores the food and moistens it in preparation for digestion.

The stomach is divided into two parts. The first part is the **proventriculus**. The walls of the proventriculus secrete gastric fluid that mixes with the food. The gastric fluid contains digestive enzymes. The second division of the stomach, the **gizzard**, then receives the food. The gizzard is composed of two hard plates that rub against one another, crushing the food between them. Breaking the food into smaller pieces helps digest the food.

After leaving the gizzard, the partially digested food passes into the intestine. The intestine absorbs usable food. Undigestible food passes into the rectum and finally out through the cloaca.

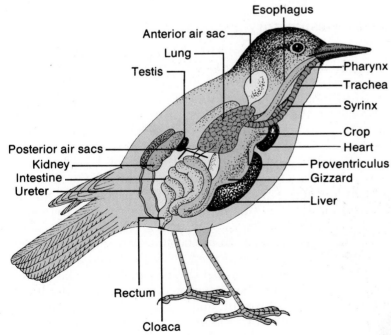

Figure 34.9 The internal anatomy of a male bird

The digestive process is incredibly quick. A bird can eat a berry and evacuate the seed from its body within 12 minutes. Such efficient digestion has two advantages. It allows the bird to process a large amount of food in a short time. It also quickly eliminates unusable food, which would add to the weight of the bird during flight.

The large quantities of food ingested by birds, combined with their feather insulation, provide the means to regulate their body temperatures internally. This characteristic, called **warm-bloodedness**, is generally not found in reptiles or amphibians. Recall that most reptiles maintain their body temperatures by absorbing or releasing heat to the surrounding environment. Warm-bloodedness allows birds to remain active even in very cold temperatures.

Warm-bloodedness requires more food in order to fuel the higher rate of metabolism. Since they must have a constantly large supply of food, many birds **migrate**, or move to another location, each winter when food is scarce. They return in the spring, when food is more plentiful.

Recall from Chapter 7 that animals obtain energy by the process of respiration. In respiration, molecules of digested food combine with oxygen in the mitochondria, forming ATP. Therefore, in addition to having a large food requirement, birds also require a large supply of oxygen. The respiratory and circulatory systems provide this oxygen.

34–7 Respiratory System

The respiratory system contains **air sacs** in addition to lungs and airways. The air sacs fill many spaces in the body cavity and even in some of the hollow bones. Air sacs allow a bird to inhale a large volume of air at one time.

Air enters the respiratory system through the nares in a bird's beak. It travels through the pharynx, larynx, trachea, and **syrinx,** or the bird's voice box. Below the syrinx the trachea branches into two tubes called bronchi. Each **bronchus** passes through a lung and enters a posterior air sac. Smaller bronchi branch off the main bronchi in the lungs, leading to the anterior air sacs. Gas exchange occurs through the small bronchi.

While air is traveling from the lungs to the anterior air sacs after inhaling, oxygen is entering the blood and carbon dioxide is entering the bronchi. When the bird exhales, the oxygen-rich air from the posterior air sacs enters the lungs through the small bronchi, and again gas exchange occurs. Thus, the bird, unlike other animals, exchanges carbon dioxide for oxygen both during inhalation and exhalation.

34–8 Circulatory System

Once oxygen has entered the bloodstream, it must be pumped to all the tissues of the body. This task is accomplished by the heart. The heart of the bird, shown in Figure 34.10, contains four distinct chambers: two atria and two ventricles. The atria are thin walled. The ventricles are thick walled and muscular. Their function is to pump the blood.

The complete separation of the ventricles divides the heart into two separate pumps. The right side pumps deoxygenated blood from the body to the lungs, where it gains oxygen and loses carbon dioxide. The left side of the heart receives oxygenated blood from the lungs and pumps it through the aorta to the rest of the body. Thus the four-chambered heart does not allow oxygenated blood to mix with deoxygenated blood. The tissues of the body receive only blood that is rich in oxygen. This is especially important for an animal with a high oxygen requirement.

34–9 Excretory System

The excretory system of a bird is simple. Uric acid is a nitrogenous waste product left over from the breakdown of proteins. The two kidneys, which are located toward the back of the bird's body, filter uric acid out of the blood. When uric acid leaves the kidneys, it enters paired ureters. The ureters empty directly into the cloaca, from which uric acid leaves the body along with the digestive wastes. What is the advantage of having no urinary bladder to a bird?

34–10 Nervous System

A bird's nervous system is highly developed. Compared to a reptile of the same body weight, a bird's brain is 6 to 11 times larger than the reptile's. In order to compensate for the weight of the brain, the cranium, or brain case, must be very thin. This prevents the bird from being too heavy at the head end during flight.

The olfactory lobes of birds are quite small. This is not surprising, since birds have very little sense of smell. The optic lobes are quite large, enabling birds to have a keen sense of vision.

The cerebrum is greatly enlarged, allowing complex behavior. In addition to being the seat of learned and unlearned behavior, the cerebrum is also the center for the controls that allow a bird to hop, fly, and swim. The cerebellum, which controls muscular coordination, is well developed. The medulla controls functions such as breathing. It lies at the base of the brain and joins the upper end of the spinal cord.

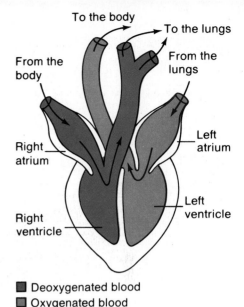

■ Deoxygenated blood
■ Oxygenated blood

Figure 34.10 Birds have four-chambered hearts.

Figure 34.11 The brain of a bird shows a small area devoted to the sense of smell (olfactory lobes).

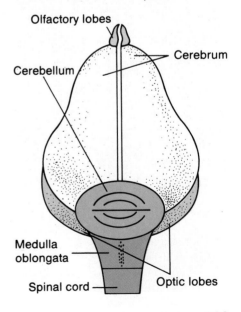

34–11 Reproduction

The female bird has only one ovary. As birds evolved the other ovary was probably lost as an adaptation for less weight during flight. Eggs develop in the ovary and leave through the oviduct.

The testes of the male bird lie above its kidneys. The sperm leave the testes by small tubes called the **vas deferens**, which lead to the cloaca.

When breeding season arrives, nest building begins. Nests are usually as inconspicuous as possible. Conspicuous nests would attract unwanted visitors. The type of nest a bird builds depends upon its species, where it lives, and the materials available. Kingfishers nest in holes in riverbanks. Tailor birds in India "sew" together the leaves of a tree, using plant fibers as thread. The male hornbill seals his mate and their eggs into a hole in a tree by covering the hole with mud. He leaves only a small opening, through which he passes food to his mate.

Once the nest has been built, the birds mate. When two birds mate, the male mounts the female so that their cloacas touch. Sperm from the male enter the female. The sperm can survive inside the female for long periods of time. One mating may be enough to fertilize many eggs.

Like reptiles, birds have internal fertilization. Fertilization occurs in the upper part of the oviduct. The newly fertilized egg consists of a yolk, on which rests the tiny embryo. The yolk contains fats and proteins that provide nutrients for the embryo. After fertilization, glands in the walls of the oviduct secrete substances that surround the zygote and yolk.

Figure 34.12 Nesting behavior varies greatly among birds. Nesting in a tree is a behavior commonly associated with birds. The kingfisher builds its nest in the side of a riverbank.

First, the white, or **albumen**, is laid down. This contains protein and is another food source for the developing bird. Strands of a stringy material called **chalaza** [kah-LAY-zah] suspend the embryo from the ends of the egg. This keeps the embryo from pressing against the wall of the egg. An outer membrane and a shell are secreted around the white by a gland. Additional glands deposit pigment on the shell.

A bird lays the fully formed egg less than two days after fertilization. A fertilized egg is shown in Figure 34.13. The shell protects the developing embryo without closing off the embryo from its environment. The shell has pores through which oxygen and carbon dioxide can pass.

Even as an embryo, a bird must maintain a high body temperature. Therefore, the parents must **incubate** the eggs, or keep them warm. In some species only the mother sits on the eggs. In other species both parents share the brooding. A few species have developed alternatives to sitting on eggs, such as burying them in rotting plant matter or in volcanic ash. The North American cowbird lays its look-alike eggs in the nest of another species, tricking the foster parent into incubating and feeding the cowbird's young.

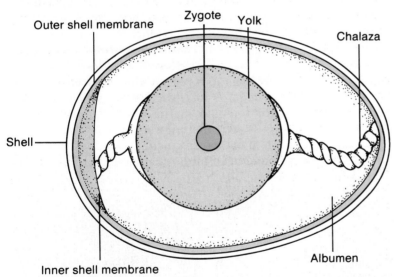

Figure 34.13 The internal structure of a fertilized egg

In preparation for incubation, a parent bird will loosen or pull a patch of feathers from the part of its chest that will contact the eggs. Beneath the skin of this **brood patch** the blood vessels enlarge, bringing heat to the surface of the skin that is in contact with the eggs.

The period necessary for incubation varies with the size of the bird. The larger the bird, the longer the time required for incubation. Incubation times range from about two weeks to almost two months.

34–12   Embryo Development

When fertilization has occured and the egg is warm enough, development proceeds. The zygote, which begins as a speck on the yolk, divides until the resulting cells cover the surface of the yolk. The cells develop into different types of tissues and organs. The heart, the first organ to develop, is visible and functioning after three days in the chick embryo.

A membrane grows out of the embryo's digestive system, enveloping the yolk. This membrane, called the yolk sac, produces digestive enzymes. The enzymes digest the food in the yolk. Blood vessels in the yolk sac deliver the digested food to the embryo. As the embryo grows, the yolk decreases in size. Like a reptilian egg, a bird's egg also contains three membranes besides the yolk sac. They are the amnion, the allantois, and the chorion.

The development of a chick embryo is shown in Figure 34.14. When the embryo has completed its growth within the shell, it pecks at the shell with a special structure called an **egg tooth**. The embryo eventually cracks the shell and continues pecking until the shell cracks enough for the young bird to emerge. The egg tooth disappears soon after hatching.

The number of eggs a bird species lays depends in part upon how much care the newly hatched birds will require. If the young birds require much care, few eggs will be laid. If one or more eggs are lost before incubation begins, the female will lay more eggs to replace them. Even if the entire **clutch**, or group of eggs, is lost, the female will replace all of them, if it is not too late in the breeding season. Cool temperatures do not harm the embryos during early stages of development. In most birds, incubation does not begin until all the eggs have been laid. All the eggs hatch at about the same time.

Figure 34.14 The development of a chick embryo from zygote to hatching takes about 21 days.

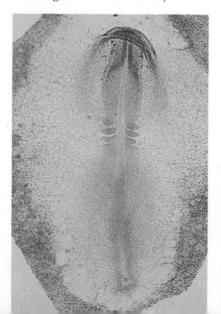
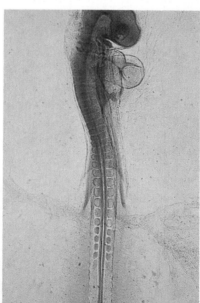
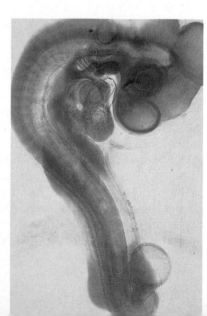

Figure 34.15 *Left:* Swans are precocial birds that lay large numbers of eggs and produce young that are downy and well developed. *Right:* Warblers are altricial birds that lay few eggs and produce young that are almost featherless.

Some birds, called **precocial** [pree-KOH-shel] birds, are quite advanced in their development when they hatch. They have down coats, can feed themselves, hop, and swim. Ducks, chickens, and swans are examples of precocial birds.

Most birds belong to another group, called the **altricial** [al-TRIH-shuhl] birds. Altricial birds are quite helpless at hatching. They are blind, often naked, and completely dependent upon their parents. The female of an altricial species lays fewer eggs than that of a precocial species. Blackbirds, nuthatches, and pigeons are examples of altricial birds.

In altricial species, the parents feed the fast-growing young, bring them water in their beaks, clean the nest, warm the young birds, and shield them from sun and rain. As you might expect, precocial birds take longer to develop in the egg than altricial birds do.

Whether precocial or altricial, a bird's first down coat is dull in color. Such coloring allows the young bird to blend with its surroundings.

When birds leave the nest, parents may produce another clutch of eggs in the same breeding season. Sometimes a pair of birds can even produce three families in one breeding season.

Checkpoint

1. What term is used to describe a bird's ability to regulate its body temperature internally?
2. What is the function of the gizzard?
3. Which structures increase the volume of air that can be inhaled at one time?
4. What do scientists call birds that hatch in a helpless state?

CHAPTER REVIEW

Summary

- *Archaeopteryx* showed characteristics of both reptiles and birds. It had feathers and wings, but its bones were heavy and it had teeth. *Archaeopteryx* could climb, but was probably unable to fly by flapping its wings. Scientists believe that it was an ancestor of modern birds.
- All birds have feathers. A body covering of feathers aids in flight, insulation, and communication with other birds. Other characteristics of birds include warm-bloodedness, development from amniotic eggs, and internal fertilization.
- Birds also have well-developed senses of hearing and sight, stand on two feet, and have forelimbs modified into wings.
- Adaptations of a bird's internal anatomy for flight include a respiratory system containing air sacs that increase the amount of air that a bird can inhale at one time.
- Birds have a four-chambered heart and an efficient circulatory system, which deliver large amounts of oxygen to the flight muscles. Other adaptations that allow birds to fly include quick digestion and excretion to eliminate excess weight, a hollow skeleton, a simple reproductive system, and a highly developed brain.
- Birds vary in their breeding habits and the care of their young. Many birds have elaborate courtship behavior and build nests.
- The egg white and yolk provide nutrients for the growing embryo. The amniotic egg resembles that of a reptile.
- Incubation periods vary depending on the size of the bird. Birds may be classified as altricial or precocial depending on the amount of care a newly-hatched bird requires.

Vocabulary

air sacs	gizzard
albumen	incubate
altricial	keel
Archaeopteryx	migrate
barbs	molting
barbules	nares
bronchus	precocial
brood patch	proventriculus
chalaza	quill feathers
clutch	shaft
contour feathers	syrinx
crop	vas deferens
down feathers	warm-bloodedness
egg tooth	

Review

1. Name three bird structures made of keratin.
2. Which two of the bird's senses are best developed?
3. Name a feature of a male bird that is used to attract a mate.
4. What feature did *Archaeopteryx* have that classifies it as a bird?
5. What feature of a bird's skeleton makes it lighter than the skeletons of most other vertebrates?
6. How do air sacs help a bird in flight?
7. What is the first organ to develop in the chick embryo?
8. When did *Archaeopteryx* live?
9. Which is *not* a function of feathers? (a) attracting a mate (b) balancing during flight (c) feeding of the young (d) signaling to other birds (e) maintaining high body temperature
10. The function of the chalaza is (a) to provide the embryo food, (b) to hold moisture, (c) to camouflage the egg, (d) to keep the embryo from pressing against the walls of the egg.

11. Which of the following is *not* a membrane in the bird's egg? (a) yolk (b) yolk sac (c) allantois (d) amnion

Match the structure in the left column with its function in the right column.

12. down feathers
13. contour feathers
14. quill feathers
15. gizzard
16. keel
17. air sacs
18. shell

a. provides for the attachment of flight muscles
b. provides for balance and steering in flight
c. provides insulation
d. increases the amount of air inhaled
e. grinding up food
f. protects embryo
g. speeds digestion
h. provides for streamlining during flight

Match the bird characteristic on the left with the correct statement on the right.

19. has webbed feet
20. has a long incubation period
21. lays few eggs per clutch
22. has short, wide wings
23. has a long, slender beak
24. male has brilliant coloring

a. lives on or near water
b. lives in congested area
c. offspring are precocial
d. offspring are altricial
e. sucks nectar from flowers
f. male does not sit on eggs

Interpret and Apply

1. Compare altricial and precocial birds.
2. List several differences between birds and reptiles.
3. Compare the beaks of nectar feeders and nutcrackers.
4. Name several characteristics that lighten the bird for flight.

5. Place the following events in the correct order:
   a. addition of albumen and shell
   b. fertilization
   c. hatching
   d. incubation
   e. egg laying
   f. mating
   g. nest building
6. Name, in order, the parts of a bird's digestive system through which food passes.

Challenge

1. Name several structures that are found in birds but not in other types of vertebrates. How are these structures an advantage to a bird?
2. Which bird has a longer incubation period, a hummingbird or an ostrich?
3. What would happen to a bird whose feather barbules lacked hooks?
4. Make a table comparing the following characteristics of reptiles, *Archaeopteryx*, and birds: bone structure, tail, (if present), mouth, body covering, forelimbs, keel.
5. How is warm-bloodedness an advantage to birds?

Projects

1. Obtain a field guide to the birds in your area. Using binoculars or field glasses, identify as many birds as possible. Keep a record of those you see.
2. Obtain a Rock Cornish game hen, chicken, quail, or other small bird from a grocery store. Boil it for several hours until the meat comes off the bones easily. Remove the meat, trying to keep the skeleton intact. Locate and identify the keel, pelvic and pectoral girdles (including the wishbone), both sets of limbs, and the vertebrae. Can you find the cranium? Why or why not?

35 Mammals

Mare with foal

The foal in the photograph above is nursing. Its food is the milk that is produced by its mother's mammary glands. Animals that provide milk for their young are called mammals.

Milk is the most nourishing of all foods. It contains all of the nutrients necessary for the growth of a young mammal. About 85 percent of milk is water. The rest of the liquid is composed of carbohydrates, fats, proteins, and vitamins. The major carbohydrate in milk is the sugar lactose. Lactose gives milk its sweet taste. Milk is also rich in minerals such as calcium and phosphorus, which are necessary for the growth of bones, teeth, and other tissues.

The milk of all mammals contains the same nutrients, but the proportions vary from species to species. The milk of each species is well suited to the needs of its developing young.

Besides providing milk, all mammals care for their young after birth. Large mammals may care for their offspring for several years. Human families are an extreme example of parental care. Some human parents care for their children for nearly 20 years.

Characteristics of Mammals

Mammals represent the most advanced group of vertebrates. Many aspects of mammalian structure and function differ from those of other classes of vertebrates. The structure of one highly successful mammal — the human — is considered in detail in Unit 7. A few structural features are so striking that they bear emphasizing here. These features include the brain, heart, body covering, and development of young.

35–1 Common Features of Mammals

Mammals have the most complex brains of all the vertebrates. The cerebrum is the largest structure of the mammalian brain. The large cerebrum allows mammals to perform complex types of behavior. The capacity of the mammalian brain is further increased because its surface is folded upon itself in ridges and grooves called **convolutions**. This folding fits more surface area into the unexpandable volume of the bony skull. The cerebellum is also large and convoluted in mammals. The senses of hearing and smell are typically well developed.

Like birds, mammals are warm-blooded. Also like birds, mammals have four-chambered hearts. Complete separation of oxygenated and deoxygenated blood ensures a good supply of oxygenated blood to the body tissues. This oxygen supply is essential for the maintenance of warm-bloodedness.

Mammals breathe with well developed lungs. Their intake of air is aided by a strong muscle between the lungs and the abdomen called the **diaphragm**.

All mammals have some hair. The hair covering and the air layer trapped beneath the hair prevent mammals from losing body heat. This contributes to their success as warm-blooded animals. Many aquatic mammals have lost much of their hair as a streamlining adaptation. Their warmth comes from a thick layer of **blubber**, or fat, beneath their skin.

Mammalian skin contains four unique types of glands. The most important of these are the **mammary glands**. Milk secreted from these glands provides nourishment for the young. Sweat glands help to regulate the body temperature and rid the body of wastes. **Sebaceous** [sih-BAY-shuhs] **glands** lubricate the hair and skin. Scent glands produce chemical substances that help mammals communicate with each other.

Most mammals have highly developed teeth. The diversity of mammalian teeth reflects the great variety of mammalian diets.

CONCEPTS
- structural characteristics of mammals
- development of young mammals

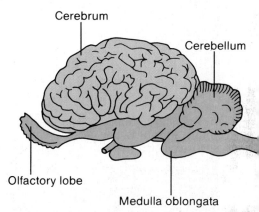

Figure 35.1 The convolutions of the mammalian cerebrum greatly increase the capacity of the brain.

35–2 Mammalian Development

Mammals, like reptiles and birds, reproduce by internal fertilization. With few exceptions, mammals do not lay eggs. Most mammals bear live young. In most mammals the embryo develops in a muscular organ called the **uterus**. Thus the developing embryo is protected by its mother's body.

After birth, the young continue to receive maternal care. Their nutrition is from milk, which they obtain from their mother's mammary glands. In addition to providing their food, the mother protects them from natural enemies and teaches them to find their own food. Generally, the more complex behavior a mammal is capable of, the longer its period of association with its mother after birth.

This trend reaches its extreme in humans. Born after nine months of development within the mother, an infant is helpless and totally dependent at birth. In the many years spent after birth with his or her parents, the young human learns amazingly complex social and intellectual behaviors.

Figure 35.2 Mammals protect their young after birth and teach them survival skills.

Checkpoint

1. What is the advantage of a convoluted cerebrum?
2. Name five unique features of mammalian skin and body covering.
3. What substance is produced in mammary glands?

Monotremes and Marsupials

Scientists divide the thousands of species of mammals into three groups on the basis of their method of reproduction. These groups are the monotremes, the marsupials, and the placentals.

Monotremes, the most primitive of the living mammals, lay eggs and incubate them in a birdlike fashion. **Marsupials** are the pouched mammals. They bear tiny, premature young. These bee-sized young leave the mother's uterus and crawl up to the pouch. Here they attach to nipples and complete their development. These two groups are found mainly in Australia, New Guinea, New Zealand, and Tasmania.

Although both monotremes and marsupials are primitive groups, they are not closely related. Scientists think that the reptilian ancestors of monotremes were different from the reptilian ancestors of marsupials and all other mammals.

35–3 Characteristics of Monotremes

Like all mammals, monotremes are covered with hair. They are warm-blooded and produce milk that nourishes their young. As in reptiles and birds, their cloaca serves excretory and reproductive functions. Fertilization is internal but the embryos develop externally in eggs. The eggs are incubated.

The heads of monotremes are remarkably birdlike in appearance. They have long, leathery, beaklike extensions of the face. The adults are toothless and lack external ears.

There are only three species of monotremes. The duck-billed platypus and the two species of spiny anteaters are restricted to New Guinea, Australia, and Tasmania.

The duck-billed platypus is a small mammal about the size of a large squirrel. The platypus is semi-aquatic. It has webbed feet tipped with claws. When swimming, it paddles with its forefeet and steers with its hind feet. It uses it leathery bill to probe for crustaceans and plants that live at the bottom of the water. The claws are used for burrowing when on land.

In the platypus, warm-bloodedness is incompletely developed. Its body temperature fluctuates but averages about 30°C. The brain of the platypus is small and has a smooth surface.

After the female platypus mates, she digs a long burrow. At the end of the burrow she lays two eggs on a bed of moist leaves. The female platypus curls her body around the eggs during the 10-day incubation period. The platypus lacks nipples. Milk for the young is produced by sweat glands on the female's underside. When the young hatch, they are nourished

Figure 35.3 The duck-billed platypus is a monotreme, or egg-laying mammal.

Figure 35.4 The spiny anteater shown is a monotreme. Other kinds of anteaters are placental mammals.

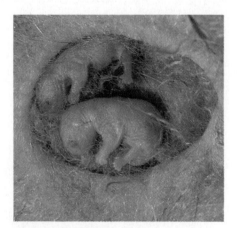

Figure 35.5 Born after a 5–6 week gestation period, opossums crawl from the uterus into the pouch and attach to nipples. The young will continue to develop in the pouch for several months.

by licking milk from the mother's fur.

The two spiny anteater species are covered with coarse hair and sturdy spines. Their masses range from 2 to 10 kilograms. Spiny anteaters have large, convoluted brains. Their powerful limbs are tipped with claws adapted for digging. They escape predators by burrowing rapidly into the ground. Spiny anteaters have long slender snouts. When foraging, they turn over stones and break into termite and ant nests. Anteaters capture their prey with their long sticky tongues.

The female spiny anteater lays a single leathery egg, which she incubates in a pouch on her belly. The young are helpless when they hatch and remain in the pouch until their spines form.

35–4 Characteristics of Marsupials

Fertilization is internal in marsupials. Development of embryos begins in the mother's uterus. The embryos have tiny yolk sacs, which provide only a limited food supply. Therefore, the young are born very early in development.

At birth the tiny marsupial young crawl from the mother's uterus, through her cloaca and fur, and into the pouch. There the young attach to the nipples of the mammary glands. The pouch protects the young. This pouch is the most striking characteristic of marsupial mammals. Milk from the nipples provides nourishment until the young are mature enough to be independent of the mother. The length of time spent in the pouch depends upon the species.

35–5 Representative Marsupials

Opossums are the only North American marsupials. They are active at night and live mostly in rural areas. They eat small birds and mammals, eggs, and insects. The opossum has the shortest period of **gestation**, or development within the mother's body, of any mammal known. The young are born only $12\frac{1}{2}$ days after fertilization. Six to 24 young are born at a time. They crawl through the mother's fur and into the pouch, where they attach to the nipples. After spending several weeks in the pouch, the young leave the pouch but still cling to their mother's fur.

There are many species of opossums in Central and South America. One type, called the water opossum, has a pouch with a muscle that can close the pouch the way that strings close a drawstring bag. The mother can then submerge herself, still keeping the young marsupials dry. They can remain in the pouch underwater for several minutes because they can tolerate high levels of carbon dioxide.

The marsupial mole is a rodentlike marsupial that lives in Australia. Since it is a burrowing animal, its pouch opens at the posterior end of its body. This protects the young in the pouch when the mother burrows through the dirt.

The koala, a large, slow-moving marsupial, lives in eucalyptus trees. It eats the leaves of only a few species of eucalyptus trees. Only 1 koala is born at a time. It spends 6 months in its mother's pouch, and another 6 on her back.

Figure 35.6 Red kangaroos, which stand as tall as people, are the largest kangaroos.

BIOLOGY INSIGHTS

Many marsupial mammals in Australia are remarkably similar to placental mammals in North America. For example, there are marsupial wolves, mice, and moles. This similarity is the result of convergent evolution. Convergent evolution occurs when organisms are subjected to similar selective pressures.

Perhaps the best known of the marsupials are the kangaroos. Kangaroos are grass eaters. Smaller kangaroos are called wallabies. They have enormous, powerful hind legs. Their large tail helps them balance when they hop. They can hop as fast as 60 kilometers per hour and can jump over fences nearly 3 meters high.

The red kangaroo's reproductive pattern is unusual. At any time in her adult life, the female may have 3 dependent young. One is an embryo in the uterus, 1 is a newborn in the pouch, and 1 is an older offspring that lives outside the pouch but returns to nurse. When the older offspring becomes completely independent of the mother, the younger one becomes a part-time resident of the pouch. The embryo then leaves the uterus and lives full-time in the pouch. At this time, the female mates again, producing another embryo.

Checkpoint

1. How does the platypus find food?
2. Where do the spiny anteater's eggs mature?
3. What is unique about the development of marsupial young?
4. What marsupial lives in North America?

Placental Mammals

Placental mammals are the most successful and abundant group of living mammals. Both marsupials and placentals give birth to live young. The major difference between these two groups is the way the young are nourished before birth. The developing marsupials leave the uterus so early that they do not always survive the journey to the pouch. Placental young remain inside the uterus until they are much more developed.

In some placentals, such as the horses shown in the opening photo of the chapter, the young are able to walk and feed themselves within hours after birth. A newborn whale can swim as soon as it is born.

35–6   Characteristics of Placental Mammals

A special structure allows the young of the placental mammals to remain inside their mothers' bodies until they develop enough to withstand environmental hazards. The structure is called the **placenta**. The placenta is a flattened organ that is rich in blood vessels. The placenta is connected to the unborn animal by an **umbilical cord**.

The placenta, which has a convoluted surface, lies next to the wall of the uterus, which also has a convoluted surface. The convolutions greatly increase the surface areas of the placenta and uterine wall that contact each other. Through these points of contact, materials are exchanged between the mother and the young. Blood does not cross the placenta, but oxygen and food from the mother's blood do. There is also reverse traffic as carbon dioxide and nitrogen wastes from the embryo travel through the umbilical cord, through the placenta, and into the mother's uterus. The mother's blood removes the waste products from the uterus. The mother's kidneys excrete the waste products of the young along with those of her own body.

While the uterus contains developing young, the mother's body does not produce additional eggs. The placenta produces a chemical substance that prevents the release of more eggs. When the young are born, the placenta is also expelled from the mother's body as the afterbirth. Then the substances that prevented eggs from being released are no longer present, and the reproductive cycle begins again.

The period of gestation varies with the size of the animal. In the mouse, it is only 21 days. In the elephant, it is almost 2 years!

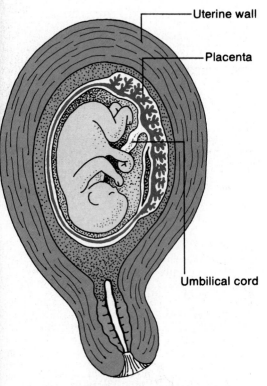

Uterine wall

Placenta

Umbilical cord

Figure 35.7 The structural features of the human placenta. The convoluted surfaces of the placenta and uterine wall allow for efficient exchange of nutrients and waste materials.

35–7 Some Types of Placentals

There are 17 orders of placental mammals. Some are very large groups, containing hundreds of different species, while others contain relatively few species. Some are found all over the world, and others are limited to a few locations. Descriptions of some of the major orders of mammals follow.

Rodentia: Rodents With about 1,700 species, the **rodents** make up the largest order of mammals. The mouse is a typical rodent. Rats and squirrels are other common rodents. Rodents live all over the world. Most rodents eat plants, but some eat insects, fish, reptiles, small mammals, and birds. They can live in trees, on the ground, in burrows, and in water.

All rodents have a pair of **incisor** teeth on each jaw, as shown in Figure 35.8. The incisors grow continuously. Only the front tooth surface has enamel on it. When the upper teeth move against the lower teeth in gnawing, part of the back surface of the upper teeth wears off. This process results in sharp, chisel-shaped teeth. There is a distinct space between the incisors and the grinding teeth in the cheeks.

One semiaquatic rodent, the beaver, is outstanding in its ability to modify its environment to suit its needs. Beavers use their sharp teeth to cut down trees and build dams across streams, thus forming deep pools. They build their homes in the water. Their large hind feet are webbed, and the openings to their eyes and ears can close when they submerge.

The largest rodents, the capybaras, live near marshes and streams in South America. They look like guinea pigs, but are as large as collies.

Mice and rats spread many diseases, such as typhus. In some parts of the world, they compete strongly with humans for grain supplies.

Lagomorpha: Rodentlike Animals Rabbits, hares, and pikas are **lagomorphs**. Lagomorphs are found throughout much of the world. They have adapted to such diverse habitats as the Arctic and the desert. They inhabit forests as well as treeless mountains.

Many people mistakenly think that rabbits and hares are rodents. Like the incisors of rodents, the lagomorph incisors are ever-growing. Lagomorphs are not considered rodents, however, due to the presence of an additional pair of incisors. Two small, peglike incisors are located behind the two larger ones.

Jackrabbits have enormous hind legs and move by bounding across open spaces. They depend upon their speed, up to 70 kilometers per hour, for survival. This is important, since the deserts in which they live do not offer them places to hide from predators.

Figure 35.8 A beaver's teeth are an adaptation for cutting down trees.

Figure 35.9 The jackrabbit has powerful hind legs that allow it to run as fast as a race horse.

Chiroptera: Bats The second largest mammalian order is the order **Chiroptera**. It contains about 850 species of bats. Bats are the only group of mammals that can fly. One is shown in Figure 35.10. They live everywhere but in the polar regions and on a few islands. The largest of all bats is the fruit bat. It has a wing span of 1.5 meters.

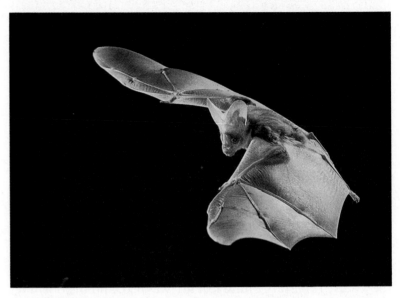

Figure 35.10 Bats are the only flying mammals. Their elongated finger bones act as supports for the wing membrane.

Four fingers support the flying membrane of a bat's wing. The sternum has developed into a keel, to which the membrane attaches. As a weight saver, the tailbones have been lost or have become very thin. The head is short and stubby, an adaptation that also reduces the bat's weight.

Most bats fly at night and guide themselves by using **echolocation**. They produce high-pitched sounds and listen for echos as sounds are reflected off objects. Bats use echolocation to avoid flying into obstacles in their path. Echolocation allows bats to capture flying insects, such as flies, mosquitoes, and moths.

Different types of bats have different diets. Food sources include insects, nectar, pollen, frogs, lizards, birds, and other bats. Vampire bats drink blood. The vampire bat's saliva contains a chemical that prevents its victim's blood from clotting. After the vampire bat has bitten an animal, such as a cow, it licks the free-flowing blood from the wound.

Young develop for a long period of time inside the mother bat. Since the mother must continue to fly during the gestation period, only 1 to 2 young are born at a time. Many young developing in the bat would make the bat too heavy for flight. A bat lives about 20 years, a long life span for such a small animal.

Mammals That Live in Water Members of many orders of mammals live in water. Most aquatic mammals are cigar-shaped, almost hairless, and have a thick layer of blubber. The blubber insulates them from the cold. Their forelimbs are usually paddle-shaped and clawless. Often no hind limbs are visible.

The order **Cetacea** is one large group of aquatic mammals. It includes whales and dolphins. The blue whale, over 30 meters long and weighing as much as 25 elephants, is the largest animal that has ever lived. Surprisingly, it feeds on vast quantities of microscopic plankton, which it filters out of the water.

Whales, like all mammals, are air-breathing. They can alternate breathing with periods of nonbreathing. A whale can remain submerged for as long as two hours. This is possible because it has about twice as many oxygen-carrying red blood cells for its weight as do land-dwelling mammals. A whale can also store oxygen in its muscles.

Figure 35.11 The manatee is a member of the order Sirenia. This animal is sometimes called a sea cow because its diet consists almost entirely of aquatic vegetation.

Carnivora: Flesh-Eating Mammals The order **Carnivora**, the flesh-eaters, contains about 280 species, most of which live on land. Carnivores include such familiar families of animals as cats, dogs, bears, raccoons, and weasels. Figure 35.12 shows a tiger. Note the long pointed teeth characteristic of carnivores. They are used for shredding flesh. Despite their name, not all members of the order limit their diet to flesh. The bears are notable for eating a wide variety of foods, including fruits and roots.

Some mammals of the order Carnivora also live in the water. Aquatic carnivores include seals, sea lions, and walruses. Although they are classified separately from animals such as whales, many similar structural characteristics permit them to follow an aquatic life.

Figure 35.12 The Bengal tiger, a carnivore, has large, powerful canine teeth.

Figure 35.13 The llama is a typical ungulate.

Ungulates: Hoofed Mammals   Two orders of mammals compose a group of animals commonly called **ungulates**, or hoofed mammals. The **Perissodactyla**, or odd-toed hoofed mammals, contain the zebras, horses, and rhinoceroses. The **Artiodactyla**, or even-toed hoofed mammals, are a far larger group including goats, sheep, pigs, hippopotamuses, camels, llamas, deer, giraffes, and the various types of cattle.

Ungulates do not have claws. Instead, they walk on the tips of their toes. Their hooves are actually modified toenails. Ungulates have wide teeth with large grinding surfaces that are useful in chewing plant material. Most ungulates are quite large. Large size gives them an advantage in fighting or escaping from predators.

Plant matter is much harder to digest than animal matter because the cells of plants are surrounded by walls of cellulose. Mammals do not have the digestive enzymes necessary to break down cellulose. However, microorganisms living in the digestive tracts of ungulates can digest cellulose. The microorganisms obtain their nourishment from the cellulose and make the contents of the cells available to the ungulates.

Some ungulates, called **ruminants**, have several compartments to their stomachs. Food that is partially digested is regurgitated, rechewed, and then passed into another compartment. When a cow "chews its cud," it is chewing regurgitated food so that it may be more fully digested.

Insectivora: Insect-Eating Animals   The roughly 400 species of **insectivores** make up an ancient order of mammals, dating from the Cretaceous period. These mammals live on all the continents but Australia and Antarctica. Insectivores are generally small mammals with long snouts. European hedgehogs, moles, and shrews are types of insectivores. Most insectivores have a well developed sense of smell.

Moles live entirely underground, so there is no need for acute vision. While the mole's eyes are small, it does have sensory organs at both ends of its body. At the front, the nose provides its sense of smell. At the rear, bristles on its tail provide it with touch sensation. Moles dig long tunnels, which act as traps for worms and insects. The mole may eat such unfortunate animals immediately. However, it may just paralyze them by a bite, and haul them away to a special storage section of the tunnel for eating later.

The pygmy shrew, weighing only 2 grams, is the smallest living mammal. It can squeeze through tunnels as narrow as a pencil.

Edentata: Toothless Mammals   The order **Edentata** includes about 30 species living in North and South America. One

Figure 35.14 The mole's long, sensitive snout has a keen sense of smell. Its powerful forelimbs are used for digging.

type, the anteater, has a long tongue covered with sticky saliva used to catch termites. The insects, swallowed whole, are ground up in the stomach.

Tree sloths are slow-moving and strictly plant-eating. Sloths live in the rain forests of South America, where they hang upside down. The sloth does not spend much time grooming itself. Algae grow in its long, coarse fur.

Armadillos are toothless animals covered with bony plates. They have sparse hair on their limbs and bellies between their bony plates. For protection, they burrow into the ground or curl up so that only their bony armor is exposed.

Primates The order **Primates** contains about 170 species of mammals. Primates have been most successful in tropical and subtropical regions. Primates include **prosimians** (lemurs, lorises, and tarsiers), monkeys, apes, and humans. The four existing types of apes are gorillas, orangutans, chimpanzees, and gibbons.

Of all the primates, only humans are fully bipedal, or able to walk on two feet. Most other primates spend much of their time in the trees.

All primates show the influence of their present or past life in the trees. They have grasping hands, agility, and excellent coordination. Most have nails, not claws, and their fingers and toes have touch-sensitive pads on the ends. Their toes are **opposable**, so that the thumb or big toe can touch the other digits. Opposable toes allow primates to grasp with their feet.

The primates' sense of smell is not as acute as that of other mammals, but their senses of hearing and vision are superior. Their eyes face forward, giving them excellent depth perception. Their eyes are also very large in proportion to their bodies.

Perhaps the most striking characteristic of primates is their enlarged cerebrum and the high level of intelligence associated with it. Primates make and use tools, have complex social systems and methods of communication, and are capable of learning complicated tasks.

Figure 35.15 For protection, an armadillo will burrow or curl up so that only its bony armor is exposed.

Figure 35.16 Primates have the ability to grasp objects with their feet.

Checkpoint

1. What structure connects the embryo of a placental mammal to the placenta?
2. What is the largest order of mammals?
3. What order of mammals contains the species with the largest cerebrums?
4. Members of what group of mammals chew their cud?

Fossil Mammals

The Age of Reptiles lasted until the end of the Mesozoic era. Fossils indicate that many mammals existed at the same time as the dinosaurs but were overshadowed by them. The extinction of the dinosaurs was the opportunity for the mammals to begin their rise to power, a position they still hold today. Mammals have dominated the land for the past 70 million years. This period is often called the Age of Mammals.

35–8   The Origin of Mammals

Even while the dinosaurs existed, some reptiles were becoming mammal-like. Yet fossils do not show the remains of an animal that was definitely a mammal until the Jurassic period, about 180 million years ago. After the dinosaurs died out, mammals flourished.

The early mammals were limited in variety. Some were opossumlike marsupials. Others were placental insectivores. Most were about the size of a large dog. They had long bodies, short legs, and five-toed feet, on which they were able to run slowly. These early mammals had long tails that were heavy at the base and relatively small heads. Their teeth indicate that they ate both plants and animals. Yet even at that early date, mammals were somewhat specialized. Some ate more meat, while others ate more vegetable matter.

By 60 million years ago, the mammals had evolved into many different forms. There were many types of hoofed ungulates, some over one meter high. There were also many types and sizes of carnivores and a few early rodents. There were even small animals that were probably the ancestors of monkeys. These species, and many more, gradually took over the environment.

35–9   The Rise of Modern Horses: An Example of Mammalian Evolution

Although early mammals were recognizable as the ancestors of modern mammals, they were different from modern forms. Over millions of years, mammals have evolved from primitive types to more specialized ones. A classical example of mammalian evolution is the evolution of the horse.

The prehistoric *Hyracotherium* and the modern horse *Equus* are shown in Figure 35.17. *Hyracotherium*, which appeared

Hyracotherium

about 65 million years ago, was only 20 to 25 centimeters high. It had 4 toes on each front foot and 3 on each hind foot. It walked on doglike feet. The head of *Hyracotherium* was small, containing small eyes set in the middle of the head. It had simple teeth, with small grinding surfaces suitable for eating soft vegetation but not for grazing on tough grass.

The modern horse *Equus* differs from *Hyracotherium* in many details. In *Equus* the number of toes on each foot has been reduced to one. The single toe has been modified into a hoof. This hard hoof aids the modern horse in running. The teeth of *Equus* are large, with an increased grinding surface permitting it to eat grass. Its eyes are set far back on the sides of the head. This adaptation allows horses to watch for predators while grazing. *Equus* is also several times larger than *Hyracotherium*.

Many fossils intermediate in form between *Hyracotherium* and *Equus* have been found. One way to interpret this evidence is to select several of the fossils and to put them in order according to age, increasing size, and decreasing toe number. People do this to demonstrate changes that were gradual in one direction. However, most modern evolutionary biologists doubt that this was the case.

Actually, many of the intermediate fossil forms of horses are found in rocks of the same age. This indicates that they lived at the same time, and that one could not have evolved directly from the other. Rather, evolutionary biologists now interpret the evidence as showing that the family tree of horses was highly branched, with most branches now extinct. Changes were not gradual and constant but occurred more rapidly during some periods. Only those horses with adaptations that were favorable in their environment were able to survive. The other forms eventually died out.

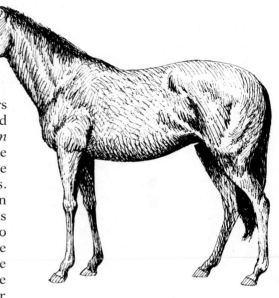

Equus

Figure 35.17 *Hyracotherium* was much smaller than modern horses and had no hooves.

Checkpoint

1. How long have mammals dominated the land?
2. Based on fossil records, when did mammals first appear on Earth?
3. What is the genus of the ancestor of modern horses?

CHAPTER REVIEW

Summary

- Mammals are warm-blooded vertebrates that feed their young milk. Milk is produced in the mammary glands of the females.

- All mammals have hair on some part of their bodies. Hair insulates the body. Mammals also have sebaceous glands, sweat glands, and scent glands. Aquatic mammals may be insulated by a layer of blubber.

- Mammals are able to maintain a constant body temperature partly because they have an efficient circulatory system, including a four-chambered heart. A diaphragm aids in respiration.

- Mammals are divided into three groups: monotremes, marsupials, and placentals. The divisions are made on the basis of their reproductive patterns.

- Monotremes are primitive mammals that lay eggs. The ability to regulate body temperature is not well developed in monotremes.

- Marsupials bear live young that later develop in a pouch on the mother's belly.

- The development of placental mammals occurs entirely within the mother's uterus. The embryo receives food and excretes wastes through the placenta.

- The placental mammals are divided into 17 orders. Humans are members of the order Primates.

- Mammal-like reptiles appeared before the dinosaurs did. After the dinosaurs vanished, mammals increased in size and variety.

- Mammals have dominated the land for 70 million years.

Vocabulary

Artiodactyla	marsupial
blubber	monotreme
Carnivora	opposable
Cetacea	Perissodactyla
Chiroptera	placenta
convolution	placental mammal
diaphragm	Primates
echolocation	prosimian
Edentata	rodent
gestation	ruminant
incisor	sebaceous gland
insectivore	umbilical cord
lagomorph	ungulate
mammary gland	uterus

Review

1. Name two characteristics mammals share with birds. Name two characteristics mammals have that birds do not.
2. Compared to most mammals, what is unusual about the method of reproduction in monotremes?
3. What muscle aids in the respiration of mammals?
4. To which two structures does the placenta attach?
5. How do bats locate their prey?
6. In what organ does the early development of marsupial embryos occur?
7. How long have mammals been the dominant form of life on Earth?
8. Which of the following mammals does *not* lay eggs? (a) duck-billed platypus (b) spiny anteater (c) sloth
9. Most marsupials live in (a) North America, (b) South America, (c) Asia, (d) Australia.

10. The first mammal-like organisms appeared (a) 500 years ago, (b) at the time of the dinosaurs, (c) before the dinosaurs, (d) about 1 million years ago.

Match the order of mammals on the left with a characteristic on the right.

11. Chiroptera	**a.** able to fly
12. Rodentia	**b.** have hoofed feet
13. Primates	**c.** have large eyes in front of face
14. Artiodactyla	**d.** have sharp teeth useful for shredding flesh
15. Carnivora	**e.** is the largest order of mammals
16. Cetacea	**f.** live in water
	g. have no teeth

Interpret and Apply

1. Compare the teeth of a carnivore with those of an ungulate. How are these teeth adapted for the animals' diets?
2. How is the marsupials' method of reproduction like that of placental mammals? How is it different?
3. Which two groups of placental mammals have teeth that grow continuously?
4. Name three orders of placental mammals that have aquatic or semiaquatic members.
5. Rabbits are classified as lagomorphs. Why aren't they classified as rodents?
6. Name three adaptations of mammals that contribute to the maintenance of a high body temperature.
7. Describe three adaptations that enable primates to live in trees.
8. Describe four adaptations that allow whales to live in the oceans.
9. In the following list, indicate whether the phrase describes monotremes, marsupials, or placental mammals. Some phrases may describe more than one group.
   a. lays eggs
   b. young develop in pouch
   c. young develop attached to placenta
   d. warm-bloodedness not well developed
   e. only one type lives in North America
   f. group to which most species of mammals belong
   g. nourish young with milk
   h. contains species *Homo sapiens*
   i. only three species exist
   j. embryos rely on yolk for food inside the mother's uterus
   k. all members lack teeth as adults
   l. cloaca serves excretory and reproductive functions

Challenge

1. Certain aspects of an animal's brain structure are associated with its intelligence. What do you think the human brain looks like? Describe its size, the relative size of the cerebrum, and the appearance of the surface of the cerebrum.
2. Apes are known to be capable of complex learning. That is, they are intelligent. Would you expect their period of dependence on their parents after birth to be long or short?
3. You discover a new type of fossil. The fossil shows that the animal was a large mammal that ate grass. In which group would you classify this new species? Explain.

Projects

1. Find out what laws exist to control mammals in your community. (Examples could include rat-control policies and leash laws for dogs.) Also find out how mammals are used in your community.
2. What products do you use on a daily basis that come from mammals?
3. Obtain a cow's heart from the butcher. Dissect it, and identify the four chambers.
4. Visit a local zoo. How many orders of mammals are represented?

Careers in Animal Husbandry

Animal husbandry is the scientific control and management of livestock. This field includes the breeding, maintaining, and marketing of healthy farm animals. There are many career opportunities related to animal husbandry.

Raising livestock is hard work. *Farmers* must provide sanitary living quarters for the animals. Disease and parasitism of one individual animal can infect an entire herd. Farmers must feed the animals special food to enhance physical development. Maintaining grazing areas and shelters is critical to the health and growth of livestock. In addition to these tasks, dairy farmers milk cows and store the milk. They use and maintain equipment for the sterilization and processing of milk. Experience in working on a farm is the best way to learn about farming.

One of the most important activities of a *veterinarian* is the care and treatment of livestock. Veterinarians maintain the health of farm animals to prevent the outbreak of diseases. The health of humans is also their concern, since some animal diseases can cause epidemics in humans as well. Veterinarians must have had at least two years of college study before going on to four years of veterinary school.

Animal breeders use the principles of genetics to determine the gene compositions of animal populations. They study the way traits are transmitted within populations. These findings are used to develop ways of breeding desirable characteristics into a population. Crossbreeding individuals from different populations is a way to achieve this goal. Improvements in strength, rate of maturity, resistance to disease, and quality of the product are economically important factors in animal husbandry. A college degree is often needed for this job.

Dairy and *animal scientists* conduct research in feeding, managing, and marketing livestock. In addition, they study the physiology of reproduction and lactation in an effort to improve livestock productivity. Animal nutrition is an important area of research. The results of these studies often improve the nutritive value of the feed and therefore the quality of the meat, milk, and eggs produced. A college degree is required for this profession.

Dairy technologists apply the principles of bacteriology and microbiology to develop new and improved methods of production, preservation, and utilization of dairy products. They research package design and dairy equipment. They study pasteurization techniques and frequently improve them. They conduct experiments in an effort to prevent bacterial growth in milk during handling and processing. To perform this job, a college education is necessary.

UNIT REVIEW

Synthesis

1. Explain how the pectoral and pelvic girdles of vertebrates have been modified as adaptations to different life-styles. Compare a perch, a bird, and a reptile.
2. Compare the body covering, or integumentary system, of bony fish, amphibians, reptiles, birds, and mammals. State how each characteristic covering is an advantage to that group of vertebrates.
3. Compare the structure of the heart and the flow of blood in a fish, a reptile, and a mammal.
4. How is internal fertilization a useful adaptation for land-dwelling vertebrates?
5. A female fish may spawn as many as one million eggs at a time. In contrast, most mammals bear only a few offspring at a time. Yet the populations of some mammals are as large as those of some fish. What adaptations allow mammals to maintain large populations while producing fewer young? Why is mammalian reproduction said to be more efficient than fish reproduction?
6. Warm-bloodedness is believed to have evolved independently in birds and in mammals. Some dinosaurs may also have been warm-blooded.
   a. Describe how the circulatory system, respiratory system, and body covering of birds and mammals contribute to the maintenance of a constant body temperature.
   b. What behavioral adaptations of reptiles allow them to regulate their body temperature?
7. Warm-bloodedness never arose among ocean-dwelling animals. What conditions of the terrestrial environment could have favored the evolution of warm-bloodedness?

Additional Reading

Buckles, Mary Parker. *Mammals of the World.* New York: Bantam Books, Inc., 1976.

Burt, William H., and Richard P. Grossenheider. *A Field Guide to the Mammals.* (The Peterson Field Guide Series) Boston: Houghton Mifflin, 1976.

Colbert, Edwin H. *The Year of the Dinosaur.* New York: Charles Scribner's Sons, 1978.

Conant, Roger. *A Field Guide to Reptiles and Amphibians of Eastern and Central North America.* (The Peterson Field Guide Series) Boston: Houghton Mifflin, 1975.

Eddy, Samuel, and James Underhill. *How to Know the Freshwater Fish.* Dubuque, IA: William C. Brown, Co., Pubs., 1978.

Elliss, Richard. *The Book of Sharks.* New York: Grosset & Dunlap, Inc., 1976.

Jenkins, Marie M. *Kangaroos, Opossums, and Other Marsupials.* New York: Holiday House, Inc., 1975.

Patent, Dorothy H. *Reptiles and How They Reproduce.* New York: Holiday House, Inc., 1977.

Peterson, Roger T. *A Field Guide to the Birds.* (The Peterson Field Guide Series) Boston: Houghton Mifflin, 1980.

Robbins, Chandler S., Bertel Bruun, and Herbert Zim. *Birds of North America: A Guide to Field Identification.* New York: Golden Press, 1983.

Smith, Hobart M. *Amphibians of North America.* (Golden Field Guide Series) New York: Western Publishing Co., Inc., 1978.

Smyth, H. Rucker. *Amphibians and Their Ways.* New York: Macmillan Publishing Co., Inc., 1971.

Stebbins, Robert C. *A Field Guide to Western Reptiles and Amphibians.* (The Peterson Field Guide Series) Boston: Houghton Mifflin, 1966.

Wheeler, Alwyn. *Fishes of the World.* New York: Macmillian Publishing Co., Inc., 1975.

Whitehead, Peter. *How Fishes Live.* New York: E.P. Dutton, 1977.

Unit Seven

The Human Body

Energy is expended in running any machine. The human body is a complex machine.

535

36 History of Human Life

Mary and Louis Leakey at Olduvai Gorge, Tanzania

Hunting for human fossils is hard work. It can be discouraging, too, since such fossils are rare. But imagine the excitement when a worker uncovers a piece of bone from an ancient human ancestor.

Mary and Louis Leakey are the scientists shown here looking for evidence of ancient human life. They and other members of their family have spent years in Africa in search of such fossils.

When a fossil is discovered in rock or sediment, scientists use special tools to remove it. Once the fossil has been removed, many experts will study it. They will try to determine its age and the characteristics of the organism from which it came.

Because of the fossil record, most scientists infer that humans today are physically different from their ancestors in the distant past. Scientists may not all make the same inferences about a fossil. In spite of disagreement, though, each new human-fossil discovery is a major event. A new piece of information has been added to the record of human life.

Distinctive Human Characteristics

Humans are members of the primate order. They share certain characteristics with all primates. Primates have opposable thumbs—the thumb can cross the palm of the hand. Both of their eyes face forward. Their brains are large. Of all the primates, apes are closest in structure to humans. Apes include gibbons, chimpanzees, orangutans, and gorillas. But there are uniquely human characteristics that separate people from apes.

In studying primate evolution, scientists sometimes compare humans and apes. In this way, scientists can identify those characteristics that are clearly human. Scientists also compare the characteristics of fossil primates to those of modern apes and humans. Some fossils have both apelike and humanlike characteristics. These fossils may be intermediate between present-day humans and their extinct primate ancestors.

The fossil evidence indicates that humans did not descend from apes. Rather, most scientists think that present-day apes and humans are both descendants of a common primate ancestor that is now extinct. This extinct, primitive primate gave rise to two lines. One led to modern humans and the other to apes. Scientists debate how long ago this common ancestor lived and what it looked like.

36–1 Structural Traits

The human skeleton has many obvious differences from that of an ape. The upright walk of the human accounts for some major skeletal differences. Vertical walking on hind limbs is called **bipedal** [by-PEHD-uhl] walking. Humans are completely bipedal. While some apes can walk upright for short distances, they usually do not.

Figure 36.1 shows the skulls of an ape and a human. Notice the opening in the skull where the spinal cord enters. This opening is called the **foramen magnum** [fuh-RAY-muhn MAG-nuhm]. In a four-legged vertebrate, this opening is at the back of the skull. In apes the foramen magnum can be found more toward the bottom of the skull. In humans the foramen magnum is at the very bottom of the skull. The location of the foramen magnum in humans allows the vertebral column to support the head during bipedal walking.

There are many other differences between ape and human skulls. The most obvious difference is in the size of the brain cavity. The human brain cavity is much larger than the ape's.

CONCEPTS
- bipedalism in humans
- unique human skeletal structure
- complexity of the human brain
- development of culture

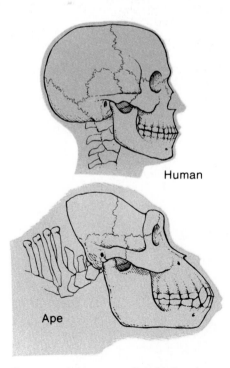

Human

Ape

Figure 36.1 How are the skulls of an ape and a human different?

The human forehead is almost vertical. The ape's forehead, on the other hand, slopes back.

The pelvic bones of apes and humans are clearly different, as shown in Figure 36.2. The human pelvis is broader than the ape's. This structure supports the internal organs and allows a bipedal posture. Sockets are positioned so that the leg bones extend vertically downward. The central opening in the human female pelvis is larger than in any other primate. When any mammal gives birth, the head of the newborn must pass through this opening. The large size of this opening in humans allows for the birth of babies with large brains.

Both apes and humans have opposable thumbs. Since humans are fully bipedal, their hands are free to hold objects. However, the thumb of humans can move farther across the hand than it can in any other primate. This allows humans to grasp and manipulate objects especially well.

The shape of the jaw is different in humans and apes. Figure 36.2 shows that the jaw of an ape — or of any other nonhuman primate — is U-shaped. The jaw of a human, however, is V-shaped. Notice also that the teeth of the ape and human are shaped differently. In addition, there are spaces between some of an ape's teeth, in contrast to human teeth. These different structures and arrangements are adaptations to different diets. Humans eat a mixed diet of plants and animals. In contrast, apes usually eat only plants.

Figure 36.2 Comparing the skeletons of apes and humans

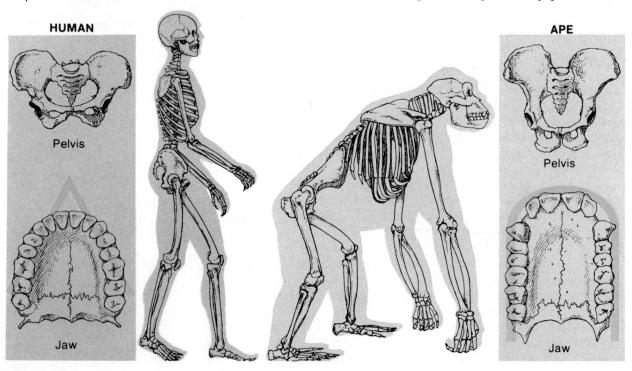

HUMAN

Pelvis

Jaw

APE

Pelvis

Jaw

36–2 Culture and the Human Brain

The human skull holds a brain larger than that of any other primate. The front part of the brain is especially well developed. The size and structure of the human brain allow it to store more information and control more complex behaviors than any other animal brain. Scientists have given the species name **Homo sapiens** to human beings. Roughly translated, the name means "thinking human."

You are at this moment reading a book, an activity only humans can perform. This activity is made possible by your brain. Gorillas and chimpanzees can learn the meaning of some words. However, complex languages are used only by *Homo sapiens.*

Figure 36.3 Language and the tools to record it have become more complex as human culture has advanced.

Because humans can speak, they can pass information on to each other. This permits the existence of complex culture. **Culture** is all the information and ways of living built up by a group of human beings. Culture is passed from one generation to the next. At best, other animals have a very limited capacity to pass on learned behavior.

One especially important part of culture is the use of tools. Tools are objects that are used to perform a job. No other animal can design and use tools as well as humans can. Bipedal posture, a large brain, and opposable thumbs all enable humans to be toolmakers.

Checkpoint

1. What term is used to describe upright walking?
2. Give two characteristics of the human skeleton that distinguish it from an ape's.
3. How is a human's thumb different from that of any other primate?
4. What is culture?
5. What factors enable humans to be toolmakers?

Human History

CONCEPTS

- fossil and cultural evidence of human origins
- characteristics of fossil hominids
- early *Homo sapiens*

Human fossils are very rare. Therefore, scientists are not certain how humans evolved. There have been almost as many hypotheses as there have been fossil discoveries. Remember that hypotheses are only trial explanations. They must be tested by further observations.

36–3 Evidence of Human History

Anthropologists [an-thruh-PAHL-uh-jihsts] are scientists who study human cultures. They attempt to learn how human cultural and physical characteristics have developed. Some anthropologists study societies that exist today. Others concentrate on prehistoric evidence of human life.

Important information can be obtained from fossil bones, particularly when the age of the bones can be measured. The size and shape of both the brain cavity and the jaw indicate how human or how apelike a fossil skull is. The position of the foramen magnum in the skull can reveal whether a primate was bipedal. So can the shapes of the pelvic and the leg bones. Anthropologists also look for evidence of culture. For example, other bones found with human bones can indicate what animals the humans hunted and ate.

Sometimes stone tools, such as knives, axes, or scrapers, are found near human bones. The number and kinds of tools tell how primitive or advanced the toolmakers were. Charcoal and burned animal bones may indicate that fire was used.

Figure 36.4 Anthropologists often gain valuable information about humans and their culture from examining burial sites. These objects were recovered from an Egyptian tomb.

36–4 *Australopithecus* Fossils

In 1924, Raymond Dart, a South African anatomy professor, discovered the unusual skull shown in Figure 36.5. The skull has a small brain cavity much like that of an ape. But the jaws are V-shaped like those of a human. The teeth are also humanlike. The opening into the skull for the spinal cord is almost at the bottom of the skull. Dart inferred from this that the animal walked upright. Dart named his discovery **Australopithecus** [aw-stray-loh-PIHTH-uh-kus] *africanus*, which means "southern primate from Africa." Modern dating techniques indicate that *Australopithecus africanus* lived between 2 and 3 million years ago.

Figure 36.5 The skull and an artist's conception of *Australopithecus*

Since 1924, many *Australopithecus* fossils have been discovered in Africa. Some of these fossils belong to species different from *Australopithecus africanus*. Among the fossils are pelvic bones that confirm that *Australopithecus* was bipedal. Yet the brain size of these fossils is much more apelike than human. The brain cavity of *Homo sapiens* is about 1,300 cubic centimeters. The average brain size for *Australopithecus* is about 500 cubic centimeters. This is slightly larger than the average chimpanzee brain. There is no evidence that any of the *Australopithecus* species used tools. Figure 36.5 shows what this animal might have looked like.

Australopithecus africanus and other *Australopithecus* species are known as hominids. The term **hominid** [HAHM-uh-nihd] refers to bipedal primates. *Homo sapiens* is the only hominid

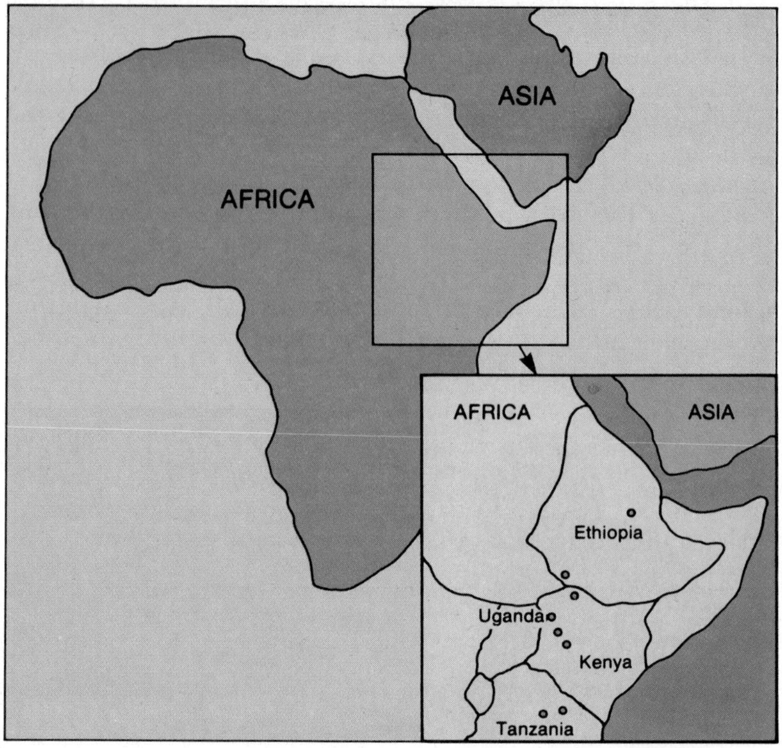

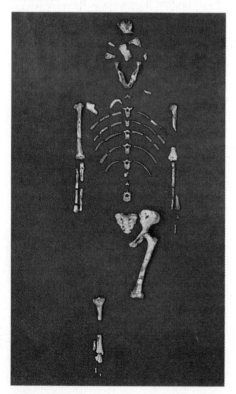

Figure 36.6 Dots indicate the locations of areas that have produced important hominid fossils.

Figure 36.7 Lucy, the oldest known hominid

alive today. All the others, including *Australopithecus* species, are extinct. Africa has been a rich source of early hominid fossils. Figure 36.6 shows the locations that have produced the most fossils. Some of the most spectacular finds have been made by members of the Leakey family.

In 1974, an American anthropologist named Donald Johanson discovered many of the bones of a small, female *Australopithecus* that he nicknamed Lucy. He gave Lucy the species name *Australopithecus afarensis*. The skeleton is shown in Figure 36.7. It is an adult female with an apelike brain and jaws. Yet the skull and the pelvis clearly show that Lucy was bipedal. Thought to be about 3.8 million years old, Lucy is the oldest known hominid.

36–5   Later Hominid Forms

All *Australopithecus* species are hominids. But they are clearly not humans. The Leakeys and others have discovered fossils that are more humanlike than *Australopithecus*. Because of their human traits, these fossils are believed to belong to the genus *Homo*. However, since they are more primitive than modern humans, they are not of the species *Homo sapiens*. The available evidence indicates that the genus *Homo* first appeared on the African continent.

In the 1950s, the Leakeys discovered a hominid fossil with a brain size of about 700 cubic centimeters, much larger than that of an *Australopithecus*. The Leakeys named this fossil **Homo habilis**. Since the fossil was found near simple stone tools, *Homo habilis* may have made and used tools. This fossil is thought to be between 1.5 and 2 million years old. *Homo habilis* may have lived at the same time as late *Australopithecus*. However, it is much more recent than the earliest *Australopithecus*.

Another species of hominid called **Homo erectus** is shown in Figure 36.8. Fossils of *Homo erectus* have been found in Africa, Europe, China, and the island of Java. The earliest of these fossils appear in rock layers about 1.5 million years old. *Homo erectus* had a brain volume of about 900 cubic centimeters. Remember that the average brain size of *Homo sapiens* is about 1,300 cubic centimeters. Many finely crafted stone tools are associated with *Homo erectus*. These hominids probably used fire. They may have lived in groups.

Figure 36.8 *Above:* An artist's conception of *Homo erectus; Left:* A comparison of the brain sizes of several hominids

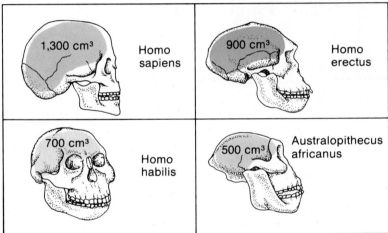

36–6   True Humans

Not all scientists agree on what makes a fossil that of a human. Average brain size, however, is one characteristic used to distinguish among various hominids. Hominid fossils of the last 100,000 years have skulls with a brain cavity that is equal in size to that of modern humans. These fossils have been placed in the species *Homo sapiens*.

Fossils of early *Homo sapiens* occur in two distinct varieties. In one group, the bones are heavy. The skull shows significant differences from the skull of modern humans. These skeletons are generally referred to as **Neanderthal** [nee-AN-duhr-thawl]. They have been discovered in caves of Europe and Asia. The other group has a skeleton more or less identical to that of

Figure 36.9 Early humans

Neanderthal

Cro-Magnon

Do You Know?
One Neanderthal fossil shows that this early human suffered from tooth decay.

Figure 36.10 Cro-Magnons decorated the walls of their caves with paintings of the animals they hunted.

modern humans. These early humans are called **Cro-Magnons**. Their bones were first discovered in France.

Figure 36.9 shows what Neanderthals and Cro-Magnons probably looked like. Neanderthals were somewhat shorter and more heavily boned than modern *Homo sapiens*. They may have belonged to a different species. But they are most often considered variations of *Homo sapiens*.

Evidence indicates that Neanderthals lived in Europe during the most recent ice ages. They were powerful hunters. They killed large woolly mammoths, cave bears, and woolly rhinoceroses inhabiting the area at the time. They made sophisticated stone tools. Neanderthals buried their dead and included small objects in the grave.

Evidence from caves in France indicates that Cro-Magnon people had complex societies. They made and used impressive stone, wood, and bone tools. Their small stone sculptures and cave paintings are beautiful and fascinating. It may never be known why cave art was created. But it is clear that the Cro-Magnons who created it were close ancestors of people who later, about six to eight thousand years ago, developed written languages and built cities.

Cro-Magnons and Neanderthals lived in the same area and at the same time. Then the Neanderthals disappeared. Scientists do not know why they vanished. One hypothesis is that the Cro-Magnons won in the struggle for food and space. Another possibility is that the Neanderthals and Cro-Magnons interbred and became genetically mixed.

Figure 36.11 Two hypotheses of the sequence of human evolution

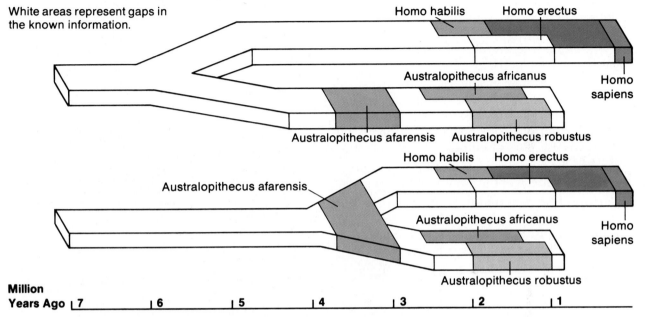

White areas represent gaps in the known information.

Homo habilis   Homo erectus
Australopithecus africanus   Homo sapiens
Australopithecus afarensis   Australopithecus robustus

Australopithecus afarensis
Homo habilis   Homo erectus
Australopithecus africanus   Homo sapiens
Australopithecus robustus

Million Years Ago |7 |6 |5 |4 |3 |2 |1

Figure 36.11 shows two interpretations of human evolution. Notice that in one hypothesis an *Australopithecus* species is believed to be the ancestor of humans. In the other hypothesis, however, *Australopithecus* is seen as an offshoot and is not in the direct line that led to humans. These hypotheses demonstrate that anthropologists disagree about which hominids descended from which ancestors. In fact, anthropologists do not even agree on which fossils belong to which species. Further evidence will be required to settle the debates.

Checkpoint

1. Name one characteristic shared by all hominids.
2. In what major structural characteristic do *Homo erectus* and *Homo sapiens* differ from each other?
3. _____ and _____ are two types of fossils that are now thought to belong to the species *Homo sapiens*.
4. Rank the following hominids in order of their brain size, beginning with the smallest: *Homo habilis, Homo sapiens, Australopithecus, Homo erectus.*
5. Which fossil hominids are believed to have used tools?

CHAPTER REVIEW

Summary

- Humans have physical features that distinguish them from other primates. These features include a large brain, a bipedal walk, fully opposable thumbs, and a large opening in the female pelvis.
- The large human brain has enabled the development of culture. The use of complex language, the making of tools, and the passing of information from one generation to the next are all part of culture.
- Fossils and evidence of culture have given scientists ideas about how humans evolved.
- Fossils of humans and their ancestors are very rare. Because of this, all hypotheses about human evolution are subject to change. New fossil evidence may support one of the existing hypotheses. Alternatively, it may lead to new interpretations.
- Hominids are bipedal primates. The oldest fossil hominids are placed in the genus *Australopithecus*. They have apelike brains and jaws. The oldest is estimated to be about 3.8 million years old.
- The first fossils that are considered to belong to the genus *Homo* are about 2 million years old. *Homo habilis* and *Homo erectus* have larger brains than *Australopithecus*. Both apparently made tools, and *Homo erectus* probably used fire.
- Neanderthals and Cro-Magnons appeared in Europe between 50,000 and 100,000 years ago. They have brains the size of modern humans. Both are generally placed in the species *Homo sapiens*. The tools made by these hominids and other evidences of their culture leave little doubt that they were fully human.

Vocabulary

anthropologist
Australopithecus
bipedal
Cro-Magnon
culture
foramen magnum

hominid
Homo erectus
Homo habilis
Homo sapiens
Neanderthal

Review

Choose the answer that best completes each of the following questions.

1. Humans are members of which order? (a) carnivores (b) mammals (c) marsupials (d) primates
2. Which of these animals has a body structure most similar to a human's? (a) chimpanzee (b) monkey (c) whale (d) seal
3. Which of the following is *not* fully bipedal? (a) gorilla (b) *Australopithecus africanus* (c) "Lucy" (d) *Homo erectus*
4. In humans, where in the skull is the foramen magnum located? (a) at the back (b) at the bottom (c) in the front (d) none of these
5. The human jaw (a) is U-shaped, (b) is V-shaped, (c) has more teeth than the ape's, (d) has fewer teeth than the ape's.
6. The term for the information and ways of living built up by a group of humans is (a) bipedalism, (b) education, (c) culture, (d) technology.
7. Most fossils of very early hominids have been found in (a) Australia, (b) northern Europe, (c) Greece, (d) Africa.
8. Scientists who study human cultures, past and present, are called (a) biologists, (b) comparative anatomists, (c) evolutionists, (d) anthropologists.
9. Which of these bones can show whether a fossil primate was bipedal? (a) skull (b) pelvic bones (c) leg bones (d) all of these

10. *Australopithecus* was similar to an ape in (a) the size of its brain cavity, (b) its manner of walking, (c) the shape of its jaw, (d) the location of the foramen magnum.
11. The oldest known hominid fossil is about how old? (a) 50,000 years (b) 100,000 years (c) 1.6 million years (d) 3.8 million years
12. The species name of all modern humans is (a) *Homo erectus*, (b) *Homo habilis*, (c) *Homo sapiens*, (d) none of these.

Interpret and Apply

1. Put the following events in order, according to the time when they occurred. The earliest event will be numbered *1*, and the most recent will be *5*.
   a. evolution of bipedal walk
   b. creation of cave paintings
   c. existence of a kind of primate who would become the ancestor of both apes and humans
   d. first use of tools
   e. existence of *Homo erectus*

Answer each of the following questions.

2. Describe two significant differences between the skull of an ape and the skull of a human.
3. What is the significance of the location of the foramen magnum?
4. The opening in the human female pelvis is large. Why is size important?
5. Why is it wrong to state that humans evolved from apes?
6. Which is more humanlike — *Australopithecus* or *Homo habilis*? What characteristics account for this?
7. What primary feature would place a fossil in the species *Homo sapiens*?
8. What are the two hypotheses for the disappearance of the Neanderthals?
9. What evidence shows that Cro-Magnons had a complex society?
10. For about how many years have bipedal primates existed? What fossil provides the evidence for this?
11. Scientists do not all agree on how humans evolved. Why is this so?

Challenge

1. Explain how a large brain, opposable thumbs, and erect posture all help humans to make and use tools.
2. What evidence puts *Homo erectus* in the genus *Homo*? Why isn't it in the species *Homo sapiens*?
3. Make and complete a chart like the one below.

Apes and Humans

Characteristics in Common	Characteristics Unique to Humans

4. You discover a fossil adult skull in the desert. The brain cavity is 480 cubic centimeters. The jaw is V-shaped. The opening for the vertebral column is located at the bottom of the skull. The fossil is about 2.5 million years old.
   a. Is this fossil a hominid? What evidence supports your conclusion?
   b. What genus do you think this fossil should be in? Explain.

Projects

1. Find out about the methods used by anthropologists to excavate and date human fossil material.
2. In 1912, an amateur scientist uncovered some bones in England. These bone fragments came to be known as Piltdown Man. For about 50 years these bones were considered to be real fossils. In the 1950s, scientists discovered that the fossils were a hoax. Find out about Piltdown Man and why it was so different from the hominid fossils that were uncovered in Africa during this period.
3. Find out how early humans made and used stone tools.

37 Bones, Muscles, and Skin

A high-jumper

Athletes move with skill and grace that are remarkable. A high-jumper must move with great speed, strength, and concentration to achieve the height necessary for the jump. Such a feat takes years to perfect.

In contrast, walking seems simple. Most people can do it without even thinking. However, have you ever watched a baby learn to walk? If so, you may appreciate how hard a task walking really is. Babies go through months of toddling before they can walk really well.

Any movement, no matter how simple it may seem, is actually a complicated process. Body movements are carried out by muscles. Motion occurs when muscles move parts of the skeleton.

In the human body, many kinds of cells work together in complex ways. Bone, muscles, and skin are three parts of this system. They give the body form, support, and protection. They also make possible a baby's first step and an athlete's leap.

The Human Skeleton

The internal skeleton of all vertebrates serves many functions. It supports the body and protects internal organs. Along with muscles, the skeleton enables the body to move. In addition, cells in the bones store and release important minerals. Also, within many bones, millions of blood cells are made every second of every day.

Like all parts of the body, the skeleton is made up of tissues. The human body is constructed of four basic types of tissue. These are shown in Figure 37.1. **Nerve tissue** makes up the brain, spinal cord, and nerves. Together, these form the communication system of the body. **Connective tissues** connect and support parts of the body. These include bone, cartilage, fat, and blood. **Muscle tissue** is responsible for movement. **Epithelial** [ehp-uh-THEE-lee-uhl] **tissue** covers interior and exterior body surfaces.

CONCEPTS

- structure of bone and cartilage
- composition of the skeleton
- different types of joints

Figure 37.1 The basic tissues of the human body

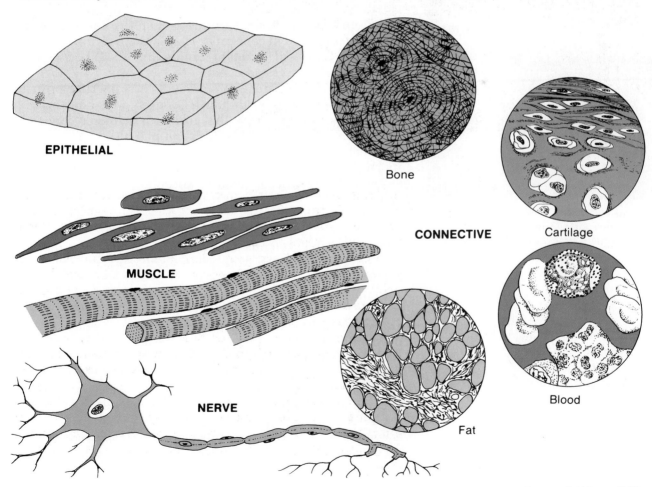

EPITHELIAL

Bone

MUSCLE

CONNECTIVE Cartilage

NERVE

Fat

Blood

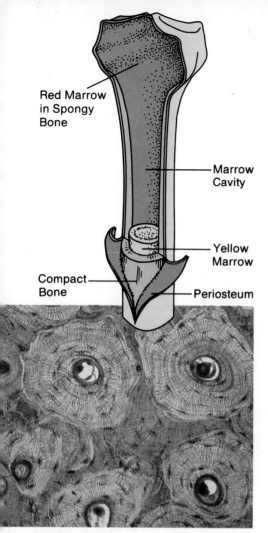

Red Marrow in Spongy Bone

Marrow Cavity

Yellow Marrow

Compact Bone

Periosteum

Figure 37.2 *Top:* The internal structure of a long bone; *Bottom:* A photomicrograph of compact bone

Do You Know?

It may take a broken bone four times longer to heal in an adult than in a child.

37–1 Bone and Cartilage

Bone is one type of connective tissue. Figure 37.2 shows the internal structure of one of the long bones from an adult human. A very tough membrane called the **periosteum** [pehr-ee-AHS-tee-uhm] surrounds and protects all bones. Muscles attach to the periosteum. Bone-forming cells are also present in the periosteum. These are responsible for bone growth.

Beneath the periosteum is a hard, dense material called compact bone. Beneath the compact bone, particularly at the knobby ends, is spongy bone.

Within the hollow spaces of spongy bone is a substance called **marrow**. Red marrow fills the spaces of most spongy bone. Most blood cells are made in the red marrow. Certain bones, such as the long bones of the arms and legs, have a central cavity filled with yellow marrow, blood vessels, and nerves. Yellow marrow is primarily fat tissue.

Figure 37.2 shows the microscopic structure of bone. Compact bone is made up of bone cells called **osteocytes** [AHS-tee-uh-sytz]. Osteocytes are surrounded by a nonliving material called **matrix**, which they secrete around themselves. Osteocytes are arranged in concentric rings around channels called **Haversian** [huh-VUHR-zhuhn] **canals.** Small blood vessels run through each Haversian canal.

Bone matrix contains large amounts of a fiberlike protein called **collagen** [KAHL-uh-juhn]. Collagen gives bone matrix strength in the same way that iron rods reinforce concrete. Osteocytes deposit crystals of calcium phosphate and calcium carbonate around the collagen fibers. These crystals give bone its hardness. Osteocytes and bone matrix are involved in the storage and release of calcium and phosphorus. These two elements are necessary for the functioning of many body tissues.

Cartilage is another kind of connective tissue that makes up parts of the skeleton. You can feel cartilage in your ears or the tip of your nose. Notice how flexible it is. Unlike bone, cartilage has no minerals.

In the early stages of a human embryo, most of the skeleton is made of cartilage. Some cartilage will remain for the person's entire life. However, most gradually becomes bone. As the developing human grows, the cartilage cells are gradually replaced by osteocytes. These secrete calcium compounds and other minerals. **Ossification** [ahs-uh-fuh-KAY-shuhn] is the term for the process of bone formation. Most ossification is complete by the time a person is 20 years old.

Like other living tissue, bone grows and repairs itself. When a bone is broken, osteocytes next to the break produce new matrix material. To mend properly, the broken ends must be held motionless together. Vitamins and minerals are necessary for bone growth and repair. Humans must eat foods containing calcium to maintain healthy bones. Dairy products are rich sources of calcium. Vitamin D is also needed because it enables bone to absorb calcium from the blood.

37–2 Joints of the Human Skeleton

Figure 37.3 shows the human skeleton. The central column of the skeleton is made up of the skull, vertebral column, and rib cage. The remaining bones, including those of the arms and legs, are attached to this central skeleton.

Joints occur where two or more bones come together. Anatomists classify joints according to the kind of movement they allow. **Immovable joints** allow no movement. Most of the skull bones are fused together at such joints.

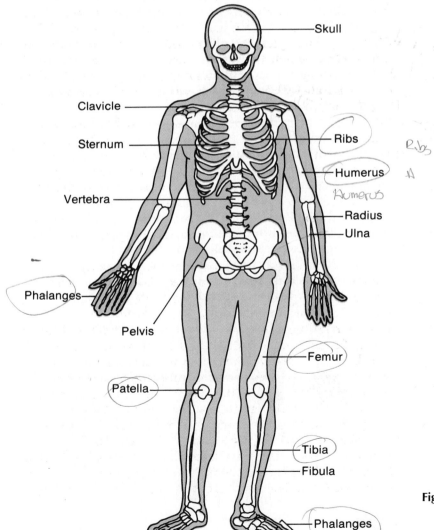

Figure 37.3 The human skeleton

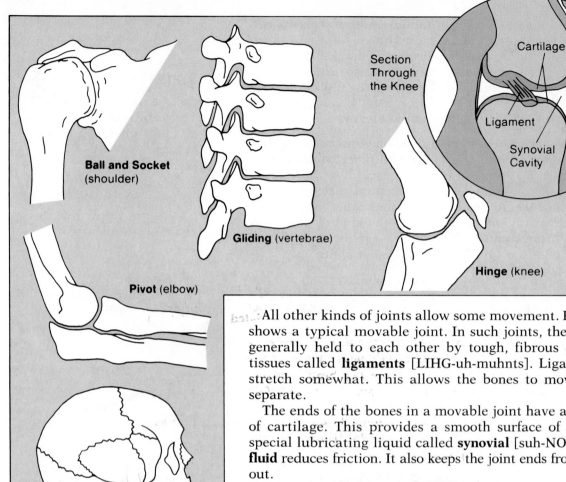

Ball and Socket (shoulder)

Gliding (vertebrae)

Pivot (elbow)

Section Through the Knee

Cartilage

Ligament

Synovial Cavity

Hinge (knee)

Immovable (skull)

Figure 37.4 Joints occur where two or more bones come together.

All other kinds of joints allow some movement. Figure 37.4 shows a typical movable joint. In such joints, the bones are generally held to each other by tough, fibrous connective tissues called **ligaments** [LIHG-uh-muhnts]. Ligaments can stretch somewhat. This allows the bones to move but not separate.

The ends of the bones in a movable joint have a thin layer of cartilage. This provides a smooth surface of contact. A special lubricating liquid called **synovial** [suh-NOH-vee-uhl] **fluid** reduces friction. It also keeps the joint ends from wearing out.

Figure 37.4 shows some specific movable joints. The joints between vertebrae are examples of **gliding joints**. Pads of cartilage called **vertebral disks** allow limited twisting, turning, and sliding between vertebrae.

Hinge joints can bend in only one direction. The knee is such a joint. A **ball-and-socket joint**, such as the one at the shoulder, allows movement in many different directions. Ball-and-socket joints allow the widest range of movement of any joint.

Checkpoint

1. List the main tissue types of the human body.
2. Identify the tough membrane that covers the bones.
3. What is the material secreted by osteocytes?
4. What is the protein that gives strength to bone?
5. What is the lubricating fluid of joints called?
6. What kind of joint is the knee?

Muscles and Skin

Muscle tissue is able to contract. It is this contraction that brings about motion. When your body moves, muscles do the work.

The muscles and other body tissues are covered and protected by the skin. In addition, the skin helps the body regulate internal temperature and sense its external environment.

37–3   Skeletal Muscle

There are three main types of muscles — skeletal, smooth, and cardiac. Most of the muscle in the body is **skeletal muscle**. It is called skeletal because it attaches to bone. It makes bones move. Skeletal muscle has a striped appearance when viewed with a microscope, as shown in Figure 37.5. Muscle with these characteristic stripes, or striations, is called **striated muscle**.

Both skeletal and smooth muscles contract when they receive impulses from nerves. In the case of skeletal muscle, these nerve impulses come from the parts of the brain that are under your conscious control. Skeletal muscles are therefore called **voluntary muscles**.

Figure 37.5 shows how a large skeletal muscle is constructed from muscle cells. Each cell has many nuclei. A single muscle cell can sometimes be almost half a meter long.

Do You Know?
Skeletal muscles make up about half of your entire weight.

Figure 37.5 *Left:* The structure of skeletal muscle; *Right:* A photomicrograph of skeletal muscle

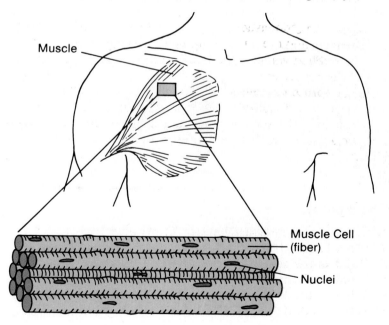

Muscle

Muscle Cell (fiber)

Nuclei

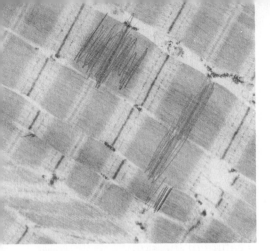

Figure 37.6 An electron micrograph of myofibrils. The Z-bands (dark lines) separate the myofibrils into sarcomeres.

A muscle cell is also known as a fiber. Within each fiber are many smaller units called **myofibrils** [my-oh-FYB-ruhlz]. Each myofibril contains many threadlike protein filaments that are lined up in a highly organized way. The appearance of myofibrils in the electron microscope is shown in Figure 37.6. Dark lines called Z-bands separate each myofibril into a number of identical-looking units called **sarcomeres** [SAHR-kuh-meerz]. Within each sarcomere are a number of threadlike protein filaments.

Figure 37.7 shows sarcomeres in a relaxed muscle and in a contracted muscle. Compare the two carefully. The central filaments in each sarcomere are thicker than the filaments that attach to the Z-band. The thick filaments are made of a protein called **myosin** [MY-uh-suhn]. **Actin** is the major protein making up the thin filaments.

Each myosin molecule in the thick filament has a large head. This forms a bridge across to an actin molecule in a thin filament. Using the energy of ATP molecules, myosin bridges can pull the thin filaments toward the center of the sarcomere. This pulls the Z-bands closer together and shortens the entire sarcomere. The shortening of each sarcomere makes the fiber contract.

A muscle fiber either contracts fully or doesn't contract at all. This type of reaction is known as an all-or-none response. A whole muscle, however, does not have an all-or-none response. It can contract at different strengths. The intensity of a whole muscle's contraction is determined by the number of its fibers that contract. The more fibers that contract, the stronger the whole muscle's contraction.

Figure 37.7 When muscle contracts, the actin filaments of each sarcomere are pulled toward the middle, and the entire sarcomere shortens. Notice that the length of the actin and myosin filaments remains the same.

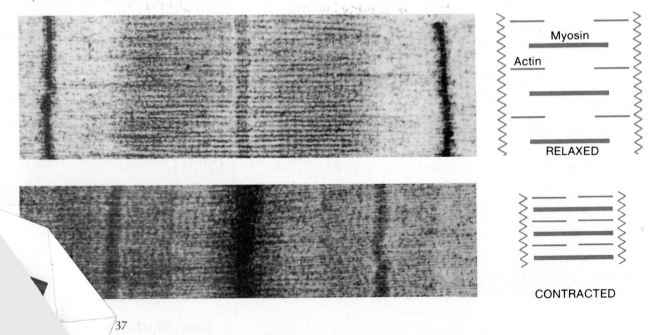

Myosin

Actin

RELAXED

CONTRACTED

37–4 Chemistry of Skeletal Muscle

The movement of actin and myosin filaments requires the breakdown of ATP. Normal respiration in muscle-cell mitochondria supplies enough ATP for moderate activity. During strenuous exercise, however, muscles need far more ATP. To support increased work, the mitochondria need more glucose and oxygen. The heart and breathing rates speed up. But it may take as long as a minute for the extra fuel and oxygen to get to the muscles.

To provide fuel immediately, the carbohydrate glycogen is stored in most muscles. It can be quickly broken down to provide the energy for ATP synthesis. Normally, cells need oxygen to break down carbohydrates and synthesize ATP. However, this breakdown of glycogen can take place without oxygen in the process of lactic acid fermentation. The end product of anaerobic glycogen breakdown is lactic acid. During heavy exercise, lactic acid accumulates in the muscle.

When the heartbeat and breathing become stronger, they supply the cells with more oxygen. When you stop exercising, you continue to breathe hard for a while. The extra oxygen is used to convert most of the lactic acid back to glycogen.

37–5 Movement of Joints

Muscles are attached to bones by strong **tendons** made of connective tissue. Most skeletal muscles are attached to two bones. During contraction, only one of these bones usually moves. The **origin** of the muscle is the place where it attaches to the nonmoving bone. The **insertion** is the place where it attaches to the moving bone.

Figure 37.8 illustrates how muscles move the lower arm. When you bend your elbow, it is the biceps muscle that does the work. The origin of the biceps is the top of the upper arm bone. The insertion is on a bone of the lower arm. When your biceps contracts, your lower arm is brought up. To straighten your arm, you use the triceps muscle. The biceps then relaxes. Bending a joint is called flexion; straightening a joint is called extension.

The biceps and triceps form an **antagonistic pair** of muscles. When one of the pair contracts, the other usually relaxes. Each member of an antagonistic pair usually moves the bone in a direction opposite to that of the other member. If both members of an antagonistic pair contract at the same time, the joint does not move. This is the basis of one kind of exercise called isometric contraction. Most skeletal muscles are members of antagonistic pairs. Complex motions require many sets of such muscles at each joint.

Figure 37.8 Using an antagonistic pair of muscles

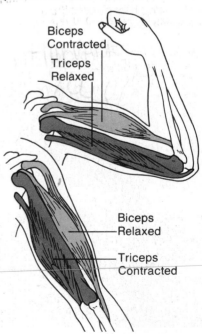

Biceps Contracted
Triceps Relaxed

Biceps Relaxed

Triceps Contracted

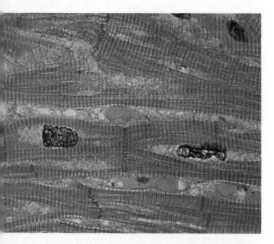

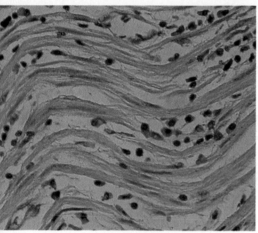

Figure 37.9 *Top:* Cardiac muscle; *Bottom:* Smooth muscle

37-6 Cardiac Muscle and Smooth Muscle

The heart is made of **cardiac muscle**, as shown in Figure 37.9. Compare the structure of cardiac muscle with that of skeletal muscle in Figure 37.5. The sarcomeres are similar in both kinds of muscle. But cardiac-muscle cells are much shorter than skeletal-muscle cells. They join end to end at the dark lines seen in the photograph. Cardiac-muscle cells also have more mitochondria.

Cardiac muscle has a much different function than skeletal muscle. For one thing, cardiac muscle is involuntary. **Involuntary muscle** is under the control of automatic signals produced by the organism. You cannot control your heartbeat as you control the muscles that move your bones.

Cardiac muscle does not tire as easily as skeletal muscle. If you open and close your fist 70 times a minute, your muscles will fatigue quickly. Yet cardiac muscle contracts and relaxes at this rate all day long every day of your life. This requires a constant supply of ATP. The large number of mitochondria provides the necessary ATP.

The **smooth muscle** shown in Figure 37.9 is a third type of muscle tissue. Each cell has a single nucleus. The cell is long, thin, and tapered at both ends. Actin and myosin fibers are present in the cytoplasm. However, they are not arranged in repeating units as they are in skeletal and cardiac muscle.

Smooth muscle occurs primarily in internal organs. For example, contractions of smooth muscle move food through the digestive system. The walls of many blood vessels contain smooth muscle. They regulate the flow of blood. The functioning of smooth muscle is generally involuntary.

37-7 Structure and Function of Human Skin

Human skin is composed of two basic layers of tissue. The outermost tissue, called **epidermis**, lies on top of the thicker **dermis**. Figure 37.10 shows a cross section through human skin.

The epidermis is made of many layers of epithelial cells. The cells in the lowest layer undergo constant mitosis. The new cells that result are pushed toward the surface. The uppermost layer consists of dead cells. These cells form the protective surface of the skin. This barrier prevents harmful chemicals and microorganisms from entering the body. The epidermis also protects the body from harmful ultraviolet radiation.

The dermis contains several types of connective tissue. One type, **adipose** [AD-uh-pohs] **tissue**, is made of fat cells. The body stores fat in these cells. Also located within the dermis are **hair follicles**. Each follicle produces a hair. Next to every

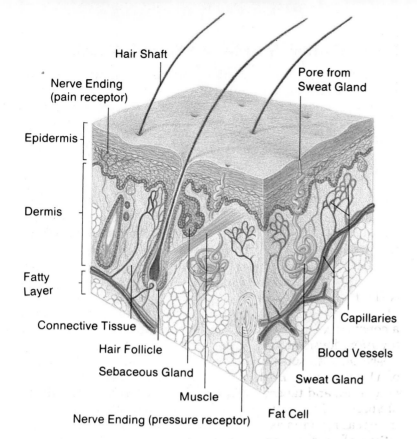

Hair Shaft

Nerve Ending (pain receptor)

Epidermis

Dermis

Fatty Layer

Connective Tissue

Hair Follicle

Sebaceous Gland

Muscle

Nerve Ending (pressure receptor)

Pore from Sweat Gland

Capillaries

Blood Vessels

Sweat Gland

Fat Cell

Figure 37.10 A cross section of human skin

hair follicle is a **sebaceous** [sih-BAY-shuhs] **gland**. Oil from these glands helps prevent the skin's outer layer from drying and cracking. The dermis also contains the **sweat glands**. When the body becomes heated, sweat glands secrete water onto the skin. The evaporation of sweat helps to cool the body. The skin helps maintain homeostasis by regulating heat loss.

Finally, the dermis contains many nerve endings. These are sensitive to pressure, touch, heat, cold, and pain. Through these senses your brain receives a great deal of information from the environment.

Do You Know?

Each square centimeter of skin has about 3 million cells and over 5 meters of blood vessels.

Checkpoint

1. What are the two major proteins found in sarcomeres?
2. Muscles are attached to bones by _____.
3. What is the term for a pair of muscles that move a joint in opposite directions?
4. During vigorous exercise, the breakdown of what substance provides the energy needed for ATP synthesis?
5. What is the scientific term for heart muscle?
6. Name the two basic layers that make up the skin.

CHAPTER REVIEW

Summary

- Bone and cartilage are two types of connective tissue that make up the human skeleton. Bones are made by osteocytes, which secrete matrix around themselves. Collagen and minerals give bone strength and hardness.
- During ossification, bone replaces cartilage. Bone needs vitamins and minerals for growth and repair.
- The central column of the human skeleton consists of the skull, vertebrae, and rib cage. The bones of the arms and legs extend from this central column.
- Bones come together at joints. Joints in the skeleton can be classified according to the amount and type of motion characteristic of the joint.
- Muscle tissue causes body motion by contracting.
- Skeletal muscle, which appears striped under the microscope, moves the skeleton.
- Individual muscle cells contain filaments of actin and myosin. These are responsible for the contraction of muscle.
- Muscle contraction requires ATP. During strenuous exercise, ATP is produced by the breakdown of glycogen. Oxygen is not used in this process.
- Tendons attach muscles to bone. Muscles move joints by acting in antagonistic pairs.
- Cardiac muscle is found in the heart. It has a large number of mitochondria. These supply the energy for nonstop muscle activity.
- Smooth-muscle cells are tapered; each contains one nucleus. Smooth muscle occurs mainly in internal organs. The action of smooth muscle is involuntary.
- The skin of the body consists of two basic layers, the epidermis and the dermis. The skin protects the body. It also regulates body temperature and picks up information from the environment.

Vocabulary

actin	matrix
adipose tissue	muscle tissue
antagonistic pair	myofibril
ball-and-socket joint	myosin
cardiac muscle	nerve tissue
collagen	origin
connective tissue	ossification
dermis	osteocyte
epidermis	periosteum
epithelial tissue	sarcomere
gliding joint	sebaceous gland
hair follicle	skeletal muscle
Haversian canal	smooth muscle
hinge joint	striated muscle
immovable joint	sweat gland
insertion	synovial fluid
involuntary muscle	tendon
ligament	vertebral disk
marrow	voluntary muscle

Review

1. To which of the four basic tissue types do bone and cartilage belong?
2. Which of the four basic tissue types can contract?
3. Name the channels in bone through which blood vessels run.
4. What kind of joint is most common in the skull? What kind of joint is the shoulder?

5. In the human embryo, the skeleton is first made of what substance?

6. What is another name for the living cells of bone?

7. Name the three different types of muscle.

8. What are the parts of the central column of the skeleton?

9. What two important elements are stored and released by bone cells?

In questions 10–14, match the structure in the left column with its function in the right column.

10. ligament
11. sebaceous gland
12. glycogen
13. tendon
14. periosteum

a. attaches a skeletal muscle to a bone
b. holds bones together in joints
c. forms a tough, protective covering over bone
d. secretes oil onto the skin
e. can be broken down to provide energy for contracting muscles

Interpret and Apply

1. Besides the skeleton, what parts of the body are made mainly of connective tissue?

2. What does bone marrow contribute to the blood?

3. How are the properties of cartilage different from those of bone?

4. Describe how cartilage changes to bone.

5. Which of the three muscle types is (are) voluntary? Involuntary?

6. What is meant by the term *all-or-none response*? How does this apply to the action of muscle fibers?

7. What is the significance of the large number of mitochondria in cardiac-muscle cells?

8. How does sweating help maintain homeostasis?

9. Compare the movement of a ball-and-socket joint with that of a hinge joint.

Challenge

1. Ligaments contain a great deal of elastin, a protein that can stretch and return to its original length. Tendons have mostly collagen and very little elastin. How does the composition of these two types of connective tissue reflect their function?

2. Explain why the rate of your breathing and heartbeat doesn't decrease for several minutes after you stop exercising.

3. Suppose the biceps muscle were removed. What kind of arm motion would then be impossible?

4. A structure called the iris controls the amount of light entering your eye. The iris is controlled by muscles. Are these muscles skeletal, smooth, or cardiac? Are they voluntary or involuntary? Explain.

5. Suppose your skin were not sensitive to pressure or pain. What might happen to the muscles and internal organs beneath the skin?

6. By the time you are 20 years old, most of your bones will have stopped growing. However, you will continue to need calcium and vitamin D all your life. Why do you think this is so?

Projects

1. Take a trip to the meat section of a supermarket. Find out what muscles and bones are found in various cuts of beef, pork, and lamb. Clean and examine discarded bones. To see the internal structure of bone, look at bones cut in cross sections.

2. Find out which common sports injuries involve bones, joints, and muscles. Report on how these injuries can be prevented. Explain the treatment used when these injuries occur.

3. Learn what fingerprints are and how they can be used for purposes of identification. Make a chart of the important characteristics fingerprint experts use in identifying an unknown set of fingerprints.

38 Digestion and Nutrition

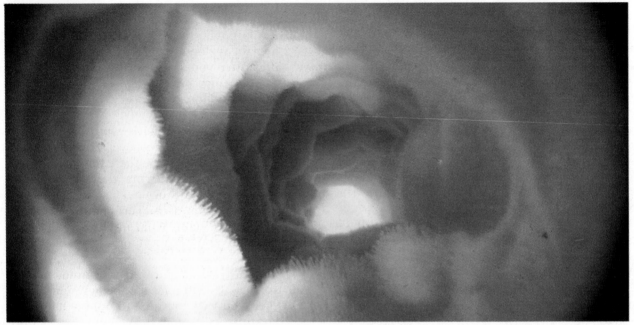

Part of the small intestine

This structure looks like part of a cave. Actually, though, it is a section of a human digestive tract. You might think of your digestive system as a very long, complicated passageway that is open at both ends. The passage twists and turns. Its structure changes from place to place. As food passes through, various organs contribute to the process by which food is digested.

A section of the small intestine is shown here. This organ absorbs food that has been broken down into small molecules. These molecules pass into the blood. In the blood, they are carried to all parts of the body. Every body cell receives nourishment in this way.

Notice the interior surface of the small intestine. There are hundreds of thousands of fingerlike projections. These projections create an enormous surface for absorbing substances. The total surface area of this organ is about 300 square meters. That's about the same area as a tennis court! Through this huge surface, your body gets the food it needs to carry out life processes.

The Mouth, Esophagus, and Stomach

The food you eat comes from organisms that were once alive. It is an extremely complex mixture of proteins, carbohydrates, lipids, and other substances. Food must be broken down into small molecules that can pass into your cells. **Digestion** is the process of reducing food to small molecules that can be absorbed into the body.

During digestion, food passes through a long tubelike structure. This tube is called the **alimentary** [al-uh-MENT-uh-ree] **canal**. It begins at the mouth and ends at the anus. Different parts of the alimentary canal are modified into specialized organs. Each of these has a specific function.

Chemical and mechanical processes are involved in digestion. Both chemical and mechanical digestion occur in most parts of the digestive system.

Chemical digestion is the chemical breakdown of large molecules into small ones. Remember that certain large molecules can be broken down into small molecules by combining with water. This process is known as hydrolysis. Proteins are eventually broken down into amino acids. Polysaccharides break down to form simple sugars, mainly glucose. Triglycerides are hydrolyzed into fatty acids and glycerol. Many digestive enzymes are necessary to hydrolyze these large molecules.

Mechanical digestion is the physical breakdown of food into small particles. Chewing and muscular churning both accomplish this. Mechanical digestion speeds up chemical digestion by exposing large amounts of food to digestive enzymes. Figure 38.1 shows how mechanical digestion works. Suppose the cube was a piece of cheese. Only the molecules on the surface would be exposed to digestive enzymes. But if the cube of cheese was cut repeatedly, more surface area would be created. Greater numbers of food molecules could then be hydrolyzed by enzymes.

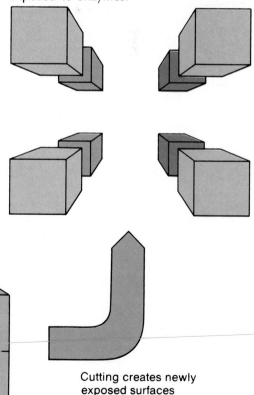

Figure 38.1 The mechanical processes of chewing and churning food increase the surface area that is exposed to enzymes.

Mechanical digestion

Cutting creates newly exposed surfaces

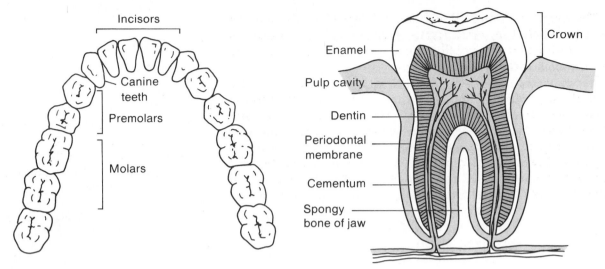

Figure 38.2 *Left:* The arrangement of teeth in the mouth; *Right:* A cross section of a human molar.

38–1   The Mouth

Food's passage through the alimentary canal begins in the mouth. Mechanical digestion begins here as the teeth chew and grind food. Figure 38.2 shows the teeth of an adult human. In the middle of each jaw are two flat **incisors** [ihn-SY-zurz]. They cut chunks of food from larger pieces. The pointed **canine teeth** pierce and tear food. The **premolars** are next to the canine teeth. After these come the **molars**. Both the premolars and molars have flat surfaces adapted for grinding.

The structure of a typical tooth shows each tooth has roots that extend into the bone of the jaw. The neck of the tooth extends through the gums, the tissue covering the jawbones. The tooth crown is the exposed chewing surface.

Inside each tooth is a pulp cavity that contains nerves and blood vessels. Surrounding the pulp cavity is a hard, bonelike material called **dentin**. The dentin of the roots is covered by a thin layer of harder material called **cementum**. The crown of the tooth is covered by the hardest material in the body, **enamel**. The **periodontal** [pehr-ee-oh-DAHNT-l] **membrane** anchors roots to the jawbone. This membrane is made of fibrous connective tissue.

Several secretions are added to food in the mouth. **Mucus**, which moistens the food, comes from cells lining the mouth. Mucus makes food easier to swallow. Three pairs of salivary glands add **saliva** to food. Like mucus, saliva lubricates food. In addition, saliva contains the enzyme **amylase** [AM-uh-lays]. Amylase breaks down starch, mainly into the disaccharide maltose.

The tongue is a muscular organ. It keeps food where it can be chewed by the teeth. It also pushes food to the back of the mouth when you swallow. In addition, your sense of taste is located mostly on the tongue.

The process of swallowing involves complex muscular action. It is illustrated in Figure 38.3. First, food is forced into the large area at the back of the mouth called the **pharynx** [FAR-ingks]. From the pharynx, muscles push food down the throat. The food passes the point where the air passage to the lungs branches from the food tube. A structure called the **epiglottis** [ehp-ih-GLAHT-ihs] closes over the air passage each time you swallow. This prevents food from entering the lungs.

Figure 38.3 How does the epiglottis prevent food from entering the lungs?

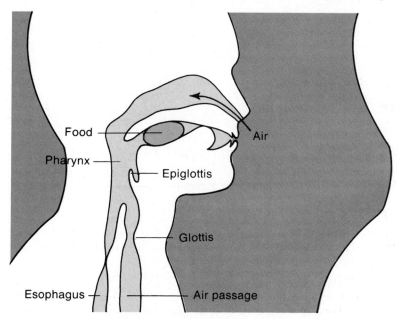

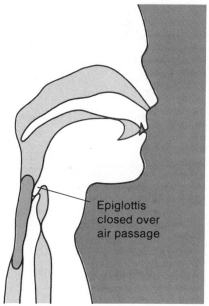

38–2 The Esophagus

As it is swallowed, food passes from the pharynx to the **esophagus** [ih-SAHF-uh-guhs]. The esophagus carries food from the mouth to the stomach. In some ways, the wall of the esophagus is typical of the entire alimentary canal's structure. The layers of cells that line the tube are called the **mucosa** [myoo-KOH-suh]. As the name *mucosa* indicates, these layers contain many mucus-secreting cells. The lubricated esophagus lining eases the passage of food. The hollow interior space of the alimentary canal is the **lumen** [LOO-muhn].

Beneath the mucosa are two layers of muscle. In the innermost layer, muscle fibers wrap around the esophagus. The fibers of the outermost layer, however, run the length of the esophagus.

Do You Know?
In adults, the alimentary canal is over 8 meters long.

These muscle layers alternately relax and contract. This causes the esophagus to squeeze together in places. These narrowings move along the length of the esophagus in waves. Food is pushed ahead of these waves. **Peristalsis** [pehr-uh-STAWL-sihs] is the name for this rhythmic muscular action. This is how food moves through much of the digestive system.

38–3   The Stomach

Figure 38.4 shows the entire digestive system of the human. The stomach is the large J-shaped organ at the end of the esophagus, on the left side of the body. When food reaches

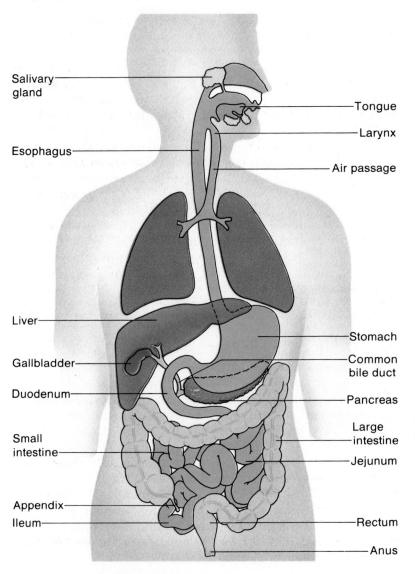

Figure 38.4 The anatomy of the human digestive system

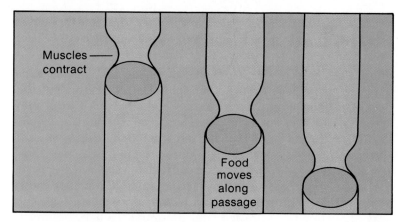

Figure 38.5 The muscular contractions of peristalsis move food through the digestive system.

the end of the esophagus, it goes past a sphincter muscle. A **sphincter** [SFIHNGK-tuhr] is a circular smooth muscle that closes a tube when it contracts. The sphincter relaxes and allows food to enter the stomach. A second sphincter muscle is located at the end of the stomach. The two sphincters together keep food within the stomach. When the second sphincter relaxes, partially digested food moves out of the stomach.

There are three kinds of cells in the stomach mucosa. One kind secretes mucus. Another kind secretes enzymes. The third secretes hydrochloric acid and water. The enzymes, water, and hydrochloric acid combine to form **gastric juice**.

Hydrochloric acid is a strong acid. It helps break up connective tissue and cell membranes in food. Hydrochloric acid also kills many harmful bacteria.

The enzymes produced by the stomach are mostly **proteases** [PROH-tee-ays-ehz]. Proteases break down proteins. The principal stomach protease is called pepsin. It breaks down protein into polypeptides. Protein digestion begins in the stomach.

Chemical digestion by gastric juice is aided by mechanical digestion. The food churns for several hours. After this, most food is the consistency of a thick soup.

Do You Know?
Pepsin can function only in an acid environment such as that of the stomach.

Checkpoint

1. What are the two types of digestion?
2. What is the term for the tubelike structure through which food passes during digestion?
3. Name four different kinds of teeth found in humans.
4. What kind of molecule is broken down by an enzyme in saliva?
5. What structure keeps food from entering the air passage?
6. What is the function of peristalsis?

- sections of the small intestine
- pancreatic enzymes and the digestion of proteins, starches, and fats
- bile's role as an emulsifier
- structural adaptations of the small intestine for absorption
- completion of chemical digestion and absorption in the small intestine
- the large intestine's function in absorbing water and eliminating wastes

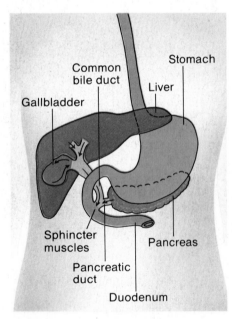

Figure 38.6 Bile, produced in the liver, travels to the gallbladder for storage. During digestion, bile is released into the duodenum to emulsify fats.

Do You Know?
One component of bile is a chemical left over from the destruction of old red blood cells. This chemical gives bile a brilliant yellow color.

The Small and Large Intestines

After the food in the stomach has reached the proper consistency, it passes through the sphincter at the end of the stomach. Food begins to move through the **small intestine**. If the small intestine was stretched out, it would be about six meters long. This is where most chemical digestion and absorption of food molecules occurs. The pancreas and liver are digestive organs associated with the small intestine.

The first part of the small intestine is called the **duodenum** [doo-uh-DEE-nuhm]. It is about 20 centimeters long. The next 2.5 meters is called the **jejunum** [juh-JOO-nuhm]. The **ileum** [IHL-ee-uhm] is the name given to the last half of the small intestine. There is no clear division between any of these sections.

The final stages of digestion happen in the large intestine. Water is absorbed there. Finally, undigested wastes are expelled from the body.

38–4 The Pancreas and Liver

The pancreas and the liver are shown in Figure 38.6. These two organs aid the digestive process. However, they are not themselves part of the alimentary canal. The **pancreas** [PANG-kree-uhs] has two principal functions. First, it produces hormones that regulate the homeostasis of blood glucose. Second, it produces **pancreatic juice**. This passes into the duodenum through the pancreatic duct. Pancreatic juice neutralizes the acidic stomach contents before they move into the rest of the small intestine.

Pancreatic juice also contains a number of digestive enzymes. Among them are several different proteases. They continue the protein digestion begun in the stomach, breaking polypeptides into smaller chains.

The pancreas also secretes a **lipase**. This type of enzyme breaks fat molecules, or triglycerides, into fatty acids and glycerol. An amylase in pancreatic juice is similar in function to the one secreted by the salivary glands.

The liver has many functions. It changes surplus glucose into glycogen, a polysaccharide. The liver stores this glycogen until it is needed by the body. The liver also produces a complex fluid called **bile** that is used in digestion.

Bile contains no enzymes. It does, however, have substances that aid in the digestion of fats, or lipids. Recall that lipids do not dissolve in water. Just as oil does not dissolve in vinegar in salad dressing, lipids in your diet do not dissolve in the watery gastric juice. An emulsifier is a chemical that breaks fats and oils into extremely tiny droplets. Emulsifiers in bile act on fats and oils in the intestine. Pancreatic lipase can then digest the lipids much faster.

Bile travels through ducts to the **gallbladder**, where it is stored. During digestion, the gallbladder releases bile into the duodenum through the **common bile duct**. These structures and their relationship to the pancreatic duct are shown in Figure 38.6.

38–5   The Structure of the Small Intestine

The interior of the small intestine has an enormous surface area. This adaptation allows for the absorption of a very large amount of food molecules. Figure 38.7 shows how the mucosa of the small intestine is folded. These folds make the surface area of the small intestine twice as large as it would otherwise be. The tiny fingerlike projections from these folds are called **villi** [VIHL-eye]. The villi increase the surface area by another factor of ten.

Figure 38.7 also shows the structure of a single villus. There are vessels within the villus. Most of these are blood vessels. In addition, there is a central tube called a **lacteal** [LAK-tee-uhl]. Lacteals absorb fats. Lacteals are part of the lymphatic system, which is discussed in Chapter 40.

Each villus is covered by a single layer of epithelial cells. Food molecules in the intestine must pass through these epithelial cells before reaching the blood vessels and lacteals. The plasma membrane of each epithelial cell is folded into many tiny projections called microvilli. Like the folds of the mucosa and the projections of the villi, the microvilli increase the surface area of the small intestine.

BIOLOGY INSIGHTS

The numerous villi and microvilli in the small intestine greatly increase the organ's surface-to-volume ratio. A larger surface area increases the rate at which absorption may occur. Thus the function of the villi and microvilli is similar to that of the root hairs in plant roots.

Figure 38.7 *Top:* A scanning electron micrograph of villi; *Left:* The arrangement of tissues in the small intestine; *Right:* Villus structure showing microvilli

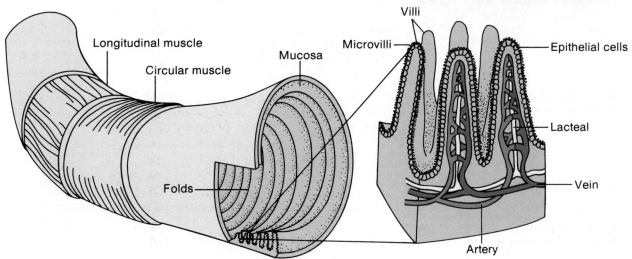

38–6 The Function of the Small Intestine

In the duodenum, food leaving the stomach is mixed with bile and pancreatic juice. This souplike mixture then moves through the jejunum and the ileum.

Cells of the intestinal epithelium itself also produce a number of digestive enzymes. These enzymes, unlike those of the pancreas, are not released into the lumen. Rather, they stay embedded in the cell membranes of the epithelial cells. Among these enzymes are **peptidases** [PEP-tih-day-sehz]. They break short polypeptides into individual amino acids. Several other epithelial enzymes break disaccharides into monosaccharides. **Maltase**, for example, breaks maltose into two molecules of glucose. Maltose is produced when amylase digests starch. Many enzymes are produced during digestion. Figure 38.8 summarizes their origin and function.

In the jejunum, most of what takes place is chemical digestion. Small molecules are absorbed through the villi and into the blood vessels. When food reaches the ileum, most chemical digestion is complete. Absorption predominates for the remainder of the trip through the small intestine. Some food molecules move through the epithelium of the small intestine by simple diffusion. Others, however, are actively transported across the epithelial-cell membranes.

By this time, the food that was taken into the body has been fully broken down. Polysaccharides have been broken down into simple sugars. Proteins have been split into amino acids. Fats have been hydrolyzed to fatty acids and glycerol.

Once sugars and amino acids cross the epithelial cell layer, they move into the bloodstream. Blood leaves the small intestine and goes directly to the liver. The liver removes excess glucose from the blood and stores it as glycogen. Glucose will be returned to the blood as cells require it. The liver also removes amino acids from the blood.

Fatty acids and glycerol follow a different path. These molecules pass into the intestinal epithelial cells. They are immediately converted back to triglycerides, or fat molecules. Triglycerides then move into the lacteals. Lacteals connect

Figure 38.8 The origin and functions of some digestive enzymes

Enzyme	Origin	Function
Amylase	Salivary glands, pancreas	Starch breakdown
Pepsin (a protease)	Stomach	Protein breakdown
Trypsin (a protease)	Pancreas	Further breakdown of protein
Lipase	Pancreas	Fat breakdown
Peptidase	Intestinal epithelium	Breakdown of short polypeptides
Maltase	Intestinal epithelium	Maltose breakdown

1. **Mouth** Teeth are used to crush food

2. **Salivary Glands** Enzymes are secreted to begin the digestion of starch

3. **Esophagus** Food is moved to the stomach through peristalsis

4. **Stomach** The churning of food and the action of gastric juice begins the digestion of proteins

5. **Liver** Bile is produced here and surplus glucose is changed to glycogen

6. **Gallbladder** Bile is stored here until its release into the small intestine to emulsify fats

7. **Pancreas** Pancreatic juice is produced here to neutralize acidic stomach contents, further digest protein, and break down triglycerides into fatty acids and glycerol

8. **Small Intestine** Intestinal juice is secreted to digest carbohydrates, fats, and proteins. Digested food is absorbed and carried by the blood cells

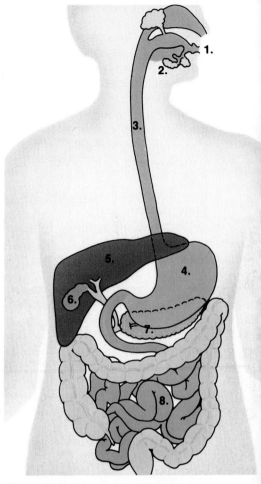

Figure 38.9 Summary of digestion

with a system of vessels that bypass the liver. These vessels empty directly into the bloodstream.

38–7 The Large Intestine

The large intestine gets its name from its diameter rather than from its length. The large intestine is only about two meters long. However, it is approximately twice as wide as the small intestine. The large intestine is also known as the **colon** [KOH-luhn].

Where the small and large intestine join, there is a small projection called the **appendix**. This structure has no known function in humans. However, in some plant-eating animals like rabbits, it helps digest cellulose.

One major function of the large intestine is to absorb water from the lumen. The amount of water in the body must remain reasonably constant. Solid, indigestible wastes called **feces** remain after water is absorbed.

The last 20 or 30 centimeters of the colon are called the **rectum**. Feces are stored there until they are eliminated from the body through the anus.

Checkpoint

1. What are the three sections of the small intestine?
2. What are villi?
3. What kinds of vessels are found within villi?
4. What enzymes are produced by the pancreas?
5. What is another name for the large intestine?
6. What is a major function of the large intestine?

- the food calorie as a unit of food energy
- carbohydrates and fats as high-energy foods
- importance of proteins in the structure and function of the body
- essential amino acids and complete protein
- importance of vitamins, minerals, and water
- malnutrition and obesity

Figure 38.10 Energy to fuel the body is derived from the breakdown of chemical bonds in food.

Do You Know?

A gram of carbohydrate contains about 4 food calories. A gram of fat, in contrast, contains about 9.

Nutrition

Food supplies your body with energy. It also provides materials for growth, maintenance, and replacement of tissues. Certain food substances are needed for various chemical reactions within cells. Nutrition is the process by which organisms obtain and use food.

Those chemicals that you eat or drink to grow and remain healthy are called **nutrients**. There are two classes of nutrients: those that can provide energy and those that cannot. Energy-supplying nutrients include carbohydrates, fats, and proteins. Vitamins, minerals, and water are the nutrients that do not provide energy.

The energy content of food is measured in **food calories**, or kilocalories. A calorie is actually a unit of energy. It is the amount of energy necessary to raise the temperature of one gram of water one degree Celsius. One thousand calories is equal to one kilocalorie, or one food calorie. When nutritionists list the calories in foods, they are actually referring to kilocalories.

Food molecules all contain chemical bonds. When these bonds are broken, energy is released. The food-calorie content of a food indicates how much energy will be released after the food is completely broken down.

38–8   Carbohydrates and Fats

Carbohydrates are used mainly to supply energy. Digestion of most carbohydrates results in the simple sugar glucose. In the process of respiration, glucose combines with oxygen. The compound ATP is produced, which provides the cells with usable energy. The most common carbohydrates in food are sugars, starches, and cellulose.

Sugars are relatively small molecules. Some sugars, such as glucose, fructose, and galactose, are monosaccharides. Disaccharides are two monosaccharides that are chemically bonded together. Sucrose, maltose, and lactose are disaccharides. Sugars occur naturally in fruits.

Sugar molecules sometimes join to form long-chain polysaccharides called starches. These take longer to digest than smaller carbohydrates. Grains and grain products, such as rice and bread, contain large amounts of starch. So do certain vegetables, such as potatoes.

Another polysaccharide is cellulose, which forms the cell walls of plant cells. Humans cannot digest cellulose. However, cellulose is important in the diet. It provides fiber, or roughage, against which the intestinal muscles push. This motion causes food to move more quickly through the alimentary canal.

When you eat digestible carbohydrates, the body first uses them to satisfy immediate energy needs. Carbohydrates not used immediately may be converted to fat.

The fats you eat are mostly in the form of triglycerides. Each triglyceride molecule is composed of three fatty acids attached to a molecule of glycerol. Like carbohydrates, fats provide the body with energy. However, fat contains far more food calories per unit of mass than do carbohydrates. Unlike most carbohydrates, fats can be stored in the body. They can be used when the body needs energy.

The body uses fat for other things besides energy. Fat forms part of the cell membrane. Fat is necessary for the conduction of nerve impulses. Also, certain vitamins are found only in fatty foods. Foods that are rich in fats include margarine, butter, salad oils, cheeses, and many meats.

38–9   Proteins

Proteins are the third group of nutrients that can provide energy. Their primary use, however, is not to supply the body with energy. They make up much of the structure of cells. Thus they are needed for growth and repair of cells. Protein molecules also take a major part in governing chemical reactions in the body. Enzymes, for example, are proteins.

Like carbohydrates and fats, proteins contain the elements carbon, hydrogen, and oxygen. In addition, they contain nitrogen. As you learned in Chapter 4, proteins are made up of chains of amino acids. During digestion, the amino acids are separated from each other. They are carried to the cells via the bloodstream. After the amino acids are in the cells, they are reassembled to make new proteins. Milk, meats, fish, eggs, dried beans, and cheeses are good sources of protein.

There are 20 amino acids commonly found in humans. Of these, eight must be obtained from food. These are called essential amino acids. The body can synthesize the remaining amino acids from these eight.

Unless the body has all the essential amino acids at the same time, it cannot make proteins. The body cannot store amino acids. Thus they are wasted.

Certain foods, sometimes called complete-protein foods, contain all the essential amino acids. If you eat one of these foods, you will have all the essential amino acids at one time. Meat, fish, poultry, milk, cheese, and eggs are complete protein foods.

Other foods contain some, but not all, of the essential amino acids. Soy beans, for example, lack valine and methionine.

Figure 38.11 Marathon runners often eat large amounts of carbohydrates before a race.

Rice does not have isoleucine or lysine. Eaten separately, neither would provide the body with usable protein-building material. But if you eat soy beans and rice together, they supply all the essential amino acids.

38–10   Vitamins, Minerals, and Water

Vitamins, minerals, and water are nutrients that do not supply the body with energy. Instead, they perform other functions.

Vitamins are usually coenzymes. Such molecules are necessary for various chemical reactions to occur in the body. The functions and food sources of various vitamins are described in the facing table.

If vitamins are missing from the diet, serious conditions can result. These are called **deficiency diseases**. For example, people develop scurvy when they do not have enough vitamin C for a long time. Their gums swell and bleed. Their teeth fall out, and their joints become sore. Without enough vitamin D, children may develop rickets. The bones become soft, and bone deformities result.

Vitamins can be divided into two groups on the basis of the substances in which they dissolve. The water-soluble vitamins dissolve in water. They include vitamin C and the members of the vitamin-B complex. Water-soluble vitamins can be lost from foods if they are exposed to water for too long. Overcooking also destroys vitamins.

The other group contains vitamins that dissolve in fat. It includes vitamins A, D, E, and K. These fat-soluble vitamins are found in foods that contain fat.

If you take vitamin pills, can you be less careful about your choice of foods? Nutritionists think not. Vitamin pills do not contain the other important nutrients found in foods.

Minerals are inorganic substances — that is, they do not contain carbon. The minerals in your diet have many functions. For example, they maintain the acid-base balance in the body. They help regulate the amount of water in the blood. They are important parts of many body structures, such as bone and red blood cells. Many life processes could not take place without minerals. Calcium, sodium, iron, and phosphorus are some important minerals. The functions of various minerals are outlined in the facing table.

You obtain water by drinking it. It is also present in many foods. Water has many functions in the body. Most are related to water's role as a solvent. It dissolves food materials, so that they can pass into the bloodstream. Most of the body's chemical reactions occur in water solutions.

Do You Know?

Limes contain vitamin C. In the eighteenth century, British sailors on long voyages discovered that eating limes prevented scurvy. That's why a British sailor is called a Limey.

Do You Know?

Soaking potatoes in water actually removes most of the vitamin C.

DIETARY VITAMINS

Vitamin	Source	Function	Symptoms of Deficiency
A	Egg yolks, butter, green and yellow vegetables, organ meats, fish liver oils	Growth, healthy skin and eyes	Night blindness, changes in epithelial cells, retarded growth
B_1 (thiamin)	Seafood, poultry, meats, whole or enriched grains, green vegetables, milk, soy beans	Carbohydrate metabolism; growth; heart, muscle, and nerve function	Retarded growth, beri-beri, nerve disorders, fatigue
B_2 (riboflavin)	Milk, eggs, poultry, yeast, meats, soy beans, green vegetables	Carbohydrate metabolism, growth	Retarded growth, premature aging
Niacin	Leafy vegetables, peanut butter, potatoes, whole or enriched grain, fish, poultry, meats, tomatoes	Growth, carbohydrate metabolism, digestion, nerve function	Digestive and nervous disturbances
B_{12}	Liver	Production of red blood cells, nerve function	Anemia
C (ascorbic acid)	Citrus fruit, tomatoes, leafy vegetables	Growth, healthy gums	Sore gums, susceptibility to bruising
D	Milk, liver, eggs, fish liver oils	Growth, calcium and phosphate metabolism	Poor tooth development, rickets
E (tocopherol)	Vegetable oils, butter, milk, leafy vegetables	Protects cell membranes, reproductive function	Unknown
K	Green vegetables, tomatoes, soy bean oil; most made by intestinal bacteria	Blood clotting, liver function	Hemorrhaging

DIETARY MINERALS

Mineral	Source	Function	Symptoms of Deficiency
Calcium	Milk and other dairy products, bean curd, dark green vegetables	Tooth and bone formation, nerve transmission, muscle contraction	Rickets, osteoporosis
Phosphorus	Most foods	Bone development, transfer of energy in cells	Unknown
Sodium	Meats, dairy products, salt	Nerve transmission, muscle contraction	Dehydration, shock
Chlorine	Salt	Formation of HCl	Abnormal contraction of muscles
Potassium	Fruits	Regulation of heart beat, maintenance of water balance, nerve transmission	Heart dysfunction
Magnesium	Nuts, grains, dark green vegetables, seafood, chocolate	Catalyst for ATP formation	Weakness, mental confusion
Iodine	Seafood, iodized salt	Thyroid activity	Goiter
Iron	Meats, dark green vegetables, dried fruits	Hemoglobin formation	Anemia

Figure 38.12 The four food groups

38–11 The Importance of a Balanced Diet

Solon, a Greek philosopher who lived thousands of years ago, said, "Nothing in excess." His advice, applied to nutrition, still holds true today.

Nutritionists generally divide the sources of nutrients into four groups. These are the meat group, the milk group, the fruit and vegetable group, and the cereal-grain group. Foods in the meat group, as shown in Figure 38.12, include meat, fish, poultry, eggs, and legumes. The legumes, often called meat substitutes, include beans, peas, and peanuts. Besides milk, the milk group contains cheese and yogurt.

The fruit and vegetable group, as the name implies, includes all fruits and vegetables. They may be fresh, frozen, canned, or dried. The cereal group includes grains and grain products. Among these are bread, cereal, rice, pasta, and tortillas. To achieve a balanced diet, you should eat foods from each group every day. Nutritionists also recommend eating a wide variety of foods.

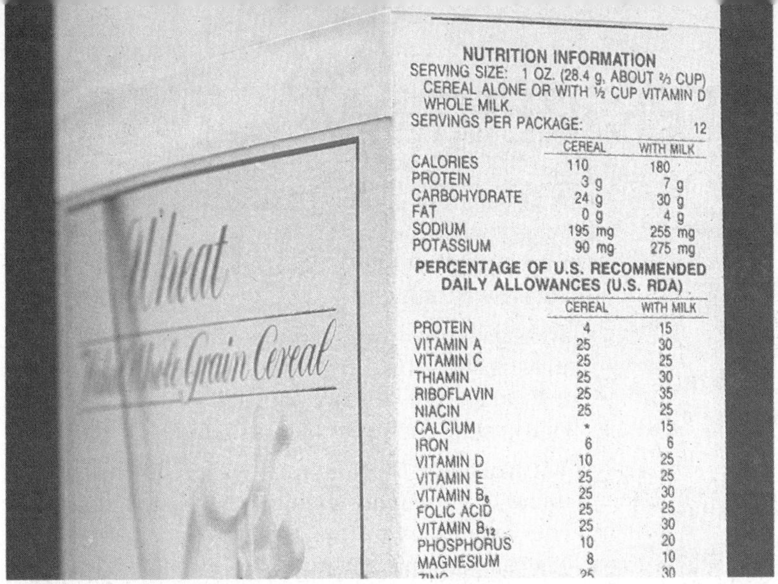

```
NUTRITION INFORMATION
SERVING SIZE:  1 OZ. (28.4 g, ABOUT ⅔ CUP)
    CEREAL ALONE OR WITH ½ CUP VITAMIN D
    WHOLE MILK.
SERVINGS PER PACKAGE:                    12
```

	CEREAL	WITH MILK
CALORIES	110	180
PROTEIN	3 g	7 g
CARBOHYDRATE	24 g	30 g
FAT	0 g	4 g
SODIUM	195 mg	255 mg
POTASSIUM	90 mg	275 mg

```
PERCENTAGE OF U.S. RECOMMENDED
    DAILY ALLOWANCES (U.S. RDA)
```

	CEREAL	WITH MILK
PROTEIN	4	15
VITAMIN A	25	30
VITAMIN C	25	25
THIAMIN	25	30
RIBOFLAVIN	25	35
NIACIN	25	25
CALCIUM	*	15
IRON	6	6
VITAMIN D	10	25
VITAMIN E	25	25
VITAMIN B₆	25	30
FOLIC ACID	25	25
VITAMIN B₁₂	25	30
PHOSPHORUS	10	20
MAGNESIUM	8	10
ZINC	25	30

Figure 38.13 Reading the nutritional information provided on the labels of the foods can help you select a balanced diet.

People who do not eat a balanced diet can develop health problems. The most serious of these is **malnutrition**. This occurs when people do not get enough of the right kinds of food. It affects about a sixth of the world's population. Millions of people are actually starving to death.

Undernourished people have a higher chance of getting diseases. Poor diets also harm the growth and development of children. For example, if babies do not get enough protein, brain damage can occur.

Obesity is a condition characterized by excessive body fat. While usually not as serious as undernourishment, obesity is also unhealthy. Overweight people frequently have health problems. Among them are diabetes and heart disease.

To lose weight, people often go on diets. A well-planned, nutritionally balanced diet can be very helpful. However, some fad diets lack important nutrients. In addition, it is dangerous to lose too much weight. If your calorie intake is too low, your body cannot function properly.

Proper nutrition is important. A balanced, moderate diet is necessary for good health.

Checkpoint

1. What are the three classes of energy-providing nutrients?
2. What is meant by *essential amino acids?*
3. Name one body structure in which minerals are important.
4. What causes scurvy?
5. What are the four basic food groups?
6. What can happen to babies who do not get enough protein?
7. Identify two health problems associated with being overweight.

CHAPTER REVIEW

Summary

- Digestion reduces food to smaller and smaller particles. Both mechanical and chemical digestion occur in the alimentary canal.

- In the mouth, the teeth and tongue begin mechanical digestion. Amylase begins the digestion of starch.

- Food moves from the mouth to the stomach via the esophagus. Peristalsis causes the movement of food through the alimentary canal.

- Gastric juice in the stomach contains water, enzymes, and hydrochloric acid. Proteases begin the digestion of proteins.

- Most chemical digestion takes place in the small intestine. The three parts of this structure are the duodenum, the jejunum, and the ileum.

- The pancreas produces pancreatic juice, which is transported to the duodenum. Pancreatic juice contains proteases, an amylase, and a lipase.

- The liver produces bile, which aids in fat digestion. Bile is stored in the gallbladder. During digestion, it is released into the duodenum.

- Folds, villi, and microvilli give the small intestine an enormous surface area. This allows the absorption of a large amount of digested food.

- Cells in the intestinal epithelium contain enzymes that function in the final stages of chemical digestion. By the time chemical digestion is complete, complex carbohydrates have been hydrolyzed into simple sugars. Proteins have been split into amino acids, and fats to fatty acids and glycerol.

- The large intestine absorbs water from the material remaining after digestion is complete. Undigested food is expelled from the body as feces.

- Nutrients are those substances that you eat to grow and remain healthy. Food energy is measured in food calories, which are equal to kilocalories.

- Energy-supplying foods include carbohydrates, fats, and proteins. Carbohydrates and fats are high-energy foods. Proteins are used primarily for growth and repair of cells.

- Vitamins, minerals, and water do not supply energy. However, they are necessary for many life processes.

- A balanced diet includes foods from four main groups. These are meats and related foods; dairy products; fruits and vegetables; and cereal and grains.

Vocabulary

alimentary canal	lipase
amylase	lumen
appendix	malnutrition
bile	maltase
canine tooth	mechanical digestion
cementum	mineral
chemical digestion	molar
colon	mucosa
common bile duct	mucus
deficiency disease	nutrient
dentin	pancreas
digestion	pancreatic juice
duodenum	peptidase
enamel	periodontal
epiglottis	membrane
esophagus	peristalsis
feces	pharynx
food calorie	premolar
gallbladder	protease
gastric juice	rectum
ileum	saliva
incisor	small intestine
jejunum	sphincter
lacteal	villi
large intestine	vitamin

Review

1. Which type of digestion do the teeth carry out — mechanical or chemical? How do they do this?
2. What are the three hard substances found in teeth?
3. What does a sphincter muscle do?
4. What kind of molecules does lipase act on?
5. What substance undergoes chemical digestion in the stomach?
6. What substances are found in gastric juice?
7. Name the three parts of the small intestine.
8. What is the term for the fingerlike projections of the small intestine's wall?
9. Name one enzyme produced by the cells of the intestinal epithelium.
10. What is another name for the large intestine?
11. What is the meaning of *nutrient?*
12. How many calories are in a food calorie?
13. What simple sugar generally results from the digestion of carbohydrates?
14. Why is cellulose important in the diet?
15. Which type of high-energy food can be stored in the body?
16. To which food group do eggs belong?
17. What fraction of the world's population suffers from malnutrition?

Interpret and Apply

1. Explain how the structures of the different kinds of teeth are adapted to different functions.
2. In the small intestine, which is more important — mechanical or chemical digestion? Explain.
3. Describe the process of peristalsis.
4. What would happen if the stomach had no sphincter muscles?
5. Why is the large surface area of the small intestine important?
6. What happens to fatty acids and glycerol after they pass into the intestinal epithelial cells?
7. What must happen for energy to be released from food molecules?

8. Complete protein foods must contain at least how many amino acids?
9. Why can fad diets be dangerous?
10. Which kind of protein does tuna fish contain — complete or incomplete? Explain.

Challenge

1. Is bile involved in chemical digestion or mechanical digestion? Explain.
2. What might happen during swallowing if the epiglottis were not present?
3. A person can survive without a gallbladder, but not without a liver. Why?
4. The small intestine is about the only part of the alimentary canal that cannot be completely removed surgically. Explain why you cannot live without this organ.
5. Proteins that come from plants are incomplete. Strict vegetarians will not eat any foods except plants or plant products. How do they obtain complete protein?
6. People can survive a short time without most nutrients, but they must have water regularly. Why do you think this is so?

Projects

1. Find out about the Heimlich maneuver. This procedure is used to dislodge a piece of food that is stuck in the throat. Learn when the procedure should be used and how it is done.
2. Do library research to learn about Dr. James Beaumont and his patient Alexis St. Martin. How did they contribute to an understanding of the human digestive system?
3. Plan a week's meals, three per day. Each day's menu should include two servings from the meat group, two from the milk group, four from the fruit and vegetable group, and four from the grain group.
4. Find out how your community provides food for people who otherwise wouldn't have an adequate diet. Include programs sponsored by schools, churches, private citizens, and the government.

39 Respiration and Excretion

Astronaut attached to life support

In the coming years, people may routinely venture into space. No one, however, can enter this hostile environment without taking along a piece of Earth's atmosphere. Humans cannot exist without oxygen. When astronauts venture into space they obtain this necessary gas from their space suits and the spacecraft. Without oxygen, an astronaut could not survive more than a few minutes.

The importance of oxygen becomes obvious when it is not easily available. Like a spacecraft, your body needs energy to operate. Oxygen is needed for the release of this energy. Before you can use oxygen, though, it must reach your cells. This happens in specific, highly organized steps. Each breath you take is part of the process.

As your cells use oxygen during respiration, they produce waste products. These wastes must be removed from your body. Thus respiration and excretion are related processes. They are every bit as precise and controlled as the launching of a spacecraft.

Respiration

The term *respiration* can mean different things. In common use, it may refer just to breathing. This is the action of moving air into and out of the lungs. To a biologist, respiration is the whole process in which the cells of an organism receive oxygen and release carbon dioxide. As part of this process, energy is released from food molecules.

Respiration can be divided into three general processes. **External respiration** is the exchange of gases between the atmosphere and the blood. This takes place in the lungs. Here oxygen diffuses from the air into the blood, and carbon dioxide diffuses from the blood into the air.

Gas exchange between the blood and the body cells is called **internal respiration**. Oxygen and carbon dioxide move in opposite directions. Oxygen diffuses from the blood into the cells. Carbon dioxide, on the other hand, diffuses out of the cells and into the blood.

Finally, the chemical process that takes place in the mitochondria of your cells is called **cellular respiration**. In this process, oxygen combines chemically with food molecules, and energy is released. This energy is stored in ATP. Carbon dioxide and water are produced as waste products.

CONCEPTS
- internal and external respiration
- anatomy and function of respiratory organs
- mechanics of breathing
- breathing rate

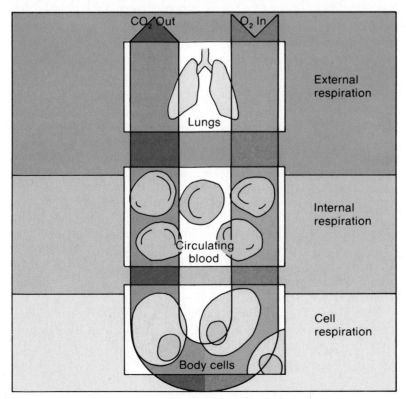

Figure 39.1 In each of these processes cells receive oxygen and release carbon dioxide.

39–1 The Human Respiratory Structures

Like fish gills, human lungs are thin, extensively folded tissues where the external environment comes close to circulating blood. But unlike gills, lungs exchange gases with air instead of water. In addition, lungs are located deep inside the body. They depend on a single tube to carry air in and out.

Figure 39.2 shows the upper part of the respiratory system. Air enters the lungs mainly through the nose. The nasal cavity contains many bony projections. These create a large surface area. Soft epithelial tissue covers these projections. The epithelium contains many tiny blood vessels called **capillaries**. Mucus-secreting cells are also present.

In the nasal passages, most dust, bacteria, and other particles are removed from air because they stick to the mucus. Cilia gradually move the mucus to the back of the throat. There the mucus is removed by being swallowed. Nasal blood capillaries add moisture to incoming dry air and warmth to cold air. This prevents damage to delicate lung tissue.

Both the nasal passage and the mouth open into the pharynx. If the nasal passages are blocked, air can reach the lungs through the mouth. The mouth, however, is not as effective in cleaning and warming air.

In the neck, the **trachea** [TRAY-kee-uh], or windpipe, branches from the pharynx. Recall that the epiglottis prevents food from entering the trachea when you swallow. Just below the epiglottis is the **larynx** [LAR-ingks], or voice box. Here a pair of **vocal cords** stretch across the trachea. They are made of tough connective tissue. When you force air past the vocal cords, they vibrate. This is how you create sound. The trachea has cartilage rings that keep it from collapsing.

Figure 39.2 shows that the trachea carries air into the right and left **bronchi** [BRONG-ky] (singular, *bronchus*). Within the lungs, the bronchi branch into finer and finer tubes called **bronchioles** [BRONG-kee-ohlz]. At the end of each bronchiole is a cluster of microscopic, balloonlike air sacs. These are called **alveoli** [al-VEE-uh-leye] (singular, *alveolus*).

Like the nasal cavity, the lining of the trachea, bronchi, and bronchioles contains cells that secrete mucus. Any particles that get past the nasal passages usually stick to this mucus. In addition, coughing helps to keep large objects out of the lungs. Thus many adaptations improve the quality of the air that finally reaches the alveoli.

The **lungs** are the large saclike organs in which external respiration takes place. Each lung is surrounded by a double membrane called the **pleura** [PLOOR-uh]. The outer pleura is attached to the chest wall. The inner pleura is attached

Do You Know?

The length and tension of the vocal cords determine the pitch of the voice. When the cords are short and tense, high notes result. Low notes are produced when the cords are long and relaxed.

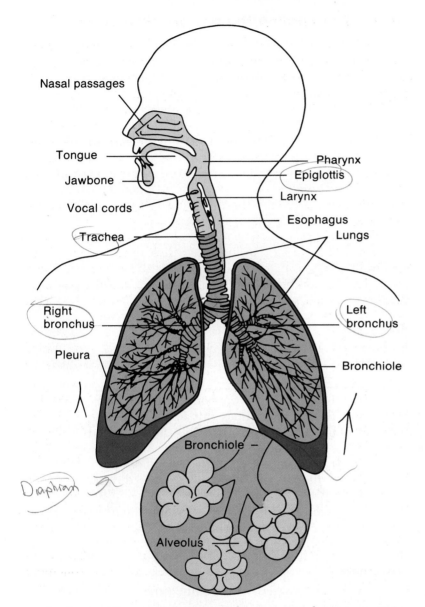

Figure 39.2 The anatomy of the upper and lower respiratory tract

Nasal passages

Tongue

Jawbone

Vocal cords

Trachea

Pharynx

Epiglottis

Larynx

Esophagus

Lungs

Right bronchus

Left bronchus

Pleura

Bronchiole

Diaphram

Bronchiole

Alveolus

to the lungs. The space between the two membranes contains a lubricating fluid. This allows the lungs to move freely. The heart occupies the space between the two lungs.

A large blood vessel carries blood from the heart to the lungs. This vessel branches into tiny capillaries in the lungs. Another large vessel then returns blood to the heart.

Occasionally bacteria and viruses invade the air passages. When bacteria or viruses penetrate into the lungs, pneumonia can result. The alveoli in the infected lungs secrete a watery fluid. The fluid interferes with the diffusion of oxygen into the body.

39–2   Gas Exchange

The alveoli are surrounded by capillaries, as shown in Figure 39.3. The walls of the alveoli are thin and moist. Gases can easily diffuse across the alveolar membrane. External respiration takes place across the alveoli.

Air is a mixture of gases. Approximately 80 percent of air is nitrogen, and about 20 percent is oxygen. Very small amounts of other gases are also present. Carbon dioxide, for example, makes up about 0.03 percent of air.

Figure 39.3 The exchange of oxygen and carbon dioxide occurs across the alveolar membrane.

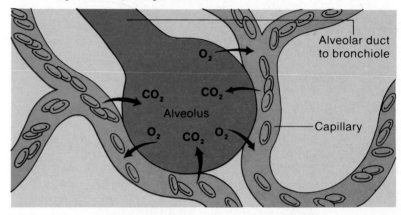

In external respiration, oxygen from the air moves into the blood in the lungs. Carbon dioxide moves from the blood into the air. Why does this happen? Before blood enters the lungs, it has given up oxygen to the body cells. At this point, the blood is low in oxygen, or **deoxygenated** [dee-AHK-suh-juh-nay-tuhd]. The level of oxygen is higher in alveolar air than in the blood, so oxygen diffuses from the air into the blood.

Deoxygenated blood is rich in carbon dioxide, which the blood has picked up from the body cells. There is more carbon dioxide in this blood than in alveolar air. Therefore, carbon dioxide diffuses out of the blood and into the air in the alveoli.

The blood leaving the lungs is rich in oxygen. This blood is said to be **oxygenated**. At the same time, its carbon dioxide content is relatively low.

Internal respiration occurs when blood reaches the body cells. During cellular respiration, cells constantly use oxygen and produce carbon dioxide. Thus the concentration of oxygen is always less in the cytoplasm of body cells than in the blood. Therefore, oxygen diffuses from the blood into the cells.

During cellular respiration carbon dioxide accumulates in cell cytoplasm. There is more carbon dioxide in the cytoplasm than there is in the blood. Carbon dioxide diffuses out of the cells into the blood. Blood leaving the body cells is therefore

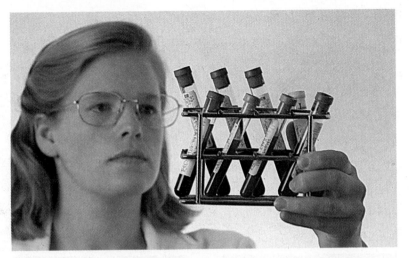

rich in carbon dioxide but low in oxygen. It returns to the lungs to repeat the cycle.

How are gases carried in the blood? A small amount of oxygen dissolves in the blood plasma. However, most oxygen molecules bind to molecules of the protein called **hemoglobin** [HEE-muh-gloh-buhn]. Hemoglobin molecules are located in the red cells. Hemoglobin with oxygen attached gives blood a bright red color. In contrast, deoxygenated blood is a dull purplish red. This is the color of hemoglobin without oxygen attached.

Like oxygen, a small amount of carbon dioxide dissolves in the blood plasma. Some carbon dioxide attaches to hemoglobin molecules in the red blood cells. However, most of the carbon dioxide reacts with water in the cytoplasm of the red blood cells. Carbonic acid, or H_2CO_3, is formed. An enzyme speeds this reaction.

Like all acids, carbonic acid forms hydrogen ions when it dissolves in water. As shown in the following equation, it also forms HCO_3^-, or bicarbonate, ions.

$$CO_2 + H_2O \xrightarrow{\text{enzyme}} H_2CO_3 \longrightarrow H^+ + HCO_3^-$$

H^+ and HCO_3^- ions accumulate in the red cells and diffuse into the plasma. In the lungs, bicarbonate ions change back to carbon dioxide.

39–3   The Mechanism of Breathing

To give the body a fresh supply of oxygen, air in the lungs must be constantly replaced. This happens when you breathe. **Inspiration** is the phase of breathing during which air is taken into the lungs, or inhaled. During **expiration**, air is expelled from the lungs, or exhaled.

Figure 39.5 *Left:* When the diaphragm contracts, air pressure decreases, causing the lungs to fill with air and expand. *Right:* When the diaphragm relaxes, increased air pressure causes the lungs to deflate.

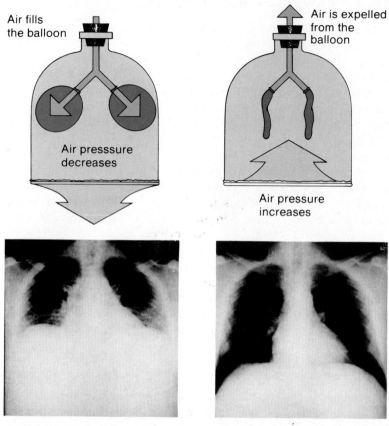

Figure 39.5 shows a model of how the lungs work. When the elastic sheet is pulled down, air pressure in the space around the balloons decreases. This causes outside air to rush into the balloons. Pushing the elastic sheet up increases the air pressure in the space. This forces air out of the balloons.

Your lungs work in a similar way. The lungs are like the balloons. The **diaphragm** [DY-uh-fram] is a large, dome-shaped muscle that separates the chest cavity from the abdomen. When you inhale, the diaphragm contracts. During contraction, the diaphragm flattens out. At the same time, muscles move the ribs up and out.

Both of these muscle actions increase the volume of the thoracic cavity. As in the model, increased volume reduces pressure in the pleural fluid. Air rushes into the lungs. As air rushes in, the walls of the alveoli stretch.

When you exhale, the diaphragm relaxes. It returns to its dome shape. Rib muscles also relax. Both movements reduce the volume of the thoracic cavity. Pressure on the pleural fluid increases, and air rushes out of the lungs. Like the rubber of a stretched balloon, the walls of the alveoli return to their smaller size. These actions force air out of the lungs.

39–4 Control of Breathing Rate

The rib muscles and the diaphragm are striated muscles. As such, they can be under voluntary control. You can choose to take deep breaths or shallow breaths. You can even choose to stop breathing for a short time. Eventually, however, your automatic controls take over, and you gasp for air. Most of the time, breathing is an unconscious response. The rib muscles and diaphragm are automatically stimulated by several nerves. These nerves bring impulses from a **breathing center** deep in the brain.

Breathing rate depends on activity level. When you sleep, your breathing slows. When you exercise, your breathing speeds up. These changes in rate are logical. During sleep, your cells burn less oxygen and produce less carbon dioxide than when you are awake and active.

Control of breathing rate is complex. A group of cells in the brain is connected to the breathing center. These nerve cells constantly monitor the carbon dioxide content of the blood. When blood carbon dioxide increases, for example, these cells send messages to the breathing center. The breathing center, in turn, sends nerve impulses that increase the rate of breathing.

Figure 39.6 During strenuous exercise, much CO_2 is released into the blood. The increase of CO_2 in the blood causes the breathing center to send impulses to increase the breathing rate.

Checkpoint

1. What is the scientific term for the exchange of gases between alveolar air and the blood?
2. The trachea divides into two air passages. What are they called?
3. Another name for the voice box is the _____.
4. What two body spaces does the diaphragm separate?
5. Where is hemoglobin found in the blood?
6. What happens to the breathing rate when the level of carbon dioxide in the blood increases?

CONCEPTS

- lungs, liver, and kidneys as organs of excretion
- structure of kidneys
- structure of nephrons
- how nephrons function
- water and salt balance in the body

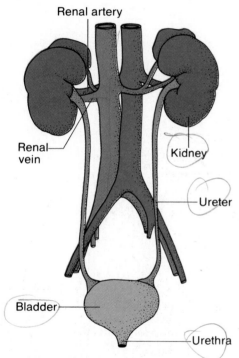

Figure 39.7 The anatomy of the excretory system

Do You Know?

The right kidney is usually slightly lower than the left. The reason for this is the presence of the liver on the right side of the body.

Do You Know?

The entire liquid content of blood is filtered by the kidneys 60 times each day.

The Excretory System

Cellular respiration produces carbon dioxide as one of its wastes. Metabolic processes produce other chemicals that are of no use to the cell. These waste substances may even be harmful. **Excretion** is the process of getting harmful or useless molecules out of cells and out of the organism.

39–5   The Organs of Excretion

The lungs are excretory organs that remove carbon dioxide from the body. The liver is an excretory organ too. It removes the products of red-blood cell breakdown by means of bile. The liver is also the major organ where amino acids are broken down. When the liver metabolizes amino acids, it produces the molecule **urea** [yoo-REE-uh], which contains nitrogen. In high concentration, urea can be poisonous to cells.

The **kidneys** filter urea and excess salts from the blood. They are the main excretory organs of your body. Every day, about 180 liters of fluid from the blood are filtered through the kidneys.

Your kidneys excrete urea from the body in urine. Urine is mostly water. It contains small amounts of dissolved urea and salts, with traces of other substances. The kidneys also help to maintain proper water balance in the body.

Figure 39.7 shows the kidneys to be a pair of bean-shaped organs flanking the lower part of the vertebral column. The **renal arteries** carry blood into the kidneys. Purified blood leaves the kidneys through the **renal veins**. Blood leaving the kidneys has less urea and slightly less water than when it entered the kidneys.

Urine is produced by the kidneys. It flows through a tube called the **ureter** [YOOR-uht-uhr] to a storage organ called the **bladder**. The bladder empties to the outside of the body through a single tube, the **urethra** [yoo-REE-thruh].

Figure 39.8 shows the internal structure of the kidney. The outermost layer is called the **renal cortex** [REE-nuhl KAWR-teks]. Below the cortex is the **renal medulla** [muh-DUHL-uh]. The filtration of blood and the formation of urine take place in the cortex and medulla. Urine collects in a large cavity called the **renal pelvis**. The ureter drains urine from there.

39–6   The Nephron: Structure

The renal cortex and medulla are made of over a million microscopic units called **nephrons** [NEF-rahnz]. Figure 39.8 shows one nephron.

In the kidneys the renal artery branches into many smaller vessels. Each of these ends in a group of capillaries called a **glomerulus** [gloh-MEHR-yuh-luhs]. The glomerulus sits inside a cuplike structure called a **Bowman's capsule**. All the Bowman's capsules and glomeruli of the kidney are located in the renal cortex.

Each Bowman's capsule is at the beginning of a long continuous tube. Sections of this tube differ in structure and function. Just behind the Bowman's capsule is the twisted **proximal tubule**. This leads into the **loop of Henle** [HEHN-lee]. The loop of Henle dips into the medulla and then returns to the cortex. There it becomes the **distal tubule**. The distal tubule then drains into the **collecting duct**. The collecting duct goes through the medulla and opens into the renal pelvis.

Use Figure 39.8 to trace the path of a molecule as it travels through the kidney. Note how a molecule in a Bowman's capsule can eventually be excreted through the urethra.

Do You Know?

If all the water that entered the Bowman's capsules were excreted, you would lose your entire supply of water in five hours.

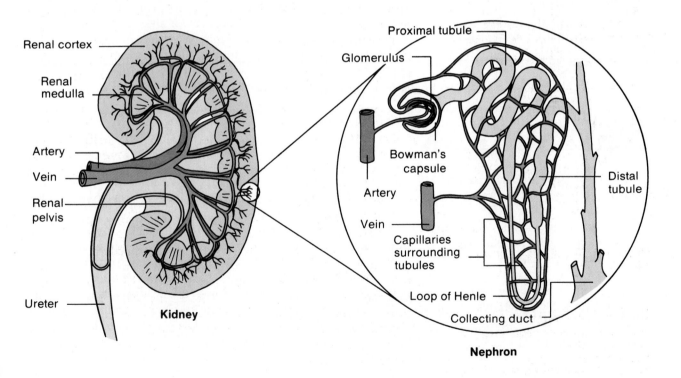

Figure 39.8 *Left:* The internal structure of a kidney. *Right:* The structure of a nephron.

39–7 The Nephron: Function

The membranes of the glomeruli and the Bowman's capsules are permeable to small molecules and ions. Some water, ions, sugar, amino acids, and urea move from the blood into the Bowman's capsules. In fact, over 180 liters of water and 600 grams of sodium are filtered into the Bowman's capsules every 24 hours. Your body contains only about 35 to 40 liters of water. Obviously, little of the water that enters the Bowman's capsules is excreted from the body.

As the fluid travels from the Bowman's capsule to the collecting duct, its composition changes. The blood recovers many substances from the fluid in the nephron by active transport. Recall that in active transport, membranes use energy to pump substances against the direction in which they would normally move by diffusion. Glucose, amino acids, and sodium are returned to the blood by active transport. Much of the urea, however, remains in the tubules.

Cells in the proximal tubule, distal tubule, and collecting ducts pump sodium ions back into the blood capillaries. Water molecules follow the sodium ions by osmosis. In this way, the body recovers over 99 percent of the water and sodium that is filtered into the Bowman's capsules.

After this reabsorption process, the fluid reaches the kidney pelvis. It is now **urine**, which consists mainly of the water that has not been reabsorbed, some salts, and urea.

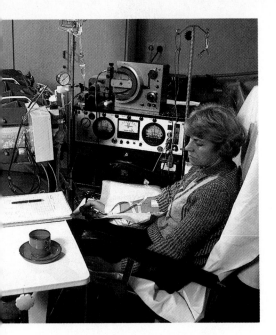

Figure 39.9 During the dialysis process, a machine performs many of the functions of a normal kidney.

NEWSBREAK

Like all organs, kidneys usually last a lifetime. Sometimes, though, kidneys fail and can no longer remove waste products from the blood efficiently. Kidney dialysis can help many people whose kidneys do not function. In dialysis, a patient's blood is passed through a machine that removes wastes much as a kidney would. However, the procedure takes several hours and must be repeated every few days.

Another solution for kidney failure is to replace nonfunctioning kidneys with healthy ones. Kidney transplants are not uncommon nowadays. But sometimes transplants fail because of the body's immune response. In this reaction, which is described in Chapter 41, the body attacks and kills cells foreign to it. Transplant patients are usually given drugs to suppress the immune response. Unfortunately, these drugs severely weaken the body's ability to fight disease.

Recently a new drug called cyclosporin A has greatly improved the outlook for organ transplants. The drug is produced from fungi that grow in the soil. No one knows how cyclosporin A works, but it somehow prevents the body from rejecting transplanted organs. And it apparently does not impair the body's ability to kill disease-causing organisms.

Without cyclosporin A, only about 50 percent of kidney transplants are successful. With the drug, 90 percent work. This decrease in transplant rejections has made scientists optimistic about transplant medicine.

39–8 Homeostasis of Body Fluids

All the cells of your body are surrounded by a watery tissue fluid. This fluid contains dissolved salts. For cells to function properly, the concentration of salts in this fluid must always be about the same. If your body loses or takes in too much water, the salt concentration of tissue fluid can change. Salt in the diet can also affect the concentration of tissue fluid. So can loss of salt through excretion. However, homeostatic mechanisms keep the composition of tissue fluid more or less constant. The kidneys are an important part of this process.

There are four principal ways your body loses water. Air entering the lungs is moistened. About one liter of this moisture is lost each day as you exhale. Another 100 milliliters of water are lost daily in feces. On an average day, about 50 milliliters of water evaporate as perspiration. The kidneys excrete about another liter of water.

Within limits, the kidneys can control the amount of water that reaches the bladder. For example, consider what happens when you perspire a lot. Under these conditions, membranes of the kidney tubules become very permeable to water. Most of the water in the tubules is reabsorbed into the blood. There is little water for urine formation. Therefore, the volume of urine is low. The color is darker than usual, because the dissolved materials are more highly concentrated.

On the other hand, what happens when you drink excess water? The cells of the distal tubule and the collecting duct become impermeable to water. Water stays within these tubules. The resulting urine is high in volume and pale in color.

Another complex and poorly understood mechanism controls the amount of sodium pumped out of the tubules. The kidneys can change the amount of salt excreted in the urine. By this means, they help to control the salt balance of the tissue fluid.

BIOLOGY INSIGHTS

The means by which the kidneys control the concentrations of substances in the blood provide an excellent example of the importance of membranes in homeostasis.

Checkpoint

1. What are the tubes that carry urine from the kidneys to the bladder?
2. What is the name of the tube that carries urine from the bladder to the outside?
3. The kidney is made of many units called _____.
4. Name the cup-shaped structure that receives water and other materials from blood in the glomerulus.
5. Under what condition do you produce concentrated urine in small volumes?

CHAPTER REVIEW

Summary

- External respiration, which is the exchange of gases between the atmosphere and the blood, takes place in the lungs. Internal respiration is the exchange of gases between the blood and the body cells. Cellular respiration is the chemical combination of oxygen with food molecules, resulting in the release of energy. Carbon dioxide is produced during this process.

- Air travels through the nose, trachea, and bronchi before entering the lungs. In the lungs, the bronchi branch into bronchioles. A cluster of microscopic alveoli is at the end of each bronchiole. Before air reaches the alveoli, it is filtered, moistened, and warmed.

- Oxygen diffuses through the walls of the alveoli. Most of it attaches to hemoglobin molecules in red blood cells. These cells carry the oxygen to the body cells.

- Carbon dioxide is transported mainly as bicarbonate ions in blood plasma. It moves from the body cells to the lungs. There it diffuses from the blood into the alveoli.

- Breathing is controlled by muscles. When you inhale, the ribs move up and out, and the diaphragm contracts and flattens. This increases the volume of the thoracic cavity, and air rushes into the lungs. When you exhale, the diaphragm and rib muscles relax. The thoracic cavity becomes smaller, forcing air out of the lungs.

- Breathing rate is controlled by cells in the breathing center of the brain. The rate of breathing is determined mainly by the concentration of carbon dioxide in the blood.

- The lungs and liver both function in excretion. The lungs remove carbon dioxide. The liver produces the waste product urea.

- The kidneys remove urea from the blood and excrete it in urine. Urine flows through the ureters and is stored in the bladder. It leaves the body through the urethra.

- The kidneys contain millions of nephrons. Each nephron contains a group of capillaries called the glomerulus. The glomerulus sits inside the cuplike Bowman's capsule. A series of tubules connect the Bowman's capsule to the renal pelvis.

- Water, urea, and other materials move from the blood into the Bowman's capsule. As this liquid passes through the proximal and distal tubules, much of the water and other substances are returned to the blood. Urea mostly remains in the fluid and is excreted in urine.

- The kidneys help to control the concentration of water and salts in tissue fluid.

Vocabulary

alveoli	kidney
bladder	larynx
Bowman's capsule	loop of Henle
breathing center	lung
bronchi	nephron
bronchiole	oxygenated
capillary	pleura
cellular respiration	proximal tubule
collecting duct	renal artery
deoxygenated	renal cortex
diaphragm	renal medulla
distal tubule	renal pelvis
excretion	renal vein
expiration	trachea
external respiration	urea
glomerulus	ureter
hemoglobin	urethra
inspiration	urine
internal respiration	vocal cords

Review

1. During internal respiration, oxygen moves from _____ to _____.

2. What is the function of mucus in the nasal passages?

3. What prevents the trachea from collapsing?

4. What is the name for the double membrane surrounding the lungs?

5. What gas diffuses from the blood to the air in the alveoli?

6. What gas is carried by hemoglobin in the red blood cells?

7. When the diaphragm contracts, how does the size of the rib cage change?

8. What happens to the size of the alveoli when you exhale?

9. What is the name for the area in the brain that controls the breathing rate?

10. Urea is produced from the metabolism of what kind of molecule? *protic amino acid*

11. Of what substance is urine mostly made? *water*

12. Glomeruli and Bowman's capsules are found in what region of the kidney? *renal cortex*

13. Name the tube through which urine leaves the body. *urethra*

14. What substances pass from the blood into Bowman's capsules? *water, salts, amino acid, sugar, urea*

15. Identify four ways that your body loses water. *sweat, breathing, solid waste, urine*

Interpret and Apply

1. List the following structures in the order that a carbon-dioxide molecule would pass through them on its way from the blood to the outside of the body.

    a. bronchiole   **d.** alveolus

    b. nasal passage   **e.** bronchus

    c. trachea   **f.** pharynx

2. How are fish gills similar to human lungs? How are they different?

3. Explain the difference between external and internal respiration.

4. Why is it important that the nasal passages have such a large surface area?

5. Explain the role of the diaphragm in breathing.

6. How is oxygen transported in the blood? How is carbon dioxide transported?

7. What is the relationship between the level of body activity and the rate of breathing?

8. Why are the lungs considered to be organs of excretion?

9. Describe the process by which water returns from the kidney tubules to the blood.

10. List the following structures in the order that a urea molecule would pass through them on its way from the blood to the outside of the body.

    a. renal pelvis   **f.** urethra

    b. loop of Henle   **g.** ureter

    c. bladder   **h.** Bowman's capsule

    d. proximal tubule **i.** distal tubule

    e. collecting duct

11. Explain the process by which the kidneys get rid of excess water.

Challenge

1. If you go to sleep when your nasal passages are completely blocked because of a cold, you may wake up to find your mouth very dry. Why do you think this happens?

2. Explain the protective mechanisms that make it unlikely for a bacterial cell to reach an alveolus.

3. Explain how cellular respiration sets up the conditions under which internal respiration occurs.

4. How is active transport important in the functioning of a nephron?

5. In what ways is the blood leaving a nephron different in composition from the blood entering a nephron?

Projects

1. Find out what causes a lung to collapse and what is done to treat this condition.

2. Find out how the kidneys of the following animals differ in structure and in function from a human kidney: a freshwater fish, a saltwater fish, a kangaroo rat.

40 Circulation

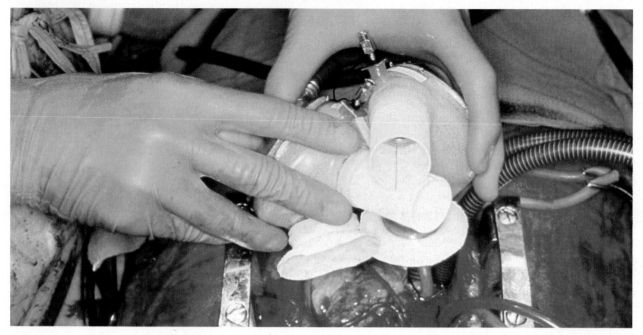

An artificial heart being implanted in an animal

The artificial heart shown here is made of plastic and metal. A research team developed this device for experiments that could eventually lead to replacing human hearts that are damaged beyond repair. The artificial heart is a marvelous piece of machinery. It may someday help many people. However, it is no match for the real thing. In present models, the power source of the artificial heart is the size of a large suitcase. Thus the power supply must be outside the body. In addition, the mechanical parts of an artificial heart can wear out.

A healthy human heart, on the other hand, keeps working for many years. It contracts about 70 times a minute, day after day. During an average person's life, the heart beats more than two and a half billion times. It pumps enough blood to fill about 2,000 swimming pools. As long as it is supplied with food and oxygen, this pumping muscle generates its own power.

The real heart is a compact, long-lasting, efficient machine. No artificial device works nearly as well.

The Heart and Blood Vessels

All organ systems depend on materials transported from other parts of the body. The blood performs this transport function. Circulation is the movement of blood through the body's blood vessels. As the word *circulation* indicates, blood travels in repeating loops. Blood always passes through the heart in each loop. The heart is the pump that keeps blood moving in one direction through the vessels. The total volume of blood in the vessels is about five liters.

Most blood vessels are microscopic. If all the tiny vessels in your body were attached end to end, they would encircle the world two and a half times.

40–1   The Heart

Figure 40.1 on the following page shows the structure of the human heart. The heart sits between the lungs and above the diaphragm. It is surrounded by a protective membrane called the **pericardium** [pehr-uh-KAHR-dee-uhm].

The human heart, like that of all other mammals, consists of four chambers. These are the left **atrium** [AY-tree-uhm], right atrium, left **ventricle** [VEHN-trih-kuhl], and right ventricle. The thin-walled atria are collecting chambers. They hold blood until it can enter the ventricles. The ventricles, with thick, muscular walls, are the pumping chambers. They do the work of moving blood around the body. The left ventricle is even larger and more muscular than the right ventricle. The left ventricle must push blood to all parts of the body. In contrast, the right ventricle pumps blood only to the nearby lungs. Valves in the heart prevent blood from flowing backward.

Deoxygenated blood returns from all parts of the body and enters the right atrium. Blood in the right atrium moves past the **tricuspid** [try-KUHS-pihd] **valve** into the relaxed right ventricle. Then the right ventricle contracts. Blood is forced up and out of the ventricle. This causes the tricuspid valve to close and the **pulmonary semilunar** [PUL-muh-nehr-ee sehm-ee-LOO-nuhr] **valve** to open. From the right ventricle, blood travels to the lungs. There it picks up oxygen.

Oxygenated blood returns to the heart from the lungs. It enters the left atrium. From the left atrium, blood moves past the **bicuspid** [by-KUHS-pihd] **valve** and enters the left ventricle. When the left ventricle contracts, blood opens the **aortic** [ay-AWR-tihk] **semilunar valve**. The bicuspid valve closes. Oxygenated blood now travels to the body. It will

- heart anatomy and function
- path of circulation in humans
- types and functions of blood vessels
- origin and function of blood pressure
- factors affecting heart rate

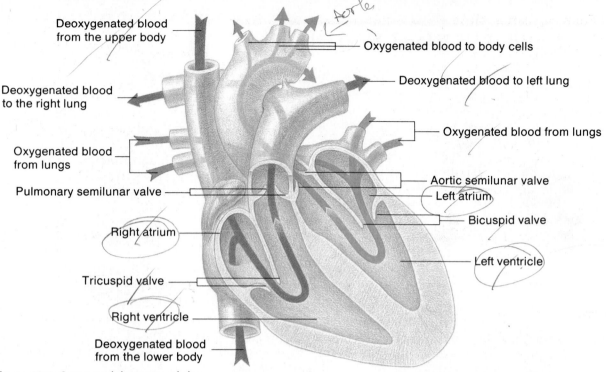

Deoxygenated blood
from the upper body

Aorta

Oxygenated blood to body cells

Deoxygenated blood
to the right lung

Deoxygenated blood to left lung

Oxygenated blood
from lungs

Oxygenated blood from lungs

Pulmonary semilunar valve

Aortic semilunar valve

Left atrium

Right atrium

Bicuspid valve

Tricuspid valve

Left ventricle

Right ventricle

Deoxygenated blood
from the lower body

Figure 40.1 Structural features of the human heart

Do You Know?

Coronary comes from the Latin word *corona,* meaning "crown." The coronary arteries received their name because they circle the heart like a crown.

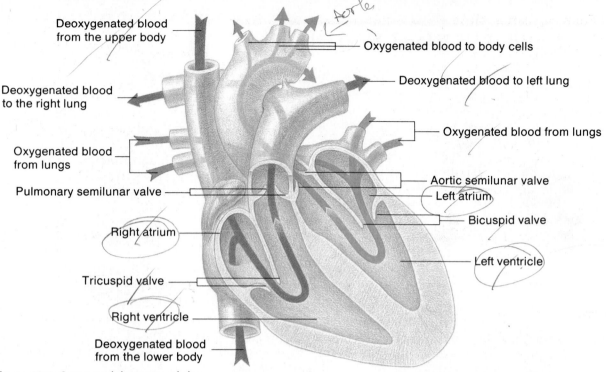

Artery

Arterioles

Heart

Capillaries

Venules

Vein

Figure 40.2 Basic vertebrate circulation pattern

return to the right side of the heart as deoxygenated blood. The blood on the right side of the heart is deoxygenated. The blood on the left side is oxygenated.

Just above the aortic semilunar valve is the opening of a vessel that carries blood to the heart muscle itself. The muscular walls of the heart are too thick to get oxygen and food directly from the blood in the heart chambers. The vessels supplying the heart make up the **coronary** [KAWR-uh-nehr-ee] **circulation**.

When heart valves close, they make characteristic sounds. Doctors listen to heart sounds for an indication of the heart's state of health. Unusual or muffled sounds often indicate defects in the heart.

40–2 The Pattern of Circulation

The blood flow in the circulatory systems of vertebrates follows the basic pattern shown in Figure 40.2. Upon leaving the heart, blood first enters an artery. An **artery** is a vessel that carries blood away from the heart and toward the body tissues. Arteries branch into smaller and smaller **arterioles** [ahr-TIHR-ee-ohlz]. Blood goes from arterioles into **capillaries**. These are the smallest vessels of the circulatory system. Exchange of materials between the blood and tissues takes place across the capillaries.

From capillaries, blood enters **venules** [VEHN-yoolz]. These tiny vessels join together to form veins. **Veins** are vessels that carry blood back toward the heart.

Figure 40.3 shows the path of blood circulation in humans. Notice that there are two loops. This is true for all mammals. In the **pulmonary circulation**, blood travels from the heart to the lungs and back to the heart. In the **systemic circulation**, blood travels from the heart to the body cells and back to the heart.

Deoxygenated blood is carried into the right side of the heart by the largest veins, the **venae cavae** [VEE-nee KAY-vee]. The right ventricle pumps blood through the pulmonary artery to the lungs. Oxygenated blood returns to the heart through the pulmonary veins. It is then pumped to the body through the **aorta**, the largest artery in the body. Figure 40.4 shows some of the major vessels of the human circulatory system.

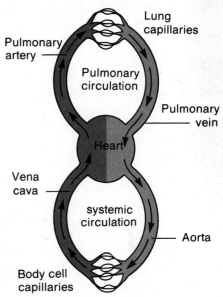

Figure 40.3 Basic pattern of human circulation

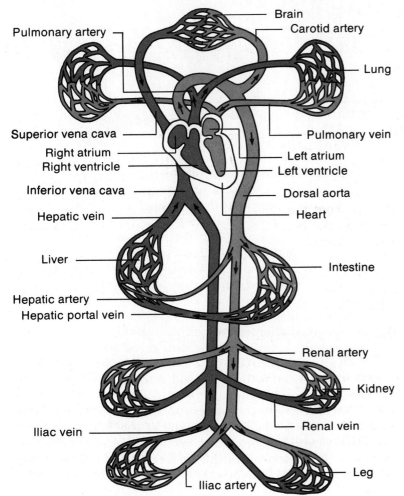

Figure 40.4 The major vessels of the human circulatory system

40–3   Blood Vessels

The structure of arteries, capillaries, and veins is shown in Figure 40.5. Notice that arteries and veins have the same number of tissue layers. Most of the layers are thicker in arteries, though. Blood in arteries is under very high pressure, since it has just come from the heart. A person can bleed to death in a few minutes from a cut artery. However, an artery's elastic layer and thick walls make it resistant to injury. The location of arteries protects them too. Arteries tend to be buried deep within the body.

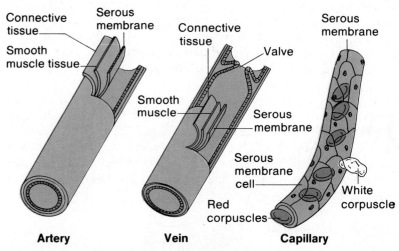

Figure 40.5 The structures of arteries, capillaries, and veins show similar features. Differences occur in the thicknesses of the vessel walls.

A capillary's wall consists of only a single layer of cells. Small molecules easily diffuse through this thin wall. It is in the capillaries, then, that the exchange of materials between the blood and tissue fluid takes place.

Blood in veins is under very little pressure. Valves occur every few centimeters in most veins. The valves are arranged so they open only when blood flows toward the heart. If blood starts to go backward, the valves close. This is shown in Figure 40.6.

A number of diseases affect the blood vessels. One common disease is **arteriosclerosis** [ahr-tihr-ee-oh-skluh-ROH-sihs]. In this disease, the artery walls become less elastic. Cholesterol, a fatty substance, builds up on the inner wall. The heart must work harder to pump blood through such arteries. A heart attack may result.

Cholesterol deposits in arteries can also trigger the formation of a blood clot. If such a clot blocks the blood flow in a coronary artery, a heart attack occurs. The heart muscle fed by the blocked artery may die from lack of oxygen. Fortunately, many heart attacks involve only a small part of the heart muscle.

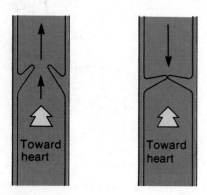

Figure 40.6 Valves in the veins allow blood to flow in only one direction — toward the heart.

40–4 Blood Pressure

Blood pressure results from the force the heart applies to the blood at any given time. Pressure is highest in arteries when the ventricles contract. Pressure drops in arteries when the ventricles relax. Contraction of the ventricles is called **systole** [SIHS-tuh-lee]. **Diastole** [dy-AS-tuh-lee] is the term for the relaxation phase. Artery walls stretch when high-pressure blood enters them during systole. The pulse you feel in your wrist is this expansion of the artery wall.

Blood pressure is usually measured in your upper arm. Pressure is given as two numbers, for example, 120/80. The larger number, the systolic pressure, is the pressure at the peak of systole. That is when the blood is moving fastest. The lower number, called diastolic pressure, is the pressure during diastole. The farther blood gets from the heart, the less pressure it has.

High blood pressure, or **hypertension**, can have many different causes. Arteriosclerosis is one. The heart of someone with arteriosclerosis must pump with greater pressure to move the blood through the restricted arteries. Hypertension is a serious condition that may result in kidney damage, heart attack, and even death. Medication and a low-salt diet are used to control hypertension.

40–5 Heartbeat Rate

Buried in the wall of the right atrium is a group of specialized cardiac-muscle cells called the **pacemaker**. These cells generate electrical impulses that make the atria and ventricles contract. The basic heartbeat rate depends on how often the pacemaker generates its signals.

Two nerves connect to the pacemaker. One nerve increases the signal rate from the pacemaker. The other slows the signal rate. At rest, your heartbeat rate slows; when you exercise, it speeds up. Sometimes a person's heart beats irregularly because of a defective pacemaker. When this happens, the person may be given an artificial pacemaker.

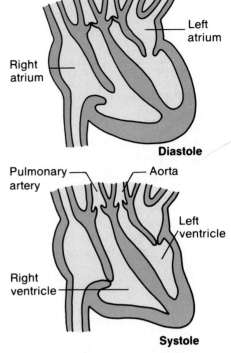

Figure 40.7 *Top:* During diastole, blood enters the ventricles from the atria. *Bottom:* During systole, blood is pumped from the heart.

Figure 40.8 An artificial pacemaker controls the heart rate electronically.

Checkpoint

1. What are the vessels that connect arteries with capillaries?
2. Which type of vessel transports blood back to the heart?
3. Into what two loops can the human circulatory system be divided?
4. Which two valves keep blood from flowing back into the ventricles?
5. What is the term for contraction of the ventricles?

Blood and Lymph

Every cell depends on blood to deliver needed substances and to carry waste materials away. About 55 percent of the blood's volume is a clear golden fluid called **plasma**. The other 45 percent consists of cells. Some liquid and cells from the blood pass out of the capillaries. These are returned to the circulation via the lymphatic system.

40–6   Blood Plasma and the Clotting of Blood

Plasma carries small molecules in solution. Among them are glucose, amino acids, carbonic acid, and urea. Some of these are needed for life processes. Others are wastes.

Approximately 6 to 8 percent of plasma is protein. Some of this protein consists of antibodies. **Antibodies** [AN-tih-bahd-eez] attack and neutralize substances that are foreign to the body. These foreign substances are usually molecules from some other living thing. Plasma also contains proteins involved in the clotting of blood. Blood clots stop the potentially dangerous flow of blood from damaged vessels.

Blood clotting is a complex process. It usually starts with structures in the plasma called **platelets** [PLAYT-lihts]. Platelets are pieces of cytoplasm that have broken off from special cells in the bone marrow. There are about 250,000 platelets per cubic millimeter of blood. When blood vessels are damaged, platelets break apart. They release a chemical into the plasma. This chemical converts a plasma protein called prothrombin into an enzyme called thrombin. Calcium ions must also be present for prothrombin to change to thrombin.

Thrombin causes changes in another blood protein, fibrinogen. In the presence of thrombin, many molecules of fibrinogen join together. They form a long, strandlike molecule called fibrin. Many strands of fibrin gather at the end of a cut vessel. They trap blood cells in a tangled mesh, or clot.

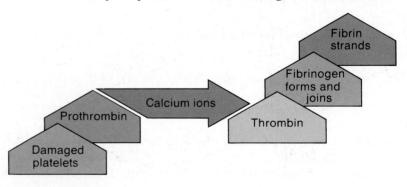

Figure 40.9 Blood clotting is a complex sequence of reactions beginning with the release of a chemical from the platelets.

Animal Anatomy:
Six Representative Organisms

Plate I

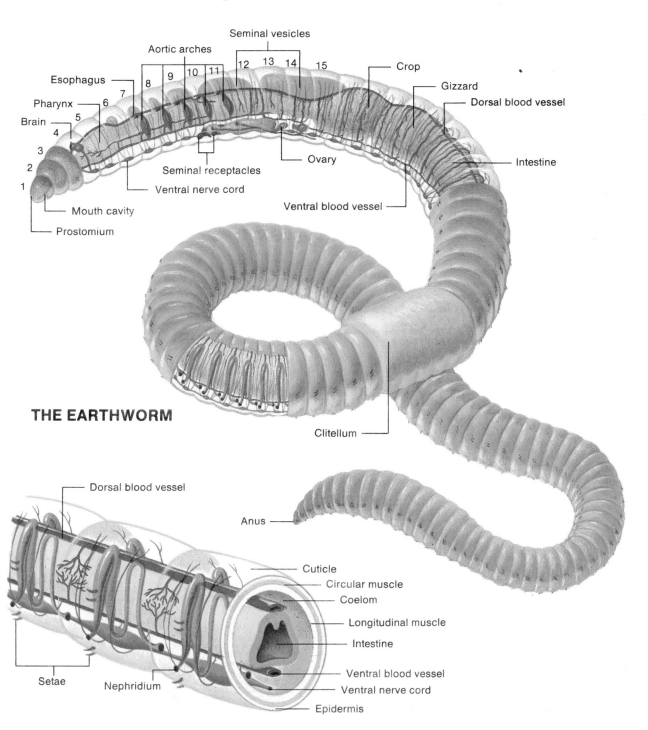

Seminal vesicles

Aortic arches

Esophagus

Pharynx

Brain

Mouth cavity

Prostomium

Seminal receptacles

Ventral nerve cord

Crop

Gizzard

Dorsal blood vessel

Ovary

Intestine

Ventral blood vessel

THE EARTHWORM

Clitellum

Dorsal blood vessel

Anus

Cuticle

Circular muscle

Coelom

Longitudinal muscle

Intestine

Ventral blood vessel

Ventral nerve cord

Setae

Nephridium

Epidermis

THE CRAYFISH

Plate II

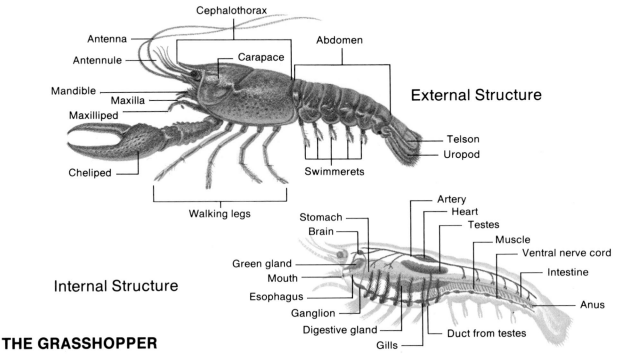

Cephalothorax

Antenna

Antennule

Carapace

Abdomen

Mandible

Maxilla

Maxilliped

External Structure

Cheliped

Telson

Uropod

Walking legs

Swimmerets

Internal Structure

Artery

Heart

Stomach

Testes

Brain

Muscle

Ventral nerve cord

Green gland

Mouth

Intestine

Esophagus

Ganglion

Anus

Digestive gland

Duct from testes

Gills

THE GRASSHOPPER

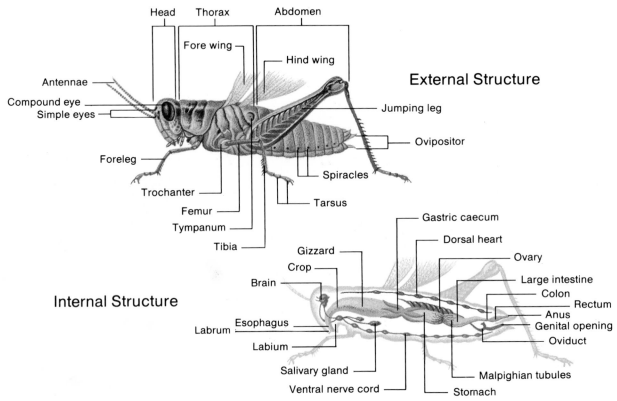

Head

Thorax

Abdomen

Fore wing

Hind wing

Antennae

External Structure

Compound eye

Simple eyes

Jumping leg

Foreleg

Ovipositor

Trochanter

Spiracles

Femur

Tarsus

Tympanum

Tibia

Gastric caecum

Dorsal heart

Gizzard

Ovary

Crop

Large intestine

Brain

Colon

Rectum

Internal Structure

Anus

Labrum

Esophagus

Genital opening

Labium

Oviduct

Salivary gland

Malpighian tubules

Ventral nerve cord

Stomach

Plate III

External Structure

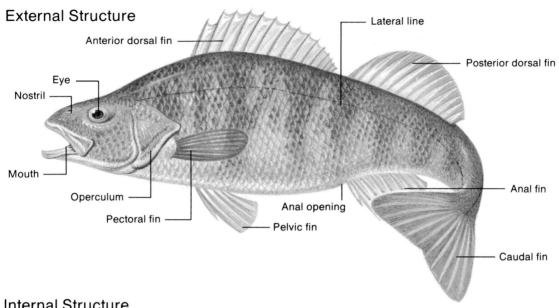

- Lateral line
- Posterior dorsal fin
- Anterior dorsal fin
- Eye
- Nostril
- Mouth
- Operculum
- Pectoral fin
- Anal opening
- Pelvic fin
- Anal fin
- Caudal fin

Internal Structure

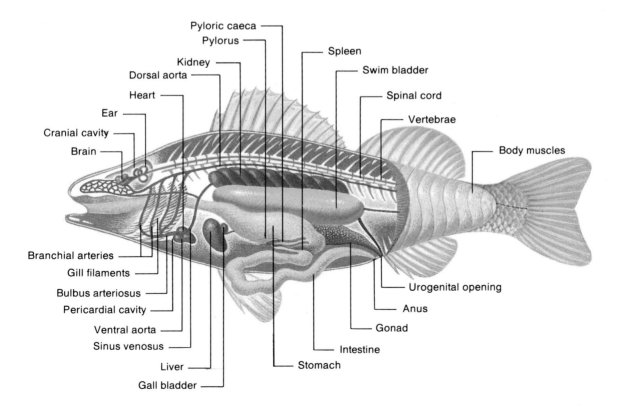

- Pyloric caeca
- Pylorus
- Kidney
- Dorsal aorta
- Heart
- Ear
- Cranial cavity
- Brain
- Spleen
- Swim bladder
- Spinal cord
- Vertebrae
- Body muscles
- Branchial arteries
- Gill filaments
- Bulbus arteriosus
- Pericardial cavity
- Ventral aorta
- Sinus venosus
- Liver
- Gall bladder
- Stomach
- Intestine
- Gonad
- Anus
- Urogenital opening

Nervous and Muscular Systems

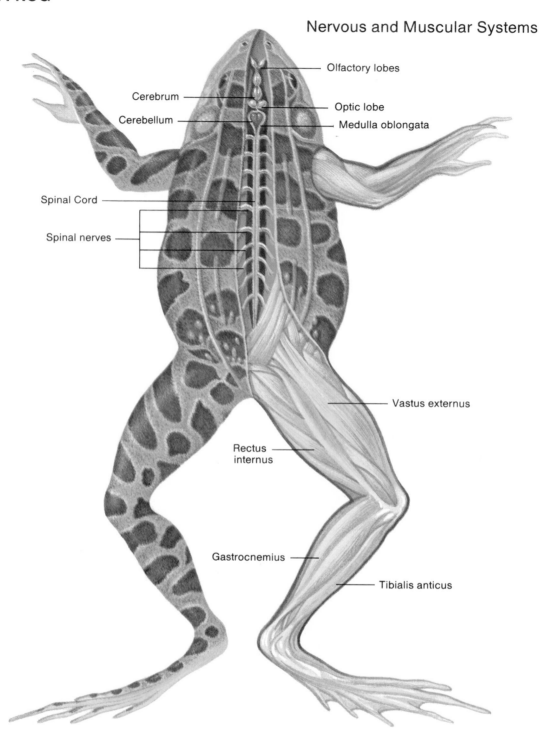

Olfactory lobes

Cerebrum

Cerebellum

Optic lobe

Medulla oblongata

Spinal Cord

Spinal nerves

Vastus externus

Rectus internus

Gastrocnemius

Tibialis anticus

Digestive System

Plate V

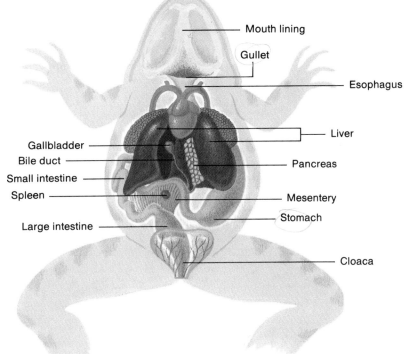

- Mouth lining
- Gullet
- Esophagus
- Liver
- Gallbladder
- Bile duct
- Pancreas
- Small intestine
- Spleen
- Mesentery
- Stomach
- Large intestine
- Cloaca

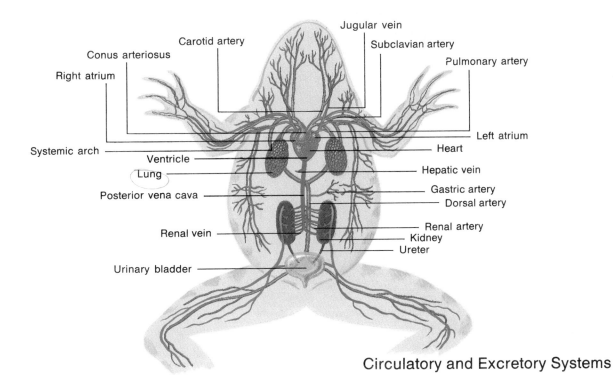

- Jugular vein
- Carotid artery
- Subclavian artery
- Conus arteriosus
- Pulmonary artery
- Right atrium
- Left atrium
- Systemic arch
- Heart
- Ventricle
- Lung
- Hepatic vein
- Posterior vena cava
- Gastric artery
- Dorsal artery
- Renal vein
- Renal artery
- Kidney
- Ureter
- Urinary bladder

Circulatory and Excretory Systems

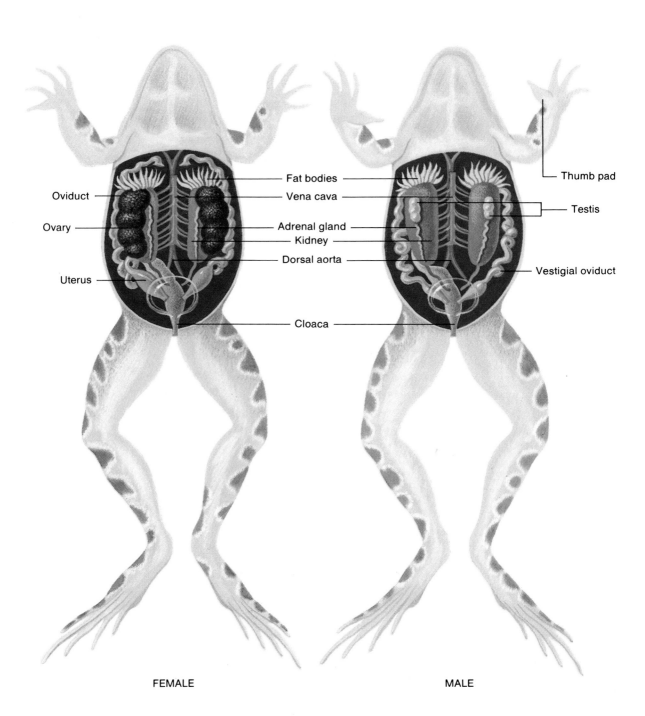

Oviduct
Ovary
Uterus

Fat bodies
Vena cava
Adrenal gland
Kidney
Dorsal aorta
Cloaca

Thumb pad
Testis
Vestigial oviduct

FEMALE

MALE

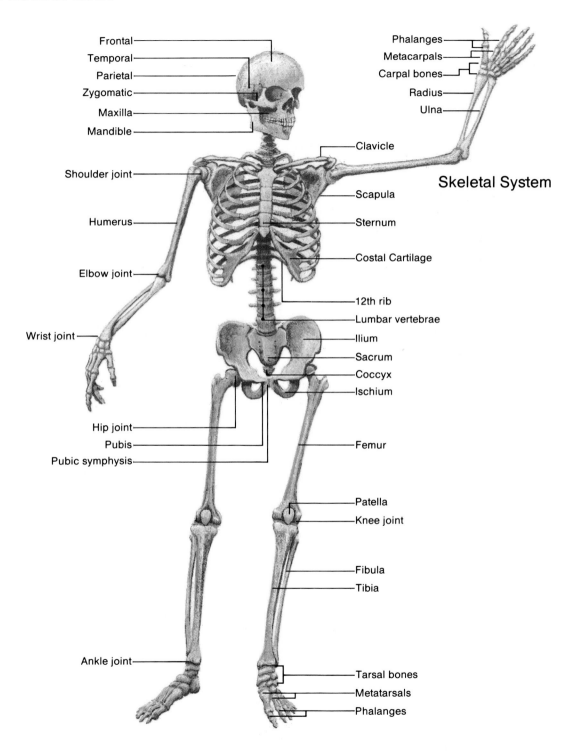

Frontal
Temporal
Parietal
Zygomatic
Maxilla
Mandible

Phalanges
Metacarpals
Carpal bones
Radius
Ulna

Shoulder joint

Clavicle

Skeletal System

Scapula

Humerus

Sternum

Costal Cartilage

Elbow joint

12th rib

Lumbar vertebrae
Ilium
Sacrum
Coccyx
Ischium

Wrist joint

Hip joint
Pubis
Pubic symphysis

Femur

Patella
Knee joint

Fibula
Tibia

Ankle joint

Tarsal bones
Metatarsals
Phalanges

Muscular Anatomy

Plate VIII

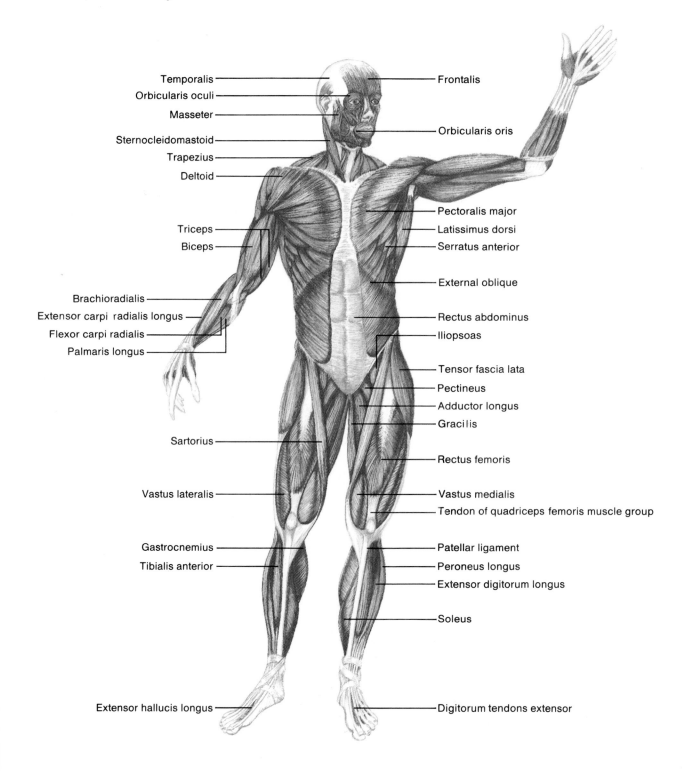

Temporalis

Orbicularis oculi

Masseter

Sternocleidomastoid

Trapezius

Deltoid

Triceps

Biceps

Brachioradialis

Extensor carpi radialis longus

Flexor carpi radialis

Palmaris longus

Sartorius

Vastus lateralis

Gastrocnemius

Tibialis anterior

Extensor hallucis longus

Frontalis

Orbicularis oris

Pectoralis major

Latissimus dorsi

Serratus anterior

External oblique

Rectus abdominus

Iliopsoas

Tensor fascia lata

Pectineus

Adductor longus

Gracilis

Rectus femoris

Vastus medialis

Tendon of quadriceps femoris muscle group

Patellar ligament

Peroneus longus

Extensor digitorum longus

Soleus

Digitorum tendons extensor

Digestive System

Plate IX

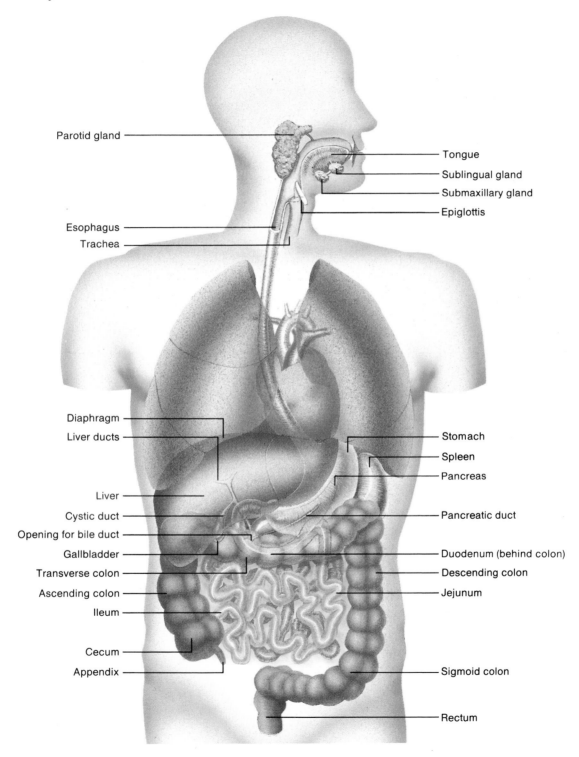

Parotid gland

Tongue

Sublingual gland

Submaxillary gland

Epiglottis

Esophagus

Trachea

Diaphragm

Liver ducts

Stomach

Spleen

Pancreas

Liver

Cystic duct

Opening for bile duct

Gallbladder

Pancreatic duct

Transverse colon

Duodenum (behind colon)

Ascending colon

Descending colon

Ileum

Jejunum

Cecum

Appendix

Sigmoid colon

Rectum

Respiratory System

Plate X

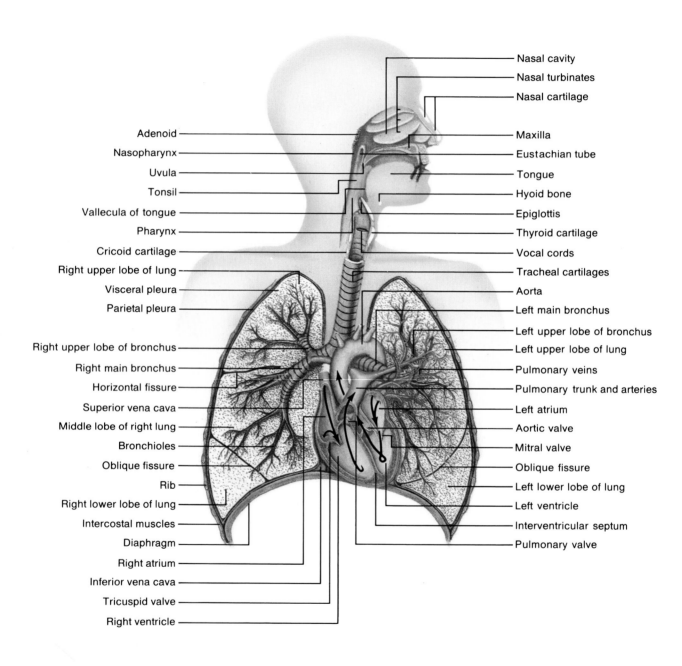

Nasal cavity

Nasal turbinates

Nasal cartilage

Adenoid

Nasopharynx

Uvula

Tonsil

Vallecula of tongue

Pharynx

Cricoid cartilage

Right upper lobe of lung

Visceral pleura

Parietal pleura

Right upper lobe of bronchus

Right main bronchus

Horizontal fissure

Superior vena cava

Middle lobe of right lung

Bronchioles

Oblique fissure

Rib

Right lower lobe of lung

Intercostal muscles

Diaphragm

Right atrium

Inferior vena cava

Tricuspid valve

Right ventricle

Maxilla

Eustachian tube

Tongue

Hyoid bone

Epiglottis

Thyroid cartilage

Vocal cords

Tracheal cartilages

Aorta

Left main bronchus

Left upper lobe of bronchus

Left upper lobe of lung

Pulmonary veins

Pulmonary trunk and arteries

Left atrium

Aortic valve

Mitral valve

Oblique fissure

Left lower lobe of lung

Left ventricle

Interventricular septum

Pulmonary valve

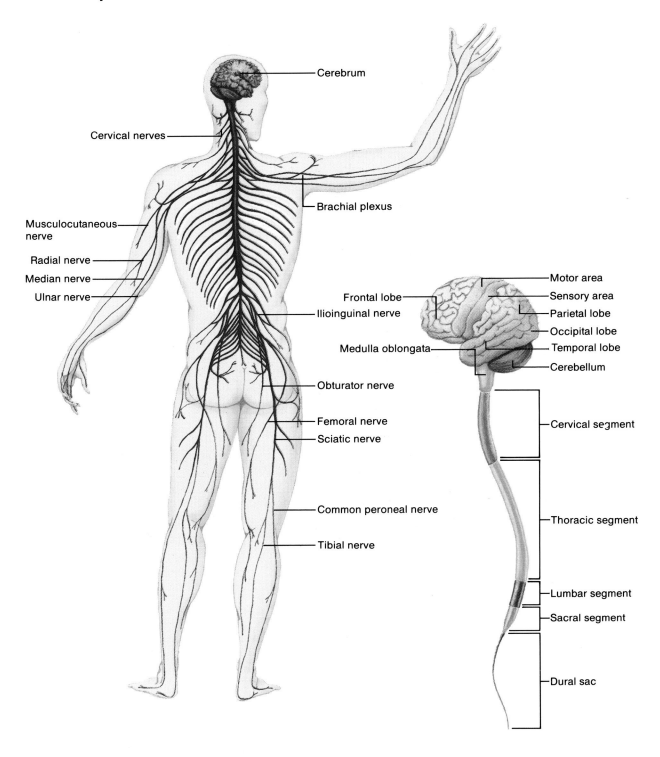

Cerebrum

Cervical nerves

Brachial plexus

Musculocutaneous nerve

Radial nerve

Median nerve

Ulnar nerve

Frontal lobe

Ilioinguinal nerve

Medulla oblongata

Motor area

Sensory area

Parietal lobe

Occipital lobe

Temporal lobe

Cerebellum

Obturator nerve

Femoral nerve

Sciatic nerve

Cervical segment

Common peroneal nerve

Tibial nerve

Thoracic segment

Lumbar segment

Sacral segment

Dural sac

Plate XII

The Ear

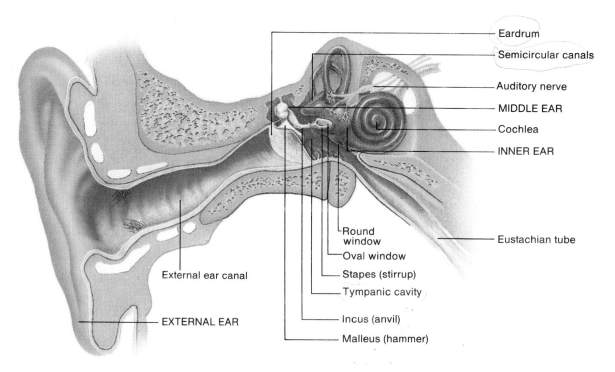

- Eardrum
- Semicircular canals
- Auditory nerve
- MIDDLE EAR
- Cochlea
- INNER EAR
- Eustachian tube
- Round window
- Oval window
- Stapes (stirrup)
- Tympanic cavity
- Incus (anvil)
- Malleus (hammer)
- External ear canal
- EXTERNAL EAR

The Eye

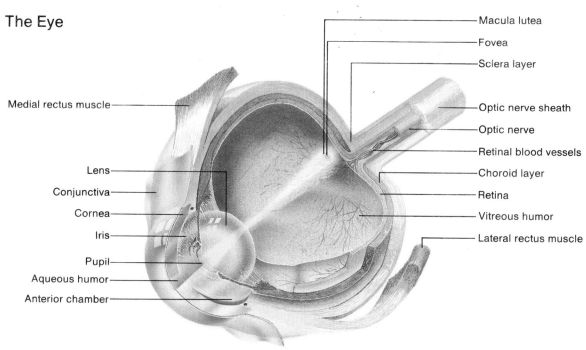

- Medial rectus muscle
- Lens
- Conjunctiva
- Cornea
- Iris
- Pupil
- Aqueous humor
- Anterior chamber
- Macula lutea
- Fovea
- Sclera layer
- Optic nerve sheath
- Optic nerve
- Retinal blood vessels
- Choroid layer
- Retina
- Vitreous humor
- Lateral rectus muscle

40–7   Red Blood Cells and Blood Types

Red blood cells, as shown in Figure 40.10, are also called **erythrocytes** [ih-RIHTH-ruh-syts]. Mature red blood cells lack nuclei. The cytoplasm of erythrocytes consists of little more than molecules of hemoglobin.

Recall that hemoglobin carries oxygen. Each erythrocyte contains more than 200 million molecules of hemoglobin. The total surface area of all your red blood cells is greater than that of a football field. Thus, the oxygen carrying capacity of the blood is enormous. There are usually between 4.5 and 5.5 million red blood cells per cubic millimeter of blood. New red blood cells are constantly being made in bone marrow.

Red blood cells also contain the proteins that determine blood type. In the early 1900s, Karl Landsteiner, an American physician, discovered that there are four major blood types. These blood types are A, B, O, and AB. Landsteiner found that whenever different types of blood were mixed, the red blood cells in the different blood samples usually clumped together. This clumping is called **agglutination** [uh-gloot-n-AY-shuhn]. When identical blood types were mixed, the clumping did not occur.

Agglutination occurs because of antigen proteins on the red-cell membranes. An **antigen** [AN-tih-juhn] is any molecule that causes the synthesis of an antibody when that molecule is injected into another organism. Figure 40.11 shows which antigens and antibodies are found in each of the four basic blood types.

Figure 40.10 A scanning electron micrograph of erythrocytes

Do You Know?
Anemia is a disorder characterized by a severe shortage of hemoglobin. As a result of this shortage, oxygen is not delivered to cells effectively.

Blood Type	Antigens Present in Red Cells	Antibodies Present in Plasma
A	A	Anti-B
B	B	Anti-A
AB	A and B	none
O	none	Anti-A and Anti-B

Figure 40.11 This chart summarizes the relationships among antigens, antibodies, and blood type.

Anti-A antibody reacts with A antigen; anti-B antibody reacts with B antigen. Notice the antibodies found in the plasma of blood types A, B, and O. Suppose a person with blood type B receives a transfusion of type A blood. The anti-A antibodies in the person's plasma will react with the A antigens on the donated red blood cells. This reaction will make the cells agglutinate. No blood type contains antibodies that will react with its own antigens.

A person with type O blood is known as a universal donor. Since type O blood has no antigens, it will not react with antibodies. Therefore, moderate amounts of it can be transfused into people of all blood types. People with type AB, on the other hand, are universal recipients. This type of blood has no blood-type antibodies. People with blood type AB can therefore receive moderate amounts of any type of blood.

Rh factors are other antigens that may be present on red blood cells. Most people have these antigens, and are said to be Rh positive. People who lack these antigens are Rh negative.

Rh factors may cause problems when a developing embryo has Rh-positive blood and the mother is Rh negative. The mother's circulatory system and the embryo's are separate. However, a few blood cells from the embryo may pass into the mother's bloodstream. Once there, they cause the production of anti-Rh antibodies. These antibodies can then pass into the baby's blood.

Usually these anti-Rh antibodies do not form until late in pregnancy, if they are produced at all. Therefore, an Rh-negative woman's first baby is generally unharmed. Once the woman has anti-Rh antibodies in her blood, though, there may be problems with later babies. These antibodies may make the baby's red blood cells agglutinate.

Fortunately, scientists have developed a way to prevent or lessen Rh problems in pregnancy. After a pregnancy, an Rh-negative woman is given an injection. A substance in the injection destroys any anti-Rh antibodies she may have produced. They will not be present, then, to harm future babies.

40–8   White Blood Cells

White blood cells, or **leukocytes** [LOO-kuh-syts], are much less common in the blood than red blood cells. There are generally between 5,000 and 9,000 white blood cells per cubic millimeter of blood. Like red blood cells, many white blood cells are made in red bone marrow. Figure 40.12 shows some different kinds of white cells. Notice that white blood cells have a large nucleus and colorless cytoplasm.

Do You Know?
Rh is short for *rhesus*. The Rh factor was first discovered in rhesus monkeys.

Figure 40.12 Different types of leukocytes

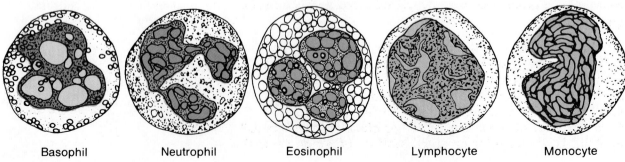

| Basophil | Neutrophil | Eosinophil | Lymphocyte | Monocyte |

White blood cells protect the body against infection by foreign organisms. White cells can be divided into two major groups. The first group, **phagocytes** [FAG-uh-syts] act like amoebas in many ways. Phagocytes move by pseudopods. When phagocytes encounter foreign material, such as a disease-causing microorganism, they surround the foreign material and digest it. The second group, **lymphocytes** [LIHM-fuh-syts], manufacture antibodies that help to combat disease organisms. White blood cells can leave the bloodstream through tiny spaces in the capillary walls. They then move over and around body cells, destroying foreign materials.

40–9   The Lymphatic System

All body cells are surrounded by **tissue fluid**. This fluid consists primarily of water and small molecules that have escaped from the capillaries. It also contains some plasma proteins and white blood cells from the circulatory system. By diffusing through tissue fluid, many materials pass between the blood and body cells.

The **lymphatic** [lihm-FAT-ihk] **system** is a network of vessels that returns tissue fluid to the blood circulation. Lymphatic vessels have thin walls. Tissue fluid readily passes into these vessels, which are found throughout the body. Once the tissue fluid is in the lymphatic vessels, it is called **lymph**.

Figure 40.13 shows the entire lymphatic system. The largest lymphatic vessels join with two large veins near the heart. At this place, lymph drains back into the circulatory system. The lymphatic system has no pump. Therefore, the system depends on one-way valves to move tissue fluid uphill from the legs and arms. As in veins, the movement of skeletal muscles helps squeeze the fluid in lymph vessels.

As you learned in Chapter 38, the lymphatic system is also involved in the absorption of fats. Another major function of the lymphatic system is combating disease. This happens in swellings in the lymph vessels called **lymph nodes**. Disease organisms are attacked there by white blood cells.

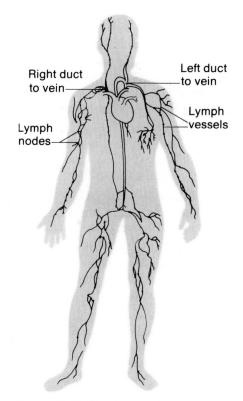

Figure 40.13 The human lymphatic system

Checkpoint

1. What protein is in the strandlike molecules of a clot?
2. What is the name for the cell-like structures that begin the clotting process?
3. What is another name for red blood cells?
4. What are the two major types of white blood cells?
5. Which type of blood has no major blood-group antigens?
6. What is the term for enlarged sections of lymph vessels?

CHAPTER REVIEW

Summary

- The heart is a muscular, four-chambered pump. It moves blood by means of rhythmic, alternating contractions of atria and ventricles. Valves in the heart keep blood from moving backward.
- Blood circulates in humans through two separate loops. The pulmonary loop takes blood from the heart to the lungs, then back to the heart. The systemic loop carries blood from the heart to the body and back.
- The structure of blood vessels reflects their function. Arteries have thick walls. Capillary walls consist of only one thin layer of cells. Veins have thin walls.
- Blood moves through arteries in spurts of alternating high and low pressure. These pressure phases correspond to the alternating contraction and relaxation of the ventricles.
- The basic heart rate is determined by the pacemaker. The body's level of activity affects the heart rate.
- Blood is a complex fluid that is about half cells and half plasma. Plasma contains many small molecules and a number of proteins. Some of these proteins, called antibodies, attach to and neutralize foreign organisms that invade the body.
- Other plasma proteins are involved in the clotting of blood. Platelets and calcium ions are also part of this complex process.
- Red blood cells are the oxygen carriers of the blood. They are produced in the bone marrow.
- Antigen molecules determine blood type and are found on the membranes of red cells. The four major blood types are A, B, AB, and O.
- White cells are present in much smaller numbers than red cells. There are two basic types of white cell, phagocytes and lymphocytes. White cells provide protection against disease.
- The lymphatic system transports tissue fluid back to the circulatory system. The lymph nodes contain many white blood cells, which destroy harmful microorganisms.

Vocabulary

agglutination	lymphocyte
antibody	pacemaker
antigen	pericardium
aorta	phagocyte
aortic semilunar	plasma
valve	platelet
arteriosclerosis	pulmonary
arteriole	circulation
artery	pulmonary semilunar
atrium	valve
bicuspid valve	Rh factor
capillary	systemic circulation
coronary circulation	systole
diastole	tissue fluid
erythrocyte	tricuspid valve
hypertension	vein
leukocyte	vena cava
lymph	ventricle
lymphatic system	venule
lymph node	

Review

Choose the best answer for each of the following questions.

1. Which of the following pumps oxygenated blood to the body? (a) vena cava (b) pulmonary artery (c) pulmonary vein (d) left ventricle
2. Blood leaving capillaries enters (a) an arteriole, (b) a vein, (c) a venule, (d) the heart.
3. Which of the following are made of a single layer of cells? (a) veins (b) arteries (c) the heart (d) capillaries

4. Deoxygenated blood leaving the heart must come from what chamber? (a) right ventricle (b) right atrium (c) the left ventricle (d) the left atrium
5. What is the valve between the two chambers on the right side of the heart called? (a) the bicuspid valve (b) the tricuspid valve (c) the pulmonary semilunar valve (d) the aortic semilunar valve
6. Relaxation of the heart ventricles is called (a) systole, (b) diastole, (c) thrombus, (d) hypertension.
7. Which part of the heart determines normal heart rate? (a) valves (b) ventricles (c) pacemaker (d) atria
8. The enzyme in blood plasma that directly causes fibrinogen to form fibrin is (a) prothrombin, (b) thrombin, (c) platelet, (d) fibrinozyme.
9. What antigen is found in type A blood? (a) A (b) B (c) O (d) anti-A
10. Which of these are very common in lymph nodes? (a) erythrocytes (b) leukocytes (c) platelets (d) Rh antigens

Interpret and Apply

1. Place the following structures in the order that a red blood cell would pass by or through after entering the right ventricle.

   a. aorta
   b. right atrium
   c. left ventricle
   d. lung capillaries
   e. venule in leg
   f. pulmonary artery
   g. vein in leg
   h. capillary in leg
   i. left atrium
   j. pulmonary vein
   k. artery in leg

2. How does the blood in the pulmonary artery differ from the blood in all the other arteries of the body?
3. Valves occur in two kinds of vessels in your body. What are they?
4. Which side of the heart pumps only deoxygenated blood?
5. Why is hypertension dangerous?

6. How do red blood cells differ in structure from all the other cells of your body?
7. What would happen if a person with type A blood received a transfusion of type B blood?
8. Why is it significant that the arteries are generally located far below the body's surface?
9. Explain how arteriosclerosis can result in high blood pressure.
10. How does tissue fluid return to the blood?

Challenge

1. Suppose a person's plasma lacked the materials necessary to convert prothrombin to thrombin. What might happen if that person received a cut?
2. Agglutination problems may occur when an Rh-negative woman is pregnant with an Rh-positive fetus. Why is there generally no problem when an Rh-positive woman carries an Rh-negative fetus?
3. Usually red blood cells are formed at the same rate that they are destroyed. After you donate blood, how do you think these two rates compare?

Projects

1. Find out about William Harvey and how he first proved in 1628 that blood circulated. In your report, describe the ideas about blood flow that were held before that time.
2. The Framingham heart study is an ongoing survey of heart disease. Learn about this project and summarize its conclusions.
3. Learn what coronary-bypass surgery is and how it helps patients with some kinds of coronary-artery disease. Report your findings to the class.
4. Once you donate blood, it can be stored and used in a variety of ways. Learn how donated blood can be broken into components with a variety of specific uses.

41 Infectious Disease in Humans

Sewage treatment plant

Most people today in the United States will live long, healthy lives. A hundred years ago, the situation was considerably different. Diseases such as typhoid fever, smallpox, and cholera claimed millions of lives each year. Today these diseases are rare or nonexistent in the United States. You may never have heard of some of them.

The control of these and other infectious diseases has been a major human triumph. Many people credit disease control to medicines and vaccines. These remarkable substances are indeed an important part of the story. But proper disposal of sewage has prevented far more diseases than all medicines combined.

Until late in the nineteenth century, people did not recognize that microorganisms in human wastes cause disease. Often bacteria from sewage got into water and food supplies. Sickness frequently resulted.

A modern sewage-treatment plant is shown above. In such plants, the bacteria in sewage are killed. Safe disposal and treatment of sewage contribute significantly to health.

Bacterial and Viral Diseases

Infectious [ihn-FEHK-shuhs] **diseases** are body disorders caused by microorganisms or viruses that can be transmitted from one person to another. Any disease-producing organism or virus is called a **pathogen** [PATH-uh-juhn]. Pathogenic organisms come from groups as different as bacteria, rickettsiae, protists, and fungi. Infectious diseases spread when pathogens are transferred from person to person.

CONCEPTS
- how bacteria cause disease
- how viruses cause disease
- transmission of infectious diseases

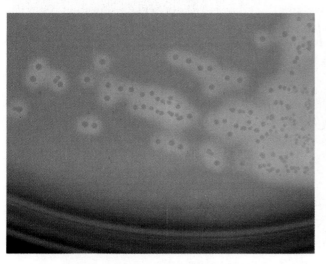
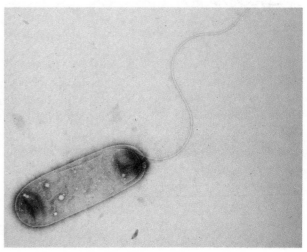

Figure 41.1 *Left:* The bacteria that cause strep infections. *Right:* The microorganisms that cause Legionnaires disease.

41–1 Bacterial Diseases

Most pathogenic bacteria cause disease by producing toxins. A **toxin** is a substance that interferes with the normal functioning of body cells.

Diphtheria and tetanus are diseases caused by bacterial toxins. Diphtheria bacilli grow and multiply in the throat. The toxin they produce is very poisonous, causing sore throat and respiratory difficulties. They can release enough toxin to cause death.

Tetanus is caused by bacteria that enter deep puncture wounds. In the body, the bacteria release a powerful neurotoxin. A **neurotoxin** [NOOR-oh-tahk-sihn] attacks nerve cells. In tetanus, nerve damage often causes rigid contraction of muscles. The jaw muscle is often affected. That is why the common name for tetanus is lockjaw.

In some diseases, toxin production occurs before the organisms enter the body. Botulism neurotoxin is an example. Spores of botulism-causing bacteria are sometimes present in foods being canned. If the food is not sterilized properly, the spores survive. The bacteria then grow inside the can and produce toxin The toxin is extremely powerful. Very small amounts can cause death. The growth of these bacteria produces a gas that often makes the can bulge. Food from swollen cans should never be eaten.

Not all bacterial diseases are caused by toxins. Some bacteria cause disease by extensively invading body tissues, damaging the tissues in the process. Tuberculosis bacteria, for example, destroy tissue in the lungs.

41-2 Viral Diseases

Viruses are smaller than bacteria. Most are not visible with light microscopes. Recall from Chapter 16 that viruses are parasites that infect living cells. They use the machinery of the host cells to reproduce. New virus particles burst from the host cells. The viruses can then infect other cells. Each type of virus infects only a specific kind of cell.

One of the most familiar of human infectious diseases, the common cold, is caused by a virus. Influenza, or flu, is another viral disease. Its symptoms include fever, muscle aches, and respiratory congestion. The virus that causes poliomyelitis, or polio, destroys cells of the nervous system. Because of damage, polio can cause paralysis and even death.

Mumps, measles, and chicken pox are all caused by viruses. These diseases are generally mild. Usually a person can contract them only once.

41-3 Disease Transmission

For a disease to be infectious, pathogens must pass from one person to another. There are three principal transmission paths for bacteria and viruses. First, pathogens may be carried through the environment by air, water, or some object such as food or silverware. Second, disease organisms can be transmitted by direct bodily contact between an infected and a noninfected person. Third, independent organisms such as insects can carry pathogens from one person to another.

Many pathogens are carried through the air when infected individuals sneeze or cough. Moisture droplets can carry bacteria and viruses into the respiratory tract of an uninfected person. Colds and flu are viral illnesses transmitted in this way. Pneumonia, strep throat, diphtheria, and tuberculosis are bacterial diseases spread through the air.

Many pathogens leave an infected person's body in solid wastes. Untreated sewage can filter into lakes, wells, or rivers. Pathogens in contaminated water may spread to uninfected people. Bacterial diseases transmitted this way include typhoid fever and cholera. Hepatitis, a viral disease of the liver, is also spread through contaminated water.

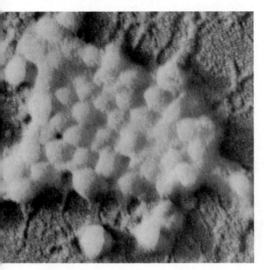

Figure 41.2 This electron micrograph shows a flu virus.

Do You Know?
Influenza means "influence" in Italian. Long ago, people believed that flu epidemics were caused by the influence of the stars.

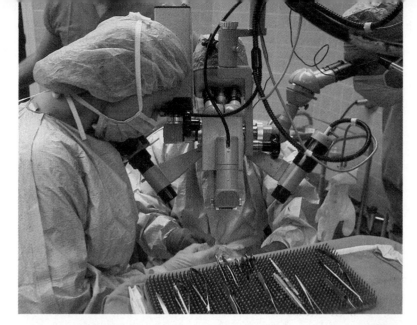

Figure 41.3 Surgical masks are worn to prevent the transmission of airborne pathogens.

Some diseases are spread by direct bodily contact. **Venereal** [vuh-NIHR-ee-uhl] **diseases**, for example, are spread by sexual contact. Syphilis and gonorrhea are venereal diseases caused by bacteria. A herpes virus causes another venereal disease.

Many diseases are transmitted to humans by other organisms. The bacteria that cause bubonic plague, for example, are passed to a person by the bite of a flea. The flea picks up the bacteria by biting an infected rat.

Each type of pathogen generally infects only certain parts of the body. If a pathogen does not reach the proper cells, it will not cause a disease. For example, even if pneumonia bacteria contaminate food, they will not cause digestive-tract disease. To make a person sick, pneumonia bacteria must get into the respiratory system.

An **epidemic** results when a disease spreads rapidly and uncontrollably. Occasionally a disease will spread over large parts of the world. In 1918–1919, an influenza epidemic killed more than 10 million people. Far fewer people were killed in World War I.

Checkpoint

1. What are disease-causing microorganisms and viruses called?
2. What is the term for a bacterial poison that affects nerve cells?
3. Name three diseases caused by viruses.
4. What is the term for a disease that spreads rapidly and uncontrollably through a population?

The Body's Defenses

Bacteria and viruses are everywhere. They are in the air, soil, and water. They are on your skin and the surfaces you touch. Fortunately, physical and chemical barriers protect your body from these pathogens.

41–4 Barriers Against Disease

Body surfaces hinder microorganisms from entering the body. Figure 41.4 shows bacteria normally present on the human skin. Most are harmless as long as they remain outside the body. Burns and cuts give bacteria and viruses access to living cells below the skin. If the skin is broken, entering organisms may grow and cause disease.

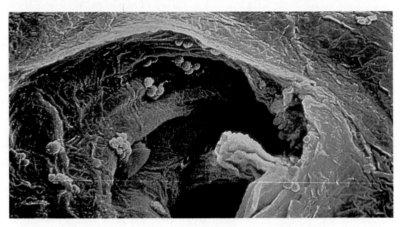

Figure 41.4 Bacteria on human skin

The mucus lining the respiratory and digestive tracts is another barrier to pathogens. It traps the bacteria and viruses in air or food. The mucus is eventually swallowed. The bacteria are destroyed by gastric juice. In addition, mucus-secreting cells produce an enzyme called **lysozyme** [LY-suh-zym]. Tear glands in the eyes also produce this enzyme. Lysozyme destroys bacteria by breaking down their cell walls.

Mucus is not as effective a barrier as skin. A number of bacteria can get through the mucus. In fact, most disease organisms gain entry through the mucus.

41–5 The Immune System

The **immune system** is a collection of cells and tissues that defend your body against pathogens. The lymphatic system, spleen, bone marrow, and thymus are the major organs of the immune system. The **thymus** [THY-muhs] is an organ

CONCEPTS

- protective function of body surfaces
- nature of the inflammation response
- function of the immune system
- antibody production

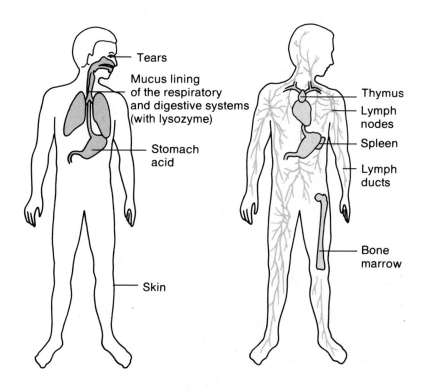

Tears

Mucus lining
of the respiratory
and digestive systems
(with lysozyme)

Stomach
acid

Skin

Thymus

Lymph
nodes

Spleen

Lymph
ducts

Bone
marrow

Figure 41.5 The body has physical barriers against invasion by microorganisms. The immune system takes over when invasion occurs.

found just beneath the breastbone. This gland is much larger in children than in adults. The thymus helps establish the immune system early in life.

The immune system goes to work when you get a cut or burn. The damaged tissue becomes swollen, red, and sore. This response is called **inflammation**. It helps destroy pathogens that enter the body at the wound.

Damaged body cells release several chemicals that cause inflammation. **Histamine** [HIHS-tuh-meen] is one of these chemicals. Histamine increases the diameter of capillaries and makes them "leakier" than usual. These expanded capillaries carry more blood and release more tissue fluid than normal. Therefore, the area where histamine is released becomes red and swollen. Many white cells collect in this area.

White blood cells are basic to the immune system. These cells are found in the blood, tissue fluid, and lymphatic system. Some are phagocytes, which destroy pathogens by surrounding and engulfing them. Other white cells are lymphocytes; certain lymphocytes make antibodies.

41–6 Antibodies

As you learned in Chapter 40, antibodies are proteins. They bind to other proteins, called antigens, found on substances foreign to the body. Protein molecules on the surface of bacteria

 BIOLOGY INSIGHTS

Response to the environment is a characteristic of all living things. The response of the immune system serves to protect the body against pathogens.

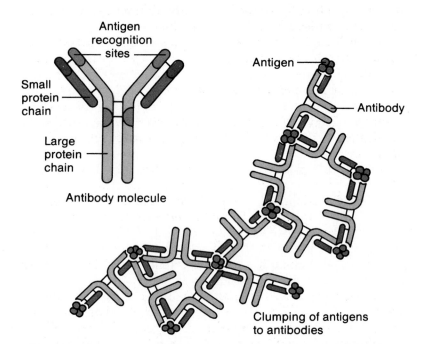

Antigen
recognition
sites

Small
protein
chain

Large
protein
chain

Antibody molecule

Antigen

Antibody

Clumping of antigens
to antibodies

Figure 41.6 Each antibody molecule has two sites that can attach to an antigen. When antibodies combine with antigens, clumping occurs.

or viruses act as antigens. Antibodies are a critical part of the body's defense.

Figure 41.6 illustrates the structure and function of antibodies. Notice that each antibody molecule has two sites that can react with antigens. One way an antibody functions is by linking many antigen molecules together in clumps. Such clumps are digested by phagocytes.

Antibodies can neutralize virus particles. To infect a cell, a virus must first be able to recognize its proper host cells. Proteins on the virus match the shape of molecules on the cell membrane of a host cell. However, antibodies can cover the recognition proteins of the virus so that the virus cannot infect a cell.

A protein called **interferon** also works against viruses. Interferon is produced by cells that have been infected by viruses. Interferon makes uninfected cells resistant to viral attack. Scientists are not exactly sure how interferon works.

41–7 B-Cells and T-Cells

Your immune system can make an antibody against any antigen. Each kind of antibody binds to only one specific type of antigen. How can the body make so many different antibodies?

Special lymphocytes called **B-cells** make antibodies. In the first year of life, a human produces an extremely large number of different B-cells, probably over a million. Each one produces

Do You Know?

Human interferon is now produced in large quantities by recombinant-DNA techniques. Scientists are testing the effectiveness of interferon against diseases as diverse as the common cold and cancer.

its own specifically shaped antibody, different from the antibodies produced by all the other B-cells.

An individual B-cell incorporates some of its antibody into the cell membrane in such a manner that the antibody faces the outside of the cell. In this way, each B-cell "advertises" the kind of antibody it can make. Suppose an antigen that has never before entered your body gets past the surface defenses. The new antigen eventually encounters a B-cell with an antibody on the surface that happens to match the shape of the antigen.

When such a match occurs, the B-cell first begins to multiply rapidly by mitosis. These divisions produce a clone consisting of millions of identical copies of the original B-cell. Then the cells in the clone begin to make and secrete large amounts of their specific antibody. The antibody molecules are then carried throughout the blood plasma and tissue fluid. The antibody can then neutralize antigen molecules. This process is diagramed in Figure 41.7.

All the B-cells in the clone can make only one kind of antibody. This antibody acts only against the type of antigen encountered by the original B-cell. If one of the B-cells in the clone contacts a different type of antigen, nothing happens.

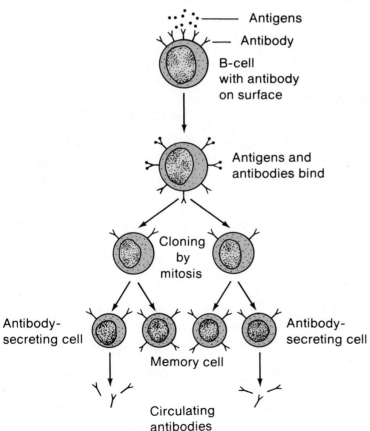

Figure 41.7 An antigen contacts a B-cell, stimulating it to begin a series of mitotic divisions that result in a clone of antibody-secreting cells.

Infectious Disease in Humans   **611**

After B-cells neutralize an antigen, some members of the clone remain in the body. These are called **memory cells**. If the same type of antigen gets into the body again, memory cells secrete large amounts of the antibody. Very quickly, all the invading antigens are destroyed. Memory cells can give you immunity to diseases such as chicken pox or mumps. **Immunity** is the ability to resist a particular disease.

T-cells are other lymphocytes important in fighting disease. Early in a person's life, T-cells pass through the thymus, where they are somehow activated. Like B-cells, T-cells clone after they attach to an antigen. They too form memory cells.

However, T-cells differ from B-cells in several ways. T-cells never release antibodies into the plasma. While B-cells respond to individual molecules, T-cells respond to whole cells. For example, T-cells will react to your own cells if they are infected by viruses. (B-cells will only react to free viruses that have not penetrated cells.) T-cells will usually attack cancer cells. T-cells also react to the cells of transplanted organs, which can cause organ rejection.

To kill the cells they attach to, T-cells release poisonous chemicals. T-cells can also release chemicals that attract phagocytes, which then destroy the foreign cells.

Do You Know?

There is evidence that the T-cells of people who get cancer do not effectively attack their cancer cells.

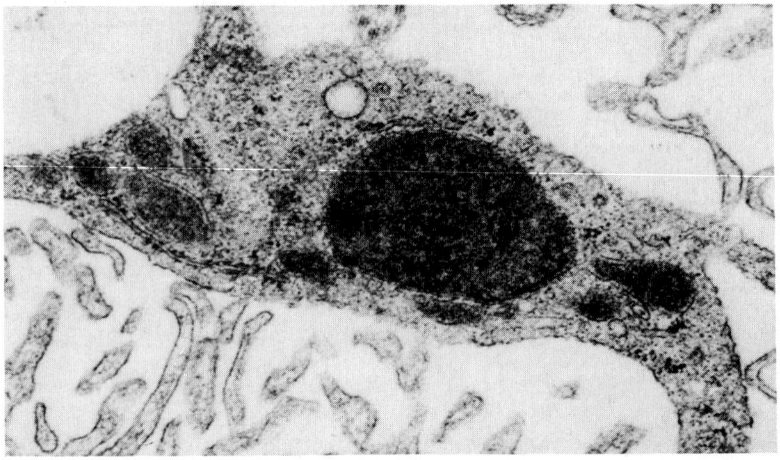

Figure 41.8 Phagocytes destroy pathogens by engulfing them.

Checkpoint

1. Identify two body-surface barriers to pathogens.
2. Red and swollen skin signals what body response?
3. What is the term for a substance that triggers the formation of antibodies?
4. What kind of lymphocyte secretes large amounts of antibodies into the plasma and tissue fluid?
5. What cells prevent reinfection by the same antigen?

Medicine and Infectious Disease

You usually need to know what causes a problem before you can solve it. Before the mid-1800s no one knew what caused infectious diseases. Therefore, few medical treatments were of any value. Slowly, scientists learned about microorganisms and the immune system. Today many diseases are cured by destroying pathogens. Diseases may often be prevented by assisting the body's own defenses.

CONCEPTS

- the germ theory of disease
- how vaccines function
- chemical treatments for bacterial disease

41–8   The Cause of Infectious Disease

Long ago, people believed that such things as evil spirits and the night air caused disease. Until the nineteenth century, no one knew exactly why sickness happened. Then Louis Pasteur developed the germ theory of disease. This theory states that microorganisms cause many diseases.

Next, somebody had to find a way to determine which pathogen caused a particular disease. In 1876, the German doctor Robert Koch did exactly that. Koch demonstrated that a particular species of bacteria causes sheep anthrax. To do this, he used a series of procedures now known as **Koch's postulates** [KAHKZ PAHS-chuh-laytz]. Koch's postulates state that the following must be done to prove that a particular microorganism causes a disease.

1. The microorganism must be found in all animals (or plants) affected by the disease.
2. The microorganism must be removed from the host and grown in a pure culture.
3. When some of the microorganisms are injected into healthy hosts, they must produce symptoms of the disease.
4. The microorganism must be found in the body of the newly infected hosts.

The next 25 years came to be known as the golden age of bacteriology. Scientists used Koch's postulates to identify the bacteria responsible for many diseases.

Do You Know?

In addition to his other accomplishments, Robert Koch discovered that the microorganisms causing African sleeping sickness are transmitted to humans by tsetse flies.

41–9   Mobilizing Body Defenses

Long before the germ theory of disease, an English doctor, Edward Jenner, discovered a way to prevent smallpox. Smallpox causes high fever and blisterlike sores. Many people died from the disease.

Jenner noticed that people working around cattle rarely contracted smallpox. They did, however, often come down with a similar but much milder disease called cowpox. Jenner concluded that cowpox made its victims immune to smallpox. In 1796, Jenner infected a child with material from a cowpox sore. The child became immune to smallpox.

Do You Know?

President Thomas Jefferson helped popularize Jenner's vaccination procedure in the United States. Jefferson inoculated his own family and about 200 other people.

Jenner called his procedure vaccination. A similar method is used today to protect people against certain diseases. The person being immunized is given a vaccine. A **vaccine** usually consists of dead or damaged pathogens that can no longer cause the disease. Though the pathogen has been weakened, its antigen molecules are still present. Vaccine triggers the production of antibodies against the pathogen's antigens. Memory cells are produced, giving long-term immunity.

Vaccines now exist for many diseases. Children are routinely immunized against diphtheria, tetanus, whooping cough, mumps, rubella, measles, and polio. Because of immunization, polio is now very rare in North America. In addition, there has not been a case of smallpox anywhere in the world for several years.

However, some diseases are not easily controlled by vaccines. The common cold is an example. Colds are caused by hundreds of different viruses. It is not practical to give people vaccines against each one.

Recommended Age	Type of Immunization
2 months	Diphtheria–tetanus–pertussis (whooping cough) vaccine (DTP), oral polio vaccine
4 months	DTP, oral polio vaccine
6 months	DTP
1 year	Tuberculin test
15 months	Measles, rubella, mumps
18 months	DTP, polio
4 to 6 years	DTP, polio
14 to 16 years	Tetanus–diphtheria (TD adult form)

Figure 41.9 Recommended ages for routine immunizations

41–10 Antibacterial Drugs

Chemotherapy is the use of chemicals to treat disease. In the early 1900s, a German chemist, Paul Ehrlich, was the first to find a chemical effective against a bacterial disease. He discovered an arsenic compound that destroyed syphilis bacteria. Unfortunately, arsenic is a poison. Ehrlich's chemical had harmful side effects.

Even so, Ehrlich's discovery led scientists to search for better chemicals to fight bacteria. In 1928, Alexander Fleming discovered the antibiotic penicillin. An **antibiotic** [an-tih-by-AHT-ihk] is a bacteria-killing substance produced in living organisms. Antibiotics are usually very effective in fighting bacterial diseases. Penicillin is still in use today. In addition, many other antibiotics have been discovered.

Today the number of available antibiotics is enormous. No single antibiotic is useful against all types of bacteria. To prescribe an effective antibiotic, doctors must identify the bacteria causing an infection. Also, bacteria undergo constant mutation. Therefore, bacteria can develop resistance to particular antibiotics. For example, some kinds of bacteria that were once killed by penicillin are now resistant to it.

Figure 41.10 The mold from which penicillin is derived

Antibiotics are not effective against viral infections. Remember that viruses reproduce by using the chemical machinery of your own cells. Any substance that interferes with this chemistry would kill your own cells along with the virus. Drugs such as aspirin may help viral-disease symptoms, such as fever. However, these drugs do not kill the viruses. Prevention is still the best way to deal with viral diseases.

Checkpoint

1. Who proposed the germ theory of disease?
2. Who developed the procedure that scientists use to show what organism is responsible for an infectious disease?
3. Identify a disease that is not easily controlled by vaccination.
4. What is the term for the use of chemicals to treat disease?
5. Name the antibiotic discovered by Alexander Fleming.

CHAPTER REVIEW

Summary

- Infectious diseases are caused by microorganisms. Many bacteria cause diseases by producing toxins.
- Viruses cause diseases by infecting host cells, multiplying, and then destroying the host cells.
- Pathogens can be transmitted from one person to another through air, water, or contaminated objects. Pathogens also may be spread through direct contact with a contagious person. Diseases also may be spread by other organisms. Epidemics result when a pathogen spreads uncontrolled through a population.
- The skin and the mucous lining of the respiratory and digestive tracts provide the primary body defenses against infection by pathogens.
- The inflammation response is the initial reaction of the immune system to invasion by foreign material.
- The immune system of the body deals with pathogens or other foreign substances that penetrate the body's primary defenses.
- B-cells are lymphocytes that make antibodies against any antigens encountered. Antibodies work by clumping antigens together and by covering the recognition sites of viruses.
- After they encounter an antigen, B-cells clone and secrete large amounts of antibodies. Memory cells remain to deal with future appearances of the same antigen.
- T-cells are lymphocytes that destroy whole cells, such as virus-infected cells and cancerous cells. T-cells secrete toxins as well as chemicals that attract phagocytes.
- Pasteur's germ theory of disease and Koch's postulates helped scientists determine the causes of infectious diseases.
- Jenner was the first to develop a successful vaccine. A vaccine is a damaged or weakened pathogen that can no longer cause disease but will cause formation of antibodies. Vaccines create immunity in the person who is vaccinated.
- Antibiotics are bacteria-killing substances produced by living organisms. None of these substances affect the growth of viruses. So far, only the immune system can deal with viral infections.

Vocabulary

antibiotic	Koch's postulates
B-cell	lysozyme
chemotherapy	memory cell
epidemic	neurotoxin
histamine	pathogen
immune system	T-cell
immunity	thymus
infectious disease	toxin
inflammation	vaccine
interferon	venereal disease

Review

1. What is histamine? How does it function in fighting pathogens?
2. What is the enzyme secreted into mucus and tears that helps prevent penetration by bacteria?
3. What happens to the bacteria that stick to the mucous membranes of the nose?
4. Identify a disease in which the bacterial toxin is produced before being taken into the body.
5. For each of the following diseases, write *B* if it is caused by bacteria and *V* if it is caused by viruses.

   a. tetanus   e. measles
   b. diphtheria   f. polio
   c. gonorrhea   g. tuberculosis
   d. cold   h. influenza

6. Name one disease that is transmitted in each of the following ways:
   a. through the air
   b. by direct contact
   c. through the bite of an insect
7. T-cells must pass through the _____ gland to be activated.
8. What kind of lymphocyte responds to viruses that are outside of cells?
9. Cowpox viruses were used by Jenner to produce immunity against what disease?
10. What family of antibacterial substances is produced by living organisms?
11. What type of cells provides a person with long-term immunity against a disease?

Interpret and Apply

1. Suppose you catch a cold. Where are you more likely to have picked up the virus from — the air or contaminated water? Explain.
2. How is botulism toxin produced?
3. Why are sewage-treatment plants so important in the control of infectious diseases?
4. Why are transplanted organs often rejected by the body?
5. How does a virus find and infect a specific kind of host cell?
6. What happens when an antigen new to the body encounters a B-cell with the corresponding antibody on its surface?
7. Why is it not possible to develop a vaccine that gives permanent immunity against the common cold?
8. A virus causing a digestive-tract illness is carried by air into the lungs. Is it likely to cause sickness? Explain.
9. Years ago, penicillin was effective against a wider variety of bacteria than it is today. Why?
10. Once people have measles, they will not get the disease again, even if they are exposed to the measles virus. Explain why this is true.
11. Why should you discard food contained in a bulging can?

Challenge

1. Describe the basic differences between the ways in which bacteria and viruses cause diseases.
2. Explain why Koch's postulates might be difficult to apply to a viral disease.
3. Why is it inappropriate for a doctor to prescribe antibiotics for a cold?
4. Doctors often do not prescribe an antibiotic until they have grown a culture of the bacteria that are causing the disease. Why?

Projects

1. Find out about the present incidence in the world of one of the following diseases: bubonic plague, cholera, malaria, typhoid fever. Where are these diseases still common? What attempts are being made to control them? Are there medical treatments for these diseases?
2. Find out about the problems faced by Jonas Salk in developing the first polio vaccine. How does the Sabin vaccine differ from the Salk vaccine? Report your findings to the class.
3. The years between 1876 and 1900 are sometimes called the golden age of bacteriology. Prepare a time-line chart that highlights the discoveries made during this period and their impact on public health.
4. Allergies are caused by defects in the immune system. Find out what goes wrong to cause an allergic response and how allergies are treated.
5. Find out the status of research in developing new vaccines for hepatitis, chicken pox, and malaria. Which vaccines are available now and which are experimental?
6. Learn what autoimmune diseases are and report your findings to the class.

42 The Nervous System and the Senses

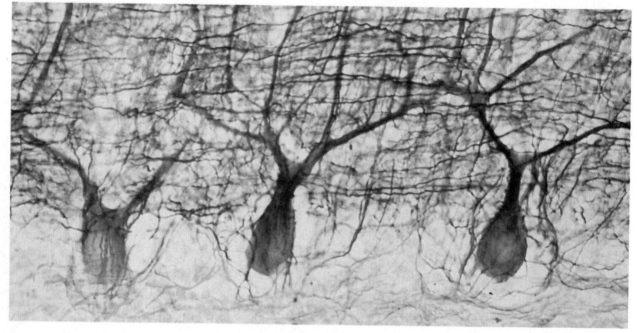

Nerve cells in the brain

What do you do if you're in an unfamiliar place and you feel thirsty? You probably ask someone where the nearest drinking fountain is. After listening to the person's directions, you set off toward the fountain. When you find it, you drink until you have quenched your thirst.

That simple act of getting a drink involves many coordinated processes. First you must recognize the feeling of thirst. Then your eyes, ears, and muscles all go into action. When you have found a fountain, you have to figure out how to make it work. Finally, you need to know when you have drunk enough water.

Your nervous system coordinated all these actions. This system consists of a vast, intricate collection of nerve cells. Some nerve cells are shown above.

The nervous system receives information from the environment. Then it causes the body parts to act on that information. It is involved in every action you perform, from sneezing to solving math problems.

The Transmission of Information

The nervous system is composed of the brain, spinal cord, and all the nerves that connect those two structures with other parts of the body. The nerves in your toes are as much a part of the nervous system as the brain is.

The nervous system has three major functions. First it receives information about the environment and the other parts of the body. Then it interprets the information it receives. Finally it makes the body respond to this information.

Consider what happens when you hear a phone ring. Nerves from your ear send a message to your brain. Your brain interprets this information as the sound of a phone ringing. Then your brain sends a message to your arm muscles. The muscles contract, and you reach out to lift the phone.

CONCEPTS
- structure and function of neurons
- nature of nerve impulses

42–1 Neurons and Nerves

The basic unit of structure and function in the nervous system is the **neuron** [NOOR-ahn], or nerve cell. A neuron carries information from one location to another. **Sensory neurons** pick up information from the environment. **Motor neurons** carry information to muscles or glands, causing them to act. **Interneurons**, also called associative neurons, carry information between two other neurons.

A typical neuron is shown in Figure 42.1. The cell body contains the nucleus and most of the cytoplasm. Many threadlike **dendrites** branch from the cell body. A long, thin fiber called an **axon** also extends from the cell body. The axon is often coated with myelin, a white, fatty material. Axons are sometimes called nerve fibers. These fibers occur in bundles called **nerves**.

The dendrites receive stimulation from the environment or from the body. If this stimulation is strong enough, a nerve **impulse**, or message, is generated in the axon. The impulse travels along the axon. From the end of the axon, a signal passes to a muscle, a gland, or the dendrites of another neuron.

A **synapse** is the junction of an axon and the structure with which it communicates. The axon does not actually touch the muscle, gland, or dendrites. There is a space of about 0.00002 millimeters between the axon and the following structure. Figure 42.1 illustrates a synapse.

42–2 The Nerve Impulse

What starts a nerve impulse? What makes it travel along a nerve fiber? Electric charges are involved in the generation

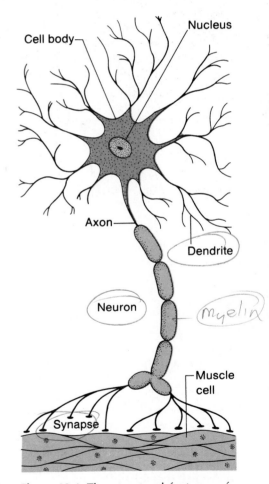

Figure 42.1 The structural features of a neuron and a synapse.

and conduction of nerve impulses. A nerve impulse is not, however, an electric current.

Remember from Chapter 3 that an ion is an electrically charged atom. Some ions carry positive charges; others are negatively charged. All cells contain dissolved ions. So does the tissue fluid outside cells. Like all cells, the neuron has a cell membrane that is selectively permeable. In other words, only certain materials can pass through the cell membrane. Because of this selective permeability, the concentration of ions is different inside and outside the cell membrane. During the neuron's resting state, there are slightly more positive charges than negative charges on the outside of the membrane. Inside the cell membrane, however, there are fewer positive than negative charges. This results in a slight difference in electrical charge between the inside and outside of the cell membrane. The membrane is said to be polarized.

A neuron receives input from the senses or other neurons. If the neuron is stimulated strongly enough, the permeability of the membrane changes. Some ions rush into the cell. Others move out. As a result, the polarity of the membrane reverses itself. The membrane becomes more positive on the inside and more negative on the outside. This is how the nerve impulse begins. The change in permeability and charge travels along the neuron from its starting point to the end of the axon. The nerve impulse travels several meters per second.

After an impulse has passed, certain ions are moved into and out of the cell by active transport. The original distribution of charges is restored. The cell membrane returns to its resting state.

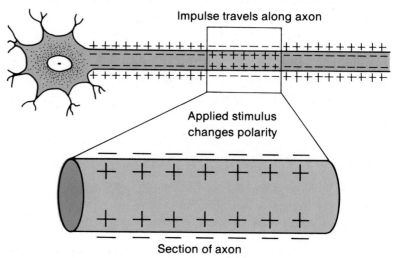

Figure 42.2 During the generation of a nerve impulse, the polarity of the nerve cell membrane becomes reversed. The nerve impulse travels the length of the axon.

Like muscle cells, neurons have an all-or-none response. Also, the impulse always has the same strength. If the stimulation is too weak, no impulse is produced. In addition, a particular neuron always conducts impulses at a particular rate, never faster or slower.

Once an impulse reaches the end of an axon, it must cross the synapse to a muscle, a gland, or another neuron. Suppose a neuron synapses on another neuron. The axon of the first neuron releases chemicals called **neurotransmitters**. Certain neurotransmitters cause an impluse in the second neuron.

Suppose that the axon of a neuron synapses with a muscle cell. To make the muscle contract, the signal must reach the muscle cell. How does this happen?

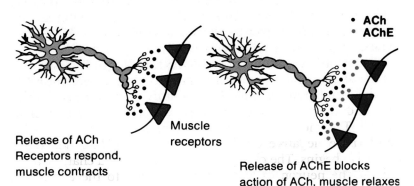

- **ACh**
- **AChE**

Release of ACh
Receptors respond,
muscle contracts

Muscle
receptors

Release of AChE blocks
action of ACh, muscle relaxes

Figure 42.3 Acetylcholinesterase deactivates acetylcholine, causing the muscle cell to relax.

When the impulse reaches the end of the axon, the axon secretes a neurotransmitter called **acetylcholine** [uh-seet-l-KOH-leen], or ACh. Molecules of ACh diffuse across the synapse to the muscle cell. When they touch special receptor molecules on the cell's membrane, the muscle cell contracts.

The ACh does not remain active for long. The muscle cell makes an enzyme called **acetylcholinesterase** [uh-seet-l-koh-luh-NEHS-tuh-rayz], or AChE. The AChE inactivates the ACh, and the muscle cell relaxes. It then contracts again if additional ACh is released by the axon next to it. Figure 42.3 shows this process.

Checkpoint

1. What is a nerve cell called?
2. What are the three structures that an axon can synapse with?
3. Which part of a nerve cell picks up stimulation from the environment?
4. Which neurotransmitter causes muscles to contract?

The Central and Peripheral Nervous Systems

Neurons make up the nervous system. The nervous system is divided into two parts, as shown in Figure 42.4. The **central nervous system** includes the brain and the spinal cord. The **peripheral nervous system** contains all the nerves that lie outside the central nervous system.

42–3 Overview of the Central Nervous System

Both the brain and spinal cord are covered by three protective membranes known as the **meninges** [muh-NIHN-jeez]. The space between the two inner meninges is filled with **cerebrospinal** [suh-ree-broh-SPEYNE-l] **fluid**. This fluid is produced in cavities within the brain. From there the fluid drains into blood vessels in the brain. Cerebrospinal fluid cushions the brain and spinal cord against shock. It also removes waste materials from the brain.

The nervous tissue of the brain and spinal cord lies under the meninges. The outer portion of the brain tissue is gray. Beneath the gray layer, the brain is white. In contrast, the spinal cord appears white on the outside and gray on the inside.

42–4 The Cerebrum

The brain of the human is very large. It contains about 12 billion neurons. Of the 12 billion, about 9 billion of them are contained in the cerebrum. The **cerebrum** [suh-REE-bruhm] is the large upper region of the human brain. The surface of the cerebrum, called the cerebral cortex, is folded into ridges and depressions called convolutions. These greatly increase the surface area.

Remember from Chapter 36 that as human evolution progressed, the brain became larger. In particular, the cerebrum became larger and more convoluted compared to the rest of the brain. The cerebral cortex controls many functions that are associated with intelligence. These include memory, creativity, and reasoning.

The cerebrum is divided into right and left halves called cerebral hemispheres. The hemispheres are connected to each other by bundles of axons. Through these axons, one side of the brain can communicate with the other. Deep folds in the cortex divide each hemisphere into four lobes. These lobes are shown in Figure 42.5.

CONCEPTS

- structure and function of the cerebrum
- functions of the cerebellum, thalamus, hypothalamus, and medulla oblongata
- structure and function of the spinal cord
- organization and functions of the peripheral nervous system

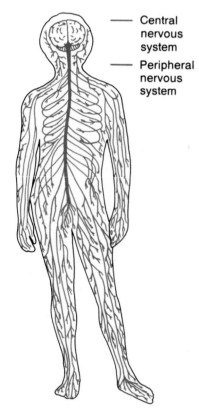

Central nervous system

Peripheral nervous system

Figure 42.4 The central and peripheral nervous systems

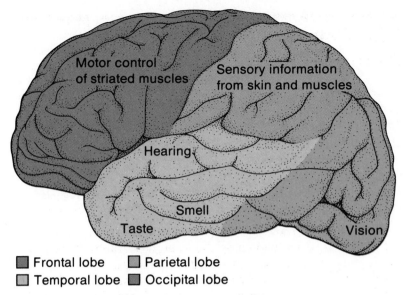

Motor control of striated muscles

Sensory information from skin and muscles

Hearing

Smell

Taste

Vision

■ Frontal lobe ■ Parietal lobe
□ Temporal lobe ■ Occipital lobe

Figure 42.5 Some functions associated with specific areas of the cerebrum

Part of the cerebrum processes information from the ears, and is thus involved in the sense of hearing. Another portion controls the skeletal muscles. The cerebrum also receives sensory input from the eyes and the skin. As you can see in Figure 42.5, the cerebrum has functions related to the senses of taste and smell.

The cerebrum receives information about the environment from the sensory neurons. The cerebrum then sends information to muscles and glands by means of motor neurons. Messages that originate in the left hemisphere of the brain cross over to neurons that control movement on the right side of the body. Messages from the right hemisphere control the left side of the body. Similarly, the left part of your brain gets information from the right side of your body. Impulses from your left side go to the brain's right hemisphere.

One hemisphere of the brain is dominant over the other. The left hemisphere is usually dominant. Left-hemisphere dominance causes a person to be right-handed. In most people, an area in the left hemisphere controls speech. The left side of the brain is also specialized for mathematics and logic. The right side is usually specialized for art and music.

42–5 Other Structures of the Brain

The **cerebellum** [sehr-uh-BEHL-uhm] lies beneath the back of the cerebrum. It too is convoluted. Signals from the motor neurons that control skeletal muscles pass from the cerebrum through the cerebellum. Here impulses from these nerves are coordinated to produce smooth motions. Without the cerebellum, only unrefined jerky movements would be possible. The cerebellum also helps maintain the balance of your body.

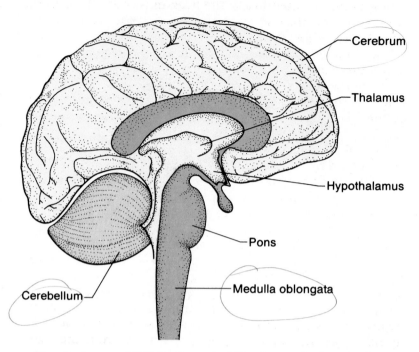

Figure 42.6 The structural features of the human brain

The **thalamus** [THAL-uh-muhs] lies beneath the cerebrum, as shown in Figure 42.6. The thalamus is a sensory relay station. It receives impulses from most sensory neurons entering the brain. Through synapses with other neurons, the thalamus directs the impulses to the parts of the cortex where they will be interpreted. In addition, the thalamus screens stimuli. If the brain received all the stimuli the body gets from the environment, it would be overwhelmed. The thalamus prevents sensory overload.

The **hypothalamus** lies beneath the thalamus. The hypothalamus controls important sensations involved in maintaining homeostasis, such as hunger and thirst. Temperature maintenance, water balance, and blood pressure are also controlled by the hypothalamus. In addition, the hypothalamus regulates the release of many hormones.

The **medulla oblongata** [muh-DUHL-luh ahb-lahn-GAHT-uh] extends down from the central part of the brain and connects to the spinal cord. The medulla oblongata controls basic life functions such as heartbeat rate and breathing. Even if a person's cerebrum and cerebellum are damaged, the medulla oblongata may enable life to continue.

42–6   The Spinal Cord

The spinal cord extends down from the medulla. Through the spinal cord, sensory and motor information passes between the brain and the other parts of the body. All sensory and motor nerves located below the neck must pass through the spinal cord on the way to the brain. A cross section of the spinal cord is shown in Figure 42.7.

The spinal cord runs through holes in the vertebrae. These bones protect the cord from injury. Perhaps you have heard of someone who had a serious accident that crushed the spinal cord. That person has lost the ability to move parts of the body below the injury. The injured person has no sensation in these body parts, either.

The spinal cord controls most reflex behavior. A **reflex** is an automatic, unthinking response to a stimulus. The brain generally does not control many simple reflex responses.

As an example of a reflex, consider your response to painful skin stimulation. Suppose you are walking barefoot on the beach, and you step on a broken shell. Within an instant of touching the shell, your foot springs up and away. The sharp edge of the shell activates certain dendrites in a sensory neuron. An impulse travels along the sensory neuron to the spinal cord. There the sensory neuron synapses with an interneuron. The interneuron, in turn, synapses with a motor neuron that sends an impulse to a muscle in your leg. The muscle contracts, and your leg pulls away from the sharp object.

Meanwhile, an impulse travels upward through the spinal cord to the cerebral cortex. However, this impulse does not reach your brain until after you have pulled your foot away. You do not feel pain until *after* you have removed your foot!

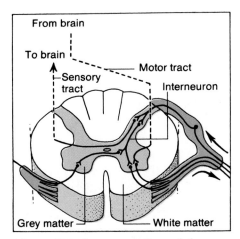

Figure 42.7 A cross-section of the spinal cord

Do You Know?

Reflexes serve a protective function. If a painful stimulus had to deliver a signal to your brain before you could act upon it, you might be severely injured in the meantime.

Figure 42.8 Certain reflex actions are controlled by the spinal cord rather than the brain. However, the brain controls the sensation of pain.

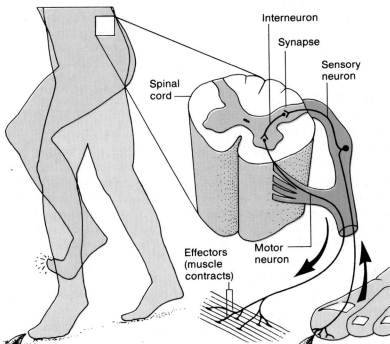

42–7   The Peripheral Nervous System

The peripheral nervous system consists of all parts of the nervous system except the brain and spinal cord. It includes the cranial and spinal nerves. The **cranial nerves** are 12 pairs of nerves that emerge from the brain. For the most part, they connect with areas in the head and face. The muscles that move the eyes and tongue are activated by cranial nerves. Cranial nerves also carry sensory information to the brain.

There are 31 pairs of **spinal nerves** that emerge from the spinal cord. Before each spinal nerve enters the spinal cord, it branches. The sensory branch goes into the dorsal portion of the gray matter of the spinal cord. The cell bodies of the sensory neurons are located just outside the spinal cord in swellings called **ganglia** [GAN-glee-uh] (singular, *ganglion*). The motor branch of each spinal nerve begins in the ventral portion of the gray matter. The cell bodies of motor neurons lie within the spinal cord and not in the ganglia.

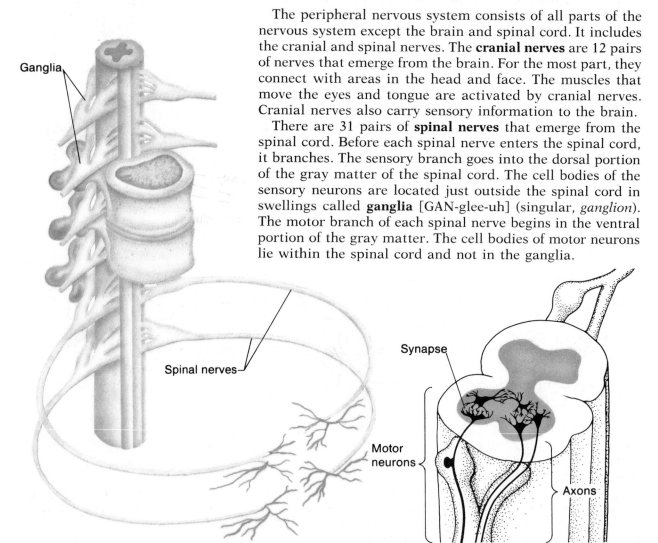

Figure 42.9 The structural features of spinal nerves

The motor neurons of the peripheral nervous system are classified into two groups. These are the somatic and the autonomic nervous systems. The **somatic** [soh-MAT-ihk] **nervous system** consists of motor neurons that connect the central nervous system to the striated, or voluntary, muscles. The neurons of the **autonomic nervous system** go to glands, smooth muscle, and cardiac muscle. These structures are not under voluntary control.

The autonomic nervous system is divided into two parts. These are the sympathetic and the parasympathetic nervous systems. The **sympathetic nervous system** is dominant in times of great stress. For example, suppose you are running

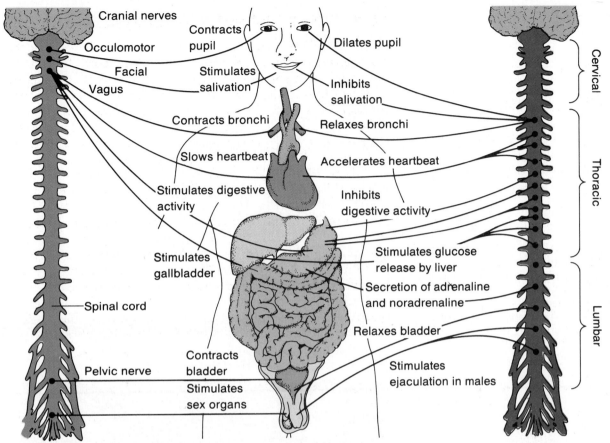

Cranial nerves
Occulomotor
Facial
Vagus

Contracts pupil
Dilates pupil
Stimulates salivation
Inhibits salivation
Contracts bronchi
Relaxes bronchi
Slows heartbeat
Accelerates heartbeat
Stimulates digestive activity
Inhibits digestive activity
Stimulates gallbladder
Stimulates glucose release by liver
Secretion of adrenaline and noradrenaline
Relaxes bladder
Contracts bladder
Stimulates ejaculation in males
Stimulates sex organs

Spinal cord
Pelvic nerve

Cervical
Thoracic
Lumbar

Autonomic nervous system

 **Sympathetic nervous system**

Parasympathetic nervous system

Figure 42.10 Functions controlled by the sympathetic and parasympathetic nerves.

in a 100-meter race. Nerve impulses make your heart speed up and your blood pressure rise. Your level of blood sugar rises, so that extra energy is available. All of these reactions enable you to move swiftly.

The **parasympathetic nervous system** counteracts the effects of the sympathetic system. After an emergency, the parasympathetic system returns the body to its normal state. The parasympathetic system is dominant under normal conditions. The vagus nerve, a cranial nerve, is the main nerve in the parasympathetic nervous system.

Checkpoint

1. What are the protective membranes that cover the brain and spinal cord?
2. Which part of the brain is the largest in humans?
3. Which cerebral hemisphere is dominant in most people?
4. Which brain part regulates body temperature?
5. What part of the nervous system coordinates most simple reflex behavior?

The Senses

The nervous system responds to events in the environment. To do this, the nervous system must have information about its environment. The senses provide this information. Traditionally, people have identified five senses: vision, hearing, smell, taste, and touch. Actually, the senses are more complex than these five categories indicate.

Each sense has specific receptors, or structures that pick up information. Each sense transmits impulses to a different region of the brain. The brain interprets these impulses as vision, hunger, or some other sensation.

Do You Know?

The different types of skin receptors are not distributed evenly over the body. Pain receptors are about 27 times more abundant than the receptors for coldness.

42-8   The Skin Senses

The skin contains receptors for touch, pain, pressure, heat, and cold. Each of these sensations has a different kind of receptor. For example, touch receptors inform the brain of even the lightest touch. Pressure receptors are buried deeper in the skin than the touch receptors. A gentle touch will not activate the pressure receptors, but firm pressure will.

Figure 42.11 Tickling activates the touch receptors in the skin.

42-9   Taste

Taste is a chemical sense, or one that is stimulated directly by chemicals. Taste receptors are located in structures called **taste buds**. Taste buds cover the top and sides of your tongue and some of the skin on your throat. Food molecules activate receptors in the taste buds. Nerve impulses are sent to the brain. The brain interprets these impulses as taste.

There are many types of taste receptors. Each type senses a different taste. Four major tastes are sweet, sour, bitter, and salty. Most foods have a blend of several different tastes. Each food stimulates more than one type of receptor.

When you have a cold, your sense of taste does not function as well as usual. The reason for this is that much of taste actually depends on the sense of smell. When your nose is blocked, your sense of smell doesn't work well.

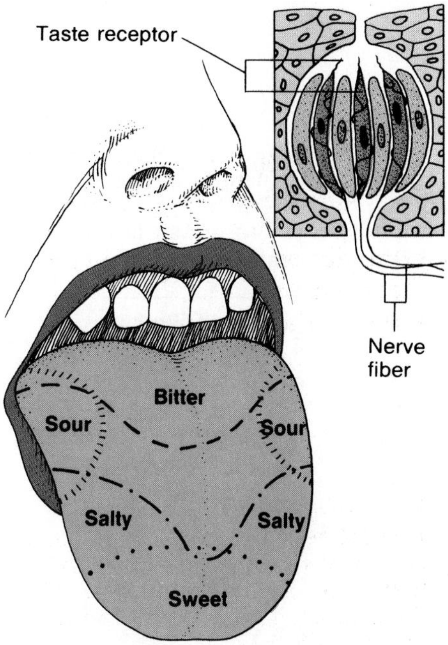

42–10 Smell

Like the sense of taste, smell is a chemical sense. Unlike taste receptors, however, the olfactory, or smell, receptors respond to molecules in the gaseous state. When you smell a substance, at least some of its molecules must be in the form of gas. The smell receptors are neurons embedded in the lining of the nose. The axons of these neurons compose the olfactory nerve, a sensory cranial nerve. The olfactory nerve sends impulses to the brain, which interprets them as smell.

42–11 Hearing and Balance

The ear is a very complex organ. It is responsible for both hearing and balance. The ear is divided into three main areas, as shown in the illustration opposite page 599. These are the outer ear, middle ear, and inner ear.

The outer ear is composed of the ear flap and the **auditory canal**. The auditory canal ends at the **tympanic** [tihm-PAN-ihk] **membrane**, or eardrum. The middle ear is on the other side of the tympanic membrane. The Eustachian tube connects the middle ear to the pharynx. The Eustachian tube contains air, which helps to equalize the pressure between the outer and middle ear.

In the middle ear there are three tiny bones in a row — the hammer, anvil, and stirrup. These bones connect the tympanic membrane with the **oval window**, a membrane-covered opening between the middle and inner ear.

The inner ear contains a coiled structure, the **cochlea** [KAHK-lee-uh]. This structure is filled with fluid. Receptor cells in the cochlea contain nerve endings. The **semicircular canals**, which are involved in the senses of balance and motion, are also in the inner ear.

Figure 42.12 Areas of response for different tastes

Do You Know?

The Eustachian tubes are named for Bartolommeo Eustachio, a sixteenth-century Italian anatomist.

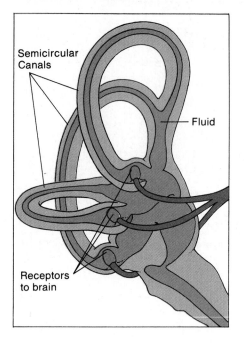

Figure 42.13 Changes in the position of the head are detected by pressure exerted on the receptors in the semicircular canals.

Semicircular Canals

Fluid

Receptors to brain

Do You Know?

In 1835, a successful corneal transplant was performed on an antelope. A British surgeon removed the cornea from a recently killed antelope and transplanted it into the eye of a blind antelope.

Sound travels through the air as waves of vibrating air molecules. When these vibrations reach the outer ear, they travel through the auditory canal. The vibrating air makes the tympanic membrane vibrate too. The tympanic membrane then passes the vibrations on to the bones in the middle ear. One after another, these bones start vibrating. The last of these bones, the stirrup, touches the oval window. The vibrating stirrup makes the membrane of the oval window vibrate. The vibration moves on to the fluid in the cochlea. This motion of the fluid stimulates the receptor cells. Sensory neurons that compose the auditory nerve send impulses to the brain. There these impulses are interpreted as sound.

In addition to hearing, the ears are involved in the sense of balance. The three semicircular canals of the inner ear are at right angles to one another, like the floor and two walls that meet at a corner of a room. This arrangement allows a person to sense motion in different planes.

The semicircular canals are filled with fluid. In addition, they contain sensory hair cells. When the head changes position, the fluid puts pressure on hairs. Sensory neurons detect the relative strength of the pressure on each hair. Neurons send impulses to the brain. These impulses communicate the position of the head.

42–12   Vision

Humans rely heavily on vision, and the human eye is well adapted for receiving light. The eye is covered by a tough outer layer. The front of this covering, the **cornea** [KOR-nee-uh], is transparent. The cornea is more curved than the eye as a whole. This curved surface bends incoming light rays.

Behind the cornea is the **iris**, the colored area of the eye. The iris contains smooth muscles. These muscles can make the iris more closed or open. This adjustment of the iris changes the size of the **pupil**, an opening in the middle of the iris. In strong light, the pupil becomes smaller, admitting less light into the eye. In dim light, the pupil becomes larger.

The **lens**, the eye's primary light-focusing structure, is behind the pupil. Muscles attach to the lens. When these muscles contract, the lens changes shape. This process allows the lens to focus light.

The light rays are focused on the **retina**, a thin membrane on the back of the eye that contains light-sensitive receptors. These receptors are called rods and cones. The **cones** are sensitive only in bright light. They can distinguish form and color very well. The **rods** are sensitive in dim light. They cannot distinguish color. Therefore, in dim light you can see only shades of gray.

You see when light reflected from an object enters the eye. The cornea and lens bend the light rays together. The rays cross and focus on the retina. The image formed on the retina is actually upside down and backward.

When light strikes the rods and cones, nerve impulses are created. Those impulses are carried by the optic nerve to the brain. In the brain, the retinal image is reversed. Therefore, you see the object right side up.

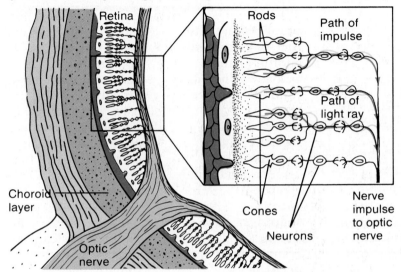

Figure 42.14 Light rays strike the rods and cones in the retina. Nerve impulses are then sent via the optic nerve to the brain.

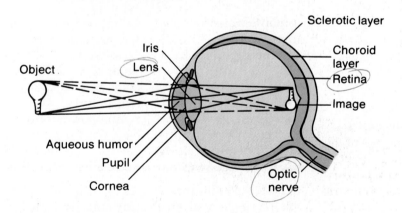

Figure 42.15 The image of an object focused on the retina is reversed. When visual impulses are interpreted by the brain, the image is reversed again.

Checkpoint

1. What five types of receptors are located in the skin?
2. In which structures are the taste receptors located?
3. What are the two chemical senses?
4. What structure is located between the outer and middle ear?
5. Which visual receptors work best in dim light?

CHAPTER REVIEW

Summary

- Neurons are the basic units of structure and function in the nervous system. Nerve impulses travel along the neuron. A signal must then cross a synapse.

- A nerve impulse is generated when stimulation reverses the polarity of the neuron's cell membrane.

- The central nervous system includes the brain and spinal cord. The peripheral nervous system contains all the nerves outside the central nervous system.

- The cerebral cortex controls many functions associated with intelligence. Different areas of the cerebrum govern different functions in the body.

- The cerebellum coordinates the movement of skeletal muscles. The thalamus screens incoming impulses and directs them to the appropriate part of the cerebral cortex. The hypothalamus and medulla oblongata regulate various behaviors and processes.

- The spinal cord is the path through which information passes between the brain and the other parts of the body. Much reflex behavior is controlled by the spinal cord.

- The somatic nervous system activates the striated muscles. The autonomic nervous system governs the glands, smooth muscle, and cardiac muscle. The sympathetic part of the autonomic nervous system is dominant in crisis situations. The parasympathetic system functions under normal conditions.

- Receptors in the skin respond to touch, pain, pressure, heat, and cold.

- Taste and smell are chemical senses.

- Sound waves pass their vibrations on to a series of structures in the ear. Stimulation of receptors causes impulses that go to the brain.

- Motion is sensed by receptors in the semicircular canals of the inner ear.

- Structures in the eye focus light on the retina. When light strikes vision receptors, impulses are sent to the brain.

Vocabulary

acetylcholine (ACh)	motor neuron
acetylcholinesterase	nerve
auditory canal	neuron
autonomic nervous	neurotransmitter
system	oval window
axon	parasympathetic
central nervous	nervous system
system	peripheral nervous
cerebellum	system
cerebrospinal fluid	pupil
cerebrum	reflex
cochlea	retina
cone	rod
cornea	semicircular canals
cranial nerve	sensory neuron
dendrite	somatic nervous
ganglia	system
hypothalamus	spinal nerve
impulse	sympathetic nervous
interneuron	system
iris	synapse
lens	taste bud
medulla oblongata	thalamus
meninges	tympanic membrane

Review

1. Identify the three types of neurons.
2. During a neuron's resting state, how do the charges inside and outside the membrane compare?
3. Identify the structures with which a neuron may synapse.
4. Which structure in the central nervous system is associated with creativity?
5. Which brain structure screens stimuli that reach the cerebrum?

6. Which parts of the body are controlled by the autonomic nervous system?
7. What does the somatic nervous system control?
8. What part of the brain controls heartbeat rate and breathing?
9. What parts of the eye bend incoming light rays?
10. How is your sense of taste related to your sense of smell?

Interpret and Apply

1. Distinguish between the functions of sensory and motor neurons.
2. What is the difference in function between acetylcholine and acetylcholinesterase?
3. Which branch of your autonomic nervous system is active when you are doing each of the following?
   a. competing in a swimming race
   b. sleeping peacefully
   c. putting out a grease fire in your kitchen
4. Describe the process by which a nerve impulse begins and travels along the neuron.
5. In the process of hearing, all the following structures are set to vibrating. Write them in the order in which they begin to vibrate.

   a. oval window
   b. anvil
   c. cochlear fluid
   d. tympanic membrane
   e. stirrup
   f. hammer

6. There are only a limited number of different taste receptors, yet humans can sense a great variety of tastes. Explain.
7. You blow a breath of air over your skin, and you feel the moving air. Which type or types of receptors will pick up this sensation?
8. In the process of vision, light passes through some, but not all, of the following structures. Which of the following structures does light pass through?

   a. retina
   b. cornea
   c. iris muscles
   d. lens
   e. optic nerve
   f. pupil

9. How does a nerve impulse cross a synapse to another neuron?
10. You accidentally touch a hot iron. You quickly move your hand away from the iron.
    a. What is the name for this type of action?
    b. Do you feel pain before you pull your hand away?
    c. Describe what happens in the central nervous system to allow you to react so quickly.
11. How is the resting membrane potential restored after a nerve impulse has passed?
12. You lift a cup off a table. Which type of nerve cell — sensory neuron, motor neuron, or interneuron — activated the muscles in your arm?

Challenge

1. What would happen if a muscle cell lacked ACh receptors? What would happen if it lacked AChE?
2. You feel hungry and remember that there are apples in the fruit bowl. You remove an apple from the bowl and eat it.
   a. Identify the part of the brain that directs each of the following actions or feelings: feeling of hunger; memory of where you put the apples; movement of arm muscles.
   b. Describe the paths of the nerve impulses involved in the following: seeing the apple in the bowl; moving your arm to pick up the apple.

Projects

1. Scientists have become very interested in the hemispheres of the brain and the functions each side seems to be specialized to perform. Use library resources to learn more about this topic.
2. Electronic devices have been developed that can enable some deaf people to hear. Do library research to learn more about these devices.

43 Chemical Regulators

The hormone adrenaline enables these fire fighters to act speedily in a crisis.

Five minutes ago, these fire fighters were sleeping peacefully. Suddenly, the alarm sounded. The fire fighters immediately sprang into action. Within 30 seconds, they were dressed. Within 1 minute, the fire fighters were on the huge truck, roaring out of the firehouse on the way to the fire. Now they are about to rescue people from inside the burning building. They must move quickly. Lost time could mean lost lives.

How can fire fighters work so speedily and efficiently? Part of the answer lies in changes that take place in the body during an emergency. The heart pumps faster. Extra blood rushes to muscles and the brain. Stored glucose is released, giving cells more energy. All of these changes allow the body to work extra hard.

The endocrine system plays a part in these changes. By means of chemicals called hormones, the endocrine system regulates the actions of various parts of the body. In a crisis, hormones switch the body into high gear. The body responds with strength and speed.

The Endocrine System

The endocrine system produces chemicals called **hormones**. By affecting certain cells, hormones regulate processes such as growth, development, metabolism, and response to crises. Hormones are secreted by **endocrine** [EHN-duh-kruhn] **glands**. The major endocrine glands of the human body are shown in Figure 43.1. Each will be discussed later.

You have already learned about other types of glands, such as salivary glands. Salivary glands have ducts, or tubes, through which saliva travels into the mouth. In contrast, endocrine glands are ductless. Hormones are secreted from endocrine glands directly into the bloodstream. In the blood they can travel to distant parts of the body. For example, a hormone produced by a gland in the head may act on cells in the feet.

The endocrine and nervous systems both regulate parts of

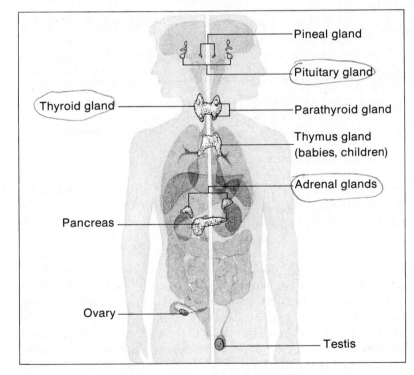

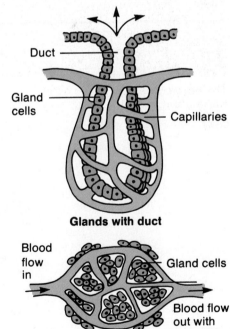

Figure 43.1 The glands of the endocrine system

Figure 43.2 Secretions from glands with ducts move through tubes. Secretions from endocrine glands are released into the bloodstream.

the body. However, there are important differences between the two. Neurons extend to the structures they control. But endocrine glands may be far from the cells they affect. Each neuron goes to only one specific structure. Hormones, in contrast, are carried throughout the body. In general, the body responds more quickly to nerve impulses than to hormones.

43–1   How Hormones Work

Each hormone comes into contact with many kinds of cells. However, only specific types of cells, or **target cells**, respond to each particular hormone.

Among the molecules on cell membranes are proteins called receptors. Each type of cell has its own kinds of receptors. A specific hormone can bind only to particular types of receptors. When hormone molecules reach a cell, they bind to the cell if the appropriate receptors are on the membrane.

The binding of some types of hormones to the cell membrane causes **cyclic AMP**, a chemical within the cell, to increase. Cyclic AMP acts as a messenger, causing the cell to produce enzymes. These enzymes catalyze chemical reactions. Each type of cell has specific chemical reactions that are set in motion by a rise in cyclic AMP.

Other types of hormones enter the cell and move into the nucleus. There they may activate genes that were inactive before. The newly active genes direct changes in the chemistry of the cell.

Prostaglandins [prahs-tuh-GLAN-duhnz] appear to play a role in some kinds of hormone action. Prostaglandins are chemicals produced by many body tissues. Like cyclic AMP, prostaglandins are thought to be messengers for hormones. They may affect the production of cyclic AMP. Scientists do not yet clearly understand the functions of all prostaglandins.

43–2   The Thyroid and Parathyroid Glands

The **thyroid gland** is an H-shaped gland located in the neck, as shown in Figure 43.1. The thyroid lies over the top part of the trachea. It produces a hormone called **thyroxine** [thy-RAHK-sihn], which regulates the rate of the body's metabolism. In most cells, thyroxine controls the rate at which glucose is oxidized.

If there is an excess of thyroxine, a condition called **hyperthyroidism** results. The metabolic rate rises. This makes the heartbeat rate, blood pressure, and body temperature rise. People with this condition may sweat heavily, become nervous, and develop bulging eyes. Hyperthyroidism can be treated with drugs that reduce thyroxine secretion. Another treatment for hyperthyroidism consists of surgically removing part of the thyroid gland.

A deficiency of thyroxine is called **hypothyroidism**. People with this condition have a lower metabolic rate than normal. They usually lack energy and may be overweight. If hypothyroidism occurs early in childhood, it can cause stunted growth and severe mental retardation. This condition is called **cretinism**. Hypothyroidism may be corrected, although not cured, with injections of thyroxine.

Thyroxine contains much iodine. If a person's diet does not have enough iodine, the thyroid gland becomes enlarged. This condition is called goiter. Goiter can be prevented by adding iodine to the diet in the form of iodized salt.

The **parathyroid glands** are four small glands on the posterior surface of the thyroid. Only eight millimeters long, they are the smallest endocrine glands. The parathyroids produce **parathyroid hormone**. This hormone regulates the levels of calcium and phosphate ions in the blood. Bones, muscles, and nerves need these ions to grow and function properly.

Do You Know?
The thyroid gland contains half the iodine in the body.

Figure 43.3 Eating seafood, which is a source of iodine, can prevent goiter.

43–3   The Adrenal Glands

An **adrenal gland** is located above each kidney. Each gland consists of two separate parts, the cortex and the medulla. The adrenal cortex, or outer portion, produces **corticoid hormones**. Some of these hormones maintain water and salt balance by regulating the absorption of those substances in the kidney tubules. Other corticoids direct the conversion of proteins to glucose. This helps maintain the proper level of sugar in the blood.

The adrenal medulla secretes **adrenaline** [uh-DREHN-l-uhn], also called epinephrine. Extreme fear, anger, pain, or cold will stimulate the adrenal medulla to produce a lot of adrenaline. Adrenaline causes widening of blood vessels in the liver, heart, and skeletal muscles. It makes the blood pressure and rate of respiration rise. It promotes the conversion of glycogen to glucose, making more energy available. The body's responses to adrenaline prepare a person either to fight danger or to flee it. Therefore, they are known as the fight-or-flight response.

43–4   The Islets of Langerhans

As you learned in Chapter 38, the pancreas secretes digestive enzymes into the digestive tract through ducts. But the pancreas is also a ductless gland. Endocrine cells are found throughout the pancreas in areas known as the **islets** [EYE-luhtz] **of Langerhans** [LANG-uhr-hans]. Different types of islet cells secrete two hormones into the bloodstream. One is **glucagon**, which converts glycogen to glucose when the concentration of glucose in the blood is low. The other hormone, **insulin**, promotes the uptake of glucose by cells and its conversion to glycogen. Glycogen is stored in the liver.

Some people's bodies do not produce enough insulin. A condition called diabetes mellitus results. Glucose accumulates in the blood and is excreted in the urine. More than the normal amount of water is excreted along with the glucose. This excessive urination, in turn, causes excessive thirst. If diabetes goes untreated for too long, coma and death may result.

Most diabetics can be treated with injections of insulin. The insulin is usually obtained from animals. However, human insulin can now be produced by the recombinant-DNA methods described in Chapter 12. In the future, most insulin used by diabetics may come from recombinant DNA.

If too much insulin is taken, insulin shock may result. The level of glucose in the blood becomes very low. As a result, the brain does not receive enough glucose to function properly. Diabetics receiving insulin treatment must carry sugary foods to eat in case insulin shock occurs.

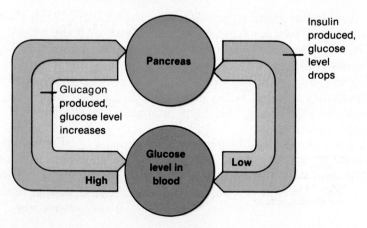

Figure 43.4 When glucose concentration in the blood increases, the pancreas produces insulin, which lowers the glucose level.

43-5 The Gonads

The **gonads** produce large amounts of sex hormones. The **ovaries** are the female gonads. The **testes** are the male gonads.

The **ovaries** produce hormones called **estrogens** [EHS-truh-juhnz], which cause the development of secondary sex characteristics. These characteristics develop during **puberty**, which occurs in the early teenage years. At this time a girl's breasts enlarge due to the development of the mammary glands. Her hips widen, she acquires an additional layer of body fat, and additional body hair. Estrogens also cause the beginning of the menstrual cycle, which is discussed in Chapter 45.

The testes produce male sex hormones, or androgens. One androgen is **testosterone** [teh-STAHS-tuh-rohn], which causes the development of male secondary sex characteristics at puberty. A boy's voice deepens and there is an increase in the growth of body hair. A rapid spurt of skeletal growth takes place.

43-6 The Pituitary Gland

The **pituitary** [puh-TOO-uh-tehr-ee] **gland** is located at the base of the brain. Both nerves and blood vessels connect the pituitary to the hypothalamus. Some pituitary hormones directly affect parts of the body. In addition, pituitary hormones determine when certain other endocrine glands release their secretions.

The pituitary gland has anterior and posterior sections. The posterior pituitary stores and releases two hormones that are produced in the hypothalamus. One of these is **oxytocin**. The other is **antidiuretic hormone**, or ADH, which is also known as vasopressin. Oxytocin causes contraction of the uterine muscles during childbirth. It also promotes the flow of milk from the mammary glands. ADH regulates the reabsorption of water in the kidney tubules. If a person does not

Do You Know?
The pituitary gland lies in a tiny pocket of the cranium called the sella turcica, meaning "Turkish saddle."

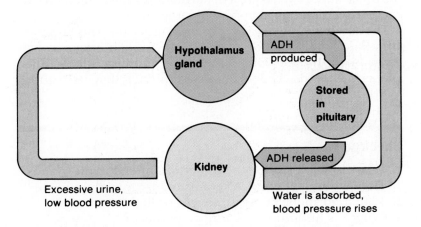

Figure 43.5 The pituitary stores and releases ADH, which is produced by the hypothalamus. ADH regulates water reabsorption and blood pressure.

Figure 43.6 An overproduction of growth hormone during childhood can result in a condition called gigantism. Dwarfism can result from the underproduction of growth hormone during childhood.

have enough ADH, much water is not reabsorbed. As a consequence, the kidneys produce an abnormally large volume of urine. ADH also regulates blood pressure by making muscles in the walls of arterioles contract.

The anterior pituitary produces **growth hormone**, which controls the growth of bones. If a child is deficient in growth hormone, extreme shortness, or dwarfism, may result. On the other hand, excess growth hormone during childhood can cause gigantism, or abnormally large stature.

The anterior pituitary also produces **prolactin**. This hormone stimulates the secretion of milk in a woman after she has given birth. In addition, the anterior pituitary affects other endocrine glands. This is discussed in the following section.

Checkpoint

1. What is the term for the secretions of endocrine glands?
2. How is the metabolic rate affected by hypothyroidism?
3. Which hormone causes the fight-or-flight response?
4. Where is antidiuretic hormone produced?

Regulation of Hormone Secretion

The body needs each hormone at some times, but not at others. An endocrine gland does not release hormones continuously. Certain signals within the body tell each endocrine gland to begin secreting hormones. Other signals stop hormone secretion. The pituitary gland is involved in many of these control mechanisms. The central nervous system is involved in others.

CONCEPTS
- functions of pituitary tropic hormones
- hormone regulation by negative feedback
- how the nervous and endocrine systems work together

43–7 Tropic Hormones and Negative Feedback

Several tropic hormones are produced by the anterior pituitary. A **tropic** [TROH-pihk] **hormone** influences the secretory activity of a specific gland. Thyrotropic hormone, for example, causes the thyroid gland to secrete thyroxine. The level of adrenocorticotropic hormone, or ACTH, determines the amount of corticoids the adrenal glands secrete. Gonadotropic hormones control the production of sex hormones by the ovaries and testes.

In a healthy person, the concentration of each hormone remains within a narrow and definite range. This is the result of negative feedback. A **negative-feedback system** is a cycle of actions in which the final event inhibits the first event. For example, an increase in substance A causes an increase in substance B. But the increase in substance B causes a decrease in substance A. So A controls the level of B, and B controls the level of A.

The relationship between ACTH and the corticoid hormones shows how negative feedback works. ACTH causes the secretion of corticoids by the adrenal cortex. High levels of corticoids inhibit the pituitary's production of ACTH. This negative-feedback system prevents the levels of corticoids from becoming too high.

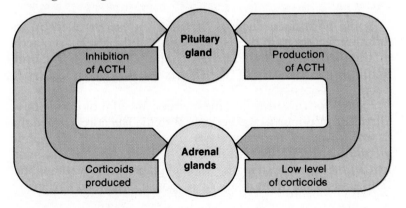

Figure 43.7 In this negative feedback system, the secretion of corticoids prevents the production of ACTH.

43–8 Interaction of the Nervous and Endocrine Systems

The endocrine and nervous systems both regulate body processes. If these systems functioned independently of one another, confusion would reign. The hypothalamus is a link between the two systems. For example, neurons from the hypothalamus communicate with the posterior pituitary. If blood is flowing at a reduced volume, the hypothalamus sends a nerve impulse to the posterior pituitary. The pituitary then secretes ADH, which causes the blood pressure to rise.

The hypothalamus also communicates with the anterior pituitary by chemical means. Certain hormones from the hypothalamus are called **releasing factors**. They stimulate the pituitary to secrete specific hormones. For example, suppose that the level of growth hormone is too low. The hypothalamus then secretes a hormone called growth-hormone releasing factor, or GHRF. When GHRF reaches the anterior pituitary, it causes the secretion of growth hormone. Figure 43.8 diagrams this process. The hypothalamus secretes releasing factors for most pituitary hormones.

> ### BIOLOGY INSIGHTS
>
> The control of most body processes is ultimately based upon a system of negative feedback. Without negative-feedback systems, the human body could not achieve homeostasis.

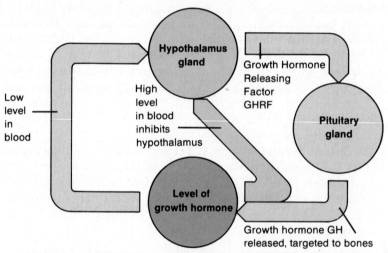

Figure 43.8 The hypothalamus produces a growth-hormone releasing factor, which stimulates the pituitary to secrete growth hormone.

Some hormones, such as prolactin, are controlled by **inhibiting factors** from the hypothalamus. If the level of prolactin in the blood is too high, the hypothalamus secretes prolactin-inhibiting factor, or PIF. PIF causes the anterior pituitary to secrete less prolactin.

Except for the pituitary, most endocrine glands do not have direct connections to the nervous system. The adrenal medulla is an exception. It receives direct input from the autonomic nervous system. When stimulated by the neurons of the sympathetic nervous system, the adrenal glands secrete adrenaline. This causes the fight-or-flight response described earlier.

Gland	Hormone	Function
Pituitary anterior lobe	Growth hormone Gonadotropic hormone ACTH Prolactin TSH	Regulates growth of bones Influences the development of sex organs and the production of hormones by the ovaries and testes Stimulates secretion of the adrenal cortex hormones Stimulates secretion of milk by the mammary glands Stimulates activity of the thyroid gland
Hypothalamus (hormones released by the anterior lobe of the pituitary)	Oxytocin ADH	Regulates blood pressure and stimulates smooth muscles Controls water absorption in the kidneys
Thyroid	Thyroxin Calcitonin	Accelerates metabolic rate Inhibits the release of calcium from bone
Parathyroids	Parathyroid hormone	Stimulates the release of calcium from bone; promotes calcium absorption by digestive tract
Adrenal cortex medulla	Corticoids Adrenaline	Regulates metabolism, salt, and water balance; controls the production of certain blood cells; influences the structure of connective tissue Causes constriction of blood vessels; increases heart action; stimulates the liver and nervous system
Pancreas	Glucagon Insulin	Stimulates the breakdown of glycogen in the liver Controls sugar storage in the liver and sugar break- down in tissues
Ovaries follicular cells	Estrogens Progesterone	Produces female secondary sex characteristics; begins growth of the uterine lining; affects adult female body functions Maintains growth of the uterine lining
Testes interstitial cells	Testosterone	Produces male secondary sex characteristics

Figure 43.9 Major hormones of some endocrine glands

Checkpoint

1. What is the term for a hormone that influences the activity of a specific gland?
2. In a negative-feedback cycle, what effect does the final action have on the first event?
3. What hormone causes the pituitary to release growth hormone?
4. What structure in the central nervous system secretes releasing factors?

CHAPTER REVIEW

Summary

- Endocrine glands are ductless. They secrete hormones that diffuse into the blood. Each hormone affects only specific types of cells. Hormones cause a series of chemical reactions within target cells.
- The thyroid gland produces the hormone thyroxine, which regulates metabolic rate.
- The parathyroid glands secrete parathyroid hormone. This hormone regulates the levels of calcium and phosphate ions in the blood.
- The adrenal cortex secretes corticoid hormones. Some corticoids regulate the absorption of water and salt in the kidney tubules. Other corticoids direct the conversion of proteins to glucose. The adrenal medulla secretes adrenaline, which prepares the body to deal with emergency situations.
- The islets of Langerhans in the pancreas secrete glucagon and insulin, which regulate the amount of glucose in the blood.
- The ovaries produce estrogen, and the testes produce testosterone. These hormones cause the development of the secondary sex characteristics.
- Oxytocin and antidiuretic hormone are both produced in the hypothalamus and stored in the pituitary. Oxytocin causes the uterus to contract during labor. ADH regulates the reabsorption of water in the kidneys. The anterior pituitary produces growth hormone, which regulates body growth.
- Various tropic hormones are produced by the anterior pituitary. These regulate other endocrine glands.
- Concentrations of hormones are regulated by negative-feedback systems.
- The hypothalamus is a link between the nervous and endocrine systems.

Vocabulary

adrenal gland
adrenaline
antidiuretic
 hormone
corticoid hormone
cretinism
cyclic AMP
endocrine gland
estrogen
glucagon
gonad
growth hormone
hormone
hyperthyroidism
hypothyroidism
inhibiting factors
insulin
islets of Langerhans

negative-feedback
 system
ovary
oxytocin
parathyroid gland
parathyroid
 hormone
pituitary gland
prolactin
prostaglandin
puberty
releasing factors
target cell
testis
testosterone
thyroid gland
thyroxine
tropic hormone

Review

In questions 1–8, match the hormone in the left column with the gland that produces or releases it in the right. Some glands produce more than one hormone.

1. insulin
2. glucagon
3. growth hormone
4. adrenaline
5. corticoids
6. oxytocin
7. ADH
8. thyroxine

a. pancreas
b. thyroid
c. anterior pituitary
d. posterior pituitary
e. adrenal cortex
f. adrenal medulla

9. What hormonal condition causes a person to become excessively tall?
10. What is meant by the term *fight-or-flight response*?
11. What causes goiter to develop?
12. What is responsible for the growth of a boy's beard during adolescence?

13. Which chemical stimulates the anterior pituitary to secrete growth hormone?
14. What characteristic distinguishes endocrine glands from other types of glands?
15. If the amount of thyroxine in the body decreases, what happens to the rate of metabolism?
16. What is the treatment for diabetes?
17. What happens when the pituitary does not produce enough ADH?
18. What is the function of a releasing factor?

Interpret and Apply

1. Identify two hormonal conditions that can prevent a person from growing to a normal height.
2. The secretions of endocrine glands can affect distant tissues. The secretions of glands with ducts, however, generally affect only nearby tissues. What accounts for this difference in effect?
3. Compare the actions of insulin and glucagon.
4. Explain how negative feedback works.
5. What is the role of cyclic AMP in hormone function?
6. What feature enables a hormone to "recognize" its target cells?
7. During childbirth, women are sometimes given injections of oxytocin. How do you think these injections affect the process of labor?
8. The pituitary has sometimes been called the master gland. Why?
9. Explain how the nervous and endocrine systems work together when the body responds to a dangerous situation.
10. What parts of the body would be affected by a deficiency in parathyroid hormones?
11. If the pituitary gland could not function, would the secondary sex characteristics develop? Explain.
12. How does the hypothalamus control blood pressure?
13. Different hormones can have similar functions. What two hormones directly affect the absorption of water in the kidneys?

14. Suppose the level of corticoids in the blood increases. How would you expect this to affect the pituitary's secretion of ACTH?

Challenge

1. In some of its functions, the hypothalamus seems to be part of the nervous system. In other functions, it seems to act as an endocrine gland. Explain.
2. Explain how the concept of negative feedback applies to the production of prolactin and PIF.
3. Which of the following situations is an example of negative feedback?
   a. An art student enters a painting in a competition. The painting wins a prize. This inspires the student to paint more pictures.
   b. The heat goes on inside a room. Once the air in the room reaches a certain temperature, the thermostat turns the heat off.
4. Why must insulin be taken by injection rather than by mouth? (Hint: Insulin is a protein.)
5. A person can live without the adrenal medulla but cannot survive without the adrenal cortex. Why do you think this is true?

Projects

1. Diabetes insipidus is a condition caused by an abnormally low level of antidiuretic hormone (vasopressin). Learn the symptoms of this disease. Find out how diabetes insipidus differs from diabetes mellitus in cause and treatment.
2. Learn how prostaglandins function in the perception of pain. Find out how aspirin is believed to affect prostaglandins.
3. Hormones have several types of molecular structures. Consult biochemistry references and diagram the molecular structures of different hormones.
4. Hypoglycemia is a condition related to hormones. Learn the nature of this condition and how it is treated.

44 Tobacco and Drugs

Opium poppies

Bright-colored poppies grow wild in many parts of the world. The kind of poppy shown here, though, is specially cultivated. Its seedpods release a milky, white juice. When dried and refined, this juice becomes the drug opium.

Since ancient times, opium has been used to relieve pain. In the *Odyssey*, the Greek poet Homer mentions that opium can ease sorrow. But people who lived long ago did not understand one important thing about opium: It is addictive. That is, a person can become physically dependent on opium. This physical dependence creates severe health and behavior problems.

Today, several drugs are obtained from the opium poppy. Some of these are painkillers. When used properly, they can relieve a toothache or make cancer easier to bear. However, all drugs derived from opium can cause addiction. One of these, heroin, is so addictive that its use is banned in the United States.

All drugs have disadvantages as well as benefits. Before they are used, their risks must be carefully considered.

Tobacco and Its Effects

It is wise to consider the consequences of smoking before you start. Careful research indicates that cigarette smoking is the chief preventable cause of illness and early death in the United States. In 1971, a law was passed prohibiting the advertising of cigarettes on radio and television. In addition, every cigarette package must contain a warning about smoking's health hazards. Yet Americans smoke 600 billion cigarettes each year.

Heavy smokers have a strong emotional need for cigarettes. This type of need is called **psychological dependence**. In contrast, a **physical dependence** exists if a person's body suffers physical problems when a drug is withdrawn. Heavy smokers develop a physical dependence on **nicotine**, a chemical in tobacco.

44-1 The Effects of Smoking

Cigarette smoke consists of gases and tiny particles. These substances harm the cilia and mucous membranes that line the breathing passages. Many smokers cough frequently. The cough is the body's effort to clear the breathing passages. Healthy cilia and mucous membranes accomplish the cleaning process automatically.

Smoke also damages the lungs. Long-term smoking can cause the walls of the alveoli to rupture, or break. As a result, the surface area for gas exchange decreases considerably, as shown in Figure 44.1. This condition, called **emphysema** [ehm-fuh-ZEE-muh], interferes with oxygen intake. Death may eventually result.

Figure 44.1 The alveoli in normal lung tissue are small. Heavy smoking ruptures alveoli, decreasing surface area for gas exchange.

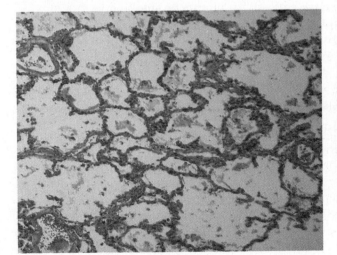
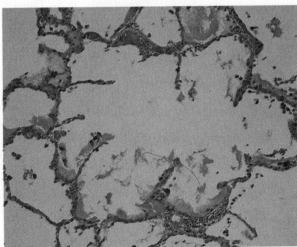

The best known result of heavy smoking is lung cancer. Chemicals in the smoke cause changes within the cells of the lungs. These changes may lead to cancer. Death from lung cancer is about ten times more frequent for smokers than for nonsmokers.

In the lungs, nicotine passes into the bloodstream. In the blood, nicotine travels to all parts of the body. Nicotine causes the blood vessels to constrict, or become narrow. When blood has to move through narrower vessels, blood pressure goes up. This puts the smoker at high risk for such problems as strokes and heart attacks. Cigarette smoking is also a factor in coronary-artery disease and arteriosclerosis.

The respiratory and circulatory systems are not the only parts of the body harmed by smoking. Cigarette smoking has been associated with ulcers in the digestive tract. Cancers of the larynx, mouth, esophagus, bladder, and pancreas have also been linked to smoking.

44-2 Factors Affecting Smoking Risks

Several factors influence the effects of smoking. The more cigarettes a person smokes, the higher the risk of tobacco-related disease. The longer a person has smoked, the greater the risk. Cigarette brands high in tars are somewhat more harmful than low-tar cigarettes. (Tars are certain irritating materials found in tobacco smoke.)

Research indicates that smoke from other people's cigarettes affects nonsmokers. A nonsmoker who spends the working day in a smoke-filled room suffers health risks. These risks are similar to those of a person who smokes about ten cigarettes a day. This discovery has stimulated a campaign by non-smokers to limit smoking in public places.

The damage caused by cigarette smoking is not always permanent. If a person stops smoking, the lungs may return to a healthier, more normal condition. However, recovery may take a long time.

Figure 44.2 Cigarette smoke can affect nonsmokers. Public areas now provide areas where smoking is not permitted.

Checkpoint

1. What chemical in tobacco causes physical dependence?
2. How does cigarette smoke affect the breathing passages?
3. What is the name of the condition in which the walls of the alveoli break?
4. How does nicotine affect blood vessels?
5. What usually happens to the lungs after a smoker gives up cigarettes?

Alcohol and Other Abused Drugs

A **drug** is a chemical substance that alters the functioning of the mind or body. Many drugs, such as antibiotics, save lives and prevent suffering. But the use of drugs is not always a good thing. When a drug interferes with a person's health or social relationships, the person is abusing the drug.

Drugs can be divided into two groups on the basis of their source. Natural drugs, such as alcohol, are obtained from living organisms. Synthetic drugs, such as amphetamines, are made in a laboratory.

44-3 Alcohol: Immediate Effects

Alcohol is the most commonly abused drug in society today. The alcohol in drinks is ethanol, C_2H_5OH. The alcohol molecule is quite small. Therefore, it enters the bloodstream quickly from the stomach, sometimes in less than two minutes. The liver metabolizes, or processes, alcohol. What happens if a person drinks more alcohol than the liver can process at one time? Some of the excess alcohol in the bloodstream is excreted by the kidneys. The lungs also excrete some, accounting for the characteristic breath of a person who has been drinking heavily. But most of the alcohol circulates in the blood until the liver can act on it.

It takes a 70-kilogram person about $1\frac{1}{2}$ hours to metabolize one typical drink, such as a can of beer. Therefore, if that person drinks more than one drink every $1\frac{1}{2}$ hours, the alcohol level in the blood will rise. The smaller the person, the slower that person metabolizes alcohol. If a person's blood alcohol level goes higher than a certain point, that person becomes intoxicated.

Alcohol affects just about every organ in the body. Alcohol is a **depressant** — a drug that slows the functioning of the nervous system. Alcohol first depresses the part of the brain that controls judgment and inhibitions. This loss of inhibition may make a person feel jolly and lively. However, it may also cause uncontrolled, unthinking behavior.

As the person drinks more, other parts of the brain become depressed. The speech and vision centers become dulled. This causes blurred vision and slurred speech. The part of the brain that controls voluntary muscles is affected next, causing a lack of coordination. Eventually, the person may lose consciousness. Figure 44.3 shows the areas of the brain affected by alcohol. Because of its effects on the brain, alcohol often plays a part in automobile accidents.

CONCEPTS
- effects of alcohol on the body
- problems associated with long-term drinking
- effects of certain natural and synthetic drugs

Do You Know?
Alcohol is produced when yeast cells convert sugar into carbon dioxide and alcohol during fermentation. Louis Pasteur discovered the process of fermentation in 1857.

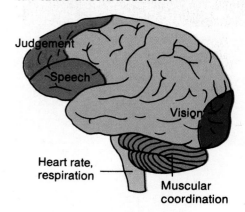

Figure 44.3 Alcohol progressively depresses different areas of the brain. Excessive amounts of alcohol can cause unconsciousness.

Judgement
Speech
Vision
Heart rate, respiration
Muscular coordination

44-4 Effects of Long-Term Drinking

Generally, people who drink only occasionally and moderately have no problem with alcohol use. But some people become physically and psychologically dependent on alcohol. This condition is the disease called **alcoholism**. Some scientists believe that a tendency toward alcoholism may be genetic. Because drinking affects behavior, alcoholics often lose their jobs. Relationships with family and friends may suffer.

Before alcoholics can be helped, they must admit their problem. Psychiatric counseling may be beneficial. Alcoholics Anonymous, a support group, has helped many people overcome drinking problems. Alcoholism can be controlled but not cured. Alcoholics cannot regulate the amount of alcohol they consume. Therefore, they must totally avoid drinking.

An alcoholic lives 12 years less than the average nonalcoholic. People who drink large amounts of alcohol over long periods risk many health problems. The esophagus, stomach, and intestine may become irritated. The pancreas and brain may be harmed. In addition, alcoholics often do not eat a properly balanced diet. Vitamin deficiencies may result. Poor nutrition may also lower the alcoholic's resistance to disease.

Cirrhosis of the liver is one possible effect of long-term drinking. Scar tissue gradually replaces healthy liver cells. The liver becomes less and less able to function. Eventually, cirrhosis can result in death.

An alcoholic may develop a severe mental condition called **alcohol psychosis** [sy-KOH-suhs]. Hallucination and serious memory failure are characteristic of alcohol psychosis. This condition may be caused partly by brain damage and partly by a deficiency of B vitamins.

44-5 Other Abused Drugs

Narcotics **Narcotics** are drugs that are often abused. Because these drugs are derived from the opium poppy, they are often called opiates. Morphine, codeine, and heroin are opiates. Like alcohol, narcotics are depressants.

All narcotics can create a strong physical dependence, or **addiction**, in the user. Codeine and morphine are sometimes prescribed for the relief of severe pain. These drugs must always be used with caution and under a doctor's direction. Heroin is so addictive that it is illegal in the United States.

Narcotics may cause euphoria, or an exaggerated feeling of well-being. After a period of use, a person develops a **tolerance** for a narcotic. This means that more of the drug is necessary to produce the same effect that a small amount once produced. Continued use results in an addiction.

The sale of narcotics is strictly controlled by law. Therefore,

Figure 44.4 A narcotic addict experiences withdrawal symptoms in trying to overcome the addiction. Drug-abuse clinics can help patients deal with the physical and emotional aspects of withdrawal.

an addict must break the law to obtain drugs. An addict's general health and personality are harmed by drug use.

If an addict stops taking narcotics, severe physical discomfort known as **withdrawal symptoms** occurs. Withdrawal symptoms include depression and loss of sleep. During withdrawal, an addict may have trouble breathing.

Marijuana Like narcotics, **marijuana** may cause euphoria. Marijuana comes from *Cannabis sativa*, a plant that seems to grow almost anywhere. Like alcohol, marijuana is a depressant and is associated with a high rate of automobile accidents. People can become emotionally dependent on marijuana; however, the drug does not cause physical dependence. The sale of marijuana is illegal in this country.

Research is being done on the long-term effects of marijuana use. Marijuana has been shown to lower sperm count. There is also evidence that marijuana smoke harms the lungs.

Cocaine **Cocaine** is another euphoria-producing drug. This drug is derived from coca plants that grow in the Andes Mountains. Cocaine probably does not cause physical dependence. However, people can become psychologically dependent on it. Cocaine is illegal except for restricted medical use.

Amphetamines **Amphetamines**, commonly known as speed or uppers, are synthetic drugs. They are **stimulants**, drugs that increase the activity of the nervous system. Many people use amphetamines in order to stay awake. Amphetamines depress the appetite, and are an ingredient in many diet pills. Amphetamines usually do not cause physical dependence but they may cause psychological dependence.

Barbiturates **Barbiturates** are also synthetic drugs. They are used as **tranquilizers**, drugs that reduce anxiety. Barbiturates are found in some sleeping pills. Prolonged use of barbiturates results in tolerance and physical dependence. Excessive use can cause brain damage and mental deterioration. Overdoses can be fatal.

Barbiturates, like many other drugs, have their proper uses. But like all drugs, they can be harmful if used improperly. The risks of all drugs should be weighed carefully against the benefits.

Figure 44.5 *Cannabis sativa*

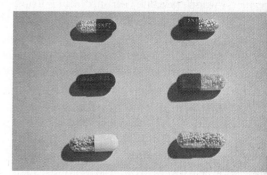

Figure 44.6 Amphetamines come in many forms.

Checkpoint

1. What is a drug?
2. Which part of the brain does alcohol affect first?
3. What is a depressant?
4. From what plant are narcotics derived?

CHAPTER REVIEW

Summary

- Heavy smokers develop both a psychological and a physical dependence on cigarettes.
- Cigarette smoke damages the breathing passages and the lungs. Cellular changes in the lungs can lead to lung cancer.
- Nicotine makes blood vessels constrict. This constriction can cause high blood pressure, stroke, and heart attack.
- The risks in cigarette smoking depend on the number of cigarettes smoked and the duration of the smoking habit. If a person stops smoking, the effects of smoking are usually reversible.
- A drug is a chemical that alters the functioning of the mind or body. Alcohol is the drug most commonly abused in the United States.
- Alcohol is a depressant. It affects judgment, vision, speech, and muscular control.
- Alcoholism is the physical and psychological dependence on alcohol. Long-term, heavy drinking may cause cirrhosis of the liver, nutritional deficiencies, and alcohol psychosis.
- Narcotics relieve pain and cause euphoria. Continued use leads to addiction. Morphine, codeine, and heroin are narcotics.
- Cocaine and marijuana are not physically addictive, but both can create a psychological dependence. Marijuana may harm the lungs and the male reproductive system.
- Amphetamines prevent drowsiness and curb the appetite. They can cause psychological dependence.
- Barbiturates are tranquilizers and sleep inducers. People can become physically dependent on barbiturates. Overdoses can be fatal.

Vocabulary

addiction
alcoholism
alcohol psychosis
amphetamine
barbiturate
cirrhosis of the liver
cocaine
depressant
drug
emphysema

marijuana
narcotics
nicotine
physical dependence
psychological dependence
stimulant
tolerance
tranquilizer
withdrawal symptoms

Review

Choose the answer that best completes each of the following questions. Write the letters of the answers on a separate sheet of paper.

1. The chief preventable cause of illness and early death in American society is (a) overeating, (b) smoking, (c) use of heroin, (d) use of tranquilizers.
2. Emphysema consists of damage to the (a) lungs, (b) nose, (c) liver, (d) brain.
3. Narcotics are produced (a) from alcohol, (b) from marijuana, (c) from the opium poppy, (d) in cigarette smoke.
4. Which of the following is *not* a risk associated with cigarette smoking? (a) cirrhosis of the liver (b) lung cancer (c) high blood pressure (d) heart attack
5. The plant *Cannabis sativa* is the source of (a) barbiturates, (b) tranquilizers, (c) marijuana, (d) all of these.
6. The chemical in cigarette smoke that can cause physical dependence is (a) tar, (b) carbon, (c) nicotine, (d) all of these.
7. Which of the following is *not* a natural drug? (a) marijuana (b) nicotine (c) cocaine (d) an amphetamine
8. Alcohol is metabolized in the (a) stomach, (b) lungs, (c) kidneys, (d) liver.

9. Which of the following does not normally create a physical dependence in the user? (a) amphetamines (b) barbiturates (c) cigarettes (d) alcohol
10. Which of the following is not a risk associated with marijuana use? (a) lung damage (b) physical dependence (c) psychological dependence (d) lowered sperm count
11. Automobile drivers who have been drinking alcohol (a) are usually very careful, (b) drive less well than they would if they had not been drinking, (c) are rarely involved in accidents, (d) never take risks while driving.
12. Prolonged use of alcohol can result in (a) dietary deficiencies, (b) cirrhosis of the liver, (c) irritation of the stomach, (d) all of these.
13. The use of which of the following drugs is illegal in the United States? (a) alcohol, (b) nicotine, (c) heroin, (d) morphine.
14. A drug that reduces anxiety is called a (a) stimulant, (b) depressant, (c) psychosis, (d) tranquilizer.

Interpret and Apply

1. Explain the difference between physical and psychological drug dependence.
2. In what ways are the effects of marijuana similar to those of narcotics? How are the effects of marijuana different from those of narcotics?
3. Morphine, codeine, and heroin all relieve pain. Morphine and codeine may be prescribed for pain relief, but use of heroin is totally illegal. Explain.
4. Explain the difference between a stimulant and a depressant.
5. Suppose you are trying to convince a friend not to start smoking. List at least three arguments you would use.
6. Explain how emphysema interferes with the exchange of gases in the lungs.
7. Why is it more difficult to stop using heroin than to stop using cocaine once a drug habit is established?

8. Describe the symptoms of withdrawal from a narcotic.
9. Explain why many smokers cough frequently.
10. What characteristic of the alcohol molecule allows it to be absorbed into the bloodstream so quickly?
11. Why does the breath of heavy drinkers have a characteristic odor?
12. Alcohol is a depressant, yet intoxicated people often seem lively and uninhibited. Explain why this happens.

Challenge

1. A person with a mass of 70 kilograms and one with a mass of 100 kilograms each drink alcohol at the same rate. Which person will become intoxicated faster? Explain.
2. How do you think the incidence of lung cancer and emphysema in an area having heavily polluted air compares to the incidence in a location having clean air? Explain.

Projects

1. Find information about Alcoholics Anonymous. Learn how the organization was founded, how it works, and what its objectives are. You might want to focus on Alateen, a group within Alcoholics Anonymous that helps teenage children of alcoholic parents.
2. One controversial way of treating heroin addicts is to substitute the drug methadone for heroin. What are the advantages and disadvantages of this method of treatment?
3. Many familiar foods, such as coffee, tea, soft drinks, and chocolate, contain the stimulant drug caffeine. Scientists are learning that caffeine is probably not as harmless as it was once thought to be. Use library materials to learn about recent scientific findings related to caffeine.
4. Hypnosis and acupuncture are sometimes used as alternatives to drugs in relieving pain. Learn how each of these methods is believed to work.

45 Human Reproduction

Similarities exist among family members due to the inheritance of genes.

"Which came first, the chicken or the egg?" That old riddle is quite impossible to solve. There must be chickens before there can be eggs, and there must be eggs before there can be chickens. Each is necessary for the other's existence.

Scientists who study the reproduction and development of organisms are called embryologists. Embryologists have a favorite saying, "The hen is the egg's way of making another egg." This saying conveys the idea that reproduction is an extremely important event in life. Without reproduction a species would die out.

Humans reproduce sexually. Because of this, each human child inherits genes from two different parents. The child is not, however, exactly like either parent. Consider the family shown here. You may notice ways in which some family members resemble each other. It is clear, though, that each of these people is unique.

All humans owe their existence to the chance union of a tiny egg with an even tinier sperm. The embryo grows and develops in its mother's body. After about 280 days, the embryo has become a baby who is ready to be born.

The Male and Female Reproductive Systems

Most human organs and organ systems are similar in the male and female. For example, only a trained eye could distinguish the thigh bone of a man from that of a woman. The structures of the male and female reproductive systems, however, are quite different, and so are their functions.

45–1 The Male Reproductive System

The gonads are reproductive organs. The male gonads are the testes, which have two functions. As you learned in Chapter 43, the testes produce male sex hormones, one of which is testosterone. They also produce gametes called **sperm**.

The testes are located in a pouch called the **scrotum**. The scrotum, which hangs outside the body cavity, is cooled by the outside air. The temperature inside the scrotum is 1.5 Celsius degrees lower than within the body cavity. Sperm need this slightly lower temperature for development.

Before a boy is born, his testes develop within his abdominal cavity. Several weeks before birth, the testes normally descend into the scrotum. Testes that fail to descend usually do not produce sperm.

CONCEPTS

- structure of the testes
- production of sperm
- structure of the female reproductive system
- ovulation and the menstrual cycle

Figure 45.1 The structural features of the male reproductive system

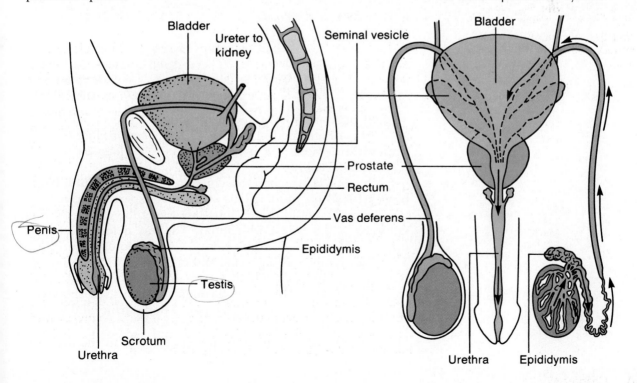

Bladder
Ureter to kidney
Seminal vesicle
Prostate
Rectum
Vas deferens
Epididymis
Penis
Testis
Scrotum
Urethra

Bladder
Urethra
Epididymis

At puberty, the testes begin to produce high levels of testosterone. The testosterone influences the testes to produce sperm by the process of meiosis. Remember from Chapter 9 that meiosis results in haploid gametes. That is, gametes have only half the number of chromosomes contained in the body cells. Human body cells contain 46 chromosomes. The gametes contain 23.

The testes contain many diploid sperm-producing cells. During sperm formation, these develop into **primary spermatocytes** [spuhr-MAT-uh-syts]. The primary spermatocytes undergo the first meiotic division. During this division, each primary spermatocyte divides into 2 **secondary spermatocytes**. In the second meiotic division, each secondary spermatocyte divides into 2 haploid cells. Each of these cells develops a flagellum and becomes a sperm cell.

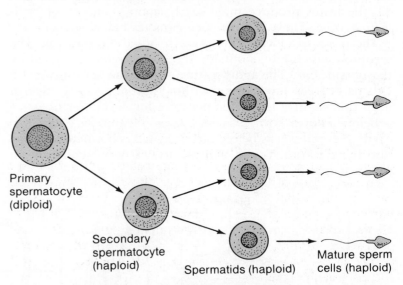

Figure 45.2 The cell division processes that produce sperm

Primary spermatocyte (diploid)

Secondary spermatocyte (haploid)

Spermatids (haploid)

Mature sperm cells (haploid)

Each primary spermatocyte produces 4 sperm cells. This process is diagramed in Figure 45.2. Sperm production continues throughout the life of the male, as long as enough testosterone is present.

Each testis is attached to a coiled tube called an **epididymis** [ep-uh-DIHD-uh-muhs]. This tube stores sperm produced in the testis. The epididymis joins another tube called the **vas deferens** [vahs DEHF-uh-ruhnz]. The vas deferens extends upward into the abdominal cavity, where it joins the urethra. The epididymis, vas deferens, and urethra form a continuous passageway through which sperm travel. The urethra goes to the outside of the body through the penis, as shown in Figure 45.1 on the preceding page. Both urine and sperm leave the body through the urethra.

As sperm cells travel from the epididymis to the urethra,

several glands add secretions, which together are known as seminal fluid. The seminal fluid carries the sperm and lubricates the passages through which sperm travel. It also gives the sperm chemical protection from the acids in urine and in the female reproductive tract. In addition, seminal fluid contains fructose, which the sperm use for energy. **Semen** consists of seminal fluid and the sperm it carries.

As shown in Figure 45.3, the head of the sperm contains the haploid nucleus. The long, thin tail is a flagellum. The anterior part of the tail contains many mitochondria. The sperm cell absorbs fructose from the seminal fluid. The mitochondria quickly convert the fructose into usable energy stored in ATP. Sperm use that energy to move their flagella, which propel them through the female reproductive tract.

Each time semen is ejaculated, or pushed out, from the body, about 100 million sperm cells are discharged. Most do not survive long. However, a small number may live for a few days in the female reproductive tract. One of these may unite with an egg.

45–2 The Female Reproductive System

The female gonads, the ovaries, lie within the abdominal cavity. They produce female hormones. They also produce the female gametes. Each female gamete is called an egg, or **ovum** (plural, *ova*). An ovum is huge compared to a sperm.

Ova are produced by meiosis, as shown in Figure 45.4. Even before a girl is born, egg-producing cells in the ovary have developed into **primary oocytes** [OH-uh-syts]. At birth, all the primary oocytes for a lifetime are present. Primary oocytes are diploid. They begin the first meiotic division but do not complete it. Ovum development does not resume until the girl reaches puberty.

When a girl becomes sexually mature, the development of

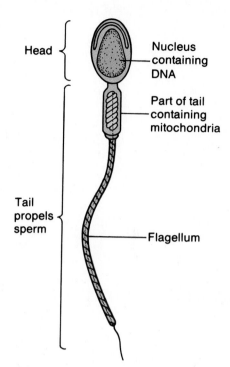

Figure 45.3 The structural features of a sperm cell

Do You Know?
At birth, the ovaries contain about 600 thousand primary oocytes. Only about 400 of these become ova.

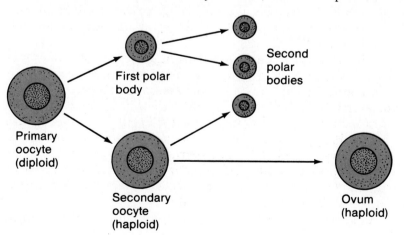

Figure 45.4 The cell division processes that produce ova

primary oocytes resumes. About every 28 days, a primary oocyte completes the first meiotic division. This division produces 2 cells of unequal size. The larger, the **secondary oocyte**, receives most of the cytoplasm. The smaller cell is called the first polar body. A **polar body** is a small cell resulting from the unequal division of cytoplasm during ovum formation.

The secondary oocyte is released from the ovary as an ovum. The second meiotic division is not actually completed until a sperm enters the ovum. After this second meiotic division, the ovum has a haploid nucleus, and a second polar body has been released. The mature ovum contains almost all the cytoplasm once found in the primary oocyte. This cytoplasm provides nourishment for the zygote if fertilization occurs.

The polar bodies produced during ovum formation do not live long. Only 1 ovum develops from each primary oocyte. In contrast, a total of 4 sperm develop from each primary spermatocyte.

Examine Figure 45.5. When an ovum leaves an ovary, it enters the abdominal cavity. It is soon drawn into the open end of a tube called an **oviduct** [OH-vuh-duhkt], which is also called a Fallopian tube in the human. The two oviducts lead into the uterus, or womb. The **uterus** [YOOT-uh-ruhs] is a hollow, fist-sized organ with thick and muscular walls.

Figure 45.5 The structural features of the female reproductive system

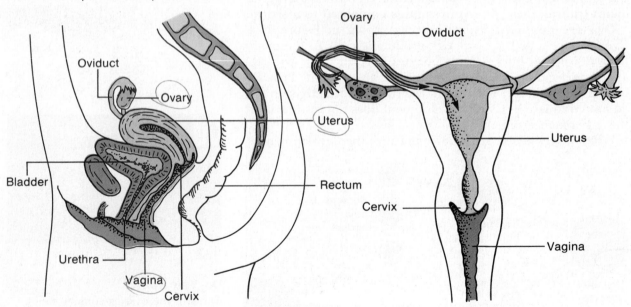

If fertilization occurs, the uterus will contain the developing embryo. The lining of the uterus is called the **endometrium** [ehn-duh-MEE-tree-uhm]. The endometrium is well supplied with blood vessels.

The narrow lower end of the uterus is known as the **cervix** [sur-vihks]. It extends downward into the **vagina** [vuh-JY-nuh], or birth canal, which leads out of the body. The vagina has two functions. It allows the entry of sperm into the female's body. It also allows the exit of the baby during birth. In the female, unlike the male, the openings of the urinary and reproductive systems are separate.

45–3 The Menstrual Cycle

Many parts of a woman's reproductive system undergo periodic changes that are controlled by hormones. These changes are known as the **menstrual** [MEHN-struhl] **cycle**. The coordination among all the parts of the system is exquisitely fine-tuned. It involves the reproductive organs and the hormones they produce. It also involves the pituitary gland. As you read about the interactions of all these parts, refer to Figure 45.6.

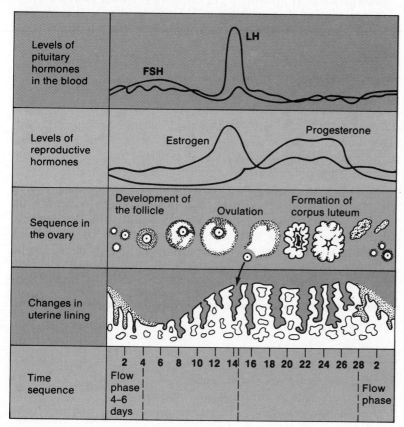

Figure 45.6 This chart shows the sequence of events and interactions among the endocrine glands throughout the menstrual cycle.

Each primary oocyte is enclosed in a structure called a **follicle**. At the beginning of the cycle, **follicle-stimulating hormone**, or FSH, is secreted by the pituitary gland. FSH travels through the bloodstream. When it reaches the ovary, it causes several follicles to grow. One of these follicles usually grows faster, and the others stop developing.

As the one follicle continues to grow, it fills with fluid. The follicle protrudes from the surface of the ovary. The growing follicle secretes the hormone estrogen. The estrogen causes the endometrium to thicken and its blood supply to increase. These changes in the endometrium prepare the uterus for pregnancy.

The growth of the follicle and the thickening of the endometrium continue for 9 or 10 days. Meanwhile, the estrogen secreted by the ovarian follicle reaches the hypothalamus. The hypothalamus then releases a tropic hormone that stimulates the pituitary to secrete **luteinizing** [LOO-tee-uhn-eyez-ihng] **hormone**, or LH.

The sudden rise of LH in the bloodstream causes the follicle to burst. The ovum is released from the follicle into the abdominal cavity. This release of the egg is called **ovulation**.

After ovulation, LH converts the follicle into a yellow structure called the **corpus luteum** [LOOT-ee-uhm]. The corpus luteum secretes the hormone **progesterone** [proh-JEHS-tuh-rohn]. The progesterone further prepares the endometrium for pregnancy. If fertilization occurs, the corpus luteum continues to secrete progesterone.

If fertilization does not occur, the ovum begins to disintegrate after about a day. The corpus luteum also begins to break down. About 11 days after ovulation, the progesterone level falls. This causes the endometrium to break down. Blood and some endometrial tissue then leave the body through the vagina. This process, called **menstruation**, lasts a few days.

While progesterone levels are high, FSH is suppressed. When the progesterone level falls, the pituitary again begins to produce FSH. Thus the cycle begins again with developing follicles. Each cycle lasts about 28 days. But the length of the cycle varies among women. Also, the length of the cycle may vary from month to month in the same woman.

Checkpoint

1. What are the two functions of the testes?
2. Which structure connects the epididymis to the urethra?
3. What does semen consist of?
4. Which hormone directly causes ovulation?
5. About how long does an entire menstrual cycle last?

Fertilization and Development

Fertilization happens when the egg nucleus and the sperm nucleus join. If this occurs, the menstrual cycle is interrupted. An embryo forms, becomes attached to the lining of the woman's uterus, and grows and develops. About 38 weeks after fertilization, development within the mother is complete. Then a baby is born.

45–4   Fertilization

When ovulation occurs, the egg is released from the ovary into the body cavity. The ends of the oviducts contain cilia. The cilia create currents that draw the egg into an oviduct. The egg is carried down the oviduct. Fertilization, if it occurs, usually takes place in the upper third of the oviduct. Recall that a fertilized egg is called a zygote.

Millions of sperm enter the reproductive tract of the woman at one time. Only a few hundred reach the oviduct. They surround the descending ovum. One sperm may penetrate the egg's outer membrane. As soon as the sperm enters the ovum, the ovum undergoes its second meiotic division. Its nucleus becomes haploid. The sperm discharges its DNA into the ovum. There, the sperm's DNA unites with the DNA in the nucleus of the egg. The union of two haploid nuclei produces a diploid cell. Immediately after this union, the egg secretes a covering, the fertilization membrane. This membrane prevents other sperm from entering the egg. Figure 45.7 shows the fertilization membrane.

CONCEPTS

- process of fertilization
- development of the embryo and embryonic membranes
- identical and fraternal twins
- factors that can harm the fetus
- process of birth

Do You Know?

Mature ova can sometimes be removed from a woman's body and fertilized outside the body. The zygote can then be placed into the woman's uterus. This technique has enabled some women with blocked oviducts to bear children.

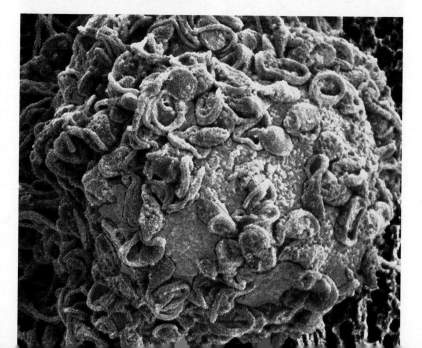

Figure 45.7 After one sperm penetrates the egg, a fertilization membrane develops, making it impossible for other sperm to enter.

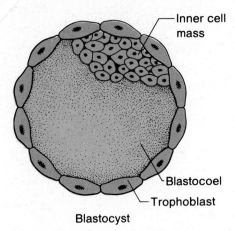

Figure 45.8 This cross section shows that the blastocyst is hollow.

45–5 Implantation and Early Development

After the egg and sperm nuclei unite, the zygote undergoes a series of rapid mitotic divisions. After a few days, the zygote has become a tiny ball of diploid cells. This ball of cells travels down the oviduct. It arrives in the uterus about four days after fertilization.

The ball of cells remains unattached in the uterus for four to six days. The cells continue to divide. A structure called a blastocyst forms. The **blastocyst** [BLAS-tuh-sihst], as shown in Figure 45.8, consists of a hollow, fluid-filled cavity surrounded by cells. A group of cells in one area of the blastocyst becomes the **inner cell mass**. The inner cell mass will become the embryo, or developing human organism. The layer of cells surrounding the cavity is called the **trophoblast** [TROH-fuh-blast]. The trophoblast will become the membranes that protect and support the embryo.

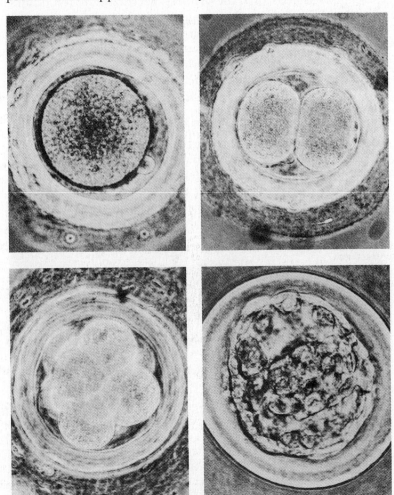

Figure 45.9 The fertilized egg divides many times, producing a mass of smaller cells. The entire mass is the same size as the single-celled egg.

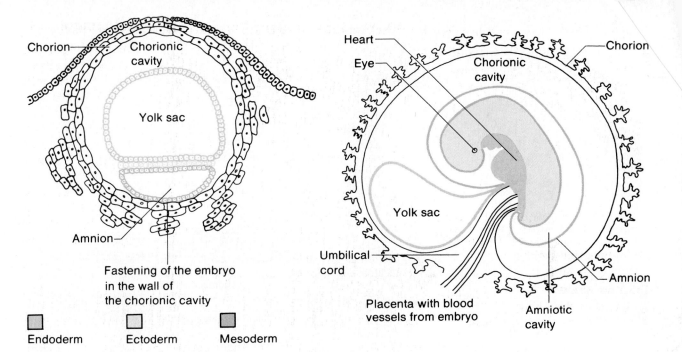

Endoderm Ectoderm Mesoderm

Figure 45.10 *Left:* A cross section showing the position of the blastocyst in the uterus. *Right:* The structural features of the embryo.

About six or seven days after fertilization, the blastocyst buries itself in the endometrium. It is completely surrounded by uterine tissue, as shown in Figure 45.10. Part of the trophoblast develops into a membrane called the **amnion** [AM-nee-ahn]. During the entire time that it is in the uterus, the embryo is enclosed in the amnion. The amnion contains amniotic fluid. This fluid cushions the embryo, protecting it against external shocks. It also prevents the embryo from sticking to the uterine wall.

Another membrane, the **chorion** [KOHR-ee-ahn], also develops from the trophoblast. The chorion is outside the amnion. The chorion has fingerlike projections called chorionic villi. Chemicals secreted by the chorionic villi destroy endometrial tissue, thus making more room in the uterus for the embryo. It also opens the capillaries in the endometrium. Blood from the mother oozes into spaces around the chorionic villi. The **placenta** [pluh-SEHNT-uh] forms where the chorionic villi embed in the endometrium. A small part of the placenta comes from the mother. However, most of it is derived from the chorion.

The embryo is attached to the placenta by the **umbilical cord**. Arteries from the embryo travel through the umbilical cord to the placenta. In the villi of the chorion, capillaries branch from these arteries. Materials pass from the blood in these capillaries into the mother's blood. Also, substances diffuse from the mother's blood into the capillaries in the villi. Umbilical veins carry the blood back to the embryo.

The embryo's circulatory system is separate from that of the mother. The embryo's blood stays within the capillaries of the chorionic villi, as shown in Figure 45.11. There is no mixing of the embryo's and the mother's bloodstreams.

The placenta carries out many functions for the embryo that other organs take care of after birth. It serves as lungs by removing oxygen from the mother's blood and by passing carbon dioxide to the mother's blood. It acts like a digestive system, bringing dissolved food from the mother's blood to the embryo. It also serves as kidneys, removing nitrogen-containing wastes from the embryo's blood. The mother's excretory system then gets rid of these wastes.

Figure 45.11 The structural features of the placenta separate the blood of the mother and embryo.

Do You Know?

Twins occur about once in 88 births. About three fourths of twins are fraternal.

Figure 45.12 *Left:* Identical twins develop separately from the same blastocyst that splits into two embryos. *Right:* Fraternal twins develop separately from two different blastocysts.

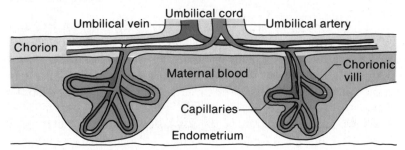

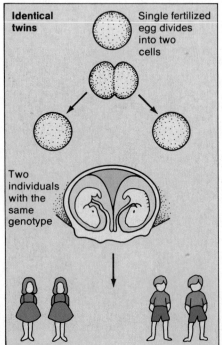

45–6 Formation of Twins

Twins may be of two types, identical or fraternal. **Identical twins** result when one embryo splits into two separate embryos. This splitting occurs very early in development, probably during the blastocyst stage. Since identical twins come from the same zygote, they each have the same genes. Therefore, they are always the same sex. Identical twins look very much like each other.

Fraternal twins result when two eggs are released, and each is fertilized by a different sperm. Each resulting zygote is the product of a different egg-and-sperm combination. Therefore, fraternal twins are not genetically identical. They may be of different sexes, and they are no more alike than are brothers and sisters born at different times.

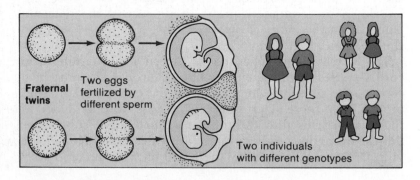

45–7 Differentiation

In the early blastocyst stage, all the cells are alike in structure and function. Soon the cells begin to move from their original position. As they do this, they become different from each other. **Differentiation** is the process in which unspecialized embryonic cells develop into specialized cells. Differentiation produces all the varied tissues and organs of the body.

The genes in each cell of the blastocyst are identical. However, not every gene in every cell is expressed. In other words, some genes in each cell are inactive. The genes a cell expresses determine the structure and function of that particular cell. Scientists do not yet know what makes cells express only certain genes.

By the eleventh day after fertilization, the inner cell mass of the blastocyst forms three **germ layers**, or groups of embryonic tissues. The inner layer is known as the **endoderm**. The middle layer is the **mesoderm**. The **ectoderm** is the outermost layer. Each germ layer gives rise to certain types of cells, tissues, and organs, as shown in Figure 45.13.

By the fourth week, the embryo has taken the form of a bent cylinder. This bending accounts for the embryo's curled-up posture. During the fourth and fifth weeks, the arms and legs begin to form. By the eighth week, fingers and toes have become distinct, as shown in Figure 45.14.

During the second month, the facial features develop. By the end of the second month, the major body structures have been established. The remainder of development within the uterus consists of growth and refinement of these structures. After the second month, the embryo is usually called a **fetus**.

Cell Layer	Tissue produced
Ectoderm	Brain Spinal cord Nerves Outer layer of skin Some parts of the eye Nose Ears
Mesoderm	Skeleton Muscles Gonads Excretory system Inner layer of skin
Endoderm	Pancreas Liver Lining of digestive system Lungs

Figure 45.13 Some of the major tissues and organs formed from the three germ layers.

Figure 45.14 *Left:* The hands and feet of a 5-week-old embryo look like paddles. *Right:* By 8 weeks distinct fingers and toes have developed.

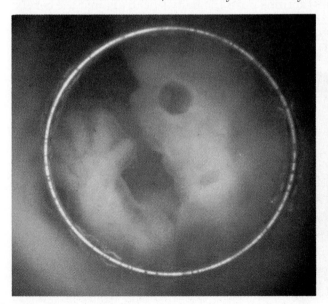
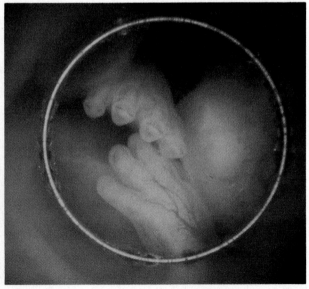

45–8   Harmful Effects on the Fetus

People used to think that the placenta prevented harmful substances from passing through the uterus into the embryo. However, scientists now know that the placenta does not act as a barrier. Whatever is in the mother's bloodstream may enter the embryo. Viruses, for example, can move from the mother into the embryo and seriously harm it. If the German-measles virus infects an embryo, it may cause deafness, blindness, or mental retardation. Drugs such as caffeine and alcohol can also pass through to the embryo, sometimes causing damage. Pregnant women are now cautioned to avoid unnecessary drugs during pregnancy.

In addition, smoking can cause problems during pregnancy. Cigarette smoke contains the harmful drug nicotine. Nicotine makes the blood vessels of the uterus become narrower. This decreases the placenta's blood supply. The embryo then receives less food from the mother. As a result, the baby's birth weight may be lowered. Low birth weight may threaten the baby's health and development.

45–9   Birth

Estrogen increases the ability of the uterine muscle to contract. During the last weeks of pregnancy, the level of estrogen rises. Oxytocin, a hormone secreted by the posterior pituitary gland, also causes contractions of the uterus. Around the thirty-eighth week after fertilization, the uterus begins to contract over and over. These repeated contractions are called **labor**.

Labor contractions push the baby's head against the cervix, stretching the cervix and finally enabling the baby to pass through it. Eventually the contractions push the baby through the vagina and out of the mother's body.

Figure 45.15 During labor the uterus contracts forcing the baby's head against the cervix. The cervix eventually dilates completely allowing the baby to pass through the birth canal.

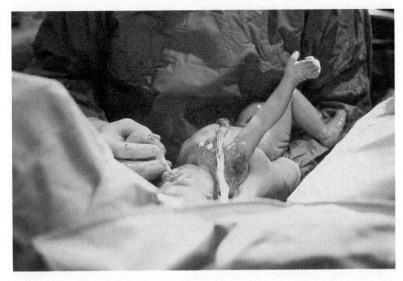

Figure 45.16 A newborn is still attached to the placenta by the umbilical cord.

At birth, the baby is still attached to the placenta by the umbilical cord. The umbilical cord is cut; the baby no longer obtains food and oxygen from the mother. Your navel is the spot where your umbilical cord was attached to your body.

While in the uterus, the fetus had no need to breathe. At birth, the lungs of the newborn are filled with amniotic fluid. The baby's first cries rid the lungs of fluid and fill them with air. The baby begins to breathe.

As soon as a baby takes a breath, his or her circulatory system changes. While a fetus is in the uterus, most of its blood bypasses the lungs. Instead of going to the lungs, blood from the right ventricle passes through a duct into the systemic circulation. This duct closes at birth. Then the right ventricle begins pumping blood to the baby's lungs.

Before birth, an opening exists between the right and left atria of a baby's heart. Normally this opening closes shortly after birth. This closing prevents oxygenated and deoxygenated blood from mixing in the heart.

During pregnancy, milk develops in the mother's breasts. A baby is born with a sucking reflex. Thus the baby is able to obtain nourishment shortly after birth.

Checkpoint

1. At which stage of its development does the embryo attach to the endometrium?
2. What fluid cushions the fetus in the uterus?
3. What structure attaches an embryo to the placenta?
4. From how many eggs do identical twins come?
5. Name the three germ layers.

CHAPTER REVIEW

Summary

- The testes produce haploid sperm. Each primary spermatocyte gives rise to four sperm cells.

- The ovaries produce haploid ova. Only one ovum develops from each primary oocyte.

- The menstrual cycle is controlled by hormones. During this cycle, an ovum develops within a follicle. An ovum is released when the follicle bursts. The endometrium of the uterus thickens in preparation for pregnancy.

- After ovulation, the follicle becomes the corpus luteum. The corpus luteum secretes progesterone, which maintains the endometrium. If fertilization does not occur, the endometrium breaks down, and menstruation occurs.

- Fertilization occurs in an oviduct. Fertilization produces a diploid zygote.

- The zygote undergoes a series of mitotic divisions, becoming a blastocyst. The blastocyst becomes implanted in the endometrium. One part of the blastocyst develops into the embryo and the other part into the membranes that surround the embryo. Two of these membranes are the amnion and chorion.

- The embryo exchanges materials with the mother through the placenta. The fetal and maternal circulatory systems are separate.

- Identical twins result when one embryo divides into two separate embryos. Fraternal twins occur when two separate sperm fertilize two different ova.

- Three different germ layers form from the blastocyst. Each of these layers gives rise to specific organs and tissues. By the end of the second month, the major body structures have formed.

- Materials can cross from the mother to the embryo through the placenta. Pregnant women should avoid smoking and taking unnecessary drugs.

- During labor, the uterus contracts over and over, pushing the baby out of the mother's body. After birth, the baby begins to breathe, and blood is pumped to the lungs. The baby derives nourishment from milk.

Vocabulary

amnion	mesoderm
blastocyst	oviduct
cervix	ovulation
chorion	ovum
corpus luteum	placenta
differentiation	polar body
ectoderm	primary oocyte
endoderm	primary
endometrium	spermatocyte
epididymis	progesterone
fetus	scrotum
follicle	secondary oocyte
follicle-stimulating	secondary
hormone	spermatocyte
fraternal twins	semen
germ layers	sperm
identical twins	trophoblast
inner cell mass	umbilical cord
labor	uterus
luteinizing hormone	vagina
menstrual cycle	vas deferens
menstruation	

Review

1. What hormone stimulates the testes to produce sperm?
2. What is the function of a sperm's flagellum?
3. What happens to the polar bodies produced in the formation of an ovum?
4. Sperm contain mitochondria. For what process do these mitochondria provide energy?
5. About how often is an ovum produced?
6. How many sperm result from the division of one primary spermatocyte? How many

ova are produced from one primary oocyte?

7. Which hormone causes the development of follicles?
8. During the menstrual cycle, what changes in the uterus prepare it for pregnancy?
9. What causes the follicle to burst and ovulation to occur?
10. What happens to the corpus luteum if fertilization occurs? What happens to it if pregnancy does not occur?
11. Once fertilization takes place, what prevents other sperm from entering an egg?
12. From what part of the blastocyst will the embryo develop? From what part will the embryonic membranes develop?
13. How does an embryo get oxygen?
14. Explain how identical twins form.
15. What is meant by differentiation?
16. What are germ layers? Name the germ layers of a human embryo.
17. Identify three things that can harm a developing embryo.
18. At what point in development does an embryo become a fetus?

Interpret and Apply

1. Explain why testes that have not descended into the scrotum cannot normally produce sperm.
2. Which sex produces more gametes in a lifetime?
3. Explain how the placenta develops.
4. Maria and Pedro are twins. What kind of twins are they, identical or fraternal? Explain.
5. Why doesn't menstruation occur if the ovum is fertilized?
6. Write the following structures in the order in which a sperm travels through them.
   a. epididymis   c. urethra
   b. testes   d. vas deferens
7. Identify two ways in which meiosis is different in men and women.
8. Identify the function of estrogen in the menstrual cycle.
9. Write the following events in the order in which they occur.
   a. formation of the amnion

b. fusion of the egg and sperm nuclei
c. implantation of the blastocyst
d. penetration of the egg by the sperm
e. labor
f. ovulation
g. formation of the fertilization membrane
10. How is a baby's circulatory system different from an embryo's?

Challenge

1. If a blastocyst separated into four equal parts and each developed independently, what would be the result?
2. What would happen if each vas deferens in a man's body was blocked?
3. Suppose a woman's oviducts were blocked. Would she produce ova? Could she become pregnant? Explain.
4. What would happen if the corpus luteum disintegrated after an ovulation that resulted in a pregnancy?
5. Explain how negative-feedback works in regulating the level of FSH during different stages of the menstrual cycle.

Projects

1. If a pregnant woman drinks too much alcohol, her baby may suffer from fetal alcohol syndrome. Write a report on this syndrome. Include such information as the effects on the baby, the incidence with which this syndrome occurs, and what can be done to prevent it.
2. Find information on the various causes of infertility. Learn what can now be done to enable certain previously infertile couples to produce children.
3. Observe the behavior of a baby less than three months old. Note the things that the baby is able to do. Then observe a one-year-old. Make a list of the differences in behavior between a one-year-old and a baby of three months.

Careers In Medicine

Professionals in the field of medical care devote their lives to healing those who are sick. Therefore, most careers in the medical field require specialized training. In addition to doctors and nurses, there are many other professionals in medicine. There are 23 major specialty fields in the medical profession. The length of the training program varies for each field.

Emergency medical technicians (EMT) must complete a 12-week course. These people are trained to perform cardiopulmonary resuscitation, remove obstructions from airways, and administer other emergency procedures until the patient can be given hospital care. A *paramedic* has had a year of experience as an EMT and has completed a one-year course. A paramedic has more responsibilities than an EMT and can, under certain conditions, take the place of a physician.

Medical illustration requires two years of training. *Medical illustrators* combine a knowledge of anatomy and physiology with artistic ability. They are needed to provide diagrams of surgical instruments and procedures for textbooks and surgical supply companies.

A technician is a specialist in the mechanical or scientific details of a particular field. *Radiology technicians* have completed two years of training. They prepare patients for X rays and operate X-ray equipment. They also assist in treating specific diseases by exposing the patient to concentrated amounts of X rays. *Medical technologists* have completed a four-year program. They perform tests of a chemical, microscopic, or bacteriologic nature. This information is used in the treatment and diagnosis of diseases.

Therapy is a branch of medicine that deals with treatment or rehabilitation of diseases without the use of drugs or surgery. Reg-

istered *respiratory therapists* have completed a five-year program. They help people with breathing problems. They work to restore the heart and lungs following complications such as cardiac failure, asthma, or emphysema. *Physical therapists* have completed a four-year program. They plan and administer physical therapy treatment programs for patients. The purpose of such therapy is to restore function, relieve pain, and prevent disability following disease, injury, or loss of body parts. *Occupational therapists* must complete a four-year program. They are responsible for planning, organizing, and conducting activity programs. These programs rehabilitate mentally, physically, or emotionally handicapped people.

The medical profession relieves human suffering and saves lives. When an epidemic or disaster strikes, the medical team is there. Medical care is provided in hospitals, clinics, private practices, nursing homes, and private homes. There are tremendous opportunities and rewards in the medical field.

UNIT REVIEW

Synthesis

1. List the characteristics that make humans different from other animals. How have these characteristics allowed humans to become such a successful species?
2. Explain how muscles and bones work together to produce movement.
3. List the four basic tissue types that make up the human body. Describe the general function of each.
4. Name and briefly describe the major functions of human skin.
5. Describe the fate of a bacon, lettuce, and tomato sandwich as it travels through your digestive system. What ultimately happens to the substances in the sandwich?
6. Name three categories of substances in the human diet that are necessary for life but that do not provide calories. Briefly describe why each of these groups is necessary.
7. Using your knowledge of the respiratory system, trace the path that an oxygen molecule would travel from the atmosphere outside your body to reach the mitochondrion of a muscle cell.
8. What is the relationship between protein in the diet and the function of human kidneys?
9. Explain how the circulatory system helps maintain the functions of the other body systems.
10. Explain how the fight-or-flight response involves both the nervous system and the endocrine system.
11. Describe how the human endocrine system and reproductive system are related.
12. Describe the role of the lymphatic system in fighting disease.
13. Describe the two-loop pattern of blood circulation in the human body. How does this pattern compare to the pattern of circulation in a human fetus? What happens to a baby's circulatory system at birth?
14. Explain how the agglutination that occurs when different blood types are mixed is similar to the process by which pathogens are neutralized within your body.

Additional Reading

Dusek, Dorothy, and Daniel Girdano. *Drugs: A Factual Account*. Reading, MA: Addison-Wesley Publishing Co., Inc., 1980.

Glasser, Ronald. *The Body is the Hero*. New York: Random House, Inc., 1976.

Goldberg, Kathy E. *The Skeleton: Fantastic Framework*. Washington, DC: U.S. News Books, 1982.

Hood, L.E., I.L. Weissman, and W.B. Wood. *Immunology*. Menlo Park, CA: Benjamin-Cummings, 1978.

Hughes, G.M. *The Vertebrate Lung*. Burlington, NC: Carolina Biological Supply Co., 1979.

Jenkins, Marie M. *Embryos and How They Develop*. New York: Holiday House, Inc., 1975.

Johanson, Donald C., and Maitland A. Edey. *Lucy: The Beginnings of Human Kind*. New York: Warner Books, Inc., 1982.

Leakey, Richard E. *The Making of Mankind*. New York: E.P. Dutton, 1981.

Longmore, Donald. *The Heart*. New York: McGraw-Hill Book Co., 1971.

McMinn, R.M. *The Human Gut*. Burlington, NC: Carolina Biological Supply Co., 1977.

Nora, James J. *The Whole Heart Book*. New York: Holt, Rinehart & Winston, 1980.

Riedman, Sarah R. *Hormones: How They Work*. New York: Abelard-Schuman Ltd., 1973.

Selim, Robert D. *Muscles: The Magic of Motion*. Washington, DC: U.S. News Books, 1982.

Unit Eight

Organisms and the Environment

Autumn landscape, Moab, Utah

46 Behavior

A bowerbird constructing his nest

The bird in the photograph above is a male bowerbird, a native of New Guinea. He has constructed a bower, or shelter, of twigs, and has painted its walls with the juice of blue berries which he has mashed with his beak. He has also collected blue objects, such as empty shotgun cartridges, with which to decorate his bower. All the other male bowerbirds in the vicinity have constructed similar nests. Each has tried to make his nest the most attractive one around. Why? It is mating season, and the males are attempting to lure females to their bowers. The more colorful the bower, the greater the chance of attracting a female.

Other birds attract mates in different ways. Some birds sing lovely songs while establishing their territory. The female birds are attracted to the area by these songs. Other birds attract females by displaying gorgeous plumage. Still others perform elaborate movements to woo potential mates.

Whatever the method, all these behaviors have a common function. The male that succeeds in attracting a mate leaves copies of his genes in the next generation.

Innate versus Learned Behavior

All organisms respond to stimuli in their environment. An organism's **behavior**, or what it does, depends not only upon the type of organism, but also upon what happens in its environment. Temperature, moisture, food supply, season of the year, and time of day all affect the behavior of an organism.

CONCEPTS

- factors affecting behavior
- characteristics of unlearned behavior

46–1   Examples of Innate and Learned Behavior

Many forms of an animal's behavior are determined genetically. **Innate behavior** is unlearned behavior that is genetically controlled. It is a predictable pattern of response, which aids in the survival and reproduction of an organism.

Reflexes are the simplest forms of innate behavior. A reflex is a response that is determined by a fixed pathway in the nervous system. All animals, including humans, have reflexes. Removing your hand from a hot object is an unlearned, survival response.

Innate behavior is not always as simple as a reflex. Digger wasps provide an example of complex behavior that is innate. By the time a female digger wasp emerges from her underground pupa, her parents have been dead for several months. The newly emerged wasp will live for only a few weeks. During this brief time, she must dig a hole for a nest, construct the nest, mate, hunt prey to place in the nest to nourish her young, and lay her eggs. There is little time for her to learn these tasks. Furthermore, there is no one to teach her. She is born knowing how to complete the tasks. Complex behaviors that are performed perfectly without learning are called **instincts**.

Figure 46.1 The digger wasp and her nest

Figure 46.2 The lioness teaches her cubs how to hunt.

Instinctive behavior patterns are often repeated within a certain time period. Behavior that is based on a 24-hour cycle is called a **circadian rhythm**. Some animals are more active during the day, others at night, and still others in twilight.

By contrast, certain behaviors are obviously learned. No one is born knowing how to solve algebra problems. **Learning** occurs when an animal's experience results in a change of behavior. Learned behavior is not determined by an organism's genes. Learning allows an animal to adapt to change.

Between the two extremes of innate and learned behavior lie many types of behavior that have elements of both. For example, consider the behavior of lion cubs and domestic kittens. Young felines spend much of their time at play, stalking imaginary prey. By the time they mature, they are competent hunters. Their play is actually practice, during which they are learning to be good hunters. But the tendency to play is not learned; it is innate. All kittens do it. Have you ever seen a baby rabbit stalking prey? It is unlikely, because rabbits do not inherit the tendency toward this behavior.

46–2   Advantages of Learned Behavior

Although it is possible to demonstrate learned behavior in organisms that are quite simple, learned behavior is much more common in organisms with more complex nervous systems. In general, the more advanced the brain, the more elaborate the patterns of learned behavior. Among the vertebrates, for example, primates show a greater capacity for learning than frogs. One reason for this is that higher organisms tend to have a longer life span than simpler organisms. If the digger wasp had to learn complex behaviors in her brief lifetime, she could not possibly complete all her tasks and produce offspring. Learning is also usually present in animals

Do You Know?

Innate behavior patterns within a species tend to be rigid. The nests of all digger wasps look identical, yet not one of them has seen the others' nests.

that receive much parental care. Lionesses actually teach their cubs how to hunt. In animals that develop without parental care, behaviors are more likely to be innate.

Another characteristic of innate behavior is that it is rigid and unchanging. If an organism knows how to build a certain type of nest, it is at a loss if the specific building materials are not available. However, if nest building is a learned behavior and the building material becomes unavailable, an organism can learn a new type of nest building.

The main advantage of learning over instinct is that it offers a greater potential for changing behaviors as conditions in the environment change. This ability is also related to the life span of an organism. If an organism lives for only a few weeks, the ability to meet a changing environment may not be necessary. On the other hand, in organisms that live for many years, the ability to change behavior as the environment changes is extremely valuable.

In contrast to organisms such as insects, humans are born quite helpless. It is a matter of years before the human brain develops completely. During the entire period of brain development, the baby depends on its parents to provide it with food, shelter, protection, and anything else it needs. But during this time of dependence, an enormous amount of learning takes place. By the time the baby becomes an adult, he or she is capable of complex behavior. Adults have the ability to modify their behavior as a response to changes in weather or food supply.

Reasoning, or rational thinking, is a type of behavior that occurs only in primates and other higher vertebrates. Reasoning is the ability to solve an unfamiliar problem without the benefit of trial and error. The classic study of reasoning involved a chimpanzee. A chimpanzee was put in a room with a bunch of bananas. The fruit was hanging from the ceiling. The chimpanzee could not reach the bananas by jumping. Eventually it figured out that by piling boxes on top of each other, it could climb high enough to reach the bananas. Although the chimpanzee had had no experience with this type of problem, it was able to use knowledge gained in other situations and apply it to this one.

Checkpoint

1. What term describes complex patterns of innate behavior?
2. What types of behaviors are usually associated with longer life spans?
3. Are reflexes innate or learned?
4. In which animals is reasoning most likely to occur?

Types of Learning

CONCEPTS
- mechanism of imprinting
- process of habituation
- how reinforcement affects behavior

Learning can involve simple or complex tasks. There are several different types of learning. These include imprinting, habituation, classical conditioning, and operant conditioning.

46–3 Imprinting

One of the simplest types of learning occurs among very young animals. It was first described by Konrad Lorenz. Lorenz is an Austrian **ethologist**, a scientist who studies the behavior of animals in their natural settings. Lorenz observed that ducklings, soon after they hatched, would follow their mother. Lorenz called this response of the ducklings to their mother **imprinting**. Imprinting is a form of learning in which an animal forms a social attachment to an organism soon after hatching or birth. Imprinting is rapid and irreversible.

Lorenz also found that if ducklings were exposed to a female of another species instead of their mother, they would follow the substitute mother. Lorenz concluded that the ducklings had imprinted on the substitute mother.

Lorenz later expanded his work to determine the conditions necessary for imprinting. He found that there was a **critical period**, a period when a duckling learns to identify its mother. This critical period occurs between 13 and 16 hours after hatching. If a substitute mother is available before or after this critical period, imprinting is not as likely to occur. By removing the mother duck and substituting himself at the critical period, Lorenz allowed the ducklings to imprint on him. The distinguished scientist walking across the lawn followed by a line of ducklings must have been an amusing sight.

Figure 46.3 These young cygnets have imprinted on their mother.

46–4　Habituation

Habituation is a form of learning in which an animal learns *not* to perform a certain behavior. Imagine that you are working in a quiet place and suddenly there is a loud noise. You may be startled to the point of jumping out of your seat. If the same noise is repeated several times during a short period, though, your response will be reduced each time. Over time, you will probably not respond to the noise at all.

46–5　Classical and Operant Conditioning

At the turn of the century, Ivan Pavlov, a Russian physiologist, studied the ways in which dogs respond to stimuli. Pavlov knew that dogs respond to the smell of food by salivating. This response is innate. By producing saliva, the dogs are preparing to digest their food.

Pavlov wanted to know if the salivation response could be triggered by a less likely stimulus. His experiment involved ringing a bell at the same time a dog was given meat. Eventually the sound of the bell was enough to stimulate salivation. Pavlov said that the dog was **conditioned** to respond to the bell. A conditioned response is a response to a stimulus that would not normally cause such a response. The type of learning, or conditioning, described by Pavlov is called **classical conditioning**.

Toward the middle of this century, the American psychologist B. F. Skinner studied another type of learning called **operant conditioning**. Skinner used pigeons in his research.

Skinner realized that if a certain behavior was followed by a **reinforcement**, or reward, the animal was more likely to repeat that behavior in the future. Skinner invented the **Skinner box**, a chamber in which he put his experimental subject. The box contained a typewriterlike key that was connected to a food supply. If the pigeon pecked at the key, it would be reinforced with food. As a result of this reinforcement, the bird learned to peck at the key until it had enough food.

Figure 46.4 In operant conditioning, a behavior is more likely to occur if it is reinforced. This pigeon spends time pecking the key. Each time it pecks, it is given food.

Checkpoint

1. What kind of biologist studies the behavior of organisms in their natural environment?
2. The type of learning in which the young learn to follow their mother is called _____.
3. When in an animal's life may imprinting occur?
4. In what form of conditioning is a desired behavior reinforced?

CONCEPTS

- levels of orientation
- complexity of courtship
- relationship between aggression and territoriality
- patterns of social behavior
- mechanisms of communication

Figure 46.5 Migration is a complex, innate behavior pattern.

Patterns of Behavior

Every animal behaves. Obviously, some behaviors are more complex than others, but there are certain basic categories of behavior that appear throughout the animal kingdom. The fact that these behavior patterns are so widespread indicates that they have evolutionary importance. Natural selection acts upon behaviors as surely as it acts upon physical characteristics. Animals with certain behavior patterns are better adapted for survival than other animals.

46–6 Orientation Behaviors

Many animals can **orient** themselves within their environment, or move from place to place. The simplest type of orientation is called **kinesis**. Kinesis is moving about without direction. For example, a wood louse increases its rate of motion when placed in an environment of low humidity. The animal's movement is nondirectional. However, it needs an atmosphere of high humidity to survive. Kinesis increases the probability that the wood louse will eventually end up in an area of higher humidity. Once this condition is met, the wood louse will stop moving.

Another type of orientation is called **taxis**, a movement directly toward or away from a source of stimulation. Moths move toward a source of light. Bloodsuckers move toward warm-blooded animals. Green turtles move toward the sea.

Compass orientation is the most complex type of orientation. It involves several elements. Some frogs, for example, find their home ponds by using the location of the pond relative to the sun, moon, and stars. But the heavenly bodies are not always in the same position; their positions change with time of day, month, and year. The frog's brain has an **internal clock**, a mechanism that allows it to compensate for the regular movements of the heavenly bodies. The frog can therefore find its home even though the "landmarks" have moved.

Animals that migrate, particularly birds, use compass orientation. Some species of birds fly thousands of miles each year, using only the stars and their internal clocks as pathfinders.

46–7 Courtship Behavior

Courtship behaviors are specialized behavior patterns that occur before mating can take place. Their function is to put both the male and the female of a species in mating condition at the same time so that copulation may occur. Courtship behavior also ensures that mating occurs only among members of the same species.

Often the endocrine system, in response to an external factor such as day length or temperature, begins to make animals responsive to mating. But finer tuning is necessary because the closeness of male and female required for copulation sometimes causes other behaviors. For example, the female spider treats the smaller male spider as prey. Without the elaborate courtship behavior, the male would not be allowed to approach the female to mate. He would be eaten first. (In some species, the female does eat the male after copulation has occurred. By that time the male has already contributed his genes. In an evolutionary sense, he has survived.)

46–8 Aggressive and Territorial Behavior

Most animals occasionally engage in **aggressive**, or fighting, behavior. Its function may be to defend young or a territory. Aggressive behavior is meant to deliver a message from one animal to another. If you approach a dog in its yard, the dog may bark loudly. Its bark indicates that you are trespassing. Bared fangs, a raised tail, erect ears and hair will confirm the threatening message.

Territoriality, the defense of a certain amount of space, is widespread in the animal kingdom. Male birds singing their glorious songs in the spring are announcing to other males that they are in possession of a certain territory. Territorial animals will use aggressive postures and vocalizations to warn other animals to stay out of their territories.

You have probably noticed male dogs urinating on objects to proclaim their territory. The urine contains chemicals called **pheromones**. The scent of the pheromones informs other dogs in the vicinity that the territory has been claimed.

Figure 46.6 This fish defends its territory vigorously.

Do You Know?

If threatened by a dog, a person should turn sideways or look away. These are submissive gestures. Direct eye contact could provoke an attack.

Territoriality has several functions. A given amount of space will provide enough food and resources for only a limited number of breeding animals. By establishing a territory, an organism is securing adequate food for its offspring. Only those animals that can secure the minimum amount of space required are able to breed successfully. Territoriality also lowers the amount of predation and disease in an area and keeps mating pairs from becoming disturbed during the mating season.

46–9 Social Behavior

Many organisms live together in groups, such as flocks of birds or packs of wolves. An organized group of animals is called a **society**. Societies are often organized into different levels of authority. An example of this behavior is the definite order of power, or **dominance hierarchy**, in certain groups of organisms. Hierarchy is established within a society of chickens by pecking action. One chicken becomes dominant to all others and is rarely challenged. Another chicken will establish its command over all but the dominant chicken. Each chicken has its place in the pecking order. This behavior promotes order and decreases aggression within the society.

Figure 46.7 A single wolf could not subdue a moose, which is so much larger than itself. When a pack of wolves work together, however, they can accomplish this task.

Animals in some societies display **cooperation**. Cooperation occurs when animals work together for a common purpose. Wolves are very cooperative animals. They are not large themselves, but the prey that they hunt is often many times larger than they are. A lone wolf cannot subdue a moose, but a pack of wolves can. It is to the advantage of every wolf in the pack to cooperate in the hunt. If a group hunt is successful, everyone eats dinner that night.

Cooperative behavior accomplishes other things too. Baboons travel in troops. A lion is unlikely to attack an entire troop

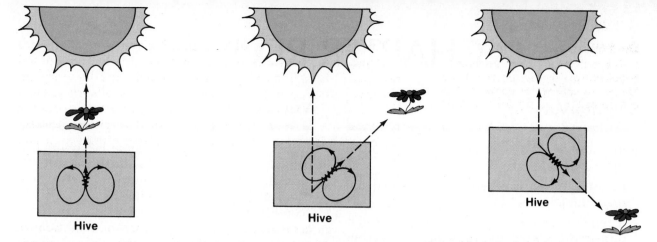

Figure 46.8 The bee dance indicates the direction, distance, and amount of available food. The cross-cuts through the figure eight point to the direction of the food source.

of baboons. But if one baboon straggles behind the other members of a troop, it is likely to be attacked and killed by a lion. Natural selection favors baboons that stay with their troop.

46–10 Communication

Communication, or the exchange of information, occurs in most societies. It can be achieved using the senses of sight, smell, hearing, and touch. The location of food is a message frequently communicated to one or more members of the society.

Karl von Frisch, a German zoologist, found that honeybees communicate the location of a food source by means of an elaborate dance. A bee dances in figure-eight circles on the wall of the hive along an imaginary vertical line. The vertical line represents the present direction of the sun in relation to the hive. The crosscut through the figure eight and the vertical line form an angle that corresponds to the angle of the food source from the sun. The distance between the food and the hive is indicated by the speed of the dance. While performing the dance, the bee moves her body from side to side. The more the bee wiggles, the more food is available.

Some messages, however, must be conveyed more rapidly. An antelope will lift its tail, displaying a white patch that signals other antelopes of the approach of a predator. A dolphin in distress will emit a series of whistles that signal healthy dolphins of its need for assistance.

Checkpoint

1. Name three types of orientation behavior.
2. What kind of behavior puts animals in a mating condition?
3. Behavior that serves to frighten other animals away is called _____ behavior.

CHAPTER REVIEW

Summary

- All animals behave in response to stimuli in their environment.
- Innate behavior is genetically controlled and predictable.
- A reflex is an innate response that is determined by a fixed pathway in the nervous system.
- An instinct is a complex pattern of innate behavior.
- Learned behavior is not genetically controlled. Therefore, learned behavior allows an organism to adapt to environmental changes.
- Learned behavior occurs most frequently among animals with highly developed nervous systems.
- Imprinting is an irreversible form of learned behavior. It occurs only during a brief critical period soon after an animal hatches or is born.
- Habituation means learning *not* to perform certain behavior.
- Classical conditioning is the act of responding to a stimulus that has previously not caused a response.
- Operant conditioning is a pattern of behavior based on reward rather than stimulus.
- Repeated patterns of behavior among animals seem to have evolutionary importance.
- Examples of behavioral patterns include orienting, courtship, aggressive and territorial behavior, cooperation, and communication.
- A dominance hierarchy establishes order in a society and reduces aggression.
- Animals communicate in many ways. It can be achieved by using the senses of sight, smell, hearing, and touch.

Vocabulary

aggressive	innate behavior
behavior	instinct
circadian rhythm	internal clock
classical	kinesis
conditioning	learning
communication	operant conditioning
compass orientation	orient
conditioned	pheromones
cooperation	reasoning
courtship behavior	reflex
critical period	reinforcement
dominance hierarchy	Skinner box
ethologist	society
habituation	taxis
imprinting	territoriality

Review

Match the scientist with the behavior he studied.

1. Von Frisch
2. Lorenz
3. Pavlov
4. Skinner

a. aggressive behavior in ants
b. communication in honeybees
c. classical conditioning in dogs
d. imprinting in ducklings
e. operant conditioning in pigeons

5. Define a reflex. Give an example of a human reflex.
6. Define instinctive behavior and give an example in animals.
7. Name an advantage of innate over learned behavior.
8. What is the main advantage of learning over instinct?
9. Name an animal that shows kinesis-type orientation.

10. What form of orientation is migration?
11. Define *taxis orientation*. Give an example of this pattern of behavior.
12. Bared fangs are common in _____ behavior.
13. Name several advantages to having fixed territories.
14. Name three species of animals that exhibit cooperation.
15. Indicate whether each of the following descriptions is characteristic of innate or learned behavior.
    a. most often present in lower animals
    b. most often present in animals with short life spans
    c. requires practice to develop
    d. often requires a teacher
    e. is rigid and unchanging
    f. includes reflexes
    g. is the most common type of behavior in humans
    h. may not be apparent at birth but requires no practice
    i. allows for adaptation and change
    j. may be influenced by rewards
    k. is genetically determined

Interpret and Apply

1. For each of the following examples, name the type of learning described.
    a. The first time a baby pets a dog, the dog snaps at the baby. The baby is afraid of dogs after that.
    b. A dog wags its tail when its master comes home each night. Its master buys a new car. The dog learns to recognize the sound of the car. Now the dog wags its tail when it hears the car.
    c. You move into a new house. It is close to a fire station, and you are awakened by sirens several times during the first few nights that you live in the house. After about a week, you stop waking up even though the sirens continue.
    d. Goose eggs were placed in the nest of a duck. Wherever the duck went, she was followed by goslings.

2. Name the general type of behavior represented by each of the following.
    a. salmon swimming upstream to spawn
    b. thousands of termites building an enormous nest together
    c. a peacock strutting past a peahen, with his tail magnificently displayed
    d. a fish assuming a threatening posture toward its reflection in an aquarium
    e. a cat arching its back, with its tail and hair erect
    f. a lizard moving from a cold place toward a warm place
3. In each of the following examples, name the stimulus and the response.
    a. After a clap of thunder, a dog dives under the bed.
    b. A cat smells tuna fish and runs into the kitchen.
    c. A baby sees its mother smile and smiles back at her.
    d. A flock of pigeons arrives after you throw a handful of popcorn on the lawn.
    e. Your mouth puckers when you suck a lemon.
    f. Your eyes tear when you chop an onion.

Challenge

1. Is the pecking order of chickens more like a democracy or a dictatorship? Explain.
2. Describe an operant-conditioning technique you could use to train your dog to come when called.
3. Name the members of a dominance hierarchy in a human society. Some ideas may be governing bodies, military officers, or employees of a factory.

Projects

1. Do research on the concept of shaping in operant conditioning. Using the technique of shaping, teach a friend to do a task such as finding a hidden object.
2. Build a maze and teach a rat (from the pet store) to run through it.

47 The Distribution of Life

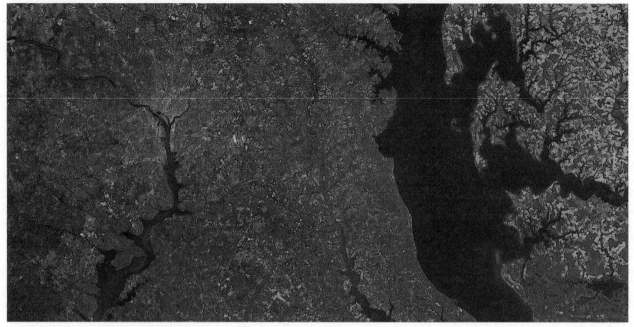

Color-enhanced Landsat photograph of Chesapeake Bay near Washington, D.C.

This photograph, taken from a satellite, shows part of Chesapeake Bay. The bay is the largest estuary in North America. Estuaries are found where the fresh water of a river mixes with the salt water of the sea. The Susquehanna River is the major river of the Chesapeake, but many other rivers, including the James and the Potomac, also feed into the bay.

Because the bay is shallow, sunlight can penetrate its depths, permitting photosynthesis to occur. The bay is also rich in nutrients. These conditions are ideal for the growth of vegetation. Plankton floats in the waters. Algae grow on the mud, sand, and rocks of the bottom. Grasses fill the surrounding marshes. This vegetation provides abundant food for many animals. Many types of fish, crustaceans, and mollusks lay their eggs in the sheltered bay, although the adults may live in the ocean. The young of so many species have their start in the bay that you could think of it as an aquatic nursery.

The amazingly high productivity of this region is due to the chance combination of many environmental factors. Anyone who has eaten crabs, oysters, or rockfish from the Chesapeake can well appreciate the results of this combination.

Biomes on Land

If you have had the opportunity to travel long distances, you know that the landscape varies from place to place. In Florida and other warm areas, palm trees are common, while in colder areas conifers are common. What causes these differences in the distribution of living things?

47–1 Physical Environment

All of the areas where organisms live make up the **biosphere** [BY-oh-sfihr]. The biosphere contains all of Earth's atmosphere, water, and soil within which life can exist.

Living organisms are affected by many environmental factors. Nonliving aspects of the environment are called **abiotic** [ay-by-OHT-ik] **factors**. Temperature, rainfall, and wind are abiotic factors. Some living things can tolerate a broad range of abiotic conditions. Others require very specific conditions. But in all cases the characteristics of the physical environment limit which life forms it will support.

The climate is the most important abiotic factor in determining what kind of vegetation can grow in an area. In polar regions the constant freezing temperatures never permit thawing of the ground, so little vegetation can grow. Close to the equator, though, continuous high temperatures allow year-round growth. Each particular plant form is best adapted to a particular climate. A large geographical area with a particular form of dominant vegetation is called a **biome**.

Just as the abiotic factors determine the dominant types of vegetation, the vegetation, in turn, influences what animals can live in an area. Thus each biome has its own characteristic types of plants and animals.

47–2 Tundra

At the extreme north and south areas of Earth are the **polar regions**. The poles are always covered with ice, permitting almost no plants to grow. A few animals are able to live at the poles, but they must rely upon the ocean for their food, since there is no food on land.

Just south of the Arctic, in the northern parts of North America, Europe, and Asia, is the **tundra**. In the tundra, the ground beneath the top meter of soil is permanently frozen. This permanently frozen ground is called **permafrost**. The soil at the surface thaws during the brief summer. Since the soil beneath is frozen, the melting snow cannot drain into the ground. Instead, it forms many shallow bogs and streams.

CONCEPTS

- how the physical environment limits the distribution of organisms
- characteristics of the major land biomes
- effects of elevation on the vegetation of mountains

Figure 47.1 The leopard seal lives in the polar regions and gets food from the ocean.

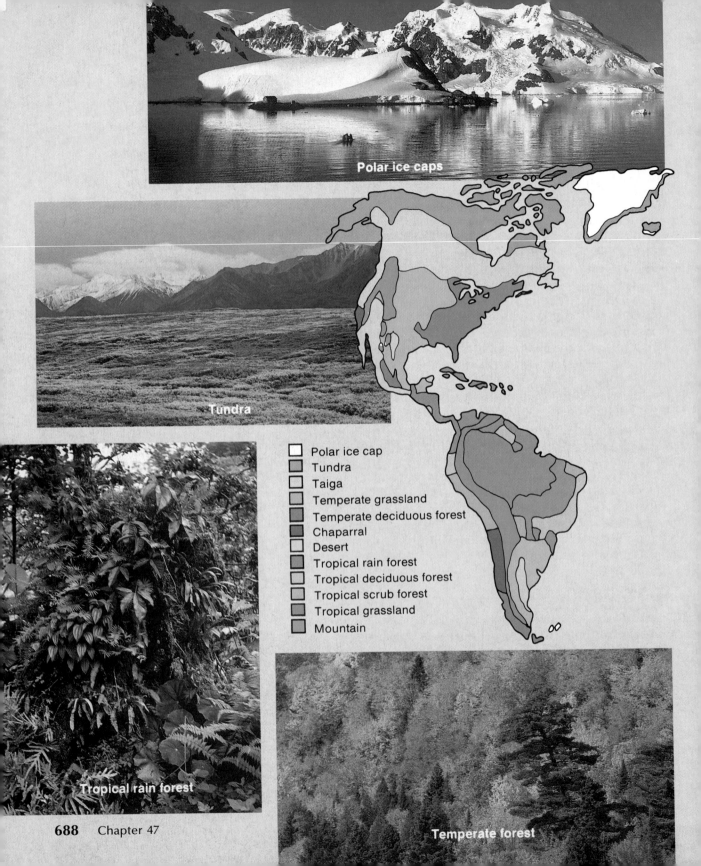

Polar ice caps

Tundra

Tropical rain forest

Temperate forest

Polar ice cap
Tundra
Taiga
Temperate grassland
Temperate deciduous forest
Chaparral
Desert
Tropical rain forest
Tropical deciduous forest
Tropical scrub forest
Tropical grassland
Mountain

Chaparral

Desert

Taiga

Grassland

Figure 47.2 *Top:* The white-phase arctic fox lives in parts of the tundra with extremely cold temperatures. *Bottom:* The blue-phase arctic fox lives in a more moderate part of the tundra.

Do You Know?
Many tundra species, such as the arctic fox, turn white in the winter. This change in color allows them to blend in with the snow.

Vegetation in the tundra rarely grows more than 10 centimeters high. The dominant vegetation consists of lichens, grasses, mosses, herbs, and low-growing woody plants. During the two-month growing season, tiny perennial flowers bloom and produce seeds.

Many birds, such as sandpipers, nest in the tundra during the summer, then migrate south in the winter. Insects, including mosquitoes, are abundant during the short summer. Most insects survive the winter as eggs or pupa. They emerge when the weather becomes warmer.

Herds of caribou and reindeer roam over the tundra. Rodents, such as lemmings, are common. Wolves and arctic foxes prey on the smaller mammals. During the summer there may be many individual animals on the tundra. But the number of species living there is low. As a rule, the closer to the poles, the fewer the number of species that live in an area.

47–3 Taiga

South of the tundra is a continuous band of forest called the **taiga** [TY-guh]. Like the tundra, the taiga has very cold winters. But summers are longer and warmer than those in the tundra. These warm periods permit the soil to thaw completely. The soil in the taiga is acidic. Bogs are common.

Conifers, especially spruce and fir trees, are the dominant vegetation. These conifers are well adapted to the snowy winters of the taiga. Their triangular shape allows snow to fall from their branches, thus preventing the branches from breaking under the weight of heavy snows.

The trees of the taiga provide food and shelter for many animals. Year-round residents include moose, lynx, porcupines, red squirrels, and many small rodents. Many of these animals hibernate during the winter, living off supplies of stored fat. Many migratory birds spend the summer in the taiga, living on the numerous insects. Flocks of seed-eating birds, such as finches, spend all year in the taiga.

On the West Coast of North America, coniferous forests extend south into milder regions. The redwood forests of the California coast are cool throughout the year, but lack the cold winters typical of the taiga.

47–4 Temperate Forests

South of the taiga are the **temperate forests**. In temperate climates, summers are long and warm, with a growing season of at least six months. Rainfall is plentiful, usually at least 100 centimeters per year.

Temperate forests in eastern North America are composed of deciduous trees, which lose their leaves in the autumn. The **deciduous forest** includes plants that grow to many different heights. The tallest trees make up the **canopy**, or leafy covering of the forest. Canopy trees, such as oak, maple, beech, and hickory, may reach heights of 30 meters.

Much of the sunlight filters through the thin leaves of the canopy to the plants below. This light allows smaller trees to form a layer called the **understory**. Redbuds and dogwoods are understory trees. Light that passes through the understory then reaches the **shrub layer**. Shade-tolerant herbs and ferns occupy the shady **herb layer** close to the forest floor. Covering the forest floor is a layer of decomposing leaves called **litter**. The leaves that fall every year decompose slowly, making the soil rich in nutrients.

The temperate forest provides food and shelter to a wide range of animals. These include gray squirrels, whitetail deer, black bears, raccoons, and opossums. Many birds, including thrushes and owls, also live in the deciduous forests.

Parts of temperate North America have seasons that are too dry to support deciduous trees. The dry summers of much of the West favor the growth of open oak or pine **woodlands**. In woodlands the trees are widely spaced and grasses grow between the trees. The dry summers and frequent fires along the foothills of Southern California favor the growth of dense thickets of shrubby trees. This kind of vegetation is called **chaparral** [shap-uh-RAL].

Figure 47.3 Ferns make up the herb layer in this coniferous forest.

47–5 Grasslands

Grasses are the dominant form of vegetation in areas that are too dry to support trees. There are **grasslands** in both temperate and tropical regions. Rainfall in the grasslands usually ranges from 25 to 75 centimeters per year. The low annual rainfall and frequent fires prevent large trees from growing in such areas.

On different continents, grasslands have different names. The *steppes* of Asia, the *pampas* of South America, the *veldts* of South Africa and the *savannas* of Africa are all grasslands. In North America, grasslands cover a huge area that extends from central Canada to the Gulf of Mexico, and west from the Mississippi River to the Rocky Mountains. The eastern area, which receives more rainfall, is called the **tallgrass prairie**. Grasses here may reach heights of 2 meters. To the west is the drier **shortgrass prairie**, or the Great Plains.

Many grasslands have thick, fertile soils that make them ideal agricultural lands. For this reason, the native vegetation of the grasslands is rarely seen. Today the grasslands of North

Figure 47.4 *Left:* The savanna region of Africa is a grassland that is the home of herds of antelope, zebras, and wildebeests. Lions and hyenas are the main predators. *Right:* The pampas region of South America.

Figure 47.5 *Top:* An orchid is an epiphyte. *Bottom:* Tropical rain forests are characterized by colorful tropical birds.

America support fields of grain, especially corn and wheat. Vast herds of bison and pronghorns once roamed over these lands. Today most of these animals have been replaced by cattle and sheep.

47–6 Tropical Rain Forests

As their name suggests, **tropical rain forests** are located close to the equator. Tropical rain forests have the most uniform conditions of any terrestrial biome. The temperature and length of day vary little from month to month. Rain falls frequently, often every day. The three major areas of tropical rain forests are the Amazon Basin in South America, the Malaysian Islands, and the Congo Basin in Africa.

Rain forests contain the greatest diversity of living organisms of any biome. The trees of the rain forest are broad-leaved evergreens. The tallest trees may reach 80 meters, but most are closer to 50 meters. The dense leaves of the canopy block most of the sun from the area below. A few very tall trees, called **emergents**, tower above the other trees of the canopy.

Most of the life in the rain forest takes place in the canopy. Ninety percent of the birds and half of the mammals are tree-dwellers. A great variety of snakes, frogs, lizards, and insects also live in the trees. In the canopy are many ferns and orchids that are supported by the boughs of the trees. These plants are called **epiphytes** [EHP-uh-fyts]. Epiphytes are not parasites; they manufacture their own food. They do, however, rely upon their host plant for support.

Because of the dense covering of the canopy, the floor of the rain forest is dark and has few shrubs or herbs. Many woody vines grow up the tall trunks, thrusting their leaves toward the light. When leaves and fruit fall to the forest floor, they are soon decomposed by bacteria, insects, and fungi. Decomposition occurs quickly and the nutrients are immediately absorbed by the trees. Therefore there is very little accumulation of organic material in the soil.

Today vast expanses of tropical rain forest are being cut for wood. Other areas are being cleared for agriculture. Unfortunately, once a rain forest is cut, the soil quickly loses its fertility. At the present rate of destruction, many rain forests will disappear within the next 50 years. This would cause the extinction of untold thousands of species.

47–7 Deserts

Deserts are the driest biomes. The rainfall in deserts is so sparse that not even grasses can thrive. Desert plants, called **xerophytes** [ZAYR-oh-fyts], are widely spaced. Rain in the desert is usually heavy and brief. The extensive root systems of some xerophytes allow them to absorb much of the water before it runs off. Plants that store water in their leaves or stems are called **succulents**. Succulents are common in many deserts.

In some deserts there are small, fast-growing herbs. After a heavy rain the seeds of these plants germinate. These plants then grow, flower, and produce seeds within a brief period. Such plants are able to tolerate the dry conditions of the desert by avoiding the periods of drought.

Deserts are subject to the most extreme daily temperature changes of any of the world's biomes. In the daytime, the air temperature may reach 40°C. But at night, the temperature may drop below freezing. Most desert animals are active only at night or in the early morning and late afternoon when it is cooler. During the heat of the day, these animals burrow underground or hide in the shade of plants.

Snakes and lizards, with their watertight skins, are well suited to life in the desert. Other desert animals include kangaroo rats, coyotes, and hawks.

You may think of deserts as being hot, for certainly many are. But there are also cold deserts. The Great Basin of North America is a cold desert. Snow and freezing temperatures are common during the winter. Scattered shrubs, especially sagebrush, are the dominant form of vegetation in the Great Basin.

47–8 Life Zones on Mountains

If you were to travel north across North America, you would encounter a variety of biomes, including taiga, tundra, and finally the polar region. This change in vegetation is a result of changes in the climate caused by changes in latitude. If you were to climb a tall mountain, you would also encounter a change in vegetation. This change in vegetation is the result

Figure 47.6 *Top:* Golden carpet is a rare succulent found in the Death Valley region of the United States. *Bottom:* Snow may fall on a desert in winter.

The Distribution of Life **693**

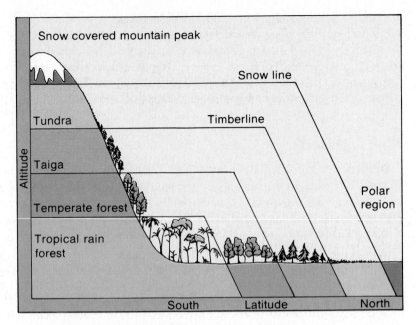

Snow covered mountain peak

Snow line

Tundra

Timberline

Taiga

Temperate forest

Polar region

Tropical rain forest

Altitude

South   Latitude   North

Figure 47.7 Changes in vegetation are affected by both latitude and altitude.

of changes in climate caused by increasing altitude. As air rises, it becomes colder. Thus the climate becomes colder and colder as you ascend.

Figure 47.7 shows the vegetation zones on a mountain. At the beginning of your climb, you would encounter deciduous trees. After climbing for a while, you would enter a forest of firs and spruce trees similar to the taiga.

Eventually you would reach a part of the mountain where it is too cold and windy for trees to survive. The point at which trees can no longer grow is called the **timberline**. Above the timberline, the vegetation resembles the low plants of the tundra. The very top of a mountain, with its high winds and scant soil, may be covered by bare rocks.

It would be a journey of many thousand kilometers to pass through all the biomes on flat land. Yet in just a day's hike on a mountain, you can see many different life zones.

Checkpoint

1. Which biome lies immediately south of the tundra?
2. What biome is responsible for the production of most of the world's grains?
3. What type of plant anchors itself to another plant rather than to the soil?
4. What term describes the upper limit of tree growth on a mountain?

Marine Biomes

Seventy percent of Earth's surface is covered by salt water. Not surprisingly, the physical environments of the oceans and seas are not uniform. Several different zones exist within the ocean environment.

CONCEPTS

- characteristics of the littoral, sublittoral, and pelagic zones
- effects of nutrient upwelling

47–9   The Littoral Zone

If you have spent any time at the seashore, you have probably noticed a stretch of sand or rocks that is covered by water at high tide but exposed to the air at low tide. The area between the low and high watermarks is called the intertidal region, or **littoral zone**.

The littoral zone is a challenging environment. It is subjected to greater variation in temperature and lighting than are other parts of the ocean. The inhabitants of the littoral zone must be able to tolerate the action of waves and periods of exposure to air.

On sandy coasts, crabs and clams burrow in the sand. In more rocky areas, organisms have other adaptations. Rockweed clings to the rocks. Its gelatinous coating gives it protection from the drying action of the sun. The rockweed provides shelter for other algae, protists, and small animals, such as limpets and snails.

Tidal rivers, or **estuaries** [ES-choo-er-eez], empty nutrient-rich waters from the land into the littoral zone. Estuaries may include saltmarshes and mudflats. The larvae of many animals, including crustaceans, mollusks, and fish, begin their lives in the protected saltmarshes of estuaries.

Figure 47.8 A tidal river exhibits a variety of life forms.

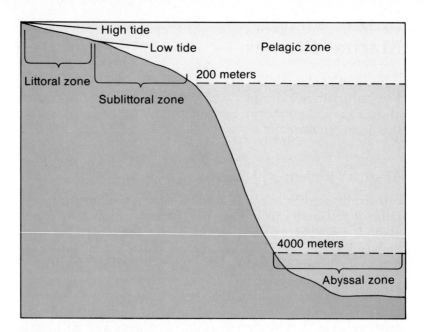

Figure 47.9 Major biomes of the sea

47–10 Sublittoral Zone

The shallow waters between the littoral zone and the edge of the continental shelves make up the **sublittoral zone**. The sublittoral zone is a more stable environment than the littoral zone. There is less variation in temperature, and the organisms are never exposed to the air. Light can penetrate to the depths, allowing the growth of both free-floating and bottom-anchored algae. These algae support a diverse group of plant-eating animals, including many fish.

The **benthic zone** is composed of the seabed in the sublittoral zone. The many organisms that live on the bottom are called **benthos**. Crabs and starfish are benthos.

In tropical areas, the sublittoral zone may contain coral reefs. Reefs are made up of the calcium carbonate deposits from the coral animals and red and green algae. The coral

Figure 47.10 In addition to their beauty, coral reefs provide shelter for a variety of organisms.

animals live in association with photosynthetic dinoflagellates. Since the dinoflagellates require light for photosynthesis, coral reefs are found only in waters less than 100 meters deep. The reef provides shelter and support for a great variety of sessile animals. Fish feed on the numerous reef inhabitants and hide in the crevices of the reef.

47–11   The Open Ocean

The open waters beyond the sublittoral zone are called the **pelagic** [puh-LAHJ-ik] **zone. Phytoplankton**, or floating photosynthetic organisms, are plentiful in the pelagic waters. Phytoplankton include diatoms, green algae, and dinoflagellates. The phytoplankton are food for crustaceans and other tiny floating heterotrophs called **zooplankton**. Fish, whales, and other free-swimming organisms feed upon the plankton. The free-swimming organisms are called **nekton**.

Light from the sun is most intense at the surface of the water. The sun's light cannot penetrate to the depths of the ocean. Red and yellow light are the first to be filtered out by the water. For this reason, when you descend into the ocean, everything appears to have a bluish cast.

The depths of the seas are called the **abyssal zone**. The abyssal zone is cold and dark. At such great depths there are no algae or phytoplankton because there is insufficient light for photosynthesis to occur. This deep water is inhabited largely by bacteria and filter feeders. These organisms feed upon material that sinks to the bottom from the upper layers of water.

The waters in different zones of the oceans do not remain forever separate from each other. Currents and temperature differences cause a process called **nutrient upwelling** to occur. Minerals released by the decomposition of organisms on the seabeds are carried upward by currents. These minerals provide nutrients for the algae. Thus the shallow and deep areas of the ocean are not independent of one another. Nutrients are provided from below, and light filters down from above. Both are necessary for supporting the rich life of the oceans.

Do You Know?

Many of the fish that live in the abyssal zone have bioluminescent organs. In some species, the light from these organs lures prey to the fish. In other species, these organs attract mates.

Checkpoint

1. Which zone of the ocean contains floating organisms?
2. What is the name for an area in which fresh water of a river mixes with the salt water of the ocean?
3. What term describes small, floating autotrophs? What term describes floating heterotrophs?
4. In what process are nutrients from the seabed carried upward to the ocean's surface?

CONCEPTS

- stages in succession of a pond
- difference between primary and secondary succession
- effects of fire on communities

Figure 47.11 Succession in a pond

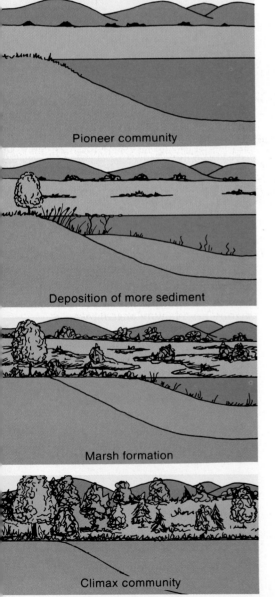

Pioneer community

Deposition of more sediment

Marsh formation

Climax community

Succession: A Change Through Time

Do you live near a pond or a wooded area? Although it may look the same to you now as it did when you were a small child, it is slowly and constantly changing. If your grandparents live in the same town as you do, the area probably looks much different now from the way it looked when they were young.

Even within a particular climate, the inhabitants of a location are not the same from one year to the next. Organisms that live in a location may change the environment by their very presence. An environment that was favorable to them when they arrived becomes less favorable to them and more favorable to other life forms. Thus one type of organism may pave the way for another. The orderly change in the inhabitants of an area through time is called **succession**.

47–12 Primary Succession

A classic illustration of succession is that of a pond. Rain carries sediment from surrounding land into the pond, filling it in and making it more shallow. Algae that live in the pond die and eventually fall to the bottom, adding organic material to the sediment. Soon underwater vascular plants such as pond weeds establish themselves in the rich bottom material. These plants make up the **pioneer community**. The pioneer plants are the first to inhabit the changing environment.

The roots of these underwater plants hold much silt, quickly building up the bottom cover of the pond. As they die, their organic matter accumulates on the bottom. The water along the edges becomes so shallow that water lilies and other floating plants replace the pioneer plants.

Eventually plants such as cattails and bullrushes replace the floating plants. These plants grow very close together, allowing the rapid buildup of sediment at their bases. A few land plants can now grow near the edges of the pond. The edges of the pond have been transformed into a marsh.

The edges of the pond gradually fill with sediment, until in time the entire pond becomes a marsh. Over time the marsh is also filled with sediment, allowing trees to grow. Thus what was once a pond becomes a forest, supporting trees and the animals they feed and shelter.

The final stage of succession in a particular area is called the **climax community**. The species that make up the climax community differ from biome to biome. In the temperate forest the climax community may contain oak and hickory trees, whereas in the taiga it may be composed of spruce and fir trees.

The change from a pond to land is called **primary succession**. Primary succession occurs when land plants colonize an area in which they have not previously grown. Primary succession also occurs when plants begin to grow on bare rocks. Succession will progress from the pioneer lichens and mosses, to low herbs, through intermediate communities, and finally to the climax community.

47–13   Secondary Succession

Sometimes a storm or fire will destroy the species growing in a climax community. When this happens, succession will proceed until there is again a climax community. Succession that occurs when an area has not been totally stripped of soil and vegetation is called **secondary succession**. Although it may take hundreds of years for a climax community to return, secondary succession occurs more rapidly than primary succession because soil has already been formed. Secondary succession also occurs when farmers abandon old fields. Eventually native species take over the land.

In some areas, fires started by lightning or human activities occasionally spread throughout an area. Such fires may kill the species in a climax stage. When this occurs, secondary succession will take place. For example, if a fire kills the spruce and fir trees in the taiga, aspen trees will soon spring up. Later, spruce and fir trees will grow up in the shade of the aspens.

Some plants are better able to survive fires than others. Grasses can easily survive fires that would kill trees. Pine trees are more fire resistant than are deciduous trees. Frequent fires favor the formation of certain types of climax communities. Some of the communities that are maintained by fires in North America include the chaparral, the southern pine forests, and the prairies.

BIOLOGY INSIGHTS

Succession usually results in an increase in the number of species living in an area. Pioneer communities typically have fewer species than climax communities. Communities with many species tend to be more stable than communities with only a few species.

Figure 47.12 Secondary succession occurred in this area after it was damaged by fire.

Checkpoint

1. What term is used to describe the orderly change of organisms in an environment over time?
2. What is the name for the first plants to inhabit a changing area?
3. What is the final stage of succession called?
4. What type of succession occurs after a fire?

CHAPTER REVIEW

Summary

- Within the biosphere, abiotic factors such as rainfall, temperature, and soil determine what plants can live in a particular area. The biosphere can be subdivided into biomes, each with a dominant type of vegetation. The vegetation types, in turn, limit what animals can live in a biome.

- The tundra contains low-growing perennials, grasses, and lichens. The ground of the tundra is permanently frozen. Few species are able to tolerate the extreme climate of the tundra.

- South of the tundra grow the coniferous forests called the taiga. The species of the taiga are able to withstand the cold dry winters of this region. The soil is thin and acidic.

- The warmer, moister climate of the temperate region is able to support the diverse vegetation of deciduous forests. The deciduous forest vegetation is layered into a canopy, understory, shrub layer, and herb layer. The soil of these forests is rich, since the leaves fall every year and decompose slowly.

- Grasslands receive less rainfall than the forests. The thick soils of the grasslands are ideal for agriculture. On this continent, most of the native grasslands have been replaced by fields of grain or herds of cattle or sheep.

- Deserts are the driest regions. Short-lived annuals survive the dry weather by growing only after heavy rains. Succulents are able to survive the dry periods by storing water.

- Tropical rain forests contain the greatest diversity of species. The warm weather and ample rainfall allow trees to grow all year. Most of the organisms live in the canopy, where there is adequate sunlight.

- Mountains often have several life zones. These life zones are similar to the biomes.

- The oceans contain various zones of life. The tidal region makes up the littoral zone. The waters between the littoral zone and the continental shelves make up the sublittoral zone. The open oceans are in the pelagic zone.

- Succession is the orderly change of organisms in an environment over time. The first plants to colonize an area make up the pioneer community. The final stage of succession is called the climax community.

- Primary succession occurs when plants colonize bare rock or other areas where there is no soil. Secondary succession occurs when plants recolonize an area in which the climax community has been disturbed.

Vocabulary

abiotic factors	permafrost
abyssal zone	phytoplankton
benthic zone	pioneer community
benthos	polar regions
biome	primary succession
biosphere	secondary succession
canopy	shortgrass prairie
chaparral	shrub layer
climax community	sublittoral zone
deciduous forest	succession
desert	succulent
emergent	taiga
epiphyte	tallgrass prairie
estuary	temperate forest
grasslands	timberline
herb layer	tropical rain forest
litter	tundra
littoral zone	woodland
nekton	understory
nutrient upwelling	xerophyte
pelagic zone	zooplankton

Review

1. List three abiotic factors that determine the distribution of biomes.

2. What term describes the depths of the ocean where no light can penetrate?
3. List the following biomes in order from highest to lowest annual temperature: (a) tundra, (b) temperate forest, (c) taiga, (d) tropical rainforest.
4. Which land biome contains the greatest diversity of species?
5. Which zone of the ocean has the most phytoplankton?
6. Name an adaptation that allows plants to live in the desert. Name an adaptation that allows animals to live in the desert.
7. How does the process of nutrient upwelling aid phytoplankton?
8. Name three biomes that are maintained by frequent fires.

In the following list, match the biome with the characteristic form of vegetation.

9. tundra
10. taiga
11. temperate forest
12. tropical rain forest
13. prairie
14. desert

a. broad-leaved evergreens, vines, and epiphytes
b. scattered shrubs and succulents
c. conifers
d. lichens, mosses, and low plants
f. continuous grasses
g. broad-leaved deciduous trees

Interpret and Apply

1. Compare the soils of the tundra and taiga.
2. Compare the soil of the grasslands to the soil of a rain forest.
3. Which biome has the least change in temperature from season to season?
4. Compare the layers of vegetation in a temperate deciduous forest to those in a tropical rain forest.
5. Place the following layers in the proper sequence, beginning with the forest floor: (a) canopy, (b) herb layer, (c) understory, (d) litter, (e) shrub layer.

6. Why are there no plants growing in the abyssal zone of the ocean?
7. During succession, the plant forms in a location are replaced by new plant forms. Does the same thing happen with animal forms?
8. What is the difference between primary and secondary succession?

In the following list, match the organism on the left to the group on the right.

9. squid
10. diatom
11. sea anemone
12. floating crustacean

a. zooplankton
b. phytoplankton
c. nekton
d. benthos

Challenge

1. You are climbing a mountain, and most of the trees that you see are deciduous. Soon the deciduous trees become smaller and less numerous. Which type of vegetation becomes dominant next?
2. Why are estuaries considered to be aquatic nurseries?

Projects

1. Read about and report on Jacques Cousteau and other pioneers of the oceans. Find out how they contributed to our knowledge of the seas. Include the technology they developed.
2. Find out the following information about the area in which you live: average yearly rainfall, average temperature, length of the growing season. What are the dominant types of vegetation in your area? In which biome do you live?
3. After a volcano erupts, the life surrounding the volcano is destroyed. Scientists have carefully observed the succession of species on bare rock following several volcanic eruptions. Research the investigations near Mt. Saint Helens or another recent volcano.

48 Ecosystems and Communities

White-collared mangabey

A monkey sits in a tree high in the canopy of an African rain forest. It plucks a ripe fruit from the tree's branch and eats the edible portion. When it is finished eating, the monkey drops the peels to the ground far below.

The leaves of the canopy form a moisture-holding cover over the ground. In the moist, warm air under the canopy, microorganisms quickly decompose the fruit peels. The organic compounds in the peels are released into the soil and air. Soon these compounds are reabsorbed by the roots of the trees in the rain forest. Thus the nutrients in the rain forest connect the monkey and the trees. These organisms are dependent upon their environment for survival.

The monkey, the fruit tree, and the microorganisms are but three of the many thousands of different organisms that live in the tropical rain forest. Each affects and is affected by the others. Everything that happens in this small part of the rain forest in some way affects all the rest of the organisms living there.

Living Communities

The distribution of vegetation in biomes is largely determined by abiotic factors, such as climate and soil. But living organisms also interact with each other. The study of the relationships between organisms and their environment is called **ecology** [ee-KOL-oh-gee]. Scientists who study ecology are called **ecologists**.

48–1 Ecosystems

All the populations of organisms in an area make up the living **community**. For example, all the plants, animals, fungi, and microorganisms in a particular meadow make up the community of that meadow. The living organisms in a community are the **biotic factors** of an ecosystem.

Living things are influenced by, and in turn influence, their abiotic environment. An **ecosystem** is a unit of the biosphere in which the community of organisms interacts with the physical environment. You could think of an ecosystem as a small part of a biome.

Usually an ecosystem has some sort of natural boundary. For example, a particular meadow in the grasslands, including its abiotic and biotic factors, is an ecosystem. So is a single tidal pool or a rotting log in a deciduous forest. For an ecosystem to exist for a long time, there must be a delicate balance between the biotic and abiotic factors.

As you learned in Chapter 5, living things are organized in levels of increasing complexity from cell through organism. As Figure 48.1 shows, an ecosystem is also a level of organization. It contains all the simpler elements and is contained by more complex systems. The most complex system of all is the biosphere, which contains all life.

CONCEPTS

- definition of an ecosystem
- the roles of producers, consumers, and decomposers in ecosystems
- difference between habitat and niche
- three ways of representing the flow of energy through an ecosystem
- forms of symbiosis

Figure 48.1 Which levels of organization of living things are lower than the ecosystem? Which are higher?

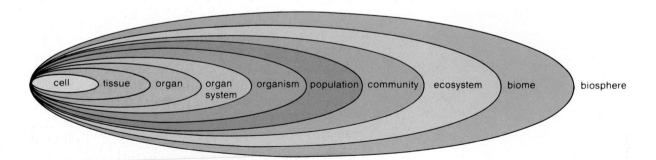

cell · tissue · organ · organ system · organism · population · community · ecosystem · biome · biosphere

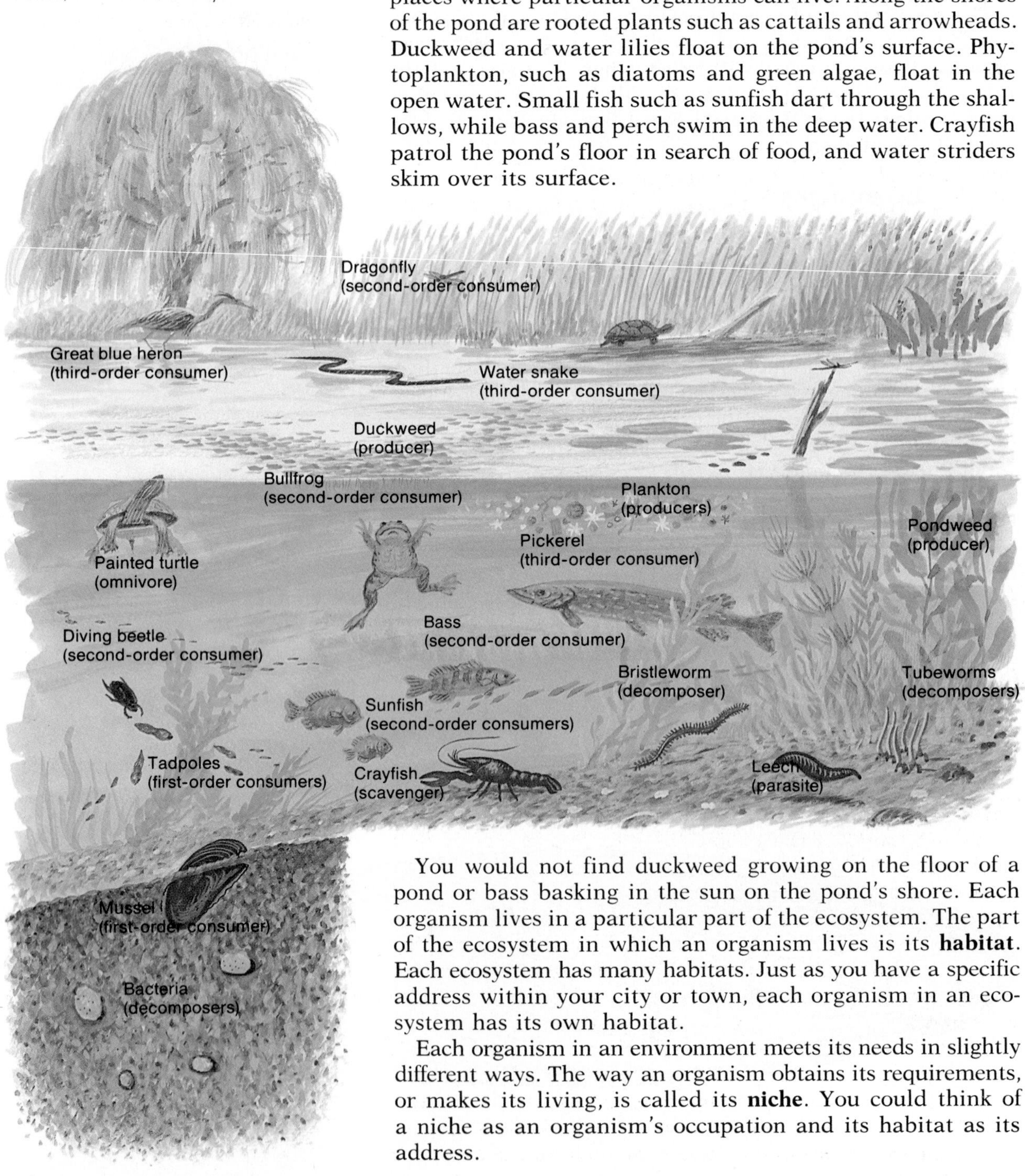

Figure 48.2 Each type of organism lives in a particular location, or habitat, within an ecosystem.

A pond is an ecosystem. Within the pond are many different places where particular organisms can live. Along the shores of the pond are rooted plants such as cattails and arrowheads. Duckweed and water lilies float on the pond's surface. Phytoplankton, such as diatoms and green algae, float in the open water. Small fish such as sunfish dart through the shallows, while bass and perch swim in the deep water. Crayfish patrol the pond's floor in search of food, and water striders skim over its surface.

Dragonfly
(second-order consumer)

Great blue heron
(third-order consumer)

Water snake
(third-order consumer)

Duckweed
(producer)

Bullfrog
(second-order consumer)

Plankton
(producers)

Painted turtle
(omnivore)

Pickerel
(third-order consumer)

Pondweed
(producer)

Diving beetle
(second-order consumer)

Bass
(second-order consumer)

Bristleworm
(decomposer)

Tubeworms
(decomposers)

Sunfish
(second-order consumers)

Tadpoles
(first-order consumers)

Crayfish
(scavenger)

Leech
(parasite)

Mussel
(first-order consumer)

Bacteria
(decomposers)

You would not find duckweed growing on the floor of a pond or bass basking in the sun on the pond's shore. Each organism lives in a particular part of the ecosystem. The part of the ecosystem in which an organism lives is its **habitat**. Each ecosystem has many habitats. Just as you have a specific address within your city or town, each organism in an ecosystem has its own habitat.

Each organism in an environment meets its needs in slightly different ways. The way an organism obtains its requirements, or makes its living, is called its **niche**. You could think of a niche as an organism's occupation and its habitat as its address.

48–3 Producers, Consumers, and Decomposers

All ecosystems require a source of energy. The organisms in an ecosystem are tied together by their need for energy. Most of the energy in ecosystems originates in the sun. Autotrophs are able to capture and store the sun's energy by the process of photosynthesis. The food-producing organisms in an ecosystem are called **producers**. The producers in a forest include the trees and shrubs.

Besides making their own food, producers provide food for all other organisms in the ecosystem. The leaves of the trees are eaten by insects such as caterpillars. When an organism gets its food from another organism, its role in the community is that of a **consumer**.

Consumers that eat only plants are called **herbivores** [UR-buh-vorz]. A caterpillar is an example of an herbivore. Consumers that eat the flesh of other animals are called **carnivores**. A bird that ate the caterpillar would be an example of a carnivore. Animals that eat both plants and animals are called **omnivores**. Raccoons and skunks are omnivores, as are humans.

A third group of organisms in the ecosystem are called **decomposers**. Decomposers, such as fungi and bacteria, feed on dead organisms and the wastes of living organisms. The chemical components of a dead organism are then released into the soil, where they are again available to the roots of the trees. Of course, bacteria and fungi do not decompose organic matter for the sake of the ecosystem. Decomposers obtain their food from the organic matter they decompose. Because they obtain their food from other organisms, decomposers are heterotrophs.

48–4 Food Chains and Webs

A **food chain** is a way of illustrating the energy relationships among organisms in an ecosystem. Figure 48.3 shows a food chain in a pond. Arrows show the direction of energy flow in the food chain.

Every food chain must begin with a producer. In a pond this producer might be the duckweed growing on the surface of the water. A duckling might eat the duckweed. A snapping turtle, in turn, could eat the duckling. Because the duckling feeds directly on the producer, it is called a **first-order consumer**.

The turtle is called a **second-order consumer** because it eats a first-order consumer. What would you call an animal that ate the turtle that ate the duckling that ate the duckweed?

Food chains exist in all ecosystems. Grass is the producer in a meadow. First-order consumers such as mice eat the

Do You Know?
Any defined area can be studied as an ecosystem. Ecologists have investigated the interactions within caves and on islands. One ecologist even studied the animals living in pools of water trapped by epiphytes.

grass. A snake that eats a mouse is a second-order consumer. A hawk that eats the snake is a third-order consumer. Consumers that actively seek out their prey, such as snapping turtles and snakes, are also called **predators**.

Figure 48.3 A pond food chain

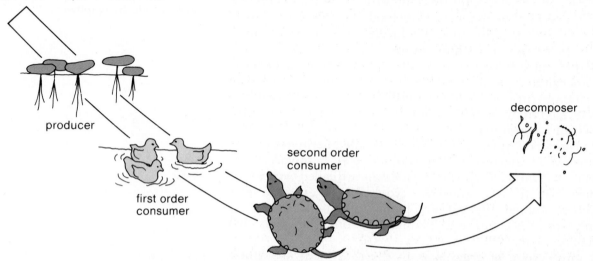

The two food chains just described are simpler than those found in most natural ecosystems. Many animals eat more than one type of food, and many plants are eaten by more than one herbivore. Thus ecosystems usually contain overlapping food chains. Several interconnected food chains, such as those shown in Figure 48.4, are called a **food web**.

Figure 48.4 A food web. How many different food chains can you trace?

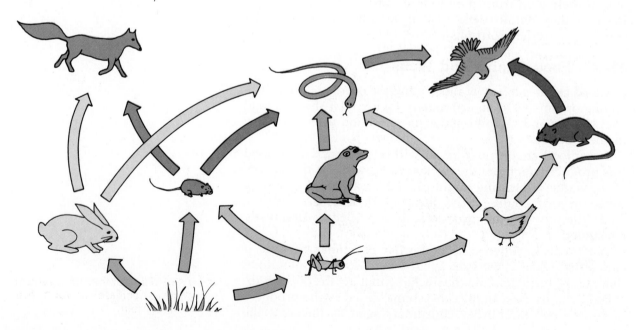

48–5 Energy Pyramids

Each time energy is converted from one form to another, some fraction of the total amount of energy is lost. Of the energy that reaches Earth as sunlight, only a fraction is captured by photosynthesis. Each time an organism is eaten, its chemical energy is transformed into cellular energy that fuels the metabolism of the consumer. Much of the energy is lost as heat. Some of the energy is lost in the digestion of food. Animals must also expend energy to capture their prey.

Only about 10 percent of the energy an organism takes in is stored in the tissues of that organism. Therefore, when a first-order consumer such as a mouse eats grass, it stores only about 10 percent of the energy available from the grass. When a second-order consumer such as a snake eats the mouse, it stores only 10 percent of the mouse's energy. This is equivalent to only 1 percent of the grass's energy. When a hawk eats a snake, the hawk stores only 10 percent of the snake's energy, or 0.1 percent of the grass's energy.

The transfer of energy in a food chain is sometimes illustrated as an **energy pyramid**, as shown in Figure 48.5. As you can see, the producers contain most of the energy in the pyramid. The first-order consumers have less energy, and the second-order consumers even less.

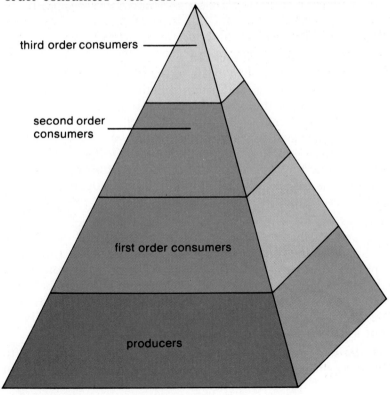

third order consumers

second order consumers

first order consumers

producers

Figure 48.5 The number of organisms in each level decreases as you move up the food chain.

In most ecosystems the producers are the most plentiful organisms. Usually the first-order consumers are less numerous than the producers because a first-order consumer must eat many producers in order to obtain enough energy. At the top of the pyramid are the top consumers, which are fewest in number.

The loss of energy in a food chain can also be shown by measuring the biomass in an ecosystem. **Biomass** is a measure of the total mass of dry organic matter produced in a given area. Figure 48.6 shows the biomass pyramid of a meadow.

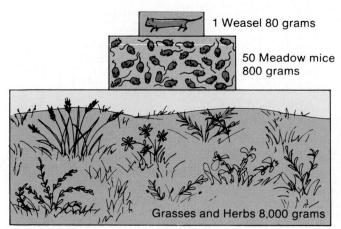

1 Weasel 80 grams

50 Meadow mice 800 grams

Grasses and Herbs 8,000 grams

Figure 48.6 As this biomass pyramid of a meadow shows, the biomass of an ecosystem decreases with each level of a food chain.

48–6 Symbiosis

All organisms are influenced by other organisms within a community. No organism exists independently of others. Some relationships between organisms benefit one type of organism without harming the other. Some relationships benefit both types of organisms.

Sometimes two types of organisms have a permanent relationship in which one depends upon the other for survival. This is called a symbiotic relationship. **Symbiosis** [sihm-by-OH-sihs] is a Greek word that means "living together." There are several types of symbioses.

Parasitism A symbiotic relationship that benefits one organism and harms another is called **parasitism**. A **parasite** is an organism that gets its nutrition from the tissues of another organism without killing it. The organism on which the parasite lives is called the **host**. Some parasites, such as tapeworms, live inside their host. Others, such as fleas, live on the surface of their host. Although parasites usually do not kill their hosts, they often weaken them.

Mutualism A symbiotic relationship that is beneficial to both organisms is called **mutualism**. Lichens are a well-known example of mutualism. Lichens consist of fungi and algae growing in close association with one another. The fungi can hold water but cannot produce their own food. The algae cannot hold water but can produce their own food when supplied with water. When the two types of organisms live together, each has enough water and enough food.

Coral reefs abound with examples of mutualism. Figure 48.7 shows a clown fish and a sea anemone. In their mutualistic relationship the brightly-colored clown fish attracts prey to the stinging tentacles of the anemone. In return, the clown fish, which is immune to the anemone's deadly sting, receives shelter from its predators.

One of the most complex examples of mutualism involves the thorn acacia, which lives in the tropical rain forest of South America, and a species of ant. When vines grow near the acacia, the ants attack by cutting through their stems and killing them. This prevents other plants from competing with the acacia. The ants also bite and sting intruding insects that could harm the acacia.

In return for this protection, the acacia leaves secrete a rich solution that the ants drink. On the tips of some leaves grow structures that are rich in proteins and vitamins. Adult ants collect these structures and feed them to their larvae. In the hollow thorns of the acacia, the ants lay their eggs and rear their young. The relationship between these two organisms has evolved to the point that neither could survive without the other.

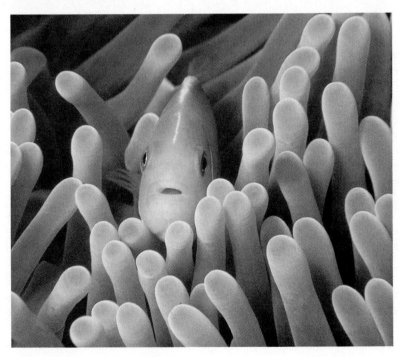

Figure 48.7 A clownfish among the tentacles of a sea anemone

Ecosystems and Communities **709**

Commensalism   **Commensalism** is a symbiotic relationship in which one organism benefits and the other is unaffected. Epiphytes that grow in the tropical rain forests are examples of commensals. Because of the lush vegetation, the rain-forest floor is too dark for most plants. By growing high on the branches of trees, the epiphytic orchids can obtain enough sunlight to carry out photosynthesis. The orchids take nothing from their host tree. Yet they depend upon the host to obtain light. The host tree is neither harmed nor helped by the epiphyte.

Another example of commensalism is that of remoras and sharks. A remora is a small fish that attaches itself to the underside of a shark. There it feeds upon leftovers from the shark's meals. The presence of the remora does not benefit the shark, but neither does it harm the shark.

48–7   Competition

Often two types of organisms require similar resources from the environment. These resources may include food, light, water, or space. When two species require the same resources, they are competing with each other to meet their needs.

If the resources in an area are limited and both species require exactly the same factors from the environment, they

NEWSBREAK

For most Americans, cooking dinner is simply a matter of turning on a stove. In many parts of the world, however, the first step in preparing dinner is to collect firewood. Yet in many places there is not enough firewood for everyone. In some developing nations the shortage of firewood is so severe that the need for firewood is a great problem. In Nepal, for example, children may spend as much as three days a week searching for firewood.

The demand for wood has resulted in the destruction of forests in many developing nations. In the Caribbean country of Haiti, for instance, over 90 percent of the forests were cut down between 1950 and 1980.

When people cut down forests, they start a chain reaction that is difficult to reverse. Without trees, the soil is exposed to wind and rain, causing erosion. Without soil, plants cannot grow and the moisture in the soil is lost. In this way a once-forested area may be transformed into a desert. Today in much of Africa, India, and the Middle East, deserts are growing while forests are shrinking.

Fortunately, people in many countries are beginning to realize the importance of preserving forest ecosystems. The best news of all comes from China, where farmers have been successful in reversing the trend. Today the Chinese are planting new forests at a rate of 1.5 million hectares a year. During the last 30 years, China has doubled its forested area. Thus, while the situation is serious, it is not hopeless. If humans today take care to maintain their forests, it is possible to stop the growth of deserts in the world.

Figure 48.8 Each kind of warbler feeds on insects in a different part of the trees. By having different niches, these closely related warblers do not compete with one another for food.

cannot continue to coexist. One species will be more successful than the other. Eventually the other species will be crowded out.

Usually similar species that have lived in the same ecosystem for a long time have evolved slightly different ways of meeting their needs. In other words, the similar species will occupy different niches.

The cormorant and the shag, two closely related seabirds, demonstrate this principle. These birds are very similar in appearance and habits. At first look it seems as though these two birds have identical ecological requirements. Both species eat fish and nest on cliffs. Yet research has shown significant differences between the two birds. The cormorant feeds in shallow harbors, while the shag feeds farther out to sea. Thus the two species are able to coexist because they do not compete directly with each other.

Checkpoint

1. What is the role of an autotroph in a food chain?
2. What name is given to heterotrophs that eat only the flesh of other animals?
3. What form of symbiosis benefits both organisms? What form of symbiosis benefits one member and has little effect on the other member?
4. What is the name given to a living community and its physical factors?

Cycles in the Biosphere

The energy in an ecosystem flows from one organism to another through food webs and chains. Once the energy is used, it is lost to the ecosystem. Energy cannot be recycled. The chemical nutrients in an ecosystem, however, can be used over and over again.

Several nutrients are especially important to the functioning of living things. Nutrients may alternate between time spent in the bodies of living things and time spent in the physical environment. The movement of these chemicals between the living and nonliving parts of the environment illustrates the close relationship of the environment and the living community. Among those nutrients recycled in an ecosystem are carbon, oxygen, phosphorus, nitrogen, and water.

48–8   The Water Cycle

Figure 48.9 illustrates the water cycle. As with any cycle, it has no beginning or end. However, it is helpful to choose a starting point, such as rainfall. When rain falls, some of it is absorbed by plants through their roots. After spending time

Figure 48.9 The water cycle

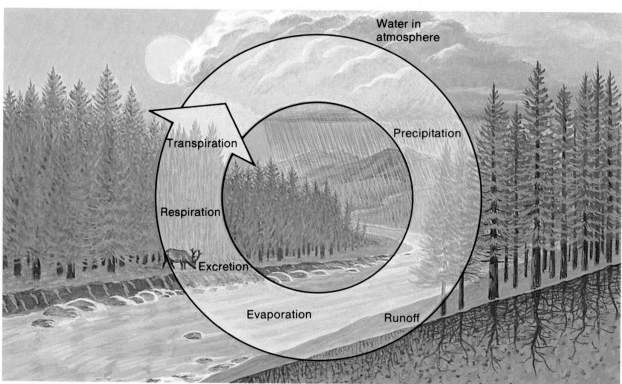

in plants, water evaporates from them in the process of transpiration. A bit of the water is drunk by animals and then released during respiration or excretion.

Some rain falls directly into ponds or streams. Some runs off the surface of the land into rivers. Some of the water filters down through the soil and flows underground. Much of the underground water eventually empties into the ocean. Water returns to the atmosphere by evaporation. When water vapor accumulates in the atmosphere as clouds it may fall once again as rain or snow.

48–9   The Carbon Cycle

Carbon alternates between its inorganic form, carbon dioxide (CO_2), in the atmosphere and its many organic forms in living things. There is also carbon dioxide dissolved in ocean water. You may think of the carbon dioxide in the atmosphere as an inorganic reservoir for all organic molecules.

The carbon cycle is shown in Figure 48.10. The process of photosynthesis takes CO_2 from its inorganic state and transforms it into complex organic molecules. During the process of respiration, the complex molecules are broken down, releasing carbon dioxide into the atmosphere again. Some of the carbon remains in organic molecules such as the cellulose

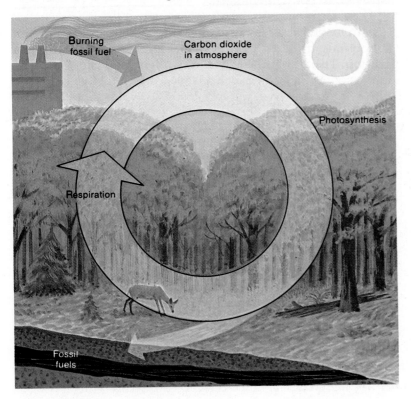

Figure 48.10 The carbon cycle

in the cell walls of plants. When animals eat plants, the carbon compounds become part of their bodies.

Some of the organic carbon is released as waste. Both the wastes and the dead bodies of plants and animals are broken down by organisms such as bacteria and fungi, which release CO_2 into the atmosphere. Thus carbon is constantly being transformed from organic to inorganic forms.

Sometimes carbon becomes involved in longer pathways. Not all dead plants and animals decompose. Some are compressed under the ground over long periods. There they are converted to fossil fuels such as coal, oil, or gas. Carbon trapped in these forms is removed from circulation in the carbon cycle for a long time — as long as millions of years. When humans burn fossil fuels, they are returning these carbon atoms to the active carbon cycle.

48–10   The Nitrogen Cycle

The element nitrogen is crucial to life because it is a component of proteins and nucleic acids. The inorganic reservoir of nitrogen is the atmosphere. Nitrogen gas (N_2) comprises 78 percent of the gas in the atmosphere, but it is not biologically active. Although you inhale large quantities of nitrogen, it leaves your body unchanged.

How does nitrogen enter the chemistry of the life processes? Certain bacteria and cyanophytes can synthesize nitrogen compounds from nitrogen gas in a process called **nitrogen fixation**. These organisms live in swollen areas called **nodules** on the roots of legumes such as clover, peas, and vetch. Some of the organisms live free in the soil or water. The **nitrogen-fixing bacteria** are capable of converting nitrogen gas to ammonium ions (NH_4^+). They then use ammonium ions to synthesize organic compounds. Some of the ammonium is excreted into the soil or water. Bacteria release some of the ammonium into the root tissues of their host plants.

Although some plants can use ammonium ions directly, other plants can use nitrogen only in the form of nitrates (NO_3^-). Other groups of bacteria, called **nitrifying bacteria**, are able to convert ammonium ions into nitrate ions, which are released into the soil. The plants are then able to obtain these nitrates to synthesize amino acids and proteins. Some of the plants are eaten by animals, which form still other proteins from the nitrogen in the plants.

When plants and animals die, bacteria and fungi decompose them, turning their nitrogen-containing molecules into ammonium and nitrate ions. Another group of bacteria, called **denitrifying bacteria**, convert nitrate ions back to nitrogen gas. The nitrogen gas is released into the atmosphere.

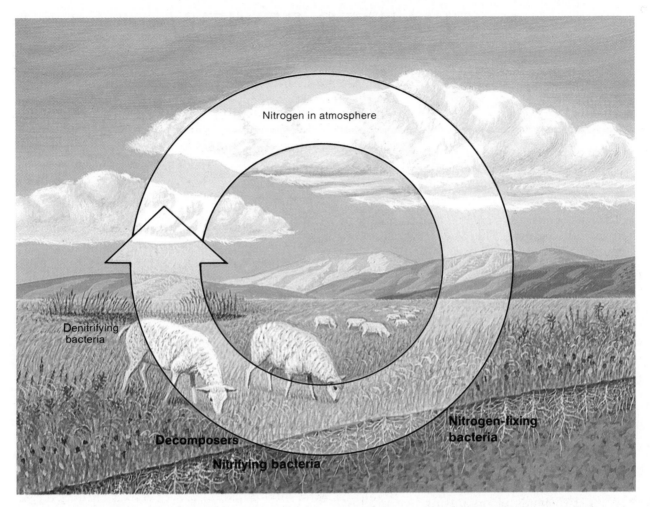

Figure 48.11 The nitrogen cycle

Like carbon, nitrogen alternates between its inorganic form in the atmosphere and its organic form in living things. As with all forms of matter, the amount of nitrogen in the biosphere is in equilibrium. Although the amount of each form of nitrogen may change from time to time, the total amount of nitrogen in the biosphere remains constant.

Checkpoint

1. By what process does water in the ocean return to the atmosphere?
2. What is the inorganic form of carbon in the carbon cycle?
3. In what process is inorganic carbon converted to organic carbon?
4. What kinds of organisms return nitrogen to the atmosphere?

CHAPTER REVIEW

Summary

- An ecosystem is a level of organization of living things. An ecosystem consists of all the organisms of a community and the abiotic factors with which they interact.

- The part of an ecosystem in which an organism lives is its habitat. The way in which an organism obtains its needs is called its niche. Two species cannot occupy the same niche.

- Most ecosystems include producers, consumers, and decomposers. These organisms rely upon each other for food and are interconnected by nutrient cycles. The interactions of the biotic and abiotic factors are maintained in a delicate balance.

- Energy flows through ecosystems in food chains or food webs. In most ecosystems producers outnumber consumers. The biomass of producers is always greater than that of the consumers. In most ecosystems, about 90 percent of the energy is lost at each level of a food chain.

- When two kinds of organisms live in close contact with each other, they are said to have a symbiotic relationship. The three types of symbioses are parasitism, mutualism, and commensalism.

- Most of the chemicals in an ecosystem are used over and over again. The path of a nutrient through the living community and the nonliving environment is called a nutrient cycle. Water, carbon, and nitrogen are three chemicals whose cycles are biologically important.

- Unlike matter, energy does not cycle. Once energy is lost to the ecosystem, it cannot be used again. Most of the energy in ecosystems ultimately comes from the sun.

Vocabulary

biomass	herbivore
biotic factor	host
carnivore	mutualism
commensalism	niche
community	nitrifying bacteria
consumer	nitrogen fixation
decomposers	nitrogen-fixing
denitrifying bacteria	bacteria
ecologist	nodule
ecology	omnivore
ecosystem	parasite
energy pyramid	parasitism
first-order consumer	predator
food chain	producers
food web	second-order
habitat	consumer
	symbiosis

Review

1. By what process does energy enter a food chain?
2. By what process is organic carbon returned to the atmosphere?
3. Which organisms convert nitrogen (N_2) into a form that is biologically usable?
4. What does a third-order consumer eat?
5. Roughly what percentage of the energy an animal consumes is stored in body tissue?
6. Give an example of two organisms in a mutualistic relationship.
7. Name two ways in which water enters the atmosphere.
8. What is the ultimate source of energy in a food chain?
9. What form of symbiosis benefits one organism and harms the other?

Interpret and Apply

1. How is a second-order consumer such as a fox dependent upon the energy of the sun?
2. What is the difference between an organism's habitat and its niche?
3. Place the following in order from most general to most specific: consumer, heterotroph, second-order consumer, wolf.
4. List three ways in which energy is lost to an ecosystem.
5. As a result of what process is carbon dioxide removed from the inorganic reservoir in the atmosphere?
6. What is the difference between a predator and a parasite?
7. Compare the flow of energy through an ecosystem to the carbon cycle. How are they related? How are they different?
8. Mistletoe is a flowering plant that grows on the branches of trees. Mistletoe must rely on its host plant for food and water. Occasionally a large number of mistletoe plants may harm their host tree. What term describes this relationship?

In the following questions, select the letter that best completes the question.

9. Which of the following processes returns carbon to the atmosphere most quickly?
   a. decomposition of dead animals
   b. formation of oil
   c. photosynthesis
   d. respiration
10. Which of the following is not the same as the others?
   a. herbivore
   b. first-order consumer
   c. second-order consumer
   d. cow
11. Which of the following would decrease the amount of CO_2 in the atmosphere?
   a. increasing the number of plants
   b. decreasing the number of plants
   c. burning of fossil fuels
   d. increasing the number of animals
12. Where are nitrogen-fixing bacteria found?
   a. in the leaves of all plants
   b. in the human digestive tract
   c. in the roots of all plants
   d. in the roots of some plants
13. Which kind of interaction between organisms is not a form of symbiosis?
   a. competition
   b. parasitism
   c. mutualism
   d. commensalism
14. Draw a food web showing the relationships of the following organisms: grasshopper, mouse, hawk, fox, grass, sparrow.

Challenge

1. How would a food web in the tundra be similar to a food web in a rain forest? How would it be different?
2. Minnows are herbivores. Bass are carnivorous fish that often feed on minnows. Which kind of fish would you expect to be more common in a pond? Explain.
3. What is the basis of ocean food chains?
4. Oxygen gas (O_2) makes up 20 percent of Earth's atmosphere. Using your knowledge of photosynthesis and respiration, draw a simple diagram of the oxygen cycle.
5. The first law of thermodynamics states that energy can neither be created nor destroyed. The second law of thermodynamics states that in every conversion of energy, some energy is lost as heat. Explain how these laws relate to the functioning of ecosystems.

Projects

1. Do library research to find out about parasites that cause life-threatening diseases in humans and in other animals. Malaria and schistosoma are two examples. Also investigate how human attempts to control malaria with DDT affected the environment. Were these efforts successful? Why or why not?

49 Population Dynamics

Common housefly, member of the
order Diptera

A single fly that follows you into the house can annoy you
to the point of your using any available object as a fly swatter.
How would you react if you encountered one trillion flies in
your house at once?

Consider the following situation. The female housefly, on
the average, lays 100 eggs at a time. Each time eggs are laid,
about half are female. A housefly can reproduce when it is
slightly less than a month old. Several generations are possible
within a year.

Suppose one female fly produced 50 female offspring, each
of which died after producing her own 50 female offspring.
After seven generations the number of flies in existence that
descended from the original fly would be over one trillion.
If all the females survived to reproduce during each generation,
the resulting number of flies after one year would be over
1.5 trillion. Swatting those flies would be a full-time job.
Think of how different life on Earth would be if the populations
of living things were able to grow unchecked.

Population Growth Patterns

A **population** is the number of organisms of a particular species living in a limited space at a given time. It is also a level of organization of living things, being composed of individual organisms. An organism has certain characteristics such as method of nutrition, body shape, and so forth. In the same way a population has its particular characteristics.

As in other aspects of ecology, the size of a population is dependent upon many external factors of the biotic and abiotic environment. As these external factors change, so do the characteristics of the population.

CONCEPTS

- biotic potential
- limiting factors of the environment
- exponential growth curve
- real growth curve
- carrying capacity

49–1 Biotic Potential

The fly population in the preceding example illustrates the biotic potential of the housefly. **Biotic potential** is the highest rate of reproduction possible for a population under ideal conditions. Fortunately flies do not achieve their biotic potential for any length of time, nor do other organisms. The biotic potential is kept in check by many limiting factors in the environment. One limiting factor is the amount of food that is available for the flies in the environment. Food is a limited resource that will only support a specific number of flies. The amount of available living space is another factor that limits population size.

Environmental resistance is the sum of all the limiting factors in the environment that prevent a population from reaching its biotic potential.

49–2 Exponential versus Real Growth

Below is an examination of the growth rate of the population of houseflies. The first female produces 50 females and 50 males. The 50 females each produce another 50 females and 50 males. If each set of females breeds once per generation, the growth of the population can be seen as the following:

Generation	Number of Flies Produced
1	100
2	5,000
3	250,000
4	12,500,000
5	625,000,000
6	31,250,000,000
7	1,562,500,000,000

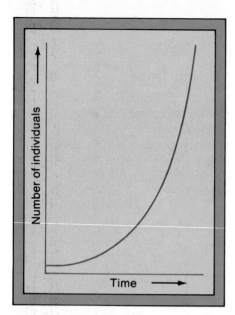

Figure 49.1 The exponential growth curve of a population shows that the population increases exponentially to an infinitely high number.

Figure 49.2 A yeast cell population levels out when its numbers reach the carrying capacity of the environment. At this point the population has reached equilibrium.

The numbers of flies in the example can be used to illustrate some concepts about population growth. However, the growth of this fly population does not represent a realistic situation. It is assumed that every fly produced lives to reproduce. It is also assumed that each female lives for only one generation. The growth rate of the fly population in the example shows exponential growth. The fly population increases 50 times with every generation. If the growth data are plotted, the resulting graph would be an exponential growth curve.

Real populations can grow exponentially for only short periods of time. Environmental resistance sets limits on the growth rate. Each population has its own unique characteristics. These are important for understanding the rate at which a population actually grows. Figure 49.2 shows a growth curve for a population of yeast cells in the laboratory. The curve is S-shaped. Growth begins at a slow rate and then increases rapidly. The rate then slows again until the curve flattens. This flattening of the curve means that the population has stopped growing. At this point the population has reached the carrying capacity of its environment. The **carrying capacity** is the limit at which the environment can support a certain population. At the carrying capacity, the population is gaining and losing individuals at the same rate. Therefore the population has reached a state of **equilibrium**.

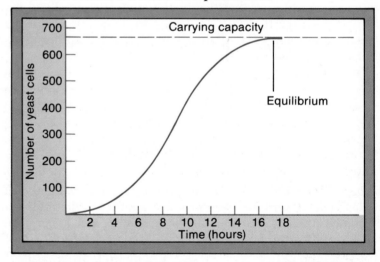

Changes in the environment can change the carrying capacity and, therefore, the point of equilibrium in the growth curve. An example of an environmental change might be the accumulation of toxic wastes or a drop in temperature.

The same environment can support different populations at different carrying capacities. For example, a pond can support a larger population of minnows than of ducks.

Figure 49.3 The size of the islands on which these animals live is one factor that affects the carrying capacity of their environment.

49–3 Factors Affecting Growth

The growth rate of a population is the direct result of factors that increase or decrease the population. Birthrate and immigration are two factors that can increase a population. The **birthrate** represents the rate at which new individuals are added to the population. The addition can be in the form of the birth of live young or the production of seeds, spores, or eggs.

Immigration of organisms also increases the size of a population. **Immigration** is the movement of organisms into a new area. You should recall from your history courses how the human population of North America changed as a result of immigration.

The **death rate** and emigration serve to reduce the size of a population. **Emigration** is the movement of organisms out of an area. Age distribution will have an effect on the number of births and deaths. Any population can be broken down into three major age groups — prereproductive, reproductive, and postreproductive. The relative numbers of each age group determine how quickly the population grows. If the prereproductive group is largest, the population will grow in the future. If the reproductive group is largest, the population will remain approximately the same size. If the postreproductive group is the largest, the population is shrinking.

Checkpoint

1. The ability of a population to reproduce at the highest possible rate is its _____.
2. The upper limit at which an environment can support a population is its _____.
3. A population is said to be at _____ when it reaches the carrying capacity of its environment.
4. Distinguish between emigration and immigration.

CONCEPTS

- density-dependent factors
- self-limiting populations
- types of competition

Figure 49.4 Crowding is a particular problem for sessile organisms such as mussels and barnacles.

Environmental Limits on Growth

It is obvious that no population maintains its biotic potential, but why not? What prevents a population from growing indefinitely? What causes a population to reach equilibrium? The answers to these questions are related to the number of organisms that occupy a given area.

49–4 Population Density

The density of a population can affect its growth rate. **Population density** is the number of organisms per unit of space. For plants and sessile aquatic organisms, space is an important limiting factor. If plants are so crowded that they do not receive enough water or light, they die. If sessile animals are so crowded that they do not receive enough food, their reproductive rate is reduced.

Parasitism increases at high density. Close physical contact can make it easier for a parasite to find a host. You may have heard that during the Middle Ages one third of the human population of Europe was wiped out by bubonic plague. The disease was caused by a microorganism found in fleas. Excessive crowding of the human population caused poor sanitary conditions. Those conditions offered ideal breeding grounds for the rats that carried the fleas.

A veterinarian knows that animals in close contact, such as the conditions found in a kennel, will be easy targets for fleas. Placing a flea-bearing animal in a kennel will provide a greater number of host organisms.

Stress also increases in crowded conditions. Mice in crowded conditions are known to neglect their young. This neglect causes the death rate to increase. In some animal populations, stress causes the level of aggression within the population to increase. Frequent fighting among members of the population is associated with hormone changes. The stress of crowding can also increase certain adrenal hormones that will decrease the reproductive hormones. As a result the reproductive rate is reduced.

Some plants are able to limit the growth of nearby plants by the production of growth-inhibiting chemicals. One such plant is the creosote bush, which grows in the deserts of the American Southwest. Creosote bushes give off a toxic substance that prevents the germination of seedlings in a circular area around them. By inhibiting the growth of nearby seedlings, the creosote bushes are probably ensuring themselves an ample supply of water. Other plants, such as walnut trees, are also known to produce growth-inhibiting chemicals.

Most populations will increase at a high rate until their rate of reproduction is checked by an external limiting factor. If diatoms are grown in a laboratory, they increase in number very quickly until crowding decreases the light available for photosynthesis. At the same time their waste products begin to interfere with their metabolism. At this point the growth rate is reduced.

There are species whose growth rate is slower when their population density is low. Oysters are an example of this type of population. Young oysters must spend part of their development attached to a hard object, usually another oyster. If oysters are scarce, younger oysters cannot develop.

Other populations, such as whales, require a certain minimum population density to support a normal rate of reproduction. If the population is too small, individuals have a difficult time finding mates.

49–5   Predation and Competition

Population growth is also limited by interactions between predators and prey. Predators are more likely to capture prey animals that are already weak from starvation or disease.

If the population density of prey organisms increases, the availability of prey can increase the carrying capacity of its predator population. A predator-prey relationship exists between the snowshoe hare and the lynx of the arctic region. Charting the relative numbers of these two animals over a long period of time shows that as the hare population increases, the lynx population follows in a cyclic pattern. An increase in the hare population increases the carrying capacity of that environment for the lynx.

The hares and the plants they eat have a relationship similar to that of the lynx and hares. The hares are the predators. An increase in the hare population would eventually be limited by the amount of available food. In addition, it has been determined that some plants eaten by hares will produce toxic substances when the plants are overgrazed. Some hares die of starvation; others are poisoned by their food source.

BIOLOGY INSIGHTS

Predator-prey relationships are not isolated pairings. Each is a part of the complex food web of the ecosystem.

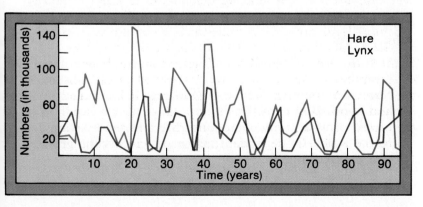

Figure 49.5 The hare and lynx populations increase and decrease in a cyclic pattern.

Figure 49.6 Having no natural predators, the prickly pear cactus spread quickly across Australia until its natural enemy, a species of moth, was introduced into the area.

Predation can have a definite effect on the structure of a population. However, studies have shown that some predators are not responsible for keeping the prey population below its carrying capacity. In the example of the lynx and hare, recent studies have shown that the hare population also rises and falls in regions where the lynx is not present. Recall that a single predator-prey relationship is one small part of a complex food web.

Like predation, competition involves the interaction between populations. **Competition** is the interaction between organisms that use one or more of the same resources. Competition can occur within a population for food, water, living space, and mates. This situation is **intraspecific competition**. As population density increases, intraspecific competition can be a significant factor in changing the structure of the population. Natural selection strengthens the population, since the fittest members survive adverse conditions. Recall how some animals react to the stress of competing for living space.

Interspecific competition exists when members of different species compete for the same resource. After careful study of populations involved in interspecific competition, the **competitive exclusion principle** was formulated. This principle states that one of the two competing species will be better able to control the use of the common resource. As a result, the other population will eventually be eliminated.

49–6   Density-Independent Factors

The factors studied previously in the chapter that affect population growth are related to the density of a population. There is another set of environmental conditions affecting a population that are independent of population density. **Density-independent factors** include weather, seasonal cycles, the actions of humans, and catastrophic events such as earthquakes and volcanoes. These factors can lower the reproductive rate of a population, and in some cases a population can be eliminated completely.

Checkpoint

1. Name a density-independent factor that limits population growth.
2. Name an organism whose growth rate is hampered by a low population density.
3. Levels of what body compounds are affected by stress?
4. Name a density-dependent factor that limits the growth of a population.

Human Population Growth

As you learned in the beginning of this chapter, the environment exerts control on the populations of all organisms. Therefore, no population of organisms ever maintains its biotic potential. One species, though, *Homo sapiens*, has found ways to overcome many of the environmental factors that limit the growth of other populations.

49-7 Growth of the Human Population

Homo sapiens appeared about 50,000 years ago. By 8000 B.C., the number of humans on Earth numbered 5.3 million. By 4000 B.C., Earth supported 86.5 million humans. During the Roman Empire, there were about 200 million humans, and by 1650 there were 545 million. Since then, the rate of growth of the human population has slowed. Even so, over 4 billion humans now populate Earth.

The fact that the population grew to such high numbers is impressive. But even more impressive is the rate of increase. It took all of prehistory and the period of history up until 1832 before there were 1 billion humans on Earth. This period included the development of tools, the rise of agriculture, the development of village-farming communities, and the industrial revolution.

Only one hundred years were necessary to double the population. In 1939, there were 2 billion humans. This rapid increase was due largely to the rise of modern medicine and sanitary practices.

It took only 20 years to add the next billion; the world population in 1960 was 3 billion. And only 15 years were needed to add yet another billion humans to the world's population. The 1975 population exceeded 4 billion.

What factors affect this rate of growth of the human population? People who study human population trends explain that the rate of growth is due to the increased gap between the birth and death rates in the human population. In other words, people are being born at a much faster rate than they are dying.

There are several reasons for the decline in the death rate. The traditional controls on human population have been minimized due to many developments in human culture. Levels of food productivity have increased due to advances in agriculture although, to be sure, starvation still occurs in many parts of the world. Stable governments have emerged, controlling large territories. This fact has resulted in limits on the amount of warfare within a given area. Sanitation

CONCEPTS

- doubling time
- human population growth rate
- the demographic transition

Do You Know?
People who study populations are called demographers.

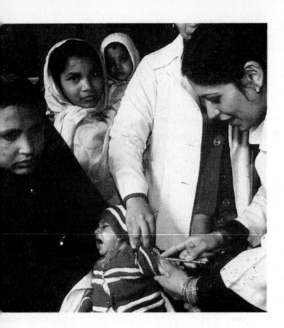

Figure 49.7 The availability of vaccines and antibiotics has lowered the death rate in nonindustrialized countries.

and personal hygiene have improved. Modern medicine and public health have greatly improved disease prevention. All of these factors have reduced the death rate.

Over the past hundred years, most industrialized nations have undergone a process called the **demographic transition**. The demographic transition is a shift from a high birthrate and a high death rate to a low birthrate and a low death rate. The gradual lowering of both the birth and death rates in industrialized countries keeps the growth of populations relatively stable.

In nonindustrialized countries, however, the situation was different. These countries experienced a rapid decline in the death rate due to the sudden availability of vaccines and antibiotics. Before the availability of these innovations, the population growth rate for these countries was 0.3 to 0.5 percent a year. The growth rate for these countries is now 2.4 to 3.5 percent a year. Although the nonindustrialized countries now have death rates comparable to those of industrialized countries, their birthrates remain high. The nonindustrialized countries have not yet completed the demographic transition. They still have high birthrates, but they now have low death rates at the same time. This combination of factors produces enormous potential for population growth. In the world today, three babies are born every second. Most of these births occur in nonindustrialized nations.

49–8 Predictions for the Future

At the current rate of population growth, 20 people are born each year for every thousand. These data represent an annual growth rate of 2 percent. At this 2 percent growth rate, the time it takes for the population to double is 35 years. This time period is called **doubling time**. The value for doubling time is not fixed. Consider the information concerning the growth of the human population presented in Section 49–7. Note that the doubling time has decreased over the last 150 years. If the current growth rate continues, by the year 2000 there will be over 6 billion humans on Earth.

In 1971, the average population density on all the land on Earth except the polar regions was 27.2 people per square kilometer. Twenty-seven people in a square kilometer may not seem very crowded, but remember that this figure is an average. Some areas are much more highly populated than others. The population density of Manhattan, for example, is about 26,000 people per square kilometer.

If the current growth trends continue, by the year 2400 the average population density on Earth will be 145,258 people per square kilometer!

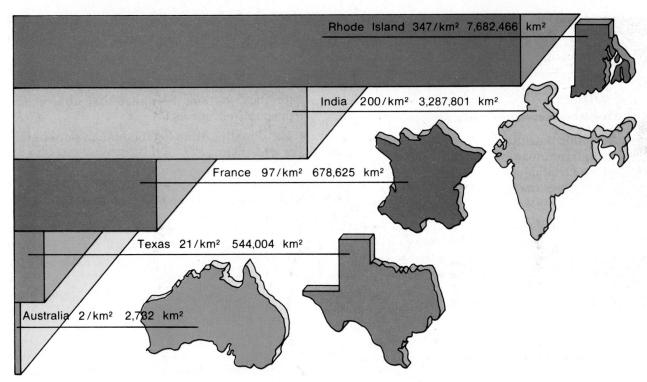

Rhode Island 347/km² 7,682,466 km²

India 200/km² 3,287,801 km²

France 97/km² 678,625 km²

Texas 21/km² 544,004 km²

Australia 2/km² 2,732 km²

Figure 49.8 Population densities vary in different parts of the world.

It is difficult to imagine a situation in which the average world population is many times more crowded than that of Manhattan, New York. In fact, most people who study human population trends do not believe that the population will ever reach that size.

Humans have managed to raise the carrying capacity of the environment by modern technology. However, most scientists agree that there is an upper limit to the number of humans that Earth can support. If the human population does not lower its birthrate, this upper limit will eventually be reached. At that point, only an increased death rate will keep the population within its biological limits.

Do You Know?

In 1968, 66% of the population lived in nonindustrialized countries. It is estimated that in the year 2000, 77% of the population will live in nonindustrialized countries.

Checkpoint

1. What is the approximate population of Earth?
2. The demographic transition consists of a shift from high birthrate and death rate to _____ birthrate and death rate.
3. What is the current annual growth rate of the human population?
4. How quickly will the human population double at its current growth rate?
5. What two ways can slow human population growth?

CHAPTER REVIEW

Summary

- The biotic potential of a population represents the maximum number of offspring that could be produced under ideal conditions. The limiting factors that make up environmental resistance counterbalance the biotic potential.
- The birth and death rates are subject to biotic and abiotic factors in the environment. A high birthrate tends to increase the size of a population. A high death rate tends to decrease the size of a population.
- Populations grow exponentially under ideal conditions.
- The growth curve shows actual increases in the size of a population over time.
- The carrying capacity of the environment causes the growth curve to level out at equilibrium. The carrying capacity is affected by changes in the environment.
- The density of a population affects the rate at which a population grows. Many limiting factors of the environment are density dependent.
- Predators have a limited effect on the size of a prey population.
- Density-independent factors such as climate and catastrophic events also change rates of population growth.
- The human population has continually increased since the appearance of humans. However, the growth rate of the population in industrialized nations has slowed.
- Humans have raised the carrying capacity of the environment due to technological advances.
- Nonindustrial nations have yet to undergo the demographic transition. The growth rate for these nations is higher than that of industrialized nations.
- The doubling time for the human population is decreasing.

Vocabulary

biotic potential	emigration
birthrate	environmental
carrying capacity	resistance
competition	equilibrium
competitive exclu-	immigration
sion principle	interspecific
death rate	competition
demographic	intraspecific
transition	competition
density-independent	population
factors	population density
doubling time	

Review

1. What is the name given to the environmental forces that prevent organisms from reaching their biotic potential?
2. What is the point of the growth curve at which the population gains individuals at the same rate as it loses individuals?
3. What effect does a high birthrate have upon population size?
4. What four components determine the growth rate of a population?
5. What prediction can be made concerning the growth of a population that is composed mostly of postreproductive individuals?
6. How does the size of a prey population affect the carrying capacity of a predator?

7. How does a low density of whales in an area affect whale population growth?
8. Name two density-dependent factors that limit a population.
9. What has happened to the current rate of human population growth?
10. Name three factors that have minimized traditional controls on the size of the human population.
11. Which part of the demographic transition has not yet occurred in nonindustrial countries?
12. How many babies are born each second?
13. What is the projected world population for the year 2000?
14. When is the human population expected to double in size?
15. How is parasitism affected by density?
16. What was the doubling time for the human population to grow from 1 billion to 2 billion?

Interpret and Apply

1. Name two density-dependent factors that can affect the population of snowshoe hares.
2. What factors prevent a population from growing exponentially for any length of time?
3. What is the relationship between population equilibrium and carrying capacity?
4. What is the relationship between carrying capacity and different populations in the same environment?
5. How does an exponential growth curve differ from a real growth curve?
6. How is aggression among animals related to hormone levels?
7. What is the relationship between interspecific competition and the competitive exclusion principle?

Challenge

1. Assume you are starting with a first generation of a single female rabbit that will produce six rabbits. These six rabbits are the second generation. If half of the rabbits produced in each generation are female and go on to produce six offspring, how many rabbits will be in the population by the fourth generation? Each female reproduces for one generation only.
2. How would providing more food affect the carrying capacity of an environment?
3. How might an increase in the lynx population affect the population of plants on which snowshoe hares feed?
4. There are currently 500 blackbirds living in a marsh. The population is growing at a rate of 10 percent per year. What will the size of the population be after 5 years?

Projects

1. Find out how scientists keep track of population size in the wild. Include such techniques as banding, trapping, and telemetry.
2. Find out if your community has any species of organisms whose populations have grown to the extent that they have become pests. If so, how is the community trying to limit their numbers?
3. Determine the density of a population in your backyard, local park, or another area near you. For example, you could find the number of earthworms per cubic meter or the number of crabgrass plants per square meter.
4. Calculate the population density of your home. Determine the number of square meters occupied by your family.

50 Humans and the Environment

Trumpeter swans, an endangered species

The human species, like all others, influences and is influenced by the physical and biological aspects of its environment. The amazing resourcefulness of humans has allowed them to populate the Arctic, the tropics, the mountains, and the deserts.

Humans have changed their environment by building cities and highways. The pioneers on this continent would barely recognize the land that they settled a few hundred years ago. Thick, rich topsoil that took thousands of years to produce has been worn away in some places by poor farming practices. Some streams and lakes are no longer sources of drinking water and fish. The air in many locations is unhealthful to breathe. The supply of fossil fuels, which took millions of years to accumulate, is being used at an alarming rate.

In the past few decades, people have begun to realize that changes must be made in the careless ways they use resources. Only then can water, air, and soil be restored to more favorable conditions. People have found and continue to discover many creative solutions to the problems of conservation.

Pollution and Its Effects

Pollution is an unfavorable change in the environment. Much pollution is caused partly or wholly by the actions of humans. Pollution causes health, social, economic, and aesthetic problems. It seems to have two causes. One is the very high population density on Earth. This high density has taxed the ability of ecosystems to rid themselves of harmful substances.

The other cause of pollution is the demand for a higher standard of living. The departure from the simple life of the past has introduced high levels of pollutants into the environment. Humans are just now becoming aware of the consequences of their increased demands upon the environment.

50–1   Water Pollution

Water is not only a necessity for human life; it is also the home of countless other species. Water has many physical and biological characteristics, and these differ for each body of water. For example, the amount of dissolved oxygen (DO) in a given body of water determines the species of fish that will be able to live in that water. Trout demand a high level of dissolved oxygen, while carp will do well at low levels.

Many factors determine the dissolved oxygen content of water and therefore its ability to support certain types of animal life. Lakes receive oxygen by diffusion from the atmosphere, and from photosynthesis of organisms in the lakes. The cloudiness of water determines how deeply sunlight can penetrate the water and therefore the depth at which photosynthesis can occur. Human sewage, animal excrement, portions of decaying plants and animals, and industrial wastes pollute water.

High levels of plant nutrients may be present in polluted water. These nutrients, which include phosphorus and nitrogen, enter the water from sewage, factories, and farms. These nutrients can cause unusually large concentrations of algae to grow. Such high concentrations are called **algal blooms**.

Eventually the plants die and are decomposed by aerobic bacteria. Of course, the oxygen used by the decomposers is not available to the fish. Therefore, species that require a high DO concentration, such as trout, disappear, and are replaced by fish that require less oxygen, such as carp. The amount of oxygen required by the bacteria to decompose the dead materials in the water is called the **biochemical oxygen demand** of the water.

Figure 50.1 The abundance of plant nutrients due to pollutants produces algal blooms in ponds and lakes.

50–2 Air Pollution

There are many ways pollutants enter the air. Tires, for example, are constantly being worn down due to friction with the roads. This friction puts an estimated 50 tons of rubber particles into the air of Los Angeles each day. Pollutants also enter the air by the vaporization of chemicals. Industries, especially those that produce metals, chemicals, paints, and rubber, add much vapor to the air.

Another source of pollutants is combustion, or burning. Complete combustion of a substance yields CO_2 as a reaction product. Incomplete combustion yields soot, CO_2, and carbon monoxide (CO) as reaction products.

Carbon dioxide absorbs heat energy that normally radiates back into space from Earth's surface. This process, called the **greenhouse effect**, is gradually causing the temperature of Earth's atmosphere to rise. Scientists estimate that, at current rates of CO_2 emission, the temperature of Earth's atmosphere could rise in 500 years. This rise in temperature could cause unusual circulation of air masses, resulting in violent storms. It could also cause the polar ice caps to melt, raising the levels of the oceans as much as 30 meters.

Another unfortunate result of burning fossil fuels, especially coal with a high sulfur content, is the presence of sulfur dioxide, SO_2, in the air. When combined with water vapor, it produces dilute sulfuric acid, H_2SO_4. This **acid rain** can kill plants, leach nutrients from the soil, and interfere with nitrogen fixation by bacteria. The acid rain that falls into lakes and streams kills fish. Also any exposed surface, including brick, stone, and metal, can be damaged by acid rain.

Industries and automobile exhaust also produce oxides of nitrogen. Nitrogen dioxide, NO_2, is a reddish-brown gas that is toxic and irritating to the breathing passages. Nitrogen oxide, NO, reduces the ability of the blood to carry oxygen.

Figure 50.2 The damage to outdoor structures and aquatic life caused by acid rain is becoming an area of major concern.

Nitrogen dioxide combines with water to form nitric acid, HNO_3, which also contributes to the acidity of rain.

Another toxic substance found in the air is lead. Lead concentration increases steadily by accumulating in organisms as it makes its way up the food chain. This process is called **biological magnification**. Lead first enters the food chain at the plant level. A high level of lead in humans can cause headaches, insomnia, anemia, and miscarriage.

50–3   Other Pollutants

Radioactive substances are used as fuel in nuclear power plants, in diagnosing and treating diseases, and in scientific research. Unfortunately, radiation can be harmful, causing genetic mutations and cancer.

Radioactive particles carried by air currents are called **radioactive fallout**. Testing nuclear weapons in the atmosphere causes fallout. Radioactive materials are easily distributed throughout the environment by biological magnification. For example, a radioactive substance falls upon soil and is taken into plants. If cows eat the plants, the substance accumulates. When humans drink milk containing the radioactive substance, it enters their bodies, concentrating in the bones. The accumulation of radiation can cause bone cancer and death.

The heavy use of petroleum harms the environment in many ways. Outflowing materials from oil refineries pollute the water. In addition, refineries are among the worst polluters of the air. Refineries often use nearby water sources for cooling, causing thermal pollution of the water. There also is the constant risk of oil spills, which spoil large areas of water by harming or killing organisms living in it.

One other pollution problem is that of **toxic waste** from the manufacture of industrial chemicals and from other industries, such as leather tanning. Many of these chemicals cannot be broken down by the biological process of decomposition. Such chemicals are **nonbiodegradable**. Chemicals that can be broken down by biological decomposition are **biodegradable**. Recent evidence indicates that buried accumulations of toxic waste cause many health problems, including birth defects and cancer.

Do You Know?
Lead fallout is estimated at 500,000 tons per year.

Figure 50.3 Toxic wastes are a byproduct in the production of many useful materials. Unsafe disposal sites have been uncovered in recent years.

Do You Know?
The government estimates that the United States produces 40 billion kilograms of toxic waste each year.

Checkpoint

1. An unfavorable change in the environment, caused by the consequences of human actions, is called _____.
2. What pollutant causes the greenhouse effect?
3. What kind of substances are used as fuel in nuclear power plants?

Conservation of Natural Resources

Soil, water, air, plants, and animals are all related. An effect upon one resource is ultimately an effect upon all resources. For this reason, efforts should be made to clean up all aspects of pollution. The quality of human life will improve, and future generations will be able to enjoy the resources of a nonpolluted Earth.

50–4   Protecting the Soil

Erosion is the wearing away of soil by wind, ice, water, and gravity. Erosion is a natural process. However, the actions of humans have increased the rate of erosion. The problems caused by erosion have made it important to find ways to decrease the rate of erosion.

One method of farming that decreases erosion is **contour plowing** on slopes. Instead of plowing straight down a slope, farmers plow across the slope. This method of plowing allows less runoff than straight plowing because each row plowed acts as a miniature dam, preventing loss of topsoil.

The planting of **cover crops** in the fall after the harvest protects the soil from the impact of rain. The roots of cover crops also help to hold the soil in place. Cover crops can be plowed under, acting as fertilizer.

Crop rotation does not prevent erosion, but it does preserve the quality of the soil. If a farmer plants the same crop each year, the crop takes the same nutrients from the soil. To avoid this problem, farmers may plant different crops on a given piece of land in alternate seasons to give the soil a chance to replenish its nutrients. Legumes such as soybeans, alfalfa, and clover are particularly important in crop rotation. The nitrogen-fixing bacteria in their roots convert nitrogen from the air into nitrate that is usable by plants. Planting legumes increases the nitrogen content of the soil.

- methods of preventing erosion
- emission-control measures
- water conservation measures
- preserving habitats
- control of animal populations

Do You Know?
An estimated 4 billion tons of eroded soil enter the streams of the United States each year. By volume, sediment is the largest water pollutant.

Figure 50.4 Contour plowing prevents erosion by reducing runoff.

50–5 Protecting the Air

Efforts are being made to reduce the pollutants that enter the air. Many cars now have engines that run on unleaded gasoline. Although it is more expensive than leaded gasoline, it is less harmful to the environment. For many years automobiles have been made with emissions control devices. These devices convert harmful compounds released by the combustion of gasoline into less harmful compounds before releasing them into the air. Frequent auto inspections will ensure that the control devices are working properly.

Industries too are being required to meet government standards with respect to the gases and particles that leave their factories. Scrubbers are emissions control devices installed in factory chimneys that remove pollutants from exhaust.

50–6 Protecting the Water

Aquifers are underground water supplies that have accumulated over thousands of years. In the United States the aquifers contain about 36,000 trillion liters of water. In addition, 16 trillion liters of water fall on the United States daily as rain and snow. However, 92 percent of this water evaporates immediately or runs off into the oceans, unused. The remaining water percolates down through the ground to supply the aquifers. Each day, Americans take 80 billion liters more out of the ground than the amount that seeps in. Also, salt from icy highways, sediment from erosion, and fertilizers and pesticides from farm runoff enter the water supply. So there are two problems: the amount of water available and the quality of the available water.

The largest single use of water in the home is the flush toilet. The standard toilet requires 19 liters of water per flush. However, new water-saving toilets requiring only 13 liters per flush have been developed.

Another water-conserving idea is gray-water recycling. Gray water is water that has been used in showering and laundering. Although not clean enough to drink, it is adequate for flushing. In the gray-water recycling system, a house would have a tank to store gray water. Pipes would lead from the gray-water tank to the toilet tank. Clean water would not have to be used for flushing.

Industries are being required to limit the harmful wastes that leave their factories and enter the water. Sewage-treatment plants are experimenting with new ways of disinfecting the water to reduce the amounts of chemicals used in purification. Also, the solid material that settles out of the water in sewage treatment plants, called **sludge**, is now distributed to farmers as a soil conditioner and fertilizer.

Do You Know?

In some areas the salt concentration in the water caused by runoff from salted icy roads is so high that people on restricted salt diets are advised to drink bottled water.

Figure 50.5 Usage of water in the home.

Activity	Number of liters used per day
Dishwashing	57
Cooking and drinking	45
Washing	49
Washing clothes	132
Bathing	303
Flushing toilets	379
Total	965

50–7   Protecting Wildlife

Extinction, or the disappearance of species from Earth, is a natural process. Species have evolved and become extinct since life began. But the actions of humans have increased the rate at which species are becoming extinct. Destruction of the natural habitats occurs when people clear the land for agricultural and other purposes. Plants and animals cannot survive when their habitats have been destroyed.

The Endangered Species Act of 1973 listed 109 species of animals that are endangered in the United States. These include bighorn sheep, lake trout, sea otters, Key deer, lake sturgeon, trumpeter swans, ivory-billed woodpeckers, and California condors.

Sometimes extreme steps are successful in saving a species from extinction. Recently there has been some success in saving the whooping cranes. The whooping cranes once lived over much of North America. As the marshes in which these birds nested were destroyed for farming, cranes became rarer and rarer. Because of loss of habitat and hunting, by the 1960's there were only 50 whooping cranes left.

Wildlife refuges have played an important role in saving the whooping cranes. A **refuge** is an area in which the wildlife is legally protected. These cranes nest in the Wood Buffalo National Park in northwestern Canada. In the winter they migrate to the Aransas National Wildlife Refuge in Texas. The governments of Canada and the United States have co-operated in saving this bird.

Captive breeding programs have also been useful in saving the whooping cranes. In 1967, eggs of whooping cranes were removed from nesting birds. These eggs were incubated and the young were raised by people. Biologists hope that some-day the captive birds can be released, thus increasing the size of the wild population. Today there are over 100 whooping cranes in the wild, showing that it is possible to remove species from the edge of extinction.

Zoos are also playing a role in saving species from extinction. In zoos, rare species are protected from starvation and predators. Occasionally a zoo is successful in breeding members of a rare species in the hope of eventually reintroducing them into the wild. The Arabian oryx is an example of an animal that owes its existence today to captive breeding programs.

Today there are many large private foundations whose purpose is to prevent the extinction of animal species. Often these foundations use their funds to buy huge parcels of land that they then declare as wildlife preserves. Animals living on these preserves are protected from loss of habitat because the land cannot be developed by humans.

Figure 50.6 The whooping crane has been saved from extinction through the establishment of refuges.

Hunting has accounted for the disappearance of very few species. Changes in habitat account for the greatest reductions in populations. In the United States hunting is carefully controlled and monitored by state and federal agencies. Hunting is now used to keep the size of animal populations below the carrying capacity of the environment. Some areas have been significantly changed by human influence. Therefore, natural controls cannot be relied upon to keep some animal populations at reasonable levels. In these cases hunting provides a humane way of controlling a population rather than allowing large numbers of animals to starve from lack of food.

Once a species has become extinct, it is gone forever. Many people feel that they should not cause the extinction of a species, and that they should actively prevent the disappearance of plants and animals from the land.

Figure 50.7 *Left:* People have provided nesting places for ducks as a step in restoring their habitats. *Right:* Peregrine falcons have been encouraged to establish nests at various places on city skyscrapers.

Checkpoint

1. Soil particles that settle on the bottom of a stream are called _____.
2. How does an endangered species differ from a species that is extinct?
3. What type of structure is used to remove pollutants from the chimneys of factories?
4. Name two sources of water pollution.
5. Name two animals in danger of extinction in the United States.

- limiting the use of nonrenewable resources
- developing renewable energy resources
- energy conservation measures

Do You Know?
Natural gas has a composition similar to that of oil but contains fewer carbon atoms.

Figure 50.8 The energy of falling water can be used to turn the turbines of an electric generator.

Figure 50.9 Passive solar homes have large windows facing the sun. Materials within the house collect the sun's energy. Solar panels are not used.

Energy Conservation

For over a decade the term *energy crisis* has been a household word. Even when people are aware that their energy resources are limited, learning ways to use less energy is another matter. But there are many ways in which people can conserve energy that they now waste. Alternative forms of energy are being explored, and some are even in use.

50–8 Alternative Energy Resources

Oil, natural gas, and coal are called **fossil fuels** because they are the remains of plants and animals that lived millions of years ago. Humans discovered that burning these substances would release the stored energy. People relied upon the energy of fossil fuels to accomplish more and more tasks. However, fossil fuels are nonrenewable resources. A **nonrenewable resource** has a limited supply.

Using alternative energy sources can cut the dependence on fossil fuels for energy. The energy of moving air or wind can be used to turn windmills and provide power. Differences in the temperatures, and therefore the densities, of different air masses are responsible for creating wind. Wind is a **renewable resource**; it cannot be used up.

Modern technology is currently dealing with ways to harness the energy of the sun to heat space and water.

Solar heating requires new considerations in architecture. One problem with solar energy is that it is so diffuse and difficult to collect. On the roof of a solar house are panels that collect and store energy from the sun. This energy is used to warm water that can transfer heat to distant parts of the house through pipes. In some climates it is practical to rely on solar energy as the sole energy source for heating air and water.

The splitting of atoms produces energy. This process, called **fission**, is the basis of nuclear energy. The energy released in fission can be converted to electricity, which can be used for any number of tasks. The technology and fuel sources such as uranium and plutonium are available to produce vast amounts of energy from the fission reaction. A few grams of fission fuel can provide the same amount of energy as tons of coal.

Though there are advantages to nuclear fission, the radioactive waste disposal problem has become very serious. States may legally ban the building of new nuclear power plants until the federal government has created safe disposal sites for radioactive waste.

50–9　Conserving Energy

As yet there is not an abundant, cheap, safe, easily usable source of energy that is available to large numbers of people.

Therefore, people are learning that putting on a wool sweater in the winter is not much more difficult than turning up the heat. Insulating homes further reduces the amount of heating fuel that is necessary, thus conserving energy.

Pilot lights on gas stoves and water heaters use energy. Many new appliances light the pilot only when the appliance is in use, allowing a substantial savings of energy.

Much energy is used in the manufacture of products such as rubber, aluminum, paper, glass, and plastic. Plastic is actually made of petroleum. Many of these materials can be recycled, or used again, after their initial use. Recycled paper, for example, can be turned into newsprint, paper towels, insulation, egg cartons, and many other products. The state of Maryland has encouraged the recycling of paper by requiring at least 25 percent of the paper purchased by the state to be recycled paper.

Recycled glass can be used in brick, glass wool, and roadbed construction. Plastic bottles can be reused to make fiberfill for jackets and sleeping bags and in carpets, wall tiles, and flooring.

It takes 95 percent less energy to make new aluminum from aluminum scrap than from raw materials. Recycling aluminum cans can yield a great energy savings. Rubber tires can be retreaded and used again and can be ground up for use in road paving. They can also be burned in a process called pyrolysis to produce usable energy. By weight, rubber produces more heat when burned than does coal.

In addition to saving energy, recycling has the advantage of keeping materials in circulation so that they do not become litter or trash. Also pollution caused in the manufacture of materials such as aluminum is avoided if most of the steps of manufacture are eliminated. Perhaps you can think of ways of recycling things that you would normally throw out.

Do You Know?
The U.S. contains 1/20 of the world's population, but uses 1/3 of the world's energy.

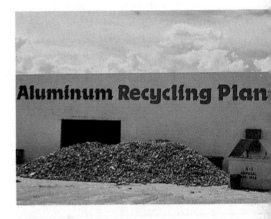

Figure 50.10 Recycling materials has become an important factor in conserving energy. Many places have laws that encourage recycling.

Checkpoint

1. Name three fossil fuels.
2. An energy source that cannot be used up is called ＿＿＿.
3. Which type of energy is obtained from fission?
4. Is solar energy renewable or nonrenewable?
5. Name three materials that can be recycled.
6. State three ecological advantages of recycling.

CHAPTER REVIEW

Summary

- Pollution affects the amount of dissolved oxygen in water. The habitat of aquatic organisms is altered if the amount of dissolved oxygen is less than the biochemical oxygen demand.
- Pollutants enter the atmosphere from a variety of sources such as the vaporization and combustion of substances.
- An increased level of CO_2 in the atmosphere causes the greenhouse effect.
- The combustion of some fossil fuels releases the sulfur and nitrogen compounds that combine with water to produce acid rain.
- Radioactive substances accumulate as they move through the food chain.
- Oil refineries can cause air and water pollution.
- The illegal disposal of toxic waste has presented a health problem.
- Conserving the soil involves a number of farming practices that can reduce erosion.
- Air pollutants from exhausts are being reduced by various pollution-control devices.
- The size of underground water supplies is being reduced, since the demand for water is exceeding the rate at which the aquifers are being replenished.
- Various water-conservation measures can be adopted in the home. Among them are using water-saving devices and gray-water recycling.
- Controls on industrial water pollutants have started to improve water quality.
- Destruction of habitat is the most important cause of extinction.
- The establishment of refuges and breeding programs is preventing the extinction of some species.
- Hunting can be a humane way of keeping some species from exceeding their carrying capacity.
- Fossil fuels are a nonrenewable resource. It is advantageous to find alternative energy sources that are renewable.
- Falling water, wind, and solar energy are renewable resources that can provide energy on a limited basis.
- The splitting of atoms, fission, provides a tremendous amount of energy. However, the use of nuclear fuels requires extensive safety precautions and a solution to the problem of nuclear waste disposal.
- Conserving energy is based on the actions of individuals. Lowering thermostats in winter, insulating homes, recycling, and purchasing energy-efficient appliances and cars all contribute to energy conservation.

Vocabulary

acid rain	fission
algal bloom	fossil fuel
aquifer	greenhouse effect
biochemical oxygen	nonbiodegradable
demand	nonrenewable
biodegradable	resource
biological	pollution
magnification	radioactive fallout
contour plowing	refuge
cover crop	renewable resource
crop rotation	sludge
erosion	toxic waste
extinction	

Review

1. How do suspended particles in water lower the rate of photosynthesis in the water?

2. What happens to the biochemical oxygen demand as the amount of plant material in the water increases?
3. Name three air pollutants.
4. What are the two acids contained in acid rain?
5. What are the products of incomplete combustion?
6. What are two possible long-range consequences of the greenhouse effect?
7. What is the relationship between lead and the principle of biological magnification?
8. What are two harmful effects of radiation?
9. What are two harmful effects of long-term exposure to toxic wastes?
10. How does shipping oil across the water in large quantities pose a threat to the environment?
11. What measures have been taken to ensure the survival of the whooping cranes?

Match the conservation practice with the resource it is meant to preserve.

12. air
13. soil
14. water
15. wildlife
16. energy

a. flow restrictors for shower heads
b. emission control on automobiles
c. fuel-efficient cars
d. crop rotation
e. breeding programs for condors

17. Which of the following energy sources is renewable? (a) coal (b) oil (c) natural gas (d) solar energy
18. How does contour plowing protect the soil from erosion?
19. Name an animal that was saved from extinction by a zoo breeding program.
20. What are legumes?

Interpret and Apply

1. What is the relationship between pollution and human population density?

2. How are aquifers, topsoil, and oil reserves similar?
3. What is the relationship between radioactive fallout and biological magnification?
4. Trout no longer live in a lake in which they were once common. What may this indicate about the DO level in the lake?
5. Why do farmers plant cover crops?
6. Why is controlled hunting considered humane?

Challenge

1. Why is flat land in less danger of eroding than hilly land?
2. You have a choice between bicycling and riding in a car to school. Name all the advantages of each transportation method.
3. A grassy area now occupies several areas uphill from a stream. There are plans to replace the grassy area with a parking lot. How would a parking lot change the stream? How could the parking lot be built without damaging the stream?

Projects

1. Talk with community representatives of local industries and learn what they have done to curb pollution. Find out what the clean-up costs were and if they have future production plans.
2. List three ways in which your family is contributing to pollution. Then list three ways that you could reduce the pollution your family creates.
3. Asbestos is a carcinogen that was once heavily used. Find out where it was used and what the effects have been on people who worked with asbestos.
4. Research the history of the development of the national park system.
5. Find out what materials can be recycled in your area.
6. List ways in which your family is conserving energy.

Careers In Ecology

Ecology is a branch of biology that deals with the relationship between organisms and their habitat. *Wildlife management* is a career that deals with the preservation and protection of wildlife. A college degree is often needed in this field. Wildlife managers must know the habitat requirements for the reproduction and survival of many species of birds and animals. They must therefore supervise habitats. In addition, they must conduct population surveys. When a species or habitat is at risk, managers must provide protection.

Fisheries managers are knowledgeable about fish and their habitat requirements. The level of dissolved oxygen, the water temperature, the number of aquatic plants, and the presence of pollutants in the water are critical to the existence of fish. Managers must also know techniques for collecting, fertilizing, and incubating spawn. This process enables managers to stock fish in waterways. Jobs in fisheries management often require a college degree.

A *forester* manages forest land and its resources. To be a forester, one must have a college degree in a related area. Some foresters work for the government in maintaining national and state forests. They aid in planning and implementing projects for the control of flooding, soil erosion, and tree diseases. They also work with park and recreation managers in the economic and recreational development of forests. Other foresters are employed by private paper or furniture companies that use wood products. The major job of industrial foresters is the development of reforestation projects in the areas where timber has been removed.

Soil conservationists study soil composition. They too must have a college degree. They conduct surveys of areas for prospective urban development, crop rotation, terracing, and reforestation in an effort to conserve soil and water. They often participate in environmental studies to evaluate the effects of strip-mining and industrial waste disposal.

Aquatic biologists study animals and plants living in the water. They analyze environmental conditions that affect animals and

plants. They monitor water for evidence of abnormal salt levels, thermal pollution, acidity, and the amount of dissolved oxygen. They must have a college degree.

Pollution-control technicians perform tasks that monitor the environment. The technician training programs vary in length. These technicians collect samples of air, water, and soil to be analyzed. They conduct physical and chemical tests in the field and lab. By using a pH meter, microscope, spectrophotometer, centrifuge, and other equipment, they can determine the chemical composition of the pollutant.

UNIT REVIEW

Synthesis

1. Would you expect to find more kinds of plants at the top of a mountain or at the bottom? Explain.
2. How is the flow of energy through an ecosystem connected to the flow of nutrients in that ecosystem? What is the major difference between the flow of energy and the flow of nutrients?
3. During the 1950s and 1960s, high concentrations of the pesticide DDT caused the populations of hawks and other birds of prey to decline drastically. Using an energy pyramid, describe how pesticides that are sprayed on crops can become concentrated in birds of prey.
4. Why has the human population been able to grow so rapidly during the last two or three centuries? Do you think that humans have exceeded the carrying capacity of their environment? State the evidence that supports your conclusion.
5. Describe two ways in which the high growth rate of human populations is related to the current problems of pollution.
6. Describe the process by which the behavior of a predator, such as a fox, can influence the evolution of its prey, such as a rabbit.
7. Would you describe the effect of a caterpillar's eating the leaves of a tree as more similar to the effect of a predator or a parasite? Explain.
8. Some people have suggested that if the human population continues to increase, it may become necessary for humans to stop eating meat. Why would eating only fruits and vegetables be an advantage?
9. Tropical and temperate forests are composed of different layers of vegetation. What limiting factor or factors cause these layers? Does vertical layering occur in the oceans? If so, what limiting factor or factors cause layering in the oceans?

Additional Reading

Attenborough, David. *Life on Earth*. Boston: Little, Brown & Co., 1983.

Boorer, Michael. *The Living Earth: Forest Life*. New York: Danbury Press, 1975.

Carson, Rachel. *The Silent Spring*. Boston: Houghton Mifflin, 1962.

Cousteau, Jacques-Yves, and Philippe Diole. *Life and Death in a Coral Sea*. Reading, MA: Addison-Wesley Publishing Co., Inc., 1978.

Duffey, Eric. *The Living Earth: Grassland Life*. New York: Danbury Press, 1975.

Emmel, Thomas. *An Introduction to Ecology and Population Biology*. New York: W.W. Norton & Co., Inc., 1973.

Lorenz, Konrad Z. *King Solomon's Ring*. New York: Harper & Row Pubs., Inc., 1979.

Oates, John. *The Living Earth: Web of Life*. New York: Danbury Press, 1975.

Odum, Eugene P. *Ecology*. New York: Holt, Rinehart & Winston, 1975.

Patent, Dorothy H. *How Insects Communicate*. New York: Holiday House, Inc., 1975.

Pringle, Laurence. *The Gentle Desert: Exploring an Ecosystem*. New York: Macmillan Publishing Co., Inc., 1977.

Silverberg, Robert. *The World within the Tide Pool*. Dallas, TX: Weybridge Publishing Co., 1972.

Sparks, John. *The Living Earth: The Air around Us*. New York: Danbury Press, 1975.

Street, Philip. *Animal Migration and Navigation*. New York: Charles Scribner's Sons, 1976.

Warner, William W. *Beautiful Swimmers: Watermen, Crabs, and the Chesapeake Bay*. New York: Penguin Books, 1977.

Appendix

A Key to Five Kingdom Classification

Kingdom Monera

Bacteria and cyanophytes (blue-green algae). Prokaryotes.

Subkingdom Schizophyta

Bacteria. Most are unicellular and colonial. Most have cell walls made of murein. Motile forms move by flagella or gliding. Heterotrophic, chemosynthetic, or autotrophic. Aerobic and anaerobic species. Most reproduce by binary fission.

Phylum Eubacteria

True bacteria. Three basic shapes: bacillus (rod-shaped), coccus (spherical), and spirillum (spiral-shaped). Motile forms have flagella. Some form endospores. *Diplococci pneumoniae, Escherichia coli, Streptococci lactis*.

Phylum Myxobacteria

Slime or gliding bacteria. Rod-shaped organisms. Move by secreting a slimy substance on which the organisms glide. Feed on decaying organic matter. Reproduction involves individual cells joining to form a mass from which multicellular, spore-containing fruiting bodies arise. *Stigmatella aurantiaca, Myxococcus*.

Phylum Chlamydobacteria

Mycelial bacteria. Filamentous. Reproduction is asexual by fragmentation, fission, or budding. Several species used in the production of antibiotics. *Streptomyces, Actinomyces*.

Phylum Spirochaete

Spiral-shaped bacteria. Some are parasites of humans and other vertebrates. Others are free-living in mud and water. Most free-living forms are anaerobes. *Treponema pallidum* (causes syphilis), *Cristispira*.

Phylum Rickettsia

Rod-shaped parasites. Most live within the cells of arthropods such as mites, ticks, and lice. Rocky Mountain spotted fever is caused by several species of rickettsiae. *Rickettsia typhi* (causes typhus).

Phylum Mycoplasma

The smallest living organisms known. Lack cell walls. Parasites within cells of humans and other animals. *Mycoplasma pneumoniae* (causes pneumonia).

Subkingdom Cyanophyta

Phylum Cyanophyta

Blue-green algae. Rod-shaped or spherical. Many are multicellular filaments. Most are nonmotile; some filamentous forms move by secreting slime on which they glide. Autotrophic. Chlorophyll present. Lack chloroplasts. Some capable of nitrogen fixation. *Anabaena, Nostoc, Oscillatoria, Spirulina*.

Kingdom Protista

Unicellular and colonial eukaryotes. Plantlike forms primarily autotrophic. Animal-like heterotrophs, some of which are parasitic. Most move by cilia, flagella, or pseudopodia; however, some species are immotile. Asexual and sexual reproduction.

Phylum Pyrrophyta

Dinoflagellates. Plantlike protists inhabit fresh and salt water. Mostly unicellular with two flagella of equal length. Many have cell walls containing cellulose. Photosynthetic species contain chlorophyll. Most are free-living and bioluminescent. Food stored as starch or oil. Asexual reproduction by longitudinal cell division. Some heterotrophic species are responsible for red tide. *Gymnodinium, Gonyaulax* (cause red tide).

Phylum Euglenophyta

Euglena. Plantlike protists. Found mainly in fresh water. One long and one short flagella. Lack cell walls and are capable of euglenoid movement. Most have chloroplasts and are autotrophic. Asexual reproduction by cell division. Light-sensitive eyespot. *Phacus, Euglena*.

Phylum Chrysophyta

Golden-brown algae; yellow-green algae; diatoms. Plantlike protists, primarily autotrophic. Most have cell walls made of pectin and silicon. Most lack flagella. Found in fresh water, salt water and in wet areas attached to rocks and wood. Sexual reproduction is common, yet asexual reproduction is dominant. Decay-resistant bodies leave deposits of diatomaceous earth. *Chromulina, Botrydium, Pleurosigma*.

Phylum Mastigophora

Flagellates. Animal-like protists. Most have one or two flagella, lack outer walls, and reproduce asexually by mitosis and cell division. Most are free-living. Some are parasites in humans and other animals, and have complex life cycles. *Trypanosoma, Trichonympha*.

Phylum Sarcodina

Amoeboid. Aquatic, animal-like protists. Pseudopods used in movement and feeding. Some are parasites of humans and animals. Some secrete hard shells of calcium carbonate or silicon. Most reproduce asexually by mitosis and cell division. Sexual reproduction involves the formation of gametes. *Amoeba*, foraminiferans, radiolarians, and heliozoans.

Phylum Sporozoa

Malarial parasites. Animal-like protists that lack cilia and flagella as adults. Parasites in humans and other animals. Asexual and sexual reproductive phases. Form spores by fission. *Plasmodium vivax, Gregarina.*

Phylum Ciliophora

Ciliates. Aquatic, animal-like protists. Most highly specialized. Movement by cilia. Most free-living. Micronu-clei and macronuclei present. Have oral groove, anal pore, and produce trichocysts. Asexual reproduction by mitosis and cell division. Sexual reproduction by conjugation in which genetic material is exchanged. *Paramecium, Stentor, Vorticella, Spirostomum.*

Kingdom Fungi

Eukaryotic heterotrophs. Some unicellular forms. Most are multicellular and multinucleate. Most have cell walls made of chitin. Body composed of filamentous hyphae that join to form a mycelium. Either saprophytes or parasites. Parasitic forms found mostly on plants.

Subkingdom Gymnomycota

Acellular and cellular slime molds. Found on damp soil and decaying matter. Mobile, soft-cell wall, amoebalike phase. Spore producing, fruiting body phase.

Phylum Myxomycota

Acellular (plasmodial) slime molds. In plasmodial stage, individual cells join to produce a multicellular plasmodium. Fruiting stage produces numerous fruiting bodies with sporangia. The sporangia release spores that produce flagellated gametes. Sexual reproduction. *Arcyria, Diderma.*

Phylum Acrasiomycota

Cellular slime molds. Unicellular, free-living amoeboid cells join to form a sluglike, multicellular organism in which each cell functions independently. This organism produces a fruiting body which releases spores. Spore walls contain cellulose. Asexual reproduction. *Acrasia, Coenonia.*

Subkingdom Dimastigomycota

Water molds, white rusts, and downy mildews.

Phylum Oomycota

Most are found in soil and fresh water. Cell walls of cellulose. Coenocytic, aquatic saprobes. Some terrestrial species are parasites on plants, attached by the extension of hyphae into the host's tissues. Flagellated zoospores produced in asexual reproduction. Sexual reproduction involves the formation of antheridia and oogonia on hyphae. *Phytophthora, Plasmopara, Saprolegnia.*

Subkingdom Eumycota

True fungi; hyphae form a mycelium; cell walls made of chitin; flagella absent in most.

Phylum Zygomycetes

Conjugating molds. Most are terrestrial saprophytes. Coenocytic hyphae. Asexual reproduction by vertical extension of hyphae and formation of spores. Sexual reproduction involves the joining of two hyphae of different genetic types to form a zygospore. Zygospores can remain dormant for long periods. *Rhizopus* (bread mold).

Phylum Ascomycetes

Sac fungi. Asexual reproduction involves the formation of conidiospores. During sexual cycle, a saclike ascus containing haploid ascospores is produced. Includes unicellular yeasts; and lichens, which are usually composed of an ascomycete and a green algae. *Saccharomyces* (baker's yeast), *Neurospora* (red bread mold).

Phylum Basidiomycetes

Club fungi. Sexual reproductive structure is the club-shaped basidium. After meiosis, stalks suspending basidiospores form on the edge of the basidium. Includes rusts and smuts, which are parasites on plants; and puffballs, mushrooms, toadstools, and bracket fungi. *Agaricus* (field mushrooms), *Puccinia* (wheat rust).

Phylum Deuteromycetes

Imperfect fungi. Sexual reproduction has never been observed. Develop from spores that are produced asexually. Includes some species that are parasites on plants and animals. *Alternaria* (causes one type of potato blight), *Trichophyton* (athlete's foot fungus), *Penicillium* (blue and green molds).

Kingdom Plantae

Eukaryotic. Most are multicellular and nonmotile. Photosynthetic, chlorophyll in chloroplasts. Cell walls made of cellulose. Life cycle involves a haploid gametophyte generation alternating with a diploid sporophyte.

Subkingdom Rhodophycophyta
Division Rhodophyta
Red algae. Nonvascular. Mostly multicellular and marine. Food stored as a starchlike substance. Asexual reproduction by formation of nonmotile spores. Sexual reproduction is oogamous; sperm are not flagellated. Most live at great depths. *Chondrus* (Irish moss).

Subkingdom Phaeophycophyta
Division Phaeophyta
Brown algae. Nonvascular. Multicellular, mainly marine. Some achieve great lengths and have sieve tubes. Three regions of plant body: holdfast, stipe, and blade. Food stored as a carbohydrate called laminarin. Asexual reproduction by zoospores. Isogamous and heterogamous species. Flagellated sperm and spore cells. *Fucus* (rockweed), *Alaria* (kelp), *Laminaria*.

Subkingdom Euchlorophyta
Division Chlorophyta
Green algae. Nonvascular. Unicellular, colonial, and multicellular; motile and nonmotile forms. Mostly freshwater, but some marine and terrestrial species. Specialized tissues. Asexual reproduction by cell division or by formation of zoospores. Includes isogamous, oogamous, and heterogamous sexually-reproducing species. Sperm flagellated. *Chlamydomonas*, *Volvox*, *Ulva*, *Acetabularia*.

Division Bryophyta
Amphibious. Found in damp places on land. Nonvascular. No true roots; attach by means of rhizoids. Sexual reproduction is oogamous. Flagellated sperm require water to achieve fertilization. Spores develop in a sporangium. Gametophyte is dominant generation.
Class Musci: Mosses. Asexual reproduction often by fragmentation. Leafy gametophyte. Sporophyte is parasitic on gametophyte, and performs some photosynthesis. *Polytrichum* (haircap moss), *Bryum* (silver moss).
Class Hepaticae: Liverworts. Asexual reproduction involves gemmae. Stalky sporophyte produces haploid spores. *Marchantia*.

Division Tracheophyta
Plants with vascular tissue consisting of xylem and phloem. Most have true roots specialized for water absorption, stems, and leaves. Sporophyte is dominant generation. Gametophyte is independent in some groups.
Subdivision Psilopsida: Whiskferns. Oldest vascular plants.
No true roots; unicellular rhizoids act as roots. No true leaves; photosynthesis takes place in stems. Some vascular tissue. Gametophyte has both antheridia and archegonia. Only two living genera: *Psilotum*, *Tmesipteris*.
Subdivision Lycopsida: Club mosses. True roots, stems, and leaves. Most have tiny leaves that act as sporangia. Some species produce two kinds of spores: microspores and megaspores. Gametophyte is independent. Sperm biflagellate. *Isotes*, *Lycopodium*, *Selaginella*.
Subdivision Sphenopsida: Horsetails. Stems are jointed and hollow. Scalelike leaves appear in whorls. Dominant sporophyte produces only one type of spore. Gametophyte independent and produces only antheridia, or both antheridia and archegonia. Water required for flagellated sperm to fertilize egg. One genus: *Equisetum*.
Subdivision Pteropsida: Ferns and tree ferns. Well-developed vascular system. Sporangia develop on undersides of leaves or on specialized leaves. Sporophyte produces one kind of spore. Gametophyte is independent and reduced; produces archegonia or antheridia, or both. Sperm are flagellated and need water for fertilization. *Anemia*, *Azolla* (water fern), *Botrychium*.
Subdivision Spermatophyta: Seed plants. Gametophyte generation greatly reduced, dependent, and non-photosynthetic. Fertilization does not require water.
Class Gymnospermae: Non-flowering seed plants. Seed not enclosed within a fruit. Sporophyte produces two kinds of spores. Male microspores give rise to pollen. Pollen carried by wind fertilizes female megaspores.
Order Ginkgoales: Trees with fanlike leaves. One living species: *Ginkgo biloba* (maidenhair tree).
Order Cycadales: Leaves are palmlike. Stem is woody and vascular. *Cycas* (sago palm), *Stangeria*.
Order Coniferales: Mostly cone-bearing trees. Leaves are needles or scales. Most produce two kinds of spores. *Cedrus* (cedar), *Tsuga* (hemlock), *Pinus* (pines).
Order Gnetales: Cone-bearing plants, usually found in deserts. Cones lack tough covering. Three living genera: *Ephedra*, *Gnetum*, *Welwitschia*.

Class Angiospermae: Reproductive structures are flowers instead of the cones. Sporophyte is dominant generation. Produce two kinds of spores. Fruit, which contain seeds, develop from the ovaries.
Subclass Monocotyledonae: Monocots. One cotyledon in embryo. Leaves have parallel veins. Vascular bundles are scattered throughout stems. Flower parts occur in threes and multiples of threes. Corn, lily, tulip, wheat.
Subclass Dicotyledonae: Dicots. Two cotyledons in embryo. Leaves have petioles and veins are branched. Most have stems with vascular cambium, and achieve secondary growth. Vascular bundles form a circle and are sometimes fused. Flower parts occur in fours and fives. Oak, maple, rose, bean, tomato, dandelion.

Kingdom Animalia

Multicellular, heterotrophic, and eukaryotic. Most have tissue, organ, and organ system levels of development. Reproduction in most involves the union of a flagellated sperm and a nonmotile egg to form a zygote. Two types of development are possible: zygote-embryo-adult; or zygote-embryo-larva-adult.

Subkingdom Parazoa

Cell specialization and very simple tissue organization.

Phylum Porifera

Sponges. Most asymmetrical and marine. Filter feeders. All reproduce asexually by fragmentation. Some sexually reproducing hermaphrodites. Larva are free-swimming; adults are sessile. Lack nerve cells. Two body layers: epidermis and mesenchyme. Epidermis is embedded with pores. Mesenchyme has spicules of calcium carbonate or silica and ameboid and flagellated cells. Classes based on type of skeletal material: calcium carbonate and silicon dioxide.

Subkingdom Eumetazoa

Tissues, organs, and organ systems. Believed to have originated from ciliates.

Phylum Coelenterata

Radial symmetry. Mostly marine and carnivorous. All have nerve cells and nematocysts. Lack a central nervous system. Body with two cell layers: endoderm and ectoderm, and a digestive cavity. Two body patterns: sessile polyps and free-swimming medusae.

Class Hydrozoa: Hydra. Alternate polyp and medusae stages, with polyp as dominant form. Medusae move by somersaulting. *Hydra, Tubularia.*

Class Schyphozoa: Jellyfish. Medusa is dominant form. Most move by drifting. Separate sexes. *Physalia* (Portuguese-man-of-war), *Atolla* (crown jellyfish).

Class Anthozoa: Corals and anemones. Exist only as polyps. Asexual reproduction by budding. Sexual reproduction with fertilization taking place internally. Corals have walls of calcium carbonate. Anemones stun prey with their nematocysts. *Metridium* (plumose anemone), *Antipathes* (black coral), *Coralium* (red coral).

Phylum Platyhelminthes

Flatworms. Bilateral symmetry. Definite head. Tissue specialization and organ systems. Acoelomate. Circulatory and respiratory systems absent. Three germ layers: endoderm, mesoderm, and ectoderm. Oxygen taken in by diffusion. Excretory system and gastrovascular cavity present. Sensory and nerve cells at anterior end. Hermaphrodites.

Class Turbellaria: Free-living flatworms. Mostly aquatic. Move by secreting mucus layer and beating cilia. Are photonegative and have chemoreceptors. Asexual repro-

duction by fragmentation or fission. Sexual reproduction with internal fertilization. Lay eggs. External development. *Dugesia, Procotyla fluviatilis* (freshwater planaria).

Class Trematoda: Flukes. Parasites on vertebrates including humans, freshwater and marine fishes. Suckers on anterior end used to attach to host. *Schistosoma* (blood fluke), *Clonorchis* (Chinese liver fluke).

Class Cestoda: Tapeworms. Adults are parasites in the intestines of vertebrates. Lack mouth or digestive cavity. Asexual reproduction by budding. Male and female reproductive organs contained in the proglottids. *Echinococcus* (dog tapeworm), *Taenia solium* (pork tapeworm).

Phylum Aschelminthes

Bilateral symmetry. Pseudocoelomate. Tough outer covering. Three germ layers: endoderm, mesoderm, and ectoderm. Lack respiratory and circulatory systems. Digestive tract present. Separate sexes.

Class Nematoda: Roundworms. Unsegmented. Outer covering is a cuticle of protein. Most are free-living in soil or water. Some are parasites in plants and animals. Fertilization is internal, and development takes place externally. Include hookworms and pinworms. *Trichinella* (causes trichinosis).

Class Rotifera: Aquatic, microscopic organisms. Outer covering is made of chitin. Most are free-living, others are symbiotic or parasitic. Cilia at anterior end used to sweep food into mouth. Asexual and sexual reproduction. Asexual females reproduce parthenogenetically. *Albertia* (parasite in annelids), *Chromogaster.*

Phylum Annelida

Segmented worms. Coelomate. Aquatic and terrestrial. Nervous, digestive, excretory, and closed circulatory systems present. Head and nephridia.

Class Oligochaeta: Bristle-footed worms. Mostly terrestrial. Move by grasping with bristlelike feet and contracting muscular body wall. Respiration takes place through body surface. Skin cells are sensitive to touch and moisture. Hermaphrodites, but not self-fertilizing. *Megascolides* (giant earthworm), *Lumbricus* (earthworm).

Class Hirudinea: Blood suckers or leeches. Most are found in fresh water, but some are marine or terrestrial. Most are external parasites on invertebrate and vertebrate hosts to which they attach with anterior or posterior suckers. Secrete the substance hirudin, which prevents blood from clotting. Hermaphrodites, but not self-fertilizing. *Macrobdella* (American medicinal leech).

Class Polychaeta: Paddle-footed worms, or marine bristle worms. Most live in tubes on the ocean floor. Each segment has a pair of bristles used in respiration and locomotion. Separate sexes and external fertilization. *Aphrodite* (sea mouse), *Nereis* (clam worm).

Phylum Mollusca

Mollusks. Bilateral symmetry. Coelomate. Mostly marine. Soft-bodied with either a hard outer shell or an internal shell. Three body parts: foot, visceral mass, and mantle. A heart, and digestive, excretory, and open circulatory systems are present. Gills present. In the majority of mollusks the sexes are separate.

Class Gastropoda: Larva has bilateral symmetry. Most have a single, coiled shell; others are shell-less. Most are marine, but there are freshwater and terrestrial species. Most have a radula used to obtain food. Chemoreceptors, touch receptors, and eyes. Abalones, periwinkles, slugs, whelks.

Class Pelycopoda: Marine. Bivalve shell is joined laterally. Muscular foot is used for burrowing. Most are sessile, filter-feeding herbivores. Cells sensitive to touch, chemicals, and light. Clams, mussels, oysters, scallops.

Class Cephalopoda: Marine. Most lack shells. Large head with eyes, mouth, and well-developed brain. Mouth is surrounded by tentacles. Locomotion by jet propulsion using siphon. Only class of mollusks with a closed circulatory system. Cuttlefish, octopus, squid, *Nautilus* (chambered nautilus).

Phylum Arthropoda

Bilateral symmetry. Hemocoel. Aerial, aquatic, and terrestrial species. Jointed appendages attached to segmented exoskeleton made of chitin. Muscle, nervous, excretory, and open circulatory systems. Separate sexes with internal fertilization in most. Two subphyla.

Subphylum Chelicerata: Cephalothorax and abdomen. Lack antennae and jaws. Six pairs of appendages: fanglike chelicera, sensory pedipalps, and four pairs of walking legs.

Class Meristomata: Horseshoe crabs. Aquatic. Five or six pairs of appendages that act as gills. A long spikelike tail called a telson. External fertilization. All members are of the genus *Limulus*.

Class Arachnida: Mostly terrestrial. Book lungs or tracheae used in respiration. Most are carnivores. Food is partially predigested externally. Simple eyes. Mites, ticks, scorpions, daddy longlegs, spiders.

Subphylum Mandibulata: One or two pairs of antennae; mandibles and maxillae; and three or more pairs of walking legs. Most have compound eyes.

Class Crustacea: Most are aquatic, free-living, and motile. Some with head, thorax, and abdomen. Others with cephalothorax and abdomen. Cuticle embedded with calcium deposits. Three or more pairs of legs, two pairs of antennae, one pair of mandibles, and two pairs of maxillae. Gills used in respiration. Crayfish, lobsters, shrimp, crabs, barnacles, pill bugs, sowbugs.

Class Chilopoda: Centipedes. Terrestrial, found under rocks and leaves. Two body regions: head and trunk. Simple unfused body segments. One pair of antennae and one pair of legs per segment. Trachea used in respiration. Carnivores; poison claws used for capturing prey. *Scholopendra, Lithobius*.

Class Diplopoda: Millipedes. Terrestrial, found under rocks and leaves. Two body regions: head and trunk. Simple eyes. One pair of antennae. Each abdominal segment has two pairs of legs and two pairs of spiracles. Trachea used in respiration. Herbivores; feed on decaying organic matter. *Polydesmus, Julus*.

Class Insecta: Insects. Three body regions: head, thorax, and abdomen. One pair of antennae, and three pairs of mouth parts. Three pairs of legs attached to thorax. One to two pairs of wings attached to thorax in some spe-

cies. Tracheal system and spiracles used in respiration. Capable of flight. Nearly all are terrestrial. Bees, mosquitoes, flies.

Phylum Echinodermata

Bilaterally symmetrical larva. Most adults are radially symmetrical. Marine. Internal skeleton made of calcareous plates. Spinelike projections on skin surface. Tube feet used for movement and grasping in most. Complete digestive, nervous, and water vascular systems. Lack head, brain, and segmentation. Separate sexes.

Class Crinoidea: Oldest class of echinoderms. Some free-swimming. Most are sessile with a long stalk used for attachment. Five or more featherlike arms with feeding grooves. Ciliated tube feet for feeding and respiration. Sea lilies, feather stars.

Class Asteroidea: Most have five arms, some have more. Free-moving. Outer surface covered with spines. Skin gills used in respiration. Lack centralized nervous system. Region at tip of each arm sensitive to light and touch. Each arm contains a digestive gland. Suctional tube feet used for locomotion and feeding. Starfish.

Class Enchinoidea: Both radially and bilaterally symmetrical members. Armless and free-swimming. Body is spherical and oval in most. Some have a body covering of spines. Suctional tube feet for locomotion and respiration. Sea urchins, sand dollars.

Class Ophiuroidea: Most have long, thin arms. Tube feet used as sensory organs and for feeding. Locomotion is by movement of arms. Brittle stars, serpent stars, basket stars.

Class Holothuroidea: Elongated, leatherlike body is surrounded by five rows of tube feet. Some tube feet used for locomotion. Tentacles surround mouth region. Lack arms. Sea cucumbers.

Phylum Hemichordata

Bilaterally symmetrical. Coelomate. Wormlike, marine organisms that usually live in U-shaped burrows. Gill slits in pharynx; solid nerve cord. Three body regions: probiscus, collar, and trunk. Develop from eggs, and some have a ciliated larval stage. Open circulatory system. True coelom. Acorn worms, pterobranchs.

Phylum Chordata

Bilaterally symmetrical. Gill slits in pharynx, dorsal hollow nerve cord, notochord, and tail are present at some stage of the life cycle. All are capable of sexual reproduction. Endoskeleton. True coelom present. Muscle and nerve tissue segmented.

Subphylum Urochordata: Marine. Dorsal hollow nerve cord and tail in free-swimming larval stage. Adults have gill slits. Most adults are sessile filter-feeders with open circulatory systems. Lack brain. *Salpa, Oikopleura* (tunicates).

Subphylum Cephalochordata: Marine. Fishlike filter-feeders. Adults have a notochord, gill slits, and dorsal hollow nerve cord. Free-swimming, but most lead a sedentary life. Lack brain. *Amphioxus* (lancelet).

Subphylum Vertebrata: Notochord present in embryo. In most adults, this is replaced by flexible vertebral column or backbone made of cartilage or bone. Brain development. Closed circulatory system. Aerial, terrestrial, and aquatic members.

Class Agnatha: Jawless fishes. Aquatic; eel-like. Notochord present throughout life. Part of the skeleton made of cartilage. Lack bones, scales, and fins. Some are parasites on other fish. Suckerlike mouth and rasping tongue. Lamprey, hagfish.

Class Chondrichthyes: Fishes with cartilaginous skeletons. Notochord replaced by vertebrae in adult. Movable jaw attached to the skull. Skin covered with teethlike scales. Lack swim bladders and lungs. Well-developed sensory system called the lateral line is present. Paired pectoral and pelvic fins. Tail fin usually asymmetrical. Internal fertilization; eggs have protective, leathery shells. Sharks, rays, skates.

Class Osteichthyes: Bony fishes. Paired pectoral and pelvic fins. Tail fin usually symmetrical. Fins designed for greater maneuverability. Scales, lateral line, and balance organ present. Many have swim bladder. Four gills on each side have one common opening. External fertilization in most. Herring, salmon, sturgeon, eel.

Class Amphibia: Amphibians. Aquatic and terrestrial. Moist, scaleless, vascular skin used as a means of respiration. Gills in aquatic larval stage; adults have lungs. Tetrapod. Internal fertilization in some. Most lay small eggs covered with a jellylike layer in water. Carnivorous. Frogs, salamanders.

Class Reptilia: Reptiles. Dry skin covered with scales; lungs and usually a three-chambered heart. Most are carnivores. Tetrapod. Internal fertilization. Reproduce on land by laying eggs. Embryo develops in an amniote egg, which has a leatherlike shell. Legs are designed for rapid movement. Snakes, turtles, alligators, lizards.

Class Aves: Birds. Body covering of feathers. Feathers aid in flight in most species. Hollow bones. Teeth replaced by beak. Spongy lungs and air sacs. Scales on legs. Four-chambered heart. Able to maintain constant body temperature. Tetrapod. Internal fertilization. Embryo matures in a protected egg. Ostriches, ducks, owls, penguins, songbirds.

Class Mammalia: Mammals. Body covering of hair. Milk produced in mammary glands. Specialized teeth. Lungs. Able to maintain a high and constant body temperature. Muscular diaphragm. Four-chambered heart. Tetrapod. Sexual reproduction. Most bear live young. Highly developed brain. Platypus, opossum, bats, rabbits.

Subclass Prototheria: Monotremes. Young develop externally in eggs with leathery shells. Cloaca present. Imperfect temperature regulation. Duckbilled platypus, spiny anteater.

Subclass Metatheria: Marsupials. Young born prematurely. They crawl into a pouch where they complete their development. Lack a true placenta. Kangaroo, koala bear, opossum.

Subclass Eutheria: Placental mammals. Embryo attached to uterus by a highly vascular organ called the placenta. Aquatic and terrestrial members. Bat, elephant, seal.

749

Glossary

A

abdomen: the body region posterior to the thorax of arthropods (p. 416); a region in vertebrates between the thorax and pelvis containing many internal organs

abiogenesis: the obsolete idea that living things can arise directly from nonliving material; spontaneous generation (p. 26)

abiotic factor: a physical or nonliving aspect of the environment that affects an organism (p. 687)

abscission: the separation of a leaf, flower, seed, or fruit from a stem (p. 365)

abscission layer: a thin layer of cells at the base of a petiole that forms at the end of a growing season and causes abscission to occur (p. 364)

absorption: the process by which substances such as food and oxygen pass through a body membrane (p. 69)

abyssal zone: deepest part of the ocean where light does not penetrate, with depths generally greater than 1000 meters (p. 697)

accessory pigments: pigments in plant cells capable of absorbing some wavelengths of light (p. 104)

acetic acid: a carbon compound with the formula CH_3COOH that can be produced from the breakdown of pyruvic acid prior to the citric-acid cycle (p. 98)

acetylcholine: a compound with the formula $C_7H_{17}O_3N$ that functions in the transmission of nerve impulses (p. 621)

acetylcholinesterase: an enzyme that blocks the function of acetylcholine (p. 621)

acetyl CoA: a coenzyme with the formula $C_{23}H_{39}O_{17}N_7P_3S$ that is formed when acetic acid reacts with coenzyme A at the start of the citric acid cycle (p. 98)

achene: a dry fruit with a seed enclosed in a thin hard layer formed from the ovary wall (p. 348)

acid: a substance that releases hydrogen ions when mixed with water (p. 46)

acid rain: a type of pollution caused by the combination of sulfur oxides and nitrogen oxides with water vapor in the atmosphere to produce dilute acid solutions that fall to Earth as precipitation (p. 732)

acquired characteristics: traits that an organism develops during its lifetime (p. 208)

actin: a protein that is the main component of the thin filaments in a muscle myofibril (p. 554)

activation energy: the initial energy required to begin a chemical reaction (p. 60)

active site: the portion of an enzyme molecule that reacts with a substrate (p. 60)

active transport: movement of particles across a membrane that requires cellular energy (p. 90)

adaptation: an inherited trait that promotes survival and reproduction for a species (p. 208); the process of becoming better suited to the environment (p. 24)

adaptive radiation: evolution of many diverse groups from a common ancestor (p. 216)

addiction: a strong physical or psychological dependence on a drug (p. 650)

adenine: a nitrogen base with the formula $C_5H_5N_5$ found in DNA and RNA (p. 111)

adhesion: an attraction between unlike molecules due to intermolecular forces (p. 334)

adipose tissue: connective tissue specialized to store fat (p. 556)

ADP (adenosine diphosphate): a coenzyme composed of adenine, ribose, and two molecules of phosphoric acid that can be converted to ATP (p. 63)

adrenal gland: an endocrine gland located above each kidney that secretes corticoid hormones and adrenaline (p. 637)

adrenaline: a hormone secreted by the adrenal medulla that acts to increase blood pressure by stimulating heart action and constriction of some blood vessels; also called epinephrine (p. 637)

adventitious root: any root that grows from a part of the plant that is not the primary root (p. 327)

aerobic: requiring oxygen (p. 97)

aestivation: a period of inactivity and reduced metabolism during summer (p. 480)

agar: a material found in a red algae that is used in laboratories to grow bacteria and fungi (p. 238)

agglutination: the clumping of an antigen with an antibody (p. 599)

aggregate fruit: a type of fruit that develops from many different ovaries in a single flower (p. 347)

aggressive behavior: dominant or fighting behavior (p. 681)

air sac: an organ of gas exchange that opens off the trachea in insects and birds (p. 431)

albumen: a protein-rich substance laid down around the yolk in a bird's egg (p. 511)

alcohol: a compound having an -OH group attached to one or more carbon atoms (p. 52)

alcoholic fermentation: the anaerobic decomposition of glucose to produce alcohol and carbon dioxide (p. 101)

alcoholism: a condition characterized by physical and psychological dependence on alcohol (p. 650)

algin: a gummy substance in brown algae that is used in the manufacture of latex and ice cream (p. 291)

alimentary canal: the tube through which food passes; in humans it includes the mouth, pharynx, esophagus, stomach, and intestine (p. 561)

allantois: an extraembryonic membrane that aids in respiration and excretion for embryos of birds, reptiles, and some mammals (p. 488)

alleles: different forms of a gene that code for slightly different traits (p. 133)

alternation of generations: a life cycle of certain plants and animals in which an asexually reproducing generation is followed by a sexually reproducing generation (p. 286)

altricial: young that are not developmentally advanced and are helpless when hatched (p. 513)

alveoli: microscopic air sacs at the end of each bronchiole in the lungs (p. 580)

amino acid: an organic acid with one or more attached amino groups ($-NH_2$) that is the building block of proteins (p. 58)

amino group: a functional group having the formula $-NH_2$ (p. 53)

amniocentesis: a procedure by which a small amount of amniotic fluid is withdrawn during pregnancy to detect genetic defects (p. 172)

amnion: a fluid-filled sac that encloses an embryo and protects it (p. 172)

amniotic fluid: the liquid contained inside the amniotic sac (p. 172)

amoebocyte: an unspecialized cell type having several functions in sponges (p. 378)

amphetamine: a group of drugs that act as stimulants on the central nervous system (p. 651)

amylase: an enzyme that breaks down starch and glycogen (p. 562)

anaerobic: not requiring oxygen (p. 97)

anal fin: a single fin located ventrally near the tail of bony fish (p. 460)

anal pore: the structure in paramecia through which undigested material is expelled from the cell (p. 263)

anaphase: the third stage of mitosis in which the chromatids move to opposite poles of the cell (p. 120)

angiosperm: a flowering plant (p. 308)

annual: a plant that lives for only one growing season (p. 361)

antagonist pair: two muscles working in opposition so that as one contracts the other relaxes (p. 555)

antenna: sensory appendage in mandibulate arthropods (p. 420)

anterior: situated toward the front part of an animal (p. 377)

anther: the part of a flower stamen that bears the pollen (p. 341)

antheridium: a sperm-producing structure found in some plants (p. 289)

anthropologist: a scientist who studies human cultures and origins (p. 540)

antibiotic: a substance produced synthetically and in living organisms that inhibits the growth of or destroys bacteria and other microorganisms (p. 244)

antibody: a specific protein formed in response to a virus or other foreign materials in the blood or tissues (p. 598)

anticodon: three nucleotide bases found on each transfer RNA that code for a specific amino acid and complement the codon on messenger RNA (p. 116)

antidiuretic hormone (ADH): a hormone produced by the hypothalamus that regulates the reabsorption of water in the kidney; also called vasopressin (p. 639)

antigen: any substance that causes the formation of antibodies (p. 599)

anus: posterior opening of the alimentary canal through which undigested material is expelled from the body (p. 375)

aorta: a large artery leading from the heart (p. 431)

aortic semilunar valve: valve in the heart at the base of the aorta (p. 593)

apical dominance: the retardation of lateral bud growth caused by the presence of the terminal bud (p. 363)

apical meristem: unspecialized cells that divide to produce new cells at root or stem tips (p. 298)

appendage: any structure that grows out from the main part of the body (p. 415)

appendicular skeleton: the pelvic and pectoral girdles and limb bones in vertebrates (p. 448)

appendix: a small projection from the large intestine that helps digest cellulose in some animals but has no function in humans (p. 569)

aquifer: permeable rock yielding an underground water supply (p. 735)

Archaeopteryx: an extinct fossilized animal that represents a transition between reptiles and birds (p. 501)

archegonium: an egg-producing reproductive structure in mosses (p. 292)

arteriole: a small artery (p. 594)

arteriosclerosis: a disease in which the walls of the blood vessels thicken and harden (p. 596)

artery: a blood vessel that carries blood away from the heart (p. 462)

ascus: a saclike reproductive structure that produces spores in certain fungi (p. 274)

asexual reproduction: a method of producing offspring without the joining of two gametes (p. 139)

assay: the qualitative or quantitative determination of the components of a drug (p. 172)

assortative mating: reproduction in which some organisms are more likely to mate with similar organisms rather than dissimilar ones (p. 197)

astral rays: fibrils that form around the centriole during mitosis (p. 120)

asymmetrical: lacking any regular shape (p. 376)

atom: the smallest particle of an element that has all the properties of the element (p. 37)

atomic mass: the mass of a neutral atom (p. 39)

atomic mass unit: a unit for expressing the mass of an atom in which one atomic mass unit equals 1/12 the mass of a carbon-12 atom (p. 38)

atomic number: the number of protons in the nucleus of an atom (p. 38)

ATP (adenosine triphosphate): a compound that stores the energy needed for all cellular activities (p. 63)

atrium: the heart chamber that receives blood from veins in vertebrates; the auricle (p. 462)

auditory canal: the outer ear canal leading to the eardrum (p. 629)

autonomic nervous system: motor neurons that connect the central nervous system to smooth muscles, cardiac muscles, and glands (p. 626)

autosome: any chromosome other than the sex chromosomes (p. 147)

autotroph: an organism that can produce its own food from simple substances (p. 20)

auxin: a plant hormone (p. 358)

axial filament: a series of fibers that are part of a cilium or flagellum (p. 244)

axial skeleton: the skull, vertebral column and rib cage in vertebrates (p. 448)

axolotl: a type of larval salamander capable of reproducing (p. 482)

axon: a long, thin branch of a neuron that carries impulses away from the cell body (p. 619)

B

bacilli: rod-shaped bacteria (p. 242)

bacteriophage: a virus that infects bacteria (p. 247)

bacterium: a very small, unicellular heterotrophic moneran (p. 236)

balanced equation: a chemical equation in which the number of each kind of atom in the reactants and products is the same (p. 47)

ball and socket joint: a type of joint allowing movement in many different directions (p. 552)

barb: a branch from the central shaft of a feather (p. 502)

barbiturate: any of a group of depressant drugs used to induce sleep or relaxation (p. 651)

barbules: tiny hooks that connect the barbs of a feather (p. 502)

bark: all the tissue outside the vascular cambium in a woody stem (p. 331)

basal disk: a specialized area of a sessile organism where a polyp attaches to a surface (p. 382)

base: any substance that combines with hydrogen ions to form a salt and water (p. 46)

base deletion: a mutation in which a nucleotide base is lost from the DNA sequence (p. 156)

base insertion: a mutation in which an extra nucleotide base is added to the DNA sequence (p. 156)

base-pairing rule: the statement that in DNA and RNA each base pairs with only one other base (p. 112)

basidium: a club-shaped reproductive structure that forms spores in certain fungi (p. 276)

B-cell: an antibody-producing lymphocyte (p. 610)

behavior: all the activity of an organism (p. 675)

benthic zone: the ocean floor in the sublittoral zone (p. 696)

benthos: organisms that live on the ocean floor (p. 696)

bicuspid valve: a valve in the heart between the left atrium and left ventricle (p. 593)

biennial: a plant that lives for two growing seasons (p. 361)

bilateral symmetry: a type of symmetry in which an organism can be divided into two mirror images along a single plane (p. 377)

bile: a substance produced by the liver that aids in the digestion of fat (p. 474)

bile duct: a tube that transports bile from the gall bladder to the duodenum (p. 474)

binary fission: cell division in bacteria in which there is no formation of spindle fibers and no chromosomal condensation (p. 238)

binomial nomenclature: a two-name system of naming organisms by genus and species (p. 222)

biochemical oxygen demand: the amount of dissolved oxygen required by bacteria to decompose dead organic materials in a body of water (p. 731)

biodegradable: capable of being broken down by biological decomposition (p. 733)

biogenesis: the idea that all living things arise from other similar living things of the same type (p. 31)

biological magnification: the accumulation of a substance in the tissues of organisms belonging to the same food chain (p. 733)

biologists: scientists who investigate living things (p. 3)

biology: the study of living things (p. 3)

bioluminescence: the ability of a living organism to emit light (p. 257)

biomass: a measure of the total mass of organic matter present in a given area (p. 708)

biome: a large geographical area with characteristic life forms (p. 687)

biosphere: the life zone of Earth that includes the lower atmosphere, land, and water to a depth of 2 kilometers (p. 687)

biosynthesis: the process of producing more complex molecules from simple ones in living organisms (p. 69)

biotic factor: a living organism in the environment that affects another organism (p. 703)

biotic potential: the highest rate of reproduction for a population under ideal conditions (p. 719)

bipedal: walking on two limbs (p. 537)

bipinnaria: a larval stage in echinoderms (p. 409)

birth rate: the rate at which new individuals are added to a population (p. 721)

bivalve: a body plan with two shells hinged together which occurs in some mollusks, crustaceans, and brachiopods (p. 407)

blade: leaf like part of nonvascular plants (p. 291); the flattened portion of a vascular leaf (p. 313)

blastocyst: a stage in the growth of the blastula that is characteristic of placental mammals (p. 662)

blastopore: opening into the gastrula stage of a developing embryo (p. 375)

blastula: a hollow sphere of cells that is an early stage in the development of an embryo (p. 375)

blood: a liquid that consists of plasma and cells which functions as an exchange medium, bringing cells food and oxygen and removing wastes (p. 396)

blubber: a thick layer of fat in some aquatic mammals (p. 517)

bone: a hard inflexible material that makes up the endoskeleton of most vertebrates (p. 448)

book lung: an organ of gas exchange with folds like the pages of a book found in many arachnids (p. 417)

Bowman's capsule: a cuplike part of a nephron in the kidney of all higher vertebrates (p. 587)

brain: a collection of neurons located anteriorly that acts as a control center for body processes (p. 387)

breathing center: a portion of the medulla oblongata that controls breathing (p. 585)

bronchi: two large tubes branching from the trachea (p. 580)

bronchiole: tiny branches of the bronchi in the lungs (p. 580)

bronchus: one of two large tubes branching from the trachea (p. 580)

brood patch: an area of enlarged blood vessels in a bird's chest that functions during incubation for warmth (p. 511)

budding: a type of asexual reproduction in which a small group of cells grows from the body of an adult to become another individual (p. 379); a type of grafting in which the scion is a bud (p. 351)

bud scale: a small, thick, modified leaf that protects a bud (p. 329)

bulb: a short, underground stem surrounded by numerous fleshy leaves (p. 332)

bundle sheath: a layer of tightly packed cells around a leaf vein (p. 316)

C

caeca: blind pouches branching from the stomach in insects (p. 430)

calyx: a group of modified leaves that surrounds the developing flower bud (p. 341)

camouflage: any means of blending with the environment (p. 434)

canine tooth: a pointed tooth used for tearing and piercing (p. 562)

canopy: the leafy covering of a forest provided by the tallest trees (p. 691)

capillaries: microscopic blood vessels having thin walls through which gas and nutrient exchange occurs (p. 462)

capillary water: a loose film of water around soil particles (p. 333)

capsule: a structure in mosses bearing seeds or spores (p. 292)

carapace: a section of exoskeleton covering the cephalothorax in crustaceans (p. 421); the upper or dorsal part of a turtle shell (p. 493)

carbohydrate: an organic molecule made of carbon, hydrogen, and oxygen that can be classified as a sugar, starch, or cellulose (p. 54)

carbon fixation: the second stage of photosynthesis in which carbon dioxide is converted into sugar molecules (p. 103)

cardiac muscle: the muscle that makes up the heart in vertebrates (p. 556)

carnivore: an animal that consumes other animals for food (p. 406)

carpel: a structure consisting of a single ovary, style, and stigma (p. 341)

carrier: an individual that is heterozygous for a recessive trait (p. 163)

carrying capacity: the limit at which the environment can support a certain population (p. 720)

cartilage: a specialized connective tissue that is strong but flexible and composes some part of the endoskeleton in all vertebrates (p. 448)

catalyst: a substance that changes the rate of a chemical reaction but can be recovered unchanged after the reaction (p. 60)

caudal fin: a single fin located on the tail of bony fish (p. 460)

cell: the basic structural and functional unit of a living organism (p. 23)

cell plate: a structure formed at the equator of a dividing plant cell during cytokinesis (p. 123)

cellular respiration: the process of converting food energy into a form usable by cells that takes place in the mitochondria (p. 69)

cellulose: a polysaccharide that makes up most of a cell wall in plants (p. 55)

cell wall: a semi-rigid structure lying outside of the plasma membrane in plant cells (p. 76)

cementum: a hard layer of material just under the enamel of a tooth (p. 562)

central nervous system: the brain and spinal cord (p. 622)

centriole: a cylindrical organelle near the nucleus during interphase that moves to the spindle poles during mitosis (p. 75)

cephalization: a tendency in animal evolution toward larger brains and more complex senses in the head (p. 387)

cephalothorax: one of two main body parts in some arthropods made of a fused head and thorax (p. 416)

cerebellum: the region of the brain lying below the cerebrum and above the pons that controls muscular coordination and balance (p. 463)

cerebrospinal fluid: a fluid in the brain and spinal cord that cushions them against shock (p. 622)

cerebrum: the largest part of the human brain that is the control area for reasoning, memory, and voluntary nervous activity (p. 451)

cervix: a muscular ring of tissue at the junction of the uterus and vagina (p. 659)

chalaza: strands of a protein material that attach the yolk to the membrane lining an egg shell (p. 511)

chaparral: a vegetative formation characterized by low shrubby trees with thick waxy leaves (p. 691)

chelicerae: the first pair of appendages in arachnids that aid in feeding; modified into poison fangs in spiders (p. 416)

cheliped: a pincer-bearing appendage in crustaceans (p. 421)

chemical bond: an attractive force between atoms produced by sharing or transferring electrons (p. 41)

chemical change: a change that produces new substances with new properties (p. 36)

chemical digestion: the breakdown of food through the action of enzymes and emulsifiers (p. 561)

chemical formula: a shorthand method of using chemical symbols and numbers to represent the composition of a substance (p. 42)

chemical reaction: a reaction where bonds between atoms are broken or formed (p. 46)

chemical symbol: a one- or two-letter abbreviation used to represent each of the elements (p. 37)

chemotherapy: the use of chemicals to treat disease (p. 614)

chitin: a hard carbohydrate material found in the exoskeletons of arthropods and also in the cell walls of some fungi (p. 269)

chlorenchyma: parenchyma tissue containing chloroplasts in higher plants (p. 298)

chlorophyll: one of several green pigments in plants required for photosynthesis (p. 74)

chloroplast: a plastid containing chlorophyll (p. 74)

chordate: any organism with a notochord, dorsal nerve cord, and gill slits (p. 445)

chorion: a fetal membrane lying outside of the amnion that becomes the fetal portion of the placenta (p. 663); a thin membrane inside the shell of a laid egg (p. 488)

chromatid: a single strand of the chromosome pair formed by the splitting of a chromosome during mitosis (p. 120)

chromatin: a complex of nucleic acids and protein that composes a chromosome (p. 72)

chromoplast: a plastid containing red, orange, or yellow pigments (p. 74)

chromosomal rearrangement: mutations in which chromosomal pieces are no longer present in their original location (p. 155)

chromosome mapping: a method of determining the relative position of genes on a chromosome using information on crossing-over frequency (p. 152)

chromosomes: long strands in the nucleus that contain genetic material (p. 72)

chromosome theory: the idea that genes are located on the chromosomes (p. 142)

cilia: tiny hairlike projections; used for locomotion in some protists (p. 261); present in some tissues of multicellular organisms (p. 261)

circadian rhythm: cyclic behavior patterns with a period of 24 hours (p. 676)

circulation: the movement of blood through the body's blood vessels (p. 397)

cirrhosis of the liver: a condition in which scar tissue gradually replaces healthy liver cells (p. 650)

citric acid cycle: a series of reactions in the aerobic phase of cellular respiration that breaks down acetyl CoA to form carbon dioxide, water, and releases energy (p. 98)

class: a group of related taxonomic orders (p. 223)

classical conditioning: a form of learning in which an organism associates a previously unrelated stimulus and response (p. 679)

classify: to put objects or ideas into groups on the basis of a similarity (p. 221)

cleavage: one of the first cell divisions in a zygote (p. 375)

cleavage furrow: an infolding of the cell membrane at the beginning of cytokinesis in animal cells (p. 122)

climax community: the final stable stage of succession in a particular area (p. 698)

cline: a gradual trend in the genotype of a population that corresponds to differences in the environment (p. 190)

clitellum: a secretory area of the earthworm's body which produces the capsule during reproduction (p. 399)

cloaca: a common chamber that functions as a digestive, excretory and reproductive duct (p. 475)

clone: a group of identical cells, or a complete individual produced from a single somatic cell (p. 182)

cloning: a method of asexual reproduction in which a single somatic cell develops into a complete identical organism (p. 182)

closed circulatory system: a circulatory system in which blood is enclosed in vessels throughout the body (p. 405)

clutch: a group of bird's eggs laid at one time (p. 512)

cocci: eubacteria with spherical shapes (p. 242)

cochlea: a fluid-filled coiled tube in the middle ear receiving vibrations that stimulate the auditory nerve (p. 629)

codon: a sequence of three nucleotide bases that codes for one amino acid in a protein (p. 113)

coelom: a fluid-filled body cavity surrounded by mesoderm (p. 395)

coenzyme: a nonprotein molecule that works with an enzyme to catalyze a reaction (p. 61)

cohesion: the attraction between like molecules (p. 334)

colchicine: a chemical used to induce polyploidy in plants (p. 182)

cold-blooded: having a body temperature that varies with the temperature of the surroundings (p. 458)

coleoptile: the first leaf of a monocot that forms a protective sheath around the growing shoot (p. 357)

collagen: a fibrous protein that is found in connective tissue (p. 374)

collar cell: flagellated cell lining the interval cavities of a sponge (p. 378)

collecting duct: a tubule that drains urine from the nephron into the renal pelvis (p. 587)

collenchyma: a plant tissue specialized for strength and support (p. 299)

colon: the large intestine (p. 569)

commensalism: a symbiotic relationship in which one organism benefits and the other is unaffected (p. 710)

community: all the populations of organisms living in a specific area (p. 703)

companion cell: a type of phloem cell found in association with sieve-tube elements (p. 337)

competition: the interaction between individuals that use one or more of the same resources (p. 710)

competitive exclusion principle: one of two competing species will be better able to control the use of the common resource thus eliminating the other species (p. 724)

complete flower: a flower that has sepals, petals, stamens, and a pistil (p. 341)

compound: a substance made of two or more chemically bonded elements (p. 41)

compound eye: an eye made up of many individual light-sensitive units (p. 422)

compound leaf: a type of leaf in which many small leaflets are attached to the same petiole (p. 314)

compound microscope: a magnifying device having two lenses (p. 6)

conceptacles: reproductive organs found in brown algae (p. 291)

cone: a light-sensitive cell of the retina that responds to bright light and colors (p. 630); seed or pollen-bearing structure in gymnosperms (p. 300)

conjugation: a primitive type of sexual reproduction by the fusion of two cells for the exchange of nuclear material (p. 239)

connective tissue: a specialized group of cells that connects and supports parts of the body (p. 549)

constrictor: a snake that kills its prey by encircling and suffocating it (p. 492)

consumer: an organism that gets its food from another organism or organic matter (p. 705)

contour feathers: any of the large flight feathers or long tail feathers of a bird (p. 502)

contour plowing: a method of erosion prevention in which plowing is done across a slope (p. 734)

contractile vacuole: an organelle that maintains osmotic pressure and expels excess water from a protist (p. 255)

controlled breeding: allowing only the individuals with a selected trait to reproduce (p. 177)

controlled experiment: an experiment in which only one factor is varied (p. 10)

control subject: the part of an experiment that is used as a standard of comparison for experimental observations (p. 10)

convergent evolution: a type of evolution in which distantly related species produce descendants that resemble each other (p. 217)

convolution: a fold, twist, or coil of any organ especially the brain (p. 517)

cork: a water-resistant outer layer of cells in plant roots and stems (p. 299)

cork cambium: a layer of cells that produces water-resistant cork cells (p. 327)

corm: a short, thick fleshy underground stem (p. 332)

cornea: the transparent covering of the eye (p. 630)

corolla: the petals of a flower (p. 341)

coronary circulation: the supply of blood to the heart (p. 594)

corpus luteum: tissue that forms from a ruptured ovarian follicle and that produces progesterone (p. 660)

cortex: a food-storage area in plants that extends from the epidermis to phloem (p. 325)

corticoid hormones: hormones secreted by the adrenal cortex that help maintain water and salt balance and blood sugar level in the body (p. 637)

cotyledon: embryonic leaf of a seed plant that provides food for the young plant (p. 309)

courtship behavior: a specialized behavior pattern that occurs before mating takes place (p. 680)

covalent bond: a bond formed when two atoms share a pair of electrons (p. 43)

cover crop: planting of grasses or other plants on bare fields to protect the soil from erosion (p. 734)

cranial nerve: a nerve that branches from the brain (p. 463)

cristae: the inner membrane folds of a mitochondrion (p. 96)

crop: an enlargement at the base of the esophagus in birds that stores food before passage to the stomach (p. 507); a storage organ in the digestive system of most segmented worms (p. 397)

crop rotation: planting different crops on a given piece of land to replenish soil nutrients (p. 734)

crossing-over: exchange of parts between two homologous chromosomes (p. 151)

culture: the complex behavior patterns that distinguish a social, ethnic, or religious group (p. 539); a growth of living cells or microorganisms in a controlled environment

cuticle: a tough outer surface that protects the bodies of parasitic flatworms from the digestive action of their hosts (p. 390); a waxy covering on the epidermis of plants (p. 314)

cutting: a leaf or piece of a stem cut from a parent plant (p. 351)

cyclic AMP: a chemical produced in a cell that controls the rate of some cellular processes (p. 636)

cyst: a resting stage in the life cycle of certain parasitic flatworms characterized by the formation of a hard protective coating (p. 391)

cytokinesis: the process of cytoplasmic division in a cell (p. 122)

cytokinin: a plant hormone that stimulates cell division (p. 364)

cytoplasm: a gellike material filling all of the cell except the nucleus (p. 72)

cytosine: a nitrogen base with the formula $C_4H_5ON_3$ that is found in DNA and RNA (p. 111)

cytoskeleton: a system of microtubules and other proteins in the cytoplasm that provides internal support for the cell (p. 75)

D

data: the qualitative and quantitative observations collected during an experiment (p. 9)

day-neutral plant: a plant that is unaffected by the period of daylight (p. 364)

death rate: the rate at which individuals in a population die (p. 721)

deciduous: plants that shed their leaves annually

deciduous forest: a forest made of trees that annually shed all their leaves (p. 691)

decomposer: an organism that breaks down dead organisms for its food; saprobe (p. 236)

deficiency disease: any disorder caused by the lack of one or more vitamins, minerals, or other essential nutrients in the diet (p. 572)

deletion: a mutation in which a chromosomal segment is lost to the cytoplasm (p. 155)

demographic transition: a shift in birth and death rates that affects the size of a population (p. 726)

dendrites: finely divided branches of a neuron that carry impulses toward the cell body (p. 619)

denitrifying bacteria: bacteria that convert nitrates to nitrogen gas (p. 714)

density-independent factor: an environmental condition affecting a population that is not related to its density (p. 724)

dentin: a hard bone-like material that surrounds the pulp cavity of a tooth (p. 562)

depressant: a drug that slows the functioning of the central nervous system (p. 649)

dermis: the layer of tissue directly under the epidermis (p. 556)

desert: a biome characterized by scant rainfall and widely spaced vegetation (p. 693)

development: the stages that an organism goes through from the moment it begins life until it reaches adulthood (p. 24)

diaphragm: a large muscular sheet that separates the thoracic cavity from the abdomen (p. 517)

diastole: relaxation period between heart contractions (p. 597)

diatom: an autotrophic unicellular organism having a cell wall with a high silicon content (p. 257)

dicotyledon: a seed plant with two seed leaves or cotyledons (p. 309)

differentiation: the process of cell specialization (p. 123)

diffusion: the movement of particles from an area of higher concentration to an area of lower concentration (p. 84)

digestion: the process of reducing food to a form that can be absorbed by the body (p. 561)

dihybrid cross: a genetic cross involving two sets of traits (p. 137)

dipeptide: a molecule made of two amino acids (p. 59)

diploid: having two of each type of chromosome (p. 139)

disaccharide: a compound sugar composed of two monosaccharides (p. 55)

distal tubule: a thin tube in a nephron leading from the loop of Henle to the collecting tubules (p. 587)

division: a group of related taxonomic classes in plant classification (p. 223)

DNA (deoxyribonucleic acid): a nucleic acid composed of repeating units of deoxyribose sugar, phosphate, and nitrogen bases in a double strand formation; this substance contains the genetic information of a cell (p. 62)

dominant: a term used to describe a gene or trait that prevents the expression of a recessive trait (p. 132)

dormancy: a period of inactivity during the development of a seed or spore (p. 355)

dorsal: located near the top or back of an animal (p. 377)

dorsal aorta: the portion of the aorta extending from the left ventrical (p. 462); a large dorsal blood vessel in invertebrates.

dorsal fins: a pair of fins located along the dorsal midline of bony fish (p. 460)

dorsal nerve cord: a major nerve that lies along the notochord and becomes the brain and spinal cord in chordates (p. 445)

double bond: a covalent bond involving two pairs of electrons (p. 43)

double fertilization: in angiosperms, a type of fertilization in which one sperm nucleus fertilizes the egg and the other fertilizes the polar nuclei (p. 346)

double helix: the twisted-ladder form of DNA (p. 112)

doubling time: the time it takes for a population to double in size (p. 726)

down feathers: small feathers that insulate a bird's body against heat loss (p. 502)

Down's syndrome: congenital defects including abnormal facial features and mental retardation resulting from an extra copy of the 21st chromosome (p. 169)

drone: a male bee (p. 435)

drug: any chemical used internally or externally for the treatment, cure, or prevention of disease; a chemical that alters the functioning of the mind or body (p. 649)

duodenum: the portion of the small intestine extending from the pylorus to the jejunum (p. 474)

E

echolocation: a method of detecting prey and obstacles using reflected sound waves (p. 524)

ecology: the study of the relationship between organisms and their environment (p. 703)

ecosystem: a unit of the biosphere in which the community of organisms interacts with the environment (p. 703)

ectoderm: the outer layer of cells in an embryo or mature animal (p. 375)

egg: the female reproductive cell (p. 140)

egg tooth: a small structure on the end of a hatching bird's beak or on the tip of a hatching reptile's nose that is used in pecking through the egg shell (p. 512)

electric charge: the property of protons and electrons that causes them to attract or repel each other (p. 38)

electron: a very small, negatively charged particle that moves outside the nucleus of an atom (p. 37)

electron acceptor: a particle that can accept electrons from another particle (p. 99)

electron microscope: a microscope that uses a beam of electrons instead of light as its source of illumination (p. 7)

electron transport chain: a series of reactions in the aerobic phase of cellular respiration in which energy is transferred from high-energy electrons to ATP (p. 99)

element: a substance made of only one kind of atom (p. 37)

embryo: an early stage of a developing organism (p. 213)

embryology: the study of an organism's development from the zygote or fertilized egg stage (p. 213)

emigration: the movement of individuals out of an area (p. 721)

emphysema: a condition in which the alveoli in the lungs are ruptured, thus interfering with oxygen intake (p. 647)

enamel: a very hard layer of material that covers the crown of a tooth (p. 562)

endocrine gland: a ductless gland that pours its secretions directly into the bloodstream (p. 635)

endocytosis: the transport of materials into cells by vesicles (p. 91)

endoderm: the inner layer of cells in an embryo or mature animal (p. 375)

endodermis: the innermost ring of cortex cells in a plant root and in certain plant stems (p. 325)

endometrium: the lining of the uterus in humans (p. 659)

endoplasmic reticulum: a network of channels in the cytoplasm of a cell that functions in protein synthesis (p. 73)

endoskeleton: an internal supporting framework of an animal (p. 410)

endosperm: a triploid tissue containing stored food for the embryonic plant within a seed (p. 346)

endospore: a thick-walled cell formed by bacteria during unfavorable conditions (p. 243)

energy: the ability to do work (p. 36)

energy level: a region of space around an atomic nucleus occupied by electrons with a specific energy state (p. 42)

energy pyramid: a relationship showing the flow of energy as it is transferred through members of a food chain (p. 707)

environment: all external factors that make the surroundings of an organism (p. 20)

environmental resistance: the sum of all the limiting environmental factors that prevent a population from reaching its biotic potential (p. 719)

enzyme: a protein molecule that acts as a catalyst to speed a chemical reaction (p. 60)

epicotyl: the part of an embryonic plant above the cotyledons that will become the leaves and stem (p. 347)

epidemic: the rapid and uncontrollable spread of a disease (p. 607)

epidermis: a specialized outer layer of cells that protects and covers surfaces (p. 298)

epididymis: a coiled tube where sperm is stored leading from the testis (p. 656)

epiglottis: a flap of cartilage that closes over the trachea during swallowing (p. 563)

epiphyte: a plant that is supported by the boughs of a tree but derives moisture and nutrients from the air (p. 692)

epithelial tissue: a specialized group of cells covering exterior and interior body surfaces (p. 549)

epoch: a subdivision of geologic time (p. 201)

equilibrium: a state where the rate of particles entering and leaving a system is equal (p. 87)

era: a large division of geologic time composed of one or more periods (p. 201)

erosion: the wearing away of soil by wind, ice, water, and gravity (p. 734)

erythrocyte: a red blood cell that transports oxygen throughout the body (p. 599)

esophagus: a tube that connects the pharynx and stomach (p. 397)

estrogen: a female sex hormone secreted by the ovaries that prepares the uterine lining for a pregnancy (p. 639)

estuary: a wide area at the mouth of a river where it meets the ocean (p. 695)

ethanol: an alcohol having the formula C_2H_5OH (p. 52)

ethologist: a person who studies the behavior of animals in natural settings (p. 678)

ethylene: a compound with the formula C_2H_4 that can be produced seasonally by plants that causes leaf abscission (p. 364)

euglenoid movement: a type of locomotion in which a euglena moves by flexing its pellicle (p. 255)

eukaryote: any cell with a membrane-bound nucleus (p. 76)

eustachian tube: a canal that connects the middle ear cavity behind the tympanic membrane to the pharynx (p. 478)

evolution: the theories concerning the processes of biological and organic change in organisms such that descendents differ from their ancestors (p. 208)

excretion: the process of eliminating waste products from a cell or living organism (p. 69)

exocytosis: the transport of material out of a cell by means of vesicles (p. 91)

exoskeleton: an external supportive covering or skeleton (p. 415)

experiment: a procedure carried out under controlled conditions in order to test a hypothesis (p. 9)

experimental variable: the one factor in an experiment that is different from the control (p. 10)

expiration: the phase of breathing during which air is expelled from the lungs (p. 583)

external respiration: the exchange of gases between the atmosphere and the blood (p. 579)

extinction: the disappearance of a species from Earth (p. 736)

eyepiece: the lens in a compound microscope that magnifies the image produced by the objective lens; the ocular (p. 6)

eyespot: a small pigmented area sensitive to light (p. 254)

F

facultative anaerobe: anaerobic bacteria that can grow under aerobic and anaerobic conditions (p. 237)

family: a group of related taxonomic genera (p. 223)

fat: a triglyceride that is solid at room temperature (p. 57)

fat bodies: a mass of fatty tissue found in some larval insects and amphibians (p. 475)

fatty acid: a lipid molecule made of a long chain of carbon and hydrogen atoms with an organic acid group at one end (p. 56)

feces: the waste material eliminated by the gastrointestinal tract (p. 569)

fermentation: an anaerobic process whereby organic compounds such as carbohydrates are broken down to form products such as lactic acid or alcohol (p. 101)

fertilization: the union of two gametes to form a zygote (p. 140)

fetus: a human embryo in its later stages of development (p. 172)

F₁ generation: the first generation of offspring in a genetic cross (p. 131)

F₂ generation: the second generation of offspring in a genetic cross (p. 131)

fiddlehead: a new, tightly coiled fern frond (p. 302)

filament: a slender stalk that supports the anther (p. 341); a group of cells joined end to end as in certain algae (p. 288)

first-order consumer: an animal that feeds directly on producers; an herbivore (p. 705)

fission: a process in which one cell divides in two (p. 285); the splitting of atoms to produce energy (p. 738)

flagella: long, whiplike projections from a cell that are used for locomotion (p. 243)

flame cell: ciliated cells that help remove excess water from a turbellarian flatworm (p. 389)

flower: the reproductive structure of angiosperms (p. 341)

follicle: a small cavity in the ovary where an egg develops (p. 660)

follicle-stimulating hormone (FSH): a pituitary hormone that stimulates the growth of ovarian follicles and the ripening of an egg (p. 660)

food calorie: a unit of measure to indicate the energy content of food (p. 570)

food chain: the feeding relationships among the members of a community (p. 705)

food vacuole: an organelle in some protists that collects and digests food (p. 260)

food web: a series of interrelated food chains in an ecosystem (p. 706)

foot: a muscular organ used for locomotion in most mollusks (p. 404)

foramen magnum: the opening in the skull where the spinal cord enters (p. 537)

fossil: an imprint or remains of an organism that lived long ago (p. 201)

fossil fuel: combustible materials that are the remains of ancient, fossilized plants and animals (p. 738)

fragmentation: asexual reproduction in which pieces of a plant grow into complete new plants (p. 285)

frame-shift mutation: mutations in which a base deletion or insertion causes the genetic message to be translated incorrectly (p. 156)

fraternal twins: the offspring resulting from two eggs being fertilized by two different sperm (p. 664)

frond: a highly branched leaf of a palm or fern (p. 302)

fruit: a mature structure that develops from the ovary of a plant and surrounds the seeds (p. 347)

fruiting body: a spore-containing capsule in myxobacteria and slime molds (p. 243)

functional group: a group of atoms in an organic molecule that gives the molecule distinctive properties (p. 53)

fungi: plantlike heterotrophic organisms (p. 269)

G

gall bladder: the organ in which bile is stored (p. 474)

gamete: a haploid reproductive cell (p. 140)

gametophyte: the haploid stage of a plant in alternation of generations that produces gametes (p. 286)

ganglion: a group of nerve cell bodies outside the brain or spinal cord (p. 398)

gastric juice: a fluid in the stomach made of enzymes, water, and hydrochloric acid (p. 565)

gastrovascular cavity: the interior space of a coelenterate where digestion occurs (p. 382)

gastrula: the stage following the blastula stage during which germ layers are formed (p. 375)

gemma: asexual reproductive structures in some liverworts and mosses (p. 293)

gemmule: a type of asexual reproductive structure in sponges made of a tough-walled group of amoebocytes (p. 379)

gene: a piece of DNA that codes for a particular trait, the basic unit of heredity (p. 133)

gene frequency: the proportion of a particular allele in a population (p. 192)

gene pool: all the genes present in a population (p. 192)

generative nucleus: one of two haploid nuclei in a pollen grain (p. 344)

genetic drift: a random variation in gene frequency in a small population (p. 196)

genetic engineering: the use of recombinant DNA and cloning techniques to produce new genes (p. 184)

genetic equilibrium: a state achieved in a population when there is no change in gene frequency over a period of time (p. 195)

genetics: the study of heredity (p. 143)

genotype: the genetic makeup of an organism (p. 133)

genus: a group of similar species (p. 222)

geographic isolation: the division or separation of a population by a physical barrier such as a mountain range (p. 215)

geotropism: the growth response of a plant to gravity (p. 359)

germinate: to sprout or to begin development into a plant (p. 304)

germ layer: one of three primary layers of cells in a developing embryo that forms the ectoderm, mesoderm, or endoderm (p. 375)

gestation: period of development inside the mother's body from fertilization to birth (p. 520)

gibberellin: a plant hormone that promotes cell elongation (p. 363)

gill: an organ that functions in gas exchange in most aquatic animals (p. 405); a spokelike structure beneath the cap of a mushroom (p. 276)

gill arches: the structures that support the gill filaments in fish (p. 463)

gill rakers: structures that keep solid particles from passing through the gills in fish (p. 463)

gill slit: an opening that leads to the gills in fish; paired openings in the wall of the pharynx of chordates (p. 445)

girdling: the process of removing a ring of bark from a tree (p. 337)

gizzard: a muscular grinding organ that is part of the digestive system in segmented worms and birds (p. 397)

gliding joint: a type of joint allowing limited movement between bones (p. 552)

glomerulus: a tuft of capillaries inside the Bowman's capsule of a nephron (p. 587)

glucagon: a hormone secreted by the islets of Langerhans that converts glycogen to glucose (p. 638)

glucose: a simple sugar with the formula $C_6H_{12}O_6$ used as fuel in most living things (p. 54)

glycerol: a three-carbon alcohol molecule (p. 57)

glycogen: a carbohydrate made of glucose molecules; used as a food-storage molecule by animals (p. 55)

glycolysis: the anaerobic stage of cellular respiration in which glucose or other carbohydrate is broken down to form pyruvic acid or lactic acid (p. 97)

goiter: a condition characterized by enlargement of the thyroid gland, often caused by insufficient iodine in the diet (p. 637)

Golgi body: an organelle that prepares and stores proteins for secretion (p. 74)

gonads: the sex organs; the ovaries or testes (p. 639)

grafting: a type of vegetative propagation in which a scion of one plant is attached to the stock of another (p. 351)

grassland: a biome in which grasses are the dominant form of vegetation (p. 691)

green gland: excretory organs in the head of a crustacean (p. 421)

greenhouse effect: the process by which carbon dioxide in the atmosphere absorbs energy that normally radiates back into space, causing the temperature of the atmosphere to rise (p. 732)

growth hormone: a hormone secreted by the anterior pituitary that controls growth (p. 640)

growth medium: any substance that allows the growth and reproduction of an organism (p. 238)

growth ring: a band of xylem cells formed in one growing season (p. 330)

guanine: a nitrogen base with the formula $C_5H_5ON_5$ found in DNA and RNA (p. 111)

guard cells: crescent-shaped epidermal cells around the stoma of vascular plants that regulate stoma size (p. 315)

gullet: an extension of the oral groove in paramecia that forms food vacuoles (p. 254); the beginning of the esophagus (p. 474)

gut: the digestive tube in an embryo; the intestine (p. 388)

gymnosperm: a type of seed plant in which seeds develop unprotected on the scales of cones (p. 304)

H

habitat: the part of an ecosystem in which an organism lives (p. 704)

habituation: a form of learning in which an animal learns to ignore a stimulus upon repeated exposure to it (p. 679)

hair follicle: a small pocket in the dermis that surrounds a hair (p. 556)

half-life: the average time it takes for one half of a sample of radioactive atoms to undergo radioactive decay (p. 201)

haploid: having half of the full complement of chromosomes (p. 139)

Hardy-Weinberg principle: under certain conditions, the frequencies of alleles in a population will remain constant from generation to generation (p. 193)

Haversian canal: a channel running through bone that contains blood vessels and nerves (p. 550)

heart: a hollow muscular organ that pumps blood through an organism (p. 397)

heartwood: the central portion of an older woody stem that no longer conducts water (p. 330)

hemocyanin: a blood protein that transports oxygen in mollusks and some arthropods (p. 405)

hemoglobin: a protein in red blood cells responsible for oxygen transport (p. 397)

hemophilia: a sex-linked condition in humans in which the blood fails to clot (p. 164)

herbaceous: having no woody stem tissue; soft, green stem tissue that lives for one growing season (p. 328)

herbivore: a consumer that eats only plants (p. 406)

heredity: the passing of traits from one generation to another (p. 131)

hermaphroditic: capable of producing both eggs and sperm (p. 379)

heterocyst: nitrogen-fixing cells in some cyanophytes (p. 245)

heterotroph: an organism that cannot make its own food and must take in nourishment from its environment (p. 20)

heterotroph hypothesis: an idea proposed by A.I. Oparin that the first living thing was a heterotroph (p. 205)

heterozygous: a term used to describe an individual having unlike alleles for a trait (p. 134)

hibernation: a period of winter inactivity and reduced metabolism in certain animals (p. 480)

hilum: a scar on a seed where it was attached to the ovary (p. 347)

hinge joint: a type of joint allowing movement in only one direction (p. 552)

histamine: a substance that dilates blood vessels and increases their permeability (p. 609)

homeostasis: maintaining a constant internal environment despite changing external conditions (p. 83)

hominid: modern humans and closely-related primate ancestors (p. 541)

homologous: having similar structure and origin but having different functions in various species (p. 212); a term used to describe the chromosomes of a matching pair (p. 139)

homozygous: a term used to describe an individual with two identical alleles for a trait (p. 134)

honey guide: a pattern of stripes on a flower that directs bees to nectar (p. 345)

hormone: any chemical regulator that is secreted and transported to an area of the body where it causes a response in a tissue or an organ (p. 362)

host: the organism on or in which a parasite lives (p. 708)

Huntington's disease: a dominant genetic disorder in which a substance is produced that interferes with brain function (p. 168)

hybrid: an individual produced by crossing two pure lines (p. 131)

hybrid vigor: the increased size and strength of hybrids resulting from the cross of two inbred lines (p. 180)

hydrocarbon: any one of a group of compounds made of hydrogen and carbon (p. 52)

hydrogen acceptor: a particle that can accept hydrogen from another particle (p. 97)

hydrolysis: a chemical reaction in which a large molecule is split into two smaller molecules by the addition of a molecule of water (p. 56)

hypertension: high blood pressure (p. 597)

hyperthyroidism: a condition resulting from the production of excess thyroxine (p. 636)

hypertonic: having a higher concentration of dissolved substances than the solution to which it is compared (p. 87)

hyphae: filamentous strands filled with cytoplasm and many nuclei that make up the bodies of most true fungi (p. 269)

hypocotyl: a part of the embryonic plant between the epicotyl and the radicle (p. 347)

hypothalamus: a region of the brain that controls many of the body's internal activities that maintain homeostasis (p. 624)

hypothesis: a possible explanation for a set of observations (p. 9)

hypothyroidism: a condition resulting from the production of insufficient thyroxine (p. 636)

hypotonic: having a lower concentration of dissolved substances than the solution to which it is compared (p. 87)

I

identical twins: the result of a fertilized egg splitting into two separate embryos (p. 664)

ileum: the last half of the small intestine (p. 566)

immigration: the movement of individuals into a new area (p. 721)

immovable joint: a type of joint allowing no movement of the jointed bones (p. 551)

immune system: a collection of cells and tissues that defends the body against pathogens (p. 608)

immunity: the ability to resist a particular disease or infection (p. 612)

imperfect flower: a flower missing either stamens or a pistil (p. 341)

imprinting: a type of learning in which an animal forms a social attachment to another organism soon after birth or hatching (p. 678)

inbreeding: crossing two closely related individuals (p. 178)

inbreeding depression: a condition of poor health or decreased fertility after many generations of inbreeding (p. 179)

incisor: a sharp chisel-shaped tooth used for cutting (p. 523)

incomplete dominance: a situation in which neither allele for a trait is dominant over the other; blending (p. 136)

incomplete flower: a flower lacking sepals, petals, pistils, or stamens (p. 341)

incomplete linkage: the breaking apart of genes in the same linkage group through crossing-over of chromosomal material (p. 151)

incomplete metamorphosis: a type of metamorphosis with egg, nymph, and adult stages (p. 428)

incubate: to maintain an environment for eggs so they can mature to hatching (p. 511)

infectious disease: any body disorder caused by the invasion of a pathogen (p. 605)

inflammation: a response by damaged tissue that includes swelling, redness, soreness, and pain (p. 609)

inflorescence: a group of flowers occurring together (p. 343)

infusion: a mixture of water and food material heated to form a clear broth (p. 28)

inheritance: characteristics passed from generation to generation through the genetic material (p. 24)

inhibiting factor: any of a group of hormones produced by the hypothalamus that signals the pituitary to decrease secretion of a particular hormone (p. 642)

innate behavior: unlearned behavior that is genetically controlled (p. 675)

inorganic chemistry: the study of compounds other than hydrocarbons and their derivatives (p. 51)

insectivores: insect-eating organisms (p. 319)

insertion: the point of attachment of a muscle to a moving bone (p. 555)

inspiration: the phase of breathing during which air is taken into the lungs (p. 583)

instinct: an innate behavior involving complex responses to a stimulus (p. 675)

insulin: hormone secreted by the islets of Langerhans that functions in carbohydrate and fat metabolism (p. 184)

interferon: a blood protein thought to be effective in making some cells resistant to viral attack (p. 184)

internal clock: a mechanism in an organism allowing it to compensate for the passage of time (p. 680)

internal fertilization: a type of reproduction in which sperm is deposited directly into a female's body (p. 488)

internal respiration: the exchange of gases between the blood and the body cells (p. 579)

interneuron: a nerve cell that transmits information between two other neurons (p. 619)

interphase: the period of cell growth occurring between divisions (p. 119)

interspecific competition: competition between members of different species for the same resource (p. 724)

intestine: an organ that functions in the digestion and absorption of food (p. 394)

intraspecific competition: competition between members of a population for the same resource (p. 724)

involuntary muscle: muscle that is not under conscious control (p. 556)

ion: an electrically charged atom or group of atoms (p. 44)

ionic bond: a chemical bond between oppositely charged ions resulting from the transfer of electrons (p. 44)

ionic compound: a compound in which the atoms are held together by ionic bonds (p. 44)

iris: the colored area of the eye that regulates the amount of light admitted to the pupil (p. 630)

islets of Langerhans: endocrine cells within the pancreas that secrete insulin and glucagon (p. 638)

isogamete: gametes that are alike in size and shape (p. 288)

isogamy: reproduction by the union of like gametes (p. 288)

isotonic: having the same concentration of dissolved substances as the solution to which it is being compared (p. 88)

isotope: one of two or more forms of an atom having the same atomic number and a different atomic mass (p. 39)

J

Jacobson's organ: tiny pits inside a snake's mouth that contain odor-sensing nerve endings (p. 491)

jejunum: a short section of the small intestine between the duodenum and the ileum (p. 566)

K

karyotype: the set of a cell's chromosomes classified by number, size, and shape (p. 168)

keel: the enlarged breastbone in birds to which the flight muscles are attached (p. 506)

keratin: a fibrous protein of which hair, horns, and feathers are made (p. 487)

kidney: an organ that removes nitrogen wastes from the blood and forms urine (p. 586)

kinesis: a simple type of behavior involving undirected movement in response to a stimulus (p. 680)

kinetic energy: the energy a moving object possesses; the energy of motion (p. 36)

kinetochore: a structure connecting sister chromatids after replication (p. 120)

kingdom: the broadest division in taxomic classification (p. 223)

Klinefelter's syndrome: in males, a condition involving abnormal sexual development that results from the presence of an extra X chromosome (p. 169)

Koch's postulates: a series of procedures developed by Robert Koch to determine whether a particular microorganism causes a disease (p. 613)

L

labium: the lower lip of an insect (p. 430)

labor: a period of uterine contractions that eventually push the baby out of the vagina at birth (p. 666)

labrum: a two-lobed upper lip of an insect (p. 430)

lacteal: a lymph vessel found in the villi of the small intestine (p. 567)

lactic acid fermentation: an anaerobic process of glucose breakdown that produces lactic acid (p. 101)

large intestine: a part of the digestive system between the small intestine and rectum that absorbs water from undigestible materials (p. 569)

larva: an immature stage in the life of some animals (p. 375)

larynx: the voice box (p. 477)

lateral: the sides of a bilaterally symmetrical organism (p. 377)

lateral bud: a small side bud above each leaf scar that develops into new growth on a twig (p. 329)

lateral line: a sense organ found in fish that is sensitive to pressure changes caused by movement (p. 464)

law of independent assortment: Mendel's second law that states that pairs of alleles involved in a cross separate independently (p. 137)

law of segregation: Mendel's first law that states that each individual has two genes for every characteristic and can pass one or the other of those genes to its offspring with equal frequency and that only an offspring with two recessive genes will show the recessive trait (p. 133)

layering: a type of vegetation propagation in which roots are induced to form from a stem (p. 351)

leaf: the chief photosynthetic organ and site of transpiration in a plant (p. 300)

leaflet: one of many small blades attached to the same petiole (p. 314)

leaf scar: a mark left on a twig that indicates the attachment of a leaf in a previous season (p. 329)

learning: a change in behavior that results from experience (p. 676)

lens: a transparent protein structure behind the pupil that focuses light on the retina (p. 630); a curved piece of ground, polished material used to refract light

lenticel: a group of loosely spaced cells on a stem's surface that function in gas exchange (p. 329)

leucocyte: a white blood cell (p. 600)

leucoplast: a colorless plastid that stores starch (p. 74)

life cycle: the span of existence for an organism from gamete formation through reproduction (p. 24)

ligament: a tough, fibrous connective tissue joining bones at a joint (p. 552)

light reactions: the first stage of photosynthesis in which energy from the sun is captured as chemical energy (p. 103)

linkage group: genes that occur together on the same chromosome (p. 149)

lipase: an enzyme that breaks down fats (p. 566)

lipid: an organic molecule that will not dissolve in water but will dissolve in nonpolar substances; made of carbon, hydrogen and oxygen (p. 56)

littoral zone: the area of the shore between high tide and low tide marks; intertidal zone (p. 695)

liver: an organ that produces bile, removes toxic materials, and stores glycogen (p. 474)

long-day plant: a plant that flowers only when the photoperiod is longer than a certain critical amount (p. 364)

loop of Henle: a section of tubule between the proximal and distal tubules of a nephron (p. 587)

lumen: a hollow interior space such as the inside of a tube (p. 563)

lung: an organ that functions in gas exchange with the atmosphere (p. 406)

luteinizing hormone (LH): a pituitary hormone that causes a follicle to rupture and then become the corpus luteum (p. 660)

lymph: tissue fluid that circulates in the lymphatic vessels (p. 601)

lymphatic system: the network of lymph vessels and lymph nodes (p. 601)

lymph node: a swelling in a lymph vessel where disease organisms are removed by white blood cells (p. 601)

lymphocyte: a type of white blood cell that manufactures antibodies (p. 601)

lyse: to digest or break down (p. 247)

lysogenic virus: a type of virus that causes the total destruction of a cell (p. 248)

lysosome: a membrane-bound organelle that stores digestive enzymes (p. 75)

lysozyme: an enzyme produced by mucous-secreting cells and tear glands that destroys bacteria (p. 608)

lytic cycle: a reproductive cycle found in viruses where the host cell lyses after producing new virus particles (p. 247)

M

macromolecule: an organic molecule made of a very large number of atoms (p. 54)

macronucleus: an organelle in paramecia and other ciliated protists that manufactures RNA (p. 263)

malnutrition: a condition that occurs when a person does not get enough of the required nutrients (p. 575)

Malpighian tubules: a group of small tubes branching from the intestine of terrestrial arthropods that absorb nitrogenous wastes (p. 418)

maltase: an enzyme that breaks down the disaccharide maltose (p. 60)

maltose: a disaccharide made of two glucose molecules (p. 55)

mammary gland: a gland in female mammals that secretes milk (p. 517)

mandibles: the jaws of mandibulate arthropods used for chewing food (p. 420)

mantle: a layer of tissue over a mollusk body that secretes the shell (p. 404)

marrow: tissue in the hollows of some bones that produces blood cells or stores fat (p. 550)

marsupial: a pouched mammal (p. 519)

mass: the quantity of matter in an object (p. 38)

mass selection: choosing individuals with desired traits from a large group (p. 178)

matrix: a nonliving material secreted by osteocytes (p. 550); the fluid inside a mitochondrion (p. 96)

matter: anything that has mass and occupies space (p. 35)

maxilla: a mouth part of mandibulate arthropods (p. 420)

maxillary teeth: small teeth inside the upper mouth of frogs (p. 474)

maxilliped: an appendage in crustaceans used in feeding and sensory reception (p. 421)

mechanical digestion: the physical breakdown of food by chewing and by the muscular churning of the stomach (p. 561)

medulla oblongata: a region of the brain controlling involuntary body processes (p. 463)

medusa: a bell-shaped, free-swimming body form found in coelenterates (p. 381)

megasporangium: a female reproductive structure of the conifers that produces haploid megaspores (p. 306)

megaspore: a haploid cell giving rise to the female gametophyte in gymnosperms and angiosperms (p. 305)

meiosis: a process of cellular division in which the number of chromosomes is reduced by half (p. 140)

meiospore: a haploid spore that results from meiosis (p. 288)

melanin: a dark pigment (p. 162)

memory cell: a type of B-cell that remains in the body after infection (p. 612)

meninges: protective membranes covering the brain and spinal cord (p. 622)

menstrual cycle: monthly hormonal changes causing ovulation and preparation of the uterus for a possible pregnancy (p. 659)

menstruation: a period in the menstrual cycle in which the uterine lining breaks down and is expelled out of the body along with blood and the unfertilized egg (p. 660)

meristem: a plant tissue made of unspecialized rapidly dividing cells (p. 298)

mesenchyme: a jellylike material underneath the epidermis of a sponge (p. 378)

mesoderm: the middle layer of cells in an embryo or mature animal (p. 375)

mesoglea: a jellylike material separating the two cell layers in a coelenterate (p. 382)

mesophyll: chlorenchyma cells that contain chloroplasts (p. 315)

messenger RNA (m-RNA): a type of RNA that carries the instructions for protein synthesis from the DNA to the ribosome where it acts as a template (p. 115)

metabolism: the chemical processes of getting energy from food and using it to maintain the structure and function of a cell or of an organism (p. 23)

metamorphosis: a series of changes in form during development of an immature form to an adult (p. 428)

metaphase: the second stage of mitosis during which the chromatid pairs align at the cell's equator (p. 120)

methane: a compound made of a carbon atom covalently bonded to four hydrogen atoms (p. 51)

methanol: an alcohol having the formula CH_3OH (p. 52)

micronucleus: an organelle in paramecia that contains the chromosomes (p. 263)

microorganism: a microscopic living thing (p. 12)

micropyle: a small opening in the ovule wall through which the pollen tube enters (p. 341)

microscope: a device that provides an enlarged image of small objects (p. 5)

microsporangium: a male reproductive structure of the conifers that produces haploid microspores (p. 306)

microspore: a haploid cell giving rise to the male gametophyte or pollen grain in gymnosperms and angiosperms (p. 305)

microtubule: long, cylindrical protein structures in the cytoplasm that give support to the cell (p. 75)

middle lamella: a layer separating the primary and secondary cell walls (p. 76)

midgut: the stomach of an insect (p. 430)

migrate: to move periodically from one environment to another (p. 508)

migration: movement of individuals from one geographic area to another (p. 197)

milt: a sperm-containing fluid made by the testes in fish (p. 464)

mimicry: a protective adaptation in which one species resembles another species and is camouflaged and protected (p. 434)

mineral: any inorganic substance necessary for the proper functioning of the body (p. 572)

mitochondrion: an organelle in which energy production for the cell occurs (p. 72)

mitosis: the process in which a cell's chromosomes are duplicated and separated prior to cytoplasmic division (p. 119)

mixture: a combination of substances where each substance retains its own characteristics (p. 45)

molar: a large flat tooth used for grinding (p. 562)

molecule: two or more atoms held together by a covalent bond (p. 41)

molt: to shed the outer covering as a periodic part of growth (p. 415)

moneran: prokaryotic organism; the group includes cyanophytes and bacteria (p. 225)

monocotyledon: a seed plant with one seed leaf or cotyledon (p. 309)

monohybrid cross: a genetic cross involving only one pair of alleles (p. 137)

monosaccharide: a simple sugar (p. 54)

monosomy: missing a chromosome (p. 154)

monotreme: an egg-laying mammal (p. 519)

motor neuron: nerve cell that transmits information to a muscle or gland from the brain or spinal cord (p. 619)

mucosa: layers of cells lining the alimentary canal that secrete mucus (p. 563)

mucus: a lubricating substance secreted by mucous glands (p. 562)

multicellular: made of many cells (p. 67)

multinucleate: having many nuclei (p. 269)

multiple alleles: having three or more alternate genes that can code for a trait (p. 161)

multiple fruit: a type of fruit that develops from a single ovary of each flower in a cluster (p. 348)

murein: a nitrogen-containing polysaccharide making the cell wall in monerans (p. 235)

muscle tissue: a specialized group of contractile cells responsible for movement (p. 549)

mutagen: any agent that can increase the rate of mutations (p. 153)

mutation: a change in the genetic material that results from an error in replication of DNA (p. 153)

mutualism: a symbiotic relationship that is beneficial to both organisms (p. 708)

mycelium: a network of filamentous hyphae in fungi (p. 269)

myofibril: small fibers that make each muscle cell (p. 554)

myosin: the protein making up the thick filaments in a muscle myofibril (p. 554)

N

NAD (nicotinamide adenine dinucleotide): a coenzyme that acts as a hydrogen acceptor in cellular respiration (p. 97)

NADP (nicotinamide adenine dinucleotide phosphate): a coenzyme that acts as a hydrogen acceptor in photosynthesis (p. 105)

narcotic: a pain-killing drug (p. 650)

nares: nostrils (p. 503)

nastic movement: a plant response that is independent of the stimulus direction but is a reversible result of turgor pressure changes (p. 360)

natural selection: the process by which better adapted organisms survive and reproduce (p. 209)

nectar: a sugary fluid produced by many flowers to attract pollinators (p. 345)

needle: the modified leaf of a conifer (p. 306)

negative-feedback system: a cycle of actions in which the final event inhibits the first event (p. 641)

negative tropism: a growth response away from a stimulus (p. 358)

nekton: free-swimming organisms (p. 697)

nematocyst: a stinging cell in coelenterates (p. 382)

nephridium: an excretory structure in segmented worms (p. 397)

nephron: a tiny excretory unit of the kidney (p. 586)

nerve: a bundle of neuron fibers (p. 619)

nerve impulse: a message generated by reversing polarity at the nerve cell membrane (p. 619)

nerve tissue: a specialized group of cells capable of conducting electrical impulses and forming the communication system of the body (p. 549)

neuron: a nerve cell (p. 619)

neurotoxin: a substance that interferes with the normal functioning of neurons (p. 605)

neurotransmitter: a chemical that transmits impulses across a synapse (p. 621)

neutral: the state of being electrically balanced (p. 38)

neutron: an uncharged particle found in the nucleus of an atom (p. 37)

niche: the way an organism interacts with the biotic and abiotic factors of the environment (p. 704)

nicotine: a drug found in tobacco (p. 647)

nictitating membrane: a thin covering over the eye of some vertebrates that protects it and keeps it moist (p. 472)

nitrifying bacteria: bacteria capable of converting ammonium ions into nitrate ions (p. 714)

nitrogen fixation: a process in which certain bacteria and cyanophytes can convert atmospheric nitrogen into usable nitrogen compounds (p. 237)

node: the region of the stem where the leaf attaches (p. 313)

nodule: a swelling on the roots of some plants (p. 714)

nonbiodegradable: not capable of being broken down by biological decomposition (p. 733)

nondisjunction: the failure of homologous chromosomes to segregate during meiosis (p. 154)

nonrenewable resource: a resource that is in limited supply and cannot be replenished (p. 738)

nonvascular plant: a plant without specialized tissues for transport of food and water (p. 285)

notochord: in lower chordates and in embryos of higher vertebrates, a flexible supportive tube running the length of the dorsal side (p. 445)

nuclear membrane: the membrane surrounding the nucleus of a cell (p. 72)

nucleic acid: any of several organic acids made of phosphoric acid, sugar, and nitrogen bases (p. 62)

nucleolus: an organelle within the nucleus composed of multiple copies of ribosomal RNA (p. 72)

nucleotide: an organic molecule made of a five-carbon sugar, a phosphate group, and a nitrogen base (p. 62)

nucleus: a membrane-bound organelle containing the chromosomes (p. 72); the central part of an atom containing the protons and neutrons (p. 37)

nutrient upwelling: a process where colder, nutrient-rich water is carried up from the bottom of a body of water (p. 697)

nutrition: the process by which an organism obtains and uses food (p. 69)

nymph: an immature stage in metamorphosis that resembles an adult (p. 428)

O

obesity: a condition characterized by excessive body fat (p. 575)

objective: the lens in a compound microscope that magnifies the object being observed (p. 6)

obligate anaerobe: anaerobic bacteria that are poisoned by oxygen (p. 237)

ocular: the lens in a compound microscope that magnifies the image produced by the objective lens (p. 6)

oil: a triglyceride that remains in liquid form at room temperature (p. 57)

olfactory lobe: a part of the brain in vertebrates that pertains to smell (p. 463)

omnivore: a consumer that eats both plants and animals (p. 705)

oogamy: sexual reproduction in which the male gamete is flagellated and the female gamete is a larger, nonmotile egg cell (p. 288)

oogonium: an egg-producing structure found in some plants (p. 289)

open circulatory system: a circulatory system in which blood is not entirely contained in vessels (p. 405)

operant conditioning: a form of learning in which a certain response to a stimulus is reinforced (p. 679)

operculum: the gill cover in fish (p. 463)

opposable: working opposite each other (p. 527)

optic lobes: the parts of the brain that process visual information (p. 463)

oral groove: an opening in a paramecium through which food is ingested (p. 263)

order: a group of related taxonomic families (p. 223)

organ: a structure composed of several tissues working together to perform a function (p. 78)

organelle: an organized structure within a cell that has a specific function (p. 70)

organic acid: a hydrocarbon derivative containing a functional group having the formula $-COOH$ (p. 53)

organic chemistry: the study of carbon chain and carbon ring compounds (p. 51)

organic compound: a chemical compound containing one or more carbon atoms in chain or ring form (p. 51)

organism: any living thing (p. 19)

organ system: a group of organs working together to perform a function (p. 79)

origin: the point of attachment of a muscle to a non-moving bone (p. 555)

osmosis: the movement of water molecules across a membrane from an area of higher concentration to an area of lower concentration (p. 86)

osmotic pressure: the force created against the cell membrane by the movement of water molecules in osmosis (p. 86)

ossification: the process of bone formation in which cartilage is replaced by bone (p. 550)

osteocyte: a bone cell (p. 550)

ostia: small openings through which blood enters the heart of crustaceans and insects (p. 421)

outcrossing: crossing an inbred individual with an individual that is not closely related (p. 179)

oval window: a membrane-covered opening between the middle and inner ear (p. 629)

ovary: the female reproductive organ (p. 341)

oviduct: a tube that carries eggs from the ovary (p. 432)

oviparous: egg-laying (p. 491)

ovipositor: a structure in female insects through which fertilized eggs travel to the outside of the body (p. 432)

ovoviviparous: giving birth to live young (p. 491)

ovulation: the release of an egg from the ovary (p. 660)

ovule: a structure in the ovary of a flower that becomes a seed after fertilization (p. 341)

ovum: the female gamete or egg (p. 657)

oxytocin: a hormone produced by the hypothalamus that causes uterine contraction during labor and promotes milk flow from the mammary glands (p. 639)

P

pacemaker: a group of specialized cardiac muscle cells that generate electrical impulses, thus causing heart muscle to contract (p. 597)

palisade mesophyll: a layer of long narrow cells under the upper epidermis of a leaf (p. 315)

palmate venation: a type of venation in which several veins radiate from a single point (p. 316)

palmately compound: a type of leaf in which the leaflets join together before attaching to the petiole (p. 314)

pancreas: an organ that secretes enzymes for intestinal digestion as well as the hormones insulin and glucagon (p. 474)

pancreatic duct: a tube that transports digestive enzymes from the pancreas to the duodenum (p. 474)

pancreatic juice: a substance produced by the pancreas that contains digestive enzymes and neutralizes stomach acid in the duodenum (p. 566)

parasite: an organism that lives on or in another organism and gets nourishment from it (p. 237)

parasitism: a symbiotic relationship in which one organism lives on or in another organism, usually harming the host (p. 708)

parasympathetic nervous system: a part of the autonomic nervous system that returns the body to normal after an emergency and maintains homeostasis (p. 627)

parathyroid glands: four small endocrine glands on the surface of the thyroid that produce parathyroid hormone (p. 637)

parathyroid hormone: a hormone secreted by the parathyroid glands that regulates the levels of calcium and phosphate ions in the blood (p. 637)

parenchyma: a plant tissue specialized for storage of food (p. 298)

parthenogenesis: the development of eggs without fertilization (p. 435)

passive transport: movement of molecules across a membrane without the use of cellular energy (p. 85)

pathogen: any disease-producing organism or virus (p. 605)

pectin: a gelatinous polysaccharide that makes up the cell walls of diatoms (p. 258)

pectoral fins: a pair of fins located laterally near the gill openings in all jawed fish (p. 457)

pectoral girdle: the part of the skeleton to which the anterior limbs are attached (p. 448)

pedigree: a diagram of family relationships (p. 164)

pedipalps: the second pair of appendages in arachnids (p. 416)

pelagic zone: the open ocean (p. 697)

pellicle: a thick outer protein layer surrounding the cell membrane of a euglena and some other protists (p. 255)

pelvic fins: a pair of fins located vento-laterally in all jawed fish (p. 457)

pelvic girdle: the part of the skeleton to which the posterior limbs are attached (p. 448)

penicillin: an antibiotic produced by the fungus *Penicillium chrysogenum* (p. 14)

penis: a male reproductive organ in animals that have internal fertilization (p. 432)

pentamerous radial symmetry: a type of body plan that can be divided into five equal parts from a central axis (p. 409)

pepsin: the principal protease in the stomach (p. 565)

peptidase: an enzyme that catalyzes the hydrolysis of polypeptides into individual amino acids (p. 568)

peptide bond: a chemical bond that forms between the organic acid group of one amino acid and the amino group of another amino acid (p. 58)

perennial: a plant that lives for more than two growing seasons (p. 362)

perfect flower: a flower having both stamens and a pistil (p. 341)

pericardium: a protective membrane that surrounds the heart in humans (p. 593)

pericycle: a layer of cells around the vascular tissues from which branch roots grow (p. 326)

period: a unit of geologic time that is a subdivision of an era (p. 201)

periodontal membrane: a thin layer of fibrous connective tissue that anchors the roots of teeth to the jawbone (p. 562)

periosteum: a tough membrane surrounding all bones (p. 550)

peripheral nervous system: all of the neurons lying outside of the brain and spinal cord (p. 622)

peristalsis: a rhythmic, muscular relaxing and contracting that moves food along the digestive tract (p. 564)

peritoneum: a membrane that lines the body cavity and forms the covering of the organs in the coelom (p. 395)

permafrost: a layer of ground in the tundra that is always frozen (p. 687)

permeable: allowing a substance to pass through (p. 85)

petal: a brightly colored, modified leaf that surrounds the reproductive organs of a flower (p. 341)

petiole: the stemlike structure that connects the leaf to the stem (p. 313)

PGAL (phosphoglyceraldehyde): a three-carbon sugar that is an intermediate product of photosynthesis (p. 107)

P$_1$ generation: the first parental generation in a genetic cross (p. 131)

phagocyte: an amoebalike white blood cell that engulfs and destroys invading microorganisms (p. 601)

phagocytosis: the active engulfing of particles into the cytoplasm (p. 91)

pharynx: an extendable muscular tube used for feeding in turbellarian flatworms (p. 388); an area of the throat between the mouth and esophagus (p. 445)

phenotype: the observable appearance of an individual as a result of its genetic makeup (p. 134)

phenylketonuria (PKU): a genetic disease in which the absence of an enzyme causes a buildup of the amino acid phenylalanine (p. 170)

pheromone: a chemical released by an animal that affects the behavior of others of the same species (p. 434)

phloem: vascular tissue that transports food throughout a plant (p. 299)

phosphate group: an ion made of a phosphorous atom bonded to four oxygen atoms (p. 62)

phospholipid: a molecule composed of a lipid and a phosphate group (p. 71)

photoperiodism: the response of a plant to varying periods of light and darkness (p. 364)

photosynthesis: a process by which plants, using chlorophyll and energy from sunlight, produce carbohydrates from carbon dioxide and water (p. 20)

phototropism: the growth response of a plant to light (p. 358)

pH scale: a scale used to measure the number of hydrogen ions in a solution and therefore its acidity (p. 46)

phycocyanin: a blue photosynthetic pigment found in cyanophytes (p. 245)

phycoerythrin: a red photosynthetic pigment found in cyanophytes and red algae (p. 245)

phylogeny: the evolutionary history of a species (p. 223)

phylum: a large group of related taxonomic classes in animal classification (p. 223)

physical change: a change from one state of matter to another (p. 35)

physical dependence: a condition in which a person's body suffers physical problems when a drug is withdrawn; addiction (p. 647)

phytoplankton: tiny photosynthetic organisms that float on or near the surface of a body of water (p. 697)

pigment: any substance that reflects light to impart color (p. 103)

pineal eye: a small vestigial eye in one species of reptile (p. 494)

pinnately compound: a type of leaf in which the leaflets attach separately to the petiole (p. 314)

pinnate venation: a type of venation in which smaller veins branch off one main vein (p. 316)

pioneer community: the first organisms to inhabit a specific environment (p. 698)

pistil: the female reproductive structure of a flower (p. 341)

pith: the central part of a stem (p. 329)

pituitary gland: a small endocrine gland at the base of the brain that secretes hormones affecting all other endocrine glands (p. 478)

placenta: an organ in the uterus that exchanges materials between the mother and fetus (p. 522)

placental mammal: a mammal that nourishes developing young through the placenta (p. 522)

placoid scales: a small, spiny type of scale found in sharks (p. 458)

plankton: small, aquatic organisms that drift in seawater (p. 256)

planula: a ciliated larval type found in coelenterates (p. 381)

plasma: the fluid portion of blood that carries blood cells (p. 598)

plasma membrane: the outer boundary of a cell separating it from the environment; cell membrane (p. 71)

plasmid: a small circular piece of DNA found in bacteria (p. 183)

plasmodium: a large mass of multinucleate cytoplasm found in acellular slime molds (p. 272)

plasmolysis: loss of turgor pressure in plant cells (p. 89)

plastid: an organelle in plants that functions in photosynthesis or food storage (p. 74)

plastron: the lower or ventral shell of a turtle (p. 493)

platelet: blood cell fragments involved in clotting (p. 598)

pleura: a double membrane surrounding the lungs (p. 580)

point mutation: a mutation in which one base replaces another in the DNA chain (p. 155)

polar body: a small cell resulting from unequal cytoplasmic division (p. 658)

polar molecule: a molecule with an unbalanced charge distribution (p. 45)

polar nuclei: two haploid nuclei within the ovule of an angiosperm that fuse with one of the sperm nuclei to form endosperm (p. 343)

polar region: the areas around the north and south poles; the Arctic and Antarctic (p. 687)

poles: opposite ends (p. 120)

pollen: grains that contain the male reproductive cells of a seed-producing plant (p. 305)

pollen cone: a male reproductive structure of the conifers containing pollen-producing microsporangia (p. 306)

pollen tube: an extension of the pollen grain through which sperm nuclei travel to the egg (p. 306)

pollination: the transfer of pollen to the female reproductive structures (p. 306)

pollution: any unfavorable change in the environment caused partly or wholly by the actions of humans (p. 731)

polygenic inheritance: a condition in which characteristics are governed by more than one set of genes (p. 162)

polynomial: an expression made of several parts (p. 222)

polyp: a vase-shaped sessile body form found in coelenterates (p. 381)

polypeptide: a molecule made of three or more amino acids (p. 59)

polyploid: having extra sets of chromosomes (p. 154)

polysaccharide: a molecule made of three or more monosaccharides or simple sugars (p. 55)

polysome: a group of several ribosomes attached to a strand of messenger-RNA (p. 117)

polyunsaturated: a term used to describe an organic molecule having more than two double bonds and having less than the maximum number of hydrogen atoms (p. 57)

population: a group of interbreeding organisms that live in a particular location (p. 190)

population density: the number of individuals per unit of space (p. 722)

population genetics: the study of how genetic principles apply to an entire population (p. 191)

population sampling: a method in which data obtained from part of a population is assumed to be true for the entire population (p. 191)

porocyte: a cylindrical cell through which water enters in some sponges (p. 378)

positive tropism: a growth response toward a stimulus (p. 358)

posterior: the back part of an animal (p. 377)

potential energy: the energy an object or system has due to its position (p. 36)

precocial: a group of birds that are developmentally advanced when they hatch (p. 513)

predator: an animal that actively seeks out other animals as a source of food (p. 706)

premolar: a flat tooth located next to the canines that is used for grinding (p. 562)

pressure-flow hypothesis: the idea that food is transported through the phloem as a result of differences in pressure (p. 337)

primary cell wall: the part of a cell wall that is laid down when the cell is formed and expands as it grows (p. 76)

primary growth: the proliferation of meristematic tissue that adds length to a root (p. 324)

primary oocyte: a cell that divides in meiosis I to produce the secondary oocyte and the first polar body (p. 657)

primary spermatocyte: a cell that divides in meiosis I to produce two secondary spermatocytes (p. 656)

primary succession: ecological succession occurring in an area not previously colonized (p. 699)

primary tissue: any of the tissues in a plant that arise from the meristem (p. 324)

primate: a mammal having a very enlarged cerebrum and a complex social system (p. 527)

producer: an organism that manufactures its own food (p. 705)

product: a substance resulting from a chemical reaction (p. 46)

progesterone: a female sex hormone that maintains the uterus in a prepared state for pregnancy (p. 660)

proglottid: a segment of a tapeworm (p. 391)

prokaryote: any cell without a membrane-bound nucleus (p. 76)

prolactin: a hormone secreted by the anterior pituitary that stimulates the secretion of milk from the mammary glands (p. 640)

prophase: the first stage of mitosis in which the chromosomes contract and the spindle forms (p. 120)

prop root: a root arising from the lower end of a stem that supports the plant (p. 327)

prosimian: any of a group of primitive primates including lorises, lemurs, and tarsiers (p. 527)

prostaglandin: a chemical produced in a cell that mediates hormonal action (p. 636)

protease: any of a group of enzymes that break down protein (p. 565)

protein: a macromolecule made of amino acids bonded together by peptide bonds (p. 58)

prothallus: small algaelike gametophyte in psilopsids and ferns (p. 301)

protist: a eukaryotic organism, usually unicellular, that is not a plant or an animal (p. 224)

proton: a positively charged particle found in the nucleus of an atom (p. 37)

protonema: a filamentous stage that becomes the gametophyte in mosses (p. 292)

proventriculus: the first part of a bird's stomach that secretes gastric juices (p. 507); a sac anterior to the gizzard in earthworms

proximal tubule: a thin tube connected to Bowman's capsule in a nephron (p. 587)

pseudopod: temporary extensions of the cytoplasm in amoeboid cells that are used for locomotion or food-getting; foot of a rotifer (p. 260)

psychological dependence: a strong emotional need for a drug (p. 647)

puberty: a time, usually in the early teenage years, when the sex hormones cause the release of eggs from the ovary, sperm production in the testes, and the development of secondary sex characteristics (p. 639)

pulmonary artery: a large artery that carries blood from the heart to the lungs (p. 477)

pulmonary circulation: the passage of blood between the heart and the lungs (p. 595)

pulmonary loop: the circulation of blood between the heart and the lungs (p. 476)

pulmonary semilunar valve: valve in the heart at the base of the pulmonary artery (p. 593)

pulmonary vein: a large vein that carries blood from the lungs to the heart (p. 477)

Punnet square: a diagram used to visualize the possible results of a genetic cross (p. 134)

pupa: an immature stage in insect metamorphosis during which the tissues of the organism are completely reorganized (p. 428)

pupil: an opening in the middle of the iris that admits light into the eyeball (p. 630)

pure line: a breed of plant or animal that produces offspring with the same traits as the parents (p. 131)

pyloric caeca: pouches extending from the upper end of the intestine in fish (p. 462); a pouch that opens into the ventriculus of an insect (p. 430); one of the paired tubes in each ray of a starfish (p. 411)

pyrenoid: a starch-forming structure embedded in the chloroplast (p. 288)

pyruvic acid: a three-carbon compound that is the end product of glycolysis (p. 97)

Q

queen bee: the only egg-laying female of a hive (p. 435)

quill feathers: feathers on the wings and tail that help to stabilize a bird in flight (p. 503)

R

race: a distinct population of a species; a subspecies (p. 191)

radial symmetry: a type of symmetry in which an organism can be divided into equal halves by passing a plane through the central axis of the animal in any direction (p. 377)

radicle: the part of an embryonic plant that will become the root (p. 347)

radioactive: a term used to describe unstable atomic nuclei that break down, releasing particles and energy (p. 40)

radioactive fallout: radioactive particles carried by air currents (p. 733)

radula: a feeding device in mollusks having toothlike projections for scraping (p. 405)

RDP (ribulose diphosphate): a five-carbon sugar found in the chloroplasts that functions in carbon fixation (p. 106)

reactant: a substance entering into a chemical reaction (p. 46)

reasoning: rational thinking; the ability to solve an unfamiliar problem without any trial-and-error process (p. 677)

receptacle: the enlarged tip of a stem that supports the flower (p. 341)

recessive: a term used to describe a gene or trait that is hidden by a dominant gene (p. 132)

recombinant DNA: the new DNA that results from combining two or more types of DNA (p. 183)

rectum: the end of the large intestine (p. 569)

red blood cells: hemoglobin-containing cells that transport oxygen throughout the body (p. 476)

red-green color blindness: the inability to distinguish red from green (p. 163)

reflex: an automatic response to a stimulus (p. 625)

refuge: an area in which wildlife is legally protected (p. 736)

reinforcement: a reward used in learning situations (p. 679)

releasing factor: any of a group of hormones produced by the hypothalamus that stimulates the pituitary to secrete specific hormones (p. 642)

renal arteries: arteries bringing blood to the kidneys (p. 475)

renal cortex: the outer layer of the kidney (p. 586)

renal medulla: the inner portion of the kidney (p. 586)

renal pelvis: a cavity in the kidney in which urine collects (p. 586)

renal vein: vein taking blood from the kidneys (p. 475)

renewable resource: a resource that is unlimited in supply (p. 738)

replication: a process in which a strand of DNA is copied exactly (p. 119)

reproduction: a process by which organisms produce offspring that are similar to themselves (p. 21)

reproductive isolation: a barrier to interbreeding caused by varied breeding times or geographical factors (p. 216)

research method: a step-by-step procedure for investigating problems that includes experimentation (p. 11)

reservoir: a depression at the anterior end of a euglena where the flagella attach (p. 254)

resolving power: the ability of an instrument to separate and distinguish two objects (p. 6)

respiration: process of converting food energy into a form of energy usable by cells; the exchange of oxygen and carbon dioxide between cells and their environment (p. 96)

response: the reaction of an organism to a stimulus (p. 19)

restriction enzyme: a group of enzymes capable of separating DNA at specific points along the chain (p. 183)

retina: a thin area on the back of the eyeball containing light-sensitive receptor cells (p. 630)

R group: any of a number of functional groups that give an amino acid its identification (p. 58)

Rh factors: a type of antigen on red blood cells (p. 600)

rhizoid: rootlike structures in fungi and bryophytes (p. 273)

rhizome: a horizontal underground stem (p. 332)

rib cage: a structure formed from the ribs that protects many internal organs (p. 448)

ribosomal RNA (r-RNA): a type of RNA that makes up the ribosomes (p. 117)

ribosome: a tiny, organelle scattered throughout the cytoplasm that is responsible for protein synthesis (p. 73)

RNA (ribonucleic acid): a single-strand nucleic acid important in translating the DNA code (p. 114)

rod: a light-sensitive cell of the retina that responds in dim light (p. 630)

root: a plant organ specialized to collect water and minerals from the soil (p. 300)

root cap: a group of protective cells covering the root tip (p. 324)

root hair: a small, fingerlike projection from a root epidermis cell (p. 325)

root pressure: pressure exerted by water in the root that helps move water up the plant (p. 334)

ruminant: an ungulate having several compartments to its stomach (p. 526)

rust: a type of fungus that infects many kinds of plants, causing crop damage (p. 276)

S

saliva: a fluid produced by the salivary glands in the mouth (p. 562)

salivary gland: a group of secretory cells that produce saliva (p. 562)

samara: a type of winged fruit found in maple trees (p. 348)

saprobe: organisms that feed on dead organic matter; decomposer (p. 236)

saprophyte: an organism that absorbs its food from dead or decaying organic matter (p. 270)

sapwood: the younger portion of a woody stem that can conduct water (p. 330)

sarcomere: the region of a myofibril from one Z band to the next; the contractile unit of a muscle cell (p. 554)

saturated: a term used to describe an organic molecule that has no double bonds and that has the maximum number of hydrogen atoms bonded to each carbon atom (p. 52)

scales: small, hard, overlapping structures covering the surface of bony fish (p. 460)

scanning electron microscope: an electron microscope that displays an image of an object's surface using a beam of electrons (p. 8)

scavenger: an animal that feeds on dead organisms (p. 406)

scientific theory: a hypothesis that is supported by experimental evidence (p. 11)

scion: the part of a plant attached to the rooted stock in grafting (p. 351)

sclerenchyma: a plant tissue specialized for strength, support, and protection (p. 299)

scrotum: external sac that surrounds the testes of a mammal (p. 655)

sebaceous gland: an oil-producing gland in the epidermis (p. 517)

secondary cell wall: the portion of a cell wall that is laid down after a cell reaches its full size (p. 76)

secondary growth: the proliferation of cambium tissue that adds width to a root (p. 326)

secondary oocyte: a cell that undergoes meiosis II to produce the ovum and a second polar body (p. 658)

secondary spermatocyte: a cell that divides in meiosis II to produce sperm cells (p. 656)

secondary succession: ecological succession occurring in an area stripped of its previous community (p. 699)

second-order consumer: an animal that eats a first-order consumer (p. 705)

secretion: a process of releasing a material that is specialized to perform certain functions; secreted material (p. 74)

sedimentary rock: a type of rock made of compressed layers of sediment (p. 201)

seed: a multicellular structure containing a diploid embryonic plant and a food supply protected by a tough seed coat (p. 304)

seed coat: a tough waterproof covering around a seed (p. 304)

seed cone: a female reproductive structure of the conifers containing spore-producing megasporangia (p. 306)

segmentation: the division of the body into sections (p. 396)

selection: choosing the individuals with a desired trait as the first step in controlled breeding (p. 177)

selectively permeable: the characteristic of only allowing certain substances to pass through (p. 85)

self-limiting: a population that levels off before reaching its carrying capacity (p. 722)

self-pollination: pollination that occurs within a single flower (p. 344)

semen: a liquid made of seminal fluid and sperm (p. 657)

semicircular canals: organs that function in balance and hearing in vertebrates (p. 464)

seminal receptacle: a chamber that stores sperm in many female invertebrates (p. 418)

sensory neuron: nerve cell that transmits information from the environment to the brain or spinal cord (p. 619)

sensory palp: slender organs of taste on the labium and maxillae of insects (p. 430)

sepal: one of a group of modified leaves that protects the developing flower bud (p. 341)

sessile: living permanently attached to the substrate (p. 373)

setae: bristles on each segment of segmented worms that function in locomotion (p. 398)

sex chromosomes: one of a pair of chromosomes that carry genes to determine sex and sex-linked traits (p. 147)

sex-influenced traits: characteristics that are dominant in one sex and recessive in the other (p. 165)

sex-limited trait: a characteristic that appears only in individuals of a certain sex (p. 165)

sex-linked genes: genes located on the X chromosome (p. 150)

sex-linked traits: characteristics determined by genes on the X chromosome (p. 150)

sexual reproduction: a method of producing offspring in which two haploid gametes join to form a diploid zygote (p. 140)

shaft: a hollow tube that forms the central part of a feather (p. 502)

short-day plant: a plant that flowers only when the photoperiod is shorter than a critical amount (p. 364)

shortgrass prairie: a type of grassland in the western United States that is relatively dry (p. 691)

sickle-cell disease: a hereditary disease in which hemoglobin is abnormal and the red blood cells are shaped like sickles (p. 167)

sickle-cell trait: the condition of being heterozygous for sickle-cell disease (p. 167)

sieve tube: a vertical column of sieve tube elements (p. 336)

sieve tube element: a long thick-walled phloem cell (p. 336)

silica: a glassy material rich in silicon (p. 258)

simple eye: a light-sensitive organ in many invertebrates (p. 418)

simple fruit: a type of fruit that develops from a single ovary in a single flower (p. 347)

simple leaf: a type of leaf in which only one blade is attached to the petiole (p. 314)

simple microscope: a single lens magnifier (p. 5)

single bond: a covalent bond involving a single pair of electrons (p. 43)

sinus venosus: a sac just behind the heart in fish and frogs that collects blood as it returns to the heart (p. 462)

siphon: a nozzlelike structure of cephalopod mollusks used for rapid locomotion (p. 408)

skeletal muscle: voluntary muscle that moves bones; striated muscle (p. 553)

Skinner box: a chamber used in operant conditioning that delivers reinforcements (p. 679)

skull: a group of fused, bony plates protecting the brain (p. 448)

small intestine: a part of the digestive system between the stomach and the colon in which most chemical digestion and absorption occur (p. 567)

smooth muscle: nonstriated muscle found in many internal organs like the stomach, intestine, and blood vessels (p. 556)

society: a group of animals that live together and show a division of labor (p. 435)

solute: the substance dissolved in the solvent of a solution (p. 45)

solution: a mixture in which the individual molecules or ions are uniformly distributed (p. 45)

solvent: the substance in which another substance is dissolved (p. 45)

somatic cell: all of the body cells except the germ cells (p. 139)

somatic nervous system: motor neurons that connect the central nervous system to striated or skeletal muscles (p. 626)

sorus: a cluster of sporangia found on the underside of fern fronds (p. 302)

speciation: the formation of a new species (p. 215)

species: a group of similar organisms capable of mating and producing fertile offspring (p. 189)

sperm: male gametes made in the testes (p. 140)

spermatophyte: a seed-producing vascular plant (p. 304)

sperm nuclei: two haploid nuclei produced from the generative nucleus in the pollen tube (p. 346)

spherical symmetry: a type of symmetry in which an organism can be divided into equal halves by passing a plane in any direction through a central point (p. 377)

sphincter: a circular, smooth muscle that closes a tube when it contracts (p. 565)

spicule: a needlelike structure that provides support and protection in sponges (p. 378)

spinal nerve: a nerve that branches from the spinal cord (p. 463)

spindle: fibrils that form between the poles of a cell during mitosis (p. 120)

spine: a type of modified leaf that is very sharp and is used for protection (p. 318)

spinneret: a nozzlelike opening in the abdomen of spiders that releases silk (p. 417)

spiracle: a small opening through which air enters a terrestrial arthropod; the external opening to the trachea (p. 417)

spirilli: spiral-shaped bacteria (p. 242)

spongin: a flexible protein fiber that makes up the skeleton in some sponges (p. 380)

spongy mesophyll: a layer of loosely packed cells beneath the palisade mesophyll (p. 315)

spontaneous generation: the idea that living things can arise from nonliving material; abiogenesis (p. 26)

sporangium: spore-producing organs (p. 300)

spore: reproductive cells that originate from asexual division (p. 270)

sporophyte: the diploid stage of a plant in alternation of generations that produces spores (p. 286)

stabilizing selection: a process that maintains traits that are successful for an organism in its environment (p. 217)

stamen: the male reproductive structure of a flower (p. 341)

starch: a carbohydrate made of hundreds to thousands of glucose molecules; used as a food storage molecule by plants (p. 55)

state of matter: one of four forms in which matter can exist, the three most common being solid, liquid, or gas (p. 35)

stem: a plant organ specialized for conducting water and minerals up from the roots and food down from the leaves (p. 300)

stigma: the tip of the pistil (p. 341)

stimulant: a drug that increases the activity of the central nervous system (p. 651)

stimulus: any change in the surroundings that causes a reaction in an organism (p. 19)

stipe: the stalk of a nonvascular plant (p. 291)

stipule: small leaflike growths found at the base of some leaves (p. 313)

stock: the rooted plant used in grafting (p. 351)

stolon: a horizontal stem that grows along the surface of the ground; a horizontal hypha in fungi (p. 332)

stoma: pores found in the leaves of vascular plants (p. 315)

stomach: a hollow organ that receives food and where the process of digestion begins (p. 461)

striated muscle: voluntary muscle that moves bones: skeletal muscle (p. 553)

stroma: the enzyme-containing fluid filling chloroplasts (p. 104)

structural formula: a method of showing the bonds between atoms and the arrangement of the atoms within a molecule (p. 51)

style: the long, slender part of a pistil that supports the stigma (p. 341)

sublittoral zone: an area of shallow water from below the low tide mark to the edge of the continental shelf (p. 696)

subspecies: a distinct population of a species, a race (p. 191)

substrate: the molecule on which an enzyme acts (p. 61)

succession: a process where plant and animal species of an area change in a specific manner (p. 698)

succulent: a fleshy plant that stores water in its stems or leaves (p. 318)

survival of the fittest: a major point of Darwin's theory, that only the most fit survive to reproduce (p. 210)

sweat gland: a gland in the dermis that releases water and minerals when the body becomes overheated (p. 557)

swim bladder: a gas-filled organ that functions in depth control in fish (p. 463)

swimmeret: an appendage on the abdomen of a crustacean (p. 421)

symbiosis: a relationship in which two organisms live together in close association (p. 708)

sympathetic nervous system: a part of the autonomic nervous system that initiates responses to prepare the body for an emergency (p. 626)

synapse: the gap between an axon and the structure with which it communicates (p. 619)

synapsis: the pairing of homologous chromosomes during meiosis (p. 141)

syndrome: a group of symptoms with a single underlying cause (p. 169)

synovial fluid: a lubricating liquid found in movable joints (p. 552)

syrinx: the voice box of a bird (p. 508)

systemic circulation: the passage of blood between the heart and the rest of the body (p. 595)

systemic loop: the circulation of blood between the heart and the rest of the body (p. 476)

systole: contraction period of the heart ventricles (p. 597)

T

tadpoles: the aquatic larvae of amphibians (p. 472)

taiga: a biome characterized by coniferous forests (p. 690)

tallgrass prairie: a type of grassland in the eastern United States that receives ample rainfall (p. 691)

taproot: a single large root that often functions in food storage (p. 323)

target cell: a specific cell type that responds to a particular hormone (p. 636)

taste bud: a taste receptor on the tongue (p. 628)

taxis: a movement directly away from or toward a stimulus (p. 680)

taxonomy: the science of classifying organisms (p. 223)

T-cell: a type of lymphocyte activated by the thymus that attacks infected cells (p. 612)

telophase: the fourth stage of mitosis in which the chromosomes spread out and new nuclear membranes are formed (p. 120)

telson: the posterior segment of the abdomen in some crustaceans (p. 421)

temperate forest: a biome characterized by plentiful rain and deciduous forests (p. 690)

tendon: a strong fibrous connective tissue attaching muscles to bones (p. 555)

tendril: a type of modified leaf that is long and slender and wraps around supports as a plant climbs (p. 318)

tentacle: one of many long appendages that function in food-getting in coelenterates and cephalopod mollusks (p. 382)

terminal bud: an area of undeveloped tissues at the tip of a woody stem (p. 329)

terrapin: a freshwater turtle (p. 493)

terrestrial: living on land (p. 403)

territoriality: the defense of a certain amount of space by an organism (p. 681)

test cross: a genetic cross using a homozygous recessive type to determine whether an individual is homozygous or heterozygous dominant (p. 136)

testes: the male gonads that produce sperm and the male sex hormones (p. 383)

testosterone: a hormone produced by the testes that causes the development of male secondary sex characteristics (p. 639)

tetrad: the group of four chromatids in a replicated set of homologous chromosomes (p. 141)

tetraploid: a cell with four sets of chromosomes (p. 182)

thalamus: a region of the brain that relays and screens sensory stimuli (p. 624)

thallus: the body of a nonvascular plant (p. 285)

thigmotropism: the growth of a plant in response to touch (p. 359)

thorax: the middle section of an insect body (p. 427)

thylakoid: a tiny membrane-bound sac containing the chlorophyll in a chloroplast (p. 104)

thymine: a nitrogen base with the formula $C_5H_6N_2O_2$ found only in DNA (p. 111)

thymus: a gland located beneath the breastbone that helps establish the immune system in juveniles (p. 609)

thyroid gland: an endocrine gland on the trachea that secretes thyroxine (p. 636)

thyroxine: a hormone secreted by the thyroid gland that controls the body's metabolic rate (p. 636)

timberline: the point on a mountain slope above which trees cannot grow (p. 694)

tissue: a group of similar cells that work together to perform a function (p. 78)

tissue fluid: a liquid similar to plasma that escapes from the capillaries and bathes the body cells (p. 601)

tolerance: a condition in which more of a drug becomes necessary to produce the same effect that a small amount once produced (p. 650)

tortoise: a land-living turtle (p. 493)

toxic waste: any poisonous or carcinogenic substance (p. 733)

toxin: any substance that interferes with the normal functioning of body cells (p. 605)

trachea: the windpipe, a tube leading from the mouth to the bronchi (p. 491); a tube that opens to the outside for gas exchange in insects and spiders (p. 417)

tracheid: a long, thick-walled hollow xylem cell (p. 334)

tracheophytes: plants having vascular tissue (p. 297)

tranquilizer: a drug used to reduce anxiety (p. 651)

transcription: the process of copying the DNA code onto a strand of messenger RNA (p. 115)

transduction: a process in which a bacteriophage injects a portion of one bacterial chromosome into another bacterium (p. 248)

transfer RNA (t-RNA): a type of RNA that delivers amino acids to the messenger RNA template at the ribosomes (p. 116)

transformation: a process by which some bacteria can absorb and incorporate DNA from their surroundings (p. 240)

translation: the process of assembling amino acids into proteins at the ribosomes according to the instructions carried by messenger RNA (p. 116)

translocation: a mutation in which a chromosomal piece becomes attached to another chromosome (p. 155); the transport of food through the phloem of a vascular plant (p. 336)

transpiration: the loss of water from a plant (p. 335)

transpiration-cohesion theory: the idea that water is pulled up the xylem in a stem as a result of transpiration from the leaves and the cohesion of water molecules (p. 334)

transport protein: a protein embedded in the plasma membrane that aids the entry of a specific substance into the cell (p. 90)

trichocyst: a flask-shaped cell under the pellicle of a paramecium and other protists that can release a threadlike structure for defense or for food-getting (p. 263)

tricuspid valve: a valve in the heart between the right atrium and right ventricle (p. 593)

triglyceride: an organic molecule made of glycerol bonded to three fatty acid molecules (p. 57)

trisomy: having an extra chromosome (p. 154)

trochophore: a larval stage in mollusks and some annelids (p. 403)

trophoblast: a layer of cells in the blastocyst that will develop into the embryonic membranes (p. 662)

tropical rain forest: a biome characterized by heavy rainfall, constant warm temperatures and dense growth of many plant species (p. 692)

tropic hormone: a hormone that influences the activity of a specific gland (p. 641)

tropism: a directional growth response of a plant to an environmental stimulus (p. 358)

tube feet: a series of small suction disks used for locomotion and food-getting in echinoderms (p. 410)

tube nucleus: one of two haploid nuclei in a pollen grain (p. 344)

tuber: a swollen underground stem (p. 331)

tundra: a biome characterized by permafrost and low-growing vegetation (p. 687)

turgid: swollen with water (p. 89)

turgor pressure: osmotic pressure exerted by the contents of a plant cell against the cell wall (p. 89)

Turner's syndrome: in females a condition including abnormal sexual development, which results from the absence of one X chromosome (p. 169)

tympanic membrane: the ear of a frog (p. 472); the eardrum (p. 629)

tympanum: the hearing organ of insects (p. 429)

U

ultrasound: a technique using sound waves to locate the position of a fetus in the uterus (p. 172)

umbilical cord: a long cord that connects the fetus to the placenta (p. 522)

understory: a layer of smaller trees and plants in a deciduous forest (p. 691)

unicellular: made of only one cell (p. 67)

unsaturated: a term used to describe an organic molecule that has double bonds and therefore fewer than the maximum number of hydrogen atoms bonded to each carbon atom (p. 52)

uracil: a nitrogen base with the formula $C_4H_4N_2O_2$ found only in RNA (p. 114)

urea: a nitrogenous waste produced from the digestion of protein, the main component of urine (p. 586)

ureter: a tube that carries urine from a kidney to the bladder or cloaca (p. 475)

urethra: a tube that carries urine from the bladder and, in males, transports sperm (p. 586)

urinary bladder: a hollow organ that stores urine (p. 475)

urine: liquid waste filtered from the body by the kidneys (p. 462)

uropod: a flattened appendage at the posterior end of some crustaceans (p. 421)

uterus: muscular organ in which the embryo develops (p. 658); in many lower animals, a long tube where eggs are stored (p. 479)

V

vaccine: a solution of weakened or killed microorganisms administered to produce immunity to a disease (p. 614)

vacuole: membrane-bound, fluid-filled spaces in the cytoplasm of a cell (p. 75)

vagina: canal that leads to the uterus in female mammals; the birth canal (p. 659)

variable: any factor that can be changed or varied in an experiment (p. 10)

vasa efferentia: several fine tubes carrying sperm from the testes to the vas deferens (p. 479)

vascular bundle: a strand of xylem and phloem cells (p. 299)

vascular cambium: a thin layer of unspecialized cells that gives rise to the secondary xylem (p. 298)

vascular plant: plants that have specialized tissues for transport of food and water (p. 285)

vascular tissue: plant tissue specialized for transport of food, water, and minerals, and for support (p. 299)

vas deferens: a tube leading from the testes through which sperm travel (p. 510)

vector: any organism that carries a disease from one host to another (p. 259)

vegetative propagation: asexual reproduction in plants (p. 350)

vegetative reproduction: asexual reproduction in plants (p. 285)

vein: a blood vessel that carries blood back to the heart (p. 462); a vascular bundle in a leaf (p. 315)

vena cava: a large vein that returns blood to the heart (p. 477)

venation: the arrangement of veins in a leaf (p. 316)

venereal disease: any sexually transmitted disease (p. 607)

ventral: the underneath of an animal; in humans the front (p. 377)

ventral aorta: a large blood vessel carrying blood from the ventricle to the gills in fish (p. 462)

ventricle: the chamber that pumps blood away from the heart (p. 462); a cavity within the brain

venule: a small vein (p. 545)

vertebrae: the bony parts of the spinal column in vertebrates (p. 447)

vertebral disk: a pad of cartilage between vertebrae (p. 552)

vertebrate: an animal with a backbone

vesicle: a tiny, membrane-bound sphere within the cytoplasm of a cell (p. 74)

vessel elements: a long, wide xylem cell (p. 334)

vestigial organ: a body part that is no longer fully developed or useful (p. 212)

viable: capable of growth (p. 356)

villi: small fingerlike projections of tissue that function to increase surface area (p. 567)

viroid: short pieces of RNA, with no protein coat, that cause several plant diseases (p. 249)

virus: particles consisting of a single molecule of DNA or RNA surrounded by a protein coat; reproduces only in a host cell (p. 246)

vocal cords: the structures within the larynx that vibrate to produce sound (p. 477)

voluntary muscle: skeletal muscles under conscious control (p. 553)

vomerine teeth: very small teeth lining the margin of the upper jaw in frogs (p. 474)

W

warm-blooded: maintaining a constant internal body temperature (p. 508)

warning coloration: any brightly colored body markings of inedible insects that ward off possible predators (p. 434)

water vascular system: a series of water-filled canals in the body of an echinoderm that functions in locomotion (p. 411)

wax: a fatty acid combined with a long-chained alcohol (p. 57)

white blood cells: any one of several colorless cells that function in protecting an organism against infection (p. 476)

wilting: the loss of turgor in a plant (p. 336)

withdrawal symptoms: a characteristic group of symptoms that occurs after use of a drug has been stopped by a person that is physically dependent on a drug (p. 651)

woodland: an area of widely spaced oak or pine trees interspersed with grasses (p. 691)

worker bee: a nonreproducing female (p. 435)

X

xerophyte: a desert plant (p. 693)

xylem: vascular tissue that transports water and minerals throughout a plant (p. 299)

xylem vessel: a vertical column of vessel cells (p. 334)

Y

yolk sac: a membrane that surrounds the yolk of an egg in birds, reptiles, and mammals (p. 488)

Z

zone of elongation: an area behind the meristem where plant cells grow in length (p. 324)

zone of maturation: an area behind the zone of elongation where plant cells begin to differentiate (p. 324)

zooplankton: tiny heterotrophic organisms that float on or near the surface of a body of water (p. 697)

zoospore: flagellated spores (p. 285)

zygospore: a diploid zygote with a thick outer layer (p. 274)

zygote: a fertilized egg that results from the joining of two haploid gametes (p. 140)

INDEX

Abdomen, 416
Abiogenesis, 26, 32, 126
Abiotic factor, 687
Abscission, 364–365; *illus.*, 364, 365
Absorption, as cell process, 69; in fungi, 270; in small intestine, 568
Abyssal zone, 697
Acacia, 709
Accessory pigments, 104
Acetic acid, 98
Acetylcholine, 621; *illus.*, 621
Acetylcholinesterase, 621; *illus.*, 621
Acetyl CoA, 98
ACh, *See* Acetylcholine
AChE, *See* Acetylcholinesterase
Acid, 46; organic, 53; *illus.*, 53
Acid rain, 732, 733
Acne, 557
ACTH, *See* Adrenocorticotropic hormone
Actin, 554
Activation energy, 60
Active transport, 88–89
Adaptation, in birds, 503, 505, 506, 507, as characteristic of life, 24; and evolution, 208; of fish to water, 458, 464–465, 466–467; in insects, 433–435; to life on land, 450; in vertebrates, 450–451; *illus.*, 24
Adaptive radiation, 216–217
Addiction, 646, 647, 650
Adenine, 111, 114
Adenosine diphosphate (ADP), 63; *illus.*, 63; 96
Adenosine triphosphate (ATP), 63, 95–96, 570; and cardiac muscle, 556; and skeletal muscle, 554–555; *illus.*, 63; 96
Adenovirus, *illus.*, 246
ADH, *See* Antidiuretic hormone
Adhesion, 334–335
Adipose tissue, 556
ADP, *See* Adenosine diphosphate
Adrenal gland, 637–638, 643
Adrenaline, 637–638, 643
Adrenocorticotrophic hormone (ACTH), 641, 643; *illus.*, 641
Adventitious root, 327
Aestivation, 480
African sleeping sickness, 259
Agar, 238, 290

Agglutination, 599
Aggregate fruit, 347
Aggressive behavior, 681
Agnatha, 449, 455–456
Agriculture, 436
Agrobacterium tumefaciens, 185
Air, pollution of, 732–733; protecting, 735
Air bladder, 291
Air sac, 431, 508
Albumen, 511
Alcohol, 52; effect on fetus, 666; effects of long-term use, 650; immediate effects, 649; *illus.*, 649; *table*, 52
Alcoholic fermentation, 101
Alcoholism, 650
Alcohol psychosis, 650
Algae, blue-green, 234, 236, 244–245; brown, 290–291; classification, 225; green, 225, 287–289; red, 290; *illus.*, 16; 236; 284; 286–291
Algin, 291
Alimentary canal, 561
Allantois, 488
Allele, 133
Alligator, 494
Alternation of generations, 286, 304
Altricial bird, 513
Alveoli, 580, 581, 582, 647; *illus.*, 647
Amino acid, 58–60; structural formula, 53; *illus.*, 53
Amniocentesis, 171–173
Amnion, 172, 488, 663
Amoeba, 260–261; *illus.*, 77; 260
Amoeba proteus, 260–261; *illus.*, 260
Amoebocyte, 378
Amphetamines, 651
Amphibia, 449
Amphibians, 470–485; characteristics, 471; fossils, 483; frog, 472–480; other, 481–483; *illus.*, 471; 473; 474; 475; 476; 477; 478; 479; 481; 482; 483
Amphioxus, 447
Amylase, 562
Anaerobe, 237
Anal fin, 460
Anal pore, 263
Anaphase, meiosis, 141; mitosis, 120; *illus.*, 121
Anemia, 599
Angiosperm, 308–309; asexual

reproduction in, 348–349; sexual reproduction in, 340–347; *illus.*, 308
Animals, amphibians, 470–485; arthropods, 414–425; behavior, 674–685; birds, 500–515; cells and osmosis, 86; characteristics of, 373–377; development, 374–376; fish, 454–469; human beings, 535; insects, 426–439; mammals, 516–531; mollusks and echinoderms, 402–413; reptiles, 487–499; sponges and coelenterates, 372, 378–383, 384, 385; vertebrates, 444–453; worms, 386–401
Annelida, characteristics, 395
Annelids, 395–399; *illus.*, 395; 396
Anopheles, 264, 265
Ant, 709
Antagonistic pair, 555
Anteater, 519
Antelope, 683
Antenna, 420
Anther, 341
Antheridium, 289
Anthropologist, 540
Antibiotic, 244, 614–615
Antibody, 598, 599–600, 609–612; *illus.*, 610
Anticodon, 116
Antidiuretic hormone (ADH), 589, 639–640; *illus.*, 639
Antigen, 599–600; 609, 610, 611, 612; *illus.*, 611
Anurans, 471, 472–480
Anus, 393
Aorta, 431, 595
Aortic semilunar valve, 593
Apical dominance, 363
Apical meristem, 324
Apods, 482–483
Appendage, 415
Appendicular skeleton, 448
Appendix, 569
Aquaculture, 466
Aquifer, 735
Arabian oryx, 736
Arachnids, 416–419; *illus.*, 417; 418; 419
Archaeopteryx, 501; *illus.*, 501
Archegonia, 301
Arteriole, 594
Arteriosclerosis, 596
Artery, 462, 594; *illus.*, 597
Arthritis, 551

Carbon cycle, 713–714; *illus.*, 713

Carbon dioxide, 96, 101, 103, 582, 732

Carbon fixation, 103

Carbonic acid, 583

Carbonic anhydrase, 583

Cardiac muscle, 556

Cardiac sphincter, 565

Carnivora, 525

Carnivore, 406, 525, 705; *illus.*, 525

Carotenoid, 104

Carpel, 341

Carrier, 163

Carrying capacity, 720

Cartilage, 448, 456, 550

Catalyst, 60

Caudal fin, 460

Cell, adaptation to changing environment, 81, 84–86; building block of life, 67–69; characteristic of life, 22; differentiation, 123; diploid, 160, discovery, 67; energy, 94–109; function, 69; reproduction, 118–125; respiration, 96–100; specialization, 78, 373–374; structure, 70–76; theory, 68; *Illus.*, 22; 70; 100

Cell division, meiosis, 140–142; mitosis, 119–121, 142

Cell plate, 123; *illus.*, 123

Cell theory, 67–69

Cell wall, 76; *illus.*, 76

Cellular respiration, 579, 582

Cellulose, 55, 76; in human diet, 570–571; and osmosis, 84; *illus.*, 84

Cementum, 562

Centipede, 422–423; *illus.*, 422

Central nervous system, human, 622–625, 632–633; *illus.*, 622

Centriole, 75; *illus.*, 75; 119

Cephalization, 387, 451

Cephalocordate, 447

Cephalopod, 408

Cephalothorax, 416

Cerebellum, 463, 623

Cerebrospinal fluid, 622

Cerebrum, 451, 463, 517, 527, 622–623; *illus.*, 517; 623

Cervix, 659, 666

Cestode, 391–392; *illus.*, 391; 392

Cetacea, 525

Chalaza, 511

Chelicerae, 416

Chelicerates, 415, 416

Cheliped, 421

Chelonians, 489, 493; *illus.*, 493

Chemical bond, 41

Chemical reaction, 46–47; *illus.*, 47

Chemical symbol, 37

Chemical regulator, 634–645

Chemistry, of life, 50–65; of matter, 34–49; of skeletal muscle, 555

Chemoautotroph, 236

Chemotherapy, 614

Chilopod, 422–423, 424

Chinese liver fluke, 391

Chitin, 269

Chlamydobacteria, 244

Chlorenchyma, 298; *illus.*, 298

Chlorophyll, 74, 104; in Monera, 236

Chlorophyta, 287–289

Chloroplast, 74; *illus.*, 74; 104

Cholera, 606

Chondrichthyes, 449, 457–459

Chordate, cephalochordate, 447; characteristics, 445–446; urochordate, 446–447; vertebrates, 447–451, 452–453

Chorion, 488, 663

Chorionic villi, 663

Chromatid, 120, 141

Chromatin, 72; *illus.*, 72

Chromoplast, 74

Chromosome, 72, 110; crossing over, 151–152; diploid, 139; giant, 146; haploid, 139; homologous, 139; mapping, 152; mutation, 153–155; nondisjunction, 154, 168–169; rearrangement, 155; sex determination, 147–148; theory, 142–143, 149; *illus.*, 110; 147

Chrysophyta, 257, 258

Cilia, 261, 262, 263

Ciliophora, 259, 261–264

Circadian rhythm, 676

Circulation, 397; bird, 509; coronary, 594; earthworm, 397; frog, 476–477; grasshopper, 431–432; human, 592–603; mollusk, 405–408; open and closed systems, 405; perch, 462; pulmonary loop, 476, 595; snake, 490–491; spider, 417; systemic loop, 476, 595; vertebrate, 451; *illus.*, 593; 594; 595

Circulatory system, closed, 405; open, 405

Cirrhosis of liver, 650

Citric acid cycle, 98–99; *illus.*, 98

Class, 223

Classical conditioning, 679

Classification, 220–229; binomial nomenclature, 221–222; five-kingdom system, 225–227; levels, 222–223; modern techniques, 223–224; prokaryotes and eukaryotes, 224; three-kingdom system, 224

Cleavage, 375

Climax community, 698

Cline, 190; *illus.*, 190

Clitellum, 399

Cloaca, 475

Cloning, 182–185; *illus.*, 184

Clotting of blood, 598

Club moss, 302; *illus.*, 302

Clutch, 512

Cocaine, 651

Cocci, 242; *illus.*, 242

Cochlea, 629

Codon, 113

Coelenterates, 381–385; *illus.*, 381; 382; 383

Coelacanth, 467

Coelom, 395–396

Coenzyme, 61

Cohesion, 334

Colchicine, 182

Cold-bloodedness, 458

Coleoptile, 357

Collagen, 374, 550, 551

Collar cell, 378

Collecting duct, 587

Collenchyma, 299; *illus.*, 299

Colon, 569

Color blindness, 163

Commensalism, 710

Common bile duct, 567

Communication, 683; *illus.*, 683

Community, 698–699, 703

Companion cell, 337

Compass orientation, 680

Competition, 710–711, 724; *illus.*, 724

Competitive exclusion principle, 711, 724; *illus.*, 711

Complete flower, 341

Compound, 41–47, 48, 49

Compound eye, 422

Compound leaf, 314

Compound microscope, 6

Milt, 464
Mimicry, 434
Mineral, 572; *table*, 573
Mite, 419
Mitochondria, 72; providing ATP for cardiac muscle, 556; respiration in, 96; *illus.*, 73
Mitosis, 119–122; compared with meiosis, 142; *illus.*, 121
Molar, 562
Molecule, 41–47; active transport, 88–89; ATP and ADP, 63; diffusion, 81–83; macromolecules of life, 54–60; polar, 45
Moles, 526; *illus.*, 526
Mollusks, 402, 403–408; *illus.*, 403; 404; 405; 406
Molt, 415
Monerans, 234, 235–245, 250–251; diverse types of, 242–245; genetic material exchange, 239–240; nitrogen-fixing, 237–238; nutrition, 235–237; reproduction, 238–239; *illus., 237; 238*
Monocot, 309, 329, 342, 357; *illus.*, 357
Monohybrid cross, 137
Monosaccharide, 54; *illus.*, 54
Monotremes, 519–520; *illus.*, 519; 520
Moss, 282–293; *illus.*, 292; 293
Motor neuron, 619
Mountains, life in, 693–694; *illus.*, 694
Mouth, 562–563
Movement, characteristic of life, 19; earthworms, 398; euglenoid, 255; grasshopper, 431; human beings, 548–559; mollusks, 404; nastic, 360; paramecium, 261–262; planaria, 389; plant, 358–360; shark, 457; vertebrates, 450
Mucosa, 563, 565
Mucus, 562, 580, 608
Multicellular organisms, 206–207
Multiple alleles, 161, 162
Multiple fruit, 348
Murein, 235
Musci, 292–293; *illus.*, 292; 293
Muscle, 548, 549; antagonist pairs, 555; cardiac, 556; cells of, 554; chemistry of, 555; contraction, 554; lactic acid in, 102; moving joints, 555; need for ATP, 555, 556; skeletal, 553–555; smooth, 556; sphincter, 565; voluntary, 553; *illus.*, 553; 554; 555; 556; 557
Mushrooms, 276; *illus.*, 276
Mutagen, 153
Mutation, chromosomal, 153–155; effect on population, 195; frame-shift, 156; gene, 155–157; *illus.*, 195
Mutualism, 708–709; *illus.*, 709
Mycelium, 269
Mycobacterium, 244
Mycoplasma, 244
Mycorrhiza, 275
Myofibril, 554
Myosin, 554
Myxobacteria, 243

NAD, *See* Nicotinamide adenine dinucleotide
NADPH$_2$, 105
Narcotics, 650–651
Nares, 503
Nastic movement, 360; *illus.*, 360
Natural selection, 209–210; and cooperation, 683; in peppered moth, 214
Neanderthal, 543, 544–545; *illus.*, 543
Nectar, 345
Needham, John, 29
Needle, 306, 318
Negative-feedback system, 641; *illus.*, 641
Negative tropism, 358
Nekton, 697
Nematocyst, 382
Nematode, 393–394; parasitic, 394
Nephridium, 397
Nephron, function, 588; structure, 586–587; *illus.*, 586
Nerve, 619–621; spinal, 626; *illus.*, 626
Nerve cord, 445, 448
Nerve impulse, 619
Nerve tissue, 549
Nervous system, birds, 509; earthworm, 398; and endocrine system, 635, 642; evolution in vertebrates, 451; frog, 478; grasshopper, 431; human, 618–633; mollusk, 407, 408; perch, 463–464; planaria, 388; and respiration, 585; snake, 491; spider, 418
Neuromuscular junction, 621
Neuron, 619–621; *illus.*, 619; 620
Neurospora, 275
Neurotoxin, 605
Neurotransmitter, 621
Neutron, 37, 38, 39
Niche, 704
Nicotinamide adenine dinucleotide, (NAD), 97
Nicotinamide adenine dinucleotide phosphate (NADP$^+$), 105, 107
Nicotine, 647, 648; effect on fetus, 666
Nictitating membrane, 472
Nitric acid, 733
Nitrifying bacteria, 714
Nitrogen cycle, 714–715; *illus.*, 715
Nitrogen dioxide, 732–733
Nitrogen fixation, 237–238, 714
Node, 313
Nodule, 714
Nonbiodegradable, 733
Nondisjunction, 154; of human chromosomes, 168–169
Nonrenewable resource, 738
Nonvascular plant, 285
Nostoc, 245; *illus.*, 245
Notochord, 445
Nuclear energy, 738
Nuclear membrane, 72
Nucleic acids, 62–63; *illus.*, 62
Nucleolus, 72; *illus.*, 72
Nucleotide, 62; *illus.*, 62; 111
Nucleus, of atom, 37; of cell, 72; *illus.*, 72
Nudibranch, 406
Nutrient upwelling, 697
Nutrition, as cell process, 69; human, 570–577; in monerans, 235–237
Nymph, 428

Obesity, 575
Obligate anaerobe, 237
Ocean, life in, 695–697
Ocular, 6
Oil, 57
Olfactory lobe, 463
Omnivore, 705
Oocyte, 657–658
Oogonium, 289
Oparin, A. I., 205

Photo Credits

American Museum of Natural History: 496, 501 right

Animals, Animals: 518 left; M. Ansterman 211, 458, 459 bottom left; M. Conte 513 left; S. Dalton 524; E.R. Degginger 482 top left, 680; Fawcett 210; M. Fogden 479 top; Habicht 526 bottom; R. Kolar 179 bottom left; Z. Leszczynski 459 bottom left, 470, 471, 481 left and right, 482 right; R. Maier 130; S. Meyers 523 bottom; Oxford Scientific Films 383, 456 right, 482 bottom left, 675; R. Pearcy 196 left; M. & B. Reed 676; L. Rhodes 466; T. Rock 709; C. Roesseler 465 bottom; Dr. N. Smith 521

Anthro-Photo: Sapolsky 18

Archive Pictures, Inc.: Mark Godfrey 41

Peter Arnold, Inc.: F. Bavendom 220, 319; R. Birke 68 top right, 216 right, 288; V. Cox 731; B. Evans 284, 375 left; L. Greenberg 47 bottom; W.H. Hodge 14 left, 19 left, 331 right, 689 top, 692 center left; M. Kage 23 left, 78, 110, 232–3, 234, 252, 256 top right, 257 top and bottom, 288 top, 376 top right, 550, 599; S.J. Krasemann 689 bottom left; M. Love 375; W.H. Miller 588, 604; C.A. Morgan 35 right, 215 left, 486, 689 center right, 692 bottom left, 735; H. Pfletschinger 57, 386; E. Rescher 553; J. Rotman 459 top, 467, 696; D. Scharf 661; C. Smith 322; K. Wood/Odyseaus 387; G. Ziesler 22, 493 bottom, 692 top left

Dr. E.S. Barghoorn, Harvard University: 206

The Bettman Archive: 164, 197, 209, 222

Lee Boltin: 540

Dr. Bottone, Mt. Sinai Hospital: 14 right

The W. Atlee Burpee Company: 182

Carolina Biological Supply Co.: 72 bottom, 119–120, 123 bottom, 149 right, 168 a & b, 317, 512

Center for Disease Control, Atlanta, Georgia: 246 bottom

Drs. George B. Chapman and Maria Costa, Georgetown University: 243 top

Cleveland Museum of Natural History: 541, 542

Bruce Coleman Inc.: 500; J. & D. Bartlett 523 top, 536; R. Borland 493 top; J. Burton 143, 179 top right, 416, 493 top; B. & C. Calhoun 356; H. Darrow 419; C. Davidson 736 right; T. Deane 435; E.R. Degginger 436, 526 top; J. Dermid 422 bottom; R. Dunne 690 top; J. Elk 718; F. Erize 687; J.S. Flannery 179 top left; M. Fogden 434 top left;

J. Foot 291, 410, 722; C. & D. Frith 674; M. Kahl 335; L. Lee Rue 527 top; G.D. Lepp 157 left; J. McDonald 418, 492 right; N. Myers 527 bottom; C. Newbert 409 left, 409 right; D. Overcash 434 bottom left; D. Schwimmer 455; R.L. Sefton 380 left; J. Shaw 434 right; S. Solum 53, 282–3; K. Taylor 214, 261 left; R. Taylor 458; N.O. Tomalin 494 lower left; P. Ward 422 top; L. West 277, 436 left, 736 left

Paul Conklin: 11, 13, 169 right, 170, 305, 650

Jeff Coolidge: 538 top

Courtesy Countway Medical Library: 4 lower left, 67

Culver Pictures: 12 top, 26

Walter Dawn: 331 left, 342 top left, 349, 363 left

E.R. Degginger: 24, 34, 39, 128–9, 146, 154, 157 right, 160, 178, 189, 190, 194, 196 right, 287

Phil Degginger: 50, 449 center left

DPI: J.H. Gerard 442–3

Earth Images: T. Domico 502 all; J. Rogers 695

Earth Scenes: E.R. Degginger 268; R. Kamal 276; B. Kent 273 bottom; Oxford Scientific Films 275 top

W. Ferguson: 292, 293

Freelance Photographers Guild: G. Hunter 77 left; V. Lipka 42; R. Mackson 585; N. Mason 667; T. Tracy 15

French Government Tourist Office: 544

From *Genetic Research: A Survey of Methods and Main Results*, ©1961, Meijels Bokindustri: 177

Grand Canyon National Park: 215 right

The Granger Collection: 4 top, 5, 12 left

Grant Heilman Photography: 3, 302 center, 306, 308 center, 449 top center; J. Colwell 318 left; W. Conway 449 top right; H. Harrison 345 bottom right, 349 middle, 513 right; G. Heilman 167 top, 221, 327, 342 bottom center, 342 bottom right, 345 bottom left, 350, 358, 363 right, 464, 699; E. Heyer 137 bottom; S. Rannels 270 top; J. Rotman 225; B. Runk 104, 318 right, 342 center; Runk/Schoenberger 222 top, 224, 237, 273 top, 287 top right, 301, 302 top, 302 bottom, 308 bottom right, 316, 319, 350, 361, 362 bottom, 364 bottom, 368, 447, 449 top left, 456 left, 742 left; C. Shuman 336 right

Dr. H. E. Huxley, MRC Laboratory of Molecular Biology, Cambridge, England: 554 bottom